Festivals of Faith

Reflections on the Jewish Holidays

BOOKS BY NORMAN LAMM

A HEDGE OF ROSES
Jewish Insights into Marriage and Married Life (1966)

THE ROYAL REACH
Discourses on the Jewish Tradition and the World Today (1970)

FAITH AND DOUBT
Studies in Traditional Jewish Thought (1971; 1986; 2006)

TORAH LISHMAH
*Torah for Torah's Sake in the Works of Rabbi Hayyim of Volozhin
and his Contemporaries*
(Hebrew 1972, English 1989)

THE GOOD SOCIETY
Jewish Ethics in Action (1974)

TORAH UMADDA
*The Encounter of Religious Learning and Worldly Knowledge
in the Jewish Tradition* (1990; 2010)

HALAKHOT VA-HALIKHOT (Hebrew)
*Jewish Law and the Legacy of Judaism: Essays and Inquiries
in Jewish Law* (1990)

THE SHEMA
Spirituality and Law in Judaism (1998)

THE RELIGIOUS THOUGHT OF HASIDISM
Text and Commentary (1999)

SEVENTY FACES (two volumes)
Articles of Faith (2001)

THE ROYAL TABLE
A Passover Haggadah (2010)

FESTIVALS OF FAITH
Reflections on the Jewish Holidays (2011)

Festivals of Faith

Reflections on the Jewish Holidays

by

Norman Lamm

Edited by

David Shatz

Associate Editor

Simon Posner

RIETS
Yeshiva University Press

Copyright © 2011 Orthodox Union

Library of Congress Cataloging-in-Publication Data

ISBN: 978-1-60280-174-5

Manufactured in the United States of America

Published by
RIETS
Yeshiva University Press
500 West 185th Street
New York, NY 10033

OU Press
an imprint of the Orthodox Union
11 Broadway
New York, NY 10004
www.oupress.org
oupress@ou.org

Distributed by
KTAV Publishing House, Inc.
888 Newark Avenue
Jersey City, NJ 07306
Tel. (201) 963-9524
Fax. (201) 963-0102
www.ktav.com
bernie@ktav.com

This volume is dedicated to
my beloved siblings

Moshe, Tzibby, and Miriam

who always reciprocated the love I felt for them

– N. L.

Mizmor le-Todah

This volume, as well as the previous one (*The Royal Table*) and the one to follow (*The Megillah: Majesty and Mystery*), are all based on sermons I delivered during my fifty years in the rabbinate. They remained in obscurity for many years, until I was urged by the Dean of Libraries of Yeshiva University

Pearl Berger

to allow her to place them on the internet so that others might find some interest in them. Several thousand viewers have availed themselves of this opportunity, thanks to her initiative.

Rabbi Menachem Genack

of the OU Press (and in partnership for this volume with RIETS/Yeshiva University Press) undertook to publish some of these *derashot* for the special occasions of the year in the hope and expectation that they would enhance the understanding and appreciation of these holy days, both those commemorating happy occasions and, as well, the somber fast days.

Norman Lamm

CONTENTS

Author's Preface   xi

Editor's Preface   xiii

Rosh Hashanah
1. An Alternate Route to Sanctity   3
2. "What Hast Thou in the House?"   9
3. Let There Be Light   15
4. The Sense of Shame   21
5. Three Who Cried   26
6. The Revelation of Man   32
7. If I Were a Prophet   38
8. The Greatest Trial   45

Yom Kippur
9. Hear, O Father   55
10. The Way of Honor   61
11. Passing Life By   66
12. Shoes and the Soul   73
13. Body and Soul   79
14. Everybody Is a Somebody   85
15. On to Eden   91
16. One Hour   98

Sukkot
17. Save and Prosper   107
18. Indispensability: Myth and Fact   111
19. The Illusions We Live By   116
20. The Starry Night   121
21. The Anatomy of an *Etrog*   127

22. Kohelet: Looking Too Far Ahead 133
23. Man Is More Than *Sekhakh* 140

Shemini Atzeret and Simhat Torah
24. Which Way the Wind Blows 149
25. Reworking the Past 155
26. A Simple Farewell 160

Hanukkah
27. Variations on the Hanukkah Theme 169
28. On Being Too Practical 174
29. The Lodger's Light 179
30. Half the Hanukkah Story 184
31. On the Threshold 189

Purim
32. Neither Here Nor There 193
33. Remember to Forget 200

Passover
34. The Sabbath of Greatness 207
35. With All Deliberate Speed 212
36. The Source of Darkness 219
37. On Being Responsible 223
38. Be Not Overwise: The Haggadah's Third Son in a New Light 228
39. Novelty and Renewal 233
40. Creative Remnants; or, Leaven from Heaven 238
41. Bitter-Sweet 243
42. A Past Worth Perpetuating 248
43. Passover and Human Diversity 253

Yom ha-Shoah
44. Death Has No Future: The Holocaust and Jewish Education 259

Yom ha-Atzma'ut and Yom Yerushalayim
45. The Illusions of Normalcy 267
46. Aspects of Creativity 273

47. God, Man, and State   278
48. In Praise of Impracticality   284
49. The Entebbe Rescue   289

Shavuot
50. There Is Religion and There Is Religion   297
51. The Torah's Mystery Man   303
52. Sinai Desanctified   309
53. Rise and Shine   314

Tish'ah Be-Av
54. When We Try to Keep God in His Place   321
55. The Veil of God   325

Epilogue   333

Index of Biblical and Rabbinic Sources   335

$\mathcal{A}$UTHOR'S $\mathcal{P}$REFACE

THIS VOLUME, CULLED MOSTLY from sermons I delivered during my twenty-five years as a congregational rabbi, and occasionally thereafter, came in response to the warm welcome that was accorded to my previous volume of commentary on the Passover Haggadah. That too was a selection from my *derashot* on themes that were timely. The current volume was edited by my dear friend and distinguished colleague, Professor David Shatz, who was personally present when the majority of these sermons were delivered at The Jewish Center in New York City.

I have named this volume "Festivals of Faith" because these festivals are all expressions of the faith of Judaism in general, each festival emphasizing a different theme of Jewish faith as explicated in the Torah and the Torah tradition. The festivals are usually biblically appointed times of *simhah*, of joy and happiness, and therefore are called *Yom Tov* (plural: *yamim tovim*), "a good day." A notable exception is *Tish'ah Be-av*, the ninth day of the Hebrew month of Av, commemorating the destruction of both Temples (and subsequently other historic tragedies) by fasting and other forms of self-denial. I included this day in a book on "festivals" because the biblical term for festival, *mo'ed* (which usually is a synonym for *simhah*, joy) is mentioned in *Eikhah*, the Book of Lamentations which is read on *Tish'ah Be-av* (Lamentations 1:15; and see *Pesahim* 77a). I will elaborate on the significance of this word in the Epilogue.

The reader will notice that I occasionally address my remarks to those who are not (yet) committed, although I imagine that the majority of my readers are well acquainted with the world of Torah and Judaism, of Bible and Talmud, of Hasidism and *Musar*. My goal is not to convert but to teach and explain and, in the process to learn something for myself – the true reward of the teacher arrives when he is forced to understand better what he undertakes to transmit to the pupil/reader.

I beg of the reader to bear in mind that these homiletic disquisitions were delivered over the course of about fifty years, during which some names or locutions changed in social and linguistic acceptability. Thus, for instance, the term "Negro" is now considered racist and must *never* be used; when I used it fifty years ago, however, it was considered acceptable, and indeed, there were no alternatives. The term "mankind" was used in the years the sermons were delivered, whereas in our time we would use "humanity." I have decided to keep these sermons substantially as they were delivered, with these warts included, if only for the sake of history. Thus, if any readers become startled by what seems like an apparent indiscretion, they may come to appreciate how idioms often improve with time.

I am pleased and honored that both Yeshiva University and the Orthodox Union have decided to co-sponsor this volume, and for this I thank two very good friends, President Richard Joel of Yeshiva and Rabbi Menachem Genack of the Orthodox Union.

NORMAN LAMM
December 22, 2010

EDITOR'S PREFACE

ANYONE WHO HAS HEARD or read sermons by Rabbi Dr. Norman Lamm is likely to consider that experience extraordinary. It takes little effort to identify the qualities that make the sermons so outstanding: the exquisite, often soaring language; the striking and pointed turns of phrase and plays on words; the elegant architecture; the cleverness and incisiveness of the *"vort,"* that is, the homiletic insight that generates the sermon's central message; the depth and emotional force of that message, its capacity to move and inspire; the range and variety of situations in human and Jewish experience to which Rabbi Lamm imaginatively applies his themes; the fluid integration of references to world culture and social phenomena; and finally, viewing the corpus as a whole, the rich diversity of themes and consistency of quality. What the written page does not capture, but captivated audiences, is Rabbi Lamm's fabulous delivery—its dynamism, drama, power, poignancy, and passion. No wonder his congregants looked forward to "sermon time" and were transfixed listeners throughout his twenty-five years in the pulpit rabbinate and beyond.

Rabbi Lamm began his rabbinic career in 1951 as Assistant Rabbi at Congregation Kehillath Jeshurun in New York City, and a few years later became Rabbi of Kodimah Congregation in Springfield, Massachusetts. From 1958-1976 he occupied the pulpit of The Jewish Center in New York City, until assuming the presidency of Yeshiva University. My family attended The Jewish Center after moving to Manhattan's Upper West Side, and we were present when many of the addresses in this volume were delivered. My work in editing this collection is an act of *hakkarat ha-tov* (expression of gratitude)—an inadequate but heartfelt way of thanking a man whose creativity and eloquence shaped my interests and perspectives from the time I was thirteen. In fact, my work on the book is a *hakkarat ha-tov* to many of the very sermons contained in these pages. Rabbi Lamm's sermons and lectures opened for me and others the world of sophisticated Jewish ideas, both their power and their beauty, and ultimately made that world my passion and profession.

I had the privilege of reviewing my initial selections with Rabbi Lamm and making the final choices with his guidance. (For me, one of the most memorable parts of the book's creation was hearing Rabbi Lamm's own comments about the individual sermons.) When deciding on selections, we were highly conscious that some of the sermons were set in particular historical circumstances: the civil rights movement of the 1960s, the Eichmann trial, the first moon landing, the early life of the State of Israel, the Entebbe rescue. Far from making the sermons dated, however, their connection to then-contemporary events demonstrates the timelessness of Torah, the power of our sacred texts to speak to what were then new and revolutionary developments—and hence to new and revolutionary developments in our own day and beyond. Furthermore, as the cliche goes, the more things change the more they remain the same. The challenge of preserving traditional values in a modern society; the morally tense pursuit of technology and scientific knowledge; the frequent eruption of brutality and inhumanity; the complexities of married life and child-parent relationships, and of youth and old age; the quest for a meaningful and inspired existence—these are always at the heart of Jewish and human concern, as are virtually all of Rabbi Lamm's other psychological, philosophical, sociological and historical themes. The sermons that address specific events are also of great importance in fulfilling *"zekhor yemot olam!"* (Deut. 32: 7)—preserving our collective memory. We learn from our variegated experiences—both present and past, this year's and those of thirty to sixty years ago—as we confront the daunting but enriching task of relating tradition to the modern world.

Some other features of this collection should be noted. *Mar'ei mekomot* (references) have been filled in, and there are minor changes in the text. Rabbi Lamm retitled certain sermons and supplied names for untitled ones. A few of the speeches, in particular those delivered at Yizkor and on Shabbat Hanukkah, culminate in appeals for institutions and organizations. Since as a rule the appeal continues the sermon's message, we have left those sections largely intact, thereby preserving the coherence and integrity of the address and preventing the text from ending abruptly. The reader should also note, as Rabbi Lamm explains in his preface, that because we seek to capture a historical atmosphere, we have preserved the vocabulary of the times even though language has evolved in a more refined and sensitive direction. Finally, after experimenting with thematic organizations of the material for each section, we decided to present each holiday's sermons in chronological order. An exception is a *Shabbat Ha-Gadol* sermon, which appears first in the Passover section although it was given after others included under that heading. The date of each selection is given at the bottom of its first page. Two recent selections originally appeared in publications of Yeshiva University's Center for The Jewish Future, and one address was delivered while Rabbi Lamm was the university's president.

Variety is a hallmark of this collection. As the index reveals, of the nearly 320 traditional texts that Rabbi Lamm quotes, only eighteen appear in more than one sermon (usually for different purposes and with different interpretations), and only one quoted text appears in more than two sermons. In addition, if one were to formulate the main moral of each sermon, the *musar haskel*, one would realize that virtually every sermon has a fresh message. Thus, while obviously some themes recur and there is a consistency of orientation, in almost every presentation Rabbi Lamm provides novelty—*hiddush*—as regards both text and message.

The sermons also exhibit the varied ways in which *derashot* can be constructed to lead up to their main message or moral. Some utilize the classic model of question and answer, perplexity and resolution, *kashya* and *terutz*. Thus: Why do we commemorate the re-consecration of the Temple by the Maccabees, but not its original building by Solomon? Why did Mount Sinai lose its sanctity after the Torah was given? Some speeches mine the symbolic meaning of contrasting terms or categories—consecration of the new month by *re'iyyah* (sight) vs. consecration by *heshbon* (calculation); priest vs. prophet; *pitttam* vs. *oketz* (in an etrog); novelty vs. renewal. On occasion, Rabbi Lamm develops an extended metaphorical application of vivid phrases in a biblical narrative: Elisha's dialogue with a panic-stricken woman, or the episode of the four lepers who enter the camp of Aram. He shows how laws can have metaphorical applications: laws about *sekhakh* and the *sukkah* walls, or about the lodger who must fulfill the mitzvah of Hanukkah lights, or about the placement of the menorah, or about finding lost objects.[1] Some sermons provide fresh twists to familiar idioms, some explicate cryptic *midrashim*, some explain puzzling laws, some interpret human psychology; all, however, in the service of a compelling *musar*

---

1. Rabbi Lamm writes: "Moral instruction is available to Jews not only in the Hummash, not only in Aggadah and Midrash, but, sometimes, in Halakhah. If we look closely and carefully enough, we will discover the grand themes of human destiny even in legal technicalities, profound human wisdom even in halakhic discourses. All it requires is imagination, a sense of allegory, some homiletic license, and a readiness to find beautiful insights in unlikely places" (this volume, p. 140).

haskel. These varied modes of *derush* (my list is not exhaustive) are all time-hallowed and venerable, but an awareness of the differences between them may heighten the reader's sensitivity to and appreciation of Rabbi Lamm's proclivity for diversity of format and focus.

✶✶✶✶✶

I am delighted that Rabbi Simon Posner, Executive Editor of OU Press, agreed to serve as Associate Editor of this volume. His meticulous work and sound judgment contributed to the book immeasurably, and working with him was a pleasure. Rabbi Menachem Genack, General Editor of OU Press, along with its Managing Editor, Rabbi Gil Student, and David Olivestone, National Director of Planning & Communications for the OU, all helped move the volume from conception to birth. We also thank Rabbi Daniel Feldman and Rabbi Yona Reiss of RIETS/Yeshiva University Press for their participation in the project. We are grateful as well to Bernard Scharfstein and Adam Bengal of KTAV Publishing for their characteristic cooperation, responsiveness, and congeniality.

Meira Mintz, as always, displayed remarkable efficiency, speed, dependability and skill in various roles—editing, locating *mar'ei mekomot*, checking proofs, and preparing the index. Rabbi Dov Karoll and Rabbi Dovid Mintz assisted significantly in reviewing the material and providing *mar'ei mekomot*. We also thank Professors David Berger, Yitzhak Berger, Shalom Carmy, Richard Hidary, Ephraim Kanarfogel, Shnayer Z. Leiman, and Joshua Zimmerman, along with Rabbi Mark Dratch, Allen Friedman, Rabbi Hillel Rachmani, Rabbi Dr. Jacob J. Schacter, Chani Shatz, Rabbi Tzvi Sinensky, and Rabbi Reuven Ziegler. Hilda Tejada of the Office of the Chancellor, Yeshiva University, provided valuable technical help.

The community owes thanks to Pearl Berger, Dean of Libraries at Yeshiva University, who some years ago had the wonderful idea of assembling Rabbi Lamm's sermons to post on the Lamm Heritage website at Yeshiva University, which enabled us to put together this collection.

My final acknowledgment is deeply personal. My brother Howard Shatz, Project Manager at Data Conversion Laboratory in Queens, New York, who of course also grew up in The Jewish Center and for whom work on this volume likewise was a labor of love, played a vital role in the book's production. Howard personally oversaw Data Conversion Laboratory's excellent work in converting the pdf's of the original sermon pages into accurate Word files—

a complex, painstaking process—and also edited several files himself to ensure accuracy. Working together on this project means much to both of us and to our sister Golda Reena and her husband Henry I. Rothman (who are among the book's sponsors), and would have meant much to our dear parents of blessed memory. In fact, Rabbi Lamm told me that he regularly typed the sermons in full partly because my father z"l and some other shul members requested copies. In a sense, therefore, *avinu ve-morenu* Meyer Shatz helped make this book possible, and we, in publishing the sermons, have closed the circle that he began.

Derush (feebly translated as "homiletics") is an art form. We hope that *be-ezrat Hashem*, the works in *Festivals of Faith* will edify and inspire a wide audience as it showcases *derush* at its very best.

DAVID SHATZ
December 30, 2010

Rosh Hashanah

AN ALTERNATE ROUTE TO SANCTITY

THIS EVENING, WITH THE prayers for *Selihot*, forgiveness, we anticipate and prepare for the High Holy Days, which are our Jewish New Year. The first day of the year, with us Jews as with no other people, is an occasion for *kedushah*, or sanctity.

The reason for this sanctity is twofold. For not only is the coming Rosh Hashanah the first *day* of the year, and therefore the Day of Judgment, but it is also the first day of the first *month* of the year. And Rosh Hodesh, the new moon, was always preceded by a sanctification by the Jewish court.

So that on this *Selihot* night, in preparation for the first Rosh Hodesh of the New Year, it behooves us to speak of the institution of *Kiddush ha-Hodesh*, the sanctification of the New Moon, the holiness of the Jewish time-cycle, the preparation for sanctity. For all our festivals, all the ceremonies and sacrifices and devotions, depended and do now depend on the beginning of the month as determined by the *molad ha-levanah*, or the first appearance of any part of the new moon.

Many years ago, before the preparation of the calendar by astronomic calculation, which was able to foretell every *molad* almost unto eternity, the Jewish court announced the new moon and declared the Rosh Hodesh *al pi ha-re'iyyah*, "by sight." This means that witnesses would testify in court that they had seen the appearance of the new moon with their own eyes. It was the era of intimate knowledge of God's world, when people would be witnesses to the birth of a month, and *Beit Din* was the godfather of the New Moon. *Kiddush al pi re'iyyah*: sanctification as a result of sight, of first-hand, intimate observation.

After the power of the courts was weakened, after exile struck at the roots of our people, a new method of *Kiddush ha-Hodesh* was introduced: *Kiddush al*

5713 (1953)

pi heshbon—sanctification, not through observation, but by calculation. It was, as it is even today, a foolproof method, intellectually conceived by using the tools of mathematics. No longer was it necessary, indeed possible, to perform *kiddush al pi re'iyyah*. It was now *kiddush al pi heshbon*, an alternate route to sanctity.

Now, I have no desire or intention to go into a mathematical evaluation of these two systems. But I do want to comment on the moral content of the symbols which *re'iyyah* and *heshbon* really are. What do these two represent to us, and what is the significance of the replacement of observation by calculation? *Re'iyyah*, observation, represented man's intimate contact with real life. The complexities and the superficialities of modern life were still a long way off. A Jew, in these early days, was able to be a good and dynamic and wonderful Jew even without being a scholar. He was able to feel and see and touch the life-stream of Jewish life. He was at one with the quintessence of Jewishness. Modern thinkers use a big word for this: They say that such people had an intimate "existential acquaintance" with the life they so loved. But then the trunk was severed from its roots; the Jew was uprooted from his native Jewish soil, both physically and culturally. He was in all senses suddenly in exile. Jewishness by feeling it, life by actual observation, *kiddush al pi re'iyyah*, was now only a glorious ideal. Life was becoming complex, the atmosphere they breathed was intensely un-Jewish, a thick pea-soup fog of strange isms and ideologies blurred their *re'iyyah*, their vision and powers of observation. And once *re'iyyah* was ruled out, the Jew had to rely upon a different method to preserve his identity, to remain loyal to his heritage. And so he followed another route on which to reach the *kiddush*, the sanctity of Jewish life. He utilized *kiddush al pi heshbon*, calculation, intellectual exercise. He wrote and read his profound religious experiences. If he could not quench his thirst for Judaism through *re'iyyah*, then he took to the giant tomes of the Talmud, where *heshbon*, calculation, the sublime intricacies of detailed logic, reigned supreme and gave expression to his innermost yearnings. It was *heshbon* which now gave sanctity and holiness to life. Once upon a time, a complete *am ha-aretz*, an abysmal ignoramus, was also able to be a good Jew, because he was able to see, to observe. Today *re'iyyah* is obsolete. How much Judaism can one contract in Times Square? Did the Hatam Sofer ever tread on the concrete of 34th Street? Was the voice of a young scholar expounding "a Rambam" ever heard in the chambers of the 42nd Street Library? Can one indeed observe Jewishness in Yankee Stadium or Manhattan

Center? If, therefore, *re'iyyah* is a thing of past, then *heshbon*, study, becomes the issue of the present and the safeguard of the future.

The Hasidim interpreted the *mishnah* in *Avot* (2:1), *Ethics of the Fathers*, similarly: *Da mah le-malah mimmekha*—know what is above you, what transpired in days gone by. *Ayin ro'ah*—once it was possible for a Jew to *see* Godliness in his everyday existence. Then, with the degeneration which is time's, that wonderful faculty was ossified, and instead came *ozen shoma'at*, the hearing ear. People, though they saw not, at least *heard* from those who had seen. But then this too passed, and a generation arose which neither saw nor heard. And to salvage what was left they resorted to *ve-khol ma'asekha ba-sefer nikhtavim*, they read books voraciously, they took to study and learning and tried to gain by *heshbon*, by intellectual inculcation, what they were unable to attain by sight or hearing. If the home is empty of something for the Jew to observe, and the streets supply him with nothing which he should hear, then he must turn to the yeshivah and the *beit ha-midrash*, to the *sefer* and the *heshbon*.

Two prophets beheld visions, and they clearly represent these two facets of Jewish life of which we have been speaking. The vision of Isaiah was a vision of *re'iyyah*, whilst the corresponding vision of Ezekiel was one of *heshbon*. Both beheld the *Ma'aseh Merkavah*, the vision of the Divine Palace, of Godly grandeur. And each, in his lofty prophetic ecstasy, enunciated his holiest and profoundest feelings at that time. These two statements have been incorporated by us in our daily liturgy, and in one of the most sacred selections.

Isaiah, who prophesied to a people living on its own soil, serene in its security, at a time when the Temple was still in its glory, saw a vision much different from that of Ezekiel. Isaiah saw a stationary, grandiose Throne upon which the glory of God rested. And *ve-shulav mele'im et ha-heikhal* (Is. 6:1), the corners of God's garment filled the palace. Godliness was everywhere evident, it could be sensed by even the most insensitive. It was an era when the reward and punishment ordained by God was immediately evident, so that when a King Uzziah defied the Torah and put his hand into the *Kodesh ha-Kodashim*, the inner sanctum, it immediately turned leprous as an open and unconcealed and immediate message that God was displeased (II Chr. 26). It was an era when *ve-ha-bayit yimmalei ashan* (Is. 6:4), the world was filled with the experience and knowledge of Godliness as a closed house is thoroughly filled with smoke from a fire. It was a period of intense and intimate *re'iyyah*, observation. And so Isaiah exclaimed, *Kadosh Kadosh Kadosh Hashem Tzeva'ot, melo khol ha-*

aretz kevodo (6:3), the entire world is filled with His holiness. Wherever you go, wherever you reside and whither you travel, God is to be experienced.

Ezekiel too saw a vision of the *Merkavah*, the Divine Chariot or Palace. It was an entirely different vision, however, for he preached in an entirely different environment. Ezekiel, first of all, did not speak to a people secure in its own homeland. He spoke to a people in exile, to the Jews in Babylon. He preached to a people who no longer were able to draw inspiration from a Temple, for in its place stood the heathen temples of Ba'al and Marduk. The Jews were then a people who were becoming thoroughly Babylonianized, and at best hyphenated Babylonians. And it was amongst such people that Ezekiel attempted to behold the vision of a *Merkavah*, a people whose "vision" was blurred, who had lost contact with the realities of Jewishness, who had forgotten the art of *kiddush al pi re'iyyah*. And even then Ezekiel saw the great sight; he too, like Isaiah, beheld a *merkavah*. But it was a different type of *merkavah*! For the vision of Isaiah was stationary, rooted to the healthy soil of Israel, where observation was still the mode of Jewish life. The *merkavah*, the chariot, of Ezekiel, however, had a new feature. It was fitted with *ofanim*, with wheels. For great visions were not permanent in this sort of environment. Like an ordinary chariot on wheels, which can go rolling down the hillside with one push, the Chariot of Ezekiel too represented this shiftiness, this ephemeral quality, this impermanence and transitoriness. It was not a trustworthy vision which can survive the vicissitudes of life. *Va-tissa'eni ruah*, the prophet's heavenly vision is swept away from him by the strange winds which blow so menacingly in his exile. A new cult of accommodationism and mode of sophistication has pervaded the atmosphere of Babylonian Jewry, and these strange winds carry away the prophetic vision of glory. The prophet now senses keenly the terrible emptiness of his people. They have lost their *merkavah*, their sense of Divinity. *Va-eshma aharai kol ra'ash gadol*, he hears a great noise, rushing in to fill up the void left by the vanishing *merkavah* (Ezek. 3:12). Nature abhors even a spiritual vacuum. Instead of the Vision of Glory, there is now only *ra'ash*, noise, empty prattle, meaningless shouting. The soft music of glory has been replaced by the grinding of machines, the hollow bellowing of "civilization." How tragic! The strange winds of the Exile have torn away the vision of the *merkavah* from the Jews, and they remain only with the loud noises of the then "modern" life—empty, hollow, un-Jewish. There is nothing left for the young Babylonian Jew to see, for the *merkavah* is gone, the sanctity of his Jewry is in jeopardy, and so, the prophet worries, there is no longer *kiddush al pi re'iyyah*. Yet Ezekiel does not despair. For if *kiddush al pi re'iyyah* has proved impossible, there always remains *kiddush al pi heshbon*; if his people cannot personally, by their innate powers of observation, *see* Judaism, then they must *study* it in order to live it. And so, where Isaiah saw the spirit of God filling the entire *Heikhal*, the entire land in its length and breadth, and exclaimed, *Kadosh kadosh kadosh Hashem Tzeva'ot, melo khol ha-aretz kevodo*, Ezekiel announces, *Barukh kevod Hashem mi-mekomo*, Blessed be the Name of God from His place. We must take to the "place of God," to the synagogue and the school, for if we cannot see our heritage alive in our homes and our places of business, then the *beit ha-midrash*, with its complicated *heshbon*, must be our source of Godliness. If not *melo khol ha-aretz*, then at least *mi-mekomo*; if not *kiddush al pi re'iyyah*, then *kiddush al pi heshbon*. And how interesting it is that this very same Ezekiel is known in history as the founder of the institution of the synagogue!

In our day, *re'iyyah* has largely failed us. Observation is not a sufficient route to sanctity. Looking about me in this synagogue, I feel happy to see the Jews who are here. But how less inspiring this sight is than it should be, than it was years ago. Remember, if you will, the *Selihot* of many years ago. We were inspired by our observations, moved by the tightly packed synagogue, stirred by the saintly faces of worshipers wet with tears, the tears of piety and the paleness of awe. We were pitched into the mood of sanctity by the plaintive sound of venerable men with patriarchal beards crying, *Al tashlikheni mi-lefanekha, ve-ruah kodshekha al tikkah mimmenni*, "O God, cast us not away and do not withdraw Thy holy spirit from our midst" (cf. Ps. 51:13). We felt the fear and awe of the season as sensitive women, trembling on the urge of oncoming old age, with its doubts and dangers and insecurities and dependency on children, wailed in prayer, *Al tashlikhenu le-et ziknah, kikhlot kohenu al ta'azvenu*, "Cast us not away, O God, at the time of old age, when our strength is spent, do not forsake us" (cf. Ps. 71:9).

That was *kiddush al pi re'iyyah*. We have lost that direct, intimate approach to the sanctity of the coming days. But there still remains an alternate route to sanctity—*heshbon*: the *heshbon ha-nefesh*, calculation of the soul, reckoning with the self, introspection: Where have I erred, how have I sinned, why did I not do my God-ordained duty? How can I better my actions toward my religion, behavior toward family and friends?

The *heshbon* of business—the calculation of honest accounting, of integrity in finances. And finally the *heshbon* of which we previously spoke, the *heshbon* of reading and studying and listening and thinking. The *heshbon* of prayer, the synagogue and school.

Your presence here tonight proves that you have found the alternate route to sanctity. Continue on it. Be with us on the holidays, on Shabbat, every day.

Let us hope and pray that God's forgiveness will be extended to us, that His sanctity will emanate *mi-mekomo* and fill *kol ha-aretz*, and that all of us and all of Israel will be blessed with a good, happy, and blessed year to come.

"What Hast Thou in the House?"

In the fourth chapter of the Second Book of Kings, we read of a most interesting episode in the life of the prophet Elisha, the famed successor to Elijah. It is a moving account of the dire poverty of our people in ancient Israel, and of the heart-warming response of one of the great early prophets.

Ve-ishah ahat mi-neshei benei ha-nevi'im tza'akah el Elisha lemor (II Kings 4:1), the widow of one of the young prophets cried unto Elisha, saying: My husband has died, and you know that he was a God-fearing man. And now tragedy has struck my family again: *Ve-ha-nosheh ba lakahat et shenei yeladai lo la-avadim,* the creditor has come to demand his payment, and because I have nothing, he wants to take my two children away as bondsmen, as slaves. And Elisha said to her, "What shall I do for you? *Haggidi li, mah yesh lakh ba-bayit?* "Tell me, what hast thou in the house?" And she answered, *Ein le-shifhatekha kol ba-bayit,* "I have nothing in my house," *ki im asukh shemen,* "save for one pot of oil." The prophet then told her to gather into her home all the empty vessels she could borrow and a miracle would occur: she would pour from the one pot of oil into all the others and they would fill up from it. This she could sell, pay her debt, and thus save her family.

Why do I tell you this story on this holy day of Rosh Hashanah? Because, as in all of Torah, I see in it not only a delicious piece of the history of our people in ancient days, but also a parable for our own times. I see in it the outlines of a stirring message for 1960 that ought to make us leave this House of God today troubled and disturbed, dissatisfied with ourselves and discontent, so that by next year at this time we can achieve a new and more elevated kind of happiness and peace.

The meaning of this parable is important today because this day we begin a New Year; because today we must each of us make a *heshbon ha-nefesh,* a

5721 (1960)

reckoning with ourselves. It is especially relevant on Rosh Hashanah because both our Torah reading and our *haftarah* deal with the great human question of one's children, of the perpetuation of our people and the future of our faith.

The widow in the parable, to my mind, voices a heart-rending complaint that many Jewish parents feel today. "The creditor is come to take unto him my two children as bondsmen." Who amongst us has not felt a twinge of worry deep within him about the Jewish future of his or her children? Who has not looked at his children and wondered if his own parents would ever have anything in common with them, if indeed he himself will have much in common with them? Who amongst us has not feared, that as we send off our children to college, they may return with a non-Jewish mate, that indeed, once the Bar Mitzvah is done, all contact with Judaism is ended? There are so many demands upon our children! We want to keep them on a high moral plane, but there comes the *nosheh,* the creditor, and demands our children to conform to the street—nay, to the gutter! You want your children to live decently, morally? No, says the *nosheh* called The Street; I want them as slaves to my standards. I will flaunt Kinseyan statistics before them, and from every billboard and every movie I will tell them that everyone is doing it. I will make them feel like outsiders and call them "squares" if they dare resist. Do you want your children to learn the virtue of happiness with their lot in life? There comes the *nosheh* in the form of the advertising industry and lays claim to your children's peace of mind. Henceforth, you must no longer be a *sameah be-helko*, content with what you have materially. I will create new wants for you, I will make you a slave to new needs, you will behold the Joneses and realize that you cannot live without a foreign car and cannot be happy until you too own an outboard motor boat.

You want your child not to be Jewishly illiterate, but how can you get him to attend a Jewish school, certainly beyond the magic age of thirteen, when the whole of society rises like an enraged creditor and with a hoarse cry declares that your children belong to it, not to you? Little League makes demands, music lessons come first, entertainment takes its toll, all of our popular culture stakes out its claims on the child first. Try to teach your child that the most important thing is to continue to be a Jew and that you would regard it as an unmitigated tragedy if he were to marry out of the fold, and there are forces in our society that will tell him that his parents are really bigots, that for one as sophisticated as he is, such ideas are nonsense, that we are living in a free country, that, after all, love conquers all. "The creditor is come to take unto him my two children to be bondsmen," modern parents cry together with the widow of ancient Palestine. As she turned to Elisha, so do we turn to the rabbis, to the synagogue, and we say: What shall we do? How shall we save our children?

But listen again to the exchange that follows between young widow and old prophet, and you will hear the echoes of contemporary life in that ancient dialogue. Elisha turns to the young woman and says, *Haggidi li mah yesh lakh ba-bayit.* "Tell me, what do you have in your house?" This is not only a request for information, this is a devastating accusation, a damning charge of parental neglect. Listen to her feeble answer: *Ein le-shifhatekha kol ba-bayit*—nothing, nothing at all; my home is empty, hollow, a vacuum. Absolutely nothing!

Elisha speaks to us today again. Are you worried about the demands on your children that threaten to take them away from you, to place them in a different world, to remove from them every last vestige of Yiddishkeit? Then answer this question: *Mah yesh lakh ba-bayit?* What hast thou in thy house? What kind of home do you have? Did your child ever see Jewishness lived in his home? Did he ever hear a *berakhah* pronounced over food? Did he ever see his parents open a *siddur?*

Indeed, *is* there a *siddur* in your home? Is a Jewish problem ever discussed at the table? Do you have Shabbat in your home? Is there true *kashrut* in the house? Did that child ever witness true love and mutual respect between parents—the sure mark of a truly Jewish home? Does that blessed union of Torah and *derekh eretz* have a welcome place in your home? *Haggidi li mah yesh lakh ba-bayit.* If you want to know why your children fall prey so easily to the creditors of society and street, first look into your own home and ask yourself how much Yiddishkeit *you* gave your child, how much you enabled him to learn by example. Parents who can offer no more than the limp confession of *ein le-shifhatekha kol ba-bayit*—nothing, my home is Jewishly empty, barren, sterile—have only themselves to blame!

Let all Jewish parents take note of this before it is too late: there is no magical formula for guaranteeing your children's remaining Jewish. A Sunday school will not do it, not even a Talmud Torah, certainly not a chat with the rabbi when it is already too late. There must be, it is true, a good, solid Jewish education in an adequate school. But even that will not do if *ein le-shifhatekha kol ba-bayit.* An empty house will breed empty Jews. A house hollow of Judaism will breed Jews with hollow hearts. For too long have American Jewish parents deluded themselves into thinking that by sending their children to school, and by sending instead of bringing them to the Junior Congregation, they can keep them Jewish. They seem to regard Judaism like one of the druggist's strong potions which are marked FOR EXTERNAL USE ONLY. Internally, they reject the prescription called Torah, and expect somehow that by rubbing in a bit of Jewish reading or storytelling externally, the plague of intermarriage and the disease of assimilation will disappear.

Our Rabbis told us that if we want to steer clear of sin, we must know what is above us: *Da mah le-malah mimmekha*—"a seeing eye and a hearing ear and all thy deeds recorded in a book" (*Avot* 2:1). They meant, of course, that if we realize that God sees all and hears all and records all, then we shall refrain from transgressing God's laws. I would perhaps add to that. If you want to stay away from *aveirah*, if you want to spare yourself the agony of alienated children and estranged grandchildren, if you want to assure the continuity of your Jewishness, then it is not enough to know what is *above* you—then you must also be aware of what is *within* you, in your very home. It must be so thoroughly Jewish that the members of your family will be able to see Jewishness with their eyes, hear it with their ears, and read it in your books. Judaism is decidedly not for "external use only." It is not only "above" but "within" you.

When I went to school, I studied French—but I never became French culturally or otherwise. I studied about Eskimos, but I never became an Eskimo. I studied Judaism, but I became a Jew only because I saw it and heard it and lived it in my parents' home. Had I not seen it there, then very likely I would have no more become a convinced Jew than I have become a Frenchman or an Eskimo.

Remember that when the young widow complained about losing her children, the prophet did not ask her if she bought them Bible stories or arranged for private lessons or had them join a Jewish boy scout troop or prepared a sumptuous Bar Mitzvah party for them. All he asked her was "What hast thou in the house?" Her tragic confession, "I have nothing in the house," made all other questions unnecessary.

Today is the Day of Judgment, the day each of us must answer for himself before our Maker. The Jewish tradition has always envisaged Rosh Hashanah as a formal trial, and we make many references to this in our prayers. Now in every trial there are witnesses. Who will be the witnesses either for or against us? Listen to what the Talmud had to say on that: *Avnei beito ve-korot beito shel adam hem me'idin bo,* "the stones or bricks and the beams of a man's house are his witnesses" (*Hagigah* 16a). The story that the bricks and beams of a man's house relate about him to the Divine Tribunal determines the outcome of the trial. Well, what kind of testimony will the bricks and beams of our houses give about us? Will they relate that they encompassed only a television set or two, but never a Jewish book? That they waved the banner of an antenna but never held aloft a mezuzah? That in their rooms there was many a cocktail party, but never any *Kiddush* or *Havdalah*? That hospitality within their confines was only for entertainment, never for charity? If we will not ourselves bravely face the challenge of "what hast thou in thy house," assuredly the house itself—the very bricks and beams—will tell the whole story. And if they won't, the destiny and future of our children will.

I hope that I have not spoken too harshly. I have not come to scold anyone, just to remind you. I speak to myself as well as to anyone else here. The future of our faith is much too important to treat it with kid gloves when we should roll up our sleeves and work with the sweat of honest toil. I would be less than honest if I did not say what I did, for I feel to the very core of my being that we shall win or lose the future not in the fight against anti-Semitism, not in approval of our Americanism by politicians, not even in the classrooms—but only in our parlors and kitchens. There, in the home, is where the future of our faith is being forged. If a rabbi fails to highlight the tragedy of the Jewishly empty home because of considerations of politeness, because he does not want to upset his people, then he might as well resign.

If I am honest with you, it is also because I am deeply convinced that there *is* a chance, and more than just a chance, for the future of Orthodox Judaism in America. It is because of my faith in you and my faith in the ability to live as a full Jew and completely participate in America and the culture of the Western world that I urge you to pay attention to your homes. For that too was the attitude of Elisha. I have been perhaps unfair to the young widow in the story, and so must remind you that she did have one thing in her house—*asukh shemen*, one pot of oil, which, our Rabbis tell us, she used to help the scholars and young prophets; it was used as a lamp for them at night (noted by Malbim in his comment to II Kings 4:3). She did not have much in her house, just this one little mitzvah—and that proved enough. With it, and with enough determination and willpower, she was able to fill up all the empty vessels, the *kelim rekim*, all that was previously empty and meaningless to her. We can do no less ourselves. Every one of us has some connection with Torah, no matter how tenuous; some link with Judaism, no matter how weak—or else we would not be here today. It is either High Holiday services or Yizkor or Shabbos candles or Yahrzeit or a kosher home or JNF box. If we have that, then we need not regard it as the last breath of a dying faith, but as the first breath of a new and vigorous revival of Judaism. It can be, not the end, but the beginning. All we need do is bring back into our homes all the *kelim rekim,* all the practices and observances of Judaism that we have abandoned as empty and meaningless and without relevance and significance for us. Let us try them once again, and let us pour into them part of the *asukh shemen,* part of the little cruse of oil that we *have* kept—the loyalty that we put into Kaddish or Yizkor, the warmth and love with which we kindle the Shabbat candles, the care and concern for the State of Israel and the Holy Land—and miracles can and will occur. Our homes will no longer be empty. Our children will thrill to new experiences and new beauty and warmth. Judaism will become not a medicine for external use only, but a vitamin for internal use, one which will make our families healthy in spirit and vibrant and vigorous in Jewishness. The loud claims of the *nosheh* will be stilled. The street and society that have clamored for our children's loyalties will be silenced. And we will be granted by the good Lord a year of health and blessings, greatest among them the blessing of knowing that our children and grandchildren are not strangers to us, aliens to all we hope and live for. *U-re'eh banim le-banekha, shalom al Yisra'el* (Ps. 128:6)—we will live to see our children's children continuing the same glorious tradition and handing over the same rich heritage to generations following, and peace will be upon Israel and upon all the world. Amen.

LET THERE BE LIGHT

ONE OF THE FASCINATING minor themes in our rabbinic literature concerning the shofar is that of confusing and confounding Satan, the devil or angel of evil. Thus, we blow the shofar all during the month of Elul *le-arbev et ha-Satan*, in order to confuse Satan as to when Rosh Hashanah falls (*Rosh ha-Shanah* 16b). Before sounding the shofar on Rosh Hashanah, we recite six verses from the Psalms, beginning with *Koli shamata*. The initial letters of these lines spell *kera Satan*, "destroy, or confound, Satan." And, finally, we sound the shofar twice, one series before the *Amidah* and another during its repetition by the cantor, again *le-arbev et ha-Satan*, to confuse Satan (see *Rosh ha-Shanah* 16b, especially the *Yerushalmi* quoted in *Tosafot*, s.v. *kedei*).

What does all this mean? Are we involved in a kind of game with the devil? Is this an echo of a non-Jewish mythology?

I believe not. I believe that there is a far deeper Jewish thought in these words, one for which the expression *le-arbev et ha-Satan* is a kind of poetic garment. This idea, of which shofar comes to remind us, is that we right-thinking, well-meaning, loyal Jews—that *we must not* be confused! Satan always seems to be better organized and more efficient. The forces of evil and tyranny on the international scene are usually far more effective and disciplined than those of democracy and peace. The Satan within each of us is usually far more competent and energetic than our *yetzer tov*, our inclination for the good.

For most people, concentration, single-mindedness, and determination are more prevalent when they are in the casino than when they are in the synagogue. On Rosh Hashanah, we are invited *le-arbev et ha-Satan*, to change roles with Satan, to confound him and, in turn, to learn from him the secret of how not to be confused.

Confusion is, indeed, the hallmark of our times. We are confused by the daily anxieties of existence, the senseless anguish and the seeming emptiness of life all about us. We are confused by the apparently suicidal inclinations of

5722 (1961)

world leaders, who explode atom bombs with no thought to the irreparable damage inflicted upon generations unborn. We are confused by the conflicting claims pressed upon us by the differing interpretations of Judaism, both those to the right of us and those to the left. We are confused by the clash of religionists and secularists in the State of Israel. We are confused by the strange kind of world in which our children are growing up—indeed, by our children themselves, their dreams and ambitions, their fears and piques, their paradoxical, ambivalent attitudes toward us—rebelliousness on the one hand, love on the other.

Those of the younger generation are especially bewildered. The intense competition of diverse doctrines and different philosophies for the mind and heart of a young person invariably leaves him or her deep in doubt and perplexity. Around his head there swirls a series of smiling salesmen, as if in some weird nightmare, each offering his product and clamoring for its acceptance. Which shall it be: Genesis or evolution? Moses or Marx? Determinism or free will? Shabbat or Ethical Culture? Neturei Karta or Ben-Gurion? Loyalty to parents and past or a clean break and new horizons? A generation is growing up that is genuinely confused.

Of course, confusion is not a good thing. Philo taught that "confusion is a most proper name for vice." Indeed, many a sinister crime in our society has been lightly dismissed as the doings of "that crazy mixed-up kid," as if confusion were some delightful affectation to be expected of an adolescent.

On Yom Kippur, we confess to the sin of confusion: *Al het she-hatanu le-fanekha be-timhon levav.* And R. David Kimhi, the great grammarian, tells us that the word *le-arbev,* "to confuse," is related to the word *erev,* "evening" or "nighttime," because then all is confused and dim (commentary to Gen. 1:5). Confusion is, surely, a darkness of the mind and heart.

And yet the person gripped in confusion ought not to despair. The fact that it is regarded as a *het,* or sin, means that it *can* be avoided or voided and banished. Confusion is often a necessary prelude to clarity and creativity. Before the world took the form its Creator ordained for it, it was *tohu va-vohu* (Gen. 1:2)—void and chaotic, all confusion. Only afterwards, after the darkness on the face of the deep, the *erev* of *irbuv,* did God command "*Yehi or*—let there be light" (Gen. 1:3)—and there was light! Creative thinkers or writers or artists know that immediately before the stroke of inspiration, there must be a period of *tohu va-vohu* and *irbuv,* of true confusion.

In this spirit and with this knowledge, let us think of how we of this confused generation ought to respond to the challenge of shofar to achieve clarity and emerge from our perplexity.

Three ways of emerging from this perplexity commend themselves to us. The first way is consciously to have a scale of values. There can be no meaningful existence unless one knows what is more important and what less so, what is right and what is wrong. In Judaism, this scale of values is not a matter for every individual to invent for himself. It is contained in the Torah. To know values, therefore, one must learn Torah. That is the first great requirement.

Of course, that sounds so self-evident as to be a truism. Yet it is not always accepted. I have more than once been exasperated in discussing this fundamental question of the values of life with young people who prefer to argue from a confusion born of ignorance, and who are dogmatically certain that they cannot be enlightened by Torah. It is remarkable how a single semester of comparative religion can qualify a youngster to pass judgment on religion without ever having to read the Bible, study the Talmud, or even glance at the inside of a *siddur*. So it must be stressed again: the first way to climb out of the web of religious confusion is to study Torah—not just to read a bit or discuss, but to study. After the *tohu va-vohu*, the chaos and the void, as we mentioned, there came the creation of light. Our Rabbis (*Bereshit Rabbah* 3:4) observed that light is mentioned five times in this portion, and they asserted that it was *ke-neged hamishah hummeshei Torah*, corresponding to the Five Books of Moses. Only through the study of Torah can there be that enlightenment that will form creative clarity out of formless chaos. Ignorance leads to a distorted scale of values and even greater confusion. Study alone can clear up perplexity.

The second way of banishing confusion also sounds deceptively simple. It is faith. By this I mean not only faith in God but faith in the soundness of your values, and faith that ultimately they will be clear to you even if now you are somewhat vague and do not understand them completely. You must have patience and confidence if you are to dissipate the clouds of confusion. When the psalmist spoke those glorious words of faith, "Even when I walk through the valley of the shadow of death, I shall fear no evil, for Thou art with me" (Ps. 23:4), he may have had our problem in mind. Even when mentally we walk through the valley of doubt and emotional perplexity, covered by the dark shadows of intellectual chaos, when our problems mount up on both sides of us like steep cliffs so that we seem dwarfed in a deep valley, even then we must not fear, for God is with us. Confusion *can* be cleared up by the faith that it *will* be cleared up.

Here we can learn a lesson from Satan, who always has faith in the persuasiveness of his case. The grafter is deeply convinced of the irresistibility of corruption. The unscrupulous advertising man knows for certainty that the shameless exploitation of sex will sell everything from cigarettes to convertibles. What we need is *le-arbev et ha-Satan*, to change roles with Satan and learn from him confidence in our convictions and values. We must not be diffident in presenting our case to the world. We must not so lack confidence in our tradition that we allow the spokesmen for Judaism to be not the genuine *gedolei Torah*, but outright secularists or half-assimilated political leaders. We must have sufficient faith in the irresistibility—and invincibility—of Torah that we will spare no effort in increasing the number and quality of day schools in the United States this year. During the year when we celebrate the Diamond Anniversary of Yeshiva University, our faith is doubly justified—and must be twice as effective. *Hashem ro'i lo ehsar*, "The Lord is my shepherd, I shall not want, or fail" (Ps. 23:1), was interpreted by one Hasidic sage to mean, "I shall never fail (*lo ehesar*) to know at every moment that the Lord is my shepherd (*Hashem ro'i*)." With this confidence and faith and patience, we can overcome our confusion.

Finally, in addition to obtaining a scale of values through the study of Torah and having faith and confidence in them, we must be prepared to live practically and decisively by these same values.

It is not enough to "have" values; one must live by them, or else they are meaningless. Just studying and having faith is not enough. One must act by them clearly and constantly. The eminent Harvard professor, the late George Foot Moore, once said that the difference between philosophy and religion is that religion does something about it. There must be a commitment in action. No young person—or even ancient person—can ever emerge from doubt or perplexity merely by pondering Judaism. You have got to take the plunge into the deep waters of the Torah and Talmud and actually swim in it, live it. You must experience Shabbat and *tefillin* and the striving for *kedushah*. You must practice *kashrut*, refrain from *lashon ha-ra* and *sha'atnez*. Unless you have tasted Judaism in actual practice, you cannot escape from your perplexity. You may study the doctor's prescription and have faith in his competence, but if you do not take the medicine, you will not get well.

In *Pirkei Avot*, we read that *az panim le-Gehinnom; bosh panim le-Gan Eden* (*Avot* 5:24). That means, literally, that a brash, brazen person will go to Gehinnom, whilst the quiet, shamefaced person will enter a more cheerful residence—Paradise. One rabbi, however, interprets this *mishnah* as a complaint rather than a prediction. Why is it, he says plaintively, that when it comes to Gehinnom, to doing evil and cooperating with Satan, we are always *az panim*, bold and decisive and brash? When it comes to Gan Eden, however, to good causes such as charity or attending the minyan or a lecture of Torah, we suddenly become *bosh panim*—shy, reticent, hesitant, withdrawn! If we are to escape the confusion of our times, we must be willing to live Judaism as decisively and as boldly as we ordinarily would be bold and decisive in indulging our own pleasures.

My words are meant for all people who are sensitive to the crises and demands of our times, but especially for young people who, in their first encounters with our bewildering civilization, still feel acutely and poignantly the anguish of confusion, the collision of cultures, and the impact of opposing standards and principles clashing head-on. To you I emphasize that you have in Judaism, the ancient-yet-new Judaism, values tested in the crucible of history and found to be durable for ages yet unborn. Throughout all vicissitudes, these values have been available to all who have been willing to study its sacred literature and discover its eternal light. Have patience with it, even as it has had patience with you and us for so long. Have faith that it will stand you and justify your loyalty to it. But above all—do it, live by it, make it an integral part of your life, now not later, today not tomorrow. That is what shofar tells you: *Ha-yom harat olam*—today is the birthday of the world. Today you create your own private world anew, and a great, noble, exciting, and meaningful world it shall be.

For those of us who agree with this proposition but who by nature tend to take their time and procrastinate, who promise themselves to think the matter through, but not right now, let me leave you with this one story told by R. Hayyim Sanzer. A poor village woman with a large family one day luckily found an egg. She called her family about her and beamingly told them the good news. "But," she said, "we are not going to eat it now. First we shall borrow a hen so that the egg will hatch. Then this new chicken will lay eggs, and they will hatch more chicks. When we have enough, we shall buy a cow, and by selling its milk, we shall be able to buy many cows, then a wagon, and then . . ." And then, to her utter dismay, the woman looked down and realized that the precious egg had fallen to the ground and broken.

Let us dispense with all the grand plans for the future. Let us put aside our well-intentioned promises and resolutions about how we shall pay attention to our Jewishness when we finish school—or when we are married—or when we have children—or when our children are grown up—or when we have retired. We must, like Abraham responding to God's command to proceed with the *akedah*, arise early in the morning. We must begin not later, but now, this moment, with an iron determination to emerge from our confusion and live by Torah. For if we wait, time passes all too quickly, and ere we know it, the egg has broken and the bubble of life has burst.

Ha-yom harat olam. Today is the birthday of the world. Today each of us must create anew the patterns of his life. With the clear call of the shofar, let us determine *le-arbev et ha-Satan*, to confound all that is evil and bring clarity to our lives. Through Torah let there be light—and may we see the light. Amen.

THE SENSE OF SHAME

WE MODERNS HAVE, TO a large extent, lost the ability to feel ashamed. Young people grow up with an attitude of sneering cynicism, and moral restraint is treated like an anachronism, an outdated inhibition. Shame is unknown. Our theaters and our entertainment places glorify profanity and immorality. But we are not shocked; we no longer have shame. Television, radio, newspapers, and magazines often publish the kind of pornography that once would have occasioned wide embarrassment and a public outcry; but today we accept it as inevitable, and no one is ashamed. People come to weddings in the synagogue dressed immodestly; Jewish organizations openly and aggressively flout the most sacred Jewish traditions; Jews, especially college professors, proudly proclaim their religious ignorance from the rooftops—and for all this there is no shame.

And yet, *bushah*, or shame, is an integral part of *teshuvah*, repentance or the genuine Jewish religious experience. Maimonides counts *bushah* as one of the fundamental aspects of repentance, the dominant theme of this holiday. It is mentioned repeatedly in our *Selihot* prayers and on Rosh Hashanah and Yom Kippur. If, then, we are ever to change for the better, if Judaism is ever to advance and Torah ever to triumph, the first thing we must do is recapture the ability to blush; we must relearn the art of feeling ashamed.

What is shame? Our inquiry is not merely for a dictionary definition. The problem of what it really is has been discussed by some of the world's greatest literary figures, psychiatrists, and philosophers. Allow me to present to you the findings of one writer who recently devoted a whole book to the subject (Helen Merrell Lynd, *On Shame and the Search for Identity*, 1958).

Shame is the feeling of a sudden loss of identity. Every man has a picture of himself as he likes to think of himself and have others think of him. When he suddenly stands exposed as something less than that, something inferior, not at all the kind of person he thought he was and others thought he was, when he

5723 (1962)

is astonished at how he has fallen short of his own ideals, when his own image of himself is cruelly jolted and disarrayed, and another, unpleasant identity is revealed—that is shame.

Shame is thus a reaction to the blow to our self-esteem, the discrepancy between our exalted view of ourselves and the sudden revelation of a lower, more vulnerable, and less worthy self. Shame is therefore relative to a person's standing in the eyes of others and, even more, in his own eyes. Mr. Average Citizen who cheats a little on his income tax is engaging in a mischievous national sport; there is no shame attached to it. But the elected official who won office on a platform of "honesty in government" and who is so apprehended—he is filled with shame. The college sophomore who cannot solve a differential equation may feel bad. The math professor who suddenly forgets how to do it is ashamed.

If you have a high image of yourself, then you feel shame when you fail that image. If you have a low image of yourself, shame is improbable, for your self-identity has not been questioned.

The root of the sense of shame is as old as the human race itself. The first human couple experienced it. In the beginning, Adam and Eve were naked, but *ve-lo yitboshashu*, "they were not ashamed" (Gen. 2:25). Later, they sinned—and they futilely looked around for something to cover themselves with, for now they were ashamed. Ashamed indeed: they thought of themselves as worthy, Adam as the *yetzir kappav* of God, the creature of God's own hands; Eve as the *em kol hai*, the mother of all life (Gen. 3:20). They inhabited Paradise; they were the most perfect of God's creatures; they spoke with God. Suddenly, rudely, crudely, they were shocked by their own failure, by their inability to resist a miserable piece of fruit—and so they were ashamed. A new and cheaper self was exposed.

And how wonderful and invaluable, how civilizing, is this sense of shame! For when we experience it, we are shaken by our failure to live up to the ideal picture of ourselves, and so we are compelled to change our real self, just discovered, and transform it so that it will conform to the higher, more ideal image we entertained. This, indeed, is the essence of *teshuvah*, repentance. That is why Maimonides teaches that after the sense of *bushah* or shame comes repentance, which attains its highest expression when a man is be able to say, "*Ani aher, ve-eini oto ha-ish*—I am another, I am no longer the same man" who committed those evil follies (*Hilkhot Teshuvah* 2:4). I have transformed my identity, my very self, my whole character, so that now I *really* am the person

I originally thought I was! No wonder the *Sefer Hasidim* taught that *ha-boshet ve-ha-emunah nitzmadot; ke-she-tistallek ahat, tistallek havertah,* "shame and faith are intertwined; take away one, and the other disappears" (ed. Margaliyot, #120, #350).

If, therefore, we moderns have largely lost the sense of *bushah*, it is not because we have a high opinion of ourselves. Quite the contrary, it is because we have too low an opinion of ourselves, because we have almost no self-esteem, no image of dignity to be jolted and hurt. Our sophisticated generation has been nurtured on Freud and weaned on Kinsey. We have been taught to expect the worst in ourselves. We have become conditioned to the beast in man, so much so that if we sometimes are confronted with a genuinely human act, we are surprised. Our problem is that we have so contemptible a view of our own inner value, our own moral worth and significance, that that which is mean and despicable seems to us to fit into the picture we have drawn of ourselves. And if there is no discrepancy, no exposure, no jolt, there can be no *bushah*, and hence there can be no impetus to grow and improve and transform ourselves.

The Sages taught (*Avot* 5:24), *Az panim le-Gehinnom; bosh panim le-Gan Eden,* "the bold-faced man to Gehinnom, the shame-faced one to Paradise." What they intended was not a prediction of things to come, but a definition packed with a moral charge.

What is it that makes a man an *az panim*, bold and audacious? It is his self-deprecation, his conviction that he deserves an existence of Gehinnom, that life is hellish, and nothing, therefore, can be expected of life, of man, or of himself. His self-denigration makes him shameless.

What makes a man a *bosh panim*, one who feels ashamed when it is right and proper and decent to experience shame? It is *le-Gan Eden*, when he values himself, when he cherishes his own soul, when he feels that Gan Eden—morality, decency, nobility—is what defines his identity and determines his goals and his aspirations.

What we need, therefore, is a greater image of our real selves, a clear definition of who we are, a nobler and more sublime self-identity. We must feel that our souls were hewn from Gan Eden, that our destiny beckons us thereto.

On Rosh Hashanah, it is this message which is taught to us by one of the three central sections of our service, and therefore one of the three central ideas of shofar: the *zikhronot*, loosely translated as "remembrances." This means not that God has a good memory, but that He knows us and is concerned with us, and that we are worthy *because* God takes notice of us. The shofar is the call which reminds us of our real self, the one we have all but abandoned. *Ki Atta zokher kol ha-nishkahot*, God remembers not only all those who are forgotten, but all those who choose to forget their selves, their souls, their divine image, their dignity and worthiness—God remembers you, He thinks each human being worthy of His notice and attention. For *ein shikhhah lifnei kisei kevodekha*, "there is no forgetting before Thy throne of glory." God brooks no *shikhhah*, no worthlessness, in His creatures. Every single human being, by virtue of being important enough to be judged by God on this *Yom ha-Din* before the divine *Kissei ha-Kavod*, throne of glory, has *kavod*, glory and dignity and value and worthiness, infinite preciousness,

Our Rabbis taught us that when people are *bayshanim*, shame-faced, capable of experiencing the sense of shame, then it is a sign that they are genuine Jews (*Yevamot* 79a). For when we realize where we stem from, what lofty origins we possess, and therefore what exalted potential stirs within our breast—that we are the *zera shel Avraham Avinu*, the seed of Abraham—then we will have enough self-esteem to be ashamed of our failures, when they occur, and so try to live up to our noble origins and our lofty destiny.

The sounding of the shofar and the theme of *zikhronot* answers for us the great and crucial question of our self-identity, the question: who are you? And the answer comes to us: you are the children of Abraham, Isaac, and Jacob, descendants of prophets and poets, visionaries and philosophers, builders of temples and martyrs for freedom, sages and saints, singers and seers. Their blood courses in your veins. Their marrow lies in your bones. Their dreams inform your ambitions. Their ideals permeate your literature. Their spirit vitalizes your heritage. Their lives are enmeshed in your tradition. *They are your real self.*

And how, therefore, can we react with anything but deep shame when we fail to act like Jews, when we fall so low that our daily lives are indistinguishable from that of a pagan: no blessing, no prayer, no kindness, no Torah?

We are, as the Arab prophet called us, "the people of the book." That is our *real* self. How, then, can we help but blush to think that we have all but abandoned "the book"—the holy Torah? That there are Jewish homes where years pass without a *Hummash* being opened up? That " the people of the book" spend communal funds on every kind of activity, but least of all for Jewish education, for teaching the Book?

Who are we? We are the teachers of morality to the world. We are the people who were charged on Sinai with those blazing words that have seared into our conscience: *Kedoshim tihyu*, "You shall be holy" (Lev. 19:2). How, then, can we help but squirm in shame when immodesty, unchastity, profanity, and vulgarity infest our social lives?

Who are we? We are a people who produced singers like King David, dreamers like Yehudah Halevi, saints like the Ba'al Shem Tov, a people distinguished by holy *tzaddikim*, people whose souls were caught up in a burning passion for the living God and striving for Him in a swirling flame with all their might and heart and soul. How, then, can we brook coldness, remoteness, smug complacency in the very midst of a house of prayer?

Who are we? We are the people who marched through the halls of history as the *am Hashem*, the people of God. Through every climate, every epoch, through all circumstances and vicissitudes, we held our heads high, for we were the priest-people, the *mamlekhet kohanim* of the world. We always were *the* teachers of religion. Should we, then, not hang our heads in shame that we have become known in this country as the *least* religious, the least observant, the most secularized of all people in this country? That the Protestants represent Protestantism, the Catholics represent Catholicism, and the Jews represent the Godless? *Elokai, boshti ve-nikhlamti*, as Ezra cried (9:6), "O God, we are ashamed and disgraced!" We who should be at the summit of religion and religious teaching and the advocacy of the word of God in society—behold how we are fallen! Shame!

Despite our failures and our frustrations, we are, essentially, a great people. It is a true image. Let us recall our historical *zikhronot*. Let this exalted image, in all its reverence and loftiness, be forever engraved in our innermost consciousness. Then we will know how to experience shame, *bushah*, when we fail our own image. Then that shame will help us rise to our true gestalt, to our true stature.

Haddesh yameinu ke-kedem—let us "renew our days as of old" (Lam. 5:21). And, having learned our true, nobler, selves, having regained the lost capacity to feel ashamed, may God grant that we never have reason to feel ashamed.

May God bless each of us and all of us with a year—many years—of *hayyim she-ein bahem bushah u-kelimah*, life in which, despite the high and noble and lofty image of dignity we have of ourselves, we will never have to experience the blush of shame.

THREE WHO CRIED

OURS IS AN AGE which has forgotten how to cry. Whether at Rosh Hashanah services or Tish'ah be-Av *kinot*, whether at a funeral or a theater, tears are conspicuous by their absence. Once upon a time, the *mahzor* was stained with tears; today, it is so white and clean—and cold. Not, unfortunately, that there is nothing to cry about. A generation which saw the finest of its sons and daughters destroyed in the most terrible massacre in recorded history; a generation which, the more it probes the heavens, the more it ignores the heart—a generation of this sort has much to cry about. How many people here today do not have their private woes, their secret sorrows?

It is rather that we have embarrassed ourselves into silence. It has become a style of the times to restrain our tears on the theory that maybe that way the pain will go away, that by refusing to display genuine emotion, the agonizing facts of our lives will be altered. But we are, nevertheless, human beings. And so the unwept tears and unexpressed emotions and unarticulated cries well up within us and seek release. What insight the Kotzker Rebbe had when he said that when a man needs to cry and wants to cry but cannot cry, that is the most heart-rending cry of all.

Granted that crying is an experience we ought not to deny ourselves. But is there not a difference in how and why people cry? Is there not a vast difference between the various types of weeping and what motivates them?

I believe there is. And Rosh Hashanah suggests three separate causes for tears, two that are vain and unfortunate, and a third that is heroic and constructive.

The three types are symbolized by three biblical characters, all women, whose tears are recalled on this holiday. They are the mother of Sisera, Hagar, and Rachel.

Sisera was a Canaanite general, leader of an army that was, so to speak, highly mechanized compared to the peasant people of Israel which it attacked.

5723 (1962)

26

This arrogant pagan warlord was defeated by the Israelites, who were led by Deborah. In Deborah's song of triumph, she paints the picture of Sisera's mother, usually overconfident, this time anxiously awaiting the return of her son (Judg. 5:28): *Be-ad ha-halon nishkafah*—she peers intently out the window, a nagging question burning within her; *maddua boshesh rikhbo lavo*—why is his chariot so late in coming, why do the wheels of his chariot tarry? She answers, soothing herself: My son and his soldiers are busy dividing the spoils of their great victory; they are splitting up the dyed cloths, the embroidered garments, the damsels of conquered Israel. But the delusion cannot last forever. The truth must emerge. Her son is dead. *Va-teyabbev*—the mother of Sisera breaks out into uncontrolled sobbing. There were one hundred sobs, tradition declares (*Tosafot Rosh ha-Shanah* 33b, citing the *Arukh*), and for this reason, we Jews on Rosh Hashanah sound a total of one hundred notes on the shofar.

A beautiful, compassionate story. A shining example of historical generosity and forgiveness—we relive the pain and anguish of the mother of our enemy. But were there no Jewish mothers who were bereaved of their sons in the same war? Was no Jewish blood spilt in our long history, no Jewish tears shed by grieving mothers?

What the Rabbis intended, I believe, was a moral of great significance: The mother of Sisera lived in a dream world. She refused to face reality and contemplate its bitter side. And when you live in a dream world, you must expect nightmares. She had imagined that her exalted position as mother of a successful conqueror inured her to pain and tragedy—that was reserved only for the contemptible enemy, Israel. She was guilty of an immoral optimism, the kind of outlook that characterizes the unthinking and arrogant of all ages. Hers was a strutting and pompous dream which collapsed under the weight of its own illusions. And this indeed is what the shofar and Rosh Hashanah remind us of: there is a *Yom ha-Din*, a day of judgment and accounting. *Al titya'esh min ha-pur'anut* (*Avot* 1:7)—do not go through life, says one interpretation, blithely ignoring consequences which you dread. He who sits on top of the world has no assurance that his world will not collapse under him. Absolute security is a myth. Life is not as certain, as guaranteed, as the haughty, unreflective mentality of the mother of Sisera lead her to believe. Beware of such vain and dangerous illusions.

Do we not know in our own lives the kind of mentality that discovers its smugness and self-confidence punctured only when it is too late? We see it in international affairs, as when our government naively assumed that Communism could never gain a foothold on this continent, so we neglected the masses of Cuba, we supported tyranny, we ignored the oppressed population—and now we have Castro and his Russian allies ninety miles off our coast. *Va-te-yabbev*...

The couple who neglect to seek advice for their serious problems, the man who ignores medical symptoms he inwardly fears, the mother who notices her children going off on the wrong path and says and does nothing—all of them lull themselves with false balm, assuring themselves that all is really well and nothing will be wrong. *Va-teyabbev*—how pitiful the tears that are so futilely shed when, later, there is divorce, and incurable illness, and a child gone astray. Broken homes, broken bodies, broken hearts—all in the inglorious tradition of Sisera's mother. Rosh Hashanah reminds us of this, tells us that nothing in life is guaranteed, that by ignoring danger, you invite it, and that better face reality now than cry vainly later.

Hagar was the second of the three who cried. We read about her in today's Torah portion. You recall that she was the servant of Sarah whom Abraham, at Sarah's behest, banished from his home. She took her child, Ishmael, into the desert, and when the water in her jug gave out, she cast the child away, pathetically saying she did not want to see him die. And *va-tissa et kolah va-tevk* (Gen. 21:16), "she raised her voice and cried." No attempt to save the child, no looking for an oasis—which factually was there, before her eyes—no real effort at changing her dangerous situation. She merely raises her voice and cries; it is the cry of desperation, a morbid, fatalistic pessimism. Hers is a "realism" that leads to resignation. Unlike Sisera's mother, she sees the "facts" only too clearly. Hagar beholds the great desert of life—and submits to it.

Rosh Hashanah reminds us of this weeping too. Just as it discourages us from harboring the dangerous illusion of total security, so it warns us off from the equally dangerous fatalism of a Hagar, the hopelessness that paralyzes all will and initiative. By recalling these tears, we learn to avoid living so that we too will be forced to shed them.

And how important that advice is. Take the matter of the danger to the future of humanity from nuclear war. Most of us are under the impression that the majority of people are indifferent to its ghastly possibility, that they never consider such horrors as real.

I believe, however, that the reverse is true. Contemporary man's attitude to the H-bomb is not that of the *em Sisera* but of Hagar. If they do not discuss it, it is because inwardly, psychologically, they have already given up and accepted it. They have surrendered and have the feeling that they are living in the end of time.

The results, morally speaking, are disastrous. If there is no future, then the present loses all value. If there is nothing to build for, there is nothing to live for. If death is certain and universal, then, like Esau, let us sell our birthright to fill our stomachs. If, as the cynics quoted by Isaiah said, *mahar namut*, "tomorrow we die" (Is. 22:13), then indeed, "let us eat and drink and be merry"—and forgo any serious purpose in life.

This, then, is the result of the Hagar mentality in its fatalism, its absolute hopelessness in the face of adversity. It is the type of mind which, seeing before it the *midbar*, is so overwhelmed by it that it stretches out and prepares to die with a whimper. And in that interval between despair and death, is it worth being temperate or sober or chaste or law-abiding or pure? The tears of Hagar and her whole frame of mind suggest a despair of which is born delinquency.

Both these approaches are dangerously wrong. A society, like an individual, which alternates between the moods of exhilaration and depression, *em Sisera* and Hagar, shows symptoms of moral mania and spiritual psychosis. Neither the one weeping nor the other is for us. Rather, it is the tears of a Jewish mother which inspire us this day.

The third woman who cried is Rachel. We read of her in tomorrow's *haftarah*, in what is one of the most moving passages and most stirring images in all literature. Jeremiah describes Mother Rachel crying from her grave over her children who are banished from their homes into exile: "Thus saith the Lord, *kol be-Ramah nishma, nehi, bekhi tamrurim*, a voice is heard in Ramah, lamentation and bitter weeping; Rachel *mevakkah al banehah*, it is Rachel weeping for her children; *me'anah le-hinnahem*, she refuses to be comforted" (Jer. 31:14). Here is a woman whose tears have moved history. Unlike Sisera's mother, they do not come from living an easy life and deluding herself into imagining that a day of reckoning will never come. Rachel lived a hard life and a brief one; she knew trouble and anguish. She sees her children going into exile and recognizes the bitterness of reality. But unlike Hagar, she refuses to bow to these realities. *Me'anah le-hinnahem*, she refuses to submit, she refuses to adjust, she refuses to accept exile and destruction as the last word. Her cry, her tears, and her protest to God are the characteristic of the Jew throughout all time. The Jewish soul beholds reality in all its ugliness but sets out to transform it. The tears of Rachel are the tears of a gallant soul who will not yield to the world but makes the world, though it take centuries, yield to it. They are not the tears of vain sentiment and self-pity, but of powerful protest; they are a sign not of weakness, but of strength; not of resignation or frustration, but of determination. The tears of an *em Sisera* or a Hagar are the end of their story; for Rachel, it is a beginning. To Rachel's cry there comes an answer: *Koh amar Hashem,* "thus saith the Lord," *min'i kolekh mi-bekhi ve-einayikh mi-dim'ah,* "refrain thy voice from weeping, and thine eyes from tears, for thy work shall be rewarded, saith the Lord, and thy children shall come back from the land of the enemy; and there is hope for thy future, saith the Lord, and *ve-shavu banim li-gevulam,* thy children shall return home" (Jer. 31:15–16). The Jewish attitude, symbolized by Rachel's crying, is one which steers clear of the extremes of ignoring facts and of surrendering to them. Judaism teaches, in the language of the Kabbalah, that the *it'aruta di-le-Eila,* the impulse from Above, or divine assistance, can only come in response to the *it'aruta di-le-tatta,* or human initiative. For God helps those who help themselves—and God help those who don't.

Has not this Rachel mentality distinguished the authentic Jew throughout the ages? Are not her heroic tears our saving grace even today? We did not rely on Britain or the United States or the League of Nations or the U.N. to take care of us, assuming with naive and idolatrous optimism that all would be well with us. We knew the harsh realities of creating an old people anew on a renewed land—with ancient enemies waiting to devour us. But Jews fought. They went into battle inspired by the tears of a Rachel who *me'anah le-hinnahem,* refusing to accept defeat, refusing to acknowledge surrender, refusing to submit to overwhelming odds. That is why *ve-shavu banim li-gevulam*; that is why there is an Israel today.

Fourteen or fifteen years ago, the great question was Palestine or the State of Israel. Today, two other central questions present themselves to us Jews, questions equally as significant as that of Israel.

The first is Russian Jewry. There is, at present, not too much we can do about it. We must recognize the brutal facts, the wily and cunning enemy we are dealing with, and the incalculably tragic results of a generation of Russian Jews denied any and all Jewish education. But we must vow never to give up hope. *Me'anah le-hinnahem.* We must apply pressure. We must talk of them and inquire about them. We must never despair, but rather prepare for their eventual release and return to the House of Israel.

But the second is one we can do much about—and that is the most momentous issue in the Jewish life of this generation—the future of American Jewry. Here the attitude we take can determine whether we shall survive and thrive or, Heaven forbid, eventually vanish without a trace.

If we adopt the genuinely Jewish approach of a Rachel, then there is hope for us. We dare not consider the complacent ideas of those who foolishly tell us that all is well and there is no cause for worry—those who, imbued with the same opiate that dulled the mind of Sisera's mother, are blind to the densely negative features of American-Jewish life: intermarriage, vast ignorance of the most elementary aspects of Judaism, a desire to mimic the non-Jews, and a growing vacuum in the lives of our children.

Yet, at the same time, we dare not take a Hagar-like attitude and assume that things are so far gone that nothing will avail. The pessimists are blind to the resurgence and growing independence of Orthodoxy; the spreading Jewish Day School movement; the growing and developing Yeshiva University; the flourishing Hebrew book industry. Either attitude—ignoring the problems and ignoring the promises, thoughtless optimism and hopeless pessimism—paralyzes all initiative and must result in national mourning.

Ours must be the tears of Rachel. Knowing reality, let us proceed to transform it to a better reality. Let everyone here decide to come to shul at *least* once a week instead of making a perfunctory three-day-a-year visit. Let every parent send his or her children to a yeshivah or day school or at least Hebrew school. Let every thinking adult leave this synagogue today determined to learn more about Judaism, about the Jewish people—about *yourselves*. Tears of determination, of *me'anah le-hinnahem*—the tears of Rachel—these shall save us.

Ha-zore'im be-dim'ah be-rinnah yiktzoru (Ps. 126:5). Those to whom tears are not the distillation of vain illusions or morbid resignation, but the dewdrops of creative moral heroism, they shall sow the seeds of hope with these tears—and reap a harvest of joy, of happiness, of *nahas* and unending blessing.

THE REVELATION OF MAN

ONE OF THE MOST POPULAR and beloved phrases in all of the *mahzor* is *ha-yom harat olam*, which we recite in response to the three times the shofar is sounded during the cantor's repetition of the *Musaf*. All the congregation joins in unison in reciting it warmly, lovingly, and reverently.

Yet there is something puzzling about it. For these words mean "Today is the birthday of the world." But what does the doctrine of the creation of the world have to do with shofar? In what way is *ha-yom harat olam* a reaction to the message of the shofar?

Perhaps we can understand it by referring to the only time that the words *harat olam* appear in the Bible—and that, in a radically different context.

The prophet Jeremiah had warned his people against engaging in treacherous power politics, and summoned them to a noble and decent ethical life lest their land be utterly destroyed. His reward for acting as a voice of conscience was that he was imprisoned, beaten, and tortured. Upon his release, he again warns of the impending doom of the nation, and, broken in body and in spirit, he utters a lament of despair which rivals in power and eloquence the greatest passages of Job. *Arur ha-yom asher yulladti bo*, he cries out, "Cursed be the day wherein I was born" (Jer. 20:14). If this must be my fate, if all my dedication and sacrifice must be so futile, then why was I ever brought into the world? Why did not God slay me before I was born; *ve-rahmah harat olam* (Jer. 20:17)—why was not my mother's pregnancy an eternal one, so that I would never have seen the light of day!

This, then, is the meaning of *harat olam* in the twentieth chapter of Jeremiah—for *harat* means not only "birth" but, more often, the conception and carrying of the child before birth; and *olam* means not only "world" but "ever," eternity. *Harat olam* in Jeremiah means the exact opposite of what it does in the *mahzor*. For the prophet, it means never being born, eternal waiting, an unending potentiality that never culminates in the creative act of birth and reality.

5724 (1963)

32

For the prayerbook, on the contrary, it means *ha-yom harat olam*, today is the birth of the world, today a new world comes into being, today we make a new, creative, dynamic beginning.

This is the choice that is given us as individuals, as Jews, as human beings on this birthday of the world. Each of us possesses wonderful native abilities and marvelous inner resources. Either we can opt for Jeremiah's *harat olam*, remaining forever with our greatest human treasures locked up within our hearts and never brought to fruition, like a child prodigy for whom a brilliant future is foretold but who never manages to translate his genius into real achievement, or we can joyously proclaim *ha-yom harat olam*, that today we shall express those capacities into reality, for today we shall fulfill ourselves by giving birth to a new and fascinating world.

And it is this, in truth, which is the response to the challenge of the shofar. For the shofar was once also a call for the liberation of slaves. Our tradition considers the words *shofar teru'ah* to be related to the word *tero'em*, and thus meaning "the shofar's call to break the chains and release the slaves" (*Zohar, Pinehas*). The shofar summons us to break the bonds of habit and indifference that keep our vast treasures locked up and our repositories of goodness and faith impounded within us, to transform the eternal waiting of Jeremiah's *harat olam* into the living immediacy of the *mahzor's ha-yom harat olam*. It is the call to release and emancipate our talents, our abilities, our greatness.

This year has been a historic one for the Negroes of our country. They have heard and responded to *their* shofar call. They have taken the decisive step from unrealized potential to a new and exhilarating reality. For the past hundred years, since the Emancipation Proclamation, all the vast talent of this great community has gone to waste. Who knows how many potential Einsteins and Oppenheimers, or George Washington Carvers or Ralph Bunches, may have been born, lived, and died unexpressed and undeveloped during this long and dark period of *harat olam*, of frustrated gestation of genius, of immense human riches always in the state of possibility and yet always coming to naught? This year, the community has decided to transform that possibility into actuality. They have announced to America: *ha-yom harat olam*, today we create a new society of dignity and honor, and even if we must lose lives of our innocent children, we shall break out of our stupor and enable our people to make their contributions to this land as freemen and the equals of all others.

I submit to you that what the Negroes have done politically, we Jews must this year do religiously. As the Divine Judge scrutinizes the records of each of us, I surmise that He will not find too many overtly evil acts that we have committed. For the major part, we shall have to answer for sins of omission. *Le-bohen levavot be-yom din, le-goleh amukkot ba-din*—on this Judgment Day, God uncovers the depths of our hearts and souls and castigates us for the inner goodness of which we were capable but never brought ourselves to express; the holiness that we could have brought to our society but somehow did not; the Word of God that struggled for release from within us but which we allowed to be silenced in the Jeremian *harat olam*.

For indeed, it is a fundamental teaching of Judaism that religion and faith are not something that need to be superimposed upon man from without, but already exist in the Jew as part of his nature and native character. The author of the *Tanya* spoke not only for Hasidism but for all of Judaism when he declared that each of us possesses an *ahavah mesuteret she-hi ahavah ha-tiv'it*, a concealed and natural love of God that strives for liberation and release (*Likkutei Amarim*, 12). The greatest talent of the Jew is his religion, his Torah.

It is an article of faith with us that in the deepest levels of the self there is a core of purity, of goodness. Beneath the cynicism lies an uncorrupted idealism; beneath the layer of envy, gems of generosity; beneath the crude will for power, the noble desire to serve; beyond the doubt and confusion, certitude and faith; within the disillusioned adult, a precious, hopeful, bright-eyed child; within the hard-boiled shell beats a soft and warm human heart.

Psychoanalysis has taught us that we hardly know what is going on in our minds. Judaism teaches us that we are usually unaware of the treasures we possess in the soul and the heart. Psychotherapy attempts to make us reveal to ourselves the subconscious. The shofar tries to make us reveal the subconscience. *Ha-yom harat olam*, today, Rosh Hashanah, we must give birth to that wonderful world of Jewishness within us.

Is not all of education, in its deepest sense, the attempt to bring out inner talents rather than just putt in external information? Do we not, as parents, constantly observe our children, looking for any creative abilities that we can help them develop? We notice a daughter who shows a slight flair for music—so we run to give her piano lessons, voice lessons, ballet lessons. A son demonstrates a knack for science; we buy books for him, enroll him in an electronics club, have him tested, purchase all kinds of equipment. And that is as it should be. Now Judaism teaches us that each and every child has an enormous gift for *ahavat Hashem*, a genius for loving Torah, for devotion to his people, for Jewish honor and dignity, a faculty for Jewish steadfastness. Shall we allow these rich endowments of their Jewish hearts to be abused by neglect, to die of malnutrition, to remain *harat olam*, eternally pregnant with the possibilities of Jewish greatness but never realized in real life? Or shall we assist them in expressing these magnificent creative abilities of the spirit? *Ha-yom harat olam.* Let us give them a Rosh Hashanah of a new life. *Ma'aleh ani aleikhem ke-illu nivretem beri'ah hadashah*, "I consider it as if you were reborn" (*Yerushalmi, Rosh ha-Shanah* 4:8).

There is something remarkable about the third of the three major sections of the *Musaf*, that of *shofarot*. It begins by relating how God, as it were, blew the shofar; the call of the ram's horn came from heaven. And it concludes on a quite different note: *Barukh attah Hashem shomea kol teru'at ammo Yisra'el be-rahamim*, "Blessed art Thou, O Lord, who heareth the sound of the shofar by His people Israel in love." Why the change?

It is, I suggest, because shofar always accompanies revelation, for revelation too is liberation—from concealment and hiding. In the beginning, the *mahzor* tells us that the shofar recalls the revelation of God at Mount Sinai, when He gave us the Torah, and that that event was accompanied by the sound of the shofar. *Attah nigleita ba-anan kevodekha*, "Thou didst reveal Thyself in a cloud of glory"; hence *u-be-kol shofar aleihem hofata*, "Amidst the blasting of the shofar didst Thou appear to them." When God emerged from within Himself, from His mysterious concealment which man could never penetrate, when He revealed His glory to Israel through the Torah, the shofar sounded. And therefore it was not man who blew the shofar, but God Himself who, as it were, was the *ba'al tokea*.

But now, on Rosh Hashanah, it is we humans who sound the shofar; He is merely *shomea kol teru'at ammo Yisra'el*, He listens to our shofar. And when we sound the shofar, then it is we who must reveal ourselves. That is what God tells us: Just as I revealed Myself to the sound of the shofar, so, now that you blow the shofar, it is up to you, O man, to reveal yourself! Let the call of shofar awaken your real, inner self, and reveal it for all the world to see. Let the shofar inspire you to tremble and to shake off the skin of sloth and cynicism and apathy which imprisons your idealism and spirituality, and let them emerge and stand revealed before your own unbelieving eyes! O Jew, *attah nigleita*, now *you* reveal your real self!

Never underestimate the Jewish heart. It is filled to the brim with sacred idealism. Never discount the *pintele Yid*—it is as alive as ever. We have all experienced at one time or another the wish that we could burst out in fervent, heartfelt prayer with *kavvanah* and *hitlahavut* and passion. Well, we can do it! According to Rav Kook, the soul is always in a state of prayer—*tefillah ha-matmedet shel ha-neshamah (Olat Re'iyyah, I:11)*. Shofar tells you to reveal that golden ability—*ha-yom*, today!—and offer your very heart as a gift to God.

What Jew does not possess the marvelous quality of *hesed*, of kindness and generosity and pity? You see a poor man stretching out his hand, and your heart instinctively moves you to help him. But then the other, external self intervenes, and you rationalize: he's probably insincere, he may be secretly wealthier than I. And so we silence our inner *hesed* and keep it in never-ending waitfulness, Jeremiah's *harat olam*. But shofar says *ha-yom harat olam*, today determine that you will be reborn, that you will give expression to those talents for goodness, and never, never turn down any request for help, for charity!

We each possess the precious quality of *ahavat Yisra'el*, love for our fellow Jews. During the difficult years of the founding of the State of Israel and its early struggle for survival, even the most alienated Jews showed the intensity of their *ahavat Yisra'el*. Yet today, we are in danger of keeping it locked up within us. If there is anything that shofar demands of us today, it is to wake up to our responsibilities to our fellow Jews in Russia. We dare not repeat the tragic error of our relative passivity during the Nazi destruction of our people. Why can we not assemble 200,000 people in a march on Washington? Why should we not storm the capital of every Western country to protest the oppression of Russian Jews, so many of whom this day risk person and reputation and livelihood to go to shul! Let us reveal our *ahavat Yisra'el* by resolving that we shall not rest until we have secured their civil and religious rights.

There is so much good in us that remains concealed, unborn within us, that shofar calls upon us to release. We are capable of deeper love for husband or wife, instead of the superficial sentiments that characterize domestic life today. We have a sense of loyalty, a knowledge that we should do more for and in the synagogue throughout the year instead of remaining strangers, alienated except for the High Holidays. We have quick, alert minds, curious intellects that we could and should use for studying Torah, attending a lecture, thinking of more serious matters. We each of us have a whole spiritual dimension that strives for birth into the real world of our personalities.

When the shofar sounds, let it become the prelude to a dramatic, momentous occasion in our lives. Let it challenge us to reveal ourselves, to break the chains of indifference and release the powers of holiness, of *kedushah*, that strain for emergence and birth. *Ha-yom harat olam*. Let us re-create ourselves, let us assist at the birth of a new spirit in the family, a new Jewish community, a new world!

Alah Elokim bi-teru'ah, Hashem be-kol shofar (Ps. 47:6). With the sounding of the shofar, let the Godly and the Divine within us emerge to new life, to new hope, to new heights.

If I Were a Prophet

Rosh Hashanah and Yom Kippur represent two great and eternal themes. Rosh Hashanah is the *yom ha-din*, the day of judgment and justice. Yom Kippur is the *yom ha-rahamim*, the day of love and compassion and forgiveness. *Din* (justice) is harsh, demanding, unswerving. *Rahamim* (love) is patient, gentle, forbearing. Both are aspects of God, and both must be ever-present in life.

Just as the two qualities are separated in time, with Rosh Hashanah emphasizing *din*, and Yom Kippur expressing *rahamim*, so are they incorporated in two types of personality in Jewish history; the *Navi* or Prophet, and the *Kohen*, the Priest.

While their functions sometimes overlap—in real life the *Navi* was somewhat of a *Kohen*, and the *Kohen* sometimes a *Navi*—in essence they are totally different; prophecy and priesthood often stand at opposite poles. The Prophet, as the man of *din*, is a radical: like Moses, chief of Prophets, he holds fast to his root ideals, and insists upon the complete and immediate application of his pure principles without compromise. The Priest, as the bearer of *rahamim*, is a realist: like Aaron, the first High Priest, he knows the conditions in which his ideals are to be lived, he appreciates the stubbornness of circumstances, the failings of flesh, and the frailty of human nature. The Prophet is the angry critic, while the Priest is the tolerant teacher. The Prophet summons man to God, while the Priest pleads with God for patience with man. Moses, the man of *din*, of justice, hurled at his people the historic divine challenge. Aaron, the man of *rahamim*, the fatherly guardian of Israel, practiced love and mercy and compassion—even while his people danced about the Golden Calf. In his passion for justice, Moses smashed the Tablets to bits. In his love and forbearance, Aaron picked up the broken pieces of his people and tried to refashion them into a self-respecting nation of God.

The rabbinate is heir to both traditions—of *din* and *rahamim*. It has historically been expected to combine both functions: that of Moses and that of

5726 (1965)

Aaron, of *Navi* and *Kohen*. The Rabbi, as interpreter of *all* of Torah, was expected to reproach his people and encourage them; criticize them and inspire them; judge them and love them.

Most of the time, *din* has been in eclipse. Rabbis have usually allowed the prophetic dimension of their vocation to be muted. They have in them much more of Aaron than of Moses; they teach, encourage, socialize, visit—but much less often do they raise their voices in harsh criticism or indignant protest. *Rahamim*, especially in modern America, brings more results than *din*. It is more attractive and also more effective. More is accomplished with friendship than with reproach, in love than in anger. Besides, prophecy is much too dangerous: prophets are usually killed by their resentful people.

Yet the Rabbi is true neither to himself nor to his congregation nor to his God if he eliminates entirely the prophetic element from his personality. Rosh Hashanah, as the *yom ha-din,* is the day that calls this prophetic dimension to mind.

On Rosh Hashanah, therefore, I wonder aloud, with you, about the great theme of *din* and the role of prophecy. Have I done justice to the historic blend of judgment and compassion, of *Kohen* and *Navi*? If I should don the mantle of the Prophet, would my people understand? Would I bring them closer to Judaism, or alienate them from God? What, indeed, would I say to you if I were more of a Prophet? What would I tell you if I were driven by a divine passion and had the fortitude to overlook amenities and ruffled feelings; if I were willing to ignore the consequences and to tell the truth as God has allowed me to see it; if I were willing to step on toes in order to elevate hearts and raise souls? Dare I, indeed, silence this spirit that agitates me?

Oh, if I were a Prophet! If I had the courage of an Isaiah and the fearlessness of a Jeremiah! I would turn to the higher social classes of American Jewry and tell them that they cheapen and vulgarize themselves when they nurture as their most powerful and most secret ambition to become Jewish WASPs, Jewish counterparts of the White Anglo-Saxon Protestants. I would accuse—without concern for this or any other season's fund-raising campaigns—many of our great national organizations of pious fraud for their myopic obsession with anti-Semitism and pleading with the Pope, when the really great danger to Jewish existence is ignorance and assimilation. I would thunder against those who have made of our *holy days* mere *holidays,* abandoning the synagogue during the most sacred festivals. I would be indignant mostly toward those who *do* come to the synagogue—who come and find nothing better to do than discuss the market or their neighbor's clothing, thereby desecrating the synagogue and making a mockery of Judaism.

Those are some of the things I might say if I were a Prophet. And they should be said, especially on this *yom ha-din*. But the Prophet is not the only authentic personality in Judaism. As a rabbi, Jewish tradition bids me incorporate as well the role of the Priest and find genuine sources of *rahamim*, of encouragement. *Hannah lahem le-Yisra'el*, do not be too harsh with the Children of Israel, our Rabbis counseled. *Im einam nevi'im, benei nevi'im hem*—they may not be Prophets, but they are the children and grandchildren of Prophets (*Pesahim* 66a). Despite all, we are God's covenanted people, the children of Abraham and Isaac and Jacob and generations of the lovers of God and Torah. We may occasionally fail, but we bear within us the genes and chromosomes of spiritual greatness. Every cell in our body contains a summary of Jewish history, a recapitulation of generations of Jewish nobility. Some of us may aspire to be Jewish WASPs, but most of us would love to be better Jews if only we were a bit stronger. It is true that we should spend many times more on education than on defense against anti-Semitism; but who can blame Jews who are still frightened only one generation after Auschwitz? Yes, people desecrate the service by their foolish conversations, but as long as they come, maybe they will learn and mature. *Hannah lahem le-Yisra'el*—let us be happy over, and not too critical of, our fellow Jews! They can certainly be redeemed!

If I were possessed only of *din*, I would castigate all those who pay tribute to Judaism and then arrogate to themselves the honorific title of "a good Jew"— the *shomer Shabbat* who is delinquent in *tzedakah;* the philanthropist who has abandoned the Sabbath; the Jew who comes to the synagogue only rarely and feels that he has thereby done his duty; and the Jew who comes daily but is a failure in *middot*, in character, forgetting that God demands clean hands and a pure heart. I would repeat to them the abrasive words of the Prophet Isaiah: *Mi bikkesh zot mi-yedkhem remot hatzerai,* "who asked this of you, that you trample My courtyard underfoot?" (Is. 1:12); that you act disloyally in home and marketplace and then dare to invade the sacred precincts of the House of God with spiritual smugness and self-righteousness!

But I am not a Prophet, I am a rabbi, and have been taught that God combines *din* and *rahamim*, and that man must do likewise. I therefore prefer to address to them the words of the psalmist: *Barukh ha-ba be-shem Hashem, berakhnukhem mi-beit Hashem* (Ps. 118:26); no matter who you are, how infrequently you come, how badly you have failed to measure up to your Jewish destiny, if you come in the right spirit, then blessed be he who comes in the name of the Lord; we bless you from the House of the Lord—bless you and welcome you most cordially, and invite you to come again and again and again. For you are our brothers and sisters, and we are all children of our Heavenly Father. No child of God is ever rejected, ever unwelcome, in the House of God.

If I were a Prophet, I would thunder against Jewish writers who see nothing but ugliness in Jewish life; against Jews with Jewish-sounding names who seek to subvert all decent society by being the chief purveyors of pornography and smut; against Jews who do not shrink from becoming slumlords; against Jewish groups that sponsor banquets serving foods that are abominations in the eyes of God; against Jewish parents who have been derelict in their duty and have raised a generation of uninspired self-centered materialists. A recent survey of college students reveals that most Catholics and half the Protestants regard as their highest ambition to serve God and their church—whereas most Jewish students consider their greatest goals the achievement of economic security and advancing their careers. No God, no Torah, no Israel, no mankind! All they can do is repeat that dull litany of selfishness, centered about the unholy trinity of I-Me-and-Myself. I would say, with Isaiah, *Hashmen lev ha-am ha-zeh* (Is. 6:10), the heart of this people is coarse, its spirit dead, its eyes blind, its soul insensitive.

The Prophet, in his passion for justice, sees all the faults and the failings. But spiritual leadership embraces the functions of both *mokhiah* and *melammed zekhut,* the critic and the defender; and the element of *rahamim* and priesthood lets me see redeeming features too. I cannot condone what the Prophet in me repudiates, what I know is unjust, in violation of *din.* But I know that this is a rootless generation, whose Jewish education was sorely neglected; that it is not in conscious revolt against God, but only acting out its ignorance imposed upon it by the past. Its sins are *shogeg,* unwitting errors, not *mezid,* malicious rejection of God and Torah. I see certain sanguine, positive factors: a marvelously generous generation that, despite its professed egotism, has created a United Jewish Appeal and Joint Distribution Committee; idealists who help underdeveloped countries and volunteer to assist backward peoples; Jews who have little idea what Torah is all about and yet give unstintingly to *yeshivot* whose functions and significance they do not truly comprehend. With the Sages of Israel, I see them as *rahamanim benei rahamanim,* merciful and compassionate people. And this compassion and goodness confirm me in my optimism and confidence about the *Jewish* future of Jews! R. Elimelekh of Lizensk offered this comment on a well-known verse from the Twenty-third Psalm (23:6), *Akh tov va-hesed yirdefuni kol yemei hayyai, ve-shavti be-beit Hashem le-orekh yamim,* usually translated, "Surely goodness and mercy shall follow me all the days of my life, and I shall dwell in the House of the Lord forever." The word *yirdefuni,* R. Elimelekh said, means not "follow," but "pursue" or "drive"; and "goodness and mercy" refers not to pleasant things happening to me from without, which would make this a plea for the soft life, but the goodness and mercy we possess within ourselves. This, then, is the meaning of the verse: surely the goodness and mercy that are within us, the benevolence and decency and charitableness that distinguish the "Jewish heart," these will drive and inspire the Jew to dwell in the House of the Lord forever, to return fully and completely to God and Torah and synagogue!

But this is not merely a professional dilemma for rabbis; for the rabbi is nothing more than a teacher. It is the Torah itself which speaks to us in two voices—that of the *Navi* and *din,* and that of the *Kohen* and *rahamim.* Some of us respond better to the direct remonstrance of the Prophet, others to the fatherly plea of the Priest. Both are the authentic voices of Judaism. Were there only the unconditional demand of *din,* some might be shocked into resentment and despair, and totally alienated from God. Were there only the gentle plea of *rahamim,* others might be lulled into paralyzing complacency, smugness, and self-righteousness. Few can bear only the white heat of the *Navi;* none ought to be exposed only to the pink cloud of the *Kohen.*

God has given us two ears; let us open both, one to the bitter but vital truths taught by the *Navi,* the other to the encouraging and patient coaxing of the *Kohen.* Indeed, let us listen with both ears to the call of the shofar. For it denotes two different themes—and both are valid and relevant.

The Prophet urges us to hide in fear and trembling at the mighty sound of the ram's horn. How did the Prophet Amos put it: *Im yittaka shofar ba-ir, ve-ha-am lo yeheradu,* "shall the shofar be sounded and the people remain unafraid?" (Amos 3:6). As surely as the sound of the shofar brought down the walls of Jericho, so the *teru'ah* today strips us before God, rips off our disguises, tears away our vacuous excuses for trying to avoid our Maker, exposes our sham to the searing light of justice, and leaves us like Adam and Eve in Eden—uncovered, ashamed, afraid, and embarrassed, as the voice of God, in the form of the shofar, thunders deafeningly in our conscience: *Ayyekkah*—where art thou? What have you done with your life? Where are you going? What is your purpose? When you were a youngster, you had great, idealistic dreams; what happened to them? Why do you flee your destiny? As we stand before God on this *yom ha-din,* the shofar should send a shiver down every spine as it confronts us with the truth we have been evading.

But there is also a view of the shofar that accords with the other tradition—that of compassion and gentleness. The shofar represents not only the awesome demand of the Lord, but also the sound of weeping—of God, as it were, crying! *Be-mistarim tivkeh nafshi,* "in the secret places doth My soul weep" (Jer. 13:17), says the Lord. Why does He weep? The great Hasidic teacher, the Maggid of Mezeritsch, once met his young grandson who was crying. "Why do you cry, my child?" he asked the youngster. "Because, grandfather, I was playing hide-and-seek with my friend, and I was hiding and waited and waited and waited—but my friend never came to look for me." "Ah," said the Maggid, "that is why God too weeps. For He waits for us to seek Him out, and He waits and waits and waits . . . and we, His children, fail to search for Him."

Be-mistarim tivkeh nafshi—the shofar is the weeping voice of God, who waits vainly, in His secret places, for us to look for Him. That is the shofar—God is not angry, but sad, pleading with us to put aside our distracting trivialities, our foolish preoccupations, and lovingly to look for Him, not to disappoint Him; for if we look, He will let Himself be found.

The shofar means both things; both must penetrate our hearts. Which will be more effective depends upon the individual constitution of each of us. But we must listen to both with all our hearts and with all our souls.

We stand at the brink of a New Year, a new life, a new world. The Prophet commands us to be loyal *avadim,* servants of the divine Judge. The Priest urges us to act like loving *banim la-Makom,* children of our Heavenly Father. It depends upon each individual whether he will react as servant or as son; whether aroused by the shofar as a mighty blast, or attracted by the shofar as a divine sobbing; whether we respond to the steel of *din* or the velvet of *rahamim.*

Ha-yom harat olam, today a new world is born; the destiny of each of us is decided anew. *Im ke-banim, im ka-avadim*: some will go forth from this day as *children* of our Heavenly Father, coaxed by the *rahamim* and tenderness of the *Kohen;* and others will walk fearlessly, driven to obey the will of the divine King as His *servants,* challenged by the ideals of justice of the *Navi.* Each of us must resolve this fateful day to answer the call of God, whether it is addressed to us in the majestic and awesome idiom of the Prophet or the patient and encouraging accents of the Priest.

And we in turn, in both capacities, implore God for a blessed New Year. *Avinu malkenu,* God is both our loving Father and our just King; *im ke-banim, rahamenu ke-rahem av al banim,* if we be like children to Thee, then treat us lovingly, as befits a Father; *ve-im ka-avadim, einenu lekha teluyot ad she-te-hanenu ve-totzi ka-or mishpatenu*—if we be servants to Thee, O divine King, we look to Thee for a judgment as clear and as shining as light itself. In either case and in both cases, bless us with a year of personal happiness and universal justice, a year of dedication to both peace and truth, a year of joy and gladness for us, for all Israel, and for all the world.

THE GREATEST TRIAL

IN THE STORY OF the *akedah*, we read that after the angel of the Lord had stayed the hand of Abraham and Isaac was released from his bonds on the altar, the angel declared: *Attah yadati ki yerei Elokim attah*, "Now I know that you are a God-fearing man" (Gen. 22:12). Rabbi Menahem Mendel of Kotzk, one of the most profound and mysterious of the Polish Hasidic leaders, asks: why the emphasis on *attah*, "now"? If the binding of Isaac at the *akedah* was the act of sacrifice that marked Abraham as a *yerei Elokim*, then the statement *attah yadati* should have come earlier in the narrative, when Abraham bound his son. Is it not out of place "now" that Isaac has been saved?

The answer of the Kotzker is nothing short of amazing, even shocking. He says that to take Isaac off the altar was many times harder for Abraham than to offer him up in the first place! It was more painful for Abraham to release Isaac than it was to bind him—and that is why the angel said *attah yadati*—only now do I know that you are really a *yerei Elokim*.

What can the Kotzker Rebbe mean by this? Certainly not that Abraham had any special pleasure in sacrificing Isaac! To cast Abraham in the role of an idealistic sadist or masochist is to misread and undo the entire meaning of the *akedah*.

Rather, the Kotzker here presents us with a new interpretation of the *akedah*, one which teaches an awesome psycho-spiritual insight. It is the nature of man, once he has taken a clear position in life, especially if he has suffered for it, not to retreat from it, but to mold the future along the doctrines of the past in order to vindicate his past. It is part of our normal psychology: when we have invested time and energy, loyalty and commitment, prestige and reputation in a certain approach, we do not want to change, we cannot change, lest we thereby declare that our entire past has been invalid and inauthentic. Self-justification of our past dictates our future.

5730 (1969)

Consider what Abraham had to invest in his initial decision to offer up his son. He had to overcome such enormous inhibitions in order to bring Isaac up on the altar. The Rabbis describe the inhuman anguish that Father Abraham had to undergo between the divine commandment and the actual binding on the altar. In those three days, he lived through three hundred years. This was his entire posterity, his beloved Isaac—and the Lord who had promised him that his seed would occupy his land now ordered him to destroy this child with his very hands! What greatness, what enormous and even inhuman devotion was required of Abraham. He had to cut out a whole part of his heart, he had to subdue the tenderest, gentlest, most powerful love—in order to obey what seemed to be such a cruel demand of his Lord. In his mind's eye, Abraham saw his son dead over and over again. As he made his way up the mountain, he rehearsed the bloody scene a thousand times. His mind ached and his heart burst and his nerves threatened to snap from the death screams of his own child, which he anticipated in such unspeakable agony. This was his beloved Isaac, and he was a warm and compassionate father, and now he had to subdue his most powerful natural instincts.

Yet Abraham followed the dictates of God and sacrificed the love of a father's heart. The love of God demands that every other love be subservient to it. And so Abraham invested in his momentous decision every fiber of his humanity and his very being. And once he had decided on his path, that was that. Having made his decision, Abraham was no longer the same man. He aged, and was now, in his own image of himself, an old and bereft father, whose light of his life had been extinguished. He cut a tragic figure in the halls of history, a man who had to choose between family and faith, between God and son, and, having chosen, would never sleep soundly again.

This, then, was what was involved in Abraham's submission to the divine command to sacrifice Isaac. At this time, after having made that historic, heart-rending, and soul-wrenching psychological decision—at this point, when Abraham held up his hand holding the knife above Isaac, he had, in the reality of his heart and mind, already sacrificed his son at the *akedah*. The pain, the suffering, the renunciation, the conflict—all of it was over. Only the anticlimax of the actual physical act remained to be done. And now, after all this, to be told to cease, because it was only a trial, a show, would have meant invalidating all that he had done, his anguish and his fear, his commitment and his pain—and especially his renunciation of his love for his child. When now the angel suddenly told him to stay his hand, he in effect told him: Abraham, you gave up that boy's life too quickly; morally, you already spilled the child's blood—and it was not really necessary. You marked yourself as a murderer in the name of a higher cause, and, after all that, you are not even going to receive the reward of knowing that your sacrifice was a real one. Who would have blamed Abraham for turning to God and saying: "God, are You playing games with me? Once I had decided to raise my hand over the *akedah*, to stretch out my hand against my son, the entire story was over for me. Couldn't You have told me before that it was only a game? Why, in Heaven's name, did You force me into a sacrifice of heroism, and then pull back and reduce a sacred drama to a pretentious gesture?" To be told to release Isaac at the last moment could very well have meant that Abraham, in his own eyes, would henceforth be the eternal fool: the man who hallucinated about God, the man who was ready to do something which he thought noble but which now seemed terrible, the man who was haunted and pursued by Heaven itself, telling him that his great sacrifice was unwanted by God, unnecessary, and therefore pointless. The angel's command not to sacrifice Isaac meant that Abraham must be prepared to embrace the role in history of a confused old man rather than, as Kierkegaard called him, the "Knight of Faith."

So it was inhumanly difficult for Abraham to invalidate his past, to risk making his whole life illegitimate—how much easier and more natural to convince himself that the angel's voice was the temptation of his fatherly love, or Satan, or his inner resistance to the divine command. But Abraham was a *yerei Elokim*, a God-fearing man. And a God-fearing man does not look to his own investment, to his own reputation, to his own sacrifice; he cares only about the will of God. He is willing to surrender the justification of his past conduct and start all over again. No matter how much pain and pride he had invested in the past, he is willing to declare it bankrupt and change. Abraham's greatness is thus more evident in obeying the angel's command to stay his hand than in God's command to sacrifice Isaac. His *not* sacrificing Isaac marks him truly as the Knight of Faith.

The Kotzker was right: binding Isaac on the altar was the act of *akedat Yitzhak*, the sacrifice of Isaac; taking him off was the act of *akedat Avraham*, the sacrifice of Abraham.

Perhaps that is why this portion is read on Rosh Hashanah—not only because tradition ascribes the event of the *akedah* to Rosh Hashanah, but because Rosh Hashanah is the time of *teshuvah*, and repentance implies the invalidation of one's ego, the confession that my past cannot and will not be justified, the admission that all that I have done and been until now is null and void. For this, indeed, is what Abraham had to do when he obeyed the voice of the angel to release Isaac: he had to say, "My enormous sacrifice of offering him up in the first place was null and void. My self-image as a heroic, tragic figure is an error. I submit to the crushing of my ego."

The shofar, symbol of the *akedah*, has ever since been the chilling summons to us to forgo self-justification, to renounce the vindication of a life in which we have built powerful superstructures on shifting sands and uncertain foundations. To say, "I was wrong, I'm willing to start all over again, to abandon my self-image, to declare myself in error, even bankrupt"—that is the greatest trial, even greater than the sacrifice of one's greatest love. But it is a challenge we cannot escape, either individually or collectively.

This affliction of self-justification hampers us at almost every juncture of life. As a rabbi who does counseling as part of his professional duties, I can say that, objectively speaking, most of the personal problems brought to my attention can be solved fairly simply. Logically, many are open-and-shut cases. What causes most of the difficulty is self-justification. A wayward husband or wrongheaded parent or child or contentious brother has followed one policy or way so long that to change would call into question his past wisdom and judgment and invalidate his character and conduct and "image" and reputation. So he decides to spend his energy perpetuating the same mistake, elevating an error to a philosophy and stubbornness to policy, and getting deeper into the same mess, because he hasn't the courage to change. But that is precisely the message of the shofar and the *akedah* it symbolizes: *attah yadati ki yerei Elokim attah*— true character requires the courage to admit that, despite your best intentions, you were wrong, and now must redirect your course of life.

Our failure to do just that is probably the major cause of our great national agony, the most humiliating episode in American history—the Vietnam War. No diabolical industrial-military complex gathered in some Pentagon basement to involve us in a bloody Asian land war. We stumbled into it, bit by bit. And then, when we realized what we had gotten into, when the public became aroused, there was a point at which we could have gotten out, but we found we did not have the courage of Abraham. We began to justify our past decisions, we threw in good money after bad money; new young lives were sacrificed on the Asian *akedah* because we would not respond to the angel's call to stay our hand, retract, and cease forthwith. So more than one father and mother is bereaved as a result.

And now, as citizens of this country, we must not shrink from another moral obligation. We must insist to our leaders that any further enormous investments in manned-landing programs in space be thoroughly debated before we stumble into it simply because the apparatus and capability exist and because not to do it would call into question the completed moon landing. It is too late now to argue whether the Man on the Moon program was worth it—ten years in which we spent $24 billion, 10 percent of our national budget, on a project of questionable scientific value (the "manned" aspect), and a decade during which we have suffered through a long Far Eastern war, a quick Middle Eastern war, several major political assassinations, student uprisings, urban crisis, racial unrest, youth rebelliousness, a sex revolution, and a runaway economy. Perhaps some will agree with the president that the landing on the moon was "the greatest day since the creation." But no one ought to agree with the vice president mindlessly and without further deliberation that now we must immediately embark upon a Man on Mars program. Man's salvation lies not in the exploration of distant planets but in alleviating pain and hunger and want on this planet.

Tik'u ba-hodesh shofar, ba-keseh le-yom haggenu (Ps. 81:4). The shofar is sounded on Rosh Hashanah *ba-keseh*, when the moon is concealed, as it always is on the first day of the lunar month. Rosh Hashanah bids us redirect our attention from Moon and Mars and all that distracts us from the real, fateful issues that trouble men and women in their daily lives. We must not permit Moon to eclipse Man.

Abraham said "*Hinneni*—I am ready" (Gen. 22:11) when he was told to stay his hand; without hesitation, he was willing to risk invalidation of his past. We must do no less. The fact that we have the technical capability and administrative apparatus necessary for such a venture farther into space should not push us into it. Just because we did so these past eight or ten years should not make us justify the Moon program by investing in a Mars program. Too many human lives may be sacrificed on the altar of that distant and barren planet. Now is the time to say "Enough!" The Moon landing salvaged our national prestige; let us now tend to our national honor—education and health and social justice and the quality of life—instead of squandering our resources on sophisticated gimmickry.

As Jews—especially as Jews—we must listen to that challenge of the *akedah*. Judaism is in trouble in America—and even in Israel. And unless we have the courage to indulge in self-criticism and openly say we were wrong in our lukewarm, tepid loyalties, our children will. Unless we abandon self-justification and invalidate our past, the next generation will abandon us. For example, there is hardly a more doctrinaire anti-Torah group than the Marxist Ha-Shomer ha-Tza'ir in Israel. Yet a year after the Six-Day War, the same group issued, for private distribution only, a conversation of its youth in which the tone was set by a young man who expressed resentment against his elders for denying him any real contact with the Jewish tradition, and thus left him both rootless and without a common language with other Jews in the Diaspora. He said, in reference to the lack of a Shabbat in his life: *Ani yakhol le-haggid be-tzurah kitzonit she-ha-hayyim shellanu shedufim. Ha-hayyim shellanu hem hol ehad arokh. . . . Anahnu hayyim hayyim afurim 365 yamim ba-shanah,* "Our lives are parched, empty. We live one long weekday; we live gray, dull lives 365 days a year." What a condemnation of parents who didn't have the guts to question their own antireligious dogma and to undo decades of commitment to the wrong ideals! They are saying the opposite of what God said to Abraham: *attah yadati*—now I know that you have no fear of God, that you are a moral coward and spiritual weakling, that you failed me! For in attempting to justify a bankrupt ideology when events screamed out against it, you bestowed on us a life that is a burden, for a life without Shabbat, without *yom tov*, without *kashrut*, without a touch of transcendence is indeed "one long weekday."

This lesson of the *akedah*, as the Rabbi of Kotzk understands it, confronts each of us, then, each in his or her personal way. None of us is perfect. Each of us has failed, in one way or another, in greater or lesser measure, to live by the highest standards and ideals of our tradition—ethically, morally, halakhically. Having chosen that way, we invest in it our logic and time and energy and pride, we are caught up in the grip of inertia. We feel we must justify our past, and thus we threaten to destroy our future. Rosh Hashanah attempts to dislodge us and to encourage us on to a new way.

No one says it is an easy task. On the contrary, it is the greatest trial of all. It is harder than sacrificing our greatest loves, for it means sacrificing our very egos, our reputations, even our identities. But we can do it. And we must do it. And having done it, we shall be liberated from the tyrannical rule of self-justification.

We enter now a New Year, a new *shanah*. The Hebrew word for "year" is related to two other meanings. *Shanah* also means "he repeated" and "he changed." Two opposites: to repeat and to change. If this is to be a *shanah tovah*, a good year, we must know what to repeat and what to change: to continue that which deserves perpetuation, and to abandon that which does not, even at the risk of self-invalidation.

May we do that, with our inherited Abrahamic courage. And then the good Lord will pass His judgment: *attah yadati ki yerei Elokim attah,* now I know that you are truly God-fearing and deserving of a *shanah tovah,* a year of health and happiness, of blessing and peace, a year of fulfillment and reconciliation, for us individually, for the State of Israel, for Jews throughout the world, and for all mankind.

Yom Kippur

HEAR, O FATHER

THE SHEMA, THE MOST celebrated and significant passage in all of Jewish literature, is one that we are required to pronounce twice every day. Yom Kippur is, of course, no exception. Yet those who are observant will have noticed that there is one slight difference between our recital of the *Shema* during the rest of the year and our reading of it on this holy day. Every other day of the year, we say, *Shema Yisra'el Hashem Elokeinu Hashem ehad,* "Hear, O Israel, the Lord is our God, the Lord is One." And then, before the passage beginning *Ve-ahavta*—thou shalt love the Lord thy God with all thy heart and all thy soul and all thy might," we recite *be-lahash,* in a soft undertone or whisper, the line *Barukh shem kevod malkhuto le-olam va-ed,* "Blessed be the name of God's glorious kingdom forever and ever." On Yom Kippur, however, we do not confine ourselves to whispering the line *Barukh shem kevod.* Instead, we recite it *be-kol ram,* in a loud voice: "Blessed be the name of His glorious kingdom forever and ever."

Why this difference? Why on Yom Kippur do we give such loud and clear expression to a sentence which we otherwise whisper in the most subdued tones?

The answer I propose to you today is, I believe, one that has a real, relevant, and terribly important message for each of us. It goes back to the two sources of the *Shema* in the Jewish tradition.

The first source of the *Shema* is well known to us. It occurs in the Bible, and consists of the words spoken by Moses to his people, Israel, in one of his very last discourses with them. Hear, my people Israel, he tells them, there is only one God in the world. And he then immediately proceeds to tell them, *Ve-ahavta,* you shall love this God with all your heart and soul and might. Moses did not mention the words *Barukh shem kevod malkhuto le-olam va-ed.* They are not at all recorded in the Bible.

5721 (1960)

The second source is in the aggadic tradition of our people, and here the *Shema* is presented in a completely different setting. Our Sages relate a most interesting and moving scene (see *Pesahim* 56a and *Midrash Aggadah* [Buber ed.] *Devarim* 6). The Patriarch Jacob, whose name is also Israel, is on his deathbed. His twelve sons surround him, ready to bid farewell to their aged father as he is about to depart from this earth. It is a tender scene—but a disturbing one. For Jacob, or Israel, is not dying peacefully. He is tossing and turning restlessly. His face seems troubled, distraught. There is something on his mind that will not let him rest, that will not let him go down peacefully into his grave. "What troubles you, father?" the children ask. "What is it that causes you all this mental pain and anguish?" Jacob's answer is straightforward. "My grandfather Abraham died leaving a good son—Isaac; but he also left a son by the name of Ishmael, who was a disgrace to him, a blot on his name. My father Isaac had two sons. I have followed in his ways; but he also left a son Esau, whose whole career did violence to all our father stood for and lived for. Now that I am about to die, I am worried—*shema yesh pesul be-mittati*. Perhaps I too am leaving a child who will rebel against God, who will offend all I have lived and died for." When the twelve sons of Jacob, called Israel, heard what was troubling their father on his deathbed, they answered as in one voice and cried out, "*Shema Yisra'el*—hear, O Father Israel, *Hashem Elokeinu Hashem ehad*, the Lord *you* have served all your life, He is our God; the tradition you inherited and bequeathed to us is the one we shall live by and hand over to our children; we shall never leave your ways or abandon the Lord God in whose service you reared us, for the Lord is One!" When Israel—Jacob—heard this affirmation of his faith by all his children, when he realized that he would leave no *pesul be-mitato*, no unworthy issue behind him, that he would be able to die in peace and in serenity, he called out in deep gratitude: *Barukh shem kevod malkhuto le-olam va-ed*, "Blessed be the name of His glorious kingdom forever and ever."

This, then, is the second source of the *Shema*. And it is this source of the *Shema* where we do find mention of the passage *Barukh shem kevod*.

What is the difference between these two versions of the origin of *Shema Yisra'el*? The *Shema* of Moses is a command to a nation; that of Jacob's children is a promise to a father. Moses' *Shema* is a theological proposition; that of Jacob's sons is a personal commitment. The first *Shema* is a declaration of ideology; the second is that which cements and unites a family. Moses recognized only one father—the Father in Heaven. Jacob's sons realized that the sense of duty toward the Heavenly Father came from a sense of obligation and love for their earthly father, Israel. While the *Shema* of Moses is intellectual, a structure of the mind, that of Jacob's sons is emotional and sentimental, stirring them to the very core of their being. In the *Shema* of Moses, the emphasis is on *Hashem ehad*, the Lord is One; in the *Shema* of the children of Father Israel, the stress is placed upon *Hashem Elokeinu*, the Lord is our God—the tradition will be continued, my father's faith will not die with him. Moses' *Shema* does not require a response; that of Jacob's children intuitively evokes the joyous, even rapturous reaction of "thank God"—*Barukh shem kevod malkhuto le-olam va-ed*.

All year long we pronounce the verse *Barukh shem kevod* softly, only *be-la-hash*, in a whisper. During the year, it is the *Shema* of Moses that predominates, the *Shema* of the intellect, the ideological *Shema* which does not evoke any response of *Barukh shem kevod*. But on Yom Kippur, we abandon the *Shema* of Moses in favor of that of the sons of Israel. On the holiest day of the year, we are not satisfied with intellectual abstractions, with theological formulations. Today we rise and with full voice, *be-kol ram*, we proclaim for all the world to hear: "*Shema Yisra'el*, Hear father, hear mother, wherever you may be today, *Hashem Elokeinu*, your God is my God. No matter that sometimes I seem to have strayed from the path onto which you guided me, that I often seem to have abandoned your heritage and forsaken your faith and neglected the richness and beauty of the Jewish tradition you passed on to me—today I promise you, father, that *Hashem Elokeinu*, your faith is my faith, your tradition is my tradition, your God is my God, your Torah is my Torah." *Hashem ehad*—this is the one Torah for which generations have lived and even given their lives, the One God whose overriding claim on our loyalties has been acknowledged by Jews throughout the ages. On Yom Kippur we return to our Father in Heaven via our fathers whom we respected and our mothers whom we loved on earth. This day our *Shema* must be more than a profession of faith; it must become a confession of fidelity, a declaration of loyalty. Kol Nidre may effectively release us from all personal vows and annul all oaths; but there is one promise, one commitment, too great and too deep, too terrible and too magnificent ever to be abrogated. It is the oath of *Shema Yisra'el*—Father, hear me now: your Lord is my God, the One God.

On this holy day, as we recall the memory of revered fathers and sweet, beloved mothers, it seems to me as if they and their parents, and all the generations who labored to bring us forth, stand breathlessly awaiting our move. I can see agony written across their foreheads and the pain of suspense in their eyes: *shema yesh pesul be-mittati.* Perhaps *my* children will forget me, my spirit, all I lived for and lived with. Perhaps in that strange new world called the space age they will ignore their responsibility to time, to their Jewish past and future; they will cut all ties to us and our Torah and tradition in favor of the glittering superficialities of their world. Perhaps their indifference to Torah will reflect disgrace and shame upon me. At this time, it becomes the duty of each of us to reassure them, so to speak, to make a promise to the past that we shall not forsake the future. We must say *Shema Yisra'el* not only as Moses said it, but with the intimacy, the personal fervor, the love and undying affection that Israel's children said it to him. What greater Yizkor can there be: What greater memorial can anyone erect for his parents than to declare to them that there is something imperishable that has survived them in us! When we can say *Shema* in that way, with that deep love and emotion, then all our past arises as one to respond to our words: *Barukh shem kevod malkhuto,* blessed be the name of God's glorious kingdom, not only for one year or one decade or one generation, but *le-olam va-ed,* forever and ever; for if such is the depth of a son's and daughter's loyalty, then the future of Torah, of Judaism, is assured. Thank God!

And then, when we have read the *Shema* in that way and proclaimed *be-kol ram,* in loud and clear tones, the *Barukh shem kevod,* our confidence that our oath to the past has been acknowledged, that our debt to parents and grand-parents, to Jewish history itself, is accepted, then we can pass safely on to the next level: *Ve-ahavta et Hashem Elokekha,* "Thou shalt love the Lord thy God." Then all our lives become suffused with a new meaning, a deeper purpose, a more elevated love and warmth that transforms us completely. For to say the *Shema* in this way is more than to agree that there is only one God. It is to change our whole way of life, to live more fully and more meaningfully to have the ennobling spirit of Torah penetrate every level of our existence. No man who has lived the *Shema* of the sons of Jacob can ever retain only half-hearted loyalty to Judaism. The *Shema* of Yom Kippur means that your loyalty to God Almighty and your love of all that is Jewish is so strong that even Heaven itself cannot shake you in your convictions!

Just recently, I read of a prayer uttered by a Jew in the Middle Ages, record-ed in the book called *Shevet Yehudah.* In English it reads something like this: "Master of all the worlds! I see that You are trying so hard to get me to abandon my faith. You bring upon me persecutions and trials and suffering and hatred, all to force me to give up being a Jew! So I want You to know, *Gottenyu,* that despite all You and Your heavenly hosts will say or do, I am a Jew and a Jew shall I remain, and nothing You can do will make me change my mind." There you have the kind of love and loyalty and magnificent pride in Jewishness that comes from the Yom Kippur *Shema*, from the awareness that Judaism is more than a set of beliefs, but a commitment to all the past and a pledge to all the future, the knowledge that if I break the continuity, then I have been treacherous to my forebears and deserted my descendants. That is why the *Shema* has always been the last words on the lips of Jewish martyrs—it was not so much the *Shema* of Moses as the *Shema* of the sons of Jacob, not so much the everyday *Shema* as the Yom Kippur *Shema*. When the Jew stood ready to offer his very life for God and Torah, all the generations of the past received him with open arms and with the triumphant welcome: *Barukh shem kevod malkhuto le-olam va-ed.*

My dear friends, we have a greater and more difficult task than dying for Torah. Our task is living for Torah. On Yom Kippur, in these sacred precincts of the synagogue, as we are about to invoke the memory of beloved parents and grandparents, we pledge ourselves anew to their great ideals. We shall not become the instruments, passive or otherwise, whereby Judaism will be dissolved. We shall not stand by idly while mitzvah after mitzvah is abandoned. We shall not close our eyes while year after year we see ourselves slipping from the firm kind of faith which alone can guarantee meaning in our lives. There is a love that strains to burst forth from our breasts, a powerful love that encompasses God and man, Torah and Israel, family and friend and stranger alike. With this love, this *ve-ahavta*, we face the past in order to be able to face the future with confidence. If we cannot in good conscience say our *Shema* as did Jacob's sons, if we cannot say it so that the response of *Barukh shem kevod* comes *be-kol ram*, then our Yizkor is meaningless. Then *we* have perhaps *remembered*, but we have failed to *remind* God; and, after all, we pray *Yizkor Elokim*, that God remember our dear ones.

The golden chain of the Jewish tradition is dangling before our eyes. The last link was placed upon it by our parents. It is swinging back and forth—the whole Jewish past waiting for you to grasp it, add on your own golden link, and then pass the chain on to your children. If you let it swing past you, you may never again have a chance to hold it, and you will have failed both your past and your future, your parents and your children. If you grasp it—then you will yourself be the newest link, the newest addition to the sacred tradition.

Grasp it. Never let it go. *Ve-ahavta et Hashem Elokekha be-khol levavekha u-ve-khol nafshekha u-ve-khol me'odekha* (Deut. 6:5). And when you have it, *ve-shinnantam le-banekha* (Deut. 6:7), pass it down to your own children and grandchildren, so that all generations can proclaim: *Barukh shem kevod malkhuto le-olam va-ed*, Blessed be the name of His glorious kingdom forever and ever.

THE WAY OF HONOR

YOM KIPPUR IS ONE of the strangest, most fascinating days of the Jewish calendar. It is a great paradox, composed of two contradictory moods. On the one hand it is *yom tzom*—a fast-day, solemn and somber. On the other hand it is *yom tov*—a festival, happy and joyous. On the one hand it is the great and awful *Yom ha-Din*, the day in which judgment is handed down on individuals, on nations, and on the entire world, a day symbolized by the *kittel*, reminiscent of the shroud which marks the inevitable end of arrogant, mortal man. On the other hand, it is a day when we affirm life, proclaiming *zakhrenu le-hayyim*, "remember us unto life," when we recite the blessing *she-heheyanu ve-kiyyemanu ve-higgi'anu la-zeman ha-zeh*, a blessing reserved for only the happiest occasions. It is *Yom Kippurim*, when we ask forgiveness for our overwhelming, crushing guilt; and, as some commentaries put it, *Yom ke-Purim*—a day as joyous and heartwarming as Purim!

All through this day which we now commence, you will find this clash of opposing moods, of conflicting themes. After our confession we recite two passages that reflect this paradox. First we shall say *Elokai, ad she-lo notzarti eini kedai*—"Oh, my God, before I was born I was unworthy; now that I am born, it is as if I were yet unborn." We emphasize the worthlessness of man's life, the vanity of his foolish illusions. Yet right afterward we begin another prayer, the first word of which is also *Elokai*—"Oh, my God." We say *Elokai, netzor leshoni me-ra ... petah libbi be-Toratekha u-be-mitzvotekha tirdof nafshi*—Oh, my God, teach me to be big enough to be silent when I am smeared by small men, when petty people aim their shafts at me. Give me a sterling character. Open my heart to the glories of Thy Torah, and let me behold the majesty of Thy *mitzvot* so that I might pursue them. What a difference! In one prayer we come to *Elokai* because we are nothing, in the other because we can become something. In one, because we are worthless, in the other because we can yet be worthy. In one, because life is just awful, in the other because God is awesome. In one we

---

Kol Nidre 5722 (1961)

follow the trend of *u-ve-khen ten pahdekha . . . al kol ma'asekha, ve-eimatekha al kol mah she-barata*—we speak of the fear and the terror that the presence of God blankets over humanity. We are caught up in trembling and anxiety. And the second represents the trend expressed in the prayer *u-ve-khen ten kavod.* We ask God to show us His glory and His honor, and instead of *pahad* and *eimah,* fear and fright, we speak of *kavod* and *tehillah* and *tikvah*—honor and praise, perfection and holiness.

Both these elements are integral parts of Judaism. Turning to God because of horror, and turning to Him because of honor—both are respectable parts of Yom Kippur. The question is: which ought we choose for ourselves? What does Torah urge upon us? Is there any difference which way I come to God, why I am in the synagogue tonight?

I believe there is a very definite difference. I believe it is a difference that will ultimately determine the meaning of your life and my life, as well as the complexion of the Jewish community for a long time to come.

This answer is not something I discovered. It was an issue a long time ago, and the Torah—the repository of the divine wisdom revealed to our race—hints at it indirectly. It has to do with a tender scene between husband and wife in a somber, tragic setting.

In one of the most touching scenes recorded in all the Bible, we find our Mother Rachel on her deathbed (Gen. 35:16–21). Here she was, a young woman in the prime of life, destined to die as she gave birth to her second child. And something remarkable happens. She is shown the child, and she says: Let him be called Ben-Oni. And next to her bed stands her husband Jacob and he says, "No, his name shall not be Ben-Oni. His name shall be Ben-Yamin." How strange! Here is Jacob, who loves his wife so dearly that he slaved for her as a shepherd for fourteen long years to win her hand, and he turns down her deathbed wish!

What really happened? Just imagine that you were present at that scene. Rachel, young, beautiful, and dying, sees her child brought before her. Bitterness and resentment well up in her heart. "Why must I die now? Who is going to wake up in the middle of the night, my child, to care for you? Strange hands are going to clothe and comfort you in the wee hours of the cold morning. Another heart will beat with delight at your happiness and success, and weep with you in your moments of failure and frustration. Someone else's hands shall rock your cradle and raise you from infancy to manhood. And you, my child, will grow up never knowing who your mother was. What of the long years ahead of you, will you ever remember that your life was brought into the world at the cost of mine? That you had a mother who ere you were born dreamed great dreams for you and loved you with a tender and great love? Therefore let your name be Ben-Oni, the son of my misery and bitterness. For if you will not remember me in the time of happiness and triumph and success, at least in the time when you will feel crushed, as if life weighs upon you like a great burden, when you will feel the sharp edge of life's griefs and tragedies, then you will remember your mother, and then I will pray to Almighty God for you. When my children's children's children will pass by this place as exiles from their homeland—as later is done at Ramah (Jer. 31:14)—they will stop here at my grave and I will weep for them, for my Ben-Oni, the children of my grief and my tragedy. Ben-Oni!"

But then her loving, devoted husband Jacob turned to her and said, "No, my dearest wife. Your tragedy hurts me deeply enough—no man can ever measure it. But don't call that child the son of your affliction. No, Rachel dear. Do not let him go through life as the sort of person who will remember his past, his mother, his tradition, his God, only during the time of *oni*, only when misery shrinks his heart, and grief oppress his soul. Let him not be the sort of man who will turn to the sacred memories of the past and the holy promises for the future only when contemplating the horrors and the terrors and the anxieties of life. Call him rather Ben-Yamin, the son of your right hand. Let him be the kind of child who will remember his mother not only in trouble, in toil, and in poverty, but also in times of happiness and exultation; not only in moments of illness, need, and death, but also at a Bar Mitzvah and a wedding. Let him turn in gratitude to the woman who gave his life when he appreciates life and when life smiles at him, when he is charmed by the delight of God's good and gracious world. For this, my dear Rachel, is the way of honor, not the way of horror. Ben-Yamin—the son of our right hand!"

Here is the example of the two conflicting trends of Yom Kippur and the choice that Jacob made and that the Torah confirmed: between Ben-Oni, turning to God because of misery and affliction, or Ben-Yamin, because of majesty and graciousness. The way of honor lies with Ben-Yamin. Both kinds of people are Jewish children; both sorrow and joy, horror and honor are part of the experience of each of us, and both are ways to God; but Ben-Yamin is a true Jewish way, the way of Jewish nobility, the way of Jewish permanence and perpetuation.

For if one comes to the synagogue and true Judaism because of Ben-Oni, because of *pahad* and *eimah*, because of the fear of death symbolized by the *kittel* and the feelings of worthlessness, then in the moments of satisfaction and peace, of health and success, he forgets God, ignores His Torah, disregards His law. There is only so much a man can take in contemplating evil and tragedy and pain; after a while he can no longer bear it and so he closes his eyes—and blinds himself to the vision of the *Ribbono shel Olam*. Most of those—though not all—who come to the synagogue because of Kaddish leave after the year of mourning has ended. Those who come because of *kedushah*, because of a quest for purpose in life, a search for the sacred and the ennobling—they remain, and they are happy, for their choice was Ben-Yamin and not Ben-Oni.

Our world today, complex and complicated as it is, offers us both alternatives. Either one can bring us to the *Ribbono shel Olam*. One way is Ben-Oni, the frightening and confusing elements of our society, for we are tottering on the brink of atomic catastrophe; our exposure to the fallout from nuclear bombs and the fear of cancer and leukemia and one hundred other diseases that come in its wake; the constant neurotic tensions of the cold wars about us; the unforgettable horrible face of an Adolf Eichmann on the television screen and the incredible hair-raising stories told by the victims who escaped—and especially the awareness that this is not a unique creature but a normal petty bureaucrat who can be turned into an archsadist, and that therefore it *can* happen again; the feeling that if a new world is being born, then, as with Rachel's child, it is being born in a deathbed, and who knows if it is worth it? *Ben-Oni!* There is no place to turn, and so we rush, willingly or unwillingly, into our Father's arms. "I came back, Dad, not because I really wanted to. But I tried to run away and became frightened. I ran out of money. I'm cold. I'm hungry. I'm sick. Here I am, Dad." So does the Ben-Oni address himself to *Avinu She-ba-Shamayim*, our Father in Heaven.

But this is not the worthy way. This can lead to Judaism, but it is not the way of honor, the one Torah recommends. If you are a prodigal son, return not because you could not face the outside world, but because you remember the loveliness of your parents' home. Come not because of the fear of death, but because of the love of true life. Come because you contemplated the *kavod* and *tehillah* and *tikvah*—the glory of God, the praise of men who devote their lives to peace, the hope that as long as there are men of eighty-five years old who are willing to go to jail for their convictions on behalf of peace and sanity, that our world can still be redeemed. Come because of the miracle that with all the weapons of destruction at our command, our world has not yet committed collective suicide; that God has given us wisdom, through science, to discover new immunities against polio and measles; that there were some few, solitary people, here and there, who were able to raise a staying hand against the sadism of the Nazis; the fact that out of the ashes of Treblinka and Buchenwald, there rose a State of Israel, even as Benjamin was a child who transformed the tragedy of Rachel's early death into the glory of her eternal posterity; the fact that there is nothing as warm and charming as the Shabbat table we knew in our parents' home and shall yet have in our own and in our children's, nothing as thrilling as a child coming home with the discovery of Jewish knowledge, nothing as satisfying as beginning every day with words of prayer. Ben-Yamin means that instead of running back to God and synagogue because all our other dreams have been dashed and crushed and transformed to nightmares, we return because that itself is our most precious and beautiful dream. We are in the synagogue tonight not because we are like spoiled children who did not succeed in running away, but because we are loyal children who are glad to be back in our Father's home.

We of the American Jewish community have an unprecedented and unparalleled opportunity to express our allegiance to Almighty God in the form of Ben-Yamin. Never before has a Jewish community so enjoyed the benefits of life, the gift of security, freedom from pogroms. Thank Heaven we need no Freedom Riders to desegregate us. We are financially secure; our greatest worry is whether we can afford a luxurious vacation, not whether we shall be able to afford a piece of bread for our children. With these great opportunities, let us not wait until, Heaven forbid, anxiety and tragedy drive us into the synagogue. Let us, rather, turn to God out of gratitude, in health, in prosperity, in satisfaction and fulfillment.

The Jewish Center is dedicated to the principle of Ben-Yamin. Our purpose is to present to our community, and especially our youth, the face of honor and happiness as a way to Torah and God. We prefer that our approach to Judaism come not through the solemnity of the shroud and the *kittel*, but through gladness and joy. Indeed we have provided for you, men and woman of our community, a lovely synagogue so that together we can thank God *she-heheyanu ve-kiyyemanu ve-higgi'anu la-zeman ha-zeh*—that we can together usher in this New Year in happiness, in loveliness, in pleasantness.

PASSING LIFE BY

A REMARKABLE CEREMONY PRECEDES the recital of the Kol Nidre. The rabbi is accompanied by two elders of the synagogue, constituting a *beit din*, and proclaims permission for the *avaryanim*, sinners, those who commit an *averah*, to join the congregation in prayer. The permission is granted on behalf of the *yeshivah shel ma'alah*, the heavenly court, and the *yeshivah shel mattah*, the court here on earth.

Why is this necessary? Is not Yom Kippur specifically made so that the sinner can pray for forgiveness? And who is not a sinner in the eyes of God? *Ki lo yizku be-einekha ba-din*—even the angels are not pure in the eyes of the Almighty. After all, for about ten times on this day we shall be reciting the *Al Het*, the confessions for the list of sins we have committed, and we shall be saying *Ashamnu, bagadnu*—that we have sinned, we have dealt falsely, and so on. In other words, each one of us can be counted amongst the *hote'im* and *poshe'im*, the true sinners. Why, then, single out that type of sinner known as an *avaryan*, he who commits the kind of sin called a *averah*, for special opprobrium? Why does he, more than the others, require special permission in order to be able to join a congregation of people who are not all the paragons of piety?

Whatever the historical reasons may be for the brief ceremony, and they are not at all clear or certain, may I commend to your attention certain contemporary implications of this proclamation.

The *hotei* or *poshea*, one who commits sins of disobedience, is involved with God. He may reject His Torah, he may know the law and rebel against it, he may be angry and defiant and shake his fists at Heaven; but there is still hope for this kind of person on Yom Kippur. We invite him to the synagogue—in fact, Yom Kippur is one day when we acknowledge that the synagogue is specifically made for such people.

But the *avaryan*, one who commits the sin called *averah*, ignores God altogether. He is neither for nor against the Torah. He just doesn't care. The word

---

Kol Nidre 5723 (1962)

averah comes from the Hebrew word *avor*, which has a number of meanings, the most significant being: "to pass by," "to go by without noticing." Therefore, we are said to commit an *averah* when we do not take God or our fellow man seriously. We are so consumed by our own petty ambitions, our trivial affairs, our little circle of woes and worries and pleasures and pains, that we never really consider the existence of religious duty or ethical obligation or moral imperative or social conscience. They simply pass us by. Great, traumatic historical events convulse our world, cry out to us to discover their meaning, beg us to transform our lives—but we are *avaryanim*, we look right through them. Life passes us by, while we remain supremely and sublimely indifferent to its consequences.

And what Jewish tradition tells us is that the *hotei* may come in and pray to God. A rebellious Jew may enter the synagogue, wrestle with his conscience, even leave unrepentant—but at least he remains involved with God. Because he has a relationship with God, because he has a relationship with his fellow men and his community, he is invited to the synagogue on this holiest night of the year, and he does not have to apologize for his presence.

But the *avaryan*, if he should stumble across the threshold of the synagogue by accident or habit or because of convention—he may not come in until two courts, two *batei din*, give him explicit sanction: the heavenly court of *yeshivah shel ma'alah*, to forgive him for ignoring God and Torah, and the earthly court, the *yeshivah shel mattah*, represented by the three elders of the congregation, to forgive him for ignoring synagogue and society, neighbor and community. On Yom Kippur, we are willing to take our chances with the rebel and the heretic and the bumptious; but we dread the dull and indifferent and self-centered. Hence, the *avaryan* needs special permission, in Heaven and on earth, before the Kol Nidre may be chanted in his presence.

Is it not true that the *avaryan* is the most dangerous of all types?

There once was a time when young people, especially in the universities, were committed to great causes. They joined picket lines, they organized mass meetings, they attended party conventions, they even participated in riots on behalf of what they considered just causes. They did not allow the great issues of their day—whether economic justice or social progress or racial equality or political integrity or religious convictions—to pass them by unaffected. They enthusiastically entered the maelstrom of life, fed by the currents of their times. Today's average college student, with the exception of those people who join the Peace Corps or those like James Meredith who have become the heroes of progress in our day, seeks only to be accepted by the proper college or graduate school, with the purpose of obtaining a secure position—not a pioneering job filled with risks and opportunities, with both the dangers and thrills of opening exciting, new horizons, but a job which will give him pension, tenure, and a lack of too much competition, Don't speak to this young man—or woman—of ideals or causes or issues. They are outside his narrow interests in his own self. *Avor*—they simply pass by someplace in the stratosphere, unconnected with his life in any real, substantial way.

As a teacher, I have that experience personally. When I meet a student who either strongly agrees with me or vociferously disagrees, I am happy, because I have engaged him; we are involved. There is a dialogue. But I am deeply distressed by the mechanical note-taker whose heart is obviously elsewhere, whose attendance is perfunctory. As a rabbi, I am delighted when people accept and agree with my sermon. I am also happy when they tell me that they disagree with this or that point. I know that at least I have reached them, that we are together involved in a search for something higher, finer, and nobler. But I am hurt by those who neither agree nor disagree, who are simply uninterested, who lie at the dead center of life and refuse to raise their heads to the tremendous issues of existence. The same is true in religion. The *hotei*, the active sinner who disobeys, may yet obey some day. But he who ignores—in other words, the *avaryan*—can never come to consider the word of God. The one who defies God is less evil than one who in his indifference doesn't even want to know of Him. The *hotei* is at least engaged in a dialogue with his Creator. The *avaryan* is silent. Whether between teacher and pupil, or husband wife, or God and man, or the individual Jew and his synagogue, to "have words," even angry words, is far superior and far preferable than not to be on speaking terms altogether.

And, unfortunately, how widespread is this disease of *averah*! American Jews have given unprecedented amounts to charity. Yet when you study the lists of the donors, you find that they add up to only a small fraction of the total Jewish community. There are, for instance, quite a number of synagogues of various sizes and kinds yet how many people are either affiliated or attend services? Some who don't may object on principle. But most simply do not care; it never even occurs to them to be interested. There are thousands upon thousands of Jews in this, the most history-making era in our thirty-five-hundred-year story, who are totally unconcerned with and unaffected by the unspeakable tragedy of European Jewry, the glory and the risks of the State of Israel, the profound changes now taking place in the worldwide Jewish community. It is an exciting, thrilling, dangerous, opportunity-filled time that we live in. Yet, except for a *krekhts* here and a little applause there, most people are *avaryanim*: life just passes them by. And it is they who need the special *hetter*, or permission, from both the heavenly court and the earthly court to pray with their fellow Jews and appear before God on this holiest day of the year.

How does one avoid *averah*? How do you learn to become responsive and hence responsible? How can you make a dent in the crust of indifference that surrounds the heart? Allow me to recommend to you a well-known passage of our Sages (*Avot* 3:1): "*Histakkel bi-sheloshah devarim ve-i attah ba li-yedei averah*—Consider three things and you will escape *averah. Da me-ayin bata*—know where you came from; *u-le-an attah holekh*—where you are going; and *lifnei mi attah atid litten din ve-heshbon*—before whom you must ultimately render an account of your life."

The first is *Da me-ayin bata,* know where you came from. Allow me to give an entirely different answer from the one offered by the Sages, but one that may possibly be more appropriate for this audience. Many people keep aloof from Torah and synagogue because of a religious inferiority feeling. They suspect that they are spiritually impotent; they simply lack a religious dimension and hence are naturally unequipped for religious commitment and involvement. To those who are *avaryarim* for this reason, Judaism says: "Know where you came from." You issue from the people who gave the Western world two religions. Your very genes and chromosomes bear the talents of a God-intoxicated people. In your veins you carry the blood not only of noble saints and distinguished religious personalities, but of ordinary men and women who, when the occasion demanded it, showed they were able to rise to martyrdom. If this is the stock you come from, then you have, even if not consciously, the talent and potentiality for a creative religious life. With that knowledge, you will not shrink from your Jewish responsibilities, and you will then avoid *averah*.

There is another type that ignores Judaism and the Jewish community because they want to "get places" in this country. They are young people who are so caught up in their ambition to make a mark in life that they presumptuously ignore their fellow Jews, fearing that their Jewishness may prove cumbersome. To them the Rabbis said; consider *le-an attah holekh*, remember where you are going: *mekom afar, rimmah ve-tole'ah*—to the grave. When man remembers the end of all men, his ambitions are blunted and he becomes much more chastened and considerate. In a wider sense, this question must be directed to all those who regard their Jewishness as standing in the way of their American and mundane ambitions. Remember where you are going. If you do not take along your Jewishness with you, if you abandon Torah, if you try to appear as un-Jewish as you can, then your end will be a bland assimilation, the graveyard of the spirit. Your children will not know who they are, they will be rootless, and their self-identity will be blurred. Spiritual depth, deep psychological wounds, and a denial of their selves and their roots—that is the result of *averah*.

But most people who ignore Torah and the Jewish community do so not because of feelings of worthlessness or ambition. They do so merely because they are busy. They are caught up in their daily affairs, which oppress them and depress them and keep them running in vicious circles. The routine of getting up in the morning, a quick breakfast, off to dull work throughout the day in an attempt to make a living, returning home, rushing out for a busy social life or to the television set . . . or, for the wife, the same day-in, day-out, year-in, year-out routine of shopping, buying, returning, preparing the household for the family—we are so taken up with the trivial details of making a living and actually living, that it never occurs to us to think of the higher demands of existence, of something transcendent and more enduring. We are too taken up with the *din ve-heshbon*, the business of everyday existence. And so to us the Jewish tradition cries out: Remember *lifnei mi attah atid litten din ve-heshbon*—before Whom you must ultimately give the true *din ve-heshbon*, the real accounting. In the long stretch of a man's life, his daily affairs sink into insignificance, and he must answer ultimate questions. Well, how are we going to do that if we continue in the way of *averah*?

The world today is torn between the forces of decency, faith, and religion, and those diametrically opposed to them. When the day comes that we stand before the heavenly court and we are asked: "What did you do about it?" will we be able to offer the excuse that we were busy with our everyday affairs? Do such excuses count, do they matter? We live in an era of great events: what have we done in an attempt to help Israel prosper? To save the remnants of those Jews now being driven out of the Asian and African countries? To help establish the sovereignty of Torah in America? To advance Jewish education amongst our children? To stem the tide of intermarriage? Shall we answer that we were too involved in the stock market? Or shopping? Or the newest fashions?

On this holiest night of the year, I plead with all of you to banish this plague of *averah* forever. God calls out to you tonight: remember Me in the way you eat, with *kashrut*; remember Me in what you want, through prayer;

remember Me in the way you work, through the observance of the Sabbath; remember Me in your dealings with your fellow men, through the observance of Jewish ethics. The synagogue calls out to you: come closer to us. Be with us not only three times a year but constantly; educate your children and educate yourself by coming to our study programs. We want you to feel that this is your synagogue. We want the synagogue to enter into you even as you enter into the synagogue. We want you to participate with us in every which way in our attempt to shape the destiny of our people in this country and throughout the world. We want you to identify with us, to be with us, to participate and involve your families with us. Break out of the vicious cycle of your petty *din ve-heshbon,* so that you may engage both God and fellow man. Do not pass the great issues of life by because you were "busy" with things which, in the long run, will appear so trivial and insignificant.

Tonight, as is our annual custom, we call upon you to contribute to the upkeep of this, your House of God. The fact of your giving, and the amount of your giving, will be an indication of how deeply you want to be involved in our programs, in our ideals, in our way of life. Those who remain silent and who fail to practice Jewish generosity are guilty of *averah.* Those who proudly announce that they will assist this synagogue in continuing its activities, they have broken through the shell of indifference. They have justified the permissiveness of the *yeshivah shel ma'alah* and the *yeshivah shel mattah.* They have shown that they are, on this Judgment Day, prepared to render a higher and nobler and greater *din ve-heshbon* to their Creator.

Let me leave you with this one story of a real event that occurred to a colleague of mine that will perhaps summarize what I have been saying.

This rabbi was returning from the funeral of a man whom he had known well. He was sitting in the car next to the man's son, a young, successful businessman. He noticed that the young man was unusually distressed and grieved even more than he had expected. "Is there anything special bothering you?" asked the rabbi of the young man. After a few moments' hesitation, the young man answered, "Yes, rabbi. There is something, very special. I shall never forgive myself. Ten minutes before father died, he picked up the telephone and tried desperately to reach me. He wanted to speak to me because he knew that his life was ebbing. He wanted to have his last words with me, his only son. And so he tried and tried and tried . . . But . . . the line was busy . . ."

Our Heavenly Father calls us today. He is trying desperately to reach us as the last moments of the year ebb away. Will your line be busy? Will you be taken with idle chatter, idle thoughts, idle excuses—or will you pick up the phone, connect yourselves to Almighty God, our Heavenly Father, and speak to Him?

Put down, I plead with you, the telephone of "weekdayishness," of everyday *din ve-heshbon*, of "busy-ness," of *averah*. Don't let the line be busy. Instead, let us listen for a Higher Voice. Your Father is calling. Let us answer—and let us respond with love and with generosity.

SHOES AND THE SOUL

ONE OF THE MORE important laws of Yom Kippur is called *neʿilat ha-sandal*—the prohibition of wearing leather shoes on this holy day. This prohibition is indeed a law, and not, in the superficial language of so many unlearned people, a "mere custom." I confess to being confused and perplexed by some of my fellow Jews. I do not understand those of them who, when they travel and visit a mosque or other places such as the Taj Mahal, have no objection to acknowledging personally the mores and customs of others, and reverently remove their footwear when required to do so; and yet, when apprised of the fact that Judaism forbids the wearing of shoes on Yom Kippur, feel constrained to act either annoyed or shy, and do not comply with the law. Yet, despite its neglect by so many, *neʿilat ha-sandal*, the prohibition of wearing leather shoes, is one of the five *innuyim*, the special prohibitions of Yom Kippur, and follows, in importance, that of fasting.

I mention this to you not, Heaven forbid, because I wish to castigate and reproach my fellow Jews. I would not want to do that on this day of divine forgiveness. Rather, it is because I want you to share with me some of the pride in our sacred heritage and glorious tradition, a pride which you will appreciate and experience all the more when you learn some of the purposes of the law of *neʿilat ha-sandal*. Allow me to mention to you three of the explanations that have been offered for this law, each of which highlights another insight of our Jewish tradition.

To understand the first reason that has been offered for the prohibition of *neʿilat ha-sandal*, allow me to refer to another aspect of Jewish lore. It is an old Jewish custom that when a man buys a new garment, his family and friends wish him well, saying, *tevalleh ve-tithadesh* or, as the expression goes in Yiddish, *tzurays gezunterheyt*—"wear it well." In other words, just as you are putting on this new garment in good health, so may God grant that you remain in good health until you wear it out. The famous commentator on the *Shulhan*

Kol Nidre 5723 (1962)

Arukh, Rama (R. Mosheh Isserles), adds (*Orah Hayyim* 223:6) that this greeting should not be extended to a man upon wearing for the first time a new pair of leather shoes. The reason—because a life had to be destroyed in order for this man to wear these shoes. And although the life that was taken was that of an animal, a being decidedly lower than man, nevertheless our consideration and reverence for life is such that we refuse to express the hope that more lives will be taken, or to pronounce a joyous blessing upon such an occasion, even if there results from it some benefit to mankind. The taking of life, even brute life, may sometimes be a necessity, but it never can be considered a virtue. (Similarly, although Judaism requires a person who performs a mitzvah for the first time to recite the joyous blessing of *she-heheyanu*, nevertheless the first time that a *shohet* performs the mitzvah of *shehitah*, he is not permitted to recite the *she-heheyanu* blessing.)

This is the reason for the law against *ne'ilat ha-sandal* on Yom Kippur. This day is the culmination, the climax, of that ten-day period in which we speak mostly of life. Every day, three times we prayed: *zakhrenu le-hayyim*, remember us unto life. We pleaded with God, requesting that He inscribe us in the Book of Life. Yom Kippur itself is, par excellence, the day when we celebrate divine compassion and mercy, a theme which we will learn once again from the Book of Jonah later this afternoon. It is the day when we acknowledge that "His compassion extends over all His creatures." On Yom Kippur, therefore, none may wear leather shoes, an object which, in order to benefit man, necessitated the end of some poor animal's life.

This life-affirming principle affects every area of Jewish teaching. Whether we speak of the ethics of nuclear testing or the morality of ending the life of a fetus, the Jewish veneration of life as the supremely precious gift of the Creator makes its influence known. I might mention, as well, the recent book *Silent Spring*, by Rachel Carson, which has recently become the center of controversy. The author maintains that as a result of the indiscriminate and excessive use of pesticides and insecticides, we are endangering wildlife on a terrifying scale. The day may yet come, she warns, when spring comes but no birds arrive with it—a frighteningly silent spring. Whether or not Miss Carson exaggerates her case, I am not competent to say. But I believe that her concern is one that could have issued from a thoroughly Jewish soul. A people which, on its holiest day, will refuse to wear shoes made of the skin of an animal, is certainly concerned that God's creatures exist without harm.

I might add that this reason for the prohibition of *ne'ilat ha-sandal* applies not only to Yom Kippur, but also to occasions of mourning, such as Tish'ah be-Av or the observance of *shiv'ah*. We show our appreciation for the life that was lost, our commiseration and personal participation in the fear and the terror and the pain that preceded it, by reverencing even the lowliest forms of life, such as those which gave us leather. Similarly, it is significant that the custom of reciting the Yizkor, which we today practice three times a year, originally was followed only on Yom Kippur. It is appropriate that the reunion of generations, the memory of lives which we loved but which are lost, should take place on the day that we proclaim by our symbolic action our appreciation for all life.

A second reason for the prohibition of wearing leather shoes on Yom Kippur was taught by my late grandfather, of blessed memory. He said that when a man wears shoes he walks straight, erect, and undeterred, unaware of and unconcerned with what he tramples underfoot. His mind does not at all perceive the terrain upon which he treads. When he walks barefoot, however, then suddenly he is aware of what he is stepping upon. Every little pebble, every blade of grass, every crevice in the sidewalk is immediately impressed upon the sole of his foot and thence upon his mind. In other words, by divesting himself of his shoes, a man opens up wide new areas of sensitivity. So that by removing our shoes on Yom Kippur, we emphasize a great human and humanitarian principle: the concern for the sensitivities, delicacies, and special feelings of other human beings. We learn suddenly that others may have subtle feelings, fears, and inhibitions which we may not appreciate, but that we ought to keep in mind at all times. When we remove our shoes we realize that we must not trample the sensitivities of others underfoot, we must not run roughshod over whole areas of life that others regard as sacred though we may ignore their importance.

Parents ought to remember that. All too often a father or mother, with all good intentions, can push a child into things for which the child is not prepared, which he secretly abhors or fears. Many a child's emotional life has been ruined by a well-meaning parent who walked over the terrain of his heart clad in stiff leather shoes—unfeeling, insensitive, indelicate. And the same is true in reverse: mature children sometimes are utterly unaware of the special new problems faced by aging parents—the blows to their pride, the new hyper-sensitivity, the sudden awareness of people once at the center of life that they are now on the periphery, and therefore the great need for being wanted and feeling important. A people which removes its shoes on Yom Kippur will learn, throughout the year, how to be on guard against trampling other people's feelings underfoot.

The third reason I wish to offer is peculiar and unique to Yom Kippur. And that is, that when Jews do *teshuvah*, when on Yom Kippur they return to our Father in Heaven, when they manifest a special religious inclination, when they spend the whole day in prayer, then not only do they themselves experience great elevation and sanctification, but they raise the whole world along with them. On Yom Kippur, when all Israel turns to God, all the world turns with them, so that even the ground we step on becomes sanctified, the very earth becomes holy (see *Menahem Tziyyon, Yom Kippurim*). And on hallowed ground it is forbidden to walk with shoes, even as God told Moses out of the Burning Bush when he first revealed Himself to him: "*Shal ne'alekha me-al raglekha*—remove your shoes from your feet, *ki ha-makom asher attah omed alav admat kodesh hu*, because the place you are standing on is hallowed ground" (Ex. 3:5). On Yom Kippur our prayer and our devotions have sanctified the ground we walk on, and therefore we remove our shoes. On this day we must feel that we are not alone in our inner love for God, in our passion for holiness, in our desire and yearning for the good and the holy and the pure. We must feel as if the whole world has come along with us, that the very earth itself can become hallowed, if we strive for greatness, for Jewishness, for Torah, with all our strength and heart and soul.

I believe that there is a special message for us moderns in this idea. There once was a time when Jews lived in ghettos. Today we are accustomed to think of ghettos in a negative manner—only of the poverty, of the oppression and the bigotry wrought against us. Yet only the ignorant would assume that that is the whole story. For life in the ghetto was also immeasurably beautiful. The Jew felt completely at home in the company of his fellow Jews. Society, the community, the very streets were receptive, friendly, hospitable. No Jew had to hide his Jewishness, no Jew ever had to be bashful about his loyalties.

Today the opposite holds true. How many Jews would be willing to take the *lulav* and *etrog* from their home to the synagogue without the feeling of self-consciousness? How many, when in company, do not feel shy, sometimes to the point of denying their better impulses, and insist upon eating only kosher? We all of us have convictions and principles, and a goodly number of us even live up to them. But we do so only at the cost of embarrassment and a feeling that we must sacrifice in order to live in accord with our conscience. We have the innate feeling that society is inhospitable to our endeavors, that the very air we breathe is unholy, that our whole milieu is hostile to everything we stand for. We feel that as religious Jews we are intruders, disturbers of the peace, aliens and outsiders who are unwelcome in a profane and vulgar society. We feel that we are *in* but not *of* this world.

But on Yom Kippur we are told to feel differently. We are bidden to imagine that all the world is a *kehillah kedoshah*, a holy community, so much so that the very earth is holy and we must therefore remove our shoes. Perhaps it is only an illusion that we create for ourselves—but it is a beautiful, a holy, a sublime illusion that is so precious that life is impossible without it. For at least twenty-four hours during the year we must imagine that all the world proclaims the glory of God; that only those who reach out for Him are entitled to feel at home in this wide world; that the earth and the air, the ocean and the seas, the mountains and the valleys and the homes within them welcome only those souls that are on fire with the love of God and prayer and Torah, that they are hospitable and friendly only to those who are God-seekers. On this one day, let all those who ignore God or deny His Torah or refuse to utter a world of prayer—let them feel that they are the intruders in God's world, they are the outsiders and the aliens and the strangers.

No wonder that all year long, after we recite the first verse of the *Shema*, we recite the next verse, "*Barukh shem kevod malkhuto le-olam va-ed*, blessed be the name of Him the glory of whose Kingdom lasts forever and ever," silently. But on this one day of Yom Kippur we proclaim it aloud. Our tradition has given a quaint reason for this, one that may sound primitive to those who consider themselves sophisticated. Yet in its very sweetness and naiveté we find a world of wisdom.

Our tradition maintains that all year long we may not read it aloud for it is a verse that is set aside for recitation by the angels. On Yom Kippur, however, all Jews are supposed to feel that they are angels, and therefore may recite it aloud.

Is not this just what we have been saying? During the rest of the year, those who are on the side of the angels, those who aspire for an angelic, heavenly type of life, must keep their peace and remain silent. On Yom Kippur, however, only those who yearn for Heaven may feel that they are the rightful citizens of this world.

Let the law of *ne'ilat ha-sandal* teach us to go through the year unafraid and uninhibited in our love of Torah and Jewishness. Let us learn from Yom

Kippur not to feel constrained to apologize for any Jewish practice or institution. Let our pride in our tradition be with us through all the year.

As we go into the New Year, inspired by memories of the past, let us remember these lessons: reverence for life, sensitivity to the feelings of others, and knowledge that this one day only those who love God are at home in His world. Let us go into the year with the famous words of our holiest prayer on our lips: *Yitgaddal ve-yitkaddash Shemeh Rabba.* We shall magnify and make holy the name of the great God, *be-alma di vera khi-re'uteh,* in the world which he has created according to His will. On Yom Kippur we create the illusion that His world is holy. During the rest of the year may we transform that illusion into a reality.

BODY AND SOUL

THIS HOUR IS DEDICATED to the memory of loved ones, especially parents, on the most sacred day of the year. It is an hour of recollection and reunion, when our minds reach back to yesteryear and our hearts respond with old love and reawakened affection as in the days of old. How freely and warmly we today affirm the Torah's commandment to honor father and mother, and the Rabbis' remark that this applies even to the memory of parents already gone from this mundane world.

It is surprising, therefore, that the first mention in the Torah of the parent-child relationship is negative. Immediately after Eve was created, the Torah already informs us: *Al ken ya'azov ish et aviv ve-et immo ve-davak be-ishto ve-hayu le-basar ehad*, "Therefore let a man leave his father and mother and cleave to his wife, and they shall became as one flesh" (Gen. 2:24). Is it not disconcerting to learn that the Torah's first judgment on the parent-child relationship is not one that encourages unity and togetherness, but, on the contrary, speaks of separation and divergence between the generations?

Moreover, as we read the history of the fathers of our people, we learn that the injunction to leave parents was not generally obeyed. Thus, when Abraham sends his servant to look for a wife for his son Isaac, he makes him swear: *Rak et beni al tashev shammah* (Gen. 24:8), "do whatever you will, but do not take my son there, away from me." Later, when Isaac meets his intended bride, Rebecca, *va-yevi'eha Yitzhak ha-ohelah Sarah immo* (Gen. 24:67), "he brings her into the tent of his mother Sarah." There is, then, a spirit of union between father and son, even between son and the memory of a deceased mother. A generation later, what is Jacob's major prayer? *Ve-shavti be-shalom el beit avi*, "May I return in peace to the house of my father" (Gen. 28:21). Before Joseph dies, he pleads with his brothers and reminds them: our father Jacob was buried with his parents in the Holy Land; therefore, *ve-ha'alitem et atzmotai mi-zeh ittekhem* (Gen.

5724 (1963)

50:25)—when I die, carry my remains, too, away from Egypt and back to the ancestral burial place.

How, then, do we account for this constant tendency of the Patriarchs to return to their parents, when the Torah tells us at the very beginning, *Al ken ya'azov ish et aviv ve-et immo*, "Therefore shall a man leave his father and his mother"?

May I commend to your attention an answer suggested by one of the greatest preachers of the past generation (conveyed to me by Rabbi Harry Wohlberg, who taught homiletics for many years at Yeshiva University, in the name of Rabbi Moshe Avigdor Amiel, who was Chief Rabbi of Tel Aviv). There are two separate words that the Torah uses for human beings. One of them is *basar*. Literally, that means "flesh." *Basar* is a term that is used for mankind from the beginning until Abraham. Thus, when the Torah refers to the all-too-human limitations of the first race of sinners, it says, *be-shaggam hu basar*, "though they be but *basar*, flesh" (Gen. 6:3). When the Lord decides to destroy the generation of the flood, He says, *ketz kol basar ba lefanai*, "the end of all people [flesh, or *basar*] has come before Me" (Gen. 6:13); as *le-shahet kol basar*, "to destroy all mankind [flesh, or *basar*]" (Gen. 6:17).

From Abraham and on, however, there is a sudden change in terminology. Man is no longer referred to as *basar*, but as *nefesh*—soul. When the Torah wishes to describe the people Abraham and Sarah had converted from paganism to the belief in God, it says, *ve-et ha-nefesh asher asu be-Haran*, "the souls they won in Haran" (Gen. 12:5). *Ten li ha-nefesh*, "give me the souls," meaning "the men" (Gen. 14:21). *Ve-nikhretah ha-nefesh ha-hi me-ammeha* (Gen. 17:14)—"that soul, *nefesh*," the person who violates the law of circumcision, "shall be cut off from his people."

And here, in this distinction between man as *basar* and man as *nefesh*, we come to an understanding of the change in the Torah's judgment. For its decision that *al ken ya'azov*, that parents and children have no relation with each other, is based only on the conception of man as mere *basar*, mere flesh. It is predicated on man's accepting a philosophy of materialism or naturalism. If humanity conceives of itself in purely materialistic terms as mere physical specimens, as machines enclosed in flesh, then indeed parents and children remain distant and remote from each other, for their relationship is merely biological. If man identifies himself as merely an advanced animal, then like the animal, which leaves its nest or den as soon as it is weaned, so man leaves his parents and their ways as soon as he no longer is dependent upon them. As long as man never transcended the level of *basar*, then the old artery-hardened *basar* of the past generation and the young, vigorous physique of the new must go their different ways. Therefore, *ve-davak be-ishto ve-hayu le-basar ehad*—they shall be one flesh, one *basar*. But if they conceive of each other as spiritual beings as well, as humans who also possess a soul, a *nefesh*, then parents and children remain linked together inextricably. The words *al ken ya'azov ish et aviv ve-et immo*, that children shall leave parents and depart from them, were meant to be valid only until the days of Abraham. But after Abraham, when Abraham's teaching had made mankind realize that it possesses a *nefesh*, a soul as well as a body, then children remained spiritually united with the generations of their forebears. For when people are conscious of their identity as *nefesh*, then the tie between them transcends the biological and there is a community of ideas and loyalty, a mutuality of ideals and faith, permanent bonds of soul and heart and mind. Then, as we are told of Abraham and Isaac, *va-yelekhu sheneihem yahdav*, "the two of them went together" (Gen. 22:8). Then, *ve-shavti be-shalom el beit avi*, "may I return in peace to the home of my father." For time inexorably corrodes *basar*, flesh; whilst *nefesh*, soul, remains supremely unaffected by the sharp edge of the passing years.

The question that confronts us in this tender and moving hour is: what standard shall we, in our modern age, maintain? We live in a time when enticements abound, urging us to slide effortlessly into easy assimilation. Which, then, shall it be: *basar* or *nefesh*? It is not that we Jews have ever deprecated material comforts. Not at all: we have always believed in enjoying God's bounty. It is, rather, a question of emphasis. Even more: it is a question of whether man shall today have *some* spiritual aspect to his personality—or none at all. And the difference as to whether one's self-identity is that of *nefesh* or *basar*, just flesh and bones or also heart and soul, is a consequential one indeed.

It has to do with the respect we accord to age itself. In a society where *nefesh* is supreme, age is honored, for the soul's wisdom and accumulated experience increase with the years. But in a society where *basar* is dominant, where material values are treated with the greatest reverence, there preeminence is given to youth, and the elderly are ignored; for *basar* disintegrates with age.

The choice between *basar* and *nefesh* has to do with the attitude of the worshiper to a service. A *nefesh*-Jew attends the whole service with equal attention, for Yizkor is considered only a part of the service. For such a person, the link with the past is not one of mere sentimentalism, conjuring up the physical form of a parent, but is part of a larger religious and spiritual context. But if the *basar* standard prevails, then the relations between that person and the generation that preceded him are merely biological or emotional, not a matter of shared principles, ideals, faith. It is paradoxical, but it is true: if the Yizkor is to be meaningful, if this hour of reunion is to be sincere and authentic, then it cannot be taken out of the context of the rest of the services. If you mean Yizkor with all your heart, then it has got to be merely one part of an entire religious devotion, and not the major part. For that is the way we express ourselves: "*Yizkor Elokim et nishmat . . .* May God remember the soul of my beloved relatives . . ." It is the soul, the spirit, the *nefesh*, that remains dominant.

The question of flesh or soul is crucial to the understanding of the nature of this day. For in this, indeed, is the main message of Yom Kippur. We fast this day, not in order to punish ourselves and thereby psychologically to relieve ourselves of the burden of guilt, but to indicate to ourselves that we can get along for twenty-four hours without *basar*—but never without *nefesh*. The fasting is not so much to deny our *basar* as to elevate and celebrate the quality of *nefesh*, our spiritual dimension. This is the essence of Yom Kippur.

And the choice of *basar* or *nefesh* standards has to do with how we relate not only to our parents, but also as parents to our children. If we desire to keep them, to live on through them, then our emphasis in our homes must be *nefesh*. If we impress them *only* with our ambitions of *basar*—success, career, wealth, social standing—and we ignore the demands of the spirit, of Torah, then we may well lose their loyalty later in life, because mundane goals take them into new social and moral currents, and with the passage of time, father and son and mother and daughter drift apart. But if the child becomes aware from earliest youth that, important as career and material comforts are—and they are important—nevertheless the most significant function of man, his destiny, his purpose for being, is *nefesh*—Torah, God, Israel—then parents and children may yet walk together, as Abraham and Isaac did: *va-yelekhu sheneihem yahdav*.

What parent does not realize that the greatest heartbreak, the most agonizing disappointment, comes when our children leave our ways, and that, contrariwise, in the long run, the blessing that counts most is that precious and indefinable quality which we call *nahas* from children! And that blessing cannot be obtained by buying things for them, only by binding our spirits with theirs; not by bribing them through pampering their *basar*, only by imbibing together of the wells of *nefesh*. Leaving, after 120 years, *insurance* and an estate will *help* children; leaving the *assurance* that there is meaning in life will not only *help* them but *hold* them for the rest of their days. Styles change, interests change, social patterns vary; but Judaism, authentic Judaism, Torah, remains a constant. Family togetherness, therefore, must emphasize the religious and spiritual dimension, over and above the merely material and social. If you want to keep your children, then the Jewish tradition tells you: emphasize observing Shabbat together as well as "going out" together; study the same *sidrah* of the week, rather than only discussing material business problems; create a community of *Kiddush* and *Havdalah*, rather than style or socializing. Otherwise, *al ken ya'azov ish et aviv ve-et immo.*

But above all, the question of *basar* or *nefesh* has to do with how we shall conduct our own lives throughout the year. Now is the time for all of us, young and old, and especially young men on the brink of their careers, to listen closely to the lofty words of the *U-Netanneh Tokef* prayer. How the poet laments the destiny and fate of man! *Emet ki attah hu yotzeram, ve-atta yodea yitzram, ki hem basar va-dam,* "In truth, as their Creator, Thou knowest their weakness to temptation, for they are but flesh and blood." *Adam yesodo me-afar ve-sofo le-afar,* "man's origin is in dust, and his bitter end is in dust." And then the *payyetan* adds three words that put into bold, stark relief the greatest tragedy of any man: *Be-nafsho yavi lahmo,* "he wins his bread with his soul, his *nefesh*." Do you see the force of his words? Man's life is but a brief respite between an eternity of silence that preceded him and an eternity of silence that follows him. Yet, with humble origin and disgraceful end, he was given a saving grace: a *nefesh*, a feeling, sensitive spirit, a bit of God, a diamond of immortality within him. And what does he do? In order to win a piece of bread, he is willing to sacrifice all that *nefesh*! He is willing to throw away his character, to destroy his personality, to yield all his most sacred principles, to give up Shabbat and *Yom Tov*—and what for? For a few crumbs! Later in life, when we have achieved that success we have so passionately searched and worked for, the fruits of this success begin to turn bitter in our mouths. And we realize, to our dismay, that we have given up so much for a piece of stale bread, for another parcel of real estate, for another big deal, for another salary increase, for another professional honor! *Be-lahmo yavi nafsho!* We surrender our souls for miserable crumbs. We give up the immortal and eternal life and the ineffable delights of the *nefesh* for the ephemeral, flighty chimerical moment of the flesh. What a tragedy! No wonder *al ken ya'azov ish et aviv ve-et immo*; if the *basar* remains a standard, then father and son have nothing to talk about, and mother and daughter have little in common. And all humans—*sofo le-afar*: a life lived and nothing accomplished. *U-motar ha-adam min ha-behemah ayin, ki ha-kol havel* (Eccl. 3:19)—if there is nothing, no *nefesh*, to distinguish man from animal, then indeed, all is vanity, and life is not worth the struggle.

But today is Yom Kippur. Today our lofty tradition tells us that our life need not be merely an insignificantly brief respite between *afar* and *afar*—but that *nefesh*, and our awareness of it, can redeem us to eternal life.

If these sacred moments of Yizkor, when we commune with our memories, are to be meaningful, then we must now rededicate ourselves to that which all of us tend to ignore during the rest of the year: the *nefesh*, the *neshamah*, that which raises man above the level of a beast, that which makes him worthy of *yizkor Elokim*, of being remembered by God. As our thoughts go back to revered father and beloved mother, let us promise them that they, we, our children, and our children's children, will ever be united through the eternal links of Israel's faith.

Ve-heshiv lev avot el banim ve-lev banim el avotam—"And the Lord shall cause the heart of the fathers to return to the sons, and the heart of the sons to their father" (Mal. 3:24).

EVERYBODY IS A SOMEBODY

I WOULD LIKE TO center my message to you this morning about a story which apparently has nothing to do with Yom Kippur, but which in fact captures the whole essence of this sacred day. It is an episode in the life of King David (I Sam. 20) which we normally read in the synagogue as the *haftarah* for the Shabbat before Rosh Hodesh.

The incident took place in the time when King Saul, the first king of Israel, was half-crazed by jealousy of the young hero David, whose popularity he considered a threat to his throne. Saul was so embittered at David that he wanted to kill him. David did not know whether or not it was safe for him to appear in the palace, and whether or not to flee. Now the eldest son of Saul and heir-apparent to the throne was Jonathan, who was the dearest friend of David. Torn between loyalty to his royal father and affection for his cherished friend, Jonathan was ultimately to give up his own claim to the throne in order to allow David to become the successor to his father, King Saul. At a particularly critical period, David asks Jonathan what to do. Jonathan tells David that he will sound out his father and see if he really intends to harm him. Meanwhile, says Jonathan, go into hiding. Three days from now, after the Rosh Hodesh feast in the palace, I will come out into the field, ostensibly to practice my archery. You hide behind the big stone Azel, David, and wait there. I will have with me a *na'ar*, a boy or servant. I will shoot three arrows in your direction, and send the boy after them. If I shoot the arrows so that they fall short of where you are, you will know that all is well, and you can come out of hiding. But if I shoot them beyond where you are hiding, then that is the signal that my father seeks to destroy you, and you must quickly flee in order to save your life.

On the second day of the palace feast, things did not go well. Saul created a terrible scene in which he accused Jonathan of plotting with David and condemned David to death as a traitor. So Jonathan left, and on the morrow, *ve-na'ar katan immo* (I Sam. 20:35)—he took the young boy with him. He aimed

5726 (1965)

85

his arrows well beyond where David was secretly stationed, and he called to the boy and said, "Go farther, hurry, the arrow is still farther on." When David saw the lad running, he knew the bad news. *Ve-ha-na'ar lo yada me'umah, akh Yehonatan ve-David yade'u et ha-davar* (v. 39)—only David and Jonathan knew the meaning of all this; the lad knew nothing. And so David and Jonathan bade each other farewell, and David went into hiding, to emerge eventually as the man upon whose head was placed the crown of Israel.

Such is the beautiful story of a noble friendship in a time when our nation was young. Yet the moral of loyalty is not the reason I have chosen to repeat it to you this morning. My reason is quite different. Allow me to explain.

Yom Kippur seems to impose an impossible burden upon us. By bidding us confess to our sins, as we do when we recite the *Al Het* and the *Ashamnu*, the Jewish tradition drives home the awesome theme of responsibility. We are responsible for every one of our moral and ethical failings. We are responsible for the neglect of Torah and Judaism. We are responsible, too, for the low spiritual and moral estate of our families. Even more, we are in some measure responsible for the sins of society: for the Bomb and its threat of mass death, for the corruption that festers in government and in business, for the filth that inundates our libraries and newsstands and theaters, for the lethal dust that chokes us and our children, for the brutality in Vietnam.

What a huge load to carry! In self-defense, we sometimes feel like saying: *Ribbono shel Olam!* What do You want from us? We are humble people. We work as hard and as honestly as we can just to keep our families going and leave something for the children. We are not famous, we have no great power, we are not in authority. If You have complaints about the Bomb, talk to the famous physicists and engineers and the international diplomats. Corruption? Speak to the president and the judges and the heads of the great corporations. Immorality? Address Yourself to the giant publishers and attorneys general and movie magnates. But we—we are without influence to change the course of events. We are small people. We may make some money, but can have no lasting effect on our own destinies, let alone that of the world. We can do nothing.

If that thought has occurred to you as a way out of the terrible responsibility urged on us by Yom Kippur; if you have had the feeling that we are just numbers, just puny statistics, just a series of holes punched on an IBM card, just helpless and anonymous blobs of protoplasm, pushed and pulled and crowded by the impersonal forces of society and nature; if you have concluded that life nowadays is such that you, as the "ordinary" man or woman, can do nothing about the really great and momentous issues in the world in general, and in the Jewish community in particular; if, in other words, you are willing to proclaim your *ir*responsibility and to issue a declaration of impotence, then the story of David and Jonathan sharply reminds you that such excuses are not only unbecoming and undignified and un-Jewish, but false and malicious!

Remember that in the biblical story of David and Jonathan there are not two but *three* main characters. Remember that not only the noble and loyal Prince Jonathan is important, and not only the young David, who is to ascend the throne and change Jewish history forever—but also the *na'ar katan*, the young lad, the ignorant boy who *lo yada me'umah*, who knew nothing of the great drama in which he was taking part—he too is a protagonist, he too deserves credit for the succession of David, for enthroning that man who was to unite the *shivtei Yisra'el*, the Israel of his day, and become the ancestor of the *Melekh ha-Mashiah*, the Messiah of the future.

How prone we are to recall only the famous names and ignore the little people, without whom nothing significant ever happens! Imagine if that young, anonymous boy, about whom we know nothing else other than that he was the servant or archery-caddy of Jonathan—imagine if he had said to himself: what do I count? What responsibility do I have to anyone for anything? And since I have no real importance in the world, why bother with such ideas as duty and loyalty? I might as well sleep late, or fail to show up, or go wandering off in a different direction! Imagine if he had been derelict in his simple duties—like so many of today's waiters who don't wait, and repairmen who don't repair, and cleaners who don't clean! How different—and how much worse!—history might have been!

Little did that youngster realize that a pair of eyes were secretly watching him that fateful day; that upon the proper accomplishment of his duty depended the future of his whole people and ultimately all the world; that his little task well done assured the safety of David, and the political and religious and spiritual destiny of thousands of his contemporaries and thousands of generations thereafter!

It is not only the princes and the heroes who play a role in history. It is not only the great and the famous upon whom the world rests. It is even a *na'ar katan*, a young lad, who, by carrying out his tasks loyally, briefly emerges from obscurity and helps redirect the course of history. He remains anonymous—but so very important!

Of such stuff is the story of all mankind made. History is the accumulation of thousands upon thousands of "lads who know not" the significance of their own deeds. The great issues are decided, in the long run, not by those in the headlines but by the thousand "little people" who do or do not follow the dictates of conscience. David could not have become the great king he was without this little boy who signaled him, without another helpful stranger who gave him bread when he was starving, without a prophet who challenged him and a wife who inspired him and countless nameless soldiers who were ready to give their lives for him. The State of Israel was not built alone by the David Ben-Gurions and Moshe Sharetts and Levi Eshkols—it was built as well by young men who died on the battlefield, and old mothers who let their sons and daughters leave the Russian Pale for the malarial swamps of Palestine, students of Talmud and loyal, religious Jews who never gave up the dream and vision of *ge'ulah*, and anonymous hundreds who invested in Israel and the thousands who once collected coins for the JNF and the millions who contribute whatever they can to UJA. Everyone who did his best played a role in Israel.

For that is indeed all that is demanded of us by God—not that we do *more* than we can, but that we do *all* that it is in our power to do. On that and on that alone are we judged. Sometimes we are called upon to make the supreme sacrifice. Usually all that Judaism demands is that we sacrifice just a little of our comfort, a little of our convenience and time and money and thought and consideration and energy. When the great Book of Life is opened in Heaven, as we read in the *U-Netanneh Tokef*, it may be true that *u-mal'akhim yehafezun*, sublime angels rush about and create a stir, but in the Book of Life, *ve-hotam yad kol adam bo*, each man's own personal, individual signature is recorded therein. Each has his own mission. That he must do: no more—but no less. When we do what God requires of us—and what is required of us is the sum and substance of the teachings of Judaism—we have fulfilled our goals and *we are important*, whether or not our names are inscribed on great monuments or in history books.

That is the theme of responsibility taught to us by Yom Kippur. Each of us could have done more in our own little way; it is when we fail that we must say *Al Het* and confess our failure. When we do that in all earnestness, we are responsible human beings. To be convinced that I am unimportant, that I simply don't count, is to be dead even though I breathe. To strive to fulfill my mission and purpose in whatever way God has allowed me, whether by raising a worthy family, charity, study, teaching, Israel, service to a great cause, is to live on and have my influence survive my own limited life.

Do you think you are without influence? Then remember that how you act toward your husband or wife at home is witnessed silently by your impressionable children, who incorporate your conduct into their character and will someday act likewise. Like the *na'ar katan* watched by David, your conduct can be the signal which will change a life. How you as a Jew act in your business or profession can have the greatest effect on some non-Jew or on some young Jewish person who is wondering whether it is worth remaining a Jew. Never underestimate it! A kind word to a person who is lonely, a smile to someone who is friendless, a compliment to someone who lacks confidence, a bit of encouragement to a child unsure of himself—you may not realize it, but it is from such little things that the future is manufactured! All the more reason, therefore, to feel personally responsible when we forget to offer that word, that smile, that encouragement!

The sainted Hafetz Hayyim told of the first time he saw a train. Who, he wondered, guides this train? Who drives it? At first, he saw very busy and official-looking people with big red caps carrying things to and from the baggage cars. Surely, he thought, these important people are the masters of the train. Then, when he discovered they were merely porters, "red caps," he noticed a big, dignified-looking gentleman in an impressive uniform collecting tickets from people. No doubt, he thought, this official owns the train—how important and solemn he appears. But when he learned he was only the ticket-collector, he turned to the man in resplendent uniform and of bushy mustache and booming voice who came marching stridently through the cars blowing a whistle. Certainly *he* guides the train. But no, he was merely the conductor. Perhaps, then, it is collectively owned and operated by all those aristocratic people in the parlor car who are so well dressed and smoke expensive cigars? No, they are only passengers. Then he came to the front car, the engine room. There he saw a man in overalls, one who seemed bedraggled, who needed a shave, who looked impoverished and insignificant, who appeared to be a manual laborer and shoved coal into the fire and pulled a few rusty switches . . . And he—this inconspicuous, anonymous, obscure fellow—he was the master of the train, upon him depended the safety of the whole train and all its passengers! The *na'ar katan* often plays the great roles!

That is the nature of the message of Yom Kippur. And that is my plea to you this holy day. Do not imagine that only the great and dramatic events are significant. In the eyes of God and in the eyes of history, we too are important if we but do all we can. For nobody is a "nobody." And everybody is a "somebody"—unless, of course, we choose to abdicate that role, that function, that responsibility.

The people we shall soon memorialize in the Yizkor may not have been famous people. Maybe they did not shake worlds. But each and every one in some measure, whether large or small, has influenced the world or some part of it. They influenced us. We influence our children, or others' children. And they, in turn, will influence others. The fact that we are here today is a tribute to them; had one link in the chain of generations been severed, we would not be Jews congregating in this *makom kadosh* today. In appreciating, therefore, the impact of the lives of our loved ones upon us, we must consider the kind of influence we shall have over the generations that will follow us. For everyone has *some* influence. We must, then, watch our step whether we like it or not; we cannot journey through life without leaving footprints, and others will follow where we go because we have marked the way.

That influence, that direction of our footprints, will be spelled out not in wealth, not in power, not in worldly fame. It will be exercised in the manner and the responsibility with which each of us carries out his assigned tasks in life. Whether we are anonymous lads, playing a supporting role in some great drama, or shabbily dressed conductors, directly guiding the destiny of hundreds of fellow passengers through life, we must be aware of our importance in the eyes of God and those who shall come after us.

Thus, and only thus, shall we emerge from death to life, from oblivion to significance. For everybody is a somebody.

ON TO EDEN

YIZKOR IS A TIME OF sacred nostalgia. For a few bittersweet moments, our hearts and minds go back to loved ones who are no longer with us. From long-buried layers of memory, we summon up the security and comfort of youth. Those of us who are now parents and even grandparents revert to a time when we were children, relieved of the burdens of responsibility, cared for and worried over and loved by those in whom we placed full trust. Others relive a happier time when a beloved husband or wife graced our lives, fulfilled our personalities, gave meaning and completion to our existence.

It is an important occasion. We need these precious moments of sentimental recollection and the reminiscence of love. They add another dimension to what might otherwise be merely a drab or prosaic or simply busy existence.

In a sense, all of the High Holiday season partakes of this yearning for the past, for better times that have gone by. From Rosh Hashanah through Yom Kippur, we recite, every day, the *Shema Kolenu* prayer, in which we repeat the words of the Torah (Lam. 5:21), *haddesh yameinu ke-kedem*, "renew our days as of old." We pray for a reversion to "the days of old," to a lovelier and more satisfying life.

Nevertheless, and this is the burden of my remarks this afternoon, while it is good to indulge such feelings, it is dangerous to overindulge them. Nostalgia is refreshing if it is a limited experience. But it cramps and even destroys our creativity if it overwhelms all the rest of life. Too often, people abandon themselves to an aching, wistful, passive worship of their past, and forgo any real effort at improving the present and securing the future. It is a profound social commentary on the fate of Judaism that for many families, the end of Jewishness and the beginning of full assimilation was marked by the reduction of all Jewish observance to the recitation of Kaddish and Yizkor. Man cannot long live by longing alone. The dream world of the past may be the playground of the imagination and sentiment. But it is also a trap that lures us with the bait of

---

5730 (1969)

bygone loves in order to neutralize whatever ambitions we might have for the active improvement of today and tomorrow.

The danger of the nostalgic experience, if overdone, is that it is an effortless and easy triumph; just by turning on my imagination, I can relocate myself in a situation in which warmth and love and affection surround me—all without exertion. But Judaism, with all its reverence for the past, is most concerned with an active existence here and now. Torah prods us on to hard work, to strenuous effort, to victories that are earned and deserved by strain and struggle and even suffering.

I believe that this is what the Rabbis had in mind in a most remarkable interpretation of the verse we cited, *haddesh yameinu ke-kedem*. Normally, that verse is translated, "renew our days as of old." But the Midrash, at the end of *Eikhah Rabbah*, understands the word *kedem* not temporally, but spatially. The word can be a time-word, "old" or "ancient," but it can also be a space-word, "east." And the Rabbis maintained that *kedem* here refers not to "days of old," but to a specific place, namely, East of Eden. In Genesis (3:24), we read that the Lord expelled Adam from the Garden of Eden, *va-yashken mi-kedem le-Gan Eden et ha-keruvim ve-et lahat herev ha-mithappekhet lishmor et derekh etz ha-hayyim*, "and He placed at the east of the Garden of Eden (*kedem* of Gan Eden) the cherubim and the flash of the turning sword in order to guard the way to the Tree of Life."

What a strange statement! We ask God to restore our days, to renew our life, as in the days of *kedem*—and the Rabbis say this refers not to the "good old days," but to the expulsion from the Garden of Eden! One would imagine that we would ask God to renew our days as they were *in* Paradise, not *after* we were chased *out* of Paradise, symbolized by East of Eden.

But this is the vital, marvelous secret which Judaism wants to teach us. Every man and every woman has his own private Gan Eden, the paradise of his dreams and his youthful ambitions. For some people it is a vision of great wealth, walking into a life where he has millions at his disposal. For others it is a great novel written without sweat, a great scientific discovery made without perspiration, the great legal theories or philosophical discourses that he will develop at the drop of a hat, or a life of love and popularity and fame and happiness and satisfaction without exertion. Often, this craving for instant success and achievement is merged with our vision of a past whose agonies we forget and which we idealize and romanticize. The delicious past becomes the symbol of our easy, private paradises.

What the Rabbis are telling us is that this sort of paradise which hangs on the gossamer threads of our imaginations and is glued together by the cement of our wish fulfillment, is something that is terribly dangerous, that if we try to enter it, we simply fall into an endless pit. Such a Gan Eden is really a Gehinnom.

Look at Adam himself. When he and Eve disported themselves in God's Paradise, they got into trouble; they submitted to all kinds of blandishments, they caused curse and conflict to come upon the world, and they began to hate each other.

It was only after God did them the favor of expelling them from the Gan Eden which He, God, had created for them, that they became human. They built a family and learned how much they really needed each other. In essence, the *human* biography of Adam, the story of man as a fully creative human being, begins only *after* the expulsion from Paradise.

So, *haddesh yameinu ke-kedem* does not mean "renew our days as of old," give us back that dream world of parental love given free, of security achieved without struggle, of a Paradise there for the asking and the wishing, but give us the courage to face life East of Eden, to throw ourselves into the fray for a fuller and finer life, to forge a new world, indeed a new paradise, after we were expelled from or pulled ourselves out of the Eden we never paid for or fought for. To create a new Paradise *mi-kedem le-Gan Eden,* east of or outside the prefabricated one, is more satisfying, more fulfilling, more noble. *Haddesh yameinu ke-kedem!*

In counseling young couples in marital disputes, one comes across many difficult situations. But the one that most disturbs and distresses me is when a young person says about a new husband or wife, "I just fell out of love with" him or her. It is the symptom of a profound malady that afflicts all too many people today, perhaps all of society. The idiom "fall in" or "fall out" of love implies effortlessness—you just tumble happily into a euphoric state of love and affection, without testing the resources of your own character, without the rigorous and tough trial of adjustment, without the trying adventure of exploring another and different personality. It implies that marriage and love are a cheap paradise. And easy come, easy go—what is acquired without strain is lost without pain.

But that is a lie—a dangerous and costly lie. To all young people of marriageable age here, I plead with you o keep this in mind. Of course, it is wonderful to fall in love. But if you do not work at developing a relationship, if you are not ready to sacrifice and give and renounce and even suffer, you may not be "falling in love," but just "falling in." In one of the *sheva berakhot*, the seven blessings recited at a wedding, we ask of God to make the young couple happy *ke-sammehakha yetzirekha be-Gan Eden mi-kedem*—as You made Your creatures Adam and Eve happy in Eden *mi-kedem*, East of Eden, after the expulsion, when they had to give up their childish illusions and struggle to *create* happiness rather than *inherit* it. In a ready-made Gan Eden, as Adam and Eve learned to their sorrow, there can be no real happiness and satisfaction. It is only after being expelled from that illusory paradise that *ve-ha-adam yada et Havah ishto* (Gen. 4:1); that in the literal sense rather than the idiomatic signification, Adam first begins to understand and to know and to recognize his wife. There is an existential closeness that develops between them, as love is reciprocated and effort is rewarded and the family is built and the human story begins.

Ten centuries ago, Sa'adyah Gaon taught that the observance of the commandments affords man happiness by way of reward. But, he asks, could not the Creator have granted us happiness without the need for performing difficult, demanding deeds? Yes, he answers. He could have—but it is in the nature of things that what is earned, worked for, strived for, gives a man much more joy and fulfillment and satisfaction than what is received merely as a gift (*Sefer Emunot ve-De'ot* III:1).

It is the failure to understand this principle that vitiates so much of the rhetoric of the younger, "Now" Generation. When, only a few short years ago, young people expressed their dissatisfaction with the status quo of society by volunteering for the Peace Corps overseas or the Domestic Peace Corps, that was admirable, a sign of idealism in its most mature expression. They were going to build a paradise—and if they did not succeed, at least they would make the world habitable, no longer a hell. But when their successors today want a society of love and peace and a "groovy" time for all—without work or sweat or pain or exertion, but only by driving to Eden in their father's car and using his expense account, then they are ready to be driven *out* of Eden much less ceremoniously than they drove in. *Haddesh yameinu ke-kedem—mi-kedem le-Gan Eden.*

For a long time, too long a time, Jewish life in this country was afflicted by the same passivism. So much of Yiddish literature and drama in the early years in America was a loving evocation of *der alter heim*, a brooding contemplation of the glory that once was. And all this time Jewish life was permitted to crumble under the onslaught of acculturation and assimilation. They dreamed of the Gan Eden of once upon a time, and failed to make that move to *kedem le-Gan Eden*, East of Eden, to active upbuilding of Jewish life and institutions. There was too much Yizkor and too little *Musaf*, too much nostalgia and too little pioneering, too much Eden and too little East of Eden.

And this, of course, is what the State of Israel is all about. It came into being when Jews stopped dreaming of Eretz Yisra'el as a primitively beautiful paradise to which Messiah was going to lead us miraculously and without any effort by us; a land flowing with milk and honey without the need for farmers and dairymen; a land in which (as Yehudah Halevi put it) the very air is filled with souls, without the necessity to build schools and persuade the skeptics and teach the ignorant. But such a paradise never existed—nor, perhaps, did it deserve to exist. The real paradise that is Eretz Yisra'el lies *mi-kedem*, East of Eden; it was drained from the swamps and built on rocks and defended against marauders and sanctified by dedication and devotion and teaching and toiling.

On Yom Kippur, certainly, we must be honest. Let us then admit it. Orthodox Jews, most of them, were wrong in giving a passive interpretation to the idea of waiting for Messiah. True, it is the pious Jew who kept the hope of a redeemed Israel alive so that it could be realized in our times. But passivity simply was not a sufficient answer. We were trapped in the vision of Eden itself, and failed to take the crucial step to East of Eden, to active work to create a viable Jewish state.

At the same time, let it be said that Israelis are making a grievous error if they allow the present grave problems of the State to distract them from the even graver spiritual problem that they will have to face sooner or later. The spiritual-cultural-religious problem will not resolve itself automatically. The great question is: will Israel really remain Jewish? This much is certain: it will not retain its uniqueness, its individuality, its very soul without a painful confrontation with the Jewish tradition and Jewish faith, without formidable, daring, and unremitting efforts to shed its secularist infatuation and come to terms with Torah and its challenges. Today we know, with the benefit of hindsight, that Zionism erred in failing to plan a program for the period that would follow the declaration of the State; it was defeated by success. Israel must plan today—despite the pressure of military threats and international cynicism and the betrayal of so many of its supposed friends—for the time when peace will come and the spiritual problems will suddenly loom large. Unless we—all of us, for the future of Judaism in the Diaspora is unthinkable without a vigorous Judaism in Israel—plan and work and struggle now for Jewish education and character and tradition and observance and faith, Gan Eden shall elude us. *Haddesh yameinu ke-kedem.*

At the end of this summer just past, General Dayan addressed the graduating class of an officers' school in Israel and offered his explanation of a biblical verse, which I think is completely correct. When God said to Jacob, *Al tira avdi Yaakov,* "do not be afraid, my servant Jacob" (Is. 44:2), that did not mean that Jacob would stay on the sidelines while God fought for him and assured him success. Not to be afraid means to be courageous, and courage is not necessary for the spectator. Fearlessness is necessary for the fighter, for the one who enters the fray and takes up arms and charges into battle. God told Jacob, in effect, that he must throw himself into the struggle to build a people and fight for the triumph of his ideals and bring God into the world, and that since he was going to be an active participant, the soldier of God, it was important to give him courage and tell him not to be afraid when things seem tough and the future looks dark.

That is an interpretation worthy of a general of Israel and a national hero. And it applies not only to military life but also to the even greater battle for the supremacy of the Jewish spirit and the integrity of the Jewish soul.

We American Jews must not falter, and more important, we must not expect miracles to save us from assimilation and ethnic obsolescence. We hold the future in our hands. Unless we resolve to give our children the maximum Jewish education—and that decidedly includes what they see at home even more than what they are taught in school—they shall remain with less than the minimum. No man can survive a divinely prepared paradise; we must be expelled. There are no heavenly guarantees for our survival as Jews. Only arduous, heroic, passionate action here and now, *mi-kedem,* East of Eden, will create the kind of society in which our families can carry on the Jewish tradition and secure the peoplehood of Israel. Easy triumphs are an illusion, and nostalgic brooding a vanity. Paradise is never inherited; it is built.

Hashivenu Hashem elekha ve-nashuvah, "Turn us to Thee, O Lord, and we shall return," or do *teshuvah.* And how does one do *teshuvah*? How does one succeed in redirecting the course of his life? Only when he prays *haddesh yameinu ke-kedem—mi-kedem le-Gan Eden,* not for a magical return to the womb of effortless convenience, the total security of infancy, but for divine help as he throws himself into the grimy battle to conquer his own paradise, to build it painstakingly and persistently, piece by piece, bit by bit.

As we recite the Yizkor, let us savor deeply of these sweet and sad sentiments of reunion, as we relive old loves and experience old pains. However, let Yizkor be, not a substitute for life, but a spur to better living; not a fruitless nostalgia, but an opportunity for refreshing re-creation at the fount of yesterday's memories, drawing the courage to build a livable today and a better tomorrow; not a petrifaction of ancient recollections, but a perpetuation of the vital heritage of the past; not just a longing look back to what was, but the lapping up of strength to face what will be. As we turn to the past and evoke love which has not grown stale, let us find the inspiration to turn, thereafter, to the future with equal love and undiminished determination.

ONE HOUR

IN ITS FORMULATION OF prayer, the Jewish tradition is somewhat more mystical than rationalistic, and its teaching strikes us intuitively as attractive and religiously valid. Normally, we assume that it makes no difference when a man prays, provided that he knows what he says and is sincere in his devotion. But Judaism tells us that there is more required than the participation of the heart and the genuineness of the spirit, although they are, of course, indispensable. A man must also know *le-khavven et ha-sha'ah*, how to guess or strike the right hour (*Berakhot* 7a).

Time, the tradition means to tell us, is not uniform. Certain hours are more accessible to particular prayers than others. Certain prayers are more suited to certain times than to others. A good prayer has its right time, and the one who prays must have a sense of the appropriateness of what he says to the time it is said. Thus, *bakkashat tzerakhim*, asking for the fulfillment of one's needs, must not be uttered on the Sabbath. Prayers celebrating God's sovereignty over nature are normally recited at the change of the day—at dawn and dusk—or the change of the month, at Rosh Hodesh. Certain propitiatory prayers, such as *Tahanun*, may not be recited at night.

In the same vein, Maimonides, in his Laws of Repentance (2: 6), tells us concerning the repentance and the prayer of individuals: "Although repentance and prayer are always appropriate, during the ten days from Rosh Hashanah to Yom Kippur they are especially beautiful and immediately accepted." This penitential period, which reaches its climax on this day, is especially suitable and appropriate for prayer.

Hence, the verse which we repeat every day during this High Holy Day season: *Avinu Malkenu, tehei ha-sha'ah ha-zot she'at rahamim ve-et ratzon mille-fanekha*, "Our Father, our King, may this hour prove to be an hour of mercy and a time of grace before Thee."

5731 (1970)

98

There are certain times that are particularly susceptible to certain movements of the spirit, and if we miss them, then those exquisite moments of spiritual efficacy and exhilaration are lost to us forever. These spiritual moments are irretrievable.

What I am trying to say is this: the world of the spirit teaches what the practical world already knows—that certain opportunities are singular; they arise, never to return. If we are wise, we know how to exploit these opportunities. If we are not, they are lost and cannot be recaptured.

The same idea has been expressed in a beautiful fashion and a different way. The Talmud teaches (*Avodah Zarah* 17a): *Rebbi* [R. Judah ha-Nassi] *bakhah ve-amar: Yesh koneh olamo be-kammah shanim, ve-yesh koneh olamo be-sha'ah ahat*—Rebbi wept and exclaimed that there are some people who must work all their lives in order to win their share in the World-to-Come, while others, whose lives may be spent in dereliction of duty, can, in one hour of strenuous and heroic effort, win their world, the World-to-Come.

The great rabbi of Lublin, Rabbi Meir Shapiro, asked a simple and obvious question: Why, if indeed a man can change his destiny in one hour, should that cause Rebbi to weep? On the contrary, he should have been overjoyed that man is afforded such opportunities that, in but one hour, he may change the course of his destiny. The Lubliner answered: Rebbi cried because it is possible for that hour to come into the life of a man and the man be unaware of it. The hour may come, the man sleeps, and the hour departs—forever. The opportunity for immortality arises for but one hour, and the hour may be lost.

It is with this in mind that I turn to the high school and college students who are here this day. You are the victims of social and economic circumstances beyond your control, which have forced you into an unnaturally prolonged adolescence. Because of this unnatural state, many of your contemporaries have fallen prey to a mass hysteria of irrationalism, disguised as noble idealism. I need not enumerate the ways in which this neurosis expresses itself. But I plead with you: Do not fall victim to it. Do not imagine that you can live a life of nonsense or abandon, leaving your religious development to later in life. No, that *sha'ah ahat*, that hour of golden opportunity, is at hand now; it may not return later on. Now, in the full flush of your strength and enthusiasm, in the full bloom of your young idealism, now is the time for you heroically to show how a true Jew lives on the campus—despite the difficulty, despite the ridicule, despite the discomfort, despite the burden of differentness it places upon you. It is almost a prophetic mission—to be the models of Jewish conduct for your peers—but it is an exciting one and a creative one. And now is the time—this hour.

As the Rabbis taught in *Avot* (2:5), *Al tomar le-ke-she-efneh eshneh, shema lo tifneh*, "Do not say that when I have time I shall study; you may never have the time."

I would direct my remarks in the same vein to young men who are at the beginning or the middle of their business or professional careers, chalking up one success after another. There is a natural tendency to become so absorbed in your work that you neglect all other portions of your personality that do not deal with the empirical and the pragmatic world. But these talents and propensities do not last forever. You will not always have the ability to develop a warm relationship with wife and children. You will not always have the kind of artistic or aesthetic bent you may now have. Above all else, remember that there is a spiritual side to personality—and I do not only refer to outward religious observances. There is an aspect of life itself that speaks of inner sensitivity, of a mystic longing, of a spiritual yearning. Do not neglect it. Now is the *sha'ah ahat* in which you must begin to develop this side of your lives. If you do not, it may very well wither away. I know that you are busy. In our period of life, busy-ness is both the blessing and the bane of our existence. Never must busy-ness allow us to neglect our own higher, nonmaterial development.

A rather depressing story was told to me by a colleague of mine. He was returning from the funeral of a dear friend in the same car with the deceased's son, who had been very close to his father. The son seemed even more upset than the circumstances called for, and much more than his personality would lead one to expect. My colleague inquired of him as to whether there was any special reason for his disturbance. "Yes," answered the young man. "I was told that shortly before he passed away, my father felt the urge to speak with me. He wanted to tell me something important. So, from his hospital bed, he picked up the telephone and rang my number. But my line was busy. By the time I was free, he was dead." *Rebbi bakhah ve-amar: Yesh koneh olamo be-kamah shanim, ve-yesh koneh olamo be-sha'ah ahat.* How sad, that during that hour, that precious and cherished and great hour—our lines are busy. And the hour never returns.

Before Yizkor, our thoughts inevitably turn to parents and children. Discord, irritation, and differences are normal in relations between parents and children. But they must never be permitted to get out of hand, to strike below the surface. To children I would say: You have your parents only for a limited time. They themselves will shortly say Yizkor for *their* parents. Make up your minds that this year will be your *sha'ah ahat*, your special time to exploit for the great Jewish and universal ideal of *Kabbed et avikha ve-et immekha*. Devote this year more than ever before to honoring and giving comfort and satisfaction to your parents—with sensitivity, with patience, with grace.

And to parents I would say: Children are really all we have. The time that we can influence them is severely limited—relatively a *sha'ah ahat*, or infrequent hours spread throughout life. Try to be wise in discharging your duties. Do not relinquish your parental role as teacher and guide. But do not bear down too hard, do not interfere with the development of a child's natural, healthy personality. If his goals are right, allow him to achieve these goals in his own way. Do not abuse and lose this golden opportunity for developing a healthy relationship with a child, a warm and loving one, that will always remain as the great source of strength for future guidance.

Now is the opportunity. Now, and perhaps never again. *Ve-im lo akhshav eimatai*—if not now, when? (*Avot* 1:14).

In all these instances, simple awareness of opportunities is insufficient. What is more important is the willingness to exploit them, to work and exert yourself in order to take advantage of opportunities.

In the first chapter of *Bava Metzia* (9a), the Talmud tells us the various laws of *metzi'ot*, finds. In one law, we are told of two people going on the way. One is a *rokhev al gabbei behemah*, riding on an animal, and the other walks, leading the animal, and they chance upon a *metzi'ah*. The rider sees it first—but the pedestrian picks it up first. Both claim the find and come to court. What is the law? The Talmud decides the Halakhah: *natelah ve-amar ani zakhiti bah zakhah*—the one who picks it up first and says "It is mine" is the rightful and legal owner.

There are many *metzi'ot* in life—in business, in family happiness, in community work, in friendship, in the simple opportunity to help someone when he most needs it. In every instance, merely being aware and articulating the opportunity does not mean that we have taken advantage of it. We must be willing to work, to labor; if you permit me the appropriate colloquialism, a man must be willing to get off his high horse in order to exploit the rare hour of opportunity.

Perhaps the most crucial instance of a *sha'ah ahat* that we dare not ignore is the possibility of a religious renaissance in the State of Israel since the Six-Day War.

Before the war, many or even most Israelis were afflicted with a dogmatic agnosticism, almost an irritating and arrogant cynicism. The war changed that for many—and it changed it deeply. One small symptom of the phenomenal change was a slim volume which has become a classic in Israel: *Siah Lohamim*, the testimony of the young paratroopers who first conquered the Western Wall. These were the children of the extreme Left kibbutzim, and yet what they had to say revealed a dimension of historical affiliation and spiritual orientation that they themselves were unaware of. Generally, the war served to detach the cynics from their cynicism, to disorient the dogmatic secularist, and has made especially the young question the wisdom of their parents, who raised them more on Marx than on Moses.

Here was an answer to our prayer, *Avinu malkenu tehei ha-sha'ah ha-zot she'at rahamim ve-et ratozon millefanekhah*. Here was the great *sha'ah ahat* for *teshuvat ha-tzibbur*, a repentance of the entire community.

Yet we have largely let it pass without exploiting it. And because of our indifference, old routines of thought and conduct, old habits of speech and deed, have returned to their former niches. The situation has unfortunately "stabilized" in the old pattern. Religious Jewry so far has failed to exploit this miraculous but rare opportunity.

Measured in historical time, fifty-eight minutes of this *sha'ah ahat* have passed; we have two minutes to go if a beginning is to be made in talking to the nonobservant portions of Israeli Jewry. The distance and the alienation between the *datiyyim* (religious) and the *hillonim* (secularists) is not only a religiously pernicious phenomenon, it is also a nationally and socially destructive threat. The fabric of the State of Israel is threatened by it. So we must make a beginning in an effort to bridge the gap between the two communities. We must not lose this *sha'ah ahat*.

Today I tell you: I take this challenge personally. I feel that I too must make my modest contribution to exploiting this great *sha'ah ahat*. For if I fail to try, then *bakhah Rebbi*—this rabbi knows that he will deserve to weep.

For this reason I am taking a three-month leave from The Jewish Center to join my effort to those of other colleagues, both rabbinic and academic, acting through several groups, primarily one called Gesher (which means "bridge"), to make this great beginning. The task is a formidable one, a difficult one, and an arduous one, that will take more than three months or three years or even ten years. But we have only a *sha'ah ahat* in which to begin.

Maybe we shall not succeed. But, as I have often said from this pulpit, there is nothing morally wrong with trying and failing; there is everything morally shameful about failing to try.

My leave from The Jewish Center will represent the combination of such opportunities. It will be a *sha'ah ahat* for young children to be exposed to life in Eretz Yisra'el, where hopefully they will learn to love it. It will be an opportunity for me to acquaint myself with Israelis, both leaders and ordinary folk, my first such genuine opportunity. And no one who aspires to any kind of leadership in the American Jewish community can afford not to know Israel. It will mean an opportunity to study and read and learn on a more sustained basis than a busy rabbinate in America affords me.

But above all else, it will be an opportunity, even if but an hour measured in the longer perspective, to try to open a dialogue between the observant and the nonobservant, between the Diaspora and the State of Israel, an attempt to present the message of Torah without political motivation, even without missionary intent, but simply with the desire to increase mutual respect between all Jews, an endeavor based on the faith and the confidence that if this mutual respect is achieved, the Torah will "sell" itself.

To the leadership of The Jewish Center and all The Center Family goes my endless appreciation for their understanding of the historic need of the novel situation of the Jewish world today.

May I assure you that, despite the beauty and the excitement of living in Jerusalem—and there is nothing quite as beautiful and exciting—I shall miss you sorely.

I shall keep all of you in mind, and when I pray at the places where our ancestors trod on the holy soil of the land of Abraham, Isaac, and Jacob, and when I approach the Wall behind which our fathers ministered in the Temple of Solomon and at the foot of which generations of our people—from royalty and priesthood to weary pilgrims and refugees—offered their deepest devotions, I shall offer my *tefillot* for each and every member of The Center Family: that when I return three months hence, *im yirtzeh Hashem*, I find the sick restored to health, the weak to strength, the mourners consoled, the lonely encouraged; that all strife will vanish and all unhappiness will disappear.

And in return, I ask you for your prayers that my work be crowned with success, and that I return *im yirtzeh Hashem* with my family reinvigorated, ready to rededicate myself to The Center, to the community, and to Torah with renewed strength.

Because I plan to leave tomorrow *im yirtzeh Hashem,* I will not have the chance to bid farewell to each of you personally. So let me address you collectively, and intend each and every one of you individually: may you be blessed with a *gemar hatimah tovah* and a *shenat hayyim ve-shalom,* a year of life and peace.

Shalom u-le-hitra'ot and *Yivarekhekha Hashem mei-Tziyyon.* May God bless you from Zion.

Avinu Malkenu, tehei ha-sha'ah ha-zot she'at rahamim ve-et ratzon mille-fanekha.

Sukkot

SAVE AND PROSPER

OUR TEXT FOR THIS morning is a familiar verse from the Psalms which we recite every Rosh Hodesh and every holiday as part of the *Hallel*, and which we recite on this festival of Sukkot as well.

That verse is, *Anna Hashem hoshi'ah na* and *Anna Hashem hatzlihah na* (Ps. 118:25). This is generally translated as "Save us, O Lord; Make us prosper, O Lord." Give us *yeshu'ah*—redemption, help, saving, and *hatzlahah*—prosperity, success.

The reason for my mentioning this verse on this particular festival is the interesting and arresting fact that on Sukkot we seem to practice discrimination and show favoritism to the *Hoshi'ah na* over the *Hatzlihah na*. When, during the *Hallel*, we hold the *lulav* and *etrog* and perform the *na'anuim*, we do so only when we recite *Hoshi'ah na*, not when we recite *Hatzlihah na*. After the *Musaf* service, we recite the prayers called *Hoshanah*. Why do we not recite *Hatzlihah na's*? Why do we prefer the *Hoshi'ah* over the *Hatzlihah*?

The answer to this seemingly simple question is in itself a major expression of Jewish *hashkafah*, of Jewish philosophy. And the answer is that *hatzlahah* indicates worldly or mundane success, financial and social prosperity, whereas *yeshu'ah* signifies spiritual eminence, religious redemption, the success of the soul. And what we learn from this is, therefore, that Judaism does not look askance at worldly success, at prosperity. It does not look with derision upon material attainments. It does not maintain, as do other religions, that the rich man can never enter the gates of Heaven. *Anna Hashem hatzlihah na* is a valid, legitimate prayer.

But at the same time, neither does Judaism teach us to center our lives about the desire for material attainments. Whether one is successful in life or not, in a material, financial sense, is simply irrelevant; it is not, in and by itself, either good or bad. What really counts is spiritual success—*yeshu'ah*, not *hat-*

5720 (1959)

zlahah. Hatzlahah is merely ephemeral, merely temporary; *yeshu'ah* is of the order of eternity.

The Midrash (*Shohar Tov*, Ps. 118, s. v. *Anna Hashem*) gives us an interesting piece of history about our verse. It tells us that it was recited responsively in the Temple at Jerusalem in days of old. *Anshei Yerushalayim omerim bifnim, "Anna Hashem hoshi'ah na," ve-anshei Yehudah omerim mi-ba-hutz, "Anna Hashem hatzlihah na."* The people who lived in Jerusalem, in the Holy City itself, would remain within the Temple and they would recite *Anna Hashem hoshi'ah na*, whereas the citizens of Judea, who lived outside the Holy City, would remain outside the Temple and respond, *Anna Hashem hatzlihah na*. Perhaps what our rabbis meant to tell us with this is more than just a historical incident. They meant to tell us that *yeshu'ah* is an inner concept, the experience of inwardness. *Hatzlahah*, however, is from without, superficial, externalized success. *Yeshu'ah* is for people of higher status of the spirit, people of loftier sanctity—the citizens of Jerusalem. *Hatzlahah*, however, while an acceptable ambition, is entertained by people who come only from Judea, but who have not yet graduated to the status of *anshei Yerushalayim*. When you look at life and at Torah and at Judaism as does an outsider, from the outside in, *mi-ba-hutz*, then all you can see in life is that which is describable as *hatzlahah*: how many adherents does this temple have, not how deep the experience; how big is the building, not how great is the effect it has upon the worshipers; how expensive are the furnishings of this temple, not how profound the religious devotion of its communicants. But when you look at Judaism *mi-bifnim*, from within as an insider of Torah, then *hatzlahah* is not banned, but *yeshu'ah* is regarded as of far greater and more transcendent significance.

That is why we, especially on this festival of Sukkot, show a decided preference for *Anna Hashem hoshi'ah na* over *Anna Hashem hatzlihah na*. It is the expression of our preference for being an insider in the holy precincts of Judaism, in the temple of Torah, than merely being an outsider or alien to the sanctities of our faith. Without rejecting worldly prosperity, we state clearly our preference for eternal *yeshu'ah,* or saving.

We find an interesting reflection in the Talmud of this Jewish outlook which prefers spiritual eminence without deprecating worldly prosperity. The Talmud relates (*Shabbat* 31a) that after a man's death, he appears before the Divine Court and is asked four questions. The first two are: "*Asakta be-piryah ve-rivyah*? Have you done your part for the perpetuation of the race and the people?" and "*Kavata ittim la-Torah*? Have you set aside regular times for the study of Torah?" But it is the next two questions which are of immediate significance to us. The third question is "*Nasata ve-natatta be-emunah*? Were you honest and faithful in your business transactions?" The final question is "*Tzippita li-yeshuʻah*? Did you constantly strive and hope for *yeshuʻah*?" Note the last questions. We are not asked if *nasata ve-natatta be-hatzlahah*, if we attained prosperity, because *hatzlahah* in *massa u-mattan*, in business, is simply irrelevant to questions of ultimate significance. All that counts after a man has finished his life and appears before the Divine Throne is that, in the process of his worldly pilgrimage, in the process of his business life, that he should have never abandoned the principle of *emunah*, of honesty and integrity and faithfulness. But when it comes to the spiritual life, to *tzippita*, to all that a man longs for and strives for and works for from the depths of his soul, there the desire for success in *yeshuʻah* is of grave importance. This represents a different accent from the popular philosophy of our day; for the popular philosophy of the day calls for success in the material attainments of life, and mere "goodness" in religion. Judaism, as we have seen, calls for "goodness," *emunah*, in business life, whereas it asks for the goal of success in spiritual happiness.

How this whole attitude toward life was expressed in the life of one great Jew, at a critical moment in the recent history of our people, is beautifully described in the biographical sketch of Rabbi Menahem Ziemba in Rabbi Jung's recent volume, *Guardians of Our Heritage.* It was the morning of December 8, 1942 in the ghetto of Warsaw, when the remaining few Jews in that ill-fated city were gripped by an overriding sense of fear and helplessness, realizing full well that they were on the brink of disaster A meeting was convened of the few remaining leaders, including statesmen, rabbis, educators, journalists, and philosophers. The majority of those gathered were completely hopeless. Historians and educators, philosophers and poets had lost all sense of hope and were divested of direction and guidance. At this critical, desperate moment, at the end of the history of the Warsaw Ghetto, all those present turned to this gentle, slender man, the *Gaʼon*, Rabbi Menahem Ziemba. He told them, "We all have one need in common. We require spiritual healing and divine guidance. I urge you to turn to Him on High for help through the medium of Torah, with its perennial message of serenity and implicit faith. What one heart cannot bear alone, a minyan of faithful hearts, in unison with our loving Father, can bear. Our sacred law teaches us that in the long run, the inward attitude is more important than outward conditions."

At that moment, one of the leftist, secularist leaders interjected, "Let us, rabbi, pray that at least our health and food provisions hold out." "Oh no!" corrected Rabbi Ziemba, gently but firmly, "Let us pray, rather, that the faith of our fathers holds out!"

Here, as a spontaneous reaction of a *Gadol be-Yisra'el*, is the philosophy which recognizes *hatzlahah* but prefers *yeshu'ah*. Of course, health and food provisions are important, but at the last gasping moment of the martyrs of the Warsaw Ghetto, the great *Ga'on* has one last prayer in mind: *yeshu'ah*, "that the faith of our fathers holds out!"

Anna Hashem hoshi'ah na and *Anna Hashem hatzlihah na* are both legitimate goals in life, but only *yeshu'ah*, not *hatzlahah*, is worthy of the *na'anu'im*, of pointing the symbolic finger of the *lulav* in all directions, showing that God is omnipresent—that the desire to succeed in His service is the overarching ambition of the Jew.

On this day, therefore, of joyous and happy dedication to the Almighty, our prayer is *Anna Hashem hatzlihah na*. Give us, O God, worldly prosperity, *hatzlahah*, for our sake, so that we have the peace of mind and the wherewithal to develop our spiritual capacities, to the end that *hoshanah le-ma'ankha Elokeinu, hoshanah*, that we will attain *yeshuah* for *Thy* sake, O Lord, our God.

INDISPENSABILITY: MYTH AND FACT

RECENTLY, I PAID TWO calls upon two different individuals. One was a condolence call to a mourner sitting *shiv'ah*. The other was a sick call to a patient in a hospital. By a remarkable coincidence, each of these told me of something he had learned from his experience, and the results were identical.

"From my experiences during this confinement, away from my normal activities," each of them told me, "I have discovered a marvelous truth. To my great relief, I now realize that I am not indispensable. I had always thought that if I took time out, away from my business or practice, all of it would collapse hopelessly. Now I see that I have been away from my office, my business, my home; and while all might have benefited somewhat by my presence, and I might have done things somewhat differently, nevertheless, my absence proved to be no disaster. It is both a welcome and a humbling thought! I am not as crucial to their survival as I thought I was! From now on, therefore, I shall give more time to my wife and my children, to discovering the wonders of the world about me, to attending to my synagogue, to developing my own mind and cultural level. I never realized I could do all these things and get away with it. Now I have learned—and not only I but my family as well will be the beneficiary of my discovery."

I believe all of us can appreciate the simple truth in these remarks. I submit to you, therefore, that the good Lord has given us an easier and more pleasant way to learn that truth than by suffering. He has given us the *sukkah* and the festival of Sukkot.

The essence of Sukkot is *Tzei mi-dirat keva ve-shev be-dirat arai* (*Sukkah* 2a)—leave your permanent home, and for seven days dwell in this temporary booth. Normally, the interpretation of the significance of this commandment points out the independence of man from his possessions. You need not have a

5724 (1963)

fine home and expensive appointments in order to survive. Consider how for seven days you can get along without them. What you do need is God, the *tzila de-mehemanuta*, the shadow of faith. Your home is not indispensable to you. (Cf. Rashbam to Lev. 23:43, and Rabbi Samson Raphael Hirsch, *Horeb*, vol. I, pp. 124 ff., Grunfeld translation.)

I prefer to interpret the meaning of Sukkot in the reverse direction, by emphasizing the converse: *you are not indispensable to your home, to your society!* When a man leaves his *dirat keva*, his lavish home and complex society, and for seven days he moves out—whether completely, or at least partially, for meals—he discovers that they survive even without his presence! By moving out from under a roof to under the *sekhakh*, he learns what the patient does in the hospital and the survivor in the house of mourning—except that he learns it through *simhah*, not anguish: that, in a great measure, the world can very well get along without him.

This is a sobering thought, for by destroying the myth of our indispensability, it makes us feel that we are not the center of the world, that we are essentially dependent beings. And it is also a liberating thought, for it assures us that we can now learn, throughout the year, to pay more attention to the things in life that are really important, and that we will not thereby be endangering the existence of the other, mundane affairs.

Perhaps, then, we ought to take a little bit of Sukkot with us through the rest of the year. Every day, a waft of the *sukkah*'s atmosphere ought to inspire us to "let go" for a short while and divert our attention to ourselves, our minds, our hearts—our *neshamah*. The world can get along without us.

Bratzlaver Hasidim offer us a remarkable suggestion: every day ought to contain at least one "dead hour." All our waking hours are so filled with "life," with nervous tensions of all sort that afflict us in the course of our daily affairs in commerce, in business, in professions, in society. Our emotions are engaged with others, our feelings entangled with them, our sensitivities inflamed with real or imaginary slights to our pride, our minds overflowing with a myriad of details and plans, worries and concerns on paying bills, satisfying employers or employees, pacifying clients or customers, meeting the competition, keeping up with the neighbors. These so-called "live" hours are so preoccupied with other people that we utterly ignore our own selves. No wonder we have so little inner peace, inner tranquility. We are "alive" so tensely, so neurotically, so busily, that we head straight for the psychiatrist's couch and for spiritual oblivion. Hence, say the Bratzlaver Hasidim, keep one little hour set aside as your "dead hour." Make no appointments, answer no phone calls, read no newspapers, keep away from radio and television, see no people, write no memos to yourself. Be "dead to the world"—and alive to yourself. Banish all your usual problems from your mind. Think of where you are going in life—or, perhaps, where life is taking you; the difference is worth thinking about. Ponder your own conduct, and what it is doing to you and to your character and personality. Project into the future—that of yourself, your children, your community. Make a *heshbon ha-nefesh* with yourself that may help you redirect and reorient your day-to-day activities. And if you are not the contemplative kind, then pull your mind out of the sucking whirlpool of daily business and elevate yourself to a new and higher kind of existence by reading that which is enduring, reviewing the *sidrah*, finding inspiration to a higher-than-animal existence through art or music, studying a *blatt gemara*—dead to the world and alive to yourself. One "dead hour" a day can make all of life worth living!

This ought to be one concrete, felicitous result of the message of Sukkot. For the Bratzlavers' "dead hour" is the essence of Sukkot: you can get away from under your *dirat keva*, from your normal routine, and into the *sukkah* under God's great heaven, without permanent damage to all the intricate goings-on in that home or office or factory, the *dirat keva*.

But when we say that Sukkot teaches us that man is not indispensable, does that mean that he is expendable, that there is no area of life where he is indeed indispensable?

No, there are areas where man is crucial, where there can be only dismal failure without him. If in his mundane affairs, his *dirat keva*, his presence is dispensable, then in the *sukkah*, symbol of the spiritual world, man is indispensable! A *sukkah* without a Jew to make *Kiddush* in it is meaningless. There is nothing holy about it. Strange as it may sound, in matters of the spirit God needs man! *Ha-Kadosh barukh Hu mit'avveh li-tefillatan shel tzaddikim* (*Yevamot* 64a)—God deeply desires the prayers of the righteous. His purposes in the world cannot be fulfilled without men—without each individual man or woman called upon by Him to contribute to the building of *malkhut Shamayim*, the Kingdom of Heaven, the God-approved society and world. If any one of us fails in his or her spiritual mission then, as our Sages were wont to say, God's Name is incomplete. Here each of us is truly indispensable.

The Talmud (*Sukkah* 53a) tells us an interesting story of the renowned Hillel at the *simhat beit ha-sho'evah*, the joyous celebration at the drawing of the waters which took place in the Temple on Sukkot.

When Hillel would reach the heights of happiness at this occasion, he would say: *Im ani kan, ha-kol kan; ve-im eini kan, mi kan,* "If I am here, everyone is here; and if I am not here, who then is here?"

A strange remark, is it not? Hillel the humble, the gentle, the meek—is this sentiment worthy of him: I am indispensable? The Jerusalem Talmud (*Sukkah* 5:4), which understood the quotation to refer to Hillel himself, therefore rightly asks: *Ve-killusin Hu tzarikh?* Does God need Hillel's praise and celebration that he should regard himself as so important? For the same reason, Rashi is moved to interpret the remark as being a quotation by Hillel of God, of the *Shekhinah.* Hillel, speaking in God's name, says, "If I am here, that is sufficient, for if I am not here, who is?" That is, nothing else counts. Yet this too is strange, for Hillel was a sage, a rabbi, and not a prophet, and hence not given to speaking of God in the first person.

Even stranger is a sentence attributed to Hillel which follows immediately upon the one mentioned (cf. Rabinowitz, *Dikdukei Soferim*): *Im attah tavo el beiti, ani avo el beitekha; ve-im attah lo tavo el beiti, ani lo avo el beitekha,* "If You, O God, will come to my home, I will come to Yours [i.e., the Temple]; but if You will not come to *my* house, I will not come to Yours." What an astonishing expression! Is Hillel striking a bargain with God, making conditions about reciprocal hospitality with Him?

I believe that Hillel was guilty neither of arrogance in saying "*im ani kan ha-kol kan*," nor of religious commercialism in saying "*im attah tavo el beiti*." What he meant was simply to teach what we have been saying: that man is *not* indispensable to the mundane world and its affairs, but *is* indispensable to the world of the spirit, of Torah, of Temple, of *Ha-Kadosh Barukh Hu.* For this is what the great Hillel said: *Im ani kan, ha-kol kan*—if I am here, in the *Beit ha-Mikdash,* in God's house; if I am here at the festival of *simhat beit ha-sho'evah,* the drawing of the waters, which tradition has understood symbolically as the drawing of the *Ruah ha-Kodesh,* the holy spirit, from its divine source; when I am involved in the life of spirituality and sanctity; then if I am here, all is well. But if I am not here, *im eini kan,* then *mi kan,* then I must feel that I am responsible for the fact that the holiness of the Temple is diminished, that the joy of the *simhah* and the whole spiritual enterprise is a failure—for here, in this House of God, I as a human am indispensable!

And then Hillel continues, not by setting conditions in negotiations, but by stating an indisputable fact of spiritual life: *im attah tavo el beiti,* when You come to my home, O God, when I understand that my home, my office, my factory, all my mundane affairs, all my successes and triumphs, all are *Your* doing, that only because You are present do my home and career exist, that it is You Who have given me the intelligence and the substance, the health and the wealth, the confidence and the *mazzal* to be what I am and have what I have, and that I am only ancillary, and my presence and services can be dispensed with; when I realize that in *beiti*, in my mundane life and the world, You are indispensable and I am not, then it is equally true that *ani avo el beitekha*, then I am important, nay indispensable, to the existence of Your house, the *Beit ha-Mikdash*, the universe of the divine spirit. When a man has grown in spiritual maturity and understanding to appreciate his real place in the world, to acknowledge God as the cause of his success, then he is great enough spiritually to be crucial to the existence of God's house. When we know we need God, He knows that He needs us! However, *im attah lo tavo el beiti*, when I am so foolish that I give You no entree to my home, when I think I can get along without You and that it is I who am indispensable, that it is my wisdom and my shrewdness that have built my house and my career and my business, then *ani lo avo el beitekha*, then I have no business in Your home, then You can get along very well without me. If man thinks he does not need God, then God knows He does not need man. The man who considers himself self-made and worships his maker is ignored by God.

Here then is an invaluable lesson for us from Sukkot: into the *sukkah* for a week's time, enough to learn that the world can get along without you, but that God cannot.

Abolishing the myth of indispensability from our daily concerns will prevent us from entertaining exaggerated notions of self-importance and will inspire us to plan those "dead hours" which can grace all of life with meaning, with serenity, with a touch of poetry. And affirming our indispensability to the spirit, to Torah, to the synagogue, to Judaism, and to God's purposes will give us a new insight into our true significance and our lofty place in the world. *Va-ani be-rov hasdekha avo beitekha.* Only when I realize that my whole life, my very self, my *ani*, my family and livelihood and joys and pleasures, all are the result of *Your* indispensable *hasadim*, Your kindness; only then *avo betekha*, do I have the right to enter Your House, Your Holy Temple, and only then may I be considered indispensable to its prevalence in the world.

The Illusions We Live By

THE HALAKHAH IS GENERALLY rich in the use of illusions, and especially in its treatment of the laws of Sukkot. There is, for instance, the law of *lavud*. This means that even if there exist empty spaces in the *sekhakh*, or the covering of the *sukkah*, if these spaces are less than three *tefahim* (about fifteen inches), then we consider the empty space as if it did not exist but was covered by branches or other *sekhakh*. *Lavud* means that we accept the illusion that any distance less than three *tefahim* does not exist; it is as if it were attached.

Another example is the law of *dofen akumah*. This means that if four cubits or less of an invalid type of covering, or *sekhakh*, was placed on the roof of the *sukkah* contiguous to the wall, we do not regard it as invalid, thereby disqualifying the entire *sekhakh*, but rather imagine that it is as if the wall were bent over and inclined for that distance, thus causing us to regard the *sukkah* as kosher.

A third example would be that of *tzurat ha-petah*. This means that if a Jew does not have sufficient material to build the requisite number of walls, then it is sufficient to place two poles on either end and a beam across them. We consider this a *tzurat ha-petah*, the figure of a doorway, and imagine that the doorway constitutes both an entrance and a wall. We accept the illusion that this empty space is really a complete wall.

One of the greatest and most distinguished scholars and preachers of modern Israel, Rabbi Moshe Avigdor Amiel *z"l* of Tel Aviv (in his famous *Derashot el Ami*), discovered a hint of this propensity for the use of illusion in *sukkot* in the Talmud's statement concerning the nature of our dwelling in *sukkot*. The Torah teaches us *ba-sukkot teshevu shiv'at yamim*, "you shall dwell in the *sukkot* for seven days" (Lev. 23:36). And the Talmud adds, *teshevu ke-ein taduru*—you shall "dwell" as if you truly "resided" in the *sukkah* (*Sukkah* 26a). We do not really change our address from home to *sukkah*; nevertheless, in our minds, in

5725 (1964)

our practice, in our will, in our intentions, we dwell in the *sukkah* as if we really lived there. All of Sukkot is a tribute to the power of a noble illusion.

Thus, the Halakhah, as a *Torat Hayyim*, a Torah of Life, tells us something about the importance of illusion in daily life. Normally, we use the word "illusion" in a pejorative sense, as a term of derision, as something which is contrary to fact, to reality, to common sense. But my thesis this morning is that that is all wrong. In many of the most significant branches of human endeavor, we make use of illusion and could not get along without it. Thus, for instance, in law we use legal fictions—as, for example, when we consider a corporation not as a collection of many people, but as an individual, collective personality. In science, we abstract "ideal systems" from reality—and that is creating an illusion. The mathematician deals with such concepts as infinity and imaginary numbers. Philosophers speak of the philosophy of *Als Ob*, the philosophy of "as if." Men of literature describe and criticize life and society by means of creative illusions.

Indeed, we live our regular lives by certain illusions—not only in the intellectual disciplines, such as law and science, but in the deepest recesses of our individual and ethnic consciousness. Without the proper illusions, life can become meaningless and a drudgery. The future is bleak, the past a confused jumble, and the present depressingly dull without the necessary illusions.

What we must know is this: that illusions are not opposed to fact. Illusions are what the facts add up to in the long run, what give us the ability to understand and interpret facts. Illusions are frequently more consonant with reality than narrow and isolated facts. Illusions are the framework of facts, that which gives them sense and meaning.

Pity the man who prides himself upon possessing "common sense," who "sticks only to facts" and who has nothing to do with sentiment or illusion. What a miserable, cold, dull, impersonal, and boring life he must lead! I do not envy the scientist who carries the laboratory, via his mind, into his home and society; who sees men as objects, as chunks of protoplasm, who thinks only in terms of numbers and size, and reduces all relationships to impersonal equations. I do not envy the businessman who, when he returns to the bosom of his family, still thinks in terms of profit and competition and marketability. He considers his wife a Juior junior partner, or perhaps vice president in charge of the home, his children as deductions, and the gifts he occasionally distributes to his family as bonuses to be reckoned in a budget. Such a family exchanges services as in a commodity market—and that is all!

Such people sterilize all beauty and sweetness out of their lives by ignoring such real and marvelous illusions as dignity and love and hope and purpose and happiness and humor. Such things cannot be weighed or measured or examined under a microscope or analyzed in a test tube or quoted on the stock page. Yet life is dull—and desperate—without them. To remove them is to take the poetry out of living.

Indeed, the poet John Ciardi, in the latest issue of *Saturday Review*, voiced this very complaint. "It is always a mistake," he writes, "to discuss poetry with a man who insists that it must make sense. . . . For the trouble with being sensible is not the sense it does or does not make, but the life it never really manages to get to. . . . [It] always manages to shut as many doors as it opens. . . . And one of the doors it always shuts, and always with a slam, is poetry." If you look only for a straight, factual message, and ignore image and illusion, then you have destroyed poetry. You cannot read Shakespeare or Wordsworth the way you read the *Wall Street Journal*. And the same holds true for music or painting or sculpture or literature.

Or take that much-abused word "love." In our sophisticated, post-Freudian, fact-ridden society, there is no great difficulty in talking about sexuality; but love is taboo and considered only a comforting illusion. Yet such "illusions" are part of a larger reality. You cannot see or touch it, buy or sell or psychoanalyze it, but it exists between devoted couples who have long transcended physical attraction; amongst people who genuinely love books or music; with committed citizens who love country or people; for authentic Jews who love God and Torah.

A narrow factualism regards integrity and honesty as illusions because "they don't pay." An idealistic appreciation of illusion, however, considers that in the long run, there *is* justice. Maybe the thief will prosper in his business; but like a worm boring its way into a luscious fruit, this same dishonesty must ultimately enter into the innermost recesses of home and family and mind, and destroy the most precious things that a man possesses: peace of mind, domestic bliss, and personal reputation.

Of course, there are some illusions that are harmful and dangerous, such as the illusion of race superiority or that might makes right. But these are *myths*: they are false and substitutes for facts. Illusions do not ignore facts; they build upon them and see them from a broader perspective.

What are some of the noble illusions that Judaism teaches? What are some of the outstanding examples of the principle of Sukkot that *teshevu ke-ein ta-duru*?

One of them is the illusion that man is basically good, that, in the words of David, *Va-tehasserehu me'at me-elohim* (Ps. 8:6), "he was created but little lower than the angels"; in other words, that man has a *neshamah*, a soul. The man who has a nose only for hard facts will not see a soul in the human personality; for this you must have an eye for larger illusions and a heart for great ideals. How silly was that Russian astronaut who, when he returned from orbit, reported that he had looked through the heavens and found no God. It is as childish as the sophomoric comment of the surgeon who announced that he had conducted a thorough search of the anatomy and discovered no soul. The best answer was provided by the wise man who replied that he had taken apart a violin and found no music! Of course, man has a *neshamah*; without it, his life is meaningless and makes no sense.

Or take the halakhic principle that every Jew has a *hezkat kashrut*—a presumption of being decent and honest. A narrow view of the facts will tell you that most people are unworthy and irresponsible. But without the illusion of man's *kashrut*, there can be no trust, no loyalty, no faith. And therefore, there can be no transactions, no marriage, and no happiness. *Teshevu ke-ein taduru*—without the proper illusions, life is unlivable.

A narrow view of the facts will tell you that Jews do not constitute one people. The Yemenite and the American Jew, the Russian Jew and the Bene Israel of India, the German Jew and the Jew from China, are completely different types. What matters is that they share a common history or aspiration or faith. These things cannot be measured and established as hard facts. Yet Judaism accepts that all Jews are one people, that they constitute *Keneset Yisra'el*. As in the *sukkah*, we accept the principle of *lavud*: even if there are gaps, and discrepancies, and big holes, and lacunae of all kinds, we assume that they are solid, attached, covered up. The Jewish people is one people. It is by virtue of such illusions that history was turned and redirected, and the State of Israel created!

Finally, there is another law of Sukkot that beautifully expresses the noble idealism that informs the Jewish mentality in its use of illusion. The Halakhah states that if a man builds his *sukkah* and makes the walls from *atzei asherah*, from the wood of a tree which was used as an idol by idol-worshipers, then the *sukkah* is invalid. The reason given is, *kattutei mikhatat shi'ureih* (see *Sukkah* 35a); since an idol must be destroyed, then we consider this wood as if it had been totally demolished, and therefore there is no *shiur*, and the wall is not big enough, since it does not even exist! Here is a heavy, solid wall before me—and the Halakhah says: it is nonexistent! What a marvelous expression of the great Jewish illusion that evil does not really exist, that all that is wicked and cruel and unseemly and anti-human can be considered unreal because, ultimately, it will be destroyed in the great triumph of the good over the evil and the holy over the profane and the pure over the defiled! The halakhic principle which accepts the illusion that idolatry is already nonexistent is the basis and expression for the great Jewish optimism that has kept us alive throughout the centuries. *Teshevu ke-ein taduru!*

The kabbalists of centuries ago devised a special recitation to be read before performing any mitzvah, such as *sukkah* or *lulav*. It reads: *Yehi ratzon she-tehei hashuvah mitzvah zo ke-illu kiyyamtihah be-khol perateha ve-dikdukeha*, "May it be Thy will that this mitzvah which I am about to perform shall be considered in Your eyes *as if* I had observed it in all its details and particulars." Indeed so! If we harbor the right illusions about life, if we live life according to the noblest ideals and observe them faithfully, then God will return the compliment, and accept the illusion *ke-ilu kiyyamtiha*, as if our noblest thoughts had been put into practice, as if our most cherished aspirations were realities, as if our errors and sins did not exist, as if our lives were lived on the highest level of humanity and Jewishness.

Teshevu ke-ein taduru—what a wonderful holiday is Sukkot, which teaches us this noble and beautiful and precious exchange of illusions! No wonder it is called *zeman simhatenu*, "the time of our happiness." May it indeed continue to be so for us, for all Israel, and for all humanity.

The Starry Night

"Religion should change with the times." I am sure that everyone in this congregation has, at one time or another, been accosted by this ubiquitous slogan. I know that I have had to contend with it ever since my first youthful venture outside my native Williamsburg.

"Religion should change with the times." This is the kind of profound platitude that everyone who utters it thinks he has invented. Like so many other clichés, which at first sight seem to possess so much wisdom and upon reflection prove utterly vacuous, this popular motto is thoroughly banal. It offers simple bromides for enormously complex problems. It issues a fog of vague and imprecise but terribly up-to-date sentiments, where clarity and analysis are called for. It has as much to offer to religious philosophy as "twinkle, twinkle little star" has to contribute to the science of astronomy.

Does this mean that we are "against change"? Of course not. To be against change is to be against life, because we are always moving, always changing, always either growing up or growing down, progressing or retrogressing. Change is the law of the universe. Life is always in flux. A great Greek philosopher once said that life is like a river, always changing and moving, and, because of its constant motion, you cannot step into the same river twice. Whereupon another Greek philosopher offered his opinion that so constant a state of flux is it in, that you cannot step into the river even once.

So we do not deny that life does change, and we do not even piously wish that it *would not* change. But we do maintain that intelligent human beings try to balance change and continuity, motion and stability. Just as complete immutability spells petrifaction and stagnation, so does constant changeability imply fickleness, unreliability, and irresponsibility. Thus, for instance, all of us want our children to change: to study, to grow physically, to better their characters, to improve their personalities. We want them to be weaned from us protective parents, to have their own careers, to marry and build their own homes, and to make their own reputations in life. But we also want them to be stable, always to remain honorable, responsible, loyal, to keep a word and a commitment once made, and to maintain throughout life their love for parents, brothers, and sisters. Is anyone ready to abandon these qualities with the facile argument that honor should change with the times? Or love should change with the times? Or friendship, or character, or integrity?

Certainly there is change. But a man cannot spiritually or psychologically survive change that is so radical, so abrupt, so unceasing that there is no continuity or stability in his life. He must have something in life that is fixed, some reference point by which to measure new ideas, new promises, new demands, and new phenomena.

That fixed point is Torah. The psalmist sang, "Thy word is a lamp unto my foot and a light unto my path" (Ps. 119:105). Of course, we use our feet to tread on different paths in life. We live neither in a forcibly imposed East European ghetto, nor in the voluntarily self-isolated communities of Western Europe, but in the open and pluralistic and technological United States—and it is an exciting and adventurous life. Our feet stake out new paths constantly. But the lamp and the light for our feet and our paths are the same—Torah and *mitzvot*. Without them we stumble, we lose our way, and our adventure turns into a horror, and the excitement into unbearable anxiety.

The more a society is in a state of change, the more it needs some anchor of permanence to give it a sense of stability. When I don my *tallit* or *tefillin*, when I hold my *lulav* and *etrog*, I suddenly am aware of myself as standing in the grand tradition of my parents and my grandparents and their grandparents before them. I perceive myself as part of a great and noble historical continuum which emerges unshaken from the vicissitudes of the various ages. These observances are both symbol and essence of my roots. And, indeed, in the performance of the Jewish *mitzvot*, I am aware of my roots such that no matter what winds may buffet my branches, no matter what storms may swirl about me, I remain firm and stable. I feel like a tree, not like a mushroom which appears out of nowhere and disappears into nothing. Thus, the *tallit* and the *tefillin*, the *lulav* and the *etrog*, *kashrut* and Shabbat, are more important here and today than they were in Volozhin or Pressburg or Hamburg of a hundred years ago. Our life in these times is obsessed by veneer, by the appeal of the new and the fashionable, by the attraction of tomorrow's style. Marshall McLuhan, for all his sensationalism, has enunciated a truth in his famous statement that "the medium is the message." Considering the proliferation of the various new media in our times, our minds are bombarded by all kinds of novel and evanescent messages, so that the timeless verities are displaced from our consciousness. We have become the generation of the spiritually dispossessed, and our own permanent values have turned unstable and illusory. We are thus perpetual adolescents, in eternal transition. With all our scorn for the hippies, we must acknowledge in gratitude that they point to a problem that is ours: they, on the margins of society, are the psychopathic symptoms of *our* inner pathology, our inner emptiness, our inner sickness. We are so caught up in change, so enamored of motion, so mercurial in our spiritual orientation, so volatile in our ethical lives, so fickle in our culture, that we are left without identity, without self, without reality. And it is against this emptiness that the hippies attempt, so pathetically, to reassert the eternal and stable truths of love and beauty and simplicity. It is a pity that their "flower power" has no roots.

In a society of this kind, we need Torah more than ever before. We need a religion which does *not* change with the times, but which offers the permanence and stability we crave. Religion should not be a mirror that reflects the crazy whirl of life's mad currents. It should be a rudder that keeps us afloat, that tells us where we are going and guides us there, that helps us attain perspective and prevents us from being overwhelmed by the empty foam of life. Were religion to change with the times, it would not be worth the effort to stay religious!

I believe that this idea is implicit in a remarkable statement of the Rabbis of the Midrash (*Yalkut Shim'oni*, Psalms, 682). They taught that *ein Melekh ha-Mashiah ba ella litten le-umot ha-olam . . . sukkah*—the King-Messiah will come to the world only to teach the nations of the world about the *sukkah*. How strange! For over two thousand years, Jews have pined away for the Messiah. For the last eight hundred years or so, we have sung daily of our hearts' deepest yearnings and proclaim courageously our *ani ma'amin*, our belief and our faith that the Messiah can come at any time, any day. And what for? To teach the gentiles how to build a *sukkah*! Did not the prophets conceive of the Messiah so much more nobly? Isaiah taught that the function of the Messiah would be to beat swords into plowshares and spears into pruning forks. Micah taught that the Messiah will establish the House of the Lord on the mountain in Jerusalem so that all nations will proclaim, "Come, let us go up to the mountain of the Lord" (Mic. 4:2). And the Rabbis of the Midrash? That the Messiah will come, gather up the nations in the UN, and teach them the prosaic laws of how to build a little *sukkah*!

What did they mean? I suggest it is this. The *sukkah* is a symbol of change. The Rabbis refer to it as *dirat arai*, a temporary abode. Its very flimsiness is an index of its temporariness. It is a symbol of the makeshift booths which our ancestors used on their journey through the Sinai wilderness. It implies, therefore, transition, transience, impermanence. The very insignificance of its *defannot*, or walls, and the requirement that the covering, or *sekhakh* be impermanent are further indications of *sukkah* as a symbol of change and transition. Now, transition is a dangerous period. Consider adolescence and the early years of marriage, or historical transition from one age to another, or economic change and displacements. At a time of this sort, disaster dogs us at every footstep, calamity is just around every corner, and man is threatened by being swept up in change and losing his moorings. A world of this kind needs a Messiah; it needs his lesson of *how to survive the sukkah!* The Messiah will teach the world what the Jews always should have known; that we can and must find stability in the midst of change and movement. The Halakhah teaches us that in order for a *sukkah* to be valid, the covering, or *sekhakh*, must not be too tightly packed. Specifically, we must be able to see the stars through the *sekhakh*. Like the ancient mariner who without instruments was able to guide himself by the stars, or like the contemporary interplanetary satellite which moves unerringly through the vast and open reaches of empty space by latching on to a star, so man, caught up in an ever-moving and ever-changing *sukkah* of life, must be able to see the stars through the *sekhakh*. That star is—Torah, faith, God.

When the artist Van Gogh was asked about his famous expressionistic painting *The Starry Night*, he said, "I felt a need of—shall I say the word?—religion, and so I went out and painted the stars." It is the very permanence of the stars and the solace they offer to an unstable society that makes them the symbol of religion. It is this fixity amidst flux that Torah offers and that the Messiah will teach.

The religion of Torah, therefore, does not change with the times. It is not subject to the whims of the public opinion poll. Its strength derives from its perennial reliability.

Nevertheless, we must also stress a corollary: that while Torah is changeless, it must always be relevant to a changing society. It must not be so changeless that it has nothing to do with man, who is always in a state of change. Judaism must address man in his changing conditions; it must speak to man of values and faith, of loyalty and honor and meaning, as they apply to *his* times and *his* society. But Judaism cannot do this if the teachers of Torah turn their backs on the rest of mankind. This is what we mean when we appeal for the relevance of Orthodox Judaism, and this is our argument with those in our own camp who would cut themselves off from modern society completely. The stars can guide man only when they are visible. If clouds of distrust and diffidence cover the stars, they are of precious little use to man. So the advocates of Torah must speak to modern man in his own idiom; they must respect his intelligence and feel with him in his misery.

When the Rabbis of old complained that *Torah munnahat be-keren zavit*, Torah lies neglected in a hidden corner (*Kiddushin* 66a), they did not mean for us to crawl into that corner with it and turn our backs on the world. Rather, they meant for us to take Torah out of that *keren zavit* and bring it into the center of the world scene, into the maelstrom of daily events, into the midst of the raging torrents of the times, and with it to offer man abiding faith and enduring stability.

Of course, by the same token, overemphasizing relevance can destroy the stable character of religion of which we speak. For instance, Reform Jews are now debating the composition of a new prayerbook. Twenty or thirty years ago they issued a new edition of their prayerbook and included special prayers for coal miners. Twenty-five years ago this was terribly relevant. Nowadays, they have discovered, the problems of coal miners are simply no longer significant; the whole issue is obsolete. When you are too relevant, you turn religion into a newspaper; and nothing is as meaningless as yesterday's news . . .

Torah, therefore, must not be a sealed book written in an ancient and undecipherable language, nor must it be a running commentary of religious journalese. It must be the *Sefer Hayyim*, the Book of Life. That is a difficult task—to be permanent and yet relevant, changeless and yet germane. It means that while affirming the unchanging nature of Halakhah, we must be able to explain it in terms of a changing society; that while teaching the *timeless* truths of Torah, we must relate them to issues that are *timely*. Above all, we must not be afraid to say that we do not have all the answers, and yet we must never cease searching for them.

In this, we of modern Orthodoxy, we who are associated with Yeshiva University, with synagogues such as The Jewish Center, with the Union of Orthodox Jewish Congregations, with journals such as *Tradition*, and movements such as Yavneh, have not always been successful. Sometimes we are too timid, sometimes too bold; sometimes too immature, often too inexperienced. But it is our sacred task to pursue the mission that has been given us. It may be that we will never perform our task to the complete and adequate satisfaction of all our critics, even of ourselves. But then, we shall work and work and work at it until the Messiah comes—and it is he who will teach the *umot ha-olam,* the nations of the world, the lesson of the *sukkah.* And if *they* are willing to learn— why, so will reluctant and recalcitrant Jews.

Perhaps, indeed, the *sukkah* of modern Orthodoxy is not what it should be. Perhaps we have not yet completely learned how to see the stars through the *sekhakh,* how to live in a world that is always changing with complete and utter loyalty to a Torah which abides eternally. But if we have failed so far, we pray, during this great and happy festival, *Ha-Rahaman hu yakim lanu et sukkat David ha-nofalet*—May the Merciful One establish for us, for once and for all, the weak and wobbling *sukkah* of David. Amen.

THE ANATOMY OF AN ETROG

THE RABBIS WERE INCLINED to read a great deal of symbolic significance into the cluster of four species, the *arba minim*, which we take in our hands in observance of the special biblical precept of this festival of Sukkot. It is in keeping with this rich tradition that we likewise indulge our imaginations and symbolically interpret certain details of this observance, particularly the laws of the Halakhah as they relate to the anatomy of the *etrog*.

At either end of the *etrog* are two small appendages. At the base or broader end, where the fruit was originally attached to the tree, is the *oketz*, or stem. At the other end of the *etrog*, where it tapers off to a narrow point, is a small, brown, bulbous appendage, which biologists call the stigma and which in Hebrew is known as *shoshanta*. That word literally means "blossom," because it is shaped like a miniature blossom and is reminiscent of the flower of the *etrog* before the fruit was produced. In more colloquial parlance, the stigma, or *shoshanta*, is called the *pittam*.

Whether the absence of either the *oketz* or the *pittam* disqualifies the *etrog* is a matter of opinion; our greatest authorities differed in their decisions. Thus, Rabbi Jacob b. Yakar maintained that our major concern is the *pittam*: if it is present, the *etrog* is valid for religious use, and if not, it is disqualified. Rabbi Isaac Halevi maintains that it is irrelevant whether or not the *etrog* contains a *shoshanta* or a *pittam*; what matters is that the *etrog* possess its *oketz* or stem. There is a third opinion, that of Rabbi Alfasi, Rambam, and Tosafot, who require both the *oketz* and the *pittam*, and invalidate the *etrog* in the absence of either one. While the details of the halakhic decision are rather intricate, we generally side with the third opinion and require the *etrog* to possess both stem and blossom (actually stigma, but following the Hebrew word *shoshanta*, we shall call it the blossom).

What do these represent? The *pittam*, as we have stated, looks like and reminds us of a blossom. It is a part of the fruit that protrudes as it grows, as if it

5729 (1968)

were pointing in the direction of growth. It represents, therefore, the youthful openness to change, newness, the state of being pliable and alert and alive, in motion and full of promise. While the *pittam* represents change and growth, the *oketz*, or stem, is that which ties the fruit to the tree itself. It therefore symbolizes rootedness, stability, continuity, and endurance. While the *pittam* points to the future, the *oketz* binds to the past. An *etrog*, to be kosher, needs both: change and stability, newness and continuity, past and future.

The halakhic reasoning for the need for these two appendages deepens this symbolic awareness. If there is no *oketz* on the *etrog*, it is disqualified because it is considered *haser*, incomplete or lacking; it is simply not a full *etrog*. If it has no *pittam*, however, it is considered *shalem*, complete, but invalidated because it does not fulfill the requirement of *hadar*, beauty. It is simply not an attractive *etrog*, and this particular fruit must be *hadar*, or beautiful: the very name *etrog* is unknown in the Bible, where it is simply called *peri etz hadar*, "the fruit of a beautiful tree" (Lev. 23:40).

To lose the *oketz*, therefore, to sever one's relations with his past and his roots, to forgo stability, is to be *haser*, deficient, to lack something organic, a part of oneself. None of us is created out of air; we all are the latest links in long chains. Whether we like it or not, each of us embody the entire past, and when we ignore that past we annihilate part of ourselves—we are *haser*, incomplete.

To be incapable of the *pittam* is to lack *hadar*, beauty. One who is not open to the future and who does not know how to change will find that his life is missing charm and freshness, vigor and color.

Judaism therefore reminds us that we must be both wholesome and handsome, complete and beautiful, *shalem* and *hadar*: our lives must possess both *oketz* and *pittam*, stem and blossom.

In youth, we all possess the *pittam* and tend to overlook the *oketz*. Youth is the time of growth, of blossoming, of change. Perhaps it is more than coincidence that the symbol of the *pittam*, the blossom, has been adopted in the peculiar idiom of contemporary youth: "flower-power!" In the obsession with change and blossoming, youth tends to ignore all that binds it to the past and to disdain those who represent such bonds. Youth is full of revolutionary fervor and idealistic enthusiasm; it is messianic and utopian. With increasing age, we tend to allow the *pittam* to wither, and become more conscious of the *oketz*: we accept membership in the established order of things, we are anxious to defend the gains of our own youth, we seek to instill a sense of tradition and contact with the past. We feel we have ourselves become part of the past that we wish to remember.

The *etrog*, therefore, reminds us of both. To those of us who are younger, it says: don't ignore the *oketz*. Without roots and stem, no flower can flourish and no beauty can endure. Do not imagine you can remain the people of the *pittam* forever; those who are today under thirty will someday be over thirty! And to those of middle age and over, the *etrog* says: do not deride the *pittam* on the *etrog* of life. There can be no real, active life without change and growth and promise and the exploration of new pathways and discovery of new horizons.

This is true even in religious life. The great Besht, founder of Hasidism, told us that we must each find our way to God through both the faith of our fathers and our own spiritual searching. In our *Amidah* prayer we invoke *Elokei Avraham* and *Elokei Yitzhak* and *Elokei Ya'akov*, "the God of Abraham and the God of Isaac and the God of Jacob." Why do we not say simply "the God of Abraham, Isaac, and Jacob"? The Besht answers: while it is true that each of the forefathers accepted God because his own father had told him about Him, because faith was part of a cherished tradition, that was not enough; he also had to discover God by his own initiative. God was indeed "the God of Abraham." But Isaac had to find Him on his own and make Him "the God of Isaac." And Jacob, though he knew of God from his father and grandfather, had to find his way to Him on his own, and make of Him "the God of Jacob." That is why we refer to the Almighty as both *Elokeinu* and *Elokei Avoteinu*, "our God" and "the God of our fathers."

This means that we must be patient with the exuberance of youth. We must recognize that it is worth practicing restraint in order to have an *etrog* with a *pittam*. Youth has too much to contribute for its zeal to be dismissed because of its excesses, because it is sometimes, or even most of the time, irritating. But that is a law of life: whoever seeks to change the status quo will step on toes and evoke opposition. The late Rabbi Y.L. Maimon used to point to the proximity of the two phrases in the prayer before the *Shema*—*oseh hadashot, ba'al milhamot*, "who does new things and is a warrior"—whoever seeks to innovate will invariably evoke opposition and a struggle will ensue. But it is worth it: there can be no kosher *etrog* without a *pittam*.

Hence, a mature personality, like a beautiful and kosher *etrog*, will have both *oketz* and *pittam*, both stem and blossom. He will cherish the past and be open to the future. Each of us possesses, in his own personality, a liberal tendency and a conservative tendency, the ability to look to the future and to look to the past, to consolidate and to innovate. Both of these are important; a full personality can afford the absence of neither.

Similarly, a mature and viable organization, such as a synagogue or a school, will likewise possess both elements, and therefore be ready for change and yet seek stability, continue old and cherished traditions, yet never be afraid to experiment with new ideas and new forms.

A nation, in order to prosper, must have both qualities. In the absence of a *pittam*, it can turn repressive and tyrannical: when it lacks an *oketz*, or roots, it becomes anarchic and wild.

Both these elements ought to be counterpoised, one against the other, in our personalities and in our community. According to Jewish law, the finest and most beautiful *etrog* is one in which the *oketz* and the *pittam* lie on one line or one axis: one against the other. The harmonious life is one in which there exists a balance between the elements of change and stability, innovation and consolidation, the old and the new, the loyalty to the past and the openness to the future. If we have too much of an *oketz* and too small a *pittam*, we become stodgy and stagnant, rigid and inflexible. If we have too big a *pittam* and too small an *oketz,* we become unsteady and erratic, vagrant and spasmodic.

Interestingly, the name *etrog* first appears in the Talmud, and linguists (see Alexander Kohut's edition of the *Arukh*) tell us that the name *etrog* comes from the Persian *tarnag*, which has two meanings: one is "beautiful," and the other, to "kindle a flame" or stoke a fire. This is probably so because the color and the shape of the *etrog* fruit are together reminiscent of a flame. So the principle of change, symbolized by the *pittam*, can be beautiful; and it can also be service-able, even as fire is. But, again like fire, it can get out of hand and burn down an entire world.

It is evident to any observer that our general society is like an e*trog* with an oversized *pittam* and a diminutive *oketz*. Our society is mobile, changing, unsteady. We are buffeted by vicissitudes and the winds of change—and this means that we must exercise extreme care and caution so that balance may be restored. According to the latest statistics, most Americans change residences every five years, and jobs almost as often, as large industries learn to pluck ex-ecutives from one community and replace them in another ever so often. The American even changes spouses with not much greater infrequency. No won-der that he experiences anxiety, an awareness that he is lacking stem and root, and he seeks to counterbalance his excessive mobility by stability in ways that are sometimes silly and empty. Witness, for instance, the passion for antique furniture, which sometimes is nothing more than socially sanctioned junk, as a way of expressing a desire to reach out to the past. Or, far sillier, the current obsession about obtaining the coat of arms that one's ancestors purportedly used.

If this is true of the general community, it is even more true of American Jewry. Large segments of the Orthodox community reveal a progressively more sterile introversion. We have become so defensive in our encounter with contemporary secular society that we embrace self-paralysis as a virtue and elevate immobility to the level of sacred doctrine. We act too often as if we were weighed down by our past and bound by our roots, impervious to both present and future. This attitude is psychologically understandable but morally indefensible.

But if the Orthodox community sometimes shows signs of too big an *oketz* and too small a *pittam*, of being too resistant to experimental approaches in education and in outer forms, there is a far greater problem in the rest of the community of an *etrog* that has an enormously large *pittam* and an *oketz* that has almost disappeared. The suburbanized Judaism of America is so grotesque as to be almost unrecognizable. In a recent study of a community that has been given the fictitious name of Lakeville, two sociologists, Marshall Sklare and Joseph Greenblum, describe the typical suburban Jew. Perhaps the best and most characteristic description is the statement to these sociologists by a woman speaking of her temple: "I think most members of this congregation don't want to be Jewish, but want to give their children more than they had, and this is the closest to nothing they can dream up." An *etrog* that is all *pittam*, with only a microscopic, artificial *oketz*! In the Jewish society of the Lakeville type, everything old must go. And yet, there is an irrational search for the stem. This kind of Jew, therefore, is willing to cast away every symbol and observance of Jewishness, but is horrified if his child wants to marry out of the faith. Logically, it makes no sense: why should he not marry a non-Jew, if his own life is non-Jewish? Yet there is a desire for the *oketz*. The Lakeville Jew has long abandoned *kashrut* as just a vestigial dietary taboo—but he cannot survive a Sunday morning without his bagels and lox. He professes no special belief in God, he certainly is embarrassed by talk of immortality, and yet he recites the Yizkor for his parents, and wants his children to memorialize him in the same manner when the time comes. So there is a minimal desire for the *oketz*, but it is so imbalanced with the *pittam* as to be weird—and also *haser:* deficient, incomplete, and invalid.

For our own good, and the good of society and the Jewish community, we must redress the balance and restore the harmony of *oketz* and *pittam*.

Some of our older prayerbooks still retain an old Yiddish prayer (*tehinah*) that was probably recited by our grandmothers before performing the mitzvah of the *arba minnim*: "May it be Thy will, our God and God of our fathers, that You forgive me for all the untoward and unattractive thoughts of my heart, in the merit of my having taken in my hand the *etrog* which was compared by our rabbis to the heart of a man."

Indeed, the *etrog* is like the heart; and the heart, like the *etrog*, must possess a harmonious blend of both elements in balance: change and stability, blossom and stem.

KOHELET:
LOOKING TOO FAR AHEAD

THE BOOK OF KOHELET is considered part of the Wisdom literature of the Bible. Like Proverbs, Job, and the Proverbs of Solomon in the Apocrypha, it is considered a book of *hokhmah*. This is appropriate for Kohelet, because tradition identifies him with King Solomon, who was the wisest of all men, the greatest *hakham* on earth.

Now, it has long been held by wise men of many ages and many climes that wisdom is a means to happiness. Socrates maintained that if people only *knew* what is right, they would *do* it, and their lives would change. This theme was continued by his student Plato, and was elaborated, in turn, by his student Aristotle, who said that in the pursuit of wisdom lies the highest and happiest life. In a more down-to-earth sense, modern man believes, as an unspoken tenet of his faith, that knowledge is redemptive, that wisdom, especially in its scientific and technological expression, can solve all problems, that *hokhmah* can make everyone happy. In truth, this certainly seems to be the case: knowledge, intelligence, good sense, talent, wisdom—what else do we possess that can help us be happy?

Yet, when we turn to Kohelet, the book of *hokhmah*, what a disappointment! *Havel havelim*, Kohelet cries out, "vanity of vanities" (Eccl. 1:1)—all is weariness, all is nonsense, nothing is of value. Kohelet is disillusioned with all those things that man usually cherishes: wealth, pleasure, the company of women, good food, even ethical living—and even *hokhmah* itself! At the end of chapter 1, he informs us that with much wisdom there comes much vexation, and "he who increases knowledge increases pain" (Eccl. 1:18). There are dozens of such statements in Kohelet, and they add up to a quite depressing view.

Actually, this picture is a bit unfair. It is true that modern man is charmingly naive when he believes that if only the scientists would desist from armaments

5729 (1968)

research and the space race and concentrate on medicine, or what is quaintly called "the science of man," they would make us all happy both physically and mentally. It is true that education is no guarantee that man will not succumb to bigotry. It is true that science and technology have brought in their wake many problems. But it is overwhelmingly truer that wisdom in its various contemporary aspects has brought us health and hygiene and longevity and convenience and sophistication. How many of us would be willing to give up these benefits of science and wisdom? On the contrary, I would say with Socrates, Plato, and Aristotle—and with the far less sophisticated modern—that wisdom does make life more pleasant, that *hokhmah* does lead to happiness.

Why then does Kohelet despair? How do we account for the fact that *hokhmah*, which usually occasions optimism, is for Kohelet a source of bitter pessimism?

The answer is that Kohelet is not a work of *hokhmah* alone. It has one added ingredient that makes all the difference: *nevu'ah*, prophecy—not in the classical biblical sense of summoning the people to God and repentance, but more in the laymen's sense of clairvoyance, of predicting and foretelling the future. And it is this which corrodes Kohelet's cheer and accounts for the gloom and dejection in the book. The author of the Aramaic translation, the Targum, appreciated this added element and included mention of it in his paraphrase at the very beginning of the book: *Kad haza Shelomoh malka de-Yisra'el*, when Solomon, King of Israel, saw, *be-ruah nevu'ah*, by means of the spirit of prophecy, that his great kingdom would be split in the civil war following his death, that the Temple that he had built and the city of Jerusalem would be devastated, and that his people Israel would languish in exile, he cried out, *Havel havalim*, "vanity of vanities": *kol mah de-torhit ana ve-David abba kolla havalu*, "all that I and my father David labored for and struggled for, all is empty and wasted and vain!"

Had Kohelet restricted himself to his great *hokhmah* alone, he would have emerged with a happy and sanguine and cheerful book, prudent perhaps, like his Book of Proverbs—but not as gloomy and even cynical as Kohelet. But the note of *nevu'ah*, looking too far ahead into the future, undid him. It made him see the fatuousness of even wisdom itself. Thus, Kohelet, the wisest of all men, cries out: "I thought to myself, *ke-mikreh ha-kesil gam ani yikreni*, what will happen to the fool will happen to me as well, the same common grave will swallow both of us, and therefore, *ve-lammah hakhamti ani az yoter*" (2:15). To give this an Anglo-Yiddish translation: "Does it pay to be smart?" In an even more frightening vein, Kohelet dourly exclaims in the verse following: "For no memory remains of the wise man or the fool forever; *be-she-kevar ha-yamim ha-ba'im ha-kol nishkah*, for as the days grow into years and the years into centuries, all is forgotten, and so does the wise man die together with the fool." Think of it—what a frightening, unthinkable thought: in two hundred years, who will know us, who will remember us? Even our descendants, even those who may bear our very own names—will they ever know we existed, will they ever recall our passions, our loves, our hates, our wants, our fears? What are we proud of today? Family, status, wealth, power? In the face of the eternity that will swallow all of us, it is *havel havalim*, utterly meaningless.

So this capacity for *nevu'ah*, for looking too far ahead, is unnerving and catastrophic. It undermines every shred of self-confidence. The knowledge of ultimate failure, of death and oblivion, blocks all progress, undercuts all aspiration, verily disembowels our lives of all significance. This dismal prophetic glimpse turns the optimism of wisdom into bitter gall, the joys of pleasure into wormwood, the triumph of money and power into dust and ashes, the pleasure of a good reputation into a mockery. Nothing lasts, nothing endures. *Hokhmah* itself is an illusion; wisdom, an empty boast. And in that case, *kol mah de-torhit ana ve-David abba,* all that we have built, all that the past generations and we have forged and created and constructed—*kolla havalu*, it is all a joke, a cruel and senseless exercise in futility.

This, then, is the difference between pure wisdom and wisdom touched by and controlled by prophecy. Wisdom approaches facts as they are in the here-and-now: circumscribed, objective, limited, maybe anticipating developments a step or two ahead—but all within the purview of mind and intellect and analysis. And wisdom, using its celebrated judgment, can settle things, make them work, establish harmony, produce efficiency. The mind gazes on the world, takes its measure, and decides that it can overcome it. Wisdom is a problem-solver, and therefore *hokhmah* leads one to happiness and to optimism.

Prophecy, however, looking far beyond the present, beyond even death, sees only endless oblivion, an infinite blank for all eternity. The prophetic intuition perceives the ultimate futility of all as the grave itself disintegrates, as the whole solar system comes to an end in the blazing flames of cosmic implosion or whimpers to its death in unspeakably cold wastes. Prophecy, therefore, is dreadfully pessimistic.

In that case, why did tradition assign Kohelet to be read on so happy a holiday as Sukkot? Who needed it? Why not some other, pleasant, wise book?

The answer comes in the closing verses of the book, which Bible critics have dismissed as a later appendage, but in which they are sadly mistaken, for this is the whole of Kohelet and its very heart and essence. *Sof davar*, "the end of the matter," after all is heard and all the evidence has been gathered, is "fear God, and *et mitzvotav shemor*, observe His commandments, *ki zeh kol ha-adam*, for this is the whole of man" (Eccl. 12:13). "Over every act shall God pass judgment, for every forgotten thing shall He remember, whether good or bad" (Eccl. 12:14).

What does this mean? Permit me to use a felicitous phraseology suggested by a writer in a recent issue of *Fortune Magazine.* This writer tells us that once upon a time, America was guilty of a "bright perception"—of excessive cheerfulness and optimism, as it swept its incipient, ugly problems under the national carpet. Nowadays, we have veered to the other extreme. We are guilty of a "dark perception"; we see only gloom, we consider ourselves hopelessly trapped. Neither of these, we are told, is correct. What we need is a "clear perception."

In these terms, we may say that wisdom alone is not enough, that by itself it offers us only a one-sided "bright perception." Wisdom looks down, deeply, too much down and too deep; but it is blind to the anguish of death and frustration and to the anxiety of approaching nothingness. Prophecy alone is also inadequate; it gives us an equally one-sided view, the "dark perception." It looks too far ahead, and is so obsessed with the beyond that it fails to see the here-and-now; so taken up with the forest that it cannot see the trees on the landscape of life. What we require is a spiritually "clear perception": *et mitzvotav shemor*, the fear of God and the observance of Torah and *mitzvot!* For here is something that transcends and includes both wisdom and prophecy—*ki zeh kol ha-adam*, it is the *whole* of man—and corrects the faults of each.

Torah, unlike wisdom, does not look *down*; and unlike prophecy, does not look *ahead.* Rather, to continue the metaphor of direction, it looks *up.* Torah requires an upward glance: *Torah min ha-shamayim*, Torah comes from heaven—or, as Hasidism teaches, Torah itself is *shamayim!* Torah encompasses both wisdom and prophecy, and much more. It tells us that both the bright perception of wisdom and the dark perception of prophecy are illusions, because man is not caught inextricably in nature. Man can have a connection with God, he can be raised above the natural law, he need not be trapped in the endless cycle of life and death, there is something in man that allows him to be plucked out of the maelstrom of the world and elevated to such heights that wisdom cannot fully understand him and prophecy cannot fully predict him.

It does this by telling us two things: first, that God knows and cares. And that He knows all and considers all means that nothing that happens to us is forgotten, that everything, no matter how minor—*al kol nelam* (Eccl. 12:14)—remains with God forever, even after earth and sun have been burnt into cinders of nuclear ash.

But that is not enough. For God to remember does not yet grace our lives with meaning. Therefore the second point: in order for us to derive significance for our lives both here-and-now and forever, in order for us to be able to use and enjoy our wisdom and pleasure and money and love and influence and escape the threat of oblivion and obscurity, we have got to *respond* to God's care, we have got to incorporate His concern into our actual lives, we have got to elevate ourselves above world and nature and the web of illusions and frustrations that threatens to ensnare us.

When man performs a mitzvah, he in effect raises himself and his environment to the order of eternal significance in God's eyes, to a level which lasts forever; he incorporates himself into Torah, which is both *from* Heaven and *is* Heaven, and which therefore cannot be ravaged by temporal disintegration.

For instance, take the beauties of nature. Wisdom tells us how gorgeous, how complex, how useful, how interrelated is the whole natural world—live it fully! Science investigates it; philosophy exclaims upon its aesthetics. Prophecy responds coldly: So what? All passeth away. The endless cycles mean that it is all meaningless. It is sham. It is illusion. Torah responds: You both are wrong. Man should enjoy beauty and nature, but not as an automatic activity. It requires the act of being *mekaddesh*, sanctifying beauty, and then its significance will endure even after the physical objects which we treasure rot and decay. Thus, when man takes the *arba minim*, the cluster of species on Sukkot, and cherishes their quality of *hadar*, beauty, that beauty lasts forever, and every appreciation of beauty in his life is exalted thereby, to endure endlessly.

Or take the consolation of wealth—and what a consolation wealth can be! Wisdom says: use it, enjoy it, build with it, invest it, multiply it, live comfortably. Prophecy offers its rejoinder with a cynical smile: *havel havalim*, how empty, how vain, how foolish. Torah answers: you are both mistaken. Wealth should be used and enjoyed—but first, sanctified! This is done by giving *tzedakah*, by being generous to others, by imparting of your substance to those who need it. In that manner, such money as one gives lasts forever; indeed, the money that one gives away is the only money that one really possesses forever. In the eyes of the eternal God, such money is never spent. Even if a man who gives *tzedakah* should lose his fortune tomorrow or die the day after, his act of generosity survives forever.

Or take love, of wife or child or parents or friends. Wisdom approves: it is psychologically healthy and socially necessary. Prophecy is skeptical: love itself is ephemeral and transient and cannot last beyond the lives of the lovers. Torah disagrees with both. Love must be turned into mitzvah; it must be graced with *kedushah*, sanctity, and thus made to endure forever. Love deeply and well and selflessly, and it becomes a thing of beauty and holiness for all time, defeating death and surviving the grave. Such love survives even after the lovers have perished.

Or take pleasure. Interestingly, wisdom and prophecy draw opposite conclusions from the same premises. Wisdom, echoing the Greek philosopher Epicurus, says that the fact of death should lead us to indulge in pleasure: eat, drink, and be merry, for tomorrow you die. Prophecy draws the exactly opposite conclusion: our eventual death makes all our pleasures and joys not only temporary and farcical, but even uninteresting. Torah rejects both. Of course we must enjoy life and its pleasures. The Jerusalem Talmud says that we shall have to answer in the other world for all the legitimate pleasures we failed to enjoy in this world (*Yerushalmi, Kiddushin* 4:12). But it must come through the context of mitzvah, and this sacred framework will sharpen our pleasures, make them fuller and more perfect and more meaningful. On this holiday of Sukkot, we emphasize the ideal of pleasure and happiness, of *simhah*. The Torah tells us "*ve-samahta*—you shall be happy" (Deut. 16:14). But, as the Rabbis in effect added, we can be happy ourselves only if we read that word also as *ve-simmahta*, you shall *make* happy. (See *Yalkut Shim'oni, Re'eh* 997.) You must give happiness to God's four wards, the *ger*, the *Levi*, the *yatom*, and the *almanah*, the stranger and the Levite and the orphan and the widow, and then God will grant happiness to your four wards, *binkha, bittekha, avdekha, va-amatkha*, your children and your household. Doing that, such *simhah* truly endures, even if it is merely the pleasure of *basar ve-yayin, dagim ve-khol mat'ammim*, of physical indulgence. Never mind sickness and death; such dedicated and consecrated *simhah* outlasts the world itself, because it is *ve-samahta lifnei Hashem Elokekha*, happiness "before the Lord thy God," happiness that remains eternally with the Eternal.

So that we have an O. Henry ending for Solomon's Kohelet. Kohelet looks ahead, too far ahead, and his combined wisdom and prophecy declare *Havel havalim*—what a waste! There is no real sense of achievement: *kol mah de-*

torhit ana ve-David abba kolla havalu. All the rest of the book is a spelling-out of the implications of the very beginning in a dirge of disillusionment, of painful disappointment with wealth and wisdom and power and love and pleasure. The bright perception of wisdom turns into the dark perception of prophecy. But at the very end, *sof davar*, after all has been heard, wisdom and prophecy are overcome in the fullness of man created in the image of God, and the clear perception emerges: *et mitzvotav shemor*, incorporating into our lives the will of God.

Solomon, then, need not fall into the doldrums because of civil war and the destruction and the exile of his people, not only because of their ultimate redemption, but because a life of mitzvah is in itself well spent, because God remembers all and cares about all. It is this knowledge that looks deeper than wisdom and farther than prophecy by looking up to our Father in Heaven.

MAN IS MORE THAN SEKHAKH

MORAL INSTRUCTION IS AVAILABLE to us Jews not only in the *Hummash*, not only in Aggadah and Midrash, but, sometimes, in Halakhah. If we look closely and carefully enough, we will discover the grand themes of human destiny even in legal technicalities, profound human wisdom even in halakhic discourses. All it requires is imagination, a sense of allegory, some homiletic license, and a readiness to find beautiful insights in unlikely places.

With this in mind, I commend your attention to the halakhic requirements of the *sekhakh*, the boughs and branches we use to cover the *sukkah*. The Halakhah lays down three conditions for the *sekhakh* to be kosher, or valid. The first of these is that it must be *tzomeah min ha-aretz*—it must grow from the earth. Thus, it must be an item such as branches or wood, but not metal or plastic. Second, it must be *talush*, cut off from the ground. Hence, one may not build a *sukkah* underneath the overhanging branches of a tree, attempting to use those branches and leaves as *sekhakh*, for they are connected to the tree, which is connected to the earth. Third, the *sekhakh* must be *eino ra'ui le-kabbel tum'ah*—it must be such that it cannot contract ritual defilement. According to the Halakhah, the only objects that can become *tamei* (impure) are artifacts that have specific functions, such as vessels or pots or pans or ladders. For this reason one may not use for *sekhakh* such items as ladders, grass mats, or wooden doors or frames, even though they are made of material that grows from the earth and is severed from the earth, because, as functional objects, they can contract impurity.

Now, the *sukkah* symbolizes transience, impermanence, the weak and the feeble. It is the sparse and provisional roof of the wanderer's hut in the great desert. The three laws of *sekhakh*, therefore, are associated with mortality and finitude, with that which cannot survive.

But man is more than *sekhakh*! Man seeks permanence and endurance. All of life is, in a sense, the effort to overcome death. So much of life is a dis-

5733 (1972)

140

guised attempt to achieve immortality, whether in healthy ways or in sick ways, whether in the form of great contributions to scholarship and philanthropy, or simple social climbing and publicity seeking. We want to continue, to survive, to conquer the temporary and the ephemeral. Hence, to accomplish this, we must strive for the very opposite of the three laws of *sekhakh*. If, indeed, man is more than *sekhakh*, he must go beyond *aretz*, *talush*, and *eino mekabbel tum'ah*.

Unlike *sekhakh*, man must transcend *aretz*, earth, the symbol of purely material existence. Now, I am not arguing for the medieval notion that humans are caught in the vise of an enormous conflict between matter and spirit, and that they must choose spirit and reject matter. (That theme really goes back beyond the Middle Ages to ancient days, to the ancient movement known as Gnosticism.) It is not an idea I would recommend to moderns or to anyone. Judaism by no means considers the material world as all bad. But neither should we submit to the equally mistaken and even more disastrous idea that has seized us in modern days—that there is nothing more to life and existence than this material world. This is a stifling and stultifying idea. It is based upon an immature skepticism that distorts the meaning of science when it insists in its name that only that is real which can be proved experimentally. We have been brainwashed with the theory that man is nothing more than an aggregate of molecules. For our contemporary materialism has indoctrinated us with a fallacious set of equations: that man equals animal, and animal equals machine, and machine equals chemicals, the kind that are found in the earth. Man, we are told to conclude, is exclusively a *tzomeah min ha-aretz*, nothing more than a product of the earth, with no additional dimensions to him.

However, if we are going to submit to this kind of scientific reductionism, we must go the whole way and ask: and what are chemicals made from? And so on. And the answer would be: chemicals are atoms, and atoms are a form of congealed energy, and energy is, after all, simply an abstraction, a set of mathematical formulae. So, in a way, we have this terrifying pseudoscientific conclusion: man is just a set of abstractions. Or, if you will: man is nothing! Not even *sekhakh*!

A brief sermon is not a place to subject materialistic concepts to critical analysis. But it is important to note that the philosophy of man as *tzomeah min ha-aretz* is on the wane today. In Russia, the authorities are alarmed at the reemergence of signs of religious interest after six decades of state materialism and atheism. In the United States, where materialism is always officially disavowed but where it is effectively the underpinning of "the American way of life," the younger generation is revolting against the endless money-mania and possessions-obsessions of their elders and their cult of affluence. In Israel, the children of kibbutzniks who exchanged their Judaism for an idealistic Marxian materialism are now rejecting materialism and searching for something deeper and higher; they are going beyond *aretz* and looking for that which points to *shamayim,* to heaven. And social thinkers and philosophers of the first rank in the Western world have developed a new interest in and respect for transcendence, for that which lies beyond immediate sense experience, beyond this world alone.

The second requirement of *sekhakh* is that it be *talush,* severed from the ground, cut off from its origin. By the same token, if man is more than *sekhakh,* then his redeeming quality must be that he remain *mehubbar,* rooted and fixed in a framework of value and meaning, in a ground of *Weltanschauung.* For man to be human, he must recognize himself as a link in an ongoing chain; he must see himself as part of the continuum of human history. He must remember the legend on certain coupons and tickets: NO GOOD IF DETACHED!

Change there must be—but change *in* something, *relative* to something, *out* of something. One of the failures of the counter-culture, the "now generation," is its rootlessness. It is not based on and rooted in and attached to a past or a tradition. The counter-culture considers this a virtue; it holds itself free and liberated and emancipated because of its lack of connection to the past. But in truth it is as free as a piece of straw floating in the air, or, as David said of the *rasha* (evil man) in his first psalm, *ka-motz asher tiddefennu ruah*—like chaff driven by the wind (Ps. 1:4). Its rejection of the whole of the human past and inherited culture leaves it without any cultural equilibrium, without any psychological or spiritual rootage, and therefore incapable of making a creative contribution to human development. It is merely adrift. And instability is a symptom, not an ideal.

I remember a story (which is probably apocryphal, but nonetheless contains a great deal of truth) that was told shortly after the first session of the United Nations. According to this story, one delegation was housed in a hotel, and after they left at the end of the session, the manager of the hotel discovered that all the faucets were missing. Upon investigation, he discovered that these men of the desert were fascinated by these contraptions called faucets, which, when turned on, magically allow water to emerge in full force. They therefore decided to take the faucets home with them to the desert, so that they could turn them on and thereby allow water to flow freely in the very desert.

What I am trying to say is that man, to be human, must be *mehubbar* to a reservoir of culture and tradition and history, lest his currents of life run dry.

This is, after all, the sum and substance of what we mean by Jewish education. Jewish education contains such elements as learning Hebrew and learning *Hummash* and learning the Talmud, and these are very important, but they are not the most significant object of Jewish education. Our central purpose is to give growing young Jews the feeling of a rootage in a great Jewish past, an awareness of being *mehubbar*—connected to and growing out of the greatness of Jewish history, so that even if they stray from the path, they will know what it is they are leaving and they will recognize that to which they ought to return.

Finally, the third qualification for *sekhakh* is that it be *eino ra'ui le-kabbel tum'ah*, not capable of contracting impurity. Hence, by the criterion we have established, a man should be *ra'ui le-kabbel tum'ah*, capable of contracting impurity. I take this to mean that man must be ready to risk and dare in order to achieve and accomplish.

The kabbalists have taught us that only that can achieve *kedushah* (sanctity) which can contract *tum'ah* (impurity). So man himself is the main source of sanctification in the world; but when he loses his soul and returns it to his Creator, his body is a corpse which is considered halakhically *avi avot ha-tum'ah*, the most potent source of defilement.

There is a powerful and dangerous idea on the loose here: that only by risking *tum'ah* can you achieve *kedushah*; that only by daring to lose can you win; that only by taking chances with failure can you succeed. The gambler's instinct can, of course, be taken to an extreme and turn into a disease. But without some element of hazard and risk, we are paralyzed and inert and can never make any progress.

The State of Israel would not be here today if those men meeting in Tel Aviv in 1948 at the session of the Va'ad Le'umi had not hazarded monumental failure in declaring independence—as a fledgling group without any experience in statecraft and any of the appurtenances of statehood. It was only because they were *ra'ui le-kabbel tum'ah*, willing to embrace the possibilities of catastrophic failure, that Israel was created and became a *kiddush shem Shamayim be-rabbim*, a public and historic sanctification of God's Name.

A leader of any kind of group must venture beyond the limits of caution and occasionally dare to speak out and declare his vision of the truth, even if he runs the risk of losing some of his followers. The alternative is to be a consensus leader, who merely does what the people want; but such a person is not a leader, but merely an administrator. All progress, all change, involves the possibility of failure. But without it, we are as good as dead. To be truly human, we must act responsibly—with equal emphasis on both: *act*, and *responsibly*. Young people are usually more active, frequently without a sense of responsibility. Middle-aged and older people are most often responsible, but usually fail to act when they should. The wise person is both—active and responsible, And if man is more than *sekhakh*, he must be *ra'ui le-kabbel tum'ah*, ready to embrace defeat in order to try for victory, for triumph, for conquest.

So there are times when we should strike out boldly. Think about it: the lesson of Sukkot, that man must be more than *sekhakh*, does not say that you should do things merely for the sake of novelty or to chase away boredom. But there are times when we want to do something which we think is right and proper, and we have assessed the possibilities of success and the possibilities of failure, the desirability of the former and the consequences of the latter, and logically we know we ought to take a chance. But we are frightened, we are apprehensive, we are too comfortable, we prefer our inertia. At such a time, Sukkot calls out to us and says: risk *tum'ah*, go ahead and innovate, experiment, make the move, go on *aliyyah*, emigrate, change your job, speak out, change your mind, do that which is new—and do not be afraid of failure, of risk, of danger, of criticism or derision! Take a chance!

The great achievement of man is to be *tahor* (pure) while he is *ra'ui le-kabbel tum'ah* (capable of becoming impure).

These, then, are the three qualities that are requisite for man in order for him to be more than *sekhakh* but to endure meaningfully. First, he must acknowledge more than material existence, more than *aretz*, but be open to the transcendental and the spiritual. Second, he must be rooted in a great past and see himself as a link in the chain of history and culture and tradition. Third, he must be willing to be *ra'ui le-kabbel tum'ah*—that is, to venture and hazard and risk and dare.

That is how man can become more than *sekhakh*, more than the weak and feeble and temporary *sekhakh*. This is so according to the rabbi of the Talmud who considered our *sukkah* to be the physical counterpart of the huts that were used by our ancestors in the desert. But man becomes more *like* the *sukkah* according to the opinion of another rabbi of the Talmud, who maintains that our *sukkot* are symbols not of the physical huts used in the desert, but of the *ananei ha-kavod*, the divine clouds of glory which protectively covered our ancestors during their peregrinations in the great desert (see *Sukkah* 11b).

In this sense, man becomes more *like* the *sukkah* and its *sekhakh* by raising his head above the ground of materialism, by locating himself in a great past, and by striving for greatness while willing to risk failure, he becomes worthy of being enveloped and covered by *ananei ha-kavod*, the clouds of glory.

Shemini Atzeret
and
Simhat Torah

WHICH WAY THE WIND BLOWS

THE DISTINGUISHING FEATURE OF every Jewish holiday is *simhah*, joy or happiness. The Torah commands us: *Ve-hayita akh sameah*, "And thou shalt be altogether joyful" (Deut. 16:15).

Now, while this particular commandment is included in the Torah's legislation of the festival of Sukkot, there is no reason to restrict it to that holiday. Indeed, the mitzvah of *simhah* applies to every holiday. It is somewhat astonishing, therefore, to discover that the Talmud finds it necessary to apply the requirement of *simhah* specifically to the present holiday, Shemini Atzeret. Thus, the Talmud says (*Sukkah* 48a), "*le-rabbot leilei yom tov ha-aharon le-simhah*,"— that the commandment to be happy on the holiday includes not only the first days of Sukkot, but the last days—which means Shemini Atzeret—as well.

(What makes this talmudic statement even more surprising is the fact that the word *akh*, as in *ve-hayita akh sameah*, is usually understood *le-ma'et*, "to exclude." That is, the word *akh*, or "only," usually means to restrict what follows. In this case, however, the Talmud understands it in the reverse, *le-rabbot*: You must be happy not only on the first day of the holiday, but *le-rabbot*, it must be inclusive and extend to the last holiday as well.)

Why the necessity for emphasizing *simhah* even on *Shemini Atzeret*?

Perhaps we can understand it from a story that the Talmud elsewhere tells (*Yoma* 21b) of a popular custom that used to take place as soon as the entire Sukkot holiday, including Shemini Atzeret, was over and done with. People would gather about the Temple, and *ha-kol tzafin le-ashan ha-ma'arakhah*—everyone would peer intently at the column of smoke that would rise from the altar, where the logs were burning so as to provide a source of fire for the sacrificial service. As the column of smoke rose, all eyes would be glued to it, to see which way the wind would blow it. If the column would blow to the north, then the poor were happy and the well-to-do farmers were sad, for a north wind indicated that there would be early rain that season, and their produce

---

5727 (1966)

was in danger of rotting, and they would therefore have to sell their harvest at a low price. If the column tended to the south, the poor were sad and the farmers were happy, because a south wind indicated late rain, and therefore the fruit and wheat could be kept until the prices rose steeply. If it was an east wind, everyone would be happy, for nature would balance perfectly for everyone. If there was a west wind, everyone was sad, for it indicated probable drought and famine.

Now we may understand the need for the emphasis on being happy even on Shemini Atzeret. For as soon as the holiday was over, people would rush to find out which way the wind was blowing. And so, quite naturally, even during the holiday itself, in anticipation of this event, the peace of mind, the quiet and serene joy that are so essential for the holiday, would already begin to vanish. During the holiday itself, the mind of the Jew and his heart would begin to concentrate not on *ve-hayita akh sameah*, "be altogether joyful" before God, but on, which way does the wind blow? The Rabbis of the Talmud, therefore, took special caution and went to special pains to remind us that we must banish such anticipation of worry from our hearts, and as long as we are in the midst of the festival, we ought to retain a full and complete sense of *simhah*.

The same teaching applies with no less force and relevance to us in the mid-twentieth century than it did to our ancestors during the Second Commonwealth, for we, too, are constantly concerned about which way the wind blows. Here we are, toward the end of a marvelous and joyous holiday. Yet, can anyone doubt that in the minds of so many of us, during our services this morning, and during the rest of the afternoon to come, the major concern is not the meaning of our prayers or the attainment of true joy, but worry about tomorrow and the day after? We are still in the midst of Shemini Atzeret, and already we are worrying: will it be an economy of boom or bust, will the stock market be bullish or bearish, will the economy go up or down, will we experience recovery or recession? Everyone has his theory, and everyone anxiously awaits some sign of which way the wind blows.

But under such conditions, even if the ultimate result is favorable, the worry and the tenseness, the anxiety and the concern in anticipation, frequently vitiate whatever benefits may obtain later on. In addition, such worry in advance destroys the sanctity of *yom tov*, it empties the holy day of its content of holiness. The Rabbis therefore remind us, *Ve-hayita akh sameah, le-rabbot leilei yom tov ha-aharon le-simhah.* Hold off your worries, postpone your problems, delay your anxieties. It is still *yom tov*, and we must be observant of the commandment to experience joy even on the eve of the day when we return to office and marketplace and start wondering about what the future will bring, about which way the wind will blow that column of smoke in its many modern guises.

This is more than just good advice or a wise recommendation. To experience *simhah* on the holiday is nothing less than a mitzvah, a commandment. To declare happiness a commandment presupposes a major psychological principle: that joy is the result not only of external circumstances, but of an inner orientation. Whether I am happy or not depends not only upon whether my needs are fulfilled by the world, but also upon whether I know what to want and how to react to the world. In other words, my personal disposition can be controlled by an act of my will. My state of mind is not an infinitely plastic piece of clay molded by outside events; it is something that I can create if I exercise enough control.

That is a hard doctrine to accept. Most of us would prefer to believe that our happiness or unhappiness is the result of what life brings us, and that if we lack happiness, it is exclusively the result of our miserable fate and we are the unwilling victims of cruel circumstances. Now there is no doubt that *simhah* is to a very large extent decided by the conditions of the world in which I find myself, but not totally and exclusively so. There is a story that Hasidim tell of one of their great teachers, and that the Mitnaggedim tell of one of *their* great rabbis—and this in itself is evidence of the authentic Jewishness of the story, whether or not it literally occurred. The great rabbi and sage about whom the story is told was in the midst of dancing on Simhat Torah, filled with heavenly and rhapsodic *simhah*. Suddenly a student came into the singing and dancing crowd and furtively handed the rabbi a telegram. The rabbi glanced at it, blanched, and returned forthwith to the dancing and singing. The messenger was stunned, for the telegram had informed the rabbi that his only daughter had been killed in a distant city. The rabbi continued in his state of joy and happiness until the day was done and the *Havdalah* recited; after which he burst out in uncontrollable weeping and mourning. What a superb illustration of self-control: mourning is forbidden on the holiday, and therefore the rabbi was able to will himself into a state of *simhah*, holding off his deeply felt grief until the *yom tov* had passed.

Some will say that this is incredibly inhuman; I will agree only that it is far greater than what is normal. Certainly, few of us could hope ever to attain such a degree of mastery over our own instincts—may the Lord spare us from such tragedy! But the same principle is available and accessible to each and every one of us in modified form. We can, indeed, exercise *some* form of control over our state of mind. We may indeed will to be happy, to be joyous, to experience *simhah*. We can, if we want to strongly enough, emerge from the doldrums of self-pity and achieve a state of tranquility or serenity.

Business worries, professional concerns, even family problems should never be allowed to gain the upper hand over our inner equilibrium. That they often do does not mean that they always must. *Ve-hayita akh sameah*—we must remain happy and joyous even at a critical period when the future is unknown and mysterious and we do not yet know which way the wind will blow. No wonder that today we recited the special prayers for *geshem*, for rain, which is a symbol of prosperity. One would imagine that if the prayers were answered affirmatively by God, there would be no cause for any further concern by us. Yet as soon as the cantor will announce with a flourish that it is God who is *mashiv ha-ruah u-morid ha-geshem*, who makes the wind blow in the right direction and gives us abundant *geshem*, we will all call out: "*li-berakhah ve-lo li-kelalah*"—may it be for blessing and not, Heaven forbid, for a curse. Why is this necessary? Because even prosperity can be a curse if, in the course of achieving it, we worry ourselves to distraction. It is a truism that not everyone who is rich is happy. It is not often appreciated that in the very process of amassing wealth, one often sacrifices his personal *simhah* on the altar of affluence. Our prayer, therefore, is that we be the recipients of God's gift of wind blowing in the right direction, that of *geshem*, but *li-verakhah ve-lo li-kelalah*—may we achieve it in a blessed way, not in an accursed way. May we attain our heart's desire for prosperity, but not at the cost of personal *simhah*. May we each achieve our professional goals, whether of fame or fortune, without at the same time ignoring a wife, neglecting children, abdicating character and principles, and forgetting about the spiritual dimension of life.

I expect that there are some who will take exception to what I have been saying. It is an altogether expected reaction of the sophisticated intellectual of today to dismiss with contempt any concern by religion for the peace of mind and serenity of ordinary folk, and to consider such concern contaminated by the dubious doctrines of Norman Vincent Peale. However, such reactions notwithstanding, the Torah is interested that we experience *simhah*, that the tempest within the heart be stilled, that during Shabbat and *yom tov* we enjoy a quiet and sacred serenity. There is, after all, a certain limited validity to the irenic, or pacifying, quality of religious faith. A calm mind is no less desirable for one's spiritual welfare than a healthy body.

Nevertheless, we must confess that if this were the end of the story, our critics would be justified. If religion is meant only to give us happiness and peace of mind and tranquility, then it is not religion; it is nothing more than a sublimated tranquilizer. Even in the course of counseling us to will ourselves into a state of *simhah* and postpone our worrying about which way the wind will blow, the Torah inculcates us with a spiritual and ethical principle of the greatest significance.

For how, indeed, shall we go about developing this state of mind called *simhah* at a time when we are consciously enmeshed in worrying about the future?

The answer that Judaism offers is of the utmost importance: it tells us that the more concerned you are with your own happiness, the less likely you are to achieve it. For the constant pursuit of one's own happiness means that *simhah* is defined in a purely egoistical fashion: How can *I* be happy? But "If I am for myself, who am I?" (*Avot* 1:14). This way leads only to frustration and bitterness. True *simhah* is attained only when I forget about myself, only when I lose myself, only when my concern is with making others happy. That is why the commandment to experience *simhah* on *yom tov* is coupled, in the Torah, with the commandment to provide for the joy and happiness of the poor and the widow, of the orphan and the stranger and the Levite.

Perhaps the best example is the joyous last day of the festival which we shall observe tomorrow, Simhat Torah. What does that mean, to be happy with the Torah? Rabbi Shneur Zalman of Liadi explained that Simhat Torah means not only to be happy with the Torah, but, even more, *le-sammeah et ha-Torah*—to make the Torah happy, to provide the opportunity for *simhah* to the One who gave the Torah! Thus, on this day we determine to live our lives so that we give God the occasion for *nahas*, that we make Him happy: *yismah Hashem bema'asav* (Ps. 104:31). Then we shall be the prime recipients of this divine gift of *simhah*.

For indeed, when we forget about the satisfaction of our own desires and concentrate instead upon making the Torah happy, upon affording *nahas* to the Almighty, then we shall find that our lives are fulfilled—no matter which way the wind blows! A life of service is the way to a life of serenity. Living according to Torah will lead to a life of tranquility. Devotion to Judaism brings you unexpected joys. In the striving for holiness we will discover the possibilities of happiness.

Tomorrow's worries will, eventually, become yesterday's forgotten trivia. No matter which way the wind blows, it will soon dissipate itself and vanish.

But true *simhah*, as we have defined it, lasts forever; for if it is achieved by means of *1e-sammeah et ha-Torah*, of making the Torah happy, and the Torah is eternal, then our *simhah* is eternal too.

If we are concerned about receiving *nahas* from our own children, let us attempt, in our own lives, to grant that same blessing of *nahas* retroactively to our parents and grandparents whom we shall shortly memorialize in our Yizkor prayers. If we want God to make us happy, it is we who must first make Him happy.

Let us, on this great and wonderful day, cease worrying about tomorrow and commence being grateful for today and yesterday; for herein lies the secret of *simhah*.

REWORKING THE PAST

LAST WEEK, I MET a man whom I had not seen for six or seven years. I recognized him, but I did not recognize him. I was puzzled. Then I realized the source of my confusion: he had grown a beard in the interim. Because of the beard, I did not recognize him, and because of the beard I did recognize him. The reason for this was because he now looked startlingly like his late father!

In discussing this with him, I appreciated his inner feelings. He thought to himself: I am now a mature man, and spent a good part of my life carving out for myself my own life, my own personality, my own niche. Now I want to recapture my father's image and make it my own, not only psychologically and spiritually but, if at all possible, even physically.

This otherwise unimportant encounter brought to my mind the problem of two forces that strive for supremacy within each of us: continuity vs. discontinuity, rootedness in the past vs. innovation and novelty, reverence for the old vs. the search for the new. In Hebrew, we might refer to these as *hemshekh* (continuity) vs. *hiddush* (innovation). This phenomenon is well-nigh universal.

It is in this sense that I consider Shemini Atzeret a metaphor for man. For Shemini Atzeret, according to the Halakhah, has a rather hybrid nature. In one sense, it is merely a continuation of the Sukkot holiday, of which it is the eighth day. In another sense, it is an independent and autonomous holiday in its own right. Thus, the Halakhah teaches that in all ways it is part of Sukkot, except for six laws—represented by the acrostic פז"ר קש"ב—in which it is *hag bifnei atzmo*, a holiday by itself (*Sukkah* 47b–48a). Hence, like the eighth day of Passover, there is no special mitzvah of appearing in the Temple, as there is on the three pilgrim festivals. And in this sense, it is merely the end of Sukkot. But unlike Passover, we recite the *She-hehiyyanu* on Shemini Atzeret, because it *is* a holiday in its own right. Thus, too, we can understand the two different versions of the name for this festival in the prayerbook. In some prayerbooks, we refer to this day as *Yom ha-shemini, atzeret ha-hag ha-zeh*—"the eighth and concluding

---

5736 (1975) (Yizkor)

day of this [Sukkot] festival." Other prayerbooks read *Yom ha-shemini Hag ha-Atzeret ha-zeh*—"the eighth day which is the Atzeret festival," emphasizing its autonomy and separateness, not as *hemshekh* but as *hiddush*. So that Shemini Atzeret in itself symbolizes the tension between the old and the new, between continuity and autonomy, between the unbroken continuum of the past and the bold assertion of independence into the future.

I do not necessarily refer only to the rebellious rejection of religion and tradition, although that certainly would be an illustration of what I am talking about. Rather, I am more interested in the fact that even in religious consciousness itself, both tendencies prevail. The Israelites at the shore of the Red Sea sang, "This is my God and I will glorify Him," and in the same sentence, "the God of my fathers and I will exalt Him" (Ex. 15:2). We approach God both as new human beings, expressing our own unique, spiritual quest, and as children of a long tradition and an ancient heritage who come with the past as our credentials. We ourselves, in our prayers, refer to God as *Elokeinu*, "our God," and *Elokei avotenu*, "the God of our fathers." David, in the *Hallel* we have been reciting all week long, says, *Annah Hashem ki ani avdekha, ani avdekha ben amatekha, pittahta le-moserai*, "O Lord, I am Thy servant, Thy servant the son of Thy handmaid, Thou hast loosened my bonds" (Ps. 116:16). It is when a religious individual appreciates that he is both the servant of God as a separate human being, and also the servant of God because he is descended from a long line of servants of God, that he can experience a sense of liberation and redemption.

The Shemini Atzeret metaphor, this dual nature of the day, refers not only to man, but to every day of life. Every single day when we wake up, we are presented with the problem of *hemshekh* vs. *hiddush*, of continuity vs. striking out in new directions. We can't very well ignore all of the past; that would be sheer irresponsibility. We have to pay old debts, and collect them as well; we nurse old resentments, and try to cherish old loves and loyalties. It is difficult indeed, and also not advisable, to break all the old patterns of conduct. At the same time, if a day is to be meaningful, one must feel that there is some open-endedness to it. It reminds me of the line in the song, "Today is the first day of the rest of your life." Every day, *every* new day, must hold the promise of openness, opportunity, surprise, novelty.

In this sense, the Shemini Atzeret metaphor is essentially the biography of man. A baby knows only *hemshekh*, only Sukkot. He conceives of his mother as an extension of himself, of his very own body. As a youngster, he sees himself as organically part of the family, no matter how tense and divisive it may be. When he comes into adolescence, he begins to assert himself; he follows the פז"ר קש"ב of autonomous development toward a personality that is *hag bifnei atzmo*, a festival in its own right. Later on, if he is wise, he will have the perspicacity to appropriate both: the continuation of the past, even while he develops his own self.

For indeed, both are necessary. If we conceive of ourselves only as *hag bifnei atzmo* and assert only our independence, we are insecure and rootless; we are floating monads in an ocean of loneliness. But if we are only part of the past, if we see ourselves only as *hemshekh*, then we turn stale, staid, and stodgy. In the conflict and tensions between the both, we have the beginnings of creativity.

But true and full creativity is achieved not by mere adjudication of the conflicting claims of each tendency, not only by striking a balance or compromise between *hemshekh* and *hiddush*, between the continuation of one's parent's life and the development of one's own integrity. Rather, creativity comes in the combination of both tendencies into a new synthesis: so that *as himself*, as a person who is unique and independent, a man can *rework and redeem the past!* What I am trying to express is an apparently irrational idea, but one that is beautiful and exciting and so very Jewish: *Ha-hayyim mekhapperim al ha-metim*—the living can atone for the dead (*Tanhuma, Ha'azinu* 1; *Beit Yosef, Orah Hayyim* 284:7); children can make up for their parents. In a world which declares, with spurious claim to scientific credentials, that the future is determined and closed, we Jews, so curiously, proclaim that even the past is not closed and dead. The past can still be saved, it can still be vindicated! The very idea of *teshuvah* (repentance) itself partakes of this irrationality: the spiritual attainment of the present can actually change the record of the past. (This thesis, challenging the idea of "necessity," has been expounded by an alienated Jew, Lev Shestov, in his book, *Athens and Jerusalem*.)

The Midrash teaches: *Kol ha-etzim kesherim le-ma'arakhah hutz mi-shel zayit ve-shel gefen, she-ha-shemen ve-ha-yayin kerevin le-gabbei mizbeah. Hitzilu ha-perot et ha-ilanot.* "All kinds of wood from all kinds of trees may be used to build the fire on the altar, except for the wood of the olive tree and the vine, because olive oil and wine are used in the sacrificial service. Hence, *the fruit have saved the trees*" (*Pesikta Zutra*, Lev., 4b).

It is the application to the vegetable world of the principle of *ha-hayyim mikhapperim al ha-metim*, of children who can change the lives of parents already gone to their eternal reward.

Mentioning this Midrash, the Ramban (commentary to Torah, Gen. 12:32) adds: *Ve-khen matzinu be-Avraham, she-hitzil et Terah,* "Thus do we find that Abraham saved his father, Terah," who otherwise would have been condemned to eternal perdition, so that Terah should merit the life of eternity. Even Abraham, the great iconoclast, the one who began the greatest revolution in the spiritual history of mankind, did not entirely break off from the past. Indeed, he went back, as an independent human being of tremendous personal achievement, and improved the past, saved his father, redeemed all that had gone before!

In the *haftarah* of Shemini Atzeret, we continue the *haftarah* of the second day of Sukkot. Both of them speak of Solomon's dedication of the Temple he built in Jerusalem. Who built the Temple? Solomon. Who consecrated it? Solomon. Yet all through his great prayer and blessing, Solomon remembers and reminds his people that it was his father David who envisioned it, who dreamt of it, who planned for it.

The whole chapter concludes with the verse which relates the events of that historic dedication to the day of Shemini Atzeret: *Ba-yom ha-shemini shillah et ha-am va-yevarekhu et ha-melekh va-yelekhu le-oholeihem semehim ve-tovei lev al kol ha-tovah asher asah Hashem le-Dovid avdo u-le-Yisra'el ammo.* "On the eighth day, he [Solomon] sent the people away, and they blessed the king. And they went to their tents happy and glad of heart because of all the goodness that the Lord had done to His servant David and to His people Israel" (I Kings 8:66).

The Sages ask (*Shabbat* 30a): We can understand the "goodness" that God had done to Israel (the Midrash describes the felicity which came upon the people that night). But what goodness was done to David, who had been long dead? And the Midrash answers: When Solomon wanted, at this event of dedication and consecration, to bring the *aron* (ark) into the inner sanctum of the Temple, the gates of the Temple cleaved one to another and would not open. Solomon tried every means at his disposal to open them, but to no avail. He recited twenty-four psalms, but there was no response. He then decided to command the doors to open by exclaiming, *Se'u she'arim rasheikhem,* "O gates, lift up your heads" (Ps. 24:7), but he received no response to his royal command. But then, when he said the words *Al tashev penei meshihekha, zakhrah le-hasdei David avdekha,* "Do not reject Thy anointed, remember the grace of Thy servant David" (II Chr. 6:42), he was immediately answered and the doors opened. At that moment, the face of the enemies of David turned black as a pot on the stove, and all Israel knew that the Holy One had forgiven David because of that sin (i.e., the sin of Uriah and Batsheba).

So Solomon showed the world: a son can, by virtue of his very own talents, open the doors to his father's Temple; he can bring in his own autonomous *kedushah* to his father's sanctuary. A son can redeem his father's reputation, restore his father's standing in the eyes of God and man!

If a man is, like Shemini Atzeret, a *hag bifnei atzmo*, a holiday in its own right, he can, as such, enhance all of Sukkot, whose latest link he is. Creativity, therefore, consists in being and developing your own self, and then using those talents to reveal and fulfill and ennoble the past out of which you emerged and which is an ineradicable part of yourself.

Is not this the meaning of Kaddish? By virtue of a child's arising and declaring *kedushat Hashem*, the sanctity of the Divine Name, by living the right kind of life, he atones for his parents who already are departed from this earthly scene.

So if a son is more devout or more scholarly or has more moral sensitivity than a parent, he is at one and the same time "doing his own thing" and carrying over the past into the future on a new plateau, on a higher *niveau*—enhancing the past, while revealing its true roots and latent potencies, demonstrating that his parents must have possessed such potential qualities of devoutness or scholarship or ethical sensitivity or charitableness that only now are being expressed in the life of the son or the daughter.

So Shemini Atzeret expresses not only the tension between *hemshekh* and *hiddush*, between continuity and autonomous innovation, but also the concept of *tikkun*, of transformation and restoration and improvement of the past.

As a "holiday in its own right," Shemini Atzeret becomes an *atzeret*, a closing factor for all of Sukkot, tying it up, integrating it, revealing its new dimensions and its concealed sanctity.

It is with such thoughts that we prepare for Yizkor. We are different from our parents, and that is as it should be. In so many ways we *are* our parents, and that is as it should be. But above all else, how we live, how we give, how we conduct our homes and our businesses and our lives, how we study Torah and how we relate to the People of Israel and especially to God, can fulfill the unrealized dreams of our parents, can express their hidden powers, can atone for their blemishes, and can bring a new ark into the temples of their memory.

A Simple Farewell

The theme that dominates these days is that of farewell.

Shemini Atzeret comes at the tail end of the Sukkot holiday, which itself is the conclusion of the whole High Holiday season, including Rosh Hashanah and Yom Kippur. The Rabbis explain Shemini Atzeret, this one-day celebration at the end of the holiday season, as a special day set aside by God. He may be compared, they say, to a king who invited his children for a feast for a number of days. When the time came for him to take leave of them, he said to them, *Beni be-bakkashah mikkem, ikkevu immi yom ehad, kashah alai pereidatkhem,* "My children, please stay with me for a while, even for only one more day; it is so difficult to take leave of you" (Rashi to Lev. 23:36).

And the biblical figure who dominates this holiday, when we read the last portion of the Torah, is of course Moses, delivering his last discourse and then facing his death.

There is something particularly pathetic about Moses in this role. He is a man who looms larger than life itself. Yet his death is so very human! He wants so desperately to live, that he is even reduced to begging: *Va-ethanan el Hashem,* "And I pleaded with the Lord at that time, saying . . . let me, please, cross over and see that good land" (Deut. 3:23).

The Rabbis fill in the gaps in this biblical account of the dialogue between God and Moses, and they add that Moses said: "If I cannot come in as the leader, let me come in at the end of the procession as an ordinary Jew. And if I cannot come in alive, let me at least come in dead, to be buried in the promised land" (*Sifra, Be-midbar,* 135; *Mekhilta, Amalek,* 22).

But the divine response was, No! *Ve-shammah lo ta'avor* (Deut. 34:4), "you shall not cross over there." Moreover, the tradition adds, Moses wrote the last

---

This is the last sermon I preached in the rabbinate before assuming the presidency of Yeshiva University.—N.L.

5737 (1976)

words of the Torah by himself, with his quill dipped into an ink made of his own tears (*Bava Batra* 15a). *Va-yamat sham Mosheh,* "And Moses died there"— there, on the plains of Moab, not in his Promised Land (Deut. 34:5).

When the Rabbis approach this story of the death of Moses, they make a number of interesting remarks, one of which (in *Sotah* 14a) has always astonished me. "Rabbi Samlai taught: The Torah begins with an act of loving-kindness (*gemilut hasadim*), and concludes with an act of loving-kindness. It begins with *gemilut hasadim,* as it is written, 'And the Lord God made for Adam and for his wife garments of skins, and clothed them' (Gen. 3:21). And it ends with *gemilut hasadim,* as it is written, 'And He buried him in the valley' (Deut. 34:6)."

Now, I can understand why the Rabbis saw the beginning of the Torah as characterized by divine charitableness. Providing clothing for primitive man was a way of giving him warmth, protection against the elements—and, even more, a sense of dignity which raised man above the natural order and elevated him above the animals. Clothing is a response to a sense of shame, and that is one of the things that makes mankind human.

But how, and why should the verse "And He buried him in the valley" be regarded as *gemilut hasadim,* an act of divine loving-kindness?

I can imagine that if some medieval churchman had written this story, it would have offered a script in which Moses bodily ascends to Heaven, in the company of a chorus of singing angels, leaving only a halo to mark the spot of his ascension. Had Mohammedans reworked this story, they would have had Moses charging the Gates of Heaven, his sword held aloft, whilst astride a white Arabian steed. A Greek tragedian would have brought Moses' life to a grand, tragic, smashing climax—perhaps a duel with Satan, who finally pierces the heart of Moses, which gushes forth blood endlessly, across the ages. A modern scenario for Moses would have had him awarded him a Nobel Prize; or, as our country recently did for George Washington, posthumously granted him the rank of a six-star general; or invited him to address the assembled United Nations from the same rostrum that was dignified by the appearance of Yasir Arafat.

Instead, the Bible offers us nothing but an utterly simple farewell. No act of bravery, no dramatic climax—Moses just lies down and dies.

The Midrash describes the scene in a manner that is pathetic in its simplicity (*Sifra, Ha'azinu* 339). God says to Moses, "Moses, lie down." And Moses lies down. "Moses, fold your hands across your chest." And Moses folds his hands across his chest. "Moses, close your eyes." And Moses closes his eyes. Whereupon, God softly kisses Moses, and thus withdraws his soul from his body. And so, Moses is dead. No witnesses, no audience, no long list of obituaries in the *New York Times*, no fancy mausoleum, no unveiling in the company of family and friends. Instead, no one knows his burial place until this very day. For thirty days the people mourned him. At the end of this period, "And the days of the mourning for Moses came to an end." Finis, it is all over.

And this, according to the Rabbis, is an act of *gemilut hasadim*, of loving-kindness!

My own intuitive feeling has always been that this was an unkind cut, a cruel blow. This powerful, titanic figure, this Moses who flouted the might of Egypt and forced the Pharaoh and his empire to their knees, who gathered up this pitiful group of slaves and molded a nation out of them, who dealt a mortal blow to the hold of paganism on the ancient world and turned civilization around, ushering in a new age—this historic giant was reduced to begging for a few more days of life! I find it heartbreaking that Moses must plead for these extra favors. I can almost imagine what went on in Moses' heart, if not on his lips: "God, I gave my sweat and my blood for this people, I suffered through every kind of agony because of them and received nothing in turn but ingratitude. Shall I be deprived of this one bit of pleasure? This obstreperous and obstinate people, who never forgave me for elevating them to greatness, who awarded my forty years of service with rebelliousness and accusations against me—accusing me of adultery, of stealing their donkeys—may I not even have the privilege of seeing their felicity? And God, was it I who wanted this mission? Did I not respond to you (Ex. 4:13), *shelah na be-yad tishlah*—send them through someone else, but leave me alone? Was it not You who insisted that I be their shepherd? Will you now deny me this one bit of *nahas*, this one last act of satisfaction? Kill me if You will, O Lord, but at least bury me there!" And the answer comes: No! *Ve-shammah lo ta'avor*—You shall not cross over; and the Lord buried him in the valley. Not even on the mountaintop, but down deep, in the valley!

And this, the Rabbis tell us, is *sofah gemilut hasadim*, the charitable and loving way in which the Bible ends! How can we account for their interpretation?

I suggest three ways in which to understand this rabbinic tradition.

First, the *gemilut hasadim* the Rabbis refer to was not an act of loving-kindness for Moses, but for all the rest of mankind, for all of posterity, for you and for me. They are teaching us that life's work is never done, that no career is ever perfect, that no achievement is ever complete. There are always faults, always gaps, always lacunae, always flaws in the painting and chips in the statues that we build and conceive of. It is not only a sobering thought, but also a consolation to all the rest of us, that even a Moses was not perfect, even a Moses did not reach his Promised Land, even a Moses was not fully successful.

Had Moses completely succeeded and attained the full realization of his vision by crossing into the Promised Land, life would have become unbearable for the rest of us. Knowing that perfection is humanly possible, and full success is humanly attainable, it would have made nervous wrecks of us, even those who are not obsessively compulsive. It is, therefore, a *gemilut hasadim* to us when we recognize, through the biography of Moses, that failure and imperfection are essentials of the human condition. With the knowledge that no life and no endeavor can be perfect, even that of a Moses, we can allay our anxieties about our own imperfections, our own lack of full achievement and absolute success. Hence, *sofah gemilut hasadim*, this story at the end of the Torah is indeed an act of charity to all of mankind.

The second answer would be that the utterly simple farewell of Moses was an act of *gemilut hasadim* primarily for Joshua, the successor of Moses.

As is, it was extremely difficult for any man to follow a Moses. I do not envy a Joshua! Anything but a simple farewell would have made it literally impossible for a Joshua to function as a leader and for the loyalties of the people to be transferred from Moses to Joshua. A triumphant march into Eretz Israel, capping Moses' prophetic career with a brilliant victory, or even a dramatic death, would have rendered the transition from Moses to Joshua virtually impossible.

So it was an act of *gemilut hasadim* for Joshua—and also for the Children of Israel—that Moses' death was undramatic and uneventful. Even more, it was in this sense an act of kindness for Moses too, for his goal was not to enhance his own reputation and add to his own prestige, not caring what went on after him—*après moi le deluge*. His goal was the eternity of Israel and the perpetuation of Torah. By having his last wish denied, by understating his death, Providence assured that his mission would continue, his life's work would be perpetuated. *Gemilut hasadim!*

Third, and finally, the simple farewell was an act of loving-kindness to Moses by virtue of its very simplicity. Why? Because Moses needed no heroic act to signify heroic ends, for all his life was an exercise in heroic holiness. His quiet, uneventful death highlighted and emphasized by contrast the dramatic quality and the heroic texture of his whole life. Courage and valor were his everyday companions. Hardihood of spirit, fortitude of character, firmness of backbone were his daily experience and daily equipment. He needed no closing act, no grand finale, no heroics or histrionics, for no death could be as great as his life, as impressive as his teachings.

When a man is remembered for one act, no matter what it be, he has lived for but a moment. But if he is remembered for his whole life, he has achieved immortality.

No wonder that the Torah says of Moses that *lo kahatah eino ve-lo nas leho*, "his eye was not dimmed and his vigor was not abated" (Deut. 34:7). Moses was too busy living to begin to die. The Rabbis tell us that he ascended the fifteen steps to the peak of Mount Nebo, where he died, *bi-pesi'ah ahat*, in one quick step or leap (*Sotah* 13b). His end came quickly and simply. It was not really death, but simply the cessation of life.

To appreciate why this was a *gemilut hasadim*, an act of loving-kindness, consider what would have happened had he experienced a dramatic death, whether of victory or of defeat. This man Moses, who spent his life reproaching his people, urging them to repentance, disturbing their peace, goading them, restlessly prodding them on from level to level, denying them peace of mind— all his life would have been vitiated by a dramatic farewell that would have been the only thing the Israelites remembered! The Israelites would have been all too prone to forget his whole life, all his teachings, all of his message, all the annoy- ing irritations that constituted Moses' mission, in favor of mythologizing and dramatizing and reenacting his death.

It was therefore a favor to Moses to force him to a simple farewell, and thus perpetuate the nobility of his whole life and his whole prophetic career.

Indeed, no parent wants to be remembered only for the way he died, no matter how noble; he wants the whole of his life and what he lived for to be perpetuated. No teacher wants to be remembered only by his last lecture, no rabbi by his last sermon.

To summarize, then, this simple farewell was *gemilut hasadim* for three rea- sons. First, it was an act of kindness to all men and women thereafter, in order to reassure us that no life or career is perfect, that we must do the best we can and be grateful for it.

Second, it was an act of *gemilut hasadim* to Joshua—and even to Israel and Moses himself—to make it possible for someone else to begin with a fair chance for success, and not impose upon the successor the excessive burden of a glorious climax of a predecessor.

Finally, it was an act of *gemilut hasadim* to Moses, so that the dramatic conclusion not obscure and outshine the far more significant achievements of his whole life, not to let the people forget his historic service.

So, the theme of farewell is suffused with charity and gentleness and goodness.

God, as it were, closes the holiday somewhat sadly: *Kashah alai pereidat-khem*, "it is difficult for Me to say farewell to you," and yet hopefully and warmly: *Ikkevu me'at*, "stay on for a while," brace yourself for the long winter to come, and wait for the next *yamim tovim*, the next festivals, to begin.

And the Books of Moses, like the life and mission of Moses, come to an end.

Somewhat sadly and longingly, but also lovingly and hopefully—and even joyously, with *simhah* on this Simhat Torah—we close the book of Moses, and open up the next one, the book of Moses' successor Joshua, and we listen intently and hear and respond, with our hearts full of devotion and sensitivity and the purest of sentiment, to the words *Rak hazak ve-ematz me'od*, "Be very strong and courageous" (Josh. 1: 7).

And may God bless you all.

Hanukkah

Variations on the Hanukkah Theme

Tonight, immediately after the Sabbath is over, we shall be confronted with the observance of two precious *mitzvot*: the kindling of the Hanukkah candles, for Hanukkah begins tonight; and the *Havdalah*, which marks the end of Sabbath. The question of which shall be performed first is one which engaged the attention of some of the most illustrious latter-day talmudic sages, and the solution most Jews have accepted is one which, implicitly and indirectly, expresses a great idea in Jewish ethics and moral philosophy.

The *Shulhan Arukh* and Rama (R. Mosheh Isserles, the chief commentator on it) record with approval the custom of kindling the Hanukkah light first, and only then reciting the *Havdalah* (*Orah Hayyim* 681:2). Other authorities, such as the author of *Turei Zahav* (Taz), and many others, emphatically disagree. They insist that we ought to recite the *Havdalah* first and only afterwards light the Hanukkah candles.

While the controversy involves a large number of proofs and counterproofs of halakhic dialectic, which are too involved to present completely at this time, it will, however, be worth our while to examine the basic ideas involved in this controversy.

The *Shulhan Arukh,* Rama, and all those who insist upon the precedence of Hanukkah candles over *Havdalah* base their verdict largely upon the principle of *pirsumei nissa,* the "publicizing of the miracle." The Hanukkah candles, after all, are reminders of the miracles God performed for our ancestors *ba-yamim ha-hem ba-zeman ha-zeh*—"in those days, at this time": the cruse of oil that lasted eight days, the victory of the sainted few over the diabolical many, and so on. Basic to the mitzvah of *ner Hanukkah* is this concept of *pirsumei nissa*—to make the divine miracle known amongst all peoples. That is why we are to place the Hanukkah candles in a conspicuous place—windows, doorways, and

5719 (1958)

so on. Therefore, since *pirsumei nissa* is basic to the whole festival of Hanukkah, it requires of us to proclaim the miracle of Hanukkah as soon as the holiday begins—before any other activity, sacred or profane, is undertaken. Before eating or drinking, or even *Havdalah,* we are to light the Hanukkah candles, and by this act of performing the mitzvah before any other, we achieve *pirsumei nissa.* We let everyone know the greatness of the miracle, one which causes us to hurry and rush to perform the commandment.

The Taz and other *posekim,* however, require *Havdalah* before kindling the Hanukkah lights because they make use of a different and, they maintain, more fundamental principle, and that is the talmudic rule of *tadir ve-she-eino tadir, tadir kodem*: if I have before me two *mitzvot* to perform, and one is *tadir,* or constant, namely a frequent mitzvah—salient, observed regularly and periodically at set intervals, while the other is *eino tadir,* an irregular mitzvah, performed infrequently, at only rare times, then *tadir kodem*—the usual, regular, more frequent mitzvah comes first. Hence, since *Havdalah* is *tadir,* because it is observed every single week of the year, whereas kindling the Hanukkah lights is *eino tadir,* for it is observed only during the eight-day period of the year, *Havdalah* takes priority over *Ner Hanukkah.*

Reduced to its essentials, then, this halakhic controversy is based upon a clash of two principles: *pirsumei nissa,* the dramatization and publication of the unusual, the supernatural; and *tadir kodem,* the precedence of the regular, the constant, the usual, and the well-known.

It is remarkable that in our current practice we reflect both contradictory opinions. Faced with these two opposing decisions, the great majority of observant Jews have reconciled the two views by distinguishing between the synagogue and the home. In the synagogue we follow the practice of the *Shulhan Arukh* and Rama, and we light the Hanukkah lights first, thus emphasizing the principle of *pirsumei nissa;* and at home we usually follow the verdict of the Taz, making *Havdalah* first, and thus giving greater weight to the rule of *tadir ve-she-eino tadir, tadir kodem* (that is, the usual, the regular, the periodic is more important and thus comes first).

It is amazing how, in deciding between two technical halakhic opinions, the Jewish masses of men, women, and children have indirectly and perhaps unconsciously expressed a whole view of life, a substantial philosophy of Judaism in its public and private aspects. For the concepts of *pirsumei nissa* and *tadir kodem* are two fundamental approaches to life—on the one hand, the need for *pirsum,* for publicizing, for the demonstration of the unusual, the dramatic, and the record-shattering; and on the other hand, the transcendent importance of constancy, of *tadir*, of the prosaic, regular, and bland routine of the religious life. What our people did by its reconciliation of these two opposing views is to say that each one is valid, each one has its importance, but each has its own place: in the synagogue, in the public domain, in the open arena of Jewish life, there we kindle Hanukkah lights before *Havdalah*; there we recognize the value of *pirsumei nissa*, of emphasizing the dramatic, the unusual, the outstanding, the miraculous. But at home, *be-tzin'ah*, in the privacy of one's hearth and family, there, while *pirsum* is recognized as important, the value of *tadir* is far more significant and necessary. There we must first be sure that our daily lives, in both ritual and ethics—*bein adam la-Makom* and *bein adam la-havero*—are regulated by the divine word through the wisdom of Torah. There we need not and ought not play up the spectacular and the dramatic; that can wait for later. First, one must be a good Jew in the daily, ordinary, and therefore realistic and reliable sense.

There is no doubt that *pirsumei nissa* has an honored place in life; and in the public arena of communal Jewish life it has priority. No one doubts the value of the dramatic, the strikingly aesthetic, the unusual and the miraculous. In order to influence the broad masses you must resort to the striking, the dramatic. Public relations is a neutral technique which can be cheap and vulgar, but pressed into dignified service for religious truth, it can be noble and worthy. The *Hakhel*—the great mass gathering at the end of the *shemittah* year—served the purpose of dramatizing allegiance to Torah. The pageantry surrounding the harvesting and the offering of the *omer* in Temple days dramatically attracted attention to the debt man owes God for the bounties of nature. A public newspaper highlights not the everyday humdrum of living, both its noble and ignoble features, but rather *pirsumei nissa*, the sensational and the outstanding. We do not call mass rallies for the observance of *kashrut* or *kibbud av va-em*. We do so for Bonds helping the miracle called Israel, and United Jewish Appeal for saving human lives all over the world. This *pirsumei nissa* is emphasized in the synagogue, in public, and in the media—and that is as it should be. It serves a high educational and noble purpose.

But it is a grievous error for anyone to imagine that what holds true for the stage is true for the quotidian routines of daily Jewish living, that techniques invented to capture the attention of the public are proper for the quiet privacy of the home. That is decidedly not so. In the home we make *Havdalah* before kindling Hanukkah lights. In the home we give priority to the *tadir*, the regular and constant actions, over the *pirsumei nissa.* In the home—that is where the great work of solid, basic training in Godliness must go on without flash and flourish. When God first gave the Torah to Israel, it was in a most dramatic setting—thunder and lightning, then universal silence, and then the loud boom of the first commandment. Over 600,000 people gathered about the smoking Mount Sinai. But while the drama of *Mattan Torah* is appropriate to a large public, the slow and hard labor of *kiyyum ha-Torah,* the observance of the Torah life in all the nooks and crannies, must go on incessantly and without fanfare in the private life of each individual Jew. It was because Jews forgot this that the tablets were broken and Moses had to ascend Mount Sinai a second time, but now without any theophany, without an admiring yet stunned audience, and without the dramatic sound-and-light effects. It was the soft, ongoing labor of *tadir,* not the celebratory flourish of *pirsum.* Ordinary Jews then learned how Torah must be observed punctiliously, in their own lives, and that is why *these* tablets were not destroyed.

The prophet Elijah too had to learn this lesson. Remember his challenge to the priests of the Ba'al atop Mount Carmel (I Kings 18)? What powerful drama—with the bearded, mantled prophet of God appearing out of the desert to take on hundreds of idolatrous priests, challenging them to invoke the Ba'al to bring fire down and consume the sacrificial flesh! How thrillingly miraculous was the prayer of Elijah as the multitude gasped at the sudden bolt of fire out of the Heavens, the consuming of the sacrifice, the prostration of the masses as they called out *Hashem Hu ha-Elokim.* God performed the miracle before *all* the people because it was didactically necessary, an opportunity for an educational experience. It deflected them from Ba'al worship and brought them to Torah. *Pirsumei nissa* belongs to the assembled public, in front of the masses, in the crowded synagogue.

But do you recall what happens immediately afterwards to Elijah, in the chapter that follows at the end of the First Book of Kings and the beginning of the Second? He flees from the evil king and queen, Ahab and Jezebel, and hides out in the desert—alone, solitary, no other human in sight. "I am alone here," he complains to God (I Kings 19:10). Elijah had been overly impressed and thus spoiled by the *pirsumei nissa,* the histrionic, the admiring crowds and the mass demonstrations. He could no longer be satisfied with the *tadir,* the ongoing uneventful task of prophecy without the crisis-to-crisis living, the daily grind, the regular and grueling task of serving God alone, in privacy. That is why God shows the prophet the whole panorama of dramatic, mighty natural phenomena—the mighty winds, the powerful thunder, and the fire. Of each of these, God proclaims to Elijah, "Not in fire is God to be found" and the same for the stormy winds and the thunder (I Kings 19:11–12). Not in the spectacular can God always be found. Where then? In the *kol demamah dakkah* (19:12), in the still, steady, quiet, simple, regular labor of character-building, of living honorably and honestly, and perceiving the will of God in prosaic daily life, the worship of God in the mode of *tadir*.

When the audience has gone home and the klieg lights are dimmed, when the noise has petered out and silence reigns, and all that can be heard is the *kol demamah dakkah* of one's heartbeat and the pulse of his conscience—that is when we leave *pirsumei nissa* and dedicate ourselves to the *tadir,* the regular and the unpretentious. That is when we give preference to *Havdalah,* to first distinguishing good from evil, sacred from profane, noble from vulgar, so that every year and every month and every day and every minute must be consecrated to God and His Torah, either by studying it or by living it with fealty and dignity.

This is a rewarding thought that Hanukkah teaches us by taking second place to *Havdalah* in our homes tonight. It reminds us that we ought not to feel disappointed if we do not experience the kind of unusual sensation or uplift at home that we do when we attend rallies. It encourages us to continue on our modest paths of *tadir,* quietly observing God's Torah, of developing nobility of character, of building a family and serving our fellow man, of bringing even a little light into the lives of our loved ones and into the heart of the stranger. It reminds us that if we dedicate ourselves to the sacred pattern of the Torah's *mitzvot,* then surely the *pirsumei nissa* will come eventually, for there is a heroism in this modesty of daily Jewish life, a heroism and a poetry and a dramatic quality that makes itself felt not in a momentary clap of thunder, not as an extraordinary revelation, but as a long and slow but beautiful symphony that we first begin to appreciate as we go on with the accumulation of years of such harmonious living *tadir* in the service of God and man. Then, when *Havdalah* gives way to Hanukkah, does the miracle of the commonplace become evident, then do we realize that there is a heroism in modesty, that the ordinary possesses its own kind of extraordinary music of the soul, and that silence can be more meaningful than the most persuasive oratory.

"Not by power nor by might, but by the spirit, saith the Lord of Hosts" (Zech. 4:6).

Then we discover that ultimately *Havdalah* yields to Hanukkah.

ON BEING TOO PRACTICAL

ON THIS LAST DAY of Hanukkah, the second Shabbat Hanukkah this year, we direct our attention to a question concerning the entire festival. Why is it that we make such a festive holiday, filled with prayer and thanksgiving, with the lighting of candles and the singing of songs, for the cleansing and the purifying of the Second Temple, which was rededicated in the year 155 before the common era, and we have no equivalent or comparable festival to celebrate the initial building of the First Temple by Solomon many hundreds of years earlier? Was not Solomon's first great campaign, building the sanctuary which his father, David, had foreseen, at least as important as what seems a subsequent minor detail in the history of the Temple?

The answer lies in the difference between building and rebuilding, between constructing and reconstructing, between dedicating and rededicating. When there is a new movement, a new campaign, a new idea, a new vision, anything that has with it the power of novelty, then it is almost assured of freshness and vigor and enthusiasm. The decision to build something new is not a spiritually difficult achievement. Everyone is anxious, everyone is aroused, everyone is excited. The people involved in such a project generally move forward with a great surge of strength and spirit.

But the decision to rebuild, that is far more difficult. To approach a pile of rubble and try to make of it a habitable home; patiently to pick up the pieces of the past and paste them together; to take the tattered ruins of a former majesty and somehow restore them; to patch together what time and circumstance have ravaged—for this the masses have little enthusiasm, less spirit, and no patience.

Thus, when King Solomon took it upon himself to build a new *Beit ha-Mikdash*, it was a comparatively easy enterprise. He was able to ride on the crest of popular appeal and mass sentiment. But when, many hundreds of years later, the Maccabees returned to a desecrated Temple, to a sanctuary that had been profaned in the eyes of the people, to restore to its old eminence a *Beit*

5721 (1960)

174

ha-Mikdash which was already an old story to the citizenry of Jerusalem, when they had to reconsecrate what had been defiled, that was a great achievement; for they could not count upon mass movement and popular sentiments. Their project required enormous vision, tremendous courage, vast inner resources, and iron conviction.

Hence the reward of the Maccabees is greater than that of King Solomon. Their task was more heroic because of the very prosaic nature which inheres in every task of rebuilding as opposed to the romantic, attractive enterprise of building for the first time. We therefore celebrate Hanukkah in honor of the Maccabean achievement of rededication, while we have no comparable holiday commemorating Solomon's achievement. We give historical rewards for the zeal of undertaking a task which would no doubt have frightened weaker souls and dissuaded them by the threat of faded glory, tired emotions, and second-hand sentiment.

This difference we have noted between the Maccabean and the Solomonic ages is evident in all phases of life. Take the young Bar Mitzvah boy, when he is first called to ascend the pulpit and recite the blessing over the Torah. No matter how poor his background, no matter how inadequate his education, I have no doubt that in the heart of any young Bar Mitzvah boy with any sensitivity whatever, there is some kind of stirring of idealism, of devotion and dedication and love of Torah and love of God. But take the same young man after a number of years have gone by and he has gone the way of all Jewish teenage men. When you approach the same youngster, when he is now in high school or college or shortly thereafter, how difficult it is to reinspire him, rekindle in him the same love and devotion and idealism.

Or take a young couple on the eve of their wedding. The love of a young man for his wife, and vice versa, on the wedding day is by all means genuine and authentic. The romance of life is a very real thing in their lives. But that same couple, after a number of years have gone by, and life has somehow become stale and routinized—how difficult it is to recapture the spark of an old love.

Or take, for that matter, the spirit that all of us felt in May of 1948 when the State of Israel was established. Do you recall that electric excitement and passionate loyalty that all of us felt, that sense of historic destiny and living through a great historic moment? How difficult a task to re-evoke from within ourselves that same excitement and loyalty today, after eleven or twelve years have gone by.

So, *le-hahazir atarah le-yoshenah*—to restore the crown of Torah to its former eminence is a far more demanding task, and therefore far more rewarding, than fashioning it in the first place.

And perhaps this will explain the strange *haftarah* we read this morning, and the remarkable difference between the *haftarah* of last week, the first Shabbat Hanukkah, and that of this week, the second Shabbat Hanukkah. The *haftarah* of last week was full of vision, sparkling with the prophetic message, with overtones of song and undertones of greatness: *Rani ve-simhi bat Tziyyon,* "Shout with song and be joyful, O daughter of Zion" (Zech. 2:14). The prophet announced: *Ki lo be-hayil ve-lo ba-koah ki im be-ruhi amar ha-Shem Tzeva'ot,* "For not by might nor by power but by My Spirit, saith the Lord of Hosts" (4:6). And the *haftarah* ends up on the great note of *teshu'ot hen hen lah,* "shouts of grace and charm" (4:7).

Compare that now to the unusual *haftarah* we just read today (from chapter 7 of the First Book of Kings [I Kings 7:41–50]): "And Hiram made the pots and the shovels and the basins . . . the two pillars and two bowls of the capitals that were on top of the pillars . . . ten bases, and ten lavers on the bases . . . and the pots and the shovels and the basins . . . and the lamps and the tongs and the cups and the snuffers and the basins and the pans and the firepans, and the hinges for the doors . . ."

What do we have here? Is this the message of the *haftarah* that is supposed to inspire us with a prophetic vision? Is there here, by any stretch of the imagination, an inspiring message which is to send us, the worshipers, home with a renewed and invigorated spirit? Is there here anything more than a mundane list of dull details in the appointments of the Temple?

And the reason for the distinction between the two *haftarah*s lies in the difference in emphasis needed when building or rebuilding, when starting upon a new task or re-starting a task of reconstruction. When engaging upon a new campaign, you already are assured of idealism—you need realism. Your spirit is then provided for, and you must therefore remind the participants not of the necessity of inspiration, but of the need to be practical.

Thus, in this morning's *haftarah,* when all the people were thoroughly inspired, when their spirits were raised and reached the high point of excitement, at this time King Solomon had to remind his people: "It is true that you have before your eyes a fiery vision, a glowing ideal, a glorious picture of a new Temple to Almighty God; but remember that all this fire and this glow and this glory will be nothing more than a flash in the pan if not for the pots and the pans and the basins and the shovels and the lavers." All the poetry of religion is without meaning, and without the ability to survive, unless it is based upon the prose of hard work which makes the foundations of a religious life. Religion cannot appear only in the beautiful white linen of the vestments of the high priests; it must also put on overalls and roll up its sleeves and lay the foundation for the real, good, honest, durable, ethical life. Our *haftarah* therefore acts as a control and a check on the runaway spirits and unbridled enthusiasm. It complements the exhilarating idealism of which we read last week, by rooting it to reality. It reminds the idealist to be practical.

When, however, you are engaged in restoring something old, in a second attempt, in rebuilding, when you know well enough the practical difficulties, then you must emphasize the romantic element, the nobility and the loftiness of the project. Hanukkah, the holiday of rededication, thus requires an emphasis not on the need of being practical, but the need of being spirited and enthusiastic and filled with zeal. If anything, in the enterprise of rededicating and rebuilding, people are often too practical. They are over-acquainted with the real practical difficulties. And that danger of being too practical, over-involved and over-entangled in mundane details, keeps them from submitting to the overpowering grasp of inspiration. Such people need, not today's *haftarah*, but last week's: *Ki lo be-hayil ve-lo be-koah ki im be-ruhi amar Hashem Tzeva'ot*: Return to your youthful idealism! Overcome the inertia of the prosaic and latch on to the poetry of life! Forget for a while your practical needs, your *hayil* and *koah*, the bricks and the mortar, the fund-raising, the managerial tasks, the whole long, dull list of actual practical needs, and concentrate instead upon *ruhi*, upon the spirit of the Lord which activates the heart of each and every human being.

Both *haftarah*s are therefore important for the total picture: the real and the ideal, the practical and the poetical, the inspiring aspirations of a Zechariah and the dull details of a Hiram. Each serves as a corrective, reminding us to restore to the proper balance the harmony of our emotional and spiritual lives.

For those of us who are still in the first flush of youthful zeal, it is important to take to heart the message of this week's *haftarah*; for those of us who are more mature, hardened by life's experiences, less possessed of romantic sentiments, overly inclined to be too practical, it is mandatory to remember the message of the *haftarah* of the first Shabbat Hanukkah: the emphasis not upon *hayil* and *koah*, but upon *ruhi*—the spirit. Such people must remember the message of that *haftarah*: open up your hearts and your minds once again to the blind and the mysterious, the lofty and the poetic, the beauty and nobility of life.

We American Jews, at this turn of the decade, are in need more of last week's message than this week's. We already know all that the Hirams must do: the work, the expense, the prosaic requirements, the inertia and the apathy with which we must contend. Ours is a historic duty to rebuild in the spirit of Hanukkah: to return to our sanctuaries and purify them from the defilements of the modern Hellenists, assimilation in a thousand different local accents. Ours is the historic destiny of reinvigorating religious feeling and rekindling the religious spark in Jews whose hearts have become encrusted with inertia and indifference, a reinvigoration and recrudescence sufficient to rebuild the institutions of Jewish traditional life: kosher shuls, day schools, *mikva'ot*, and most important—kosher Jews. Our age is more like that of the Maccabees than that of Solomon. We must take great care not to allow the practical to paralyze the poetical. We must not become too practical.

At the close of this festival of Hanukkah, when we read both *haftarah*s, we reemphasize for our day and our era what the Maccabees did for theirs: the power of purity, the adventure of faithfulness, the excitement and thrill of Torah. We recall to our contemporaries the excitement and suspense of each individual soul about to rescale the slopes of the spirit, to ascend the summit of Sinai where once our ancestors stood and said Amen to the voice of the Lord as it issued from the smoky mists. We too must be prepared to respond with a message of the supremacy of the spirit. *Ki lo be-hayil ve-lo ba koah ki im be-ruhi amar Hashem Tzeva'ot.*

For not by might nor by power, but by My Spirit, saith the Lord of Hosts.

THE LODGER'S LIGHT

THE *SHULHAN ARUKH* CODIFIES a *halakhah*, or law, which is not only of practical importance to those who wish to observe Hanukkah properly, but is also, as we shall later see, of wider significance.

The law concerns an *akhsenai*, or lodger, a traveler who is away from home during the Hanukkah holiday. How is he to observe the kindling of the Hanukkah lights? We read, *akhsenai she-ein madlikin alav be-veito*, a traveler who knows or suspects that his family has failed to kindle the Hanukkah candles for him at his home and who cannot, therefore, fulfill his obligations through them from a distance, can do one of two things. *Im yesh lo petah patuah le-atzmo, tzarikh le-hadlik be-pitho*, "if he has his own apartment with its own entrance, let him light his menorah at the entrance to his rooms." If, however, his accommodations are not so adequate, if he has but a small room without a separate entrance, then *tzarikh latet perutah le-ba'al ha-bayit le-hishtattef immo be-shemen shel ner Hanukkah*, he should give a coin, some money, to the inn-keeper and thereby participate with him, the owner of the house, in his lighting of the Hanukkah menorah. By giving him this monetary gift, the *akhsenai*, or lodger, becomes a partner, as it were, with the *ba'al ha-bayit*, or owner, in the mitzvah of the Hanukkah lights (*Shulhan Arukh, Orah Hayyim* 677:1).

This is an important law, especially for us American Jews, who, because of our economic position and the availability of transportation facilities in modern times, have become *akhsena'im* like never before. Our travels, both for business and pleasure, are unprecedented—and Jewish law teaches us how to remember Hanukkah no matter how far from home we are.

But there is a larger sense in which we can all be regarded as lodgers. Some two thousand years ago, the Greek Jewish philosopher Philo taught that every human being is an *akhsenai*, a traveler on the face of the earth. Man is essentially a "citizen of heaven," a divine creature with heavenly aspirations, and his celestial origin, his divine roots, make him only a temporary dweller in this

5723 (1962)

world. He merely stays a while in this world; it is not his real home, he does not "live" here. We are all, Philo teaches, merely lodgers who temporarily reside on earth.

There is a more immediate sense, however, in which the term *akhsenai* applies to us who are here today. For we are relative newcomers in this country. Despite the fact that we celebrated, not too long ago, our tercentenary, few Jews indeed can trace their ancestry in America for three hundred years. The majority of us are second-generation American Jews; a goodly number were born overseas. Certainly our cultural and sentimental affiliations, our folk memories, many of our mannerisms, go back to the lands where our families lived for so many generations—for hundreds of years. It is for good reason that, despite our love for America, our dedication and loyalty to the United States, so many of us speak nostalgically of *der alter heim,* "the old home." Nine or ten centuries of European Jewish history cannot fade from our collective memory without a trace. They leave even the most Americanized of us with the feeling that here we are *akhsena'im,* lodgers, and that our personalities, our tastes, our spiritual image were forged in the various lands of Europe which we respectively think of as the old home.

This is more than sentiment and psychology. In our own generation and the ones immediately preceding it, American Jewry was immeasurably enriched by the spiritual wealth that Jewish immigrants from Europe brought with them. Our greatest organizations, our foremost schools, our most eminent *yeshivot,* were built, inspired, developed, and sustained by Jews born and raised in Europe. American Jewry would be a tragically impoverished community today were it not for the splendid and mighty resources that European Jews contributed to our lives. Europe, until the time of the Nazis, was not only *der alter heim,* but one that overflowed with vitality and vigor.

Today, however, we can no longer look to European Jewry to provide us with reinforcements in our battle for the survival and ultimate triumph of Torah. Only two or three weeks ago, a guest speaker at The Jewish Center described the tragic plight of the remnants of European Jewry.

Today we are in the position of the lodger described in the *Shulhan Arukh—* the *akhsenai she-ein madlikin alav be-beito;* we are travelers in whose homes no light burns. It is dark, very dark, in *der alter heim.* In Lithuania, there are no *yeshivot* and there is none of the intellectual ferment that once characterized the Jewish religious aristocracy. In Poland and Galicia and Hungary, the great luminaries of Torah and Hasidism and piety no longer shine with their old brilliance. The enlightened Orthodox Jewry that once populated the cities of Germany and galvanized generations of modern Jews who remained true to Torah is no more. *Ein madlikin alav be-beito*: the light of Torah, of Judaism, is extinguished in our "old home," and darkness—a deep, tangible, deadening darkness—has settled over that continent and will keep it *Judenrein* for all eternity.

What, then, shall we "lodgers" do? Shall we be satisfied with empty complaints about the spiritual poverty that has engulfed us? Certainly not. In the words of an old proverb, recently quoted widely, "it is better to light one candle than to curse the darkness." We must do something on a wide scale to assure the continued life of the light of Torah, symbolized by the Hanukkah menorah. And, to follow the *Shulhan Arukh*, there are two ways open to us. One is *mi she-yesh lo petah patuah le-atzmo*; one who has his own resources, let him light his own lamp. He who has the intellectual capacity, the will and initiative and the freedom from mundane worries, must himself become a Torah scholar. There are those for whom the *petah*, or entrance, into the world of Torah is clear and open. Such people must devote themselves heart and soul to holding aloft the light of Torah.

But such people are few indeed. Would that there were many more! But realistically we know that their number is limited. Of course, every Jew without exception is required to study Torah to the fullest extent possible. There are no exemptions. Yet full-time devotion to creative study of Torah is, in our country and under our circumstances, the exception rather than the rule. The conditions of life for most of us are not the *petah patuah le-atzmo*; we cannot do it by ourselves.

What then is our alternative? How then shall we make sure that Judaism survives, that the light of Torah illuminates the paths of our children and our children's children, that it remains a "beacon unto the nations" (Is. 49:6)? The answer is the second alternative presented to us by Jewish law: *tzarikh latet perutah le-ba'al ha-bayit, ve-yishtattef immo be-shemen shel ner Hanukkah*. We must open up our purses and with our monetary support participate with the owner or innkeeper in the mitzvah of lighting the Hanukkah candles. And if we are the *akhsena'im*, the lodgers, then the owner of the premises, the innkeeper, is Almighty God. It is His world in which we appear as temporary lodgers. It is He who is the *ba'al ha-bayit*, and his Hanukkah menorah is the light of Torah as it is studied in the *yeshivot*. And if the lights have gone dark in "the old home," if we cannot ourselves become full students, and if we American Jews do not want to live in utter darkness, then we must join with the divine *Ba'al ha-Bayit* by contributing our *perutah*, and much more than that, for the up-keep of the sources of Torah in our day.

It is for this reason that it has become a tradition in The Jewish Center to make an appeal for the *yeshivot* in Israel on Shabbat Hanukkah. The *Ba'al ha-Bayit* of the universe calls upon us today to offer our generous support in keeping alive the *ner Hanukkah* of Judaism.

It is, to my mind, most significant that the appeal today is specifically for the *yeshivot* in the State of Israel. Torah is, of course, a blessing everywhere in the world. We have some great *yeshivot* here in America. But there is a special importance to Torah in Israel that we must never overlook. For the welfare of the *yeshivot* in Israel is a precise index of the spiritual quality of the country. Whether the *yeshivot* in Israel prosper or not, whether they have to live constantly on the brink of crisis and insolvency or not, whether the State of Israel as such learns to develop mighty spiritual energies or not, will be the test of the ages, the historical experiment as to whether our whole tradition is or is not vindicated. Our Torah implied, our prophets boldly proclaimed, our Sages taught, that the mission of the Jewish people was to establish a nation with all the appurtenances of nationhood that would yet retain in its fullness the spiritual quality of a people bound up with God—a nation that would represent to all other nations the glowing spirituality that descended upon us from Sinai. If, therefore, we have in our days succeeded in erecting a state that is politically independent and viable, with the whole apparatus of statehood, but that is spiritually impotent, religiously weak, in which the menorah of Judaism is dim to the point of uselessness, then the whole experiment of Judaism throughout the ages will be declared by the world and by history to be a failure. If, however, we can succeed in the spiritual realm even as we have in the political; if we can feed the *shemen* fuel to the menorah of Torah in Israel even as we have and are feeding the fuel of economic viability to its industries, then we shall stand vindicated before the bar of history. Then all the world will acknowledge that the mission of Israel has not been in vain. Then all the prophets of Israel shall be in our debt, for we will have justified their faith that a people can live in this world and yet not suffer inevitable corruption—and not the least of them, the prophet Zechariah, who declared, as we read in today's *haftarah*, *lo be-hayil ve-lo be-koah ki im be-ruhi, amar Hashem Tzeva'ot*, "not by power, neither by might, but by My spirit, saith the Lord of Hosts" (Zech. 4:6). If we can keep alive that Spirit, that Light, through the Israeli *yeshivot*, then the State of Israel as a whole is a success. If not, Heaven forbid, then the whole vast enterprise will have been a tragic failure. It will have proved that Torah was made for *galut*, not for a free and proud people.

The story is told of a man who sued a railroad because his car was crushed by an oncoming train and the flagman, whose job it was to warn away motorists, had failed to do so. The flagman, however, testified that he had waved the lantern at the crossing, and the railroad was, on the basis of his testimony, acquitted. After the trial, the railroad's attorney asked the flagman why he had been so nervous and jittery during his testimony, since everything appeared so clear and obviously in favor of the company. He replied, "Because I was afraid they were going to ask me if the lantern was lit!"

Through United Jewish Appeal and Bonds for Israel, through the noble sacrifices of countless pioneers and young soldiers, we have forged in our day a great lantern: the State of Israel. It has all the requisite trappings of a modern state. Now let it not be said that we have made ourselves a lantern and have forgotten to kindle it. A dark lantern is as bad as none at all.

An unlit menorah is not sufficient. If the light is missing, if there is no *ruah*, if there is no Torah, then we are in desperate trouble.

Today we call upon all members and friends of the Center Family to respond generously to this appeal to kindle the lights of Israel, to support its eminent *yeshivot*. By doing so, you will be giving the whole experiment of rebuilding Israel both meaning and dignity.

If we want God to answer our prayers for *or hadash al Tziyyon ta'ir*, "make a new light shine upon Zion," then we must first make it possible for the old light of Torah to shine forth *from Zion: Ki mi-Tziyyon tetzei Torah u-devar Hashem mi-Yerushalayim*, "For from Zion shall go forth the Torah, and the Word of the Lord from Jerusalem" (Is. 2:3).

Akhsenai she-ein madlikin alav be-beito tzarikh latet perutah le-ba'al ha-bayit le-hishtattef immo be-shemen shel ner Hanukkah. The *Ba'al ha-Bayit* of the world waits for us to join Him in the grand and historic partnership of keeping alive the *ner Hanukkah*, the light of Torah, as represented by the great Israeli *yeshivot*. Let us join Him without hesitation, so that light and happiness be our lot and that of our children forever after.

HALF THE HANUKKAH STORY

TWO THEMES ARE CENTRAL to the festival of Hanukkah which we welcome this week. They are, first, the *nes milhamah*, the miraculous victory of the few over the many and the weak over the strong as the Jews repulsed the Syrian-Greeks and reestablished their independence. The second theme is *nes shemen*, the miracle of the oil, which burned in the Temple for eight days although the supply was sufficient for only one day. The *nes milhamah* represents the success of the military and political enterprise of the Maccabees, whilst the *nes shemen*, the miracle of the oil, symbolizes the victory of the eternal Jewish spirit. Which of these is emphasized is usually an index to one's *Weltanschauung*. Thus, for instance, secular Zionism spoke only of the *nes milhamah*, the military victory, because it was interested in establishing the nationalistic base of modern Jewry. The Talmud, however, asking "What is Hanukkah?" answered with the *nes shemen*, with the story of the miracle of the oil (*Shabbat* 21b). In this way, the Rabbis demonstrated their unhappiness with the whole Hasmonean dynasty, descendants of the original Maccabees who became Sadducees, denied the Oral Law, and persecuted the Pharisees.

Yet it cannot be denied that both of these themes are integral parts of Judaism. Unlike Christianity, we never relegated religion to a realm apart from life, we never assented to the bifurcation between that which belongs to God and that which belongs to Caesar. Religion was a crucial part, indeed the very motive, of the war against the Syrian-Greeks. And unlike the purely nationalistic interpretation of Hanukkah, we proclaim with the prophet (whose words we shall read next Sabbath), "For not by power nor by might, but by My spirit, saith the Lord of Hosts" (Zech. 4:6). In fact, the Maccabean war was, to a large extent, not a revolution against alien invaders as much as a civil war against Hellenistic Jews who wanted to strip Israel of its Jewish heritage. Hence, Hanukkah symbolizes a victory through military means for spiritual ends. That is

5728 (1967)

why Rabbinic sources tell of both themes, the *Pesikta* speaking of the *nes mil-hamah* (*Pesikta Rabbati* 6) and the gemara speaking of the *nes shemen*.

It is interesting that the dual themes adumbrated in the Hanukkah narrative are anticipated in the *sidrah* we read today. Young Joseph has two dreams (Gen. 37:5–9), the first of these equivalent to the n*es milhamah*, and the second reminiscent of the *nes shemen*. In the first dream he sees himself and his brothers *me'almim alummim*, binding their sheaves in the field, and the sheaves of the brothers bow down to his sheaf. This is clearly a materialistic dream; he wants to take over the food industry and corner the grain market. The second dream is a more spiritual and cosmic one: it is a dream of *shemesh ve-ha-kokhavim*, the sun and the stars and the attainment of spiritual preeminence.

Even more interesting are the reactions that these dreams evoke. When Joseph tells his brothers about his dream of the *alummim*, we read: *va-yosifu od seno oto*, they hated him even more. When he tells them about his dream of the sun and the stars, we read: *va-yekanne'u bo ehav*, his brothers were jealous of him. The material dream evokes *sin'ah*, hatred; the spiritual dream arouses *kin'ah*, jealousy. We Jews are hated for our *nes milhamah*, and we are envied for our *nes shemen*.

The State of Israel, in our day, has fulfilled the first dream. The *alummim* of the State of Israel, its farms and its fields, its towns and villages and cities, are comparatively safe and secure. We have achieved a miraculous victory in *milhamah*, the recent war. The result has been predictable—*sin'ah*, hatred. Let us not be blind to the nucleus of animosity that is latent even in the admiration which has been expressed for the State of Israel as a result of its military successes. Perhaps I am naive, but I have abiding "faith" in the silent anti-Semitic potential within a good deal of this expression of worldwide applause for Israel. The best proof—General de Gaulle, whose press has protested his remarks, but whose countrymen seem more and more to have responded by reverting to their old anti-Semitism. The general declared that Israel is "a warlike state bent upon expansion," and that Jews are "an elite people, sure of itself and dominating." Why? Because Israel dared to succeed without first begging his leave. How revealing is his further comment: "Jews provoke ill will in certain countries and at certain times." There it is: *sin'ah*, hatred, provoked by the success of our *alummim*, by the accomplishment of our *nes milhamah*. Throughout the ages non-Jews have circumscribed our areas of endeavor. They gave us no farms for our *alummim*, and then hated us when we overcame these limitations nevertheless. They pushed us into moneylending, and detested us when we became bankers. They allowed only the very uppermost echelons of our young people to get themselves a university education, and then they declared their hatred for us when this group succeeded in producing the world's leading financiers and scientists, doctors and men of culture. They confined us to squalid ghettos and expected to crush our dignity—but they were furious when we emerged with our dignity intact, when, in the words of Joseph's dream, *ve-hinneh ka-mah alummati ve-gam nitzavah*, "our sheaf stood upright, unbent, unsubmissive." Their hostility was boundless when all their oppression resulted in our possessing a fabulously noble religion, a cultural level second to none, and a superb moral life. Definitely, in general, we are "elite, sure of ourselves, and dominating." No people that has had to endure what has been wished upon us, and has survived with our quality, is anything less than "elite" and "sure of itself." Hence our heritage of *sin'ah*, the ill-will we have "provoked" in so much of the world.

But now that Israel, for itself and all the Jewish people, has fulfilled the first dream, the time has come to realize the second, the vision of *shemesh ve-kokhavim*. Now, just as we have earned the world's *sin'ah*, we must deserve its *kin'ah*.

What is *kin'ah*? It is not envy pure and simple. Some modern scholars (Brown, Driver, and Briggs in their *Hebrew and English Lexicon of the Old Testament*) relate the Hebrew word *kin'ah* to the Arabic root *kanaa*, which means "to turn red," as with a dye. In other words, it means "to blush, to be embarrassed." The Hebrew *kin'ah* is thus a rather complex phenomenon; one of its components is the feeling of embarrassment, of self-criticism, which results in an awareness of one's shortcomings as he measures himself against the object of his *kin'ah* and which, therefore, may hopefully lead him to transcend himself and inspire him to greater achievement. To inspire such creative *kin'ah* is, in essence, a moral task and an educational function. What our duty is at the present stage of our history is to arouse the world's *kin'ah*, and thus make the rest of the world yearn for our spiritual achievements, for our miracle of oil, and thereby prove the correctness of our Sages' statement, *kin'at soferim tarbeh hokhmah*, that envy (in the sense of creative *kin'ah*) amongst scholars can only increase wisdom in the world (*Bava Batra* 21a).

Indeed, just as Joseph beheld his first *sin'ah*-inspiring material dream, and afterwards rose to his *kin'ah*-provoking spiritual vision, so, too, the miracles of Hanukkah are sequential: first there was the *nes milhamah*, and then later came the *nes shemen*. This is reflected in our *Al ha-Nissim* prayer which we recite all through Hanukkah. We thank God for the miracle of our victory, for having given over *gibborim be-yad halashim, rabbim be-yad me'attim,* "the strong in the hands of the weak, and the many in the hands of the few," *ve-ahar ken,* "and afterwards," *ba'u banekha li-devir beitekha,* "Thy children came into Thy holy habitation," cleansed Thy Temple, purified Thy sanctuary, and kindled lights in Thy holy courts.

I submit that those two little words *ve-ahar ken,* "and afterwards," define the position of world Jewry today. We have finished one half the Hanukkah story. We have accomplished the *nes milhamah,* the miracle of military victory, and now we must proceed to the *nes shemen,* the miracle of the conquest of the Jewish spirit. We have realized the dream of the *alummim;* next we must proceed to the inspiring vision of the *shemesh ve-kokhavim.*

Can it be done? Most certainly! I am more optimistic now than I have ever been before in my life that this, indeed, can be achieved. As an example, permit me to bring to your attention a revealing report in this past week's *Ma'ariv,* one of the leading newspapers in Israel. One of its most distinguished reporters, Geulah Cohen, interviewed General Ariel Sharon, who is one of the most popular heroes of the young generation of Israelis, and is widely known by the affectionate nickname Arik. Arik, the commander of the Negev and the conqueror of the Sinai, might well be called the quintessential sabra. In the course of the interview, he was asked, "I understand that when you came to the Western Wall, a Hasid gave you a pair of *tefillin* and asked you to wear them and that you did so. How come, why so suddenly?" The self-confident Arik for the first time turned somewhat shy. "Yes," he answered, "I did do just that." And here follows a remarkable insight: "I do not identify myself," said Arik, "with those who hate religion. On the contrary, I respect those who believe. Indeed, I believe in those who believe. I am genuinely sorry that I was never taught enough about Judaism. Thus, when I came to the Wall, I had very deep feelings that I wanted to express, but to my dismay I discovered that *li ein millim; la-yehudi ha-dati yesh,* I had no words, whereas the religious Jew does!"

This recognition is a historic achievement. Now it becomes our sacred duty, the sacred duty of all religious Jews, to give the Ariks the "words," the spiritual wherewithal to continue to the next glorious chapter in the Jewish history of our times. Let us give them, and our American Jewish youth, the stuff with which to finish the second half of the Hanukkah story, with which to perform the second miracle, that of the *nes shemen;* with which to realize Joseph's second dream; with which to excite mankind's envy, its creative *kin'ah* of our spiritual and moral success, and not only be afraid and hostile because of our material and martial conquests.

Then, having made this second dream a miraculous reality and having provoked the world to emulate our moral attainment, will we be able, with complete justification, to conclude the *Al ha-Nissim* prayer with the words *le-hodot u-le-hallel le-shimkha ha-gadol,* now we may thank and praise the great name of Almighty God for ever and ever.

ON THE THRESHOLD

IN ITS DISCUSSION OF the proper placement of the Hanukkah menorah, the Talmud (*Shabbat* 22a) decides in favor of R. Shmuel mi-Difti: one must place the menorah at the left of the doorpost as one enters, with the mezuzah on the right. Maimonides codifies this *halakhah* almost verbatim (*Hilkhot Hanukkah* 4:7).

But what drove the Talmud and the Rambam to focus on the *petah ha-bayit*, the entrance to the house? What makes the doorpost or threshold so important in the Halakhah? If indeed the point is that one must feel surrounded by *mitzvot*, why not declare that one must kindle the menorah while wearing a *tallit*, or use some other method to feel enveloped in the sanctity of the *mitzvot*? This is not dissimilar to the question posed by the *Penei Yehoshua*, namely, why does the gemara posit that the mitzvah of Hanukkah refers specifically to the home, the *bayit*, treating this particular mitzvah differently from every other mitzvah we must perform with our bodies and which refer to us as individuals, not to our homes?

I suggest that the threshold, the *petah ha-bayit*, is a symbol of instability and doubt, of confusion and diffidence. On the threshold, a person stands between inside and outside, undecided as to whether he is to go in or out. The threshold as such a symbol is found often in the Tanakh. In the Joseph story (Gen. 43:18), the brothers are frightened as they are ushered into the palace of Joseph. They approach the official in charge as they speak to him from the *petah ha-bayit*. They are hesitant, wavering between protesting and keeping silent. When Lot goes out to face the angry mob (Gen. 19:6), he speaks to them from the threshold of his house, unsure of how to treat this unholy gathering of Sodomites, uncertain as to whether or not he will survive the encounter. Earlier yet, when Cain is irate at the divine reaction to his offering, he is told that if he will not improve his ways, sin will crouch at his *petah*—again the symbol of

5770 (2009)

uncertainty. Man is always vacillating between yielding to the blandishments of the *yetzer ha-ra* and heroically overcoming his lust.

So does Hanukkah contain this symbol of the irresolute. The Rambam, in his *Iggeret ha-Shemad*, writes of the harsh evil decrees promulgated by the Greek authorities, "one of which was that one should not shut the door of his *petah ha-bayit* lest he exploit the privacy of his home to perform *mitzvot*." This left the Jews of that era in deep and frightening doubt: to yield to the Greeks and avoid death, or to defy them and keep the faith? Hence the connection between Hanukkah and the threshold.

To return to our original theme: the threshold now has two supports, as it were—the mezuzah to the right and the Hanukkah menorah to the left. The mezuzah represents the inside of the house, guarding all that has been taken within. Thus, it is affixed to the right upon entering, not upon exiting. The Halakhah also insists that the entrance must contain a door in order to fulfill properly the mitzvah of mezuzah. The mezuzah, as it were, pleads for a closed door so that it may guard the interior of the home and all that has been stored in it and keep it safe from the imprecations of a pagan world. The Hanukkah lights, on the other hand, argue for an open-door policy, for their function is *pirsumei nissa*, to illuminate the "street" or outside with the sanctity that issues from within. This collision on the threshold—whether to shut the doors and guard what we already have within, or to open the doors wide to allow us to share the blessings of Torah with the outside world—this clash of opposing tendencies is what creates within us that tension. It is only when we have the two *mitzvot* around us that we can properly weigh and measure and know when to open the doors to the outside world, to absorb from it what is good and true and beautiful, and when to shut the doors tight against the falsehood and profanation of an ungodly world and its nefarious influences.

Purim

NEITHER HERE NOR THERE

TOWARD THE END OF the Book of Esther, which we shall read this week, we are told that after their miraculous deliverance the Jews accepted upon themselves the observance of Purim forever after. *Kiyyemu ve-kibbelu*, the Jews "confirmed and took upon themselves" and their children after them to observe these two days of Purim (Esth. 9:27).

Now, logic dictates that the two key verbs should be in reverse order: not *kiyyemu ve-kibbelu*, but *kibbelu ve-kiyyemu*, first "took upon themselves," accepted, and only then "confirmed" what they had previously accepted. It is probably because of this inversion of the proper order in our verse that the Rabbis read a special meaning into this term in a famous passage in the Talmud (*Shabbat* 88a). When the Lord revealed Himself at Sinai and gave the Torah, they tell us, *kafah aleihem har ke-gigit*—He, as it were, lifted up the mountain and held it over the heads of the Israelites gathered below as if it were a cask, and He said to them: "If you accept the Torah, good and well; but if not, *sham tehei kevuratkhem*, I shall drop the mountain on your heads, and here shall be your burial place." Moreover, the Rabbis then drew the conclusions from this that the Israelites were coerced into accepting the Torah. R. Aha b. Ya'akov maintained that if this is the case, then *moda'ah rabbah le-Oraita*—this becomes a strong protest against the obligatory nature of the Torah; it is "giving notice" to God that the Torah is not permanently binding, for the Torah is in the nature of a contract between God and Israel, and a contract signed under duress is invalid.

The other Rabbis of the Talmud treated this objection with great seriousness. Thus, Rava agreed that, indeed, the Torah given at Sinai was not obligatory because of the reason stated, that *moda'ah rabbah le-Oraita*; but, Rava adds: *af al pi ken, hadar kibbeluha bi-yemei Ahashverosh*, the Israelites reaffirmed the Torah voluntarily in the days of the Purim event, for it is written:

Shabbat *Parashat Zakhor* 5728 (1968)

kiyyemu ve-kibbelu, that the Israelites "confirmed" and then "accepted," which means: *kiyyemu mah she-kibbelu kevar*—after the Purim incident the Israelites confirmed what they had long ago accepted; that is, now, after their deliverance from Haman, they affirmed their voluntary acceptance of the Torah, which they originally had been forced to accept at Sinai. Therefore, since the days of Mordecai and Esther, we no longer possess the claim of *moda'ah rabbah le-Oraita*, of denying the obligatory nature of Torah because we accepted it originally under duress; for we affirmed it out of our own free will in the days of the Purim episode.

What does all this mean? The Rabbis offer us a double insight into both theology and psychology.

A moral act is authentic only if it issues out of genuine freedom of choice. The Torah is meaningful only if man is free to accept it or reject it. Spiritual life is senseless where it is coerced. "See," the Torah tells us, "I give you this day life and death, benediction and malediction, *u-vaharta ba-hayyim*, and you shall choose life." God gives us the alternative, and we are free to choose.

Therefore, if I am forced at gun point to violate the Sabbath, I cannot be held responsible for my action. I am not guilty, because my act partakes of the nature of *ones*, compulsion. But coercion can be not only physical but also psychological, as when a man performs a criminal act in a seizure of insanity or other mental distress. Both the physical and the psychological deeds are characterized as *ones*. Even more so, extreme spiritual excitement also implies a denial of freedom and therefore lack of responsibility. Hence, if suddenly I am confronted by the vision of an angel who commands me to perform a certain mitzvah even at great risk to myself, and I proceed heroically to do just that, no credit can be given to me for my act. My freedom to decline pursuit of the mitzvah has almost vanished as a result of my unusual spiritual experience.

Thus, too, Israel at the foot of Sinai was engulfed in the historic theophany; they heard the voice of God directly in the great revelation of Torah. Of course, under the impress of such revelation, they accepted the Torah; they would have been insane not to. The felicitous and full confrontation with God elevates man to the highest ecstasy. But it robs from him his freedom to say no, to decline, to deny. And as long as man does not have the option of saying no, his yes has no merit. If he does not have the alternative to deny, then his faith is no great virtue. Faith and belief and submission and renunciation are all meaningful only in the presence of the moral freedom to do just the opposite.

Therefore, when I am faced with extremely happy circumstances, my freedom is diminished; even as it is when I am faced with a very harsh situation. When God honors me with His direct revelation, when I am privileged to hear His *Anokhi*, "I am the Lord thy God," directly from Him, I am as unable to disbelieve and disobey as when He twists my arm and threatens me with complete extinction—*sham tehei kevuratkhem*—if I do not accept the Torah. God's promises and His threats, the blessing of His presence and the threat of His wrath, are both coercive and force me to do His will under duress, without making a free choice of my own. Only a demon in human form would have done otherwise.

This, I believe, is what the Rabbis meant by their interpretation of Sinai as *kafah aleihem har ke-gigit*. They did not mean that literally and physically God raised a mountain over the heads of the assembled Israelites and threatened to squash them underneath. They did mean to indicate thereby that the very fact of God's direct revelation was so overwhelming that Israel had no choice but to accept His Torah, as if He had literally raised a mountain over their heads. The common element, in both the symbol and what it represents, is a lack of freedom to do otherwise. For this reason the Rabbis conceded that *moda'ah rabbah le-Oraita*. Since the acceptance of the Torah was not voluntary, since we were morally coerced and spiritually forced and psychologically compelled to do what we did, then the Torah lacks that binding nature which can come only from free choice. Israel had no choice at Sinai; therefore, the contract called Torah cannot be considered obligatory.

I suggest that just as the felicity of God's presence is coercive and curbs the freedom to disobey, so too the opposite, the tragedy of His absence, is coercive, and denies us the freedom to obey and believe. And just as when God reveals Himself it is as if He threatened us with *sham tehei kevuratkhem*, making our obedience mechanical and not virtuous, so too when He withdraws from us and abandons us, it requires a superhuman act of faith to believe, obey, pray, and repent. We are not morally responsible for lack of faith brought on by existential coercion.

Not long after the biblical *tokhahah*, the long list of horrible dooms predicted for Israel, we read the terrifying words: *ve-amar ba-yom ha-hu, al ki ein Elokai be-kirbi metza'uni ha-ra'ot ha-elleh*, "and Israel shall say on that day, because God is not in the midst of me have all these evils befallen me" (Deut. 31:18). What does this mean? The commentator Ovadyah Seforno interprets it as the absence of God, the *silluk Shekhinah*, the withdrawal of the Divine Presence. This *silluk Shekhinah* will make Israel despair of prayer and repentance, and this despair will result in a further estrangement of Israel from God. Now, this kind of irreligion is not a heresy by choice, it is not a denial that issues from freedom. It is a coerced faithlessness. There are times when man is so stricken and pursued, so plagued and pilloried, that we dare not blame him for giving up his hope in God. Not everyone is a Job who can proclaim, *lu yikteleni lo ayahel,* "Though He slay me, yet will I trust in Him" (Job 13:15).

When Elijah will come and proclaim the beginning of redemption, when the Messiah will appear and usher in the new age of universal peace and righteousness, when God will reveal Himself once again in the renewal of the institution of prophecy, at that time there will be no virtue in the return of Jews to Torah and the return of mankind to the canons of decency. For they will not have acted out of freedom, but out of moral compulsion and spiritual coercion. Similarly, we cannot really blame the victim of the concentration camp who called upon God out of his misery and received no answer, who was himself witness to the ultimate debasement of man created in the image of God. We cannot condemn him for abandoning religion, much as we would prefer that he emulate those few hardy souls who were able to survive the Holocaust with their faith intact. For both the presence and the absence of God, the *silluk Shekhinah* and the *giluy Shekhinah*, take away my freedom from me. In one case I am forced to accept Torah; in the other, to reject it. Under such conditions, *moda'ah rabbah le-Oraita.*

However, if freedom is denied to us in both revelation and withdrawal, if there is no praise for believing in God in the time of His presence and no blame for doubting Him during His absence, if both fortune and misfortune, happiness and tragedy, are equally coercive, if in each set of circumstances our attitude to Torah is considered involuntary—when then do we accept Torah out of freedom, and when is our loyalty praiseworthy and our *kabbalat ha-Torah* valid? The answer is: When God is neither present or absent; when He neither conceals nor reveals Himself; when Fortune neither smiles at us nor frowns at us. In a word, our freedom is greatest when life is neither here nor there! For then, and only then, do we have genuine options: to accept God and Torah, or to deny them; to choose the way of life and blessing, or the way of death and evil.

And it is this situation, that of "neither here nor there," that prevailed during the Purim episode. The victory of the Jews over Haman and the frustration of his nefarious plot was a surprising triumph and showed that God had not abandoned us; but there were no overt miracles either, no clear and indisputable proof that God was present and responsible for our victory. That is why the Book of Esther is included in the Bible and yet is the only book in which the Name of God is not mentioned. That is why the Rabbis maintain that the very name "Esther" is indicative of the hiding of God, the lack of His full revelation and presence. The *Megillah* itself is described in the Book of Esther as *divrei shalom ve-emet*, "words of peace and truth"(Esth. 9:30). By *emet*, or truth, is meant the action of God directing the forces of history. Intelligent and wise people reading the Megillah, or experiencing it during that generation, know that all that has occurred is the result of the actions of God "Whose seal is Truth." All the improbable events leading to the redemption of Israel were obviously the providential design of the God of Israel. But it was just as possible for one less endowed with spiritual insight to interpret all the events as *shalom*, peace, as a result of fortuitous events helped by the stupidity of the Persian king, the arrogance of Haman, and the wisdom of Mordecai: a diplomatic exploitation of unusually happy circumstances. Thus, the astounding victory was natural enough; there was no supernatural intervention in the affairs of the Jews of Persia. Therefore, the Purim story was "neither here nor there." So Jews were free, authentically free, to interpret the events of that historical episode as they wished. Hence, if—as they did—they turned to God and accepted the Torah, this was a genuine and binding choice: *kiyyemu ve-kibbelu*. The first time, at Sinai, they accepted the Torah but without the freedom to reject it, and it therefore represented a *moda'ah rabbah le-Oraita*, a protest against its obligatory nature because of the lack of freedom; but now, *kiyyemu mah she-kibbelu kevar*, they confirmed in freedom what they had previously accepted out of compulsion.

This lesson should not be lost on us in our individual lives. It is often said that in crisis, in the extraordinary moments of life, you can test the true character of a man. I do not believe that this is true, except if his reaction is contrary to expectations. If a man, for instance, responds heroically at a time of tragedy, he may be commended. But if he falls apart in extreme adversity, he cannot be condemned; he simply was not free to do otherwise. The same holds true in reverse situations. One who is friendly and charitable as a result of the miraculous recovery of a sick child may not yet be considered a man of nobility and generosity. He has almost been forced into charm and sweetness by his overwhelming sense of relief and gratitude.

When, then, can we tell what a man is really like? When may he be held morally accountable for his acts, and considered either guilty or praiseworthy? When he is free. And he is free when things are neither here nor there, when he is subject neither to elation nor depression, neither to the distress of adversity nor to the uplift of felicity.

It is in the Purims of life, when we have no clear proof that God is with us or against us, that there is a special virtue to accepting the Torah. Those who come to the synagogue and pray only on occasions of *simhah*, or when reciting the Kaddish, are doing the right thing. But the real test comes after the *simhah* or the eleven months of Kaddish—then, when things are neither here nor there, is the religious fiber of a personality tested. And not only is it tested, but at that time the decisions are more meaningful, more enduring, more lasting; for then the act of *kiyyemu*, confirmation, has *kiyyum*—enduring quality.

That is why I am not always happy with the famous statement of Rabbi Samson Raphael Hirsch that "the Jewish calendar is the catechism of the Jew." This might possibly be interpreted as saying that the high moments of *simhah* and the low moments of *tzarah* define the Jew's life. But I prefer the ordinary to the extraordinary. The real test of *kabbalat ha-Torah* is not Shavuot but Purim. The real test of loyalty is not on Passover with its manifest miracles, but on Hanukkah, which is more in the category of "neither here nor there." What is accepted in high moments or rejected in low moments does not always last the great majority of moments and hours, of days and months and years, when we live neither on the mountains nor in the valleys but on the boring plateaus; when the days in the office and the evenings at home follow each other in dull succession. Then does our commitment have the greatest value, the strongest effect. Then it deserves the highest praise.

Halakhah is the discipline of the Jew in his daily routines. The Western mentality has not always understood the Halakhah. The Halakhah teaches man to acquire faith, to search for God, to sanctify himself, in the hundred and one prosaic acts of everyday existence when man is seized neither by joy nor sorrow, neither by love nor hate. It does not trust the religious experience of narcotic ecstasy, the easy religion of LSD, the attractive luxury of following the guru to India and meditating in silence—nor does it condemn the despair of the man who murmurs against God out of his misery. It challenges us to holiness in the course of a life which is neither here nor there. And when we respond to Halakhah's call, when we answer with the act of *kiyyemu ve-kibbelu*, it stands us in good stead and keeps us level-headed and stout-hearted even in the extremes of life.

In decades past, in the horror of the Holocaust, we experienced many a moment when it seemed that God had abandoned us and forsaken us. Now we look forward to the vision of the renewal of prophecy and our manifest redemption when God will reveal Himself directly to us once again.

But now, in between these two poles, these two extreme ages, we live in Purim-type days, times that are neither here nor there religiously and spiritually.

Now, above all other times, we have both the freedom and the responsibility to confirm with all our hearts and all our souls the rousing declaration of ancient days, the *na'aseh ve-nishma*.

Let it be said of us, as it was said of the generation of Mordecai: *kiyyemu ve-kibbelu ha-Yehudim aleihem ve-al zar'am*, that we confirmed and accepted Torah and tradition upon ourselves and our children.

And then it shall be said of us, as it was said of Mordecai himself (Esth. 10:3), that we shall be *gadol la-yehudim ve-ratzui le-rov ehav*, great Jews, beloved by the majority of our brethren, *doresh tov le-ammo, ve-dover shalom le-khol zar'o*, seeking only the welfare of our people, speaking only peace to all our children and descendants after us.

REMEMBER TO FORGET

MEMORY AND FORGETFULNESS ARE subjects for study by psychologists, neurologists, and cyberneticians. It is for them to learn and explain the "how" of these processes, the mechanisms, the dynamics.

But these themes are also the substance of spiritual life. Many commandments of the Torah refer to remembering and forgetting. We are commanded to remember, amongst other things: the Sabbath; the day we left the Land of Egypt; what the Lord did to Miriam—and, thus, the teaching that no one is infallible; how we angered the Lord in the desert—and, therefore, to be aware of our own penchant for ingratitude.

Similarly, there are commandments concerning forgetfulness. Most prominent is the commandment of *shikhhah*—that if one has harvested his field and forgotten a corner, he should not return to it but must leave that forgotten corner for the poor (Deut. 25:19). Even more paradoxical is a commandment to forget (although it is not worded explicitly in that manner). We must forget grudges, insults, hurt. *Lo tikkom ve-lo tittor*—you shall not take revenge, you shall not bear a grudge (Lev. 19:18). Forgetfulness is even considered a blessing.

Our Rabbis teach us: *gezerah al ha-met sheyishtakkah min ha-lev*, "it is ordained that the dead be forgotten from the heart" (*Bereshit Rabbah* 84:19). R. Bahya ben Asher pointed out that this is a great blessing, for if man were always to remember the dead, he soon would be laden with such grief that he could not survive emotionally or spiritually (commentary to Gen. 37:35).

But most often, and most usually, forgetfulness is regarded as an evil, as a sin. Thus, the Rabbis taught, *Ha-shokheah davar ehad mi-mishnato ma'aleh alav ha-katuv ke-illu mithayyev be-nafsho*, "If one forgets a single item from his studies, Scripture considers it as if he were guilty with his life" (*Avot* 3:10).

And, of course, the source of all these commandments is the one which gives the Shabbat before Purim its special distinction and its very name: Shab-

---

Parashat Ki Tetzei 5734 (1974)

bat Zakhor. *Zakhor et asher asah lekha Amalek . . . lo tishkah* (Deut. 25:17–19)—remember what Amalek, that barbaric and savage tribe, did to you . . . you shall not forget.

But this commandment not to forget is problematic. After all, everyone forgets. Forgetting is natural, it is part of both our psychological and our physiological selves; it is not a volitional or deliberate act. How, then, can the Torah consider it a sin if we forget?

Permit me to recommend to you an answer suggested by R. Yitzhak Meir, the Gerer Rebbe, known to posterity by the name of his great halakhic work, *Hiddushei ha-Rim*. Forgetfulness, he says, often depends upon man. For we are not speaking here of simple recollection of facts, but the kind of forgetfulness that implies the emptying out of the mind, the catharsis of the heart of its most basic spiritual principles, of the very props of its identity. And this kind of *shikhhah* is contingent upon *ga'avah*; it is a forgetfulness which has its roots in man's arrogance.

When a man's mind is preoccupied with himself, he has little place for what is really important—and he forgets it. Hence we read (Deut. 8:14): *Ve-ram le-vavekha ve-shakhahta et Hashem Elokekha ha-motzi'akha me-Eretz Mitzrayim mi-beit avadim*, "And thy heart shall be lifted up, and thou wilt forget the Lord thy God who taketh thee out of the Land of Egypt, out of the house of slaves."

Similarly, we are commanded to remember and not to forget Amalek. Now, the numerical value of the Hebrew word Amalek is 240—the very same numerical value as the word *ram*, the heart being lifted, raised, exalted, supercilious! When man is filled with conceit, he falters and forgets.

Too much ego results in too little memory. An absent mind is the result of a swelled head. A high demeanor results in a low recall. If *ram*, you will forget *Amalek*. It is the arithmetic of mind and character.

Indeed, this is a human, if not a specifically Jewish, weakness. Rav Kook has taught us in effect that the root of all evils is that we forget who we are, our higher selves. We turn cynical and act as if man is only an amalgam of base drives, of ego-satisfactions, of sexual and material grasping. We forget that, in addition, man is capable of noble action, of sublime sentiment, of self-sacrifice. When we forget that, we are in desperate trouble. (See *Orot ha-Kodesh* III:97.)

Most Jews who assimilate today, so unlike those of the early and middle parts of this century, do not do so primarily because of self-hatred, but because of a massive act of ethnic forgetfulness. And such national absent-mindedness, such forgetting of our higher identity, is often the result of *ve-ram levavekha*.

Our memory is weakened by excessive affluence and too much self-confidence. We American Jews act as if our liberties and successes are self-evidently our right. We act as if our good fortune is deserved. And so *ve-ram levavekha* leads to *ve-shakhahta*. And what do we most often forget? Amalek!

I read recently that a Swedish gentile woman, who has several times been proposed for the Nobel Peace Prize because of the hundreds of Jews she saved during the Nazi period, said in an interview that only once in her life did she entertain hatred for a fleeting moment. It occurred during a visit she paid to Yad Vashem, the Holocaust museum, in Jerusalem. She overheard an American Jew say to the guide: "I don't understand why they didn't fight? Why weren't they real men?" She was seized with anger, and said to him: "You look fat and prosperous! Have you ever been hungry a day in your life? Do you have any idea what it is like to be starved almost to insanity, surrounded by powerful enemies, aware that no one in the world cares for you—and you have the un-mitigated nerve to ask that question?"

I confess that in reading the interview, I shared her hatred—but only for a fleeting moment. One cannot hate fools. One can only have contempt for them.

Certainly, we are subject to that weakness of forgetting time and again. Only a year ago Israelis—and Jews throughout the world—were afflicted by overconfidence, and the Yom Kippur War was the result. I should hope that we Jews are bright enough to have learned from this experience.

Most important, one of the things we must never dare to forget is the contemporary Amalek, the Holocaust. The news that the younger generation of Germans does not want to be reminded of it, that they feel they did not participate in it, comes as no surprise to me. But Jews must never fall into the trap of *ve-ram levavekha* and so forget Amalek. Remember and do not forget! The Holocaust must constantly be part of our education, commemoration, and motivation for further study and spiritual development.

Conversely, too, if we remember Amalek, that will lead to a realistic assessment of ourselves, and we shall be able to avoid the pitfall of a "lifted heart."

The United States and all the Western world are today in the doldrums. We are all of us in a pessimistic mood about the economy, something which affects each and every one of us. If the Lord helps, and we all escape economic disaster—if it will be, as we say in Yiddish, *afgekumen mit a shrek*, "escaped with a scare"—then perhaps we will have learned to rid ourselves of the cultural and psychological and moral signs of decadence in our culture, all these corruptions the result of *ve-ram levavekha*, overconfidence inspired by affluence.

So the *Hiddushei ha-Rim* has given us an unforgettable *Devar Torah* about forgetfulness and arrogance.

It is a lesson worthy of our deep thought and meditation. Remember it, do not forget.

Passover

THE SABBATH OF GREATNESS

MANY REASONS HAVE BEEN offered as to why this Sabbath before the holiday of Passover is known by the name Shabbat ha-Gadol. Allow me to commend to your attention one such reason, which I find particularly significant. The author of the *Tur*, one of the greatest legal codes of Judaism, maintains that our Sabbath is known as Shabbat ha-Gadol *lefi she-na'aseh bo nes gadol*—because a great miracle was performed on this day (*Tur, Orah Hayyim* 430). It was on this day of the year that the Jews were liberated from Egypt, that they summoned up the courage to take the lambs that were tied to their doorposts and slaughter them as sacrifices to Almighty God. This act outraged the Egyptians, for whom the lamb was a divinity. They were stunned by the effrontery of these miserable Hebrew slaves who dared, in the presence of their masters, to exert their own religious independence. And yet, *ve-lo hayu rasha'in lomar lahem davar*, the Egyptians could not and did not say a word in an attempt to stop the Israelites. Because of this *nes gadol*, this great miracle, the Sabbath was called Shabbat ha-Gadol, the great Sabbath.

This is, indeed, a beautiful explanation. But there is something troubling about it. Granted that the silence of the Egyptians, their sudden paralysis, was a true miracle. But what makes this a "great" miracle? Why *gadol*? This was an era which saw the miracles of the Exodus from Egypt, the ten plagues, and the splitting of the Red Sea. Were these miracles not at least equally great? How does one measure the size or significance of miracles?

I believe the answer can be most instructive. For *nes gadol* refers not to the silence of the Egyptians, but to the miracle of Jewish character. What we celebrate is not a great miracle, but the miracle of greatness. And I refer not only to the courageous defiance exercised by the Jews in Egypt, but to an even more

This *derashah* is based upon a theme suggested by Rabbi Joseph M. Baumol.— N. L.

Shabbat ha-Gadol 5722 (1962)

significant fact. The other miracles of which we read and which we celebrate allowed the Israelites to escape and survive, but in the process the Egyptian enemy was hurt, injured, or killed. The plagues caused a great deal of pain for the Egyptians, and the splitting of the Red Sea was followed by the drowning of the hordes of Pharaoh. This miracle, however, involved no injury to the enemy. The Jews grew and rose in stature, but no one was hurt. It was not the kind of bravado or courage that is expressed in doing violence to one's neighbor. Shabbat ha-Gadol celebrates *nes gadol*, the magic and the miracle of genuine greatness achieved by our people. This was real *gadlut*: greatness from within, not at someone else's expense.

The story is told of the great saint and sage R. Israel Salanter was walking in the street one day and encountered two boys who had been fighting with each other. The stronger had thrown the weaker into a ditch at the side of the road. "What is going on?" asked the rabbi. The stronger boy answered, "We had an argument as to which of us is taller. So I threw him into a ditch to prove to him that I am taller than he." "Foolish boy," replied the rabbi, "could you not have achieved the same purpose by standing on a chair rather than throwing him into a ditch?"

What the rabbi was teaching was a secret of true greatness. *Gadlut* consists of achieving eminence without crushing another human being.

And oh, how rare is that quality of *nes gadol*, the miracle of greatness. Everyone wants to be great, and so few know the Jewish secret of greatness. The big powers all want to appear great and acceptable in the eyes of the uncommitted bloc of Afro-Asian nations. It is a national policy of our government to try to gain in popularity amongst the new nations. It is not for us here to decide the validity of this principle. But I know that many Americans were saddened when Adlai Stevenson, the American ambassador to the U.N., this past week chastised the State of Israel for defending itself against Syrian attacks. He seems to be afflicted with what has become a traditional liberal blindness—the inability or unwillingness to discriminate between the hooligan's attack and the victim's defense. It is of one piece with a popular liberal attitude that expends much more energy and sentiment in defending the murderer from punishment than in preventing the victim from having suffered in the first place. We were saddened and disappointed when Ambassador Stevenson—who, according to the British press, acted without authorization of and to the chagrin of the State Department—attempted to act big in the eyes of the Arabs and their friends by reproaching the loneliest of all nations. No eloquence and no humor can disguise the *katnut*, the smallness of spirit, of a man who, rather than stand on a chair, will throw Israel into a diplomatic ditch.

And the same lesson holds true for all of us. It is true for the State of Israel, which also often finds that it suffers from overpoliticization, with the partisanship of its political parties often exceeding all bounds. Political consciousness of the citizenry is good, but when each individual party—and this holds true for all of them—tries to gain in prestige and power at the expense of all others, by belittling and scandalizing others, then the State itself begins to suffer.

It holds true for American Jewish organizations, where the progress of American Jewry is all too often stifled because of the unwillingness of the various organizations to unify or at least cooperate, not so much to protect their own autonomy as to make sure that the other organizations do not receive credit and power.

As individuals, Shabbat ha-Gadol reminds us that the way to greatness in business should never come by crushing competitors. In our professions we should not attempt to achieve prestige by hurting colleagues. The concept of *nes gadol* teaches each of us not only how to act, but also how to think; in our innermost hearts, we should measure our own success or failure not relative to our neighbors, but by absolute standards. We must, each of us, attempt to grow great by ourselves, not only by comparison to the smallness of others.

But granted the negative aspect of this definition of *gadlut* or greatness, that it must not come at the expense of others, what is the positive or affirmative definition? What do we mean when we say that one must grow big by himself and through himself?

Perhaps the Talmud can help us here. In discussing the laws of *metzi'ah*, or finds, talmudic law is that if one finds an object which has no distinguishing marks and is unclaimed, he may keep it. If he is a child, a *katan*, the *metzi'ah* belongs to his father or guardian. If he is a *gadol*, an adult, then it belongs to himself. And yet, the Talmud maintains, *Lo katan katan mammash ve-lo gadol gadol mammash* (*Bava Metzi'a* 12b)—whereas "child" and "adult" normally refer to chronology or physical development, that is, before or after the age of thirteen, that does not hold true in this context. *Katan* or *ketannim* with regard to finds is not a question of age, but a question of independence. A minor, or *katan*, is one *ha-somekh al shulhan aviv o shulhan shel aherim*—who literally relies or leans on the table of his father or on the table of others. A *gadol*, or adult, is one who has his own table, who supports himself.

I believe this is more than an economic definition in Jewish financial law. It is a lesson for all of life. To be *gadol*, great, means to be yourself, to draw upon your own spiritual resources, to live true to your own destiny and character. A spiritual *katan* will beg for crumbs from the tables of others; one who has achieved *gadlut* will repair to his own table, no matter how sparse the food may be.

In Egypt, throughout their servitude, our ancestors were in the category of those who "rely on the table of others." They had assimilated Egyptian life and values, Egyptian culture and religion. They had sunk to spiritual minority, or *katnut*, and this kind of *katnut* cannot be redeemed or healed by plagues or the splitting of seas or political independence. What was needed was nothing less than a miracle—the *nes gadol*, the miracle of genuine greatness by an act which affirms the spiritual self, a rallying to unique Jewish destiny and image and character, a courageous cutting of the cultural umbilical cord which tied the Jewish victims to their Egyptian persecutors. This was achieved through *shehitat eloheihem*, through the slaughtering of the Egyptians' gods and the rejection of their idolatry, which until that time had been accepted by the Israelites. This was the miracle of Jewish greatness. No one else was hurt, and it was an act of spiritual independence.

This is a teaching which holds true universally. He who lives by leave of another, he who satisfies his cultural hunger by crumbs from strange tables, he who seeks esteem by alien standards—he is a *katan*. The abject conformist, the servile status-seeker, the eternal *mah yafisnik*—these are *ketannim* in long trousers. Jews whose lifelong ambition it is to imitate non-Jews, Jewish movements and doctrines which pine for crumbs from the tables of secularism or Unitarianism, from Deweyism or Marxism—and there are such movements here and overseas—are minors with big vocabularies. Those who are willing to settle for Jewish statehood, but are ready to abandon all attempts at the greater aspiration for Jewish selfhood, they suffer from stunted spiritual growth.

The first promise that God gave to the first Jew, Abraham, was *Ve-e'eskha le-goy gadol*, "And I shall make you into a great nation" (Gen. 12:2). God did not mean *goy gadol* insofar as numbers or power is concerned; we Jews have never had much of either. He meant a nation of genuine greatness. And that is why later, when God tells Abraham of the future bitter exile of his descendants in Egypt, He gives him the greatest consolation: *Ve-aharei khen yetze'u bi-rekhush gadol* (Gen 15:14). This is usually translated, "And afterwards they will leave with great wealth." I believe the real translation is, "And afterwards they will leave with a *wealth of greatness.*" Great wealth is an ordinary ambition; a wealth of greatness is the extraordinary Jewish aspiration.

Our *haftarah* for today concludes with a promise by the Almighty: *Hinneh anokhi sholeah lakhem et Eliyyah ha-navi lifnei bo yom Hashem ha-gadol ve-ha-nora,* "Behold, I shall send to you the prophet Elijah before the coming of the great and terrible day of the Lord" (Mal. 3:23). We have a choice: *gadol* or *nora,* great or terrible. We live in a world where decisions must be made. We live in a world where Elijah calls out to us as he did to the Jews gathered about him at Mount Carmel, saying, "How long will you waver?"

In our world, there can be no wavering and no indecisiveness. It is either/or: either be Jewish and great, or cringe at the tables of others and *nora,* terrible. The world we live in will not permit leisurely smallness. Judaism cannot survive with pettiness of the spirit and the immaturity of Jewish mindlessness. If we return to Torah and tradition, we can ourselves forge the *nes* of *gadol.* If, Heaven forbid, we do not, we must face and expect the terrible failure of *katnut.*

On Shabbat ha-Gadol, we strive for the experience of *yom Hashem ha-gadol,* and by once again becoming a *goy gadol,* we will be able to bequeath to our children and children's children a *rekhush gadol,* a heritage of authentic greatness.

Ve-heshiv lev avot al banim, ve-lev banim al avotam—"And the Lord shall cause the heart of the fathers to return to the sons, and the heart of the sons to their father" (Mal. 3:24).

WITH ALL DELIBERATE SPEED

MODERN LIFE CATCHES UP each of us in its whirlpool of frenzied activity, making a virtue of speed and causing each of us to rush madly through the frenzied activities of each and every day. So unnerving is this fast pace that we seek desperately for some haven, for some place of refuge where we can slow down, breathe easier, and find a bit of peace. And for this peace and calm we naturally turn to religion, to shul, to Torah. We hope for the still, small voice of religion to reassure us and soothe our keyed-up souls.

And yet if that is all we seek of Torah, we are going to be very disappointed. Quite to the contrary, the message of Passover is not "slow down" but "speed up." The key word of all of Pesah is the Hebrew word *hippazon*—haste, hurry. The first *korban Pesah* was to be eaten with loins girded, with feet in shoes, with staff in hand: *Va-akhaltem oto be-hippazon*, "and you shall eat it in haste," *Pesah hu la-Shem*, "it is the Lord's Passover" (Ex. 12:11). The very matzah we eat is a symbol of rushing; there is no time for the dough to rise, and so we have matzah instead of bread. According to Maimonides (*Guide for the Perplexed* III:46), not only the matzah and the eating of the Passover lamb were results of *hippazon*, but all of the Passover ritual reflects this hastiness. We are forbidden to break a bone of the *korban* because, says Maimonides, we must act as if we have no time for a leisurely meal. It is because of rushing that we may not cook but only roast the lamb. We must eat only in one house, and not go visiting from house to house the night of the Seder—because we must rush through the meal. The *afikoman* must be eaten before midnight. And in Maimonides' version of the Haggadah text he presents at the end of *Hilkhot Hametz u-Matzah*, he begins the whole recital with the words *bi-vehilu yatzanu mi-Mitzrayim*, "we left Egypt in a hurry, in *hippazon*."

Why this emphasis on haste during Pesah? Is it only to increase our neurotic obsession with speed? Do we not rush enough during the whole year?

5718 (1958)

And the answer is that we rush, yes, but for the wrong things. We are always in a rush to make a living, but we are much too slow in making order out of life. I would use two different words to describe the right kind and the wrong kind of rushing: "hurry" and "haste." "Whoever is in a hurry," said Lord Chesterfield in 1749, "shows that the thing he is about is too big for him." Haste and hurry are very different things.

Our unhappy, mad rush through life is *hurry*—an anxious scramble to hide the void and emptiness of life and disguise it, lest we come face to face with its utter barrenness. Hurry is not what the Torah recommends on Passover. On the contrary, when it comes to hurry, Judaism tells us to take it easy and digest our meal through *hasibbah*, by reclining in aristocratic fashion. When the Torah commands *hippazon*, it means haste. It means, to use a famous phrase from the recent Supreme Court decision on integration, "all deliberate speed." It means not to waste time and fritter away our years in nonsense but to proceed directly to the core of life, to uncovering its inner meaning. The man who rushes to play cards is in a hurry. The one who rushes to shul is in haste. One rushes to waste time, the other to use it and exploit it.

I believe this is what the Talmud had in mind when it recorded the controversy between R. Akiva and R. Elazar ben Azariah (*Berakhot* 9a) as to what the Torah meant by eating the *korban Pesah* in *hippazon*. R. Elazar said that *hippazon* means to rush through the meal and finish it by midnight. R. Akiva said to rush through the meal and finish it by dawn—not *hatzot*, but *boker*. And the Talmud explains that the difference of opinion comes about because of a difference of interpretation of the word *hippazon*. R. Elazar, who sets midnight as the deadline, understands this as *hippazon de-Mitzrayim*; we rush because the Egyptians hurried us out of the land. Midnight was the time the dreaded tenth plague struck, and so they rushed us out as fast as they could. R. Akiva says the word refers to *hippazon de-Yisra'el*; we must rush not because the Egyptians chased us, but because we were ourselves anxious to make our way out of this evil land and to attain the freedom which God had promised us. And the Israelites, making haste because of their own will and understanding, were prepared to leave at dawn, at daybreak.

These two definitions represent the worthy and unworthy forms of rushing, of *hippazon*. *Hippazon de-Mitzrayim* means hurry, rushing because of external circumstances and reflecting no credit upon ourselves. *Hippazon de-Yisra'el* means haste, rushing because of our love of freedom, our cherishing God's promise. It means rushing not because of the outer force of Egyptian oppression, but because of the inner pressure for Jewish expression. Hurry is neurotic confusion; haste is noble ambition. The hurry of *hippazon de-Mitzrayim* is purposeless and the result of fear; haste is purposeful and the outgrowth of love. We are in a hurry when we are pursued by men or the shadows of men. We make haste when we are in pursuit of the Lord and His word. Hurry is an Egyptian kind of *hippazon*; haste is the Jewish brand of *hippazon*. *Hippazon de-Mitzrayim* is *ad hatzot*; it leads us to plunge into the utter blackness of midnight. *Hippazon de-Yisra'el* is *ad ha-boker*; it takes us by the hand and quickly introduces us to the bright sunshine of the spring dawn. It does not permit us to linger on in the dark. R. Elazar ben Azariah tells us that *hippazon* is *zekher le-avdut*, like *maror*; according to R. Akiva, the *hippazon* becomes *zekher le-herut*, like *hassibah*.

Most adults, afflicted as they are with the disease of hurry, hurry, and more hurry, seem to have entered a conspiracy against the children of our nation. They want to keep them in the supposed purity of their childhood as long as possible, and make the growing-up process as slow as they can. We slow down their real growing up because, as one writer put it, we Americans grossly overrate the number of karats in the so-called Golden Age of Childhood, as if we believed that the choicest thing about being a frog is being a tadpole. And so, we indulge and protect our children and extend the period of childhood to about the age of twenty or more instead of thirteen. And thus, when their minds are reaching the top level of their potential, when they are most able to think creatively, we shield them from too much mental strain. When they are most ready to accept responsibility, we deny it to them. The comparison between an American high-school student and his Russian equivalent, drawn by a famous nationwide weekly recently, is most instructive. The Russian young man is just that—a young man. He is serious, hard-working, a full student in every spare moment. There is no nonsense in his school, and the subjects he takes are those of the adult world without embellishment. The American young man is not yet a man—he is a "teenager," as we call our nation's youth whom we have kept as children instead of young adults. He seems to major in extracurricular activities and "snap courses," and is free and easy-going. His studies are a necessary evil and far from an intellectual discipline. He rarely has an intense interest in scholarship. In other words, the American adolescent does not know haste. And so there is waste, and a national emergency, and the jitters in the world of officialdom.

But if there is no haste, there is a good deal of hurry. Parents rush their children into the mad round of dating even before they are thirteen, or younger, reflecting—as some psychiatrists maintain—their own basic insecurity and desire for recognition. We push them into the hurried world of social dancing and night-clubbing while at the same time taking them out of Hebrew school because, as we say, with all that tremendous amount of work from junior high, how can he possibly take Hebrew too? We keep them from haste in the process of growing up intellectually—we are afraid they will sprain their brains; and ethically—how many teen-agers give charity—and religiously. Our Jewish tradition, however, never looked upon childhood or adolescence as a hurried whirl of fast dates. Our Rabbis cherished childhood for the *girsa de-yankuta*, for the studies they pursued then, for the fact that what is learned in childhood is better remembered later. Now, however, the modern Pharaoh and his Egyptians—Khrushchev and the Communists—have goaded America into rushing things a bit, and American educators and parents are beginning to understand that they have underestimated children and were tragically wrong in substituting hurry for haste. It will be to the eternal credit of Jewish education, and especially the Day School movement, that when other school systems in America were pushing for more hobbies and frills and all sorts of nonsense and postponing learning a second language until the eighth grade, we of the Day School were teaching a second language and culture in kindergarten! Now, of course, almost everyone in American education agrees that that is the right policy—but when we did it, it was a policy of haste, of *hippazon de-Yisra'el*. The motives were inspired by love of Torah and love of learning. My only fear is that now that America has woken up to its previous follies, it should not be stampeded into raising a generation of uncultured engineers, of IBM machines in human form. That will again be *hippazon de-Mitzrayim*, not *hippazon de-Yisra'el*. Now we must make haste, but we must not hurry. We must rush our youth culturally and religiously, for, as Hillel said, *Ve-im lo akhshav, eimataї?* (*Avot* 1:14), "If not now, when then?" But if we are tempted to hurry them, to push them into *hippazon de-Mitzrayim* in a senseless piling up of technological courses, then on Passover we caution and say: *hasibbah* too is a mitzvah. Take it easy. Make haste, but don't hurry.

Perhaps one of the most moving and pathetic documents illustrating the Jewish teaching of *hippazon* is one which was written by the famous columnist Max Lerner after the recent death of his father. Max Lerner is a great liberal, a professor, and an editor and now author as well as columnist for the *New York Post*. The article he wrote after his eighty-seven-year-old father passed away is a minor masterpiece. And yet, it seems, Max Lerner in a way tells us more about himself and *his* generation than about his father and *his* generation. His father had studied in a yeshiva in Russia and came here with his family in 1907. He went through the familiar odyssey of immigrant jobs, from one to the other, until he settled in the one of his first love: Hebrew teaching. He was, as Lerner says, a quiet man who was never a big success at anything and who did not make a great noise in the world—but he loved and was loved, and enjoyed his children. Now listen to this:

> When I saw him toward the end of his illness, while he could still talk, he asked me to bring his notebooks. They were a confusion of ledgers, journals, loose sheets, on which over the years he had written his reflections on a variety of themes, covering his life within the world . . . dealing with the early Prophets and the latter day secular figures. . . .
>
> I am, alas, an ignorant man. With all my years of schooling, I am unable to read the languages in which my father wrote, as my sons are already able to read mine. I shall save the bundle of pages on which he spent the burden of his hours, driven as he was by a strange necessity to find a garment for what he felt and dreamt. Some day, I may repair my ignorance and discover what thoughts they were that coursed through the mind of this patient, reflective man.

I wonder if you can appreciate the tragedy in these lines—indeed, I wonder if Max Lerner appreciated it when he wrote them. Here is a bright, prolific writer, who must write a daily column which is read avidly and admired by thousands, including myself; who lectures far and wide—only last year he spoke in Springfield; who teaches in a college in Massachusetts; who recently wrote a very important book on American civilization. We are not speaking now about a spoiled American youngster. We are talking about an intellect—an egghead, not a blockhead. What a fantastically busy man he must be—the daily column with the press's deadlines, the rushing to make intercity trains and airplane flights, rushing to class and back to the city, meeting with publishers . . . by all means a life of *hippazon*. And yet this man, with time for everything else, rushing for every cause, a master of the culture of this day—this man cannot understand the words of his own beloved father! This man of rush, rush, rush for everything else and a past master of the written word has never taken the trouble to learn either Hebrew or Yiddish—his father's languages. This man, who writes so knowledgeably about the politics of Nehru and the economics of Ghana, must say, "I am, alas, an ignorant man" when it comes to a simple Hebrew letter. The man who rushed to absorb so much at school, took his time when it came to his father's tongue. And so the man of *hippazon* must now write—and how profound is the shame—"Some day I may repair my ignorance and discover what thoughts coursed through the mind of this patient, reflective man." There is hurry for a deadline, hurry for another lecture tour, hurry for the latest *Congressional Record*, hurry to get out another book and grind out another article—but no rush and haste at all when it comes to understanding your own father; then, it is only "some day"! And until then, you take your time (until it is too late), and the old father who for eighty-seven years recorded his tenderest thoughts in the language of Moses and Isaiah, that old father has no son to lend him an ear; his most cherished ideas remain closed to his brilliant son, his loftiest meditations saved up so lovingly throughout the years now fall on deaf ears and are greeted with a thunderous silence—"Some day I may repair my ignorance," and meanwhile a smart, intelligent old man goes down into his grave and sinks into eternal oblivion.

I am not blaming Max Lerner, who happens to be my favorite columnist. I am blaming a whole generation of Max Lerners who, caught up in the *hippazon de-Mitzrayim*, have never learnt the *hippazon de-Yisra'el*, who hurry but are never in a haste, who feel compelled to speed in order to catch up with the fast-moving events of the day, but fail to respond to the inner needs of the Jewish self, and leave those needs for "some day."

This is a question each of us must put to himself: is my *hippazon* of the Egyptian variety or of the Jewish kind? Is my rushing hurry or haste? Is it the neurotic rush, which concentrates on the ephemeral and unimportant, or the creative rush, which centers on the eternal and the significant? Are we rushing only to make money, or also to live right? Are we in mad pursuit of entertainment, or do we make haste to fill our lives with *mitzvot u-ma'asim tovim*, with noble thoughts and deeds? In a word: are we rushing away from life or toward it? Pesah emphasizes *hippazon de-Yisra'el*, the kind of rush which will continue our tradition, which will keep open the lines of communication between past and present, not those which will cut them off. *Hippazon de-Yisra'el* means to make haste so that we may better listen to our old fathers and speak to our young children, so that all of us remain *Yisra'el*, so that neither we nor our children become *Mitzrayim*, assimilated into the common culture; so that we will not be hurled headlong into the whirling midnight of *hippazon de-Mitzrayim*, but speed quickly to a new dawn of *hippazon de-Yisra'el*.

Our life today is too fast-moving for anyone to be slow and survive. But if it has got to be fast, then it must be for that which is worthy and noble and Godly, not for that which is selfish and trivial and Godless—*hippazon de-Yisra'el* and not *hippazon de-Mitzrayim*.

To make haste in the Jewish way is, then, the message of Passover and the meaning of all its laws. Perhaps it is this very kind of Jewish haste, this *hippazon de-Yisra'el*, that was in the mind of the great sage and translator of the Bible to Aramaic, Yonatan ben Uziel, who translates the word *hippazon* (Ex. 12:11), "you shall eat it in haste," as *bi-vehilu di-Shekhinat Marei de-Alma*, as "in haste, rushed by God, Master of the World." He meant to tell us, and all of this holiday means to tell us, that when we rush because of love of God and Torah and Israel, when we rush for the sake of high ideals and noble aspirations, then God is with us—then the *Shekhinah* guides our steps and gives us speed, and then the Master of the World shares our haste with us.

On this Pesah, that is precisely what I wish every one of you: the Godly, Jewish kind of *hippazon*, the rush and haste in which the *Shekhinah* participates. In a word,

God-speed!

THE SOURCE OF DARKNESS

FROM THE VERY BEGINNINGS OF time, when Adam complained to God of his loneliness, man has regarded his solitude as a painful experience, even a curse. Modern man is especially bothered by loneliness. Despite—or maybe because of—his large cities and giant metropolises, he finds himself terribly alone in the world. He finds the silence of the universe and its indifference to his problems unbearable. He is alone and does not like it.

It is perhaps this feeling of loneliness that was the essence of the ninth plague that God brought upon the Egyptians and of which we read in this morning's *sidrah*. The *hoshekh*, or darkness, imposed a rigid and horrifying isolation upon the Egyptians. The effect of the plague is described by the Torah as *lo ra'u ish et ahiv* (Ex. 10:23), "they did not see one another." All communication between a man and his friends ceased. He had no family, no friends, no society, he was completely and utterly blacked out of any contact with any other human. How lonely! What a plague!

It is all the more surprising, therefore, to read the opinion of R. Yehudah, recorded in the Midrash, about the ninth plague (*Shemot Rabbah, Bo* 14:2). Our Sages asked, *Me-heikhan hayah ha-hoshekh ha-hu*? What was the source of that darkness? Where did it come from? What is the nature and origin of loneliness? R. Nehemiah gave a credible answer: *Me-hoshekh shel Gehinnom*. The darkness that descended upon Egypt came from the darkness of Gehinnom, from the netherworld. Loneliness is a curse; hence its origin is the place of punishment. But R. Yehudah's answer is astonishing: *Me-hoshekh shel ma'alah, shene'emar: yashet hoshekh sitro*. The source of that darkness was from Heaven, for it is written that God dwells in secret darkness (Ps. 18:12)! What an unexpected origin for a plague: God's dwelling place! Darkness comes—from Heaven!

Astonishing, yes, but in the answer by R. Yehudah we have a new insight into the problem of loneliness, and hence into the condition of man as a whole. Darkness or solitude can become the curse of loneliness, as it did when it

Parashat Bo 5719 (1959)

plagued the Egyptians and separated every man from his brother, a loneliness that prevented one from feeling with the other, from sharing his grief and his joy, his dreams and his fears. Darkness can indeed be a plague. But the same darkness can be a blessing; it can be worthy of the closest presence of God Himself. For solitude means privacy; it means not only a devastating loneliness but also that precious opportunity when a man escapes from the loud brawl of life and the constant claims of society and, in the intimate seclusion of his own soul and heart, he gets to know himself and realize that he is made in the image of God. Loneliness can be painful, but it can also be precious. The same *hoshekh* that can spell plague for a man if it seals him off from others by making him blind to the needs of his fellows, this same *hoshekh* becomes Godly when it enables a man to become more than just a social animal, more than just a member of a group, but also a full, mature, unique individual in his own right. *Yoshev be-seter elyon* (Ps. 91:1)—God dwells in the highest kind of secrecy or mystery, which cannot be penetrated by man. So must every person have an inner life, an internal *seter*, a chamber of blessed *hoshekh*, which, in its privacy, assures him of his uniqueness as a different, individual man or woman. As Longfellow once wrote, "Not in the clamor of the crowded street/ Not in the shouts and plaudits of the throng/ But in ourselves are triumph and defeat." In ourselves—that is where we can develop that brilliant darkness which has its source in God.

An American scholar recently wrote an article called "The Invasion of Privacy" in which he says that the perfect symbol of the confusion of our times is the picture window so typical of our newer houses. The picture window, he says, is more a means of letting others look in than for having the owner look out. Modern life, with its perpetual telephone calls and never-ending blare of television, with its round of constant appointments and business and social duties, represents an intrusion upon the privacy of each of us, a deliberate attack upon the citadel of personal privacy. And modern man succumbs to this attack—he opens the blinds on the picture window of his heart, seeking to reveal his deepest secrets either to an ever-widening circle of friends or to his analyst or to his priest. We are often afraid of the solitude of privacy. We often fail to realize that *hoshekh* is not only a *makkah* but also an aspect of Godliness. Educators and parents sometimes go to extremes and are appalled by a child who prefers to play by himself or think independently, and rush to impose "group games" and "doing things together" and "togetherness" upon the delicious solitude in which a child seeks to discover himself. For a child realizes that, as with the young prophet Samuel, it is within himself that a man can hear the voice of God. Society may be the stage where the *command* of God is *executed*: but the inner solitude of man is the audience chamber where we *hear* that command. How can a man be a truly good father, as God requires of him, if he does not have a few moments a day to contemplate in utter loneliness the wonder of children? How a good husband if he only acts out his role without ever thinking through his relationships in the stillness of his heart? How a good son or daughter if we never are alone long enough to realize the enormous debt we owe parents for life and love? "Woe to him who is never alone and cannot bear to be alone!"

Don Isaac Abarbanel, that great fifteenth-century Jew who was treasurer to the king of Spain until the exile in 1492, put it in sharper fashion in his comment on the first passage in *Pirkei Avot,* the *Ethics of the Fathers.* We read, *Moshe kibbel Torah mi-Sinai* (*Avot* 1:1), "Moses received the Torah from Sinai." But, asks Abarbanel, it was not from Sinai that Moses received the Law; it was from God and at Sinai. It should have been stated, *Moshe kibbel Torah be-Sinai* or *min Hashem.* The reason for *mi-Sinai,* he answers, is that the Torah *was* revealed to Moses only because of his inimitable capacity for creative solitude, only because at Sinai he isolated himself from man and with God for forty days and nights, because Sinai was the place that *niggash el ha-arafel,* that he in his loneliness approached the darkness wherein God dwelt. *Moshe kibbel Torah mi-Sinai*—Moses received the Torah *by virtue of* Sinai, because he learned the secret of Godly solitude. So solitude gave birth to Torah. So does it give birth to ideas and to thoughts and to art and to beauty and to the essence of man and to all that is noble in life.

I have never known a really creative person who did not precede the creative act with at least a moment of profound, thoughtful solitude. No really great speech or beautiful musical composition is rolled off extemporaneously; it is forged in the silence of the mind when the outside world is shut out by a Godly darkness. No brilliant idea—whether in the sciences or business—is born out of the brawl of life; it is hatched out of the stillness of a creative personality. What is inspiration? It is nothing but the product of positive and constructive silence in the innermost, inviolable chambers of a man's heart. The source of light is in this kind of darkness or solitude. And the source of this darkness is in God. It is the *hoshekh shel ma'alah.*

It is therefore of the greatest importance to all of us that even as we seek to banish the plague of loneliness, we do not drive away the blessing of privacy. We ought to regard it as sacred and protect our moments of solitude with zeal.

If, in the conditions of contemporary life, it becomes difficult to escape these intrusions upon our privacy, to enjoy the *va-yashet hoshekh sitro*, it becomes all the more important to guard it zealously. We ought to seek opportunities for this solitude of contemplation wherever and whenever we can—whether during our vacation periods, when we can afford more of this precious and delicious time; at the beginning of the day in the synagogue at minyan, when we can, in a silent *Shemoneh Esreh*, truly find that we are alone with God; any time we can wrest from our busy schedules for the sweet silence of solitude. There is a great deal of *hoshekh*-solitude in the world. The Egyptian makes of it a plague of isolation—*lo ra'u ish et ahiv*—an inability to see his fellow-men, a picture window through which others can look but he is blind to them. The Godlike, however, will make of this solitude an atmosphere of holiness, *yashet hoshekh sitro*, a creative opportunity to discover themselves and the voice of God that speaks to them, a window which does not allow others to peer within, but enables them to see their fellow men and be with them. This kind of *hoshekh* is not the plague of darkness; it comes from the Most High source of all existence. May we learn to make use of that darkness and thus bring great light into the lives of all of us.

On Being Responsible

5723(1963)

RESPONSIBILITY IS THE HALLMARK of the civilized and mature human being. One of the two things that filled the great philosopher Immanuel Kant with awe was the sense of moral responsibility in man. In an ultimate sense, to be responsible means to be religious, for an irresponsible person believes that, except for the police, there is no one to whom he has to answer for his conduct, whereas the responsible person acknowledges the existence of a higher power beyond himself to whom he must answer or respond for his life and his actions. Therefore, if one accepts that there is a God who asks and challenges and makes demands upon us, and he feels it necessary to respond to Him, then he is *responsible*.

There is yet another way in which responsibility is related to faith—not, this time, faith in God but faith in man. The Talmud tells us, *hen shellekha tzedek ve-lav shellekha tzedek* (*Bava Metzi'a* 49a)—make your yes firm and your no firm. Let people know exactly what you mean. In other words, a man must be responsible for what he says. For if he is not, the Talmud continues, then he is counted among the *mehusserei amanah*, those who lack faith, those who are faithless. Rabbi Simhah Zissel, the great light and leader of the Musar movement, asked: what is the relationship between responsibility and faith? He answered: by *mehusserei amanah* the Talmud means that the man who has no responsibility does not deserve anyone else's faith in him. He is not trustworthy. He is not faithful. Therefore, for the same reason, the *dayyan mumheh*, the righteous judge, is called in the *Hummash* by the name *elohim*—not only because he, like God, is a source of authority, but also because, like God, he is deserving of faith by others. For such people, responsibility never becomes, as the American humorist Ambrose Bierce defined it (in *The Devil's Dictionary*), "a detachable burden, easily shifted onto the shoulders of God, Faith, Fortune, Luck or one's neighbor." A man who is not counted amongst the *mehusarei amanah* keeps the responsibility on his own shoulders. There is a famous rabbinic proverb that *lefi gamla shihna*, "according to the strength of the camel is the load placed upon him" (*Bereshit Rabbah* 19:1). The bigger the man, the more responsible is he, and the more deserving of our *emunah,* or our faith in him. If, therefore, in an ultimate spiritual sense, responsibility is a religious faith in God, then in a more immediate social sense, responsibility means reliability, dependability, winning the faith of others.

But there is yet another aspect to responsibility which also reflects an element of faith, and that is faith in the future, faith in the durability of human ideals, faith that the good and the noble and the right are not a fleeting, chimerical, imaginary phenomenon, but that they will endure long after cruelty, dishonesty, and meanness will have been spent and will have perished. The great teacher, talmudic sage, and lexicographer of geonic times, Rabbi Nathan of Rome, in his renowned halakhic dictionary, the *Arukh,* analyzes the theme of responsibility, or *aharayut.* He points out that talmudic law regards real estate but not chattel as an adequate surety in any transaction. Only *karka,* land, can be used for a mortgage, can be regarded as *nekhasim she-yesh lahem aharayut,* or "responsible property"—meaning that if one offers *karka* (land) as property from which a debt can be collected, we accept it. What is the relationship between *karka* (land) and *aharayut* (responsibility)? Rabbi Nathan explains the relationship by the fact that *karka* has *aharit,* it has a future, it lasts, it continues onward. *Mittaltelin* (chattel or movables) can be destroyed. Land cannot. Therefore, says the author of the *Arukh,* the idea of *aharayut* is tied in with *aharit.* Responsibility is based upon the idea of the future.

Is this not a profoundly psychological and spiritual as well as legal and economic truth? Statesmen who think the world has no future, that its *aharit* may well be buried under a fine radioactive ash, abandon all *aharayut* for civilized international conduct. A man who feels his job has a future will execute it responsibly; otherwise, if he believes it has no *aharit,* he will feel no *aharayut* toward it. Look at the tremendous sense of responsibility that our prophets felt for our people, especially for the conduct of Israel. Because they saw ahead that this people would endure into the limitless future, they felt obligated to lead it right. No wonder the Talmud tells us that *kol ha-nevi'im kullan lo nitnabbe'u ella li-yemot ha-mashiah,* "all the prophets, in all their addresses, intended primarily the days of the coming of the Messiah" (*Berakhot* 34b)! All their words were directed to Israel's and the world's great future. All prophecy, with its demands and its reprimands, its courage and its encouragement, its avowals and its arousals, its incessant reminders to Israel of the Covenant and its sacred terms, all this sublime sense of *responsibility* comes only because the prophets knew that this people, to use the phrase of C.P. Snow, "has the future in its bones." If it has an *aharit*, then we have an *aharayut*.

This theme is of perennial significance. The Jew who believes in the future of his synagogue will feel a sense of responsibility for it. He who knows that Torah has an *aharit* will not rest, but his *aharayut*—or responsibility awareness—will move him to support *yeshivot* and all other Torah institutions. The parent who really has faith that Judaism has a future will not forfeit his responsibility to bring up his children Jewishly. It is only the *mehusserei amanah*, those who lack faith in the *aharit*, who abandon *aharayut*.

It is appropriate this day to remember the greatest, most singular expression in all of history of a sense of responsibility based upon faith in the future. This week, Jews throughout the world celebrate the twentieth anniversary of the uprising of the Warsaw Ghetto. This was an uprising which, despite the impossible odds against the heroes, was born, not of despair, but of hope, not of an attitude that we have nothing to lose, but that we have everything to gain. That is why the most recurrent phrase on the lips of all the martyrs of European Jewry was *Ani ma'amin be-emunah shelemah be-bi'at ha-mashiah*, "I believe with perfect faith in the coming of the Messiah." We believe that *Keneset Yisra'el* has an *aharit*. These gallant Jews took responsibility for the redemption of the honor of all Israel on their bowed and lean shoulders, because in their stout hearts there flourished a faith in Israel's *aharit*, a confidence in its future. This was not the daring of desperadoes. It was a heroism born of hope—hope, despite the horrors; faith, despite the facts; trust, despite the terrors; *aharayut*, *because* of the faith and the belief in *aharit*. It is because of this uniquely Jewish heroic hope that, millennia ago, a non-Jew by the name of Balaam beheld the camp of Israel and exclaimed, *U-tehi ahariti kamohu*, "may my end, my *aharit*, be like unto Israel's" (Num. 23:10)! And generations hence, all the civilized non-Jewish world will join us, year after year, in everlasting tribute to the Jewish fighters of the Warsaw Ghetto, hailing the memory of the martyrs to *aharit*. It is because of their exemplary courage and unexcelled sense of *aharayut* that, despite persecutions and oppressions, hatred and envy, a glorious *aharit* will prevail for the people of Israel.

It is this understanding of the theme of responsibility and faith in the future that makes the whole episode of the Exodus from Egypt, which we read today, so much more meaningful. Is not the behavior of the Israelites most strange? They were, after all, the direct beneficiaries of the emancipation. And yet, at the first sign of crisis, they cried out to Moses, *Ha-mibbeli ein kevarim be-Mitzrayim lekahtanu la-mut ba-midbar*, "is there a shortage of graves in Egypt that you have taken us to die in the desert?" (Ex. 14:11). Why the sarcastic innuendo?

Even stranger is the response of Moses, *Al tira'u*, "do not be afraid"; *hityatzevu u-re'u et yeshu'at Hashem*, "stand by and look at the help that God will bring you"; *Hashem yillahem lakhem ve-atem taharishun*, "the Lord will fight for you and you will be silent" (Ex. 14:13). Is this an invitation to passivity, to quietism? Is this the way to forge a free people? Is this the kind of attitude which can inspire a Warsaw Uprising or a War for Israel's Independence?

I submit that the problem that runs like a golden thread through the entire history of those days was one of responsibility. And, like all responsibility, at bottom it was a question of faith; and in this case, specifically faith in the future. The Children of Israel were never over-anxious about leaving Egypt. They were pulled out by Moses, and finally pushed out by Pharaoh. Their gift of liberty was a gratis endowment by a gracious Divinity, and so they felt no responsibility for their own fate or destiny. As a matter of fact, they did not really believe they had any noble destiny or decent fate. They considered themselves not actors in a great drama, but puppets in a show doomed to an early closing, quickly to be forgotten. Their complaint about there not being enough graves in Egypt and dying in the desert revealed specifically their lack of faith in the future, and hence their lack of any responsibility for their condition. *Tov lanu avod et Mitzrayim mi-mutenu ba-midbar* (Ex. 14:12)—better to be slaves in Egypt without responsibilities than to die in the desert without a future. They saw no *aharit*, hence felt no *aharayut*.

And the answer Moses gave was not, as is ordinarily imagined, an invitation to further irresponsibility. Quite the contrary! He said to them, *al tira'u*! Stop being afraid! If you want God to help you, if you want *yeshu'at Hashem*, do not just sit around moping, do not just stand there with folded arms. Rather, *hityatzevu*—stand up straight, stand on your own two feet, assert the strength and the courage and the sense of responsibility God has given you. Then and only then *ve-re'u et yeshu'at Hashem*, will you see the help of the Lord!

That is why R. Judah the Prince in the Midrash (*Mekhilta Be-Shallah*, 2) interprets the key phrase in Moses' response not as declarative, "The Lord will fight for you, and you may keep quiet," but as interrogatory, as a question: *Hashem yillahem lakhem ve-attem taharishun*? Do you really expect that God will fight for you while you sit by as idle spectators, doing nothing? If you want to have an *aharit*, then you must learn to accept *aharayut*; and remember: it is worth taking upon yourselves *aharayut*, because our people shall have an *aha-rit*. With these words, Moses led his people across the Red Sea, which the Lord split only after the Israelites had entered until the waters reached their nostrils. Only then, *va-yosha Hashem ba-yom ha-hu et Yisra'el mi-yad Mitzrayim* (Ex. 14:30). On that day, the day Israel acted proudly and with dignity and self-sac-rifice and responsibility, did God deliver them from the Egyptians. And if *va-yir'u ha-am et Hashem*, if "they learned to fear God," to accept the *aharayut* of Torah and *mitzvot* that He placed upon them, it was only because *va-ya'aminu ba-Shem u-be-Mosheh avdo* (Ex. 14:31), only because of faith, only because of *emunah*. It was only because of their faith in God—for responsibility implies a religious personality; because they deserved others' faith in themselves—for responsibility implies reliability; and because of their faith in the future of our Jewish ideals, the Torah of Moses, the people of the Lord—for responsibility implies faith in the future.

With this kind of responsibility, based on these kinds of faith, we too can, like our ancestors at the shore of the Red Sea, be caught up in a great song, in a life of *shirah*, a perpetual, rising *Az Yashir* of felicity, of bliss, and of peace.

BE NOT OVERWISE:
THE HAGGADAH'S THIRD SON
IN A NEW LIGHT

ONE OF THE MOST famous and beloved parts of the Haggadah concerns the Four Sons, the four types of individuals to whom the Seder's story is directed. Yet an analysis of this Jewish typology, this casting of characters, leaves us slightly confused. The four do not seem to be organized properly; they are somewhat disarrayed. Hence, while one of them, the *rasha*, is a classification of piety and ethical behavior, the other three are categorized according to intellect: the Wise Son, or *hakham*, the Simple Son, or *tam*, and the exceedingly foolish one who cannot even ask, the *she-eino yodea lish'ol*. Furthermore, why are there two types of unintelligent sons, the *tam* and the unquestioning one? Since they are both unwise, does it not mean that essentially there are only three sons, not four?

R. Yitzhak Arama, the author of *Akedat Yitzhak*, solves our problem by offering a new definition of the *tam* and presenting the Haggadah's Third Son in a new light (*Sha'ar 38 [Parashat Bo]*, s.v. *ve-hinneh*). For while the Jerusalem Talmud (*Pesahaim 10:4*) clearly declares the *tam* to be one who is faulted intellectually, calling him a *tippesh*, or fool, the *Akedat Yitzhak* maintains that he is not typed intellectually but religiously and ethically. The Four Sons are divided into two classes, he tells us. Intellectually, the *hakham* and the *she-eino yodea lish'ol* are opposed to each other: the first is wise, the second foolish. Then, however, there is the criterion of conduct. Here the *rasha* and the *tam* are counterposed: the first is wicked, the second good. The *tam* is the opposite, not of the *hakham*, but of the *rasha*. That *tam* is a complimentary word is seen from the fact that Father Jacob was called *tam* (*Ya'akov ish tam*) and that the Talmud's term for an animal that is benevolent rather than dangerous and

---

Passover 5724 (1964)

murderous is *shor tam.* The *tam,* then, is not a Simple Son or a Foolish Son, but a Wholesome Son, the pious and good and obedient one.

Thus, while the *tam* is the opposite of the *rasha,* he is also different from the one who cannot ask. For while the latter is *childish,* the former is *child-like.* While the latter is infantile, the *tam* is simple—and what a noble virtue simplicity is! The Hafetz Hayyim and the Hazon Ish and others like them were brilliant scholars, but they exuded simplicity. And, to go from the sacred to the secular, Professor Albert Einstein was not exactly a simpleton; yet how marvelously simple he was in all his ways!

Yet the *tam* is also different from the *hakham.* Despite all the praise we heap on the Wise Son, he is not unblemished. For some strange reason, which may go deep into the unconscious of our race, there has always been an instinctive element of suspicion about the *hakham.* Witness the sarcasm with which we refer to someone as "*der hakham fun der Mah Nishtanah*"!

Wisdom can, after all, be distorted. One who is only wise is always in danger of having his wisdom degraded, of becoming merely smart; and the smart man often succeeds only in outsmarting himself! One of the brightest men in biblical history was Korah—and he was trapped in his own shrewdness when he decided to lead a rebellion against Moses. Do you recall Rashi's observation: *Korah she-pikkeah hayah mah ra'ah li-shetut zo,* "Korah was so bright, what led him into this foolishness?" (commentary to Num. 16:7). Perhaps even more to the point is the added comment of the Kotzker Rebbe: *mah ra'ah li-shetut zo—lihyot pikkeah!* "What led Korah into this foolishness of being shrewd!" A *hakham* can become merely a *pikkeah,* smart; and this is foolish, for then he may outsmart himself.

The *tam,* the Wholesome or Good Son, may very well be as wise as or wiser than the *hakham.* There is only this difference: unlike the Wise Son, he has no desire to display his learning before others by asking impressive questions. He is a man without pretenses. He does not wear his *lomdut,* or scholarship, on his sleeve. And herein, indeed, lies his superiority over the *hakham!*

Every Shabbat at *Minhah* time we recite the verse *adam u-behemah toshia, Hashem;* we implore the Almighty to help both man and animal. But the Talmud (*Hullin* 5b) has another explanation, maintaining that our prayer refers to one species, man only—the kind of men *she-hen arummin be-da'at u-mesimin atzman ki-behemot,* "who are brilliant in intellect and yet act as simple as animals." What marvelous restraint that requires—to possess an acute mind and an abundance of learning, and refrain from exhibiting them to your fellow men!

The crux of the matter is not the possession of intellect, but the relative values one assigns to intellect and goodness. Thus, when Yehudah Halevi pleaded for the superiority of historical experience and personal participation over abstract reasoning, he was stating the case for the *tam* over the *hakham*. Furthermore, the ultimate test of both humanity and Jewishness, and the essential guarantee of their survival, lies not in ideal thinking but in real living. The author of the *Or ha-Hayyim*, Rabbi Joseph Yabetz, who lived during the expulsion from Spain, writes (chap. 2) that when Jews were put to the test of choosing between kissing the cross or enduring exile and even death, the sophisticated philosophizers embraced Christianity under pressure, while the masses of men and women and children, usually unsophisticated and unlearned, but who loved God and lived Judaism simply, dared to risk death and exile. He thus confirms the importance of a total view of Jewish living.

In essence, the Hasidic movement represented the emergence of the *tam,* the reaffirmation of the virtue of simplicity, of inner goodness and kindness and piety, whether or not accompanied by intellectual power. It was *not* a revolt against scholarship or intellectualism or the study of Torah; certainly Judaism, more than any other religion, places a premium upon knowledge and intellectual attainment. It *was* a protest against the overemphasis of these virtues at the expense of the inner life of the Jew, his emotions, his heart, his soul, *temimut*—the act of being a *tam*. The wholeness of personality, the integration of all experience into a simple love of and submission to God, was considered as superior to the isolated quality of *hokhmah*.

One of the greatest of all Hasidic teachers, the grandson of the Ba'al Shem Tov, R. Nahman Bratzlaver, put it this way: *ahar kol ha-hokhmot,* "after all this wisdom," one ought to discard all his sophistication and turn to the Lord in order to serve Him *bi-temimut u-bi-peshitut gamur,* "in utter wholesomeness and simplicity," *beli shum hokhmot,* "without any awareness of being wise." The greatest *hokhmah* of all, he says, is *livli lihyot hakham kelal,* not to be wise at all, for in fact there is no completely wise person in the world, for man's wisdom is still as naught compared to that of the Creator. *Ve-ha-ikkar hu, ki* "*Rahamana libba ba'i*" (Rashi, *Sanhedrin,* 106b, s.v. *revuta*); above all, the Merciful God desires man's heart—not, assuredly, in the American Jew's sense of "a good heart" excusing one from living like a Jew, but in the sense of an emotional and spiritual deepening of the experience and practice of the *mitzvot*. Hasidism is unimpressed by intellectual acrobatics. It prefers heart over mind, faith over philosophy, dedication over dialectics, love over learning. The third son, the *tam,* is thus regarded as even greater than the first, the *hakham*.

Can such a point of view be accepted today? I believe so. Our society in general suffers from an overabundance of knowledge at the expense of man's wholeness, his self, his integrity. Science reigns supreme, and colleges are impossibly crowded. Knowledge is universally acknowledged as the key to a better job and more convenient society, as power in the world of international relations. All of this is unquestionably true. Yet when the mind and its achievements are so stressed that all else is excluded, that man is considered a machine whose loves and hates and fears and passions and aspirations are trivial, then we have outsmarted ourselves, Then man is in eclipse; he is like a freak child who has an abnormally large head and undersized body and heart.

In our Jewish world, we suffer from a horrendous "*amaratzes.*" There is no doubt that we are intellectually anemic. Yet in our attempts to correct the situation we seem to be heading in the way of the *hakham* rather than the *tam.* Look in any Jewish bookshop and you will be impressed by the many new books on so-called Jewish theology. These are books by a new breed of writers for whom Jewish religious thought is a kind of fascinating game—equivalent to the Israelis' hobby of archaeology. For all their sophisticated words about the commitment to Judaism, you will rarely find one of them who comes to shul or lays the *tefillin* or is careful about *kashrut.* I have met readers of this brand of wisdom in all parts of the world—Jews who weigh every word of Buber but have never read through the Bible, even in translation!

Look through the catalogues of adult education institutes of the synagogues and fraternal organizations of our country. You will find that usually the wrong questions are being asked. There is too much *hokhmah* and too little *temimut.* I, for one, would ban all courses which contain the word "and" such as "Judaism *and* Psychiatry," "Judaism *and* Civil Rights," "Judaism *and* Democracy." Instead I would substitute the simple *mah zot* of the *tam*—the "what is it all about" of Shabbat and *kashrut* and family purity and Jewish ethical law. The answers are intellectually more profound than the other kind—and religiously much more significant! Let us not forget that it was Solomon, the wisest of all men, the *hakham mi-kol ish,* who taught: *al tithakam yoter,* "do not be overwise" (Eccl. 7:16).

The *tam,* in his way of *temimut,* is not one whit less intellectually competent than the sophisticated *hakham.* Let us emphasize this again and again. The *tam,* as the full Jew, is fully cognizant of the value of wisdom, and himself possesses learning in abundance. But he insists upon integrating learning into the totality of a responsive, religious, reverent personality. To the inquiring college student the *tam* declares: be not overwise. Religion, especially Judaism, cannot be grasped only by reading and debating, although that is necessary for any intelligent person: it must, in the final analysis, be tasted and tried. Instead of being a *hakham* and seeking proof of God's existence, be a *tam*—and offer proof, in yourself and your daily conduct, of the existence of a *man*, a human being, a Jew with a heart and a soul.

We live in a world where, unfortunately, the *rasha* reigns supreme. It is not enough, in this kind of environment, to emphasize the *hakham* alone. For while it is true that wisdom is indispensable both to general life and Jewish living, it is equally true that beyond all the complexities and subtleties that tantalize man's mind and confound his understanding there stands the simple and sublime truth of the One God, Author of all. What we need is the *tam*, one who can include wisdom in his personality and transcend it, who can possess scholarship without displaying pretentiousness, who can develop his intellect and yet, in the moment he turns to his God, abandon his self-consciousness and serve his Maker with wonder and simplicity, with love and faith.

Afilu kullanu hakhamim, kullanu zekenim, kullanu nevonim, kullanu yode'im et ha-Torah, mitzvah aleinu le-sapper bi-yetzi'at mitzrayim (Haggadah). Even if we all be wise and experienced and understanding and learned in Torah, yet we must engage in the comparatively simple and naive recitation of the Haggadah story. For all of it is the answer to the *tam's* simple question. It is the teaching that *be-hozek yad hotzi'anu Hashem mi-Mitzrayim*, that "God took us out of Egypt with a strong hand" (Ex. 13:14); and that we today too must feel gripped by His presence, knowing that God is a good Father whose powerful hand grasps ours and leads us safely through the hills and vales of life, avoiding all the traps and snares, and into the *ge'ulah shelemah*, the complete and final redemption of all Israel; and through Israel all the world.

NOVELTY AND RENEWAL

OURS IS AN AGE characterized by an insatiable appetite for the new; we literally live by the news. We jump with glee at the latest headlines, the newest models, the most recent designs, and the most up-to-date fashions. We abhor the old and the tried, and we treat with studied contempt the set and the stable. We speak derisively of "the same old thing"—it is so uninteresting!—and we greet the word "brand new" with the eager delight of a five-year-old embracing a new toy. No wonder that our childish penchant for novelty is exploited by industry for profit, so that, no matter what the true facts are, the word of the manufacturer cometh forth from Detroit every year blaring "new, new, new!" No wonder that our cities are becoming progressively uglier, and as those immense boxes with the shiny tinsel-like facades go up, they displace old historic landmarks which are wrecked indiscriminately, thus destroying whatever charm and character our cities have. Even in religion we are given to the kind of spiritual adolescence which condemns all that is old to obsolescence, so that Jewish modernist deviationism, for instance, has substituted vacuous new ceremonies and empty and artificial rituals for the landmarks of *kashrut* and Shabbat and family purity which have been thoughtlessly destroyed.

We who are Orthodox Jews, however, take exception to this fawning worship of the new. We are committed to tradition, to a sense of reverence for the glories and the sancta of the past. We do not believe that truth and values and holiness should be treated in as fickle a manner as the style of hats.

Yet it would be wrong to let the matter rest there. For, after all, does not our tradition too speak lovingly of the new? The psalmist proclaims: *Shiru la-Shem shir hadash,* "sing ye to the Lord a new song" (Ps. 96:1, 98:1, 149:1). In the Haggadah we say, *ve-nomar lefanav shirah hadashah,* "and may we recite before Him a new song." And every day we pray: *Or hadash al Tziyyon ta'ir,* "may You cause a new light to shine on Zion." Obviously Judaism is not against the new as such. It does not subscribe to a reactionary conservatism. To be traditional

---

Parashat ha-Hodesh 5725 (1965)

does not mean to submit to a spiritual hardening of the arteries. New problems demand new solutions. Some of the new solutions we have arrived at in the past several years have proved to be among the most constructive in Jewish history: the State of Israel, the Hebrew day schools with their dual programs, the Yeshiva University, organized community *kashrut*, the United Jewish Appeal These are all new, and they are all to the good for the future of our people and our faith!

The problem, therefore, is how to accommodate the new within a religion which reveres the old. It is not a question of Halakhah and the degree of change, if any, which is permissible or advisable. Rather, the issue is: how does a religion which reverences tradition deal with the all-too-human desire for newness?

Three insights commend themselves to us. First, the yearning for newness ought be applied to one's own life and spirit rather than to the outside world. Thus, the prophet Ezekiel quite properly pleads for *lev hadash ve-ruah hadashah* (Ez. 36:26), "a new heart and a new spirit," not merely for new techniques and new objects. The Halakhah declares that *ger she-nitgayyer ke-katan she-nolad dami*, "a proselyte has the status of a newborn child" (*Yevamot* 22a). And, in the same spirit, Maimonides declares that the repentant person must experience the feeling of spiritual rebirth; religiously he is a new individual (*Mishneh Torah, Hilkhot Teshuvah* 7:7).

Perhaps it is best to distinguish between these two elements of newness by using two different terms: "novelty" and "renewal." Novelty is the misuse of the inclination for newness for things, for gadgets, for "kicks." Renewal comes about when we apply the desire for newness to man himself, to achieve new insights which result in the transformation of his soul and his spirit. Novelty is extrinsic, it is a question of packaging. Renewal is intrinsic, it is a matter of content. Novelty is the seeking of thrills; renewal is the thrill of seeking. The desire for novelty is what leads a young man from a Jewish home to interdate and ultimately to intermarry. The search for renewal leads a young person from a background of little or no Jewish education to seek out Torah and *mitzvot*. If we are concerned only with novelty, then we change Judaism in order to make it palatable for most Jews. But if we seek renewal, then we try to change Jews to make them more worthy of Judaism.

The great Hasidic teacher, the Gerer Rebbe, author of the *Sefat Emet*, discovered this teaching of renewal in the great law which we read this morning and from which derives the name of this special Sabbath. The Torah commands us: *Ha-hodesh ha-zeh lakhem*, "this month is unto you" (Ex. 12:2). We are instructed to base the Jewish calendar on the moon, which revolves about the earth once in twenty-nine or thirty days, rather than on the sun, as do other people. What is the significance of this sanctification of the month as a special mitzvah? The answer he offers is the doctrine of renewal. According to the Halakhah, thirty days of usage establishes the entity of habit. Thus, for instance, if we see a friend whom we have not seen or heard from for more than thirty days, we are required to pronounce the blessing of *She-heyehanu.* It is an occasion of joy. Not having seen him for thirty days, we have become habituated to his absence, and therefore the encounter with him is something new which should prompt a blessing. Similarly, there are many blessings we must make upon witnessing marvelous natural scenes or phenomena, or chancing upon spots where miracles were performed for our ancestors or ourselves. In all these cases, if we have been there, or seen them, within thirty days, we are not required to pronounce the blessing, whereas if we have not been there for more than thirty days, we are obligated to make the *berakhah.* In all these cases (and many more instances may be cited from Jewish law), whatever we have done or have not done persistently for thirty days becomes customary for us. That is why, the author of *Sefat Emet* tells us, we must sanctify the moon, and, as it were, renew ourselves before thirty days have passed and we have become encrusted in the routine and the regular. *Ha-hodesh ha-zeh lakhem* is a commandment to experience renewal, the relief from stultifying and crippling conventionality; it is the mitzvah to redeem ourselves from wearying and fossilizing habit and paralyzing patterns. It means that we must make a conscious effort to do things differently. We must challenge ourselves, for instance, not always to sing the same songs, to extend the same greetings, to pockmark our speech with the same clichés, to respond with the same stereotyped reactions, to affect the same study habits, the same grudges and affections, the same likes and dislikes. Above all, it means not always to adhere to the same level of observance of Judaism, but always to try to reach new heights and new enthusiasm. We must never be satisfied with *mitzvat anashim melummadah*, doing things in a mechanical, heartless, soulless way. Rather, we must experience renewal, with its consequent blessings of growth and development. How much different is this from the craze for novelty! This, indeed, is the creation of what the prophet commanded, the *lev hadash ve-ruah hadashah*, the new heart and the new spirit in accordance with the will of God, rather than the search for *elohim hadashim* (Judg. 5: 8), for new gods in accordance with the whim of man.

The second insight follows upon the first. Just as the *object* of our desire for newness must be renewal, directed inwards, *to* within ourselves, so the *source* for this renewal must come *from* within. It means that we have within ourselves the hidden talents and capacities to renew ourselves.

Perhaps it is best to explain the relation of newness to talents already available by referring to the prayer mentioned previously: *Or hadash al Tziyyon ta'ir*, "May You cause a new light to shine upon Zion." The Sephardic sages, following R. Sa'adyah Gaon, deleted this phrase from our prayerbook. It appears, you recall, in the first blessing before the *Shema*, in which we praise God for having created the luminaries, the heavenly bodies. This phrase, the Sephardic sages maintained, is out of place in this blessing, for the blessing speaks of the creation of the luminaries during the six days of creation, and this particular passage appeals for a new light in the end of days; past and future, old and new, are incommensurate and cannot be included in one blessing. Nevertheless, we follow the Ashkenazic decision, formulated by R. Asher, who justifies our practice on the basis of the well-known and beautiful *aggadah* that when God created the sun and the moon and the stars, they originally were endowed with much more light than they have at present; but God set aside a great part of the light that he originally created and is keeping it for the end of days, when this light will be used to illuminate the lives of the righteous who live in accordance with the will of God. This is the *or hadash al Tziyyon* for which we pray: the release of light, in the future, from that which was already created at the beginning but has remained unused. The prayer, then, is not out of place in this blessing: the new comes from the old, the future issues from the past. Hence, the word *hadash*, "new," may properly be used in the sense of the first expression of that which was long in existence but hitherto unexpressed.

So it is with man: the great act of renewal issues from within, it is the transformation of luminous potentiality into brilliant reality. It means that we have within ourselves, unconsciously, immense reservoirs of ability and courage and untapped potentials far beyond our fondest hopes and greatest dreams. When we apply our penchant for newness not to superficial novelty, but to the renewal of our personality and spirit and character; when we break out of our old habits and molds and endeavor to reach new spiritual heights, then we will have made use of these vast resources, of which we may never have been aware, for creative and constructive ends.

Finally, the concept of renewal means not only to discover within ourselves unused treasures of personality and character, but also it bids us to undertake a new orientation, whereby we look differently at the old. In the second paragraph of the *Shema*, we are promised the rewards of heaven if we will obey the commandments "which I command you this day" (Deut. 11:13). What does "this day" mean to those generations that were not present at Sinai? Rashi, based upon the *Sifrei* (*Re'eh*, 58), answers: *she-yihyu aleikhem hadashim ke-illu shematem bo ba-yom*, that whenever you perform the commandments of the Torah, they should appear to you as fresh and as new as if you had heard them from the mouth of God, as it were, on that very day! What is old so often bores us, it elicits no response from us; whereas what is new is always more urgent and more stimulating. We are charmed by the newly-wed and saddened by the newly-dead. Whatever is new is always more invigorating, and attention-capturing. But whether a thing is old and dilapidated and uninteresting, or new and fascinating and challenging, depends primarily on your point of view! It is so with all of life: whether it is our study of Torah or our daily prayers, our daily associations, from school friends to business associates to our marriage partners—every Jewish and human obligation must be such that *she-yihyu aleikhem hadashim ke-illu shematem bo ba-yom*, we must treat them as if they have just occurred, as if they are newly developed, newly emerging, newly re-born. Then we shall be able to experience the gift and the blessing of renewal. This indeed is what the *Pesikta Rabbati* (15) meant when, in commenting upon the key phrase of our *maftir* reading, *Ha-hodesh ha-zeh lakhem* (Ex. 12:2), it links the Hebrew word for "month" with the Hebrew word for "new" (*hadash*) and says: *haddeshu ma'aseikhem*, "renew your deeds": From within your own heart and soul, find the untapped resources with which to transform your own character and personality, and look with a new light upon all the ancient blessings and hoary gifts which God has given you.

This month of Nissan, which we initiate today, is one which we hope and pray will be for us a month of renewal, in which we will sing a new song of redemption not only for all the people of Israel but for each of us individually. Our dream and our prayer is not for novelty but for renewal, for the kind of inner transformation whereby all that is precious in the past will come to life in us once again.

Such is our prayer: *haddesh yameinu ke-kedem*, "make our days new—as of old!"

Amen.

CREATIVE REMNANTS; OR, LEAVEN FROM HEAVEN

IN THIS MORNING'S *HAFTARAH*, after the immortal messianic vision of universal peace, Isaiah gives us a specific prophecy concerning the redemption of Israel. He states: *Ve-hayah ba-yom ha-hu yosif Hashem shenit yado liknot et she'ar ammo*, "And it shall be on that day that the Lord shall set His hand again for a second time to recover the remnant of his people" (Is. 11:11).

What is this *she'ar ammo*, this "remnant" of the people of Israel, of whom the prophet speaks? The *Zohar* (*Be-shallah*) informs us that the *tzaddikim*, the righteous, are always referred to as *she'ar*, a remnant—a theme also found in the Talmud: *Leit alma mitkayyema ella al inun de-avdi garmayhu shirayim*, "the world exists only by virtue of those who regard themselves as *shirayim*."

What the *Zohar* and the Talmud mean when they say that the righteous consider themselves *shirayim* can be interpreted variously. Most commentators say that *shirayim* means "leftovers." In other words, the truly righteous person is one of profound humility who considers that he has very little value indeed, no more than insignificant leftovers.

I would suggest an alternative to this explanation of *shirayim*. *Shirayim* may mean not only "leftovers," but also "relics." Since they are *tzaddikim*, righteous people, they notice the painful disparity between themselves and the civilization in which they live, the disjunction between their most cherished ideals and the unredeemed society in which these ideals suffer sore neglect. They therefore consider themselves nothing more than relics of a glorious age long past, out of joint with their times.

But I prefer a third interpretation of this concept, namely, that the truly righteous consider themselves *shirayim* in the sense of being "creative remnants." For *shirayim* have yet another function, perhaps inappropriate to the festival of Passover, but possibly excusable on this eighth day of the holiday,

5726 (1966)

when we make the transition to weekday. Once, when yeast was not as readily available in packages as it is today, the baker would take the remnant of one batch of dough and use it to sour the new batter, to initiate new fermentation. I am informed by knowledgeable friends that this process is often used today too. So that *shirayim* are those remnants which create new and healthy loaves. The *tzaddikim*, therefore, symbolize a past that is great and glorious, but without the self-deprecation suggested by the term "leftovers," and without the pessimism implied by the word "relics." Rather, they regard themselves as the ferment that will re-create past glory in the present and transmit its creative leavening into the future. This idea of *shirayim* as creative ferment means that the righteous indeed are a leaven from Heaven, a *shirayim* without which, as the *Zohar* puts it, *let alma mitkayyema*, "the world cannot exist." According to this interpretation of *shirayim*, our Rabbis speak of the crumbs of character, not the character of crumbs.

These thoughts are relevant to the Yizkor which we shall soon recite and in which we remember the past. What indeed is the relation of ourselves to this past? I do not speak of those who have consciously broken with the past, who have no use for our ancient heritage. For them, Yizkor is nothing but an exercise in syrupy sentimentalism and is essentially meaningless. But what does it mean for us who cherish what has gone before us, who see ourselves as *shirayim* of that past—not merely of parents, but of all the Jewish tradition? Indeed, according to the Bible, one of the terms used to designate a close relative is *she'er basar*—*shirayim*, as it were, of the flesh. Each of us represents the latest link in an unbroken chain of human ancestry.

Some people may regard themselves as *shirayim* in the sense of mere leftovers. They consider their marvelous background, contrast to it their impoverished present, and find nothing connecting them to the past other than pious wishes and good intentions. Maybe an attitude of this sort is good for the character in that it impresses us with humility. But it is bad for the soul; despair has never proved spiritually constructive. All of us have a tendency, not always healthy, to over-romanticize the past and, in comparison, deprecate the present.

Others may consider themselves *shirayim* in the sense of relics. They feel that they themselves have not broken faith with the past. But what of their children? If I am but a relic, then it means that I have not severed the link between my parents and myself, but that I acknowledge a break in the chain of tradition in the link below me, that between myself and my children. In any case, the great and sacred chain of tradition is ruptured, and Jewishly speaking, I am only a fossil, an unproductive relic.

But it is not enough for right-thinking people to consider themselves relics—*shirayim*. Relics were meant to be admired, not emulated; fondled, not followed. Relics speak of a past tied to the present but offer no guidance and guarantee for the future.

Our relation to our parents and to the past must conform to the third interpretation. We who are loyal to Torah may today be numerically only a remnant, but we must remain a *creative* remnant. Ours is the duty of bringing the ferment of the past into the present in order to re-create a great future which will rival the past.

This Shabbat, we shall read the first chapter of the *Ethics of the Fathers*. At the beginning of this *perek*, we shall read the statement of Shimon ha-Tzaddik, Shimon the Righteous, who taught that the world is established on three foundations: *al ha-Torah, al ha-avodah, ve-al gemilut hasadim*, "on the study of Torah, on the service of God, and on good deeds" (*Avot* 1:2). Who was this Shimon the Tzaddik who gave such noble and lofty advice? The *mishnah* tells us: Shimon the Righteous *hayah mi-sheyarei Keneset ha-Gedolah*, he was one of the *shirayim* of the Great Assembly. Indeed, a *tzaddik* is always a sort of *shirayim*, a creative remnant. Shimon the *tzaddik* was this kind of creative remnant; he represented and embodied all that was holy and precious in the Men of the Great Assembly, and carried over their sacred teachings into his contemporary life, and then enshrined them in Jewish teaching as an imperishable and priceless possession of Jewish posterity. It is only a man who considers himself *shirayim* in the sense of a creative remnant who can bequeath this kind of teaching to all eternity.

No wonder that as part of the Yizkor prayer, we say, concerning our dear departed, *Tehei nafsho tzerurah bi-tzeror ha-hayyim*, "may his soul be bound up in the bond of everlasting life." If we are not going to be merely leftovers of our parent's culture, if we shall not be but relics of all that they taught and held precious, but if we are going to be creative remnants of the world they created, then indeed we shall be continuing their bond of life forever. Even as the *shirayim* represent the remnant which brings the ferment of the past into the new batter, and from there into the next one, so the teachings of the past remain deathless and this bond of life continues from generation to generation.

All that we have said needs to be said with special emphasis concerning Orthodox Judaism in the United States of our times. When Orthodox Jews first came to this country, they stifled in an atmosphere of diffidence, in a failure of self-confidence. They gazed across the shores to Europe and knew in their hearts that they were merely *shirayim*, in the sense of leftovers.

When authentic Judaism survived to a second generation, they were astonished! Then they considered themselves relics, museum pieces that had miraculously been preserved intact, leading a kind of life that was foreign to American soil but that had somehow survived against all expectations. Others, too, regarded Orthodox Jews in America as mere relics, whose days were numbered and whose very survival was a remarkable phenomenon not expected to be duplicated.

But then there arose a new generation, and modern Orthodox Judaism in America considers itself today neither a leftover nor a relic, but a new kind of *shirayim*—a creative remnant. Those who ignore the new world cannot hope to influence it. Those who have abandoned the Jewish heritage have no influence to bring to the world. It is we who refuse to close our eyes to new conditions and new problems and new currents, and yet are determined to remain utterly loyal to the Jewish tradition and the greatness of the past without compromise—it is we who have the God-given opportunity to become the *shirayim*, the creative remnant that will ferment the batter of the present with the blessing of the past in order to create a better future.

How will this be done? Only through Torah—through nothing else. At the end of the *Ne'ilah* prayer on the holiest day of the year, we cry out, in words first written by the great Rabbi Rabbenu Gershom: *Ein shiyyur rak ha-Torah ha-zot*, "we have nothing left, no *shirayim*, save this Torah." It is Torah alone which can transform the new generation and bring it back to its Jewish greatness. When we have that, we have everything. Toward the end of Yom Kippur, we proclaim that Torah is a creative remnant which will be sufficient for the whole year to come.

But how shall we go about introducing the old leaven of our holy Torah into the new batter of this generation? The answer is that Providence has provided us with an historic instrumentality: Yeshiva University. Yeshiva is the major institution of American Orthodox Judaism, dedicated to the proposition that Judaism is neither antiquated nor hopelessly alien to this world. Wherever you will go in this country, from large city to small town, you will find the graduates of Yeshiva in pulpits and in schools, in communal agencies and in positions of lay leadership. Were it not for Yeshiva University, Judaism in this country would not only lack creativity, but it would not even be survived by a remnant.

It is for this reason that leaders and members of The Jewish Center have always been active on behalf of Yeshiva University. It is for this reason that we long ago instituted the annual appeal for Yeshiva on the eighth day of Passover. I know and hope and trust that it will not be necessary to belabor the point for you. I might mention, however, that it is absolutely and vitally necessary that you increase your pledge. Few people truly appreciate the tremendous financial pressure on Yeshiva University. Costs rise for institutions as much as, and even more than, they do for housewives and businessmen.

We appeal to you to help bring about the redemptive vision of Isaiah: *Yosif Hashem shenit yado.* Even as God, according to the prophecy of Isaiah, will raise His hand a second time again, so must we give again, this year as every year, but more so and with less hesitation. Above all—*yosif*, we must add, we must increase in accordance with the increasing needs. If we want our role to be that of *shirayim* in the sense of a creative remnant, then our contribution to Yeshiva University must not be of the nature of *shirayim* as leftovers. For the purpose of our endeavors is *liknot et she'ar ammo*, to support and strengthen and recover that part of our people which is truly *she'ar*, the *shirayim*, the creative remnant, through which and with which we shall make Torah thrive and see Israel redeemed in our lifetime.

BITTER-SWEET

THE *MAROR THAT WE* eat at the Seder is more than just a vegetable recalling the hard times inflicted upon our remote ancestors in ancient Egypt. It is the very symbol of human anguish through all the ages, and what we do with it is an expression of the Jewish philosophy of suffering as it issues out of the historical experience of the Jewish people.

Consider how astounding is our attitude toward this piece of food and how it speaks volumes to us. We do not weep when we eat it. We take this *maror*, this morsel of misery, and we recite a *berakhah* (blessing) over it, as if to say, "Thank you God for the miserable memory!" We then take this bitter herb and dip it into the *haroset*, the sweet paste of wine and nuts and fruit. Life, we say in effect, is neither all bitter nor all sweet. With rare exceptions, it is bitter-sweet, and we ought not to bemoan our fate but to bless God for it. Ever since Adam and Eve ate of the Tree of Knowledge of Good and Evil, our kabbalists teach us, good and evil have been co-mingled, and life offers us neither pure, unadulterated goodness nor pure, unredeemable wickedness. The pessimist deplores the bitter and the bad that corrupts the sweet and the good. The optimist is delighted that the sharp edge of bitterness is softened with sweetness, that there is some good everywhere.

That is why when the Jew, the eternal optimist, dips his *maror* into the *haroset* he makes a *berakhah*, a blessing. That is why, when we celebrate the *zeman herutenu*, the time of our liberation, the Jew at this time *reclines* while he eats. He plays the role of a nobleman even while the gentile majority persecutes and oppresses and embitters him. Let others laugh at the comic Jew who tells himself he is a *melekh* while he is being tormented. We know it is true. Life is bitter, but we have dipped it into the sweetness of *haroset*.

Hence, as we come to Pesah this year and every year, we relearn our lesson. Many of us enter the holiday burdened with a secret sigh, with the heart heavy, the mind distracted, and the soul sorely troubled. Yet, as Jews, we shall look for

---

Passover 5727 (1967)

the sweet, we shall perform the *tibbul maror be-haroset* and experience by sheer will the *simhat yom tov*, the happiness of the holiday.

But the message of *maror* is more than just the awareness of the bitter-sweet taste of life, more than just the idea that every black cloud has a silver lining. What *maror* means to tell us is that misery is not meaningless, that pain is not pointless punishment, that human anguish has larger dimensions, that the bitter leads to the sweet. In fact, without the foretaste of *maror*, *haroset* loses its value. There can be no sweet without bitter, no light without darkness before it, no joy without prior sadness. There can be no wealth without poverty, no faith without doubt, no freedom without slavery, no redemption without exile.

The author of the Haggadah reminds us, *Va-etten le-Esav et Har Se'ir la-reshet oto, ve-Ya'akov u-vanav yaredu Mitzrayim*, "God gave to Esau the Mount of Se'ir to inherit, but Jacob and his sons went down to Egypt." Why is this particular bit of historical information important to us? It tells us that Esau had no experience in exile, and so he later had no right to Canaan, the Holy Land. But Jacob and his children suffered the yoke of Egypt, and so they were rewarded with redemption. Their very exile entitled them to the greatest joy known to any nation in history.

R. Samson Raphael Hirsch saw this idea in a powerful, subtle, and sophisticated interpretation of the famous cry of King David in the Psalms, *Keli, Keli, lammah azavtani?* (Ps. 22:2). We usually translate this as "My God, my God, why hast Thou forsaken me?" But, asks R. Hirsch, should not so pious and saintly a Jew as King David accept his lot with love and resignation even to the point of keeping his silence if God forsakes him? He answers that King David was not asking "*why* hast Thou forsaken me," because then the Hebrew would be *maddua*; the word *lammah* means not just "why," but "wherefore." *Lammah*, for what reason, for what purpose, "*wherefore* hast Thou forsaken me?" I do not question Your deeds insofar as Your justice is concerned, but what do You want me to *do* with all of this agony? Suffering must have meaning. My question is therefore: *Keli, Keli*, my God, my God—what meaning and purpose does this particular anguish have for me? What am I expected to accomplish with it?

Hasidim tell a charming story. In the very first generation of the movement, there was a great saint known as Der Shpoler Zeide, the Shpoler Grandfather. It happened that at the Seder table, on the first night of Passover, he called upon his youngster to recite the Order of the Service, the *kaddesh u-rehatz*. In those days—and even in our days, as I remember it from my elementary yeshiva days—the youngster would not just recite the list of ten items, but would explain each one in Yiddish. He would say: *Kaddesh—az der tate kumt aheim fun shul, makht er kiddush balt, kedei die kinder zolen nisht shlafen un zei zolen fregin mah nishtannah,* "*Kaddesh* means that when Father comes home from the synagogue on Passover eve, he must make the *Kiddush* quickly so that the children not fall asleep and that they be able to ask the *Mah Nishtannah.*" Now, when the Shpoler Zeide invited his son to recite this formula, he did not say the entire thing. Instead, he merely said: "*Kaddesh*—when the father comes home from the synagogue, let him make the *Kiddush* immediately." He did not recite the rest, and the father was upset that his son had not been taught the entire explanation of *Kaddesh.*

The next day, at the table after the morning services of the first day of Pesah, the child's teacher was present, and he said that he did not think that the rest of the recitation was important. At this, the Shpoler Zeide rebuked him and said: You have no idea of the great meaning in this simple little Yiddish explanation! What does it mean? It refers not only to the father of the house—it refers to the Father in Heaven. When God, our Father in Heaven, leaves the synagogue on Passover eve and He sees His Jews so overcome with fervor and piety, He performs the *Kiddush*—not the recitation of the *Kiddush*, but *kiddushin*, marriage. He remarries, re-betroths the people of Israel. He recites once again the vow of His love for us: *Ve-erastikh li be-tzeddek u-be-mishpat be-hesed u-be-rahamim* (Hos. 2:21). And why does He do that? Here the metaphor switches, and Israel is no longer the bride, but the child, the *yeled sha'ashu'im*, the delightful child of the Almighty Father. God turns to us "so that the children not fall asleep" in their exile (*ani yeshenah—be-galut*; see *Midrash Zuta, Shir ha-Shirim* [Buber], 5), so that we do not become moribund and comatose and fall into an everlasting sleep. God seeks us out lest we become "vanishing Jews," lest we disappear in the course of persecution and our own forgetfulness. God wants us, His children, to rise up and to say to Him, *Mah nishtannah ha-laylah ha-zeh mi-kol ha-leilot*, "Why is this night so different from other nights?" Why is this exile so much colder and blacker and longer and more heart-rending and more agonizing than any other exile ever was before? *Mah nishtannah ha-laylah ha-zeh* does not mean merely "*Why* is it different," but "*wherefore* is this night so different," what purpose is served by the exile that is so long and dark, the night that is so endless, the blackness that is so bitter and so frightening? *Kedei die kinder zolen fregen mah nishtannah*—God wants us not to question Him, but to inquire after the purpose of our suffering so that we might use it creatively and nobly.

What a heroic attitude! When we ask the *Mah Nishtannah* in this manner, therefore, we are not like the defiant survivor of a storm shaking his fist angrily but vainly at the howling rains, but we are like one who, having survived the winds, abandons the dramatics of raging self-pity and sets about quietly but resolutely rebuilding his home, making it stronger than ever, and learning to appreciate what gifts God has given him. When we do that, we temper the bitter with the sweet, the *maror* with the *haroset*, and we can survive to enjoy again the bliss of God's goodness. Then we can ultimately learn even to make a *berakhah* over *maror*.

Indeed, the beauty of the Seder lies not only in its teaching of the bitter-sweet quality of life and the meaningfulness of suffering, but the further fact that evil *itself* is a source from which the good can be fashioned! Out of the very fiber of anguish we can weave the fabric of joy. It is interesting that the *korban pesah*, the sacrificial Passover lamb, had to be a *seh*, a lamb—the very animal which was the idol of the ancient Egyptians. Would it not have been more appropriate had we been commanded to offer up a goat or a deer for the paschal sacrifice? Similarly, matzah must be made from the same *hameshet minim*, the same five species that when fermented become *hametz* (*Pesahim* 35a). But why take the chance of having *hametz* contaminate our matzah? Why not make matzah out of potatoes or eggs?

The answer is that we learn that from the *avodah zarah* itself we are going to fashion the *korban la-shem*. From the very substance that can become *hametz*, we are going to make matzah; the very stuff of evil will become the means to achieve the good and the holy.

The great Ba'al Shem Tov put it this way: *Ha-ra merkavah le-tov*, "evil is a chariot which will carry us to the good." Out of evil itself we shall fashion the good life.

Does this not happen often? A man loses a loved one—a spouse, a child, or a parent—and he perpetuates the memory of his loved one by building living monuments of education or healing or Torah. From the evil has come the good.

A child is sick, and as a result his parents draw closer to each other and to him than ever before. From the bitterness comes the sweet.

A family loses its fortune and they suddenly must learn, and do learn, to subsist on inner resources of maturity and wisdom that they never knew they possessed. From the *hametz* comes the matzah.

The only daughter of a cruel, tyrannical Communist dictator who had tried to silence the very mention of God across the length and breadth of the entire globe suddenly decides that she prefers freedom and self-expression, and turns to God, whose name was not permitted to be spoken in her father's house or her father's land. It is the ultimate irony of history's inexorable revenge: out of the *avodah zarah* of Communist Russia, the Pharaoh of modern times, there comes forth renewed faith, the *korban pesah* of the contemporary age.

Let us therefore learn that life is bitter-sweet, that it is worth making a blessing over it in gratitude for the sweet, that *maror* itself has meaning and purpose, and that a creative and noble end can be fashioned out of the very stuff of suffering. Such is our destiny in this world. It is a lot that *benei horin*, free men, must accept heroically.

Let me conclude with the unfinished tale of the Shpoler Zeide. After the Rebbe expounded this interpretation of *Kaddesh* and *Mah Nishtannah*, all who heard him—and the rabbi himself—began to weep disconsolately. The floodgates had opened the dam of Jewish woe and travail, and the pent-up anguish of years gushed forth. But then the rabbi held up his hand and bade his family and friends cease their weeping. "It is true," he said, "that the night is cold, long, and dark, and we do not know why or for what reason or purpose. But when children are frightened by the dark, they sing and dance to drive the darkness away." And so the Zeide and his Hasidim locked hands, and they sang and they danced and they drove the darkness away.

A people that dips *maror* into *haroset* and makes a *berakhah* over it is never defeated by fate or by foe. A folk that can find the mellow in a morsel of misery can drive away the darkness with its own light, the outer sorrow with the inner joy.

May God grant that we learn for ourselves this bitter-sweet lesson, rising *me-avdut le-herut, mi-yagon le-simhah, u-me-evel le-yom tov, u-me-afelah le-or gadol, u-mi-shibud li-ge'ulah*, "from slavery to freedom, from woe to joy, from mourning to festivity, from darkness to light, from exile to redemption."

Ve-nomar le-fanav shirah hadashah, "let us sing before Him a new song, *Halleluyah*."

A Past Worth Perpetuating

AT THE END OF Passover, when we celebrate the redemption of the past, the Exodus from Egypt, our *haftarah* bids us turn to the future. It speaks of the coming of the Messiah, the redemption that we still await.

This connection between past and future is even more pronounced on the eighth day of Passover, when we recite the Yizkor. It is not only the remote past that we tie in with the distant future, but the immediate past that we call upon in order to summon us to greater activity and greater dedication for the days to come. And the more we investigate this relationship, the more profound and germane does it become.

The Talmud (*Sanhedrin* 98b) records a strange passage. What, asks the Talmud, will be the name of the Messiah? The answers are obscure, even startling. The school of R. Shila answered: The name of the Messiah will be *Shiloh*. The school of R. Yannai maintained that the name of the Messiah would be *Yinon*. The school of R. Hanina held that *Haninah shemo*, his name would be Hanina. Each school gave the name of its own rabbi to the Messiah!

What the Talmud is trying to tell us is that, on the one hand, the Messiah will not be a strange, unassociated, unrelated soul dropping right out of Heaven. His character will be a composite of all the finest traits of the teachers of old. And on the other hand, there is a little bit of the Messiah in everyone who has ever made a creative effort in his life. Everyone has something invaluable in his life, something unutterably precious, to contribute to the redemptive process.

It is hard for us to discern what it is that we ourselves can give to the future, to the Messiah. But those after us, contemplating us in retrospect with a sense of perspective and proportion, will be able to tell what in our lives is worth perpetuating, what we can offer to the Messiah, to the redemption.

So each school and each student examined the role of the teacher and found something unique—for a name is a symbol of uniqueness, of individuality—to the whole messianic development.

5730 (1970)

Each of us too, looking at his own origins, must find something in the past that is worth perpetuating. The naming of the Messiah is, fundamentally, an expression of the belief that there is something in the past that is worth perpetuating into a brilliant and redeeming future.

Now, this should not be taken as just another pulpit platitude. This is not the truism that it may appear to be. Were it so, the Bible would not have to remind us: *Zekhor yemot olam, binu shenot dor va-dor*, "remember the days of old, understand the years of every generation" (Deut. 32:7). Were it so, wise men and thinkers throughout the ages would not have had to remind us, as did George Santayana most recently, that those who choose to forget history are doomed to relive it.

In revolutionary periods, when all men seem to plunge back into a collective adolescence, they react against the past with a special revulsion, attempting to uproot it and destroy it and wipe out all its traces. So, for instance, is it true of the Communist revolutions of Marx and Lenin, and so is it true of today's radicals and revolutionaries, who believe that in order to build a decent society, it is necessary to eradicate everything of the past.

So, to an extent, even Zionism during its revolutionary period evinced this rejection of the past. That is why no less a personality than Ben-Gurion can state, with amazing lack of insight, that the history of the Jews ought to be reduced by two thousand years—the two thousand years that we dwelled outside of the Land of Israel.

But this is not a Jewish attitude. We Jews too know of revolution. Our vision of the messianic future is one which will result from a radical revolution. And our very birth took place in revolution. The founder of our faith, Abraham, was an iconoclast, a man who smashed the idols of the "establishment," who questioned its most fundamental premises, who revolted against his own father, who was a troublemaker of the most dangerous sort. Yet, despite the fact that he marks an abrupt break from his heathen past, we do not obliterate that past. Even on the Seder night we remember that *Terah avi Avraham*, "Terah was the father of Abraham." And one need but study the Ramban to see the reverence with which the personality of Terah—that purveyor of idolatry, that salesman of icons—is treated by the Sages of Israel. Even in *his* past they found something worth perpetuating!

So if we today are in the process of the long labor pains of what we hope and pray will be the messianic age, we must look for his names, his features, his qualities and attributes, in the lives of our teachers, parents, guides, grandparents. From the finest of the past we shall lead on to the brightest future.

Yizkor, then, is a time of such contemplation of the past for purposes of perpetuation. We shall do for our loved ones what the disciples of Rabbis Shila, Yannai, and Hanina did for their teachers. We shall evaluate silently and lovingly, remembering those features which are worthy of remembering, which are enlightening and edifying and deserve to be transmitted to the future.

And yet, there will be a note of regret in such thoughts—not sadness at the gap and the void and the emptiness in our lives which still exist over the span of the years that separate us from our loved ones, but also of our own guilt. Our nostalgia will be accompanied by the feeling that perhaps, somewhere along the line, we went astray.

Permit me to explain by means of something that my revered teacher, Rabbi Joseph B. Soloveitchik, said in a recent address.

Before God revealed to Moses his Thirteen Attributes of Grace, the revelation of His personality, of love and compassion and kindness and patience, He said to Moses something which has become, through the ages, the stuff of mystic contemplation: *Ve-ra'ita et ahorai, u-panai lo yera'u,* "You shall see My back, but My face shall not be seen" (Ex. 33:23).

What does this mean? R. Soloveitchik answers as follows: During the time of grace, when we are surrounded by love and warmth, when life is good and conditions are happy—at that time, *u-panai lo yera'u,* we don't see God's "face," we do not "face up" to our blessings, appreciate them and value them. Only later, after God's presence has passed, after the *middot ha-rahamim* are gone, only then, *va-ra'ita et ahorai,* do we see God's "back," do we begin to understand how lucky we were—and are no more; how precious our experience was—but it is now gone. Now, perhaps too late, we learn to cherish and admire what we should have acknowledged in the first place. We can only see our good fortune as one looks longingly after a train that has passed by and is already receding into the distant horizon. Ah, if only we had been able to look our good fortune, our Attributes of Mercy, in the "face," when they were present, even as we ponder their "back" as they leave us!

What young person appreciates his own youth? Despite our Freudian wisdom about the problems of youth, despite all the alienation and wretchedness of youth that we hear about today, who does not appreciate it now that it is past; who would not want it again? Of course, young people today do not appreciate it. Neither did we when we were young. It is only in retrospect, after it is gone, that it will be cherished and longed for. *Ve-ra'ita et ahorai.*

What healthy person appreciates his limbs—until, Heaven forbid, they are threatened with paralysis or amputation? What individual is thankful for his heart until it starts to give him trouble? Who knows of his lungs until his breathing becomes difficult? *U-panai lo yera'u.*

Hence, as we think of our beloved relatives, as we ponder a past worth perpetuating, even as the students gave their rabbis' names to the Messiah, we are also a bit sad: we are regretful, and we blame ourselves, for waiting until we can only see the "back" of relationships before appreciating them, for failing to value them while we were face to face with them. If only we had shown more love, more tenderness, more gratefulness to them while they were alive, to their very faces, and not only behind their backs when they are irrevocably gone! None of us is free of that feeling of pathos, of guilt. We are all of us guilty of that human failing: of waiting until the revelation of love is past and only then looking after it longingly. We are guilty of failing to appreciate it when it was with us.

So let us determine this day of Yizkor and of the reading of Isaiah's message of the Messiah that we shall try to rectify that failing when it comes to the people who are with us now; that we will not only look to the past for qualities to offer to the Messiah, and to the future, but we shall live in the present as well. From our feeling of regret as to how we treated the loved ones of the past, let us learn how to act toward our loved ones of the present. Those of us who are fortunate enough to have parents or even grandparents, men who have wives, and women who have husbands, those of us who have children or teachers or guides or friends—let us begin with a morbid thought and end with a joyous one. Let us remember that life does not last forever, that those we have with us now will not remain with us indefinitely. We have them now, but only for a limited time, so let us cherish them now. They are with us now—let us give them the maximum of joy and friendship now.

I do not mean that we must romantically exaggerate their virtues. I suggest, rather, a realistic appreciation of their good points. Even more, I mean simply to enjoy their presence; and more than that, to determine to let them know our appreciation. Now is the time to share warmth and affection and appreciation and cherishing—now, when their faces are seen, not later after their backs have irrevocably been turned to us.

Such an attitude, I dare say, will make of us the kind of people and the kind of society that will pave the way for a Messiah, and make us worthy of his appearance.

Then we shall be able to say with Isaiah in today's *haftarah*: *Ve-amar ba-yom ha-hu odekha Hashem,* "He shall say on that day, Thank you, O Lord" (Is. 12:1).

Passover and Human Diversity

One of the most popular passages of the Haggadah is that of the Four Sons. I have often wondered why I have never met any of these four "in the flesh," as it were. Is there anyone so wicked, so evil, that he has no redeeming feature whatsoever—even that of making the trains run on time? Is there a Wise Son who never committed a *faux pas*, who never uttered a foolish statement? Have we ever met a Pious Son who never sinned—in defiance of the verse in Kohelet (7:20) that "there is no man upon earth who [always] does good and never sins"? And the Son who does not know enough to ask—has he no modicum of intelligence at all?

After a few youthful years of having my curiosity seasonally piqued by this question, it occurred to me that these are archetypes, not four real, living, distinct individuals; indeed, it is extremely rare, even impossible, to find pure examples of these types in real life. Almost all people are composites of two or three or four—in fact, hundreds—of types of "sons," and in different proportions. Were the Four Sons meant to represent real people, the tradition would most likely have identified a representation for each of them. Yet this is not the case, except for Haggadah artists throughout the ages, whose fertile imaginations led them to identify and illuminate individual real people, as Wise or Wicked, Simple or Who Does Not Know Enough to Ask, in their illustrations for the Haggadah.

In that case, the passage on The Four Sons reflects Judaism's acceptance of the human propensity for internal contradictions, inconsistency, ambivalence, and paradox. This acknowledgment is more than a reluctant reconciliation with painful fact; it is, as well, a desideratum, a welcome aspect of human character. Furthermore, the selection of the Four Sons is not the only part of the Seder that reveals an understanding of ambivalence and paradox; another significant example is the prevalence of the matzah, which is considered both a sign of freedom and a sign of servitude.

5766 (2006)

The complexity of human personality was clearly recognized by the Torah and the Sages throughout history. Thus, according to *Avot de-Rebbe Natan* (1:37), man is like the beasts in three ways and like the angels in three other ways. He is partly an animal and partly a Divine Image. The moral drama of life is usually driven by the endless battle between a man's sense of righteousness and his concupiscence—his *yetzer ha-tov* and his *yetzer ha-ra*.

The Jerusalem Talmud records the law, which we follow to this day, that whoever sees large numbers of people massed together should recite the blessing "Blessed be the One who is Wise over all secrets," for just as people's faces differ one from the other, so do their characters and opinions differ one from the other (*Yerushalmi Berakhot* 9:1). The "secret" is how people of such diverse qualities and outlooks can yet coexist as part of the same multitude.

In a sense, this individual differentness is surprising, given the doctrine of the creation of man in the Image of God. If we are all created in the Divine Image, should we not all be the same? The answer is that the unity of God is not merely a matter of number but also of utter uniqueness, and it is this quality that constitutes the essence of the Divine Image that we are bidden to reflect. Hence, we are each unique despite, or perhaps because, we are created in His Image. The Talmud explains (*Sanhedrin* 38a) that the variation in humanity is a manifestation of God's glory through His ability to create many varied images from one mold. Our differentness, then, is our glory, for it is the reflection of our creation in the Divine Image that is the source of the sacredness of our individuality.

Man's rich complexity, a composite that accounts for each human as distinct and different from every other human being, thus has the potential for his noblest achievements—as well as his most disgraceful failures.

Indeed, there are times when this inconsistency is startling in the boldness of its internal clash, and the psychological and spiritual consequences of such contradictions do not warrant any benevolent interpretation or apology. As the Rabbis taught, a sin "extinguishes" a mitzvah (*Sotah* 21a). Despicable conduct is not excusable by reason of occasional or even frequent acts of goodness.

A dramatic example of the danger of such inner dissonance is that of King Solomon. The biblical Song of Songs, *Shir ha-Shirim*, contains one verse (3:11) that disturbed the Rabbis. The verse reads: "Go forth, O daughters of Zion, and gaze upon King Solomon, even upon the crown with which his mother crowned him on the day of his wedding and of the gladness of his heart."

What is it that so intrigued the Sages? "We reviewed all of Scripture and could find no reference to a crown that Batsheva made for Solomon," declares Rav Hanina bar Yitzhak (*Shir ha-Shirim Rabbah,* 3). But if Scripture provides no details, the eminent commentator Rabbi Moshe Alshikh (ad loc.) points to the Oral Law, both Talmud (*Sanhedrin* 70b) and Midrash (*Be-midbar Rabbah* 10), which offers them in abundance. According to these sources, "the day of his marriage" refers to the day King Solomon married the pagan daughter of the Egyptian Pharaoh. "The day of the gladness of his heart" refers to the day he dedicated the Holy Temple in Jerusalem.

What a remarkable—and disturbing—coincidence! The king violates the cardinal prohibition against intermarriage on the very same day that he presides over the culmination of the historic dedication of the *Beit ha-Mikdash*! To compound matters, the celebration of the wedding far exceeded that of the Temple's dedication, and Solomon overslept while all the people were awaiting him for the Temple service. His mother, upset by the sudden and uncharacteristic transgression by her royal son, punished him and bitterly reproached him with searing words of censure. Here the Alshikh adds that this very harsh rebuke was the "crown" she made for her son! "The day of painful and enforced awareness of his striking inconsistency was the gift his mother bestowed upon him."

While this account contains much aggadic hyperbole, the lesson is clear: If such glaring and calamitous disjunctiveness and inconstancy of character can afflict the biblical personality hailed as the "wisest of all men" (see I Kings 5:11), how much more so the rest of the human race!

The catastrophic inconsistency ascribed to King Solomon is shocking because of the dominating and charismatic personality of Solomon as depicted in the Tanakh. The Talmud (*Sukkah* 52a) avers that the greater the man, the greater his *yetzer ha-ra*—his libidinous capacity and his powerful negative urges. Unfortunately, the type is all too common, a universal affliction, and is not at all restricted to eminences. Consider, for instance, the man who is generous, who helps and is courteous to friends, but is humiliating and abusive to his wife and children. Or the one who prays with great intensity, but has no compunctions about cheating his employer or deceiving his customers. Or the person who eats kosher, but does not act, talk or sleep kosher. Regretfully, there is no dearth of illustrations of similar outrageous dissonance of character. In many such cases, the culprit possesses elements of each of the Four Sons, perhaps with the *Rasha*, or Wicked Son, predominating. We are all prone to inconsistency; it is universal and usually benevolent, but no one should quietly accept the kind of clash of attributes that bespeaks a horrendous violation of one's avowed principles. Magnanimity to the synagogue building fund does not excuse intermarriage, as Solomon's mother taught him. Each act stands on its own, and the owner of the fragmented character must wrestle with his spiritually split personality.

King Solomon wore many great crowns—those of royalty, wisdom, and power—but the most meaningful of all was the crown his mother gave him: her refusal to accept his weakness as incorrigible, his inconsistencies as unsolvable, and his self-indulgences as excusable simply because he built the magnificent and Holy Temple in Jerusalem. It was the crown of rebuke by a wise mother to a beloved child whose superior wisdom failed him at the most critical time of his life. Batsheva taught us all that in raising children—even adult children!—we must be honest and unsparing in our criticism. Such reproach is what parents owe their children—provided, of course, that while we are angry we must not be hostile, harsh but not mean, hurting but not hating.

Equally if not more important is the mirror that she urges us to hold up before our own eyes so that we might learn for ourselves when inconstancy, although ubiquitous, is intolerable. Or, as the author of the Haggadah implies, each of us has a bit of the *rasha* within himself or herself, but we must never let our own *rish'ut* get the best of us.

Yom ha-Shoah

Death Has No Future:
The Holocaust and
Jewish Education

ARBA'IM SHANAH AKUT BE-DOR. For forty years our generation struggled to understand the mystery of those fatal years of the Holocaust. Neither our speech nor our silence helped us to uncover the secrets of God or of man. Perhaps we shall have to wait another forty or another four hundred years, or perhaps we shall never be wise enough even to know how to react.

But events march on, and history does not permit us the luxury of endless contemplation. Hence, some reactions began to emerge fairly quickly. The first and enormously significant response to the Holocaust was the political one: the founding of the State of Israel. Powerlessness would never again be considered a Jewish virtue. The desperate struggles of the heroic Jewish fighters in Warsaw and elsewhere were metamorphosed into the pride of statehood and the military confidence of the Israeli Defense Forces. Today, the future of the Jewish people is unthinkable without the State of Israel.

Another response has been a holy, compulsive drive to record and testify. We do not want to forget, and we do not want the world to forget. We have resolved to keep the memory of our *Kedoshim* alive by demonstrations and by meetings such as this. And many of us have undertaken projects of sculpture and art and museums and exhibits to perpetuate the memory of the Six Million. As the years slip by and memory begins to fade, we desperately want to prevent their anguish and blood and cry from being swallowed up by the misty, gaping hole of eternal silence, banished from the annals of man by the Angel of Forgetfulness.

The efforts at remembering and reminding must continue. As long as so-called "revisionist historians" deny that the Holocaust occurred; as long as Babi

---

5745 (1985)

Yar and Buchenwald behind the Iron Curtain contain almost no reference to Jews; as long as it is even conceivable that an American administration which preaches more compassion for the victim than for the criminal on the domestic front, can see nothing wrong in its president honoring dead Waffen-SS while pointedly ignoring their Jewish victims in Dachau—there will be a need for Jews to remember and remind, even if we know in our hearts that the world will not long remember or want to be reminded. And let it be said here clearly and unequivocally: A courtesy call at a conveniently located concentration camp cannot compensate for the callous, obscene scandal of honoring dead Nazi killers. Surely the President's aides can arrange a visit by him to the tomb of Konrad Adenauer or some of the decent German anti-Nazis who perished at Hitler's hands for their principles.

Yet—and yet . . . these responses alone are inadequate. The problem of the Jewish people today is not the State of Israel; it will survive. The problem is not the world's conscience. I have no faith in it, though we must continue to prod and prick and provoke it. The problem of the Jewish people today is—the Jewish people. With a diminishing birth rate, an intermarriage rate exceeding 40%, Jewish illiteracy gaining ascendance daily—who says that the Holocaust is over? President Herzog of Israel estimates that we are losing 250 Jews per day! From the point of view of a massive threat to Jewish continuity, the Holocaust is open-ended.

The monster has assumed a different and more benign form, a different and bloodless shape, but its evil goal remains unchanged: a *Judenrein* world.

The Holocaust is not yet ready to be "remembered"; we are still in the midst of attempting to avoid the *final* Final Solution: a world without Jews.

In the light of this sobering, ominous reality, our responses are open to serious and deep reexamination.

I deeply sympathize with the heartfelt, sincere effort of memorial-building. But is that the Jewish way? No archaeologist has yet found a statue to the memory of R. Hanina ben Teradyon or R. Ishmael. No seeker after antiquities has yet unearthed an ancient museum to preserve the story of the victims of Masada or Beitar or R. Akiva and his martyred students—or, for that matter, the victims of the Crusades or the Inquisition or Kishinev.

Our people have historically chosen different forms of memorialization. They asked for the academy of Yavneh as a substitute for and in memory of the Holy Temple (*Gittin* 56b). They ordained days of fasting and prayer and introspection. They devised ways of expressing *zekher le-Mikdash* (reminder of the Temple) and *zekher le-hurban* (Reminder of the Destruction). They created the Talmud. In other words, they remembered the past by ensuring the future.

Museums and art have their place. In the context of an overall Jewish life, they serve as powerful instruments to recall the past for the future. But without a comprehensive wholeness, all our museums are mausoleums, our statues meaningless shards, our literature so much ephemeral gibberish.

We must seek to remember our dead, but not by being obsessed with death. We must be obsessed with life. *Lo ha-metim yehallelu Yah* ("The dead praise not the Lord" [Ps. 115:17]). The dead cannot tell their own story. Only the living can testify to them and perpetuate them: *Va-anahnu nevarekh Yah* ("But we will bless the Lord" [Ps. 115:18]). Their deaths make sense—even the sense of unspeakable and outrageous grief—only in the context of their lives. And their lives—their loves and hates, their faith and fears and culture and creativity and traditions and learning and literature and warmth and brightness and Yiddishkeit—are what we are called upon to redeem and to continue in our own lives and those of our children.

We know more or less how the Aztecs and Incas were butchered. But there is no one to mourn them today because there was no one to continue their ways and resume their story. That is bound to happen to our Six Million if we fail to ensure the continuity of our people. An extinct race has no memory. If there are no living Jews left, no one else will care about the Holocaust, and no one but a few cranky antiquarians will bother to view our art or read our literature or visit our museums.

Let me cite an example from the American-Jewish experience. There was a time when most American Jews memorialized their deceased parents by saying Kaddish for them for eleven months and on Yahrzeit and by reciting the Yizkor prayers four times a year; otherwise, their Jewishness became progressively more tenuous as they abandoned their parental lifestyles, values, and faith. What happened when these children died? For the most part, *their* children did not do for *them* what they had not done for their parents. For the most part, it was those who continued the whole rubric of Jewish life and living of their parents who also most fully cherished and reverenced their memories.

The reason for this is both profound and simple: Death has no staying power. Only life lives. Death is only past, it is over and done with. Who will remember a parent on Yizkor? Usually one who will be in shul as well on Hanukkah and Purim and Shabbat and even during the week. Those who somehow continue their parents' lives in their own lives will be there to note and recall their deaths. In a word: without life, death doesn't have a future.

At the Seder, a little less than two weeks ago, we ate a hard-boiled egg immediately before the meal as a sign of mourning. Jewish tradition teaches that since the first night of Passover always falls on the same night of the week as does Tish'ah be-Av, the egg is a token of grief for the victims of the destruction of Jerusalem and of pogroms throughout the ages. It occurs to me that not only do we eat an egg at the Seder because no Jewish *simhah* may be conducted or complete without remembering the tragedies of Jewish history, but equally so because there can be no enduring memorial to the fallen martyrs of our people unless it lies in the context of the Seder of Jewish life. Without a child to ask the *Mah Nishtannah,* there will be no adult to tell the story of *avadim hayinu.* Without *seder* or order; without the holiness of *kaddesh* or the purity of *u-rehatz*—there will be no *maggid* to tell the story of Auschwitz and relate the *maror* of Buchenwald and Belzec. And so the *hurban* will remain without a *zekher.* There can be no Tish'ah be-Av without a Pesah. And there will be no Yom ha-Shoah without the rest of the Jewish calendar.

How did Jewish tradition cherish and pay homage to its heroes? We are told of the righteous King Hezekiah that upon his death he was honored greatly by the people of Judah and Jerusalem (II Chronicles 32:33), and the Talmud *(Bava Kamma* 16b) explains that the honor that they accorded him was that *hoshivu yeshivah al kivro*—they established a school upon his grave!

That is what Jewish history and destiny call upon us to do now—before it is too late. The resources and energies and intellectual power of our best and brightest must be focused on making sure that there will be Jews remaining in the world lest the Holocaust prevail even while it is being denied. And that requires one thing above all else: a fierce, huge effort to expand Jewish education.

Let us resolve to build a school—a yeshivah, a day school, a Hebrew school, an elementary school, a high school, a school for adults, any genuine Jewish school—on the unmarked graves of every one of the million Jewish children done to death by the Nazi *Herrenvolk.* If not a yeshivah on every grave then, for Heaven's sake, at the very least one more Jewish child to learn how to be a Jew for the grave of every one child-martyr! A million more Jewish children learning how and what it is to be Jewish will accomplish more for the honor of the Holocaust martyrs than a million books or sculptures or buildings. Teach another million Jewish children over the globe the loveliness and meaningfulness and warmth of Jewishness, and you will have redeemed the million Jewish child-martyrs from the oblivion wished upon them by the Nazis. A million Jewish children to take the place of those million who perished—that is a celebration of their lives that will not make a mockery of their deaths and that will be worthy of our most heroic efforts.

Will we have the courage to save our and our children's future from the spiritual Holocaust that threatens us? Will we have the wisdom to reorder our priorities and "establish a yeshiva over the gravesites" of our *Kedoshim*—before the hearts and minds of the majority of our children themselves turn into private little graves of the Jewish spirit?

That is the fateful question that we are obliged to answer. The future of our people lies in our hands. If we do nothing but utter a sigh and shrug our shoulders with palms extended as a sign of resignation and helplessness—then we will stand accused of being passive onlookers at this bloodless Holocaust, and our guilt will parallel that of the silent spectators of the 1930's and 1940's. But if we resolve to live on despite all, if we stand Jewishly tall and put our shoulders to the wheel and teach and instruct a new generation in the ways of Yiddishkeit, then our hands will grasp the future firmly and surely, and we shall live and the *Kedoshim* will live through us.

Etz hayyim hi la-mahazikim bah (Prov. 3:18). Our Torah and our Tradition are a Tree of Life, and by holding on to them we will redeem our past and honor our people by giving them a future.

Yom ha-Atzma'ut
and
Yom Yerushalayim

THE ILLUSIONS OF NORMALCY

OUR *HAFTARAH* FOR THIS morning records one of the more fascinating chapters in the early history of our people. The city of Samaria was besieged by the army of Aram. Today Aram is Syria, and even then it was a sworn enemy of Israel. Four lepers who, in keeping with biblical law, were outside the city, found themselves near starvation. The men knew they would die if they remained where they were, but it was also no use to try to reenter the city, because they would die in the famine that reigned in the land because of the siege. Instead, therefore, they decided to take their chances and proceed to the camp of Aram. If the Arameans kill us, they reasoned, we are no worse off than we are now; and if they let us live, why then we shall survive. As they approached the enemy camp, the Bible tells us, God performed a miracle, and the sound of their approach was in the ears of the Arameans like that of a great army on the march. The Syrians were dumbfounded by the thought that the Israelite king might have hired Hittite and Egyptian mercenaries to do them battle. Thereupon the Syrians panicked, and leaving their camp upon a moment's notice, they all fled and deserted the city. When the four lepers entered the ghost city, they filled themselves with what they found—food, silver, gold, and clothing—and then they said to each other, we do not do right to care only for ourselves, for *yom besorah hu va-anahnu mahshin*, "today is a day of good tidings, and shall we be silent?" (II Kings 7:9). As patriotic Israelites, they notified the guards at the gate that they had alighted upon Aram and *ve-hinneh ein sham ish ve-kol adam*, "behold, there is no man there, neither the voice of a human being," *ki im ha-sus asur, ve-ha-hamor asur, ve-oholim ka-asher hemah*, "but the horse is tied to the stake, and the donkeys are tied, and the tents are as they were" (II Kings 7:10). Aram has suddenly been deserted, and it is the perfect time for an Israelite attack against its mortal enemy. The guards notified the king, and in this manner the four lepers were instrumental in achieving a victory of Israel over Syria.

Parashat Tazria-Metzora 5721 (1961)

This story is an interesting recollection from the Jewish past. But if it is included as a *haftarah* which is read and reread every year, then it must be more than that. It must have ramifications for all times, and it must have a special relevance for us of this day. Indeed, I believe that its message is most appropriate to us in 1961.

There comes a time in the life of a man—or the life of a people—when he or it realizes that the day is a *yom besorah*, a day of tidings, a day when an important message makes him restless, urging him to speak out. At a time of this sort, when he feels impelled to say something significant and urgent to the world, he has no right to be silent and to suppress the message which restlessly stirs within him. And one of the major things that we in our age must talk about, expose, and bring to the attention of the world is this: that our life has become such that *ki im ha-sus asur, ve-ha-hamor asur, ve-oholim ka-asher hemah*—everything seems to be functioning smoothly, there is every evidence of "business as usual," but unfortunately, *ve-hinneh ein sham ish ve-kol adam*—the *man* is missing; the voice of humanity is absent. The whole machinery of life and society seems to be so well lubricated, but at the center we do not find the humaneness; there is no feeling of compassion. There is no voice of protest raised against injustice.

Our society is essentially based upon the pattern of Aram—a deserted ghost city. Everything seems to be functioning smoothly: communications and transportation, business and finance, universities and laboratories—but at the core: *ve-hinneh ein sham ish ve-kol adam*. Instead of the warm heartbeat of individual human beings, there is only the grinding of gears and the hum of electronic machines. One of the basic ills of contemporary society is that it is so thoroughly mechanized that it has become dehumanized. The individual human being has been depreciated. Man as such has become depersonalized and has been reduced to a cog in a tremendous machine. We no longer think in terms of individuals; we think of individuals only as little units of society. We do not conceive any longer of patients, but of hospital beds. We do not concern ourselves with hungry children, we count the number of mouths we must feed. We fail to consider the unfortunate victim of an accident, and his widow and orphans; he is only one of the casualty rate on a holiday. Man has been reduced to a statistic, a thing.

Even in the ideological sense, the *ish* and the *kol adam* have been banished from life. For the last three hundred years since the onset of the modern era, a mechanistic philosophy has been dominant. According to this philosophy, all the world is a machine, all of whose parts function until they run down. Even man is a machine—and he does what he does because he *must* do it, because he has no choice, because man is a creature of habit and circumstance and necessity. He may think that he does what he *wants* to do; in truth, however, he does it because he *must* do so and not otherwise. Man is not really a free agent; he is only another screw in the great machine of the universe. He must function in his capacity mechanically, just like the *sus* and *hamor* and *oholim*. He has lost his humanity, his freedom. And as a result of this mechanistic philosophy which has banished human freedom, people have become confirmed in their irresponsibility and have learned to coat it with a respectable veneer of sophistry and sophistication.

In a world of this sort, all Jews must recognize a *yom besorah*, a time when their message is of the utmost importance if the humanity of man is to be salvaged. Israel dare not be silent. It must proclaim for all the world that man was created in the image of God, that he is a thinking and feeling human being, not a thing; that it is not true that he is just a little more advanced than the animals—rather, he is but "little lower than the angels" (Ps. 8:6). Man, Israel must teach the world, is unique. Every individual human being is absolutely irreplaceable. These are the good tidings that we must this day pronounce for all the world to hear. We must restore the value of man up to its former dignity.

The historic trial of Adolf Eichmann that is now taking place in Jerusalem has fortunately gone beyond the question of merely what to do with one man who is the greatest murderer of all times. The proceedings are beginning to turn on the crime rather than the criminal. All the material is now present for a great lesson for our generation, the generation that has grown up and matured since the war: a new insight into man and his capacity for depravity and decadence. One would think that this impact would hit the world like a ton of bricks. Instead, *ki im ha-sus asur, ve-ha-hamor asur, ve-oholim ka-asher hemah.* Everything functions normally, the buses run and the elevators go, the radio blares and the television records, newspapers are read and stock is exchanged—*ve-hinneh ein sham ish ve-kol adam*, but the humanity of man, which should make him rise to new heights of indignation, has remained essentially muted. A mass circulation magazine has even begun to complain that the news from the trial has become boring.

And listen to this most amazing example of "business as usual": a report from the *L'Osservatore Romano*. One would have expected that with the revelation anew of the terrible depths to which our culture has descended, a culture raised in Christianity and in Christian concepts and categories, that the officials of the Roman Catholic Church would bow their heads in shame and acknowledge their participation, even if indirect, in the guilt for these crimes. If not an open confession, one might at the very least have expected a sense of humility. Instead, the Vatican's official newspaper had nothing better to reveal, in the same month as the trial, but that Titus, the Roman general who destroyed the Holy Temple and ravaged Jerusalem in the year 70, felt that the Jews deserved their punishment, and that he was the instrument for their destruction. "The Jewish people were so obviously struck by divine punishment that it would indeed have been an impious action to spare them from destruction." To which *L'Osservatore Romano* adds wisely and sagely that *they* know what the sin of all Jews was: the rejection of the Christian witness and faith. At the very time that official Christianity should recognize its share in the responsibility for the horror and the shame of the twentieth century, they rewarm and rehash the old theological nonsense which has caused so much anguish in the world, which has stained so many pages of history with innocent Jewish blood! The same horses, the same donkeys, the same tents—but there is no man, the voice of humanity is lacking in the Vatican.

At a time of this sort, when sensationalist magazines are bored and pious journals are snickering, the State of Israel has a sacred historic duty to recognize that *yom besorah hu, va-anahnu mahshim,* that it has an urgent message to tell the world and that it dare not draw a curtain of silence over itself; that no matter how unwilling the world is to listen, it must drill it in again and again like the proverbial drop of water which ultimately forms a hole in the rock. It must remind the world of *ish,* of humaneness. Throughout Jewish history, we have been the ones to wake up the world to the message of humanity. From the time of Moses, of whom it is said *va-yifen koh va-khoh va-yar ki ein ish* (Ex. 2:12), "that he looked hither and yon and saw that there was no *man,*" and therefore he became the man to execute justice and righteousness, until the time of the Rabbis of the Mishnah, who proclaimed that *be-makom she-ein anashim, hishtaddel lihyot ish* (*Avot* 2:6), "in a place where there is no man, you must become that man," Jews have recognized that where others are remiss in their humaneness, we shall assert ours. How appropriate a task for the State of Israel, which this week celebrated its thirteenth birthday. Thirteen years is the time when traditionally a young lad becomes an *ish*—a man. On this Bar Mitzvah year of the State of Israel, it too must proclaim for the world the message of *ish.*

270

The second lesson to emerge from this historic trial is that without God, without Torah, without an ideal higher than man himself, man can be reduced to a very clever robot who will kill and murder efficiently as part of "obedience." He will be able to sit behind the desk, and with complete politeness to secretaries and underlings and callers, as part of his "orders" and "discipline," calmly press a button which will seal the doom of thousands and millions of his fellow men. In other words, it has revealed to us, to our new generation, that modern man has something rotten and mean in his soul, that he is the kind of being who can allow business as usual in utter disregard of the sanctity of *ish*, and without ever listening to *kol adam.*

We Orthodox Jews in a world of this sort have a historic responsibility.

We must break out of the bonds of our usual discord and wake up our fellow Jews and through them the world. We must educate, first, our own Jews, and afterwards all others, teaching that unless the Divine Image fills the human form, then man is better off dead than alive. We must teach all humanity that if you take the word *ish*, "man," and remove the middle letter, *yod*, which stands for God, what you have left is *esh*, a consuming fire, whether it be the powerful fire of the crematorium or the cataclysmic fire of the nuclear bomb. Through every available means, through school and through paper, through journal and through speech, through friendship and through example, we must teach the Torah way of life, which in practice for Jews, and in its ideals for all people, can alone bring back to man the sense of dignity which comes from the *Tzelem Elokim*, the Divine Image in which he was created. *Yom besorah hu, va-anahnu mahshim.* We must teach our fellow Jews both the grandeur of our own heritage and also the danger of a secularized, godless culture. We must tell them that if they want to assimilate, let them first know the kind of world into which they are assimilating: a sick, sick culture, the very cradle in which Nazism was nursed and weaned. For men who truly believed in God could never let orders given by mere creatures transcend such very basic and fundamental religious principles as "Thou shalt not murder." A misguided religious bigot will kill individuals in a rage of passion. But cold, white-collar, wholesale murder with scientific efficiency is possible only in a secular society in which Godlessness has allowed science to develop into deadly channels.

There is a *nega*, a plague, in the soul of modern man, man whose *sus* and *hamor* and *oholim* are cared for, but whose heart is in disarray, whose spirit is in chaos, whose soul suffers from sickening cynicism, whose core of *ish* has been obliterated, who is like the ghost city: only the ghost of a man. And our *sidrah* tells us the one effective procedure for him who suffers a *nega*, and that is *ve-huva el ha-kohen*, "he shall be brought to the priest." We must bring suffering man back to Torah, back to God, back to a sense of the sacred. For the *nega* of our times is a disease of the soul and a plague of the spirit.

If the State of Israel is to serve its historic destiny, then it must assume the role of *ish*. On the year of its Bar Mitzvah, it must attempt to achieve religious maturity. Diplomacy, military marches on Independence Day, all this is good and well; but this is not the essence of the destiny of Israel. Israel must now rise to its full historic stature and begin to fulfill the religious role which destiny gave it. There is no doubt that, religiously speaking, Israel has made mistakes in the past; only one who is blind will deny this. But, like the proud father next to his Bar Mitzvah son, we recite over Israel the *Barukh she-petarani*—blessed is God who has let us survive those years of immaturity and weakness and mistakes. We now turn to the future, a future in which Israel must return to its sacred origin.

Good wishes go out from the hearts of all Jews to the State of Israel. Like the young lad who, as his first mitzvah, learns to lay his *tefillin*, so do we wish Israel the blessings of *tefillin*. Just as the *tefillin* consists of two parts, the *shel yad* (the part that is wound on the hands) and the *shel rosh* (the part that is wound on the head), so do we hope that Israel will be strong in hand and dedicated in mind; that security and strength will be within its borders, and that dedication of mind and soul to Almighty God will be its religious greatness. In its dual capacity as a strong and peaceful nation and a holy and noble people, may the State of Israel relay its message to all the world, that the God who dwells in its midst has given every man the Divine Image, and that every human being must assert the *ish* within him and articulate the *kol adam*, the voice of humanity which God granted him. For today is a *yom besorah*, a day of proclamation of this great message, on this day we shall not be silent.

And in return, in the words of the Grace after Meals, *vi-yevasser lanu beso-rot tovot yeshuʿot ve-nehamot*, the all-merciful God, through His prophet Elijah, "will proclaim to us good tidings, tidings of salvation and consolation." Amen.

ASPECTS OF CREATIVITY

THE MOST WONDROUS MIRACLE in the course of life is the appearance of life itself—the birth of a child. If, therefore, when a child is born, he or she is greeted with *simhah*, with happiness, this is as it should be; for a child is the very highest expression of joyous creativity. No wonder the Jewish tradition teaches us that the father and mother of a child are partners with God in His creation; for the act of childbirth is the most significant creative act in human life. According to some of our classical commentators, the meaning of the biblical verse that man was created in the divine *tzelem*, the image of God, means that just as God is creative, so does man have the capacity to build and create. The most God-like of all human activities is that of creativity.

It is interesting, therefore, and somewhat perplexing, to note the somewhat remarkable law which comes at the beginning of the first of the two portions which we read this morning, namely, that a woman is considered in a state of ritual impurity, or *tum'ah*, for a specified period of time after childbirth. If, indeed, the creative act is an imitation of God, why should the act of childbirth, the most creative natural act of which a human being is capable, bring with it, as a side-effect, a state of *tum'ah*?

What the Torah wanted to teach us thereby is that every creative human act, no matter how noble, inevitably brings with it certain negative features. Destructivity is one of the aspects of creativity, for creativity is a reorientation of the *kohot ha-nefesh*; it disturbs the equilibrium of the inner workings of the soul, for what is new can be produced only by upsetting the status quo. (This idea has been elaborated psychoanalytically by Freud in *Civilization and Its Discontents*.) From the same reorganization which produces creative results there also emerge destructive consequences. You cannot have *yetzirah* without *tum'ah*. The creative act involves an area of shade, something negative, an element of pain and agony and frustration. The seed must rot for the plant to grow. When you carve wood, you must expect splinters. The sculptor must chip

---

Parashat Tazria-Metzora, 5723 (1963)

away part of the block and discard it in order for the figure that his imagination has conceived to emerge.

In the very creation of the world, according to the Kabbalah, the same principle held true: the creation was accompanied by what the Kabbalah called the *shevirat ha-kelim*, the breaking or bursting of the vessels; meaning that just as God gave life and vitality to all the world in His holiness, so did some of this life-giving holiness become entrapped and ensconced in evil. God gave rise to the world, and, as a side-effect, there arose evil as well. *Tum'ah*, or uncleanliness, accompanied the cosmic act of *yetzirah.*

The establishment of great nations, great ideas, and great institutions likewise follows this pattern. American democracy came into being at the expense of bloodshed and revolution. French democracy, a most creative element in world history, carried with it the *tum'ah* of Robespierre and the symbol of the guillotine. The people of Israel was created in the house of slavery of Egypt. And when we left, there came along with us the *erev rav*, the riffraff, those who did not deserve integration into our people. It is they who, according to the Jewish tradition, were responsible for the making of the Golden Calf and all the other sordid features that characterized the history of our people in those early days. No creation is possible without an element of impurity.

That is why the Torah gives us, in this week's *sidrah*, the laws of impurity as they relate to the *yoledet*, the mother who has just given birth to a child. The Torah wishes to inform us, by observing the most creative of all acts, childbirth, that every element of *yetzirah* has the adhesions of impurity, teaching us thereby to expect them and thus avoid their evil consequences.

Parenthood itself contains risks of impurity. Some parents imagine that their children belong to them, and fail, even in later years, to allow a child to develop as an independent personality—even as some parents fail in the opposite direction, by abandoning responsibility for guiding and directing a child by being overly permissive. How many parents really feel they have completely succeeded in raising their children without making any mistakes? In order to prepare young parents to expect mistakes, and to try to avoid them, the Torah stresses *tum'ah* right after childbirth.

Thus too it reminds the man building a business that if he does not take care, he is liable to build his business at the cost of his ethical integrity, or at the expense of his psychological tranquility. He may become so totally involved in his work that other aspects of his personality wither away. It warns the man in public life that he may create a great deal of good for the community, but if he is not aware of the principle of *tum'ah* that adheres to creativity, he may neglect his family while he pays attention to the larger human or national community. It warns the writer or the novelist that in the throes of creation and in the intense dedication necessary to produce something of enduring value, he is liable to disturb the inner recesses of the soul and to allow repressed demons to emerge; he may ignore his moral responsibilities as an artistic creator. All too often, modern writers, sometimes Jews more than others, allow their literary creations to wallow in all kinds of obscenity, all sorts of verbal *tum'ah*.

Perhaps this too is the explanation of the remarkable law in this week's *sidrah*, that the mother's period of impurity is twice as long upon the birth of a baby girl as upon the birth of a baby boy. The question of this difference in time span intrigued our Rabbis of old. When the question was addressed to R. Simeon bar Yohai, he replied, enigmatically, that when a boy is born, *ha-kol semehin bo*, everyone rejoices, and therefore seven days of impurity is sufficient. But when a girl is born, *ha-kol atzavin bah*, there is an element of sadness, and therefore the impurity lasts twice as long (*Niddah* 31b).

But what does this mean? Surely not every parent always wants a boy and not a girl—ordinary experience proves that. Even in antiquity, it was recognized that the human race could not survive without the female portion of its population.

Maharsha, the famed commentator on the Talmud, explains as follows: When a girl is born, the mother, in her own pain and agony of childbirth, realizes that this young infant will someday have to undergo the same excruciating experience, and therefore, despite all her happiness at the gift God has given her, she is already saddened because her daughter will have to repeat the same experience.

I would prefer to interpret this just a bit differently. Because creativity implies impurity, therefore the greater the creation, the longer and more intense the period of impurity, even as the greater the light, the more marked is the shadow. When it comes to this most significant of all examples of natural creativity, it is the female of the species who is more creative; it is she who gives birth, not the male. Therefore, when a daughter is born, the creative act is at its greatest and most intense, for a woman has given birth to a child who herself possesses the capacity for human creativity, in other words, the ability to give birth to yet another generation in its own time. Because the birth of a daughter is so much more creative an act than the birth of a son, the period of impurity is twice as great for the mother. Hence, the additional length of the period of *tumʿah* is not an indication of the relative value of a son or a daughter as such, but, quite to the contrary, a commentary on the greater creativity-value the Torah ascribes to womanhood.

It is with these thoughts in mind that our hearts turn in gratitude to the Almighty for having given us, fifteen years ago, the gift of the State of Israel at such a crucial point in the history of our people.

The State of Israel was the most creative achievement of our people in a national sense in the last thousand years. Not only is the State itself the creation of the people of Israel, but this creation itself possesses the potential of further creativity in generations to come. It is truly *bat Tziyyon*—the "*daughter of Zion.*" And the idea we have been expressing, that creativity inevitably has a proportionate aspect of impurity, should be for us both a source of solace and a warning.

All of us who love the State of Israel and admire it and are thankful to Heaven for it accept it as an immensely creative contribution to the life of our people. And yet anyone who refuses to surrender his critical faculties will be able to find negative features in the life of the State. Certainly, it is by no means the messianic goal and the fulfillment of the thousands of years of striving, dreaming, hoping, and prophesying of our people. The religious complexion of the State is by no means stable, and not yet that which we have prayed and hoped for. The creation of the State resulted in a sudden lessening of the idealistic fervor which brought it into being. There are other areas of shade that one can find.

What our *sidrah* of today tells us is that this is to be expected, and that it would be completely unnatural were such a historically creative act not to have a concomitant of "impurity"—and that if we are aware of this, we can look for these elements of *tumʿah* and rid ourselves of them.

How can we dispose of this spiritual impurity, this residue of *galut*, that has come along into the free State of Israel from the many lands of our dispersion?

The answer is, by following the same pattern that the Torah described for the purification of the *yoledet*, she who has given birth. One is time: The Torah specifies a number of days—no more, no less. You can't hurry up the process. You simply have to wait. Anyone who expects or expected that the State of Israel would suddenly come into being as a full-fledged messianic state was simply day-dreaming and completely out of touch with reality. It will take time until impurities that have attached themselves to us during the last one hundred years that Jewish souls have wandered off into the labyrinthine channels of strange ideals and systems are gone, and the *tum'ah* is spent, and the population of the State of Israel is ready for a great period of reawakening and *teshuvah*. Nothing can hurry the natural process of maturation and purification.

The second element is *tevilah*, immersion, purposeful purification of ourselves. It means that we must consciously seek to wash away from ourselves all the accretions of alien ideologies that have disrupted the normal development of our spiritual life in the State of Israel and in the Diaspora as well. *Ein mayim ela Torah*, "water refers to Torah." The waters of immersion, which the Torah prescribes for the mother who gave birth, symbolize the purification through Torah of the Jewish people throughout the world, they who are the mothers of the State of Israel. All Jews can rid themselves of the spiritual impurity of our times not only by waiting for the natural process to take place, but also by dipping our souls into the waters of Torah and the "Sea of Talmud." We must return to our primordial spiritual origin and there cleanse our souls and our spirit and be prepared for the great purification of the people of Israel and the State of Israel in the great and glorious future ahead of us.

The beloved president of Israel, Itzhak Ben-Zvi, of blessed memory, who passed away this week, represented both of these elements. He was, first, a leader of infinite patience, a forbearing father of his people in whose presence all tempers were stilled and troubled spirits calmed. And, second, he had a love for Torah and a deep reverence for its scholars, He was a synagogue Jew, a student of Talmud, and an *ohev Yisra'el*. He represented an element of *taharah*—of purity and purification in the life of the fledgling State. May his blessed soul return pure to its Creator.

And so our hearts turn to the Almighty in prayer that He guide the State and her leaders in the right path; that He send consolation to her grieving citizens; that He protect her from her many enemies so ominously surrounding her on all sides; that He purify her spiritual life with the *mayim tehorim* of Torah, and allow all of us to "draw the waters joyously from the wells of salvation" (Is. 12:2–3).

GOD, MAN, AND STATE

THE CONJUNCTION OF THE two *sidrot* we read today, *Tazria* and *Metzora*, is remarkable. The first speaks of birth, the second of a kind of death: *metzora hashuv ke-met*, a leper is considered as partially dead (*Midrash Tanhuma*, *Tzav* 96:13; Rashi, Num. 12:12). *Tazria* describes the joyous acceptance into the fold of a new Jew by means of *berit milah*, circumcision, while *Metzora* tells of the expulsion of the leper from the community.

Yet, these two portions are read on the same Shabbat with no interruption between them. The tension between these two opposites, this dialectic between birth and death, between pleasure and plague, between rejoicing and rejecting, speaks to us about the human condition as such and the existence of the Jew specifically. Even more, this tension contains fundamental teachings of Judaism that are relevant to the problems of the State of Israel whose eighteenth birthday we shall be celebrating this Monday.

After delineating the laws of childbirth, the Torah in the first *sidrah* gives us the laws of circumcision. The *Midrash Tanhuma* (*Tazria*, 7) relates a fascinating conversation concerning this Jewish law. We are told that Turnus Rufus, a particularly vicious Roman commander during the Hadrianic persecutions in Palestine, spoke to R. Akiva, the revered leader of our people. He asked R. Akiva: *eizeh mehem na'im*, Which is more beautiful: the work of God or the work of man? R. Akiva answered: The work of man. Turnus Rufus was visibly disturbed by the answer. He continued: Why do you circumcise your children? R. Akiva said: My first reply serves as an answer to this question as well. Whereupon R. Akiva brought before the Roman commander *shibbalim* and *geluska'ot*, stalks of wheat and loaves of good white bread. He said to the Roman: Behold, these are the works of God, and these are the works of man. Are not the works of man more beautiful and useful? Said the Roman to R. Akiva: But if God wants people to be circumcised, why are they not born circumcised? R. Akiva replied:

Parashat Tazria-Metzora 5726 (1966)

God gave the *mitzvot* to Israel *le-tzaref bahen*, to temper or purify His people thereby. (See *Bereshit Rabbah* 44:1.)

Here is the triumphant Roman commander, activist, arrogant, proud, and power-drunk. In an attitude of contempt, he faces the aged Jewish leader of this conquered people, a man who proclaims that the greatest principle of life is the study of Torah. What can these otherworldly mystics know about the world, about reality, about life? So he taunts the old rabbi: How come you circumcise your children? Do you not believe that man, as God's creation, is already born perfect?

But the Roman pagan is amazed by the response: No! All of Judaism—its philosophy, its Torah, its *mitzvot*—is based upon the premise that God withheld perfection from His creation, that He only began the task and left it to man, His *tzelem*, His "image," to complete. In Genesis, we are taught that God rested from creating the world *asher bara Elokim la'asot*, "which God created to do" (Gen. 2:3)—and R. Samson Raphael Hirsch interpreted that to mean that God created the world for *man* "to do." Therefore, R. Akiva shows Turnus Rufus the wheat stalks and the white bread, to teach him that God has created wheat because He wants man to do something with it. It is God's will that man make the created world more beautiful and more perfect. No wonder that in the Jewish view science and technology play such a positive role. No wonder that religious Jewry has contributed so mightily, throughout the ages and today as well, to the advancement of science and the control of nature.

Therefore, too, the *mitzvot*, and especially circumcision, were revealed to Israel to teach that man must act by himself in order to perfect his self and his world, and in the process *litzaref bahen*, to purify himself and fulfill all his sublime potentialities.

Indeed, R. Akiva himself exemplified this great principle. He was, on the one hand, one of the saintliest spirits in all our history. The Talmud, in imaginative grasp of the truth, tells us that when Moses ascended Mount Sinai to receive the Torah and saw the sacred soul of R. Akiva, he protested to God that Akiva was more worthy to be the bearer of Torah than he. And yet, on the other hand, it was the same R. Akiva who did not isolate himself in the academy, but became the sponsor of Bar Kokhba, the great Jewish general who led the revolution against Rome.

This, then, is what *milah* teaches us: *ma'aseh basar va-dam na'im*, the work of flesh and blood is beautiful indeed. The world is an uncompleted creation; man's fate is to finish it. It is the principle of activism. The State of Israel was built by people who perceived this Jewish principle. They were the ones who refused to stand aside, outside the stream of history, but who actively took it upon themselves to rebuild Jewish statehood. Their activity was in full keeping with the Jewish tradition as taught by the law of *milah*. More than enough Jewish blood was spilled in the effort, and the sweat and tears invested in the State shall never be forgotten.

Yet, this is only half the story. There is an opposite danger. If man is indeed a creator, then there is the peril that he will become intoxicated with power and self-delusions, that he will begin boasting and bragging and proclaiming bombastically: *kohi ve-otzem yadi*, "my own power and my own strength have performed all this" (Deut. 8:17). When he circumcises his child, he tends to forget that a healthy child is the gift of God. When he bakes his bread, he does not always realize that the wheat came from God's earth. When he builds his state, he ignores the fact that without the divine promise to Abraham and divine guidance throughout the ages there would be no Jews to build the Jewish state. When he is self-completing, he tends to become, in his imagination, self-creating. He is self-finishing and thinks that he is, therefore, self-made; and God spare us from self-made men!

To help us avoid this dangerous delusion, we have the teachings of *Metzora*. Just as *Tazria* and *milah* warn us to avoid the passivism that issues from a misunderstanding of faith, so *Metzora* and the law of *shiluah min ha-mahaneh*, the banishing of the leper outside the camp, teach us to avoid the fatal illusion that issues from faithlessness. Just as one *sidrah* tells us to circumcise the flesh and assert our manhood, so the second tells us to circumcise the heart and serve our God.

The great medieval scholar R. Elazar of Worms explains the law of *metzora*, the leper, and his banishment outside the camp by means of a comment on a famous verse in the Psalms: *adam bi-yekar ve-lo yalin nimshal ka-behemot niddmu*, "man does not abide in his glory, he is compared to the animals" (Ps. 49: 21). Man, says R. Elazar, is born naked and ignorant, without understanding and intelligence. But God puts him on his feet, grants him wisdom and insight, feeds him and clothes him and makes him great. But then man forgets and does not understand that all this glory came to him from his God. Therefore, he becomes like a *behemah*, a mere animal. An animal is not kept at home, but sent out to pasture; he is unfit to live in a truly human community. So a man who forgets God is a *metzora*, he is morally sick, and must be sent outside the camp of his peers. The leper symbolizes the man who acquires self-confidence at the cost of fidelity to God and he therefore is reduced to the role of a beast.

Man, then, must be a co-creator with God. *Tazria* teaches that man must imitate his Maker; *Metzora* reminds him not to impersonate his God, not to be an imposter. One *sidrah* stresses the virtue of human commission; the other, the virtue of human submission to God.

Indeed, in an insight brimming with tremendous significance, the eminent Italian-Jewish thinker Rabbi Mosheh of Trani finds this second principle in the commandment of *milah* itself. Just as circumcision teaches that man must act, so its particular designation for the eighth day teaches that his actions must not lead to the mere amassing of power and self-importance. Rather, man must acknowledge and reach out to the Creator of all the world. The number seven, R. Mosheh teaches, is the symbol of nature. Seven is the number of days in the week, the unit of time which establishes the rhythm of our lives. The earth itself, agriculturally, follows a seven-year cycle in Judaism, that of the *shemittah*. The number seven, therefore, stands for this world in its fullness. The number eight, however, is beyond seven: it teaches that you must transcend what seven symbolizes, you must go beyond nature and reach out for the supernatural, for God, He who creates nature. Were *milah* on the seventh day, then the duty of man would be to correct the imperfections of Nature, but forever to stay within it as nothing more than a clever animal. But *milah* was commanded for the eighth day, to teach that the purpose of all man's activity, the purpose of his work on nature, is to elevate himself beyond the perfection of body and mind, beyond the conquest of the world, beyond technology. When man controls his environment, he fulfills the number seven; when he controls his instincts, he reaches number eight. His technology is symbolized by the number seven; his theology by eight. *Milah* on the eighth day teaches that man must not only *complete* himself but must grow *beyond* himself; he must yearn and aspire to something higher. It signifies not only *milah* but *berit*; not only a surgical cut but the sign of the covenant, a contract with God sealed in blood. It means that if a human being will not strive to be more than human, he must become less than human, an animal, *nimshal ka-behemot niddemu*. Then man becomes a *metzora*, and like an animal must be sent *hutz la-mahaneh*, outside the camp of human beings.

Indeed, this is the crucial problem concerning the character of the State of Israel. Is it to be a symbol of seven, or a symbol of eight? Will it be just a natural state, or something higher, something nobler? If Israel will only be natural, a state like all others, a small sliver of real estate on the shores of the Mediterranean, considered nothing more than the creation of the Haganah and Sabra ingenuity, then it has no special claim on Jewish communities throughout the world—no more than its population warrants. It has no right to messianic pretenses. Such a conception places it *hutz la-mahaneh*, outside the purview of authentic Jewish history, an aberration. It is, then, in defiance of the covenant; it is the way of *tum'ah*, impurity. Only by fulfilling the symbol of eight, of loyalty to the covenant of God, of Torah, lies the way of *taharah*, of purity and rebirth, of joyous fulfillment of the historic dreams and prayers and prophecies of our history.

This, then, is the real problem on the eve of the eighteenth birthday of the State of Israel: Will it be *milah* or *berit*? Surgery or covenant? *Tazria* or *Metzora*? *Taharah* or *tum'ah*? Striving to be more than a natural human political entity, or falling to a mere natural group which, under the impress of secular nationalism, often becomes beastly—*nimshal ka-behemot niddemu*?

Such decisions are never made all at once. They involve long processes measured in historical time, certainly more than eighteen years. Many facts will determine the answer, and not the least of them will be the spiritual leadership in the state under the resolute stewardship of our distinguished and revered guest, His Eminence, Chief Rabbi Yehuda Unterman, may he live and be well. The enormously difficult task of Israel's spiritual leaders is to be both *responsive* to their fellow Israelis and *responsible* to our Heavenly Father. Like the *kohanim* in our *sidrah*, they must confront all Jews, the perfectly pure and the perilously impure. Sometimes it is their unhappy and tragic task to say to a man: *tamei*, impure, you must go out! Yet their greater and nobler task is to teach this same *tamei* to return, to bring Jews back into the historic community of Israel, to train all Jews in the way of the Torah's *taharah*. It is by no means a simple duty; it is, in fact, unenviably difficult. Our hopes and good wishes and our prayers for divine guidance and blessings go to Chief Rabbi Unterman and his distinguished colleagues in this historic mission.

We have spoken of *berit milah* in relation to the State of Israel. The eighteenth birthday also has another significance: *shemoneh esreh le-huppah*, the eighteenth year is traditionally the year of marriage. Let us conclude, then, by extending our wishes to Israel in a manner appropriate to both events. Let us all wish the State of Israel divine blessings: *le-Torah le-huppah u-le-ma'asim tovim*. May it be a future of Torah, in which Israel will accept the divine word and turn to its Father in Heaven. May it be the time of *huppah*, the marriage of hearts between Israel and Jews throughout the world. And then, having returned to God and to Jews throughout the world, may Israel become the shining beacon of *ma'asim tovim,* of good deeds and noble living, throughout the world and for all mankind. *Le-Torah, le-huppah u-le-ma'asim tovim.* Amen.

IN PRAISE OF IMPRACTICALITY

OUR *SIDRAH* OPENS WITH the words *Va-yedabber Hashem el Mosheh be-Har Sinai lemor*, "And the Lord spoke to Moses at Mount Sinai, saying . . ." (Lev. 25:1). What follows this introduction is a portion that deals with the laws of *shemittah*, the Sabbatical year, when the land must lie fallow and all debts be remitted.

The Rabbis were intrigued by one word in this opening verse: the word *be-har*, "on the mountain." Why the special reference to Mount Sinai at this time? The question as they phrased it has come over into Yiddish and Hebrew as an idiomatic way of saying, "What does one thing have to do with the other?" Thus, *Torat Kohanim* (*Behar*, 1:1), as quoted by Rashi: *Mah inyan shemittah etzel Har Sinai*? "What connection is there between the Sabbatical laws and Mount Sinai?" Were not all the laws and commandments enunciated at Mount Sinai? Why, then, this special mention of *shemittah* in association with Mount Sinai?

Rashi quotes the answer provided by the Rabbis. Permit me, however, to offer an alternative answer. Although Judaism is action-geared, oriented to the improvement of man and society; although it has a high moral quotient; although it addresses itself to the very real problems of imperfect man and suffering society; although, in contrast to certain other religions, it is more this-worldly; nevertheless, this concern with the real and the immediate and the empirical has a limit. Not everything in Judaism has to be as practical as an American businessman's profit-and-loss sheet or as "relevant" as the social activists and the radicals would like it to be. Judaism may not be ancient history, but neither is it journalism.

And this we see from the piquant fact that the laws of *shemittah* were given specifically at Mount Sinai. Laws known as *mitzvot ha-teluyot ba-aretz*, "commandments whose fulfillment is dependent upon the Land of Israel," were given to the people of Israel *before* they ever arrived in Eretz Yisra'el, the Land of Israel! Agricultural laws were given, in all their details, to a nomadic tribe without farms, without roots in the soil. Consider what the laws of *shemittah*

Parashat Behar 5732 (1972)

sounded like to our grandparents as they surrounded Mount Sinai, that bare desert mountain. They must have seemed weird, irrelevant, out of place, impertinent.

And yet, what was true of *shemittah* at Mount Sinai is true of all the commandments at all times. They may seem hopelessly impractical, untimely, and irrelevant to the cold-eyed and hard-headed man, and yet they are the Law of the Lord, obligatory upon Jews at all times and in all places.

Indeed, there is hardly anything as irrelevant as the piddling relevancy of the coldly practical man. Show me the man who sees only what is before his eyes, and I will show you a man who cannot see beyond his nose!

What does this praise of the impractical teach us?

First, it tells us simply that there are things that are of value in and of themselves, not only because they are instrumental or lead to other things. Thus, some of the commandments may restrain man's destructiveness. Others may lead him to improve society or his own soul or help the disadvantaged. But some are valuable simply because they were commanded by God. No other reason is necessary.

The same is true of knowledge. There are some kinds of knowledge which may lead to invention and enhance the health of man and his convenience. But science is more than technology. There is also such a thing as knowledge for its own sake, knowledge acquired in order to satisfy the natural intellectual curiosity of man.

A week ago, Apollo 16 returned from its trip to the moon. Except for those Americans who are so benumbed by the sensational that after the first time a thing is done it becomes a dreadful bore, the exploits of the astronauts kept the world enraptured. And yet consider what a monumental irrelevance the whole project is! The government spends millions of dollars, some of the brightest men in the world donate their talents, three men risk their lives—all in order to study the structure of remote rocks so that we might formulate a theory of when the moon was created and how old it is. "So what?" one might ask. And the answer is: so everything!

Yes, there may be legitimate questions about the priorities in our national budget. That is not now our concern. But without doubt, knowledge for its own sake must not be deprecated. The real point to a small man sometimes appears to be beside the point.

And the same is true in Judaism. There is the study of Torah for the sake of performance of the *mitzvot*, or the sake of cohesion of the community, or the sake of raising the level of Jewish observance. But the highest concept of Torah study remains *Torah lishmah*, Torah for its own sake. Here, too, there may be a question of priorities in determining the subject matter of Torah. But there is no denying the ultimate and high value of *Torah lishmah*, of study for its own sake.

It was the Jerusalem Talmud (*Hagigah* 2:1) that attributed to the most notorious heretic in Jewish history the opposition to "otherworldly study of Torah." Elisha ben Abuya, known as *Aher* ("the other one"), is said to have stormed into a classroom, rudely interrupted the teacher, and shouted at the students: "What are you doing here? Why are you wasting your time in such irrelevant material as Torah? You, you must be a builder; you must be a carpenter; you ought to become a fisherman, and you should be a tailor. Do something useful in your lives!" The great heretic was an eminently practical man.

Of course, I do not mean to be cute by espousing impracticality and advocating irrelevance. Total irrelevance is deadening to the spirit and results in what philosophers call solipsism—the divorce from the outside world and experience, and the introversion into oneself; and impracticality can become nothing but a semantic excuse for inefficiency and incompetence. What I do mean is that relevance is *a* good, but not the *only* one, or even the most important one. And while practicality is necessary for the execution of ideals, dreams and visions need not be pre-restrained in the Procrustean bed of a mercantile mentality.

The second point is that sometimes the apparently remote does contain highly significant and very real dimensions, but it is our narrow vision and restricted understanding that does not allow us to expose these obscure insights. *Kashrut* sometimes is ridiculed in this modern age because it appears superfluous when we consider the sanitary facilities we possess. And yet, those who understand *kashrut* realize that it has so little to do with sanitation and has so very much to say about reverence for life—and this in a world in which life is losing its value, in which the approval of abortions is moving into the encouragement of euthanasia. *Shaʿatnez* and *kilʾayim*, the prohibition against mixing various garments or seeds or animals, has always been held up as a paradigm of nonrational commandments, and yet today we realize how much they have to say to us about ecology and the preservation of the separate species of the universe. The Sabbath laws are meant not only to give us a day of rest, because Sunday in modern America can accomplish that as well. They tell us that we are not the by-products of a cosmic accident, that we owe our existence to God and must therefore curb our insufferable pride and collective arrogance.

So these and many other such illustrations remind us of the need to search beneath the surface of Judaism for teachings that are eminently pertinent.

Third, we must be future-oriented. We must have faith that what is genuinely irrelevant now may, someday, become most relevant and meaningful as a result of our ability to carry on heroically despite present irrelevance and impracticality. What today seems visionary may prove indispensable to tomorrow's very real need.

The Rabbis were fond of saying that *divrei Torah aniyyim be-makom zeh va-ashirim be-makom aher*, "the words of Torah are poor in one place and rich in another" (*Yerushalmi Rosh ha-Shanah* 3:5). By this they meant to say that sometimes the text of Torah will seem utterly narrow and superficial, teaching very little indeed. It is only when we compare it with another text, in another context, that we can appreciate how genuinely deep and insightful it really is. I would like to paraphrase that passage, switching from *makom* to *zeman*. Thus, *Divrei Torah aniyyim bi-zeman zeh va-ashirim bi-zeman aher*. It sometimes happens that the words of Torah in one epoch may seem to be thin and insignificant; it is only later, at another time that the same words stand revealed as possessing unspeakable richness of insight and teaching.

Take as the most striking example the hope for Jerusalem, whose fifth anniversary of liberation we celebrate later this week.

If we have the privilege to commemorate the reunion of people and city, of Israel and Jerusalem, we must acknowledge our debt to a hundred generations of Jews and Jewesses who since the year 70 have been wild dreamers, impractical idealists, possessed of visions impossible of execution; Jews who turned to Jerusalem three times a day in prayer; who when they ate bread thanked God for bread—and for Jerusalem; who mentioned Jerusalem when they fasted and when they feasted; who brought little packets of the dust of Jerusalem during their lifetimes in order to take it along with them in their coffins on their long journey to eternity; who arose at midnight for *Tikkun Hatzot*, to lament over Jerusalem, and at every happy occasion promised to return there.

If we *live* in Jerusalem today, it is because of those unsophisticated visionaries who wanted at least to *die* in it.

If we can visit Jerusalem *this year*, it is thanks to those otherworldly dreamers who sang out, *Le-shanah ha-ba'ah bi-Yerushalayim*, at least let us be there next year.

If we can happily laugh—*az yimmalei sehok pinu*, "then will our mouths be full of laughter" (Ps. 126:2)—it is in large measure the work of those who did not realize how irrelevant they were, how impossible their dreams were, and who prayed to return there, thus daring and braving and risking the derisive laughter of legions of practical men who simply knew that we were finished, and that Jerusalem would never become a Jewish city again.

It is only because of generations of bridegrooms who concluded every wedding by stamping on a glass, its shattering fragments recalling the *hurban Yerushalayim*, the destruction of Jerusalem, and proclaiming *Im eshkahekh Yerushalayim tishkah yemini*, "If I forget thee, O Jerusalem, let my right hand fail" (Ps. 137:5), that today we can defy the whole world, East and West, and say: Never again shall you separate us from Jerusalem, not capitalists and not communists, not Moslems and not even Christians, who have lately discovered that Jerusalem is important to them.

Jerusalem Day is a tribute to this special Jewish brand of impracticality and irrelevance.

So, *mah inyan shemittah etzel Har Sinai?* What is the association or connection between the sabbatical laws and Mount Sinai? They come to tell us, first, that not everything need be relevant; second, that not everything that appears irrelevant really is; and third, that what is irrelevant today may be the most important fact of life tomorrow.

This lesson, too, is part of the heritage of Sinai. Indeed, without it, all the rest is in jeopardy. With it, all the rest will prevail too, *bi-meherah be-yameinu, amen.*

THE ENTEBBE RESCUE

IF WE WERE TO search Scripture for an appropriate expression of our relief, joy, and thanksgiving at the heroic and brilliant rescue by Israel of the over one hundred Jewish hostages kept by Arab and German terrorists at the Entebbe Airport in Uganda, one important verse would come to mind: *ka-et ye'amer le-Ya'akov u-le-Yisra'el mah pa'al Kel,* "Now it shall be said concerning Jacob and Israel, what hath God wrought?" (Num. 23:23).

What indeed hath God wrought! How great and miraculous was the deliverance, how wondrous was the rescue! From the depths of despair, we were brought to the heights of joy and gratitude—but we are mindful of the loss of three lives, and the disappearance of one of the hostages.

Indeed, for the last several days our national mood has been reminiscent of the heady days following the Six-Day War. And yet, this very association with the Six-Day War raises problems that were debated then too. Amongst them is, should we really be thanking God for this victory, or congratulating the Israelis who risked so much and achieved so mightily? Should we be reciting the verse "What hath God wrought?" or the verse immediately following it: *Hen am ke-lavi yakum ve-kha-ari yitnassa,* "Behold, a nation arises as a lioness, and lifts up its head as a lion" (Num. 23:24)? Should we be proclaiming "What hath God wrought?" or "[Israel is] a nation that arises like a lioness and lifts up his head like a lion"? After all, it was these courageous young men who risked their lives—and the prestige of Israel—in a raid concocted so quickly and executed so brilliantly. So, which shall it be: *mah pa'al Kel* and its religious consequences; or *hen am ke-lavi yakum* and its political-military ramifications?

This is no idle speculation. Two attitudes strive for supremacy within each of us, and the two attitudes are present in our community as well. One of them,

---

This sermon was presented on July 10, 1976. Although not delivered in conjunction with a holiday, it is included here because it responds to one of the most dramatic events in Israel's history.—N. L.

Shabbat *Parashat Balak* 5736 (1976)

perhaps the minority, is what might be termed quietistic. It advocates *bittahon*, complete faith in God, to the exclusion of man's strength or power. In fact, it is somewhat contemptuous of man's activities. The other point of view, much more prevalent, is activist. It is sometimes called *hishtaddelut*, effort or initiative. It disdains appeals to faith, and comes dangerously close to the boastfulness against which Moses warned us: *kohi ve-otzem yadi asah li et ha-hayil ha-zeh*, "it is my power and the strength of my hand which has made for this success of mine" (Deut. 8:17).

The first attitude is one which responds only with the words *mah pa'al Kel*, "What hath God wrought?"; the second knows only the following verse, *hen am ke-lavi yakum*, "it is a nation which arises as a lioness."

Secularist man tends to see science and technology and all human achievement as displacing the divine in the world. The secularist mentality is such that it perceives human genius to be in competition with God's work, and holds that religion is meaningful only when science has no answer and technology no solution—as if faith in God were a function of human ignorance! It sees no reason to exclaim about what God has wrought, when it knows that achievement is a result of a nation arising like a lioness.

We have here echoes of the "secular city" debate which was current in theological circles a number of years ago. In a less sophisticated form, we can always hear such arguments and challenges as "Can you still believe in God—or in Torah, or observe the commandments—in the space age?"

Opposed to this is the outlook of religious man, who, in his faith, often fails to appreciate the importance of human creativity, of science and technology, even while he makes use of it and enjoys the benefits and advantages that it has brought to civilization. In a way, such an approach is a subtle indication that it accepts the secularist premise that man's achievements are in competition with, and seek to displace, those of God, except that we side with God in this contest and exclaim, *mah pa'al Kel*.

Neither of these positions, to my mind, is authentically Jewish. I must hasten to add that I deny as well the kind of compromise which attributes success to man and failure to God!

There *is* such a way of thinking which ascribes human vulnerability and natural cataclysms to God, and man's triumphs—to man. In the insurance industry, when we speak of natural disasters or catastrophes, we employ a euphemism "an act of God"! (Indeed, I have heard of an Orthodox Jewish insurance agent who was seeking to sell a policy to an equally pious potential client, and said to him, "Now if there should occur an act of God, God forbid . . .") Such a mentality recites *mah pa'al Kel*, "What hath God wrought," only on the occasion of bad news. But if there is economic success, or a career triumph, or a military victory, then this mentality is one which then recites *hen am ke-lavi yakum*, it is a result of my genius, my talent, my competence. But such a division of credit and blame is manifestly unfair.

What should be the authentic Jewish attitude? I believe it is that neither one is adequate! We need both verses—*mah pa'al Kel* in order to avoid the arrogance that comes from the successful exercise of human power, and *hen am ke-lavi yakum* to avoid the paralysis of human power that is often the result of spiritual passivity.

There is no fundamental contradiction between the two verses, although we must always live in the tension between them. A truly religious Jew sees God's wisdom in man's wisdom, and God's power in man's power. For God and man, according to Jewish teaching, are partners in creation, and it is God who delegated to man the role of His surrogate in the mastery of creation. If indeed man is the image of God, then man's deeds must reflect God's personality. In such a case, a manifestation of human wisdom or the benevolent use of human power for creative ends must be seen as a reflection of the character of God. No wonder that the Halakhah directs us to recite special blessings upon encountering unusually wise or powerful men, in which we declare our gratitude to God for sharing His power and wisdom with mere flesh and blood. For us, *hen am ke-lavi yakum* is a reflection of *mah pa'al Kel* .

If there is no *hishtaddelut*, if there is no human initiative—what the *Zohar* calls *it'aruta di-letatta*, "initiative from below"—the world must remain fallow, and the dark forces of nature will reign supreme in the absence of human creativity. I recall the story of a farmer in Maine who bought an old and dilapidated farm. Slowly, he repaired the sheds, plowed the land, pruned the trees and hedges, fixed up the farmhouse. After he had finished, the local parson came by for a visit and, beholding the scene of this successful renovation, said, "I am glad to see what the Lord has done to this farm." Whereupon the farmer, in typically laconic Yankee fashion, responded, "You should have seen this farm when the Lord had it alone!"

Indeed so, God insists that man become the tool for His creative work. If He has it by Himself, He will refuse to do any more with it.

Similarly, if Israel had not undertaken its brilliant exploit, we would have lost not three or four hostages, but over a hundred, Heaven forbid. Without *hen am ke-lavi yakum*, we would have had no occasion to say: *mah pa'al Kel*. Without those Israeli lions, we would not today be thanking God. Perhaps when we are next solicited for the campaign on behalf of Israel, we will not groan and moan and complain, but remember the risks that these young lads of Israel embraced when they undertook this arduous and dangerous maneuver.

And yet—and yet! Human agency alone cannot be held exclusively responsible for this miracle! I shudder to think what might have been, the untold errors and accidents and slip-ups that might have made a shambles of the entire effort and would not only have resulted in a massacre of the hostages and the would-be rescuers, but in a devastating public reaction to the futile Israeli effort. I can understand the censure of Israel by the French Pilots Association on the basis of a possible failure, although I ordinarily find it difficult to sympathize with anything French these days. Indeed, if not for *mah pa'al Kel*, we would have no occasion for pride which would lead us to exclaim *hen am ke-lavi yakum*. Without God, our lions would be of no avail.

So we offer today our warmest and most deep-felt felicitations to the Israel Defense Forces, the lions of Israel. Not only Jews, but decent people throughout the world will join us in these congratulations. This is especially true of England, which not too long ago had the uncomfortable experience of having a representative of the crown humiliated by that psychopath, Idi Amin, when the ambassador came groveling and bowing and scraping before him. Now England too can hold its head up higher and exclaim with all the world about Israel, *hen am ke-lavi yakum*.

But no less—and even infinitely more—must we offer our prayer for thanks to Almighty God and exclaim *mah pa'al Kel*, "What hath God wrought!" in so protecting and prospering our Israeli soldiers in this extremely perilous effort.

I cannot help but think, on this occasion, of how God bends man to His purposes, how little we know of what role we play in history. It seems such a short time ago that Israel was banished from UNESCO, and the representative of Lebanon came up to the rostrum of the United Nations and arrogantly crowed, "Israel is a country which belongs nowhere!" And now look at what God hath wrought: in the same week that Israel managed this brilliant coup of saving its hostages from Uganda, Lebanon is in the deepest throes of its most agonizing despair, it has effectively ceased to be a nation, it is—and I say this without any special satisfaction—a country which is a noncountry, it is itself nowhere! How ironic is the justice that God executes upon the nations of the world. *Mah pa'al Kel!*

The same coordination of an intersection between the divine and the human must always be part of our understanding of the forces of history, and this understanding must guide us in all our endeavors—not only those of Israel's military and political and economic security, but also in our efforts for Torah, whether in Israel (and I speak specifically of such great and distinguished yeshivot as Kerem B'Yavneh, on whose behalf I have come to these shores), or Jewish activity in the United States, or Jewish education in England.

In offering our congratulations to Israel and our thanks to God Almighty, in expressing both verses in profound appreciation of this historic event in which Israel proved to be so bold, so swift, so quick, and so powerful, our lesson is clear: we must learn from this heroic act to inspire ourselves to heroism in pursuit of our spiritual goals as well. And here too we must be bold and swift and quick and powerful. For so we read this afternoon in the fifth chapter of *Avot*: *Rabbi Yehudah ben Teima omer: Hevei az ka-namer ve-kal ka-nesher, ratz ka-tzevi ve-gibbor ka-ari*, "R. Judah ben Teima says: Be bold as the leopard, and swift as the eagle, and quick as the deer, and powerful as the lion. And all this must be done in order to carry out the will of our Father in Heaven" (*Avot* 5:23).

Shavuot

THERE IS RELIGION AND THERE IS RELIGION

THE BOOK OF RUTH, which is read on this Shavuot festival, offers us one of the most profound insights into the modern status of religion. By telling this extremely personal tale of love and pathos concerning three major metahistorical characters, all of them women, we are given one of the most illuminating analyses of the two kinds of religion that have vied for the control of men's consciences, souls, and destinies till this very day.

Elimelekh was a rather important person in the Palestine of about three thousand years ago. Financially, scholastically, and personally he was a well-known Jew whose name was important enough to be mentioned in a book of the Bible. One fine day Elimelekh decided to leave his homeland and emigrate to nearby Moab. Famine stalked Israel, and Elimelekh thought that he and his family would fare better in this strange land. And so he took with him his wife, Naomi, whose name means "pleasantness," and his two sons, who later married non-Jewish wives. Very soon thereafter, Elimelekh and his sons die, and they fade out of the picture as secondary and unimportant characters. The sweet but sad Naomi now decides to return to her native land, Israel, probably to die in loneliness and sorrow. She decides to take leave of her two daughters-in-law, Ruth and Orpah, and go back to what once was her home.

But the young ladies have become too attached to her to say goodbye so easily. They tell her that they share a common grief, a common tragedy, and therefore a common destiny. Both Ruth and Orpah tell Naomi that they want to accept her faith—Judaism—and return with her to Israel. We begin to sense a religious stirring in these pathetic souls who find themselves enmeshed in this intensely human drama. Naomi is moved by their expression of loyalty, but she will not hear of it. In consonance with Jewish teaching that we are not to encourage conversions to our faith, she bids them to return to their heathen

5714 (1954)

country—Moab,—to return to their parents, perhaps to remarry and begin new lives. I have passed my prime, says Naomi, and have only memories to live for, but you two are still young, and perhaps you can forget the past and find a future. Both protest that their love for their mother-in-law outweighs their desire for home, and they want to remain. Naomi again tries to dissuade them. And here the really crucial event occurs: Orpah takes leave of her mother-in-law and sister-in-law and returns to her pagan family in Moab. But Ruth, our heroine, is adamant. She will not leave her Naomi. She must become a Jewess. In the moving simplicity of all great poetry, she tells Naomi: "Where you will go, I will go; where you will sleep, I will sleep. . . . and where you will die, there I will die" (Ruth 1:16–17).

And here, as the two dim figures of Ruth and Orpah part in the early dawn of recorded history, generations and destinies move with them. A bleak, lonely, pathetic scene on the distant plains of ancient Moab, but one which initiates and summarizes the parting of the ways of two great nations. For Ruth, as our tradition explains, converted to Torah, accepted Naomi's faith, married a great Jew—the kindly, renowned, and saintly Boaz—and soon became the great-grandmother of the greatest king of Israel, whose birthday is today: King David—the noble, saintly, sweet singer of Israel who unified a nation and gave it the immortal Psalms. Orpah returned to her heathen origins, despite her original protestations, ultimately forgot that she ever even knew Naomi and Ruth, and was swallowed up in the life of Moab. And tradition here records the opposite: she became the ancestress not of kings and saints and scholars and prophets and poets, but she bore a line of descendants distinguished by their viciousness, immorality, venery, and anti-Semitism. Just as Ruth became the forerunner of King David, and the royal house of Israel, so did Orpah, her sister-in-law, become the grandmother of David's archenemy Goliath, hero of that lewd and savage people, the Philistines (*Sotah* 42b). Israel was constantly at war with the raiding Philistines, both militarily and culturally. And their eternal opposition was epitomized in the unequal battle between David and Goliath (I Sam. 17). This entire drama of nation against nation and culture against culture goes back to two young women who parted from each other in the presence of one Naomi, two young ladies who were sisters-in-law, and who, but for a turn of fate, might have remained together for all time.

And as we ponder this juxtaposition of nations—the people of David vs. the people of Goliath, the Psalms vs. the Spear, holiness vs. lewdness—we look back to their ancestors, who were sisters-in-law. And why, one wonders, was fate so good to Ruth and so harsh on Orpah? For did not Orpah, too, offer to remain with Naomi and accept Torah instead of a civilization of immorality? And the answer lies in that slight difference of attitude which usually passes unnoticed, but which moves history as effectively as a bulldozer pushing sand. Listen to the Bible describe the parting of ways of these two girls: *va-tishak Orpah la-hamotah*, "and Orpah kissed her mother-in-law," *ve-Rut davekah bah*, "whereas Ruth clung to her" (Ruth 1:14). Here was the essential difference between Ruth's and Orpah's attitudes toward Naomi and therefore Torah: Orpah only kissed, while Ruth cleaved and clung. A very slight difference, you might say. True, but one which develops and unfolds through the centuries. The clinging and deep attachment of a Ruth becomes the profound passion for Truth and the noble clinging to the God of a David and of a people, Israel. And the superficiality of Orpah, symbolized by the kiss, degenerates into the rabid and demonic wickedness of a Goliath; the lukewarm attraction becomes the very cold antipathy. Indeed, the Talmud refers to Israel as *benei devukah*, "the sons of she who clung," and to the enemies of Israel as *benei neshukah*, "the sons of she who kissed her mother-in-law" (*Sotah* 42b). And ultimately, predict the Sages, *yavo'u benei neshukah ve-yippelu be-yad benei devukah*, the clingers prevail over those who merely kiss, the Davids vanquish the Goliaths. Superficiality must always buckle and fall, when the real test comes, before the power of sincerity and the might of depth and true loyalty.

And isn't religion itself today affected by that same kind of superficiality, this form-without-content malady? Certainly, for there are two kinds of religion—the kissing and the clinging. We have got to be careful when using that word "religion." For there is religion, and there is religion. One is the *benei neshukah*, and the other, the *benei devukah*. And the differences between them are easy enough to detect. The *benei neshukah* are ever-ready with the ubiquitous and easy expression of affection. Synagogue—nice; services—beautiful; Talmud Torah or day school—necessary; *kashrut*—a fine thing for some folks. All our Jewish institutions are treated with the saccharine sweetness symbolized by the superficial and sugar-coated kiss. But the *benei devukah*, without whom these same institutions could never exist, view these things otherwise. Synagogue—not nice but urgent; services—not beautiful but profound and soul-stirring; Jewish education—not just necessary but vital, a matter of life and death; *kashrut* and *taharat ha-mishpahah* (family purity)—not just good ideas for some folks, but among the very cornerstones of our faith and survival, our way of life. The *benei neshukah* kiss the mezuzah; the *benei devukah* cling to what is written therein. The *benei neshukah* close the *siddur*, kiss it, and leave it in the synagogue; the *benei devukah* close it, take its message with them, open their hearts to it, and begin to practice it. *Benei neshukah* express affection, whilst *benei devukah* impress with passion and devotion. The *benei neshukah* are ultimately of no avail, while the *benei devukah* ultimately will prevail. *Ve-attem ha-devekim ba-Shem Elokeikhem, hayyim kulkhem ha-yom*, "And you who cling to the Lord are alive, every one of you, to this day" (Deut. 4:4).

These, then, are some of the differences between the kissing kind of religion, which has only form, only superficiality, only a saccharine sentimentalism, and the clinging kind of religion, which means meaningfulness, purpose, depth, and a hold on the core of life.

What of today? An extensive analysis of religious trends by the *New York Times* religion staff shows a return to churches, temples, and synagogues on an unprecedented scale. A return to what, we ask, to a *benei neshukah* sentimentalism with which we hope to cover up our basic dilemma, and hide the mighty wrangling of our souls; or to the *benei devukah* kind of religion, where we are going to meet ourselves directly, where we are going to go to the core of things and make of ideals and principles working things which will guide us through all situations?

I am afraid that this report is misleading. I am afraid that the return is only in name, and only to a more exaggerated sentimentalism. For if there were a real return to a clinging, fighting, powerful, and meaningful type of religion—I don't care what denomination—it would show tremendous effects on the economics and politics of our nations. A true revival of real and deep religion would not allow to go unchallenged the dumping and overproduction of butter and grain here while little children shrivel to emaciated skeletons overseas. A true and deep religious return would not allow the vulgarest demagogue in American history, Senator Joseph McCarthy, to monopolize the TV channels for so long a time over trivialities. It would base the matter on moral and ethical issues. That would be part of the results of a *benei devukah*, a clinging, Ruth-like kind of religion—as opposed to a Ruth-less one.

But what have we instead? Some kindly old senator from Vermont who thinks that he will establish a hegemony over the Christian Paradise if he introduces a bill in the Senate amending the Constitution to read that we as a nation devoutly recognize the authority and law of the man Christianity calls a god. As if a polite constitutional kiss is going to save us from heathens, Communists, Jews, and the Mau-Mau. But let us forget for a moment this travesty of Americanism—and I am inclined to think that the gentleman who introduced the bill probably regrets it by now—and this violation of the freedom of religion and separation of church and state. Let us turn to something we Jews can agree to as not violating our religious tenets. Another resolution, passed on the Senate floor—where the strangest things seem to happen nowadays—and passed on to the House with unprecedented speed, sponsored by Senator Ferguson of Michigan, would amend the Pledge of Allegiance. Instead of "one nation, indivisible," which you and I have recited since we were tots, and mispronounced as well, we shall now be required to read "one nation under God, indivisible," and so on. What a pale victory for religion! What a desecration of everything holy to any religion to proclaim it so patriotically, to reduce religion to two words, but to wait two years and hundreds of victims before beginning to realize that McCarthyism is no good—and that because of political exigencies. *Benei neshukah.* The good senator just threw a kiss to God, but we wonder if God is going to blow one back to him. And yet how enthusiastic Americans have become over this great show of religion. The president's pastor is for it in order to distinguish our pledge from Russia's. America is suddenly turning really pious—churches, veterans groups, patriotic organizations, fraternal clubs, labor unions, and, of course, Daughters of the American Revolution, are all for it. "This nation will grow in strength by this fuller acknowledgement of its faith in Almighty God," writes one sacerdotal correspondent. And how does one important correspondent summarize this mass movement to give God a coveted entree into our great American pledge? "All the various sponsors . . . agree on one thing: the widespread support the bill is receiving must bear testimony to a religious revival of significance." That is just what we disagree with! This rabbi, for one, doesn't care one iota about the entire issue. I personally thank God every day for our democracy. But I don't think that just plain verbiage, this mild and pietistic mention of God, is going to accomplish much, or that it means very much. It is only a superficial kiss; I fail to detect the clinging.

What we need, then, is a revival of the *benei devukah* kind of religion; and we here think especially of that kind of dynamic and powerful return to Torah Judaism. And we therefore appeal from this pulpit to all who have come this morning for the Yizkor services alone: try to deepen the religious spark you have. Do not make of Judaism merely a lovely demonstration of sentimentalism for dead parents. Don't come here just for an affectionate kiss to your parents' souls. Come, rather, to cling and bind your souls inalterably to the Eternal Spirit with whom they have become united. Do not be *benei neshukah,* to whom the reading of a list of names becomes metaphysically important and the wherewithal of Judaism. Become *benei devukah*, and begin to live a life of Yizkor, of remembering the Torah, source of our existence, and thus eternalizing the memories of your loved ones. Prove yourselves to be not *benei neshukah*—lukewarm, superficial, weak Jews who come for Yizkor and then run off before *Musaf*, deserting the synagogue and insulting God Almighty. Be, rather, *benei devukah*, who come to remain and then to return again more and more often until it becomes a regular habit.

The Davids and the Israelites scan over their lives, then, finding happiness, turn their eyes heavenward and thank God for having made them the sons of Ruth, who was able to cling. That is the true Yizkor. The Goliaths, their lives spent in hollowness and frustration, do not even know where to turn their eyes. To them Orpah is an unheard-of name. Memory is not her lot. She has become the forgotten mother of *benei neshukah*. As we say the Yizkor, let us resolve to return to a faith like that of the *benei devukah* of old, and may it forever redound to the credit of those parents and ancestors whom we shall now remember in love, loyalty, and everlasting devotion.

THE TORAH'S MYSTERY MAN

THE BOOK OF RUTH read on Shavuot is a beautiful and inspiring story, instructive to us in many ways. The story itself is fairly simple, and most of us are, or should be, well acquainted with it. The cast of characters is well-known: Boaz, Ruth and Naomi as the major characters, and Orpah, Elimelekh, Mahlon and Kilyon as the minor characters.

But there is one personage who makes a brief appearance in this Book (chapter 4) whom we may designate as the "Mystery Man"! The Bible doesn't even give him a name. He is an anonymous and therefore mysterious character. You recall that Boaz was determined to marry this young widow of his cousin, this Moabite girl Ruth who had embraced Judaism. Now since Ruth and her mother-in-law Naomi owned the land left to them by their respective husbands, marriage would mean that these estates would be transferred to the new husbands. Let us remember that in those days real estate had more than commercial value—it meant the family inheritance, and sentiment was supported by law in making every attempt to keep property within the family or as close to it as possible. Now while Boaz was a first cousin, there was a closer relative—the brother of Elimelekh, the father of her late husband. Before Boaz could marry her and take possession of the family property, he needed the closer relative's consent (this relative is called the *go'el* or redeemer, for he redeems the family's possessions). Boaz therefore met this man and offered him priority in purchasing the lands of father and sons. He seemed willing to do this, regardless of price. But when Boaz told him that he would also have to marry Ruth if he should redeem the land, the *go'el* hesitated, then refused. I can't do it, he said. Boaz was then next in line for the right of redemption, and that he did, and, of course, he married Ruth. From this union, four generations later, came one of the greatest Jews in our long history, King David.

Who is this relative who missed the historic opportunity to enter history? What is his name? We do not know. The Bible does not tell us. It does tell us

---

5716 (1956)

rather pointedly that it does not *want* to mention his name. When the book describes Boaz's calling to the man to offer him the chance of redemption, we read that Boaz said, "Come here such a one and sit down" (Ruth 4:1). *Peloni Almoni*—"such a one." Lawyers might translate that as "John Doe." Colloquially we might translate those words as "so-and-so," or the entire phrase in slang English would read, "and he said, hey you, come here and sit down." Translate it however you will, the Torah makes it clear that it has no wish to reveal this man's name. Evidently he doesn't deserve it. He isn't worthy of having his name mentioned as part of Torah.

We may rightly wonder at the harsh condemnation of this person by the Torah. Why did he deserve this enforced anonymity? He was, after all, willing to redeem the land of his dead brother and nephew. But he balked at taking Ruth into the bargain as a package deal and marrying her out of a sense of duty. Well, who wouldn't do just that? Are those grounds for condemnation? As a matter of fact, our Rabbis tried to pry behind this veil of secrecy and they found his true name. It was, they tell us, *Tov,* which means "good" (*Ruth Rabbah* 6:3; *Tanhuma, Behar*, 8). He was a good chap. He showed a generally good nature. There was nothing vicious about him. And yet the Torah keeps him as a mystery man, it punishes him by making him a nameless character. He remains only a faint and anonymous shadow in the gallery of sacred history. His name was never made part of eternal Torah. He was deprived of his immortality. He is known only as *Peloni Almoni*, "the other fellow, "so-and-so," "the nameless one." A goodly sort of fellow, yet severely punished. Why is that so?

Our Sages have only one explanation for that harsh decree. By playing on the word *Almoni* of the title *Peloni Almoni*, they derive the word *illem*—mute or dumb. He remains without a name *she-illem hayah be-divrei Torah* because he was mute or dumb, speechless in Torah (*Ruth Rabbah* 7:7). He was not a Torah-Jew. Some good qualities, yes, but not *a ben Torah*. When it came to Torah, he lost his tongue. He could express himself in every way but a Torah way. Had he been a Torah kind of Jew, he would not have sufficed by just being a nice chap and buying another parcel of land. He would have realized that it is sinful to despise and underrate another human being merely because she is a poor, forlorn, friendless stranger. Had he been imbued with Torah he would have reacted with love and charity to the widow and the orphan and the stranger, the non-Jew. The Rabbis suggest that his reluctance to marry Ruth was for religious reasons: that the Torah forbids marriage with a Moabite, and Ruth was a Moabite. Had he ever bothered to study Torah in detail, as a Jew ought to, he would have known the elementary principle of *Mo'avi ve-lo Mo'aviyyah* (*Yevamot* 76b)—only male Moabites could never marry into the Jewish nation; female Moabites are acceptable spouses. Once this Moabite girl had decided to embrace Judaism from her own free will and with full genuineness and sincerity, she was as thoroughly Jewish as any other Jewish woman, and a Jewish man could marry her as he could the daughter of the Chief Rabbi of Israel. But this man was *illem be-divrei Torah*, he was unfeeling in a Torah way, he was out of joint with the spirit of Torah, he was ignorant of its laws and teachings; he had no contact with it. And a man of this sort has no name, insofar as Torah is concerned. He must remain *Peloni Almoni—the* nameless one. Such a person is unworthy of having his name immortalized in the Book of Eternal Life. His name has no place in Torah.

What we mean by a "name" and what the Torah meant by it, is something infinitely more than the meaningless appellative given to a person by his parents. It refers, rather; to a spiritual identity; it is the symbol of a spiritual personality in contact with the Divine, hence with the source of all life for all eternity. A name of this kind is not *given*; it is *earned*. A name of this sort is not merely registered by some bored clerk in the city records. It is emblazoned in the sacred letters of eternity on the firmament of time. One who is, therefore, *Almoni*, strange to Torah, can never be worthy of such a name. He must remain a *Peloni Almoni*.

It is told of the famous conqueror, Alexander the Great, that he was inspecting his troops one day and espied one particularly sloppy soldier. He said to him, "soldier, what is your name?" The soldier answered, "Sir, it is Alexander." The great leader was stunned for a moment, then said to him, "well, either change your name or change your behavior." That is what we mean by a name in Torah. It is the behavior, the personality, the soul, and not the empty title that counts.

As far as we Jews are concerned as a people, we can be identified primarily through Torah. Without it we are a nameless mass. Our history, like that of other peoples, has in it elements of military ventures, politics, economics. But more than any other people, it is a history of scholarship, of Torah. It was a non-Jew—Mohammed, the founder of Islam—who called us "The People of the Book"—not just books, but *The* Book." It was a non-Jew—the famed economist Thorsten Veblen—who called Jews "eternal wayfarers in the intellectual no-man's land." It was a non-Jew—the Protestant philosopher Paul Tillich—who said that, for Christians, Jews serve the spiritual purpose of preventing the relapse of Christianity into paganism. It was a non-Jew—the King of Italy—who in 1904 told Theodor Herzl that "sometimes I have Jewish callers who wince perceptibly at the mere mention of the word Jew. That is the sort I do not like. Then I really begin talking about Jews. I am only fond of people who have no desire to appear other than they are." The King of Italy was referring to nameless Jews, those who reject the name "Jew," those who are "mute in the words of Torah." For the Jew who is not *illem be-divrei Torah* knows that the function and destiny of our people is to be a "holy nation and kingdom of priests" (Ex. 19:6). As a people we have the choice: remain with Torah and be identified with the House of David, be *benei melakhim*, princes of the spirit— or become nameless and faceless blurs in the panorama of history; the people of Boaz, or a collection of *Peloni Almoni*s.

And what holds true for our people as a whole holds true for us as individuals as well. The Kabbalah and Hasidism have maintained that the name of every Jew is *merummaz ba-Torah*, hinted at in the Torah. Here too they meant "name" as a source of spiritual identification, as an indication of a living, vibrating, pulsating, soulful personality, a religious "somebody." When you are anchored in Torah, then you are anchored in eternity. Then you are not an indistinguishable part of an anonymous mass, but a sacred, individual person.

We who are here gathered for Yizkor, for remembering those dearly beloved who have passed on to another world, we should be asking ourselves that terrific question: will we be remembered? How will we be remembered? Or better: will we deserve to be remembered? And are we worthy enough to have our names immortalized in and through Torah? Are or are we not *illemim be-divrei Torah*?

Oh, how we try to achieve that "name," that disguise for immortality! We spend a lifetime trying to "make a name for ourselves" with our peers, in our professions and societies. We leave money in our wills not so much out of charitable feelings as much as that we want our names to be engraved in bronze and hewn in stone. And how we forget that peers die, professions change, societies vanish, bronze disintegrates and stone crumbles. Names of that sort are certainly not indestructible monuments. Listen to one poet who bemoans the loss of his name:

Alone I walked on the ocean sand/A pearly shell was in my hand;

I stooped and wrote upon the sand/My name, the year, the day.

As onward from the spot I passed/One lingering look behind I cast,

A wave came rolling high and fast/And washed my lines away.

The waves of time wash names of this kind away, indeed. Try as we will, if we remain each of us an *illem be-divrei Torah,* unrooted in Judaism, then we remain as well *Peloni Almoni.* Is it not better for us to immortalize our names in and through eternal Torah, so that God Himself will not know us other than as *Peloni Almoni?*

There is a custom which we do not practice but which Hasidic congregations do, which throws this entire matter into bold relief. The custom stems from the famous *Shelah ha-Kadosh,* Rabbi Isaiah Horowitz, who recommends that in order *she-lo yishkah shemo le-Yom ha-Din,* that our names not be forgotten on Judgment Day, we should recite a verse from the Bible related to the name at the end of the daily *Shemoneh Esreh (Siddur ha-Shelah s.v. pesukim li-shemot anashim).* There is a Biblical verse for every name. Thus my own is Nahum. And the verse I recite is from Isaiah, *Nahamu nahamu ammi yomar Elokeikhem*—console, console My people, says your God (Is. 40:1). My, what that makes of an ordinary name! Even as a child I was terrifically impressed with it—a job, a mission, a destiny: console your fellow man, your fellow Jews! Let any man do that and no matter what his parents called him, God knows his name—it is not *Peloni Almoni*; it is an eternal verse which will be read and taken to the hearts of men until the end of days.

On this Yizkor Day, think back to those whom you will shortly memorialize: does he or she have a name in Torah—or must you unfortunately refer to *Peloni Almoni* a shadow of a memory about to vanish? How will we be remembered—not by children, not by friends, not by other men at all . . . but at *Yom ha-Din,* on the day of judgment, by God Himself? Will we distinguish ourselves with humility, so that our names will become merged with the glorious verse of Micah (6:8): *Ve-hatznea lekhet im Elokekha,* walk humbly with thy God? Or will we prove ourselves men and women of sincere consideration and kindness and love for others so that our names will be one with *ve-ahavta le-re'akha kamokha,* love of neighbor (Lev. 19:18)? Or will we devote our finest efforts to the betterment of our people and effecting rapprochement between Jews and their Torah, so that our names will be *beni bekhori Yisrael,* Israel is my first-born (Ex. 4:22)? Will we delve to the limits of our mental capacity into the study of Torah, so that our names will be an *etz hayyim hi la-mahazikin bah,* a tree of eternal life to those that hold it (Prov. 3:18)? Or will we do none of these things, just be *tov*, good-natured men and women. with no special distinction in Torah, no real anchorage in Jewishness, and find that our lives have been spent in nothingness and that even God has no name for us, that we will be just plain *Peloni Almoni?*

On this Shavuot day, when we recall the giving of the Torah at Sinai, the "Mystery Man" of the Book of Ruth calls to us from the dim obscurity in which he has been shrouded: Do not do what I did. Do not be *illem be-divrei Torah,* mute and speechless when it comes to Torah. Do not end your lives in a puff of anonymity. Grasp the Tree of Life which is Torah. Live it. Practice it. Overcome all hardships and express it in every aspect of your life. Do not abandon it lest God will abandon you. Jump at this opportunity for immortality. In short: make a name for yourself—through Torah, and with God.

SINAI DESANCTIFIED

IN PREPARATION FOR THE great event of revelation, or *Mattan Torah,* at Mount Sinai, the Almighty commanded Moses, *Ve-higbalta et ha-am saviv,* "and you shall set bounds unto the people round about the mountain, saying, 'Take care that you go not onto the mountain or touch even the border of it, for whoever touches the mount shall surely be put to death. . . . Whether it be beast or man, it shall not live'" (Ex. 19:12–13). And then, almost immediately thereafter, we read: *Bi-meshokh ha-yovel hemah ya'alu ba-har,* "but when the ram's horn sounds, then they may come up to the mountain" (19:13). One of the most incisive commentaries on the Torah, Rabbi Meir Simhah of Dvinsk (in *Meshekh Hokhmah,* ad loc.) observes that whereas the Almighty is quite severe in warning the people to stay away from the mountain during the time of revelation, He rather abruptly grants permission to scale the mountain thereafter. Usually, when a strong prohibition is proclaimed, some time passes before an exemption or suspension is granted. Yet here the Almighty switches from a marked prohibition to a clear permission: when the ram's horn sounds, then they shall go up onto the mountain. Why the suddenness? Why is God, as it were, so anxious to provide the *hetter* immediately after pronouncing the *issur*?

The answer our commentator provides to this question touches on one of the fundamentals of our Jewish faith that is of perennial relevance and significance. It is, he says, a protest against the pagan mentality, both ancient and modern. Every religion, pagan as well as Jewish, knows of a category it calls the holy, something known as *kedushah,* or holiness. There is, however, a vast difference between how the pagan and the Jew understand and conceive of the holy. The pagan identifies it as something magical, something objective, a miraculously inherent quality. The holy object was holy to his mind, and always will remain so—it is the religion of totem and taboo. *Kedushah* is conceived as independent of and remote from man.

5713 (1963)

To the Jew, however, *kedushah* is not at all absolute and magical. There is nothing in all the world that is holy in and of itself without being *made* holy. Holiness comes about only when God descends to meet man, and man strains to rise to meet Him. When the encounter between man and God is done, when God has withdrawn His *Shekhinah*, or Presence, and man has retired from the moment of spiritual elation, then *kedushah* vanishes.

This is why, according to our commentator, the Almighty so abruptly informed Israel of the desanctification of Mount Sinai immediately after emphasizing its holiness. *Bi-meshokh ha-yovel*, when the shofar sounds, indicating the end of revelation, then *hemah ya'alu ba-har*, let them scale the heights of the mountain and see that this is a mountain like all other mountains, with vegetation and foliage and insects and wild beasts. There is nothing inherent in the mountain to make it different from other desert mountains. Let the Israelites appreciate that God did not reveal himself at Mount Sinai because Mount Sinai is holy, but Mount Sinai is holy only because and when God revealed Himself on it. And when *Mattan Torah* is over, when God has left and man has returned from the great historic encounter, then *kedushah* disappears. To this very day we do not consider Mount Sinai holy. There is a Christian monastery on Mount Sinai—but no shul.

To put it simply, for the pagan, *kedushah* exists independent of God or man. For the Jew, *kedushah* comes only when God calls upon man or when man calls upon God. There can be no *kedushah* unless there is a *mekaddesh*—a sanctifier, someone, whether he be divine or human, to impose holiness. This is a conception of holiness which is indeed one of the most important principles of all Judaism. It is so fundamental to the life of Torah that it was made clear to us ere the first word of Torah was revealed.

Thus, the holiness of a synagogue issues from the intent of the men and women who frequent it; a synagogue is not holy in and of itself. If people come to a shul to pray and study Torah and practice *mitzvot* and submit their lives to the judgment of its teachings, it is holy. If the praying is subservient to social experience, and the study secondary to status-seeking, and the *mitzvot* are ignored and the Halakhah is compromised and people seek in the synagogue a confirmation of their prejudices and failings and religious inadequacies, the synagogue is not holy, no matter how impressive its religious architecture. In Judaism, a synagogue possesses *kedushah* not because of its furnishings, but because of its worshipers; not because of its religious art, but because of the devout hearts; not because of the money spent on it, but because of the feelings spilt in it.

According to traditional Jewish teaching, a *Sefer Torah* is holy only if the *sofer*, the scribe, was pious and his heart and mind directed to God. If the scribe is a skeptic, even a learned one, if he has reservations in his commitment to the life of Torah, then he may boast of the most beautiful handwriting and the most expensive parchment, but it is not holy; it is just another piece of fancy penmanship.

You cannot *have* a religion unless you *are* religious. There will be no Judaism unless Jews are Jewish. There is nothing sacred unless we, in our own lives and by our own conduct, sanctify it. *Kedushah* comes into being only when there is first a *mekaddesh*, someone—either God or man—willing to bestow holiness upon the object or place.

But what does it mean "to sanctify," to "be religious," to "be Jewish," to be a *mekaddesh*?

I believe the major answer is: to be dissatisfied; never to rest on your laurels; never to be complacent; never to accept the religious status quo as sufficient. In the realm of spirit and Torah, either we advance or we retreat; we can never stay in the same place. To be a *mekaddesh*, to give dignity and meaning and sanctity to all those institutions in our life and in our society that we cherish, we must resolve never to be satisfied with sentimental mementoes of a static and moribund faith, never to allow the flicker of the spirit to remain ensconced in our hearts without illuminating the world about us.

Jewish tradition, in one variant of a text in the *Tosefta* (*Sotah* 7:18), tells us that in the camp of the children of Israel in the Sinai Desert, shortly after they received the Torah on Shavuot, there were two arks. *Ehad she-yotzei immahem la-milhamah hayah bo sefer Torah, ve-ehad she-sharuy immahem ba-mahaneh hayu bo shivrei luhot.*

The ark they took with them in their wars, in their conquest of Canaan and their conversion of a land of pagan idols into a Holy Land, that ark contained the *Sefer Torah*. The ark that was stationary, that remained with them in their camp, that ark contained not a *Sefer Torah*, but the jagged remnants of the tablets of the commandments which Moses had broken in his anger at the Children of Israel, who worshiped the Golden Calf.

When the ark is conceived as being stationary; when it is not allowed to interfere in the personal strivings and adventures of a man's life; when it is kept only for its historical and sentimental or ornamental value, then it cannot contain a *Sefer Torah*. It then holds in it only *shivrei luhot*—pitiful remnants of broken commandments. These, too, have historical and sentimental value. They are a tender, moving reminder of the past. But the commandments are broken. They are irrelevant. They are spiritually meaningless. They have lost their vitality. Their ability to influence the lives of men is gone.

When, however, the ark is dynamic, when it is *yotzei immahem le-mil-hamah*, when it follows—nay, leads them in their wars, in their daily struggles for bread and shelter; when it is near to them in their moments of crisis and decision; when it forms the pattern for their dreams, the basis of their prayers, and the substance of their hopes; when it is taken along into their offices and shops and stores and factories; when it is made part-and-parcel of life and is held up as a living guide to present and future and not merely as a sentimental souvenir of an over-idealized past; then it contains no *shivrei luhot*. Then it holds within its sacred precincts the Holy Torah itself, whose parchment is beautiful in its wholeness and whose letters, though eternal, are timely.

The ark that remains in the camp, detached from and uninvolved in the Jew's life, may be ornamented, polished, and outwardly attractive. But it is merely a pretty casket for the broken corpse of a religion that once was and is no more. The ark that travels with him may be dirty with the soot of the great highway of life; it may be soiled from the tender caresses of hands stained with the grime of honest toil. But in it lies the *Sefer Torah*, a dynamic, living, pulsating heart that beats in a divine rhythm of unceasing vitality, and through which flows the life-blood of countless generations of scholars and saints, of prophets and poets, of just plain good Jews who lived Jewish lives and found favor in the eyes of God and man.

In order to be a *mekaddesh*, in order to infuse our lives with the dignity of *kedushah*, we must prefer a Torah that can fit into the suitcase of our vibrant personalities over a large and stately one that remains nobly ignored and unattended in its majestic loneliness in the ark in the synagogue,

As we prepare for the summer vacation period, let us remember that neither this synagogue nor any other will retain its *kedushah* unless each of its members and worshipers remains a *mekaddesh* throughout the summer vacation and thereafter. We cannot and must not expect that summertime is a vacation from religious responsibility and the synagogue will be awaiting us with open arms when we return without in the least diminishing its own sacred integrity.

On this holiday of Shavuot, when we commemorate the giving of Torah at Sinai, we must resolve that each of us will become a *mekaddesh* in the circles in which he travels. We must understand that our faith is not only a heritage from the past, but something that will create for us a future. We must understand that the Torah depends upon us even as much as we depend upon it. We must therefore affirm that we shall not be isolationists in our *Yiddishkeit*—we shall not keep it for ourselves, but attempt to share it with others, whether it be through personal example, through conversation, through support of *yeshivot*, or by any of its means with which we are acquainted.

May the Almighty grant that as we rise for the Yizkor and commune with our own thoughts and our own memories, we recall that great principle of Judaism: the fate of Torah depends upon us. The fate of *kedushah* depends upon us. The fate of the future depends upon us.

May we fulfill our sacred responsibilities in the eyes of God, in the eyes of man, and in the eyes of generations yet unborn.

RISE AND SHINE

ONE OF THE RESULTS of the revelation of the Torah at Mount Sinai was the fascinating effect it had on Moses himself: *U-Mosheh lo yada ki karan or panav be-dabbero itto.* As a result of the encounter with God, the face of Moses began to shine, and he himself was not aware of his radiance, or halo. So noticeable were the physical traces of this historic spiritual achievement that *va-yire'u mi-geshet elav.* Aaron and the elders and all Israel were afraid to approach Moses, so did his face glow. (See Ex. 34:29–30.)

Of course, this was a singular and unique event in the annals of mankind. Yet, in a measure of speaking, anyone who undergoes a spiritual experience of significance feels that he is in some way transformed or transfigured, and experiences a glow or radiance even if it be only internal.

People who are sincerely religious aspire to such a sensation. In addition to obedience, we inwardly yearn for some tremor, some sense of exaltation, something that will elevate us even momentarily beyond the humdrum of existence. That is especially true of the younger generation, those who look with amused contempt on the goal of achieving "the good things in life," which we, in the innocence of our youth, were told could be supplied by DuPont and a secure job. They are now benefiting from the affluence their parents' generation achieved. They take it for granted, and see that it is not all as satisfying as it was made out to be. And so they genuinely search for inspiration, for illumination, for a special feeling of transcendence. Unfortunately, they sometimes seek to satisfy these longings by artificial means—mistaking the narcotic experience for an authentically spiritual one. Yet the need and the desire are fairly universal.

How, then, does one achieve this?

Apparently, the Rabbis asked a similar question. In the Midrash (*Shemot Rabbah, Ki Tissa* 47:6) we read the question *Me-heikhan natal Mosheh karnei ha-hod,* "from whence did Moses derive the rays of glory?" And the explanation states:

5734 (1974)

314

ר' ברכיה הכהן בשם רבי שמואל אמר הלוחות היו ארכן ששה טפחים ורחבן ששה טפחים. והיה משה אוחז בטפחיים והשכינה בטפחיים וטפחיים באמצע ומשם נטל משה קרני ההוד.

R. Berakhyah says that Moses derived the rays of glory from the tablets. The tablets were six *tefahim* high and six *tefahim* wide [a *tefah* is the length of a human fist, about four inches]. Moses held on to two *tefahim* of the tablets, and the *Shekhinah* held on to the two top *tefahim* of the tablets. In the middle there were two that were ungrasped either by Moses or by God. And from those two middle *tefahim*, Moses derived his rays of glory!

I take this passage to mean that there are three areas of existence: the unattainable, the already attained, and the yet to be attained.

The two *tefahim* held by the Holy One represent the unattainable. Not everything in life is possible for man to achieve. In the nineteenth and early twentieth centuries, when our civilization was intoxicated with the heady successes of science and technology, it naively believed that anything man wanted he could achieve, given enough funding for his research projects and the brains to carry them out. But this was the social and cultural analogue of the young adolescent first feeling his muscles and overwhelmed with his potency. Maturity requires of us to banish any illusions of omnipotence. Judaism teaches us that not everything in the realm of the spirit (or any other area) is given to man to know and to attain. We are taught that humility and a sense of our physical limitations and spiritual finitude are the first step toward wisdom. Ben Sira exclaimed: *be-mufla mimmekha al tidrosh*, "in what is wondrous to thee shalt thou not inquire." The effort to wrest the secrets of God results only in dreadful failure. Over-ambitiousness in any area of life, the effort to over-reach into that which lies beyond the ken of humans, whether as a species or as individuals, leads to frustration and bitterness; not to a halo but to a hell of unhappiness.

The two *tefahim* that Moses held refers to successes already achieved. There are those, both individuals and organizations, who do nothing but revel in past accomplishments. Instead of concentrating on problems at hand, they delight in telling you about all the things they once did. This repetition, a litany of old and faded glories, is no way to achieve a halo. Stand on your dignity, and you crush it. Rest on your laurels, and you flatten them. Complacency and smugness can never lead to inspiration. Past glories and successes are significant primarily insofar as they are a springboard for future creativity.

The area of life that does lead to radiance, to the glow of deserved satisfaction, comes from the *revah ba-emtza*, the part in between, that which signifies the distance between the real and the ideal, between the possessed and the possible, between what the Israelis call *ha-ratzui ve-ha-matzui*. To try for more than I have already achieved, and push the limits of that which is at all achievable—that is the way to attain the halo of success.

So it was with Moses. The spiritual level he had already achieved was not sufficient to give him his *karnei ha-hod*, his rays of glory. The areas that were beyond human possibility, Moses was wise enough not to attempt. He did derive his radiance from his restlessness to achieve more than he did but what he yet could.

All creativity consists, therefore, of two steps: locating the two *tefahim* of empty space and reaching for it. Whether it be in music or engineering, medicine or psychology, in history or matters of the spirit, it is important to know one's limits and to push at them.

Judaism, in all its branches, has never demanded of man that he be an angel. It never sets impossible demands upon him. It is one of the foundations of our faith that Torah and Halakhah are all achievable without surpassing the limits of human ability. It is possible, always possible, to live up to the standards of Torah. Torah does not ask us to strain ourselves beyond human limitations. But neither does Torah ever allow us to feel smug and self-righteous. It seeks to inculcate in us the feeling of dissatisfaction, of restlessness with present achievement. Hasidism put it this way: if you cannot be a *tzaddik*, at least be a *hasid* of a *tzaddik*!

If there is a single community of Jews who illustrate to me this attainment of the rays of glory as a result of pushing into the two *tefahim* of empty space, it is the Russian Jews. Consider the conditions under which they live—the tyranny, the oppression, the fear, the risk. Yet, they marshal all their courage and their intelligence. They do not try to overthrow the Communist government, but they do try to get out either to Israel or to America, to reestablish their lives as Jews. Their courage, their heroism, their bravery give them a halo. When I look upon a Russian-Jewish immigrant, whether in Israel or here—and as long as I am here, I will never bring myself to pass judgment upon a Russian Jew who comes here instead of to Israel—I see, almost visibly, a halo about his head.

This concept is something that is important to all parents. In raising our children, we sometimes tend to extremes. Occasionally, we see a child as an extension of ourselves, and we try to achieve through the child what we have failed to do in our own lives. As a result, we may set goals that are too high, too exacting, too demanding, for the talents and abilities of a particular child. If we push too far, if we attempt to reach "the two *tefahim* of the Holy One," we run the risk of psychologically destroying the child and ruining his self-confidence. The other extreme is a policy of *laissez-faire*: things will take care of themselves. We then allow a child to follow his own patterns of inertia and indolence, and we remain satisfied with the "two *tefahim* of Moses." If we fail to push just a bit beyond, if we fail to inspire and to urge and to encourage the child to transcend his present level, then we are permitting him to stagnate. The proper way, on the basis of the idea we have found in this passage, is to help the child, by inspiration and example, to exploit his latent talents and interests and abilities. That is how children develop the *karnei ha-hod*, and give their parents the glow of what we call *nahas*.

But above all else, this principle applies to the principle of Torah. I know that I sound like a broken record, but I believe it is my duty to repeat this at every occasion: no one has the moral right to call himself a Torah-committed Jew if he merely observes the *mitzvot*. The most important mitzvah is *Talmud Torah*, the study of Torah. One who does not study the Torah at least once during the day and during the night—or at the very barest minimum (and this is decidedly less than the Halakhah demands) at least attend a *shi'ur*, a lecture on Talmud or Torah once a week—a person of this sort cannot call himself Torah-committed. Smugness and complacency in our own religious lives are not going to give us a feeling of satisfaction in our Judaism. Our problem is not trying too hard, but trying too little. And if we have not been attending sufficiently to the study of Torah—our *own* study of Torah, not only that of our children—perhaps these words will give us enough of a guilt feeling to try to improve our situation.

A wonderful example of this glow of satisfaction, these *karnei ha-hod*, is perhaps the feeling of warmth and enthusiasm and inspiration that came for those of us who joined in the first all-night Torah vigil on the eve of this Shavuot.

I was pleased beyond words that between seventy-five and eighty people stayed with us, studying Torah until about 1:30 or 2:00 in the morning, and that about forty-five remained all night long, culminating in the *Shaharit* services from 4:30 to 6:30 a.m. Those who joined us were not even conscious that time had passed. The text caught us up in its intellectual excitement, its spiritual insightfulness, and before we realized it, we had spent a whole night studying Torah. Everyone who was with us knows what I mean when I say that we experienced a bit, even if only infinitesimal, of the *karnei ha-hod* which Moses felt when he reached out for those two *tefahim* of empty space. We tried for empty space—for that which we had not achieved or attempted before, but which was attainable by us—and it certainly was worth it!

It is worth repeating, in this respect, a very well known Hasidic story. It is told of the saintly Hasidic master R. Zusya that when he was on his deathbed, his Hasidim noticed him weeping. "Why do you weep, O Rabbi?" they asked him. "I weep," he said, "because I fear having to come before the *Beit Din shel Malah* the Heavenly Court." The Hasidim were puzzled: "You, O Rabbi, have to fear the judgment of Heaven? Do we not all know that you have led an exemplary and saintly life?"

"No, my children, you do not understand. I am not afraid that the heavenly Judge will ask me, 'Zusya, why were you not self-sacrificing like Abraham?' I will tell Him, quite simply, 'I am not Abraham, I am only Zusya.' I am not afraid that He will say to me, 'Why were you not wise like R. Akiva?' I will tell Him, 'I do not have the intellect of R. Akiva, I am only little Zusya.' But my great and overwhelming fear is, what shall I answer when the heavenly Judge says to me, 'Zusya, why were you not *Zusya*?'"

That is the great question. No one demands that we be more than we are, more than Zusya. But what we ultimately must answer for is why we never fulfilled all our expectations, why we never exploited all our potentialities, why Zusya was not Zusya.

At this time, on Shavuot and as we approach Yizkor, we are summoned to pause for a moment of reflection: Are we wasting our energies striving for the impossible? Or are we—what is more likely—prone to be satisfied with the two *tefahim* of Moses, with what we already have, ceasing all effort and inspiration and aspiration?

It is in a precious moment of this sort that the empty space on the tablets beckons to us: reach for it, and glow. Rise—and shine.

Tish‘ah Be-Av

WHEN WE TRY TO KEEP GOD IN HIS PLACE

IF THERE IS ONE word which symbolizes and characterizes this day of Tish'ah be-Av—set aside for woe and anguish from the time of the Israelites' obstreperousness toward Moses in the desert, through the destruction of the two Temples, and from the Spanish Inquisition in 1492 to Hitler's extermination order in 1942 against Polish Jewry, all of which came on the ninth of Av, the Black Day of the Jewish calendar—that word is *eikhah*. It is a simple word, which means "how." But the peculiar poetic construction of the word *eikhah*, instead of the more usual *ekh*, has a connotation of woe, of gloom and moroseness. It is the word with which Moses in today's *sidrah* expresses his exasperation: *eikhah essa levaddi?* (Deut. 1:12), "how can I bear them alone?" Isaiah in today's *haftarah* chooses this word to bemoan the sad fate of Jerusalem: *eikhah*, "how is the faithful city become as a harlot?" (Is. 1:21). And, of course, it is the refrain of Jeremiah's dirges, his Lamentations, known in Hebrew as the *Megillah* of *Eikhah*.

The Rabbis of the Midrash were intrigued by the word, and what they say throws light not only upon the word itself but upon the broader concept which informs this day and the historic events it commemorates. Indeed, they see *eikhah* as part of a structure which expands Tish'ah be-Av from a day of national mourning into a symbol of the most crucial universal significance. They tell us: *Kol mah she-ira le-Adam ira le-Yisra'el*, "everything that happened to Adam happened to Israel" (*Yalkut Shim'oni, Eikhah*, 1001). Adam was placed by God in the Garden of Eden; Israel was brought by the Lord to Eretz Yisra'el, a Paradise in its own right. Adam was given a commandment; Israel was given 613 commandments. Adam sinned; Israel sinned. Adam was sent away and expelled; Israel was sent away and expelled into a long and bitter exile. What the Rabbis intend by this parallelism is the teaching that Israel's exile issues from

Shabbat Hazon 5724 (1964)

a human failing rather than a specifically Jewish weakness. By pointing to the identical pattern in the life of Adam and of Israel, they underscore the universal dimensions of Tish'ah be-Av.

And the final example of the parallel developments that the Sages of the Midrash offer is the climax of each of the two epics. In the case of Adam, the Almighty *konen alav ayyekkah*, wails over Adam, calling out *ayyekkah*, "where art thou?" And in the case of Israel, *konen alav eikhah*; He wails over Israel's fate, *Eikhah*, how could all this have come to pass? Both words, *ayyekkah* and *eikhah*, are essentially the same. Without the vowel signs, they are spelt the same way. God's query to Adam, *ayyekkah*, "where art thou?" bears an intimate relationship to the prophet's lamentation, *Eikhah*, "how has this come to pass?"

For indeed, the *hurban ha-Bayit*, the destruction of the Temple, recapitulates the tragedy of man in the face of God. Adam, having eaten of the Tree of Knowledge and supposedly grown more sophisticated, now flees to the cluster of trees in the midst of the Garden—and attempts to hide from God! His illegitimate grasp for knowledge has gained for him the idiotic illusion that he can set boundaries for God, keeping Him away from his own areas, and that he can erect impenetrable barriers between the domains of God and man. Adam thus invites the response of the Almighty, in syllables of searing sarcasm, "*Ayyekkah*—where art thou?" Adam, where do you think you are that you can hide from Me? What makes you think that you can declare any place in the world out of bounds for God?

Was not the Temple destroyed for the same reason? Our tradition enumerates some of the moral causes of the tragedy visited upon the Sanctuary. But all of them add up to one basic idea: the people imagined that God's presence dwells only in the Temple; elsewhere, one may do as he pleases. A man may hate his brother, so long as he prays in the *Beit ha-Mikdash*. He may exploit the worker and drive his slaves; does he not bring his sacrifices regularly to Jerusalem? This was the blasphemy of which the generation of the *hurban* was guilty; they conceived of God as imprisoned in His reverent House, and imagined that as long as one appeased Him there, He would not interfere elsewhere. But that whole philosophy is pagan, unholy, and unwholesome. That is why Isaiah, in the *haftarah* we read this morning, pours out his bitterness against those who so piously corrupt the whole vision of Torah: *Mi bikkesh zot mi-yedkhem remos hatzeraï*? (Is. 1:12), "who asked this of you [to visit the Temple]? You are but trampling My courtyard underfoot!" When you restrict God *only* to the synagogue, then He refuses to dwell *even* in the synagogue. When this is how you undermine the meaning of a Temple, then as a sign of divine displeasure, that very Temple, symbol of your profane misunderstanding, must be destroyed! For God, whether man likes it or not, peers into man's "exclusive" preserves—his office and home, his bank and theater, his marketplace and hotel—and acidly asks, *ayyekkah*, where do you think you are? You have failed to look for Me, and so *I* shall seek *you* out. And when the Almighty grimly poses the *ayyekkah*, then man must whimper in return, *Eikhah*.

Modern man repeats the same syndrome—with even more tragic results. We have eaten of the Tree of Knowledge like no generation before us—and we have found the fruits bitter; for such is the taste of radioactive ash. We have developed science and technology at an incredible pace. Yet we have become what in Jewish literature is known as *hakham le-hareia*, "wise for our own hurt." Our genius has proved an evil genius. With our increase in knowledge has come a shrinkage of wisdom; with the conquest of the universe, we have discovered that we have let our own lives lie fallow; learning to make a living, we have forgotten how to live; exploring outer space, we have ignored the thunderous silence of our inner space and inner void.

For what has all this learning and sophistication led us to? To an ever stricter seclusion of God from life. Like Adam and like our ancestors two thousand years ago and more, we have determined to incarcerate God in His reverent jail and we have declared the rest of the world forbidden to Him. What is to God is to God, but all the rest is to Caesar.

What is the name of this ideology which "respects" religion so long as it does not venture out of its prescribed sphere? It is the theory and practice of secularism. Secularism is not atheism. It is something else, though equally as bad. It agrees to the practice of religion, provided that the limits are set and that beyond them life and experience are hermetically sealed off from the influence of faith. Secularism characterizes the overwhelming majority of religions and religionists today. It accepts God—but equally as much accepts that one can hide from Him, that in some little clump of trees one can surround himself with cool shade and be free from the searing gaze of the Deity who has clumsily been permitted to escape from His House of Worship. Modern secularist man gets even with God; once He expelled us from Paradise, now we shall build ourselves a little Paradise and keep *Him* out!

But God won't go away. He won't abide by the rules that secularism has put down for the game of religion. God's a poor sport. He doesn't like to be locked up and is annoyed with those who test His claustrophobia. To the self-important secularist—the Jew who worships God in the synagogue but rejects His judgment (Halakhah) elsewhere, the man who opts only for "ritual" but ignores ethics and morality, or vice versa—God appears in all His awesome might and poses His devastating question: *Ayyekkah*, where art thou that thou thinkest to exclude Me? And when that happens, Man can but answer, from the shambles of his supermodern Paradise-playground, *Eikhah*.

The Temple is the *Beit ha-Mikdash*, the House of Holiness. And the opposite of *kedushah*, or holiness, is *hol*, the profane. The antonym of *kiddush Hashem*, the sanctification of God's Name, is *hillul Hashem*, the profanation of the Name. Rabbi Hayyim of Volozhin once explained the origin of *hillul*: the word derives from *halal*, a void, empty space. For when man acts as if God were elsewhere, not here; when his demeanor and conduct are such as to indicate his inner belief that right here and now is a *halal*, a void where God's omnipresence is countered and entrance denied Him; when man believes, or his deeds bespeak the belief, that there are places where God is and places where He is not—that is the vilest and basest profanation of His Name. It is the *hillul Hashem*, the spiritual obscenity of secularism. That is why the *Beit ha-Mikdash* must be destroyed if men distort its purpose and abuse it in the service of *hillul* rather than *kiddush*.

This then is the relevant message of Tish'ah be-Av and *Eikhah*: we must learn to avoid the mistakes of the past and the present and to acknowledge God in all existence—personal, national, and international. Even as the Temple was destroyed by *hillul*, we must rebuild it through *kiddush*.

Then, in place of *Eikhah*, will come the *pirkei nehamah*, the chapters of consolation. For instead of hiding from God and inviting His *ayyekkah*, our generation will seek Him out: *zeh dor doreshav*. And the divine answer will be: *Anokhi anokhi hu menahemkhem*, "I, yea I, will be your Consoler" (Is. 51:12).

THE VEIL OF GOD

TISH'AH BE-AV IS MORE than the commemoration of the five specific historical events mentioned in the Talmud, foremost among them the destruction of the two Temples in Jerusalem six centuries apart. It is even more than the national threnody for a string of tragedies, beginning from the earliest times and extending through the ninth of Av, 1492—the expulsion of Jews from Spain—and the same date in 1942, the signing of the extermination order against Polish Jewry by the unmentionable leader of Nazi Germany. More than these alone, Tish'ah be-Av is a condition of the divine-human dialogue; it is a quality of the relations of God and the people of Israel.

Man does not always perceive God uniformly. Sometimes, He appears close to us, nearby, concerned, sympathetic, involved in our destiny, a loving and forgiving Father. "The Lord is near to all who call upon Him" (Ps. 145:18). It is a source of joy and comfort to man when he perceives God in this fashion. But sometimes God appears infinitely remote, distant, faraway. It seems almost as if He has vanished from the world, without leaving a trace. God appears aloof, unapproachable, forbidding, uninterested, and ready to abandon man to eternal solitude. There is no greater agony for man than when God thus veils His presence, when He performs *hester panim,* the "hiding of His face" from mankind. When God, as it were, withdraws from the world and leaves man to his own resources, forsaken and at the mercy of the impersonal and brutal forces of nature and history, man's life is worse than meaningless. It is this latter condition that is described in Tish'ah be-Av.

That black day was the beginning of the long, ages-old epoch in which God and Israel disengaged from each other, when a seemingly impenetrable veil cruelly separated them. The culmination of Jeremiah's Lamentations sound this very note: *Lammah la-netzah tishkahenu, ta'azvenu le-orekh yamim* (Lam. 5:20), "Why do You forget us for an eternity, forsake us for so long a time?"

Shabbat Hazon 5725 (1965)

325

But if so many generations were born and died under the heavy cloud of this veil, this *hester panim*, since that disaster 1,895 years ago initiated this agonizingly long separation, then we are faced with two questions: First, how is it that we have not disappeared as a people? According to all the laws of historical determinism, we should have disappeared long ago. If there is no longer any relation between God and Israel, how can we account for the mystery and miracle of Israel's persistence? And second, how can we pray? Is it not futile to try to arouse One who in advance resists any communication? Moreover, how can we speak of such matters as *ahavah rabbah ahavtanu*, of God's great love for Israel?

For an answer to these questions and a solution to the whole problem of *hester panim* and Tish'ah be-Av, we may turn to a remarkable insight offered by two of the earliest giants of the Hasidic movement. The Hasidic classic, the *Benei Yissaskhar*, records two questions asked of R. Pinhas of Koretz, the disciple-colleague of the Ba'al Shem Tov, and the one answer that both gave to the two questions. (See *Ma'amarei Tammuz-Av*, #3.)

The first question concerns the well-known tradition that the Messiah is born on Tish'ah be-Av (*Midrash Eikhah Zuta* [Buber ed., version 2] 1:2). Is it not unreasonable to assert that the purest of all souls, the exalted agent of the Almighty in the long-awaited redemption of Israel, would come into this world on the very day distinguished for infamy and grief? Is not this the single most inappropriate day for such an historic event? Second, the Talmud records a most marvelous tale. It relates that when the enemy broke into the sacred precincts of the Temple and laid low its walls, they entered the inner sanctum wherein there stood the two Cherubim, the statuettes resembling the faces of young, innocent children, and from between which the voice of God would issue forth. When the enemy beheld these Cherubim, the Talmud relates, they found that the two figurines were *facing each other* (*Yoma* 54b). Now this is most unexpected, because according to Jewish tradition, the Cherubim faced each other only when Israel was obedient to God (*osin retzono shel Makom*); when Jews did not perform the will of God, the Cherubim turned *away* from each other. The destruction of the Temple was certainly the result of Israel's disobedience and rebellion. One would expect, therefore, that they would turn their faces away from each other. Why, then, were they facing one another, the sign of mutual love between God and His people?

The answer is a profound insight into the nature of love and friendship. The attachment between two people is always strongest just before they part from each other. Two friends may continue their friendship with each other on an even keel for many years. Their loyalty requires of them no outward expression, even if they do not take each other for granted. Then one of the two prepares to leave on a long, long journey. How poignant does their friendship suddenly become! With what longing do they view each other! Similarly, husband and wife are involved in the daily struggles and trivialities that cloud their true feelings for each other. But when one is about to leave for a protracted vacation or sick leave or business trip, and they know they will not be near and with each other for a painfully long period, then they suddenly rise to the very heights of mutual love and dedication, and they behold each other with new warmth and yearning and sweet sorrow. Indeed, the Halakhah declares this to be a mandatory expression of the right relationship between husband and wife: *Hayyav adam lifkod et ishto be-sha'ah she-hu yotzei la-derekh* (*Yevamot* 62b), when one is about to take leave for a long journey, he must be especially tender and loving toward his wife.

Now the love between God and Israel follows the same pattern as genuine human love. Tish'ah be-Av was the beginning of the *hester panim*, the parting of the lovers. God and Israel turned away from each other, and the great, exciting, and immensely complicated relationship between the two companions, begun in the days of Abraham, was coming to an end. But before this tragic and heartbreaking moment, there took place a last, long, lingering look, the fervent embrace of the two lovers as they were about to part. At the threshold of separation, they both experienced a great outpouring of mutual love, an intense *ahavah*, as they suddenly realized the long absence from each other that lay ahead of them; in so brief a time, they tried to crowd all the affection the opportunities for which they had ignored in the past, and all the love which would remain unrequited in the course of the future absence. That is why the Cherubim were facing each other. Certainly the Israelites were rebellious and in contempt of the will of God. But they were facing each other; God and Israel looked toward each other longingly and in lingering affection before they were pulled apart. And from this high spiritual union of God and Israel was created the soul of the Messiah! *Mashiah* was conceived in intense and rapturous love!

From this exquisitely intensified relationship *before* the long separation, we may gain a new insight into the relationship of God and Israel *during* this prolonged period of *hester panim* initiated by the destruction of the Temple. True and devoted friends never forget each other even if anger and offense have caused them to separate from one another. Of genuine friends it may never be said that "out of sight, out of mind." Where there was once deep and profound love between husband and wife, some spark of it will always remain, no matter how sorely their marriage has been tried. Absence, indeed, may make the heart grow fonder, and the old love may well be reawakened. Those who deal with marital problems have observed that often a couple will undergo legal separation, and that very absence from each other will make them realize how they need and yearn for each other—and thus lead to reunion. A father may be angry with his son, so angry that they no longer speak with each other. But the father's heart aches, his sleep is disturbed, and his heart lies awake at night waiting for his son to call, to write, to make some small gesture toward reconciliation. All these are instances of separation tense with love striving for reunion.

Such indeed is the *hester panim* that separates us from our Father in heaven. We are exiled from Him—but not alienated. We are so far—yet so close. We are separated—but not divorced. God's face is hidden, but His heart is awake. Of course, the divine love for Israel has not expired. It is that and that alone that accounts for our continued existence to this day. Certainly "with a great love hast Thou loved us"—for though we are banished, we need but call to Him and He will answer. Like a wise parent, the Almighty may punish, even expel, but never ceases to love His child!

Have we any evidence of this phenomenon in the history of Israel in our own times? I believe we do, but I approach the subject *bi-dehilu u-rehimu*, with trepidation. If one were to ask: was it worth experiencing a Holocaust which decimated one-third of our people in order to attain a State of Israel?, then not only an affirmative answer but even the very question is a blasphemy. Only a cruel, heartless jingoist could ever allow such thoughts to poison his mind. Yet the past is done and cannot be undone. History is irrevocable. We may protest it and bemoan it and regret it, but it is there despite us. A tremendous paradox emerged from the paroxysms of our times, and we must strive to understand it: during one lifetime, we have witnessed the nadir of Jewish history, the descent into the very pit, and the rebirth of Jewish independence in pride and glory.

The Holocaust was the most intense, the most dismal *hester panim* we have ever experienced. God abandoned us to the vilest scorpions that ever assumed the shape of man. From our agony and our dishonor we cried to heaven, but our cries could not pierce the metal veil, which only reflected our shrieking back upon us to mock us in our terrible loneliness and torment. Auschwitz was the device of human genius as God turned aside. Buchenwald was built by human toil and intellect as God closed His eyes.

Yet we survived the experience: crippled, maimed, decimated, disgraced, we yet trudged back from the death camps and displaced-persons camps, from the fury and the wrath, and from the shameful silence of the onlookers, to a land promised us 3,500 years ago. Providence did not allow us to be utterly destroyed. The veil of God ensconced us in misery; but through it, mysteriously, there shone a vision of love. In retrospect, right before the *hurban* of European Jewry, the State of Israel was being providentially prepared so that the survivors might emerge into new dignity. God too followed the Halakhah: *Hayyav adam lifkod et ishto be-sha'ah she-hu yotzei la-derekh*. Before He "walked out on us," before He forsook us and turned away from us, He provided for our perpetuation, for a new generation and a new life and a new spirit.

Job taught us a long time ago that there are no easy answers to the mystery of suffering. Certainly the unspeakable agonies of a whole people cannot be easily explained, much less explained away. But from the hints left to us by our Sages in the folios of the Talmud about the birth of Messiah and the position of the Cherubim, we may begin to search for direction and understanding and meaning of the history of our times and the mysterious relationship between God and Israel.

Even while intoning the sorrowful lament of Jeremiah, *Lammah la-netzah tishkahenu, ta'azvenu le-orekh yamim*, bemoaning God's aloofness and our forlornness, we recite the same prophet's words in the same Book of Lamentations as he senses intuitively that *hasdei Hashem ki lo tamnu, ki lo khalu rahamav* (Lam. 3:22), "the love of the Lord has not come to an end, His compassion has not ceased."

Epilogue

EPILOGUE

THE BULK OF THE material presented in this volume dealt with happy events in the annual cycle of the Jewish year. Festival followed festival, each reflecting another aspect of the *Yamim Tovim* (plural of *Yom Tov*)—literally, "good days," but really "Happy Days." Each of the special days discussed in this volume is a joyous occasion, an occasion of *simhah*, with two exceptions—Yom ha-Shoah (in Nissan) and *Tish'ah be-Av*, the Ninth Day of the month of Av, the day that commemorates the destruction of the two Temples in Jerusalem.

Why does the yearly holiday cycle conclude with the one month that commemorates not joy but its exact opposite—mourning, tears, grief, and sorrow?

Two answers come to mind. First, all special holy days are referred to by a number of names, primarily *hag, yom tov,* and *mo'ed*. Now the first two terms, *hag* and *yom tov*, clearly refer to happy days. *Mo'ed*, however, is neutral, connoting neither joy nor sorrow. Hence, whereas the English terms generally used to translate *mo'ed* are "holiday" or "Festival," neither is accurate. The best translation of all is: Appointed Time. The utter neutrality of this phrase proves most useful. For almost all of the biblical holidays are referred to as *mo'ed* or, in the plural, *Mo'adim*. These are celebrations; one of the standard holiday greetings is *Mo'adim le-Simhah*. And yet, the Fast of Av (*Tish'ah be-Av*) is described in Lamentations 1:15 (*Eikhah*) as *mo'ed*. This is a joyless occasion, and it is therefore appropriate, from a linguistic point of view, to assign to it a term used for both happy and sorrowful occasions.

There is, however, a second answer. The mention of *mo'ed*, as noted, comes in the book of *Eikhah*, 1:15. This is the King James translation: "The Lord hath trodden under foot all my mighty men… He hath called an assembly against me…" Now, to "call an assembly" implies setting a date—a legitimate use of the word *o'ed*. But many or most of our traditional commentators prefer to find in this word an echo of its more frequent use in the Torah, namely, a reference to joy and *simhah*. Paradoxically, therefore, they posit a reference to *simhah* in *Tish'ah be-Av* itself—perhaps an oblique note of optimism in the midst of bitter persecution and devastation. Several stories illustrative of this remarkable tendency are reported concerning no less an authority than the immortal R. Akiva who, when his colleagues—all distinguished *Tanna'im*—inclined to weep over the destruction of the (second) Temple by the Roman soldiers, instead smiled. That is because, R. Akiva explains, if the enemies, idol worshippers, were disporting themselves, then *kal va-homer* (*a fortiori*), those who do God's will are destined to enjoy freedom (*Eikhah Rabbah* 5:18).

We are the people of R. Akiva, whose holy and irrepressible spirit discovered in *mo'ed* not dejection but the seeds of joy and regeneration. Generations after R. Akiva gave up his life in an act of martyrdom, the Talmud's injunction clearly instructs us: "One should get into the habit of saying, 'All that the Merciful One does is for the good'" (*Berakhot* 60b).

How appropriate it is, therefore, that we end the Jewish holiday calendar—and hence this volume—with the *mo'ed* that lies at the very center of our Faith.

INDEX OF BIBLICAL AND RABBINIC SOURCES

Consult the Table of Contents to find a numbered list of the sermons and their page numbers.

BIBLE

Sermon number

Genesis

1:2-3 – Void and chaos before creation of light	3
1:5 (Radak) – And it was *erev*	3
2:3 (with R. Hirsch) – God rests after creating the world	47
2:24 – Man must leave his parents	13
2:25 – Adam and Eve experience shame	4
3:20 – Eve is the *em kol hai* (mother of all living things)	4
3:21 – God clothes Adam and Eve	26
3:24 – God guards Eden to the east	15
4:1 – Adam knows his wife after the expulsion	15
6:3, 13, 17 – Man is referred to as "*basar*"	13
12:2 – The promise to be a great nation	36
12:5, 15:14, 17:14 – People are referred to as "*nefesh*"	13
12:32 (Ramban) – Abraham saves Terah	25
15:14 – The promise to leave exile with great wealth	36
19:6 – Lot speaks to the Sodomites from the doorway	31
21:16 – Hagar cries as Ishmael lies dying	5
22:8 – Abraham and Isaac walk together	13
22:11-12 – God knows that Abraham is God-fearing	8
24:8 – Isaac must remain with his father	13
24:67 – Isaac brings Rebecca into his mother's tent	13
28:21 – Jacob prays to return to his father's house	13
35:16-21 – Death of Rachel the Matriarch	10

Sermon number

37:5-9 – Joseph's dreams — 30

37:35 (R. Bahya ben Asher) – Forgetting the dead is a blessing — 33

43:18 – Joseph's brothers approach the *petah ha-bayit* — 31

50:25 – Jacob asks to be buried with his fathers — 13

Exodus

2:12 – Moses sees no other man and kills the Egyptian — 45

3:5 – Moses removes shoes before approaching God — 12

4:13 – Moses asks God to send someone else to Pharoah — 26

10:23 – During plague of darkness, communication ceases — 35

12:2 – This month is unto you the first month — 39

12:11 – *Korban Pesah* eaten in haste — 35

12:11 (Yonatan ben Uziel) – Jews were rushed by God — 35

13:14 – God took us out with a strong hand — 38

14:11-13 – The Jews complain and Moses responds — 37

14:30-31 – God saves the Jews from Egypt and they fear Him — 37

15:2 – Glorify and exalt God — 25

19:6 – A holy nation and kingdom of priests — 51

19:12-13 (with *Meshekh Hokhmah*)– Barriers around Mount Sinai — 52

33:23 – Man can see only God's back, not His face — 42

34:29-30 – Moses' face glows — 53

Leviticus

19:2 – Jews are commanded to be holy — 4

19:18 – Prohibition against bearing a grudge — 33

23:36 – Dwell in *sukkot* for seven days — 19

23:36 (Rashi) – God says, "Stay with me a while" — 26

23:40 – *Peri etz hadar (etrog)* — 21

23:43 (Rashbam) – For seven days, rely on God alone — 18

25:1 (Rashi) – What is the connection between *shemittah* and Sinai? — 48

Numbers

12:12 (Rashi) – A *metzora* is considered like a dead person — 47

16:7 (Rashi) – How could Korah be so foolish — 38

23:10 – Balaam wishes to be like Israel — 37

23:23 – What hath God wrought? — 49

23:24 – The nation raises its head like a lioness — 49

Sermon number

Deuteronomy
    1:12 – Moses says, " I cannot bear them alone"   54
    3:23 – Moses prays to enter the Land   26
    4:4 – You who cling to the Lord are alive   50
    6:5 – Love God   9
    6:7 – Teach your children   9
    8:14 – Man forgets God when he attains wealth   33
    8:17 – My own strength and power achieved all this   47, 49
    11:13 (Rashi) – The commandments are received each day anew   39
    16:14 – Rejoice on the holidays   22, 24
    24:19 – Commandment of *shikhhah*   33
    25:19 – Commandment to remember Amalek   33
    31:18 (Seforno) – Withdrawal of the Divine Presence   32
    32:7 – Remember the days of old   42
    34:4-5 – God turns down Moses' request   26
    34:6 – God buries Moses   26
    34:7 – Moses' strength was not diminished   26

Joshua
    1:7 – Be very strong and courageous   26

Judges
    5:8 – Seeking new gods   39
    5:28 – Sisera's mother weeps for her son   5

I Samuel
    17 – David and Goliath   50
    20 – Jonathan saves David   14

I Kings
    7:41-50 – The building of the Temple   28
    8:66 – Solomon sends the people away   25
    13:12 – Solomon, the wisest of all men   43
    18 – Elijah fights the priests of Ba'al   27
    19:10-12 – God is found in the *kol demamah dakkah*   27

Sermon number

II Kings

    4:1-2 – Elisha and the widow   2

    7:9-10 – The lepers report that Aram has fled   45

Isaiah

    1:12 – Who asked this of you, that you trample my courtyard?   7, 54

    1:21 – How has the faithful city become as a harlot?   54

    2:3 – Torah comes forth from Zion   29

    6:1, 3 – In Isaiah's vision, Godliness is everywhere   1

    6:10 – The heart of the people is coarse   7

    11:11 – God will redeem the remnant of His people   40

    12:1 – He shall say on that day: Thank you, O Lord   42

    12:2-3 – Waters of salvation   46

    22:13 – Death is universal, so enjoy today   5

    40:1 – Console, console My people (*nahamu nahamu ammi*)   51

    44:2 – God tells Jacob to be courageous   15

    49:6 – A light unto the nations   29

    51:12 – I, yea I, will be your Consoler   54

Jeremiah

    13:17 – God weeps in secret   7

    20:14-17 – *Harat olam*—Jeremiah bemoans his birth   6

    31:14-16 – Rachel cries for her exiled children   5, 10

Ezekiel

    3:12 – In Ezekiel's vision, God is distant   1

    36:26 – A new heart and a new spirit   39

Hosea

    2:21 – God betroths Israel with justice and mercy   41

Amos

    3:6 – When the shofar is sounded, people fear   7

Micah

    4:2 – Messiah's role is to bring nations to the House of God   20

Sermon number

Zekhariah

    2:14 – Zion should rejoice   28

    4:6-7 – Not by power or might, but by God's spirit   27, 28, 29, 30

Malakhi

    3:23 – The great and terrible day of the Lord   34

    3:24 – The hearts of fathers and sons will be reunited   13, 34

Psalms

    1:4 – The wicked man is like chaff driven by wind   23

    2:9 – *tero'em be-shevet barzel*   6

    8:6 – Man is only slightly lower than the angels   19, 45

    18:12 – God dwells in secret darkness   36

    22:2 – My God, why hast thou forsaken me?   41

    23:1 – God is my shepherd, I shall not want   3

    23:4 – Trust in God even amidst confusion   3

    23:6 – Goodness and mercy shall follow me all the days of my life   7

    24:7 – O gates, lift up your heads   25

    49:21 – Man is compared to animals   47

    51:13 and 71:9 – Cast us not away   1

    81:4 – The shofar is sounded when the moon is concealed   8

    91:1 – God dwells in mystery   36

    96:1, 98:1 – Sing a new song to God   39

    104:31 – God is happy with His creation   24

    115:17-18 – The dead cannot praise God; only the living can   44

    116:16 – "I am Thy servant, the son of Thy handmaid"   25

    118:25 – *Anna Hashem hoshi 'ah na/hatzlihah na*   17

    118:26 – All sincere people are welcome into the House of the Lord   7

    119:105 – Torah as a guiding light   20

    126:2 – Then our mouths will be filled with laughter   48

    126:5 – Those who cry will reap a harvest of joy   5

    128:6 – May you live to see grandchildren   2

    145:18 – The Lord is close to all who call upon Him   55

Proverbs

    3:13 – Take hold of the Torah   44

Sermon number

Job

15:13 –Though He may slay me, I shall trust in Him   32

Song of Songs

3:11 (with Alshikh) – King Solomon's crown   43

Ruth

1:14 – The difference between Ruth and Orpah   50

1:16-17 – Your God is my God   50

4:1 – *Peloni Almoni*   51

Lamentations (*Eikhah*)

3:22 – God's love has not come to an end   55

5:20 – Why do You forget us for an eternity?   55

5:21 – Renew our days as of old (*ke-kedem*)   4, 15

Ecclesiastes

1:1 – All is vanity   22

1:18 – Knowledge increases pain   22

2:15-16 – What is the worth of wisdom?   22

3:19 – If nothing distinguishes man from animal, all is vanity   13

7:16 – Be not overwise   38

7:20 – There is no man who never sins   43

12:13-14 – Torah observance is the whole of man; God passes judgment   22

Esther

9:27 – The Jews adopt the observance of Purim (*kiyyemu ve-kibbelu*)   32

9:30 – Words of peace and truth   32

10:3 – Mordekhai was great and beloved   32

Ezra

9:6 – We are ashamed   4

II Chronicles

6:42 – Plea to remember King David   25

Sermon number

26 – Immediate punishment of King Uzziah   1
32:33 – King Hezekiah was honored after his death   44

Babylonian Talmud (Alphabetical)

Avodah Zarah

17a – Some acquire the World-to-Come in one moment   16

Avot

1:1 (Abarbanel) – Moses received the Torah *because of* Sinai   36
1:2 – The world stands on three things   40
1:7 – Do not ignore dreadful consequences   5
1:14 – If I am for myself, who am I?   24
1:14 – If not now, when?   16, 35
2:1 – Know what is above you   1, 2
2:5 – Do not say that you will study when you have time   16
2:6 – Where there is no man, you must be a man   45
3:1 – Three reminders to avoid sin   11
3:10 – Forgetfulness as a sin   33
5:23 – Be bold and swift in fulfilling the will of God   49
5:24 – The brazen go to Gehinnom, the ashamed to Gan Eden   3, 4

Bava Batra

15a – Moses wrote about his death using his tears as ink   26
21a – Jealousy among scholars increases wisdom   30

Bava Kamma

16b – A yeshivah was built over King Hezekiah's grave   44

Bava Metzi'a

9a – One who picks up and claims an item first is the owner   16
12b – The definition of adulthood   36
49a – Make both your yes and your no firm   37

Berakhot

7a – One must know how to choose the right hour   16

Sermon number

9a – The meaning of *hippazon*   35
34b – Prophecy primarily about the days of the Messiah   37

Gittin

56b – Yavneh as substitute for the Holy Temple   44

Hagigah

16a – The stones of a man's house are his witnesses   2

Hullin

5b – Men who are brilliant but simple   38

Kiddushin

66a - Torah lies neglected in a hidden corner   20

Niddah

31b (with Maharsha) – Different periods of impurity after
    birth of boy and girl   46

Pesahim

35a – Matzah made from the same species that can become *hametz*   41
56a – Jacob's sons recite the *Shema*   9
66a – Jews are the descendants of prophets   7

Rosh ha-Shanah

16b – Confusing the Satan   3
33b (Tosafot) – 100 shofar blasts parallel Sisera's mother's cries   5

Sanhedrin

38a – Variation in humanity is manifestation of God's glory   43
70b – King Solomon's marriage to Pharaoh's daughter   43
98b – The name of the Messiah   42
106b (Rashi s.v. *revuta*) – God desires man's heart   38

Sermon number

Shabbat

1b – The nature of the Hanukkah miracle   30

3a – Questions asked after death   17

22a – Menorah placed at left of the doorpost   31

30a – The goodness done to David   25

88a – Jews were compelled to accept the Torah   32

Sotah

13b – Moses dies quickly   26

14a – The Torah begins and ends with *gemilut hasadim*   26

21a – A sin extinguishes a *mitzvah*   43

42b – Orpah was the grandmother of Goliath   50

Sukkah

2a – Leave your permanent home to live in a temporary dwelling   18

11b – Purpose of the *sukkah*   23

26a – Dwell in the *sukkah* as if you resided there   19

35a – A *sukkah* made from materials worshipped as *avodah zarah*   19

47b–48a – Six laws special to *Shemini Atzeret*   25

52a – The greater the man, the greater his *yetzer ha-ra*   43

53a – If I am here, everyone is here   18

Yevamot

22a – A convert is like a newborn infant   39

62b – When leaving for a journey, one must be tender to his wife   55

64a – God desires the prayers of the righteous   18

76b – Female Moabites are acceptable spouses   51

79a – Capacity for shame a sign of Jewishness   4

Yoma

21b – The column of smoke on *Shemini Atzeret*   24

54b – The Cherubim faced each other   55

Tosefta, *Sotah* 7:18 – Two arks   52

Jerusalem Talmud

Sermon number

Berakhot 9:1 – The blessing over seeing large numbers of people   43

Hagigah 2:1 – Aher's opposition to impractical Torah study   48

Kiddushin 4:12 – Enjoy the pleasures of this world   22

Pesahim 10:4 – Calls the "*tam*" son a *tippesh*   38

Rosh ha-Shanah 3:5 – Words of the Torah are rich in one place
and poor in another   48

Rosh ha-Shanah 4:8 – Rosh Hashanah is a time of rebirth   6

Sukkah 5:4 – Does God need Hillel's praise?   18

Midrashic Literature (Midrash Rabbah first, then alphabetical)

Bereshit Rabbah

   3:4 – "Light" in Creation story parallels Torah   3

   19:1 – The load corresponds to the camel's strength   37

   84:19 – The dead are forgotten   33

Shemot Rabbah

   Bo 14:2 – The nature of the plague of darkness   36

   Ki Tissa 47:6 – Why Moses' face glowed   53

Be-midbar Rabbah 10 – King Solomon's marriage to Pharaoh's
daughter   43, 54

Eikhah Rabbah 5:21 – "*Ke-kedem*" means "like in the east"   15

Shir Ha-Shirim Rabbah 3 – King Solomon's crown   43

Ruth Rabbah

   6:3 – The redeemer's name was Tov   51

   7:7 – *Peloni Almoni* was speechless in Torah   51

Avot de-Rebbi Natan 1:37 – Man is like the beasts and the angels   43

Eikhah Zuta (Buber ed., version 2) 1:2 – Messiah is born on Tish'ah be-Av   55

Mekhilta, Be-shallah, 2 – Jews cannot be idle spectators   37

Midrash Aggadah (Buber) *Devarim* 6   9

Midrash Shohar Tov, Psalm 118 – *Hoshi'ah na* versus *hatzlihah na*   17

Midrash Zuta, Shir Ha-Shirim (Buber), 5 – We are asleep in exile   41

Pesikta Rabbati

   6 – The nature of the Hanukkah miracle   30

   15 – Renew your deeds   39

Pesikta Zutra, Lev. 4b – Acceptable trees for use on the altar   25

Sermon number

Sifra

    Be-midbar 135 – Moses pleads to enter the land   26

    Ha'azinu 339 – Moses' death   26

Sifrei, Re'eh, 58 – The commandments are received each day   39

Tanhuma

    Tzav 96:13 – A *metzora* is considered like a dead person   47

    Tazria 7 – Turnus Rufus and Rabbi Akiva discuss circumcision   47

    Ha'azinu 1 – The living atone for the dead   25

Targum to Eccl. 1:1 – Why Solomon declared "all is vanity"   22

Yalkut Shim'oni

    Re'eh, 997 – To be happy on Yom Tov, you must make others happy   22

    Psalms, 682 – The Messiah teaches the nations about *sukkah*   20

    Eikhah, 1001 – Everything that happened to Adam happened to Israel   54

Zohar

    Be-shallah – The world exists for those who view themselves

        as remnants   40

    Pinehas – The shofar calls to break bonds of slavery   6

Other Works of Halakhah and Jewish Thought

Maimonides, *Mishneh Torah*

    Hilkhot Teshuvah 2:4 – The sinner achieves a new identity   4

    Hilkhot Teshuvah 2:6 – Prayer between Rosh Hashanah and

        Yom Kippur   16

    Hilkhot Teshuvah 7:7 – Penitent is like a newborn child   39

    Hilkhot Hametz u-Matzah (Haggadah text at end) – We left Egypt

        in haste   35

    Hilkhot Hanukkah 4:7 – Menorah to the left of the doorpost   31

Maimonides, *Guide of the Perplexed* III:46 – Passover ritual reflects haste   35

Maimonides, *Iggeret Ha-Shemad* – Greek decrees   31

Akedat Yitzhak (Arama) *Sha'ar* 38 (*Parashat Bo*), s.v. *ve-hinneh* – *Tam* is

    opposite of *Rasha*, not of *Hakham*   38

Benei Yissaskhar, Ma'amarei Tammuz-Av, #3 – Why Messiah born on

    Tish'ah be-Av, and question about Cherubim   55

Menahem Tziyyon, Yom ha-Kippurim – Why we do not wear shoes

    on Yom Kippur   12

Sermon number

Or ha-Hayyim (Yabetz), chap. 2 – Philosophers embraced Christianity
  while masses did not   38
Orot ha-Kodesh (Kook) III:97 – Man forgets his true self   33
Rama, Orah Hayyim 223:6 – "Tithaddesh" not recited upon new shoes   12
Sa'adyah Ga'on, Sefer Emunot ve-De'ot III:1 – one receives more joy from
  something he has worked for   15
Sefer Hasidim (ed. Margaliyot, #120, #350) – Shame and faith intertwined   4
Shulhan Arukh
      Orah Hayyim 677:1 – The laws of a traveler on Hanukkah   29
      Orah Hayyim 681:2 – Havdalah and Hanukkah candles   27
Siddur ha-Shelah – One shoud recite a biblical verse related to his name   51
Tanya, Likkutei Amarim, 12   6
Tur, Orah Hayyim 430 – The reason for Shabbat ha-Gadol   34

Liturgy and Haggadah

Adam u-behemah toshia Hashem   38
Adam yesodo me-afar   13
Afilu kullanu hakhamim   38
Al ha-Nissim (of Hanukkah)   30
Al het   3
Al tashlikhenu   1
Anna Hashem hoshi 'ah na/hatzlihah na   17
Anna Hashem ki ani avdekha   25
Ani Ma'amin   37
Anu mattirin le-hitpallel im ha-avaryanim   11
Ashamnu   11
Avinu Malkenu tehei ha-sha'ah ha-zot. . . she 'at rahamim   16
Barukh shem kevod malkhuto le-olam va-ed (on Yom Kippur)   9, 12
Boshti ve-nikhlamti   4
Elokai ad she-lo notzarti   10
Elokai netzor leshoni me-ra   10
Elokeinu ve-Elokei avoteinu   21, 25
Emet ki attah hu yotzeram   13
The four sons of the Haggadah   38, 43
Geshem prayer   24

	Sermon number
Haddesh yameinu ke-kedem	15, 39
Ha-rahaman hu yakim lanu et sukkat Dovid ha-nofalet	20
Ha-yom harat olam	3, 6
Havdalah	27
Im ke-vanim im ka-avadim	7
Kaddish	12, 32
Ki lo yizku be-einekha ba-din	11
Le-Kel orekh din	6
Mah Nishtannah	41
Or hadash al Tziyyon ta'ir	29, 39
Oseh hadashot ba'al milhamot	21
Seder egg	44
Shema (on Yom Kippur)	9
Shiru la-Shem shir hadash	39
Shofarot	6
u-mal'akhim yehafezun. . . ve-hotam yad kol adam bo	14
U-ve-khen ten pahdekha. . . . U-ve-khen ten kavod	10
Va-etten le-Esav et Har Se'ir	41
Ve-nomar lefanav shirah hadashah	39
Yehi ratzon she-tehei hashuvah mitzvah zo. . .	19
Yom ha-shemini Hag ha-Atzeret ha-zeh	25
Yizkor sermons	9, 13–16, 24, 25, 40, 42, 50–53

GRANDES HORIZONTALES

GRANDES HORIZONTALES

The lives and legends of Marie Duplessis,
Cora Pearl, La Païva and La Présidente

Virginia Rounding

BLOOMSBURY

Published by Bloomsbury, New York and London
Distributed to the trade by Holtzbrinck Publishers

Library of Congress Cataloging-in-Publication Data has been applied for.

ISBN 1-58234-260-1

Endpapers: Bradshaw's Plan of Paris, 1855 (By permission of the British Library
[Shelfmark: Maps 16110 (86)]).

First U.S. Edition 2003

1 3 5 7 9 10 8 6 4 2

Typeset by Hewer Text Ltd, Edinburgh
Printed in Great Britain by Clays Limited, St Ives plc

For my companion of the
rue du Chemin Vert

Of such women, you know, the mould is broken. We will not see their like again.

Zed, *La Société Parisienne,*
La Librairie Illustrée, Paris, 1888

CONTENTS

Acknowledgments   xi

Introduction   The *Demi-monde*   1

Chapter One   Prostitutes and Prostitution
                    in Nineteenth-century Paris   9

Chapter Two   The Life of Marie Duplessis   31

Chapter Three   *La Dame aux camélias*   55

Chapter Four   The Creation of La Païva   75

Chapter Five   *La Femme piquée par un serpent*   97

Chapter Six   Salons   109

Chapter Seven   *Les Fleurs du mal*   133

Chapter Eight   Rebuilding   155

Chapter Nine   The Hôtel Païva   175

Chapter Ten   The English Beauty of the French Empire   195

Chapter Eleven   Putting on a Show   229

Chapter Twelve   The Collapse of Empire   253

Chapter Thirteen   *La Femme de Claude*   269

Chapter Fourteen   Last Years   285

Conclusion   Seen and Unseen   307

                    Select Bibliography   317

                    Index   329

Acknowledgments

I would particularly like to record my thanks to Thierry Savatier, great-great-nephew of Apollonie Sabatier (La Présidente), for his willingness to share his knowledge and insights about his great-great-aunt, and for furnishing me with proof copies of the relevant pages of his edition of Gautier's *Lettres à la Présidente* before publication, as well as sending me details of some documents pertaining to Marie Duplessis, auctioned in 1984. Monsieur Savatier also put me in touch with Dr Wendy Nolan Joyce, who devoted part of her PhD thesis to Madame Sabatier. Professor John Klier, Head of the Hebrew and Jewish Studies Department at University College London, gave me useful information about Jews living in Moscow in the early nineteenth century. Thanks are also due to the librarian of the Wallace Collection for access to the Collection's file on Madame Sabatier, to the Travellers' Club in Paris for access to the Hôtel Païva, and to the staff of the British Library, the London Library and the Bibliothèque Nationale. (Mention also has to be made of the man who feeds the cats in the Cimetière de Montmartre and who, for a small contribution to his cat project, will direct visitors to any grave they wish to find.)

Unless otherwise indicated in the notes, all translations from the French are my own, including those of the correspondence between Apollonie Sabatier and Charles Baudelaire and of extracts from poems by Alexandre Dumas *fils* and Théophile Gautier. I have also made a point of translating passages of the *Mémoires de Cora Pearl*, only using the 'authorised' version of *The Memoirs of Cora Pearl* when the original translation (or, rather, version) seems particularly felicitous (or at least not inaccurate).

The *Demi-monde*

T HE FOUR COURTESANS or *grandes horizontales* whose lives and legends are examined in this book were all, in differing ways, representative of the *demi-monde* in nineteenth-century Paris – that is, of that half-world midway between respectable high society and the low life of the common prostitute. *Demi-monde* is a term suggestive of twilight, of a world of shifting appearances and shadow, where nothing is quite what it seems, a world between worlds. Alexandre Dumas *fils* was the first to give the term wide currency in his play *Le Demi-monde*, first performed in March 1855, and his strictures in the introduction to a later printed edition suggest that it, and its associated *demi-mondaine* (a woman belonging to the *demi-monde*), had soon come to be used rather more widely that he had himself intended. Dumas *fils* is at pains to establish 'for dictionaries of the future'[1] that the *demi-monde* is not synonymous with the 'mob of courtesans',[2] despite the fact that this is how the term has been habitually deployed. Rather, it is the class of the *déclassé*, a word denoting a person who had fallen in social status and thus become 'declassed'. Declassed women included victims of scandal, divorcees, women separated from or abandoned by husband or lover, 'merry widows', or foreign women whom the authorities might deport when it suited them. According to Dumas *fils*, a woman could not simply choose to join the *demi-monde*; rather, the circumstances of life may mean that she arrives in it without appearing to have exercised any choice, or as a result of the choices she had made having more far-reaching consequences than she ever imagined. He asserts that the *demi-monde* is in fact made up of 'women of honourable stock who, as daughters, wives or mothers, were received and cherished as of right in the best families, and who deserted'.[3] But even Dumas *fils* does not wish to restrict the designation to such women, and so he concedes that the *demi-monde*

> also welcomes girls who started out in life with an error, women who live with a man whose name they adopt, elegant and beautiful foreigners recommended and protected by an intimate friend, under his personal responsibility, and finally all those women who had roots in legitimate society, and whose fall has love as its excuse, as its sole excuse . . .[4]

A *demi-mondaine* could not necessarily be identified by her appearance, and this could prove a difficulty for visitors to Paris. Even that most expert of Parisians, the writer Maxime Du Camp, could declare 'one does not know today whether honest women are dressing like prostitutes, or prostitutes are dressed like honest women.'[5] The *demi-monde* knew how to copy the *haut monde* (the world of high society) and yet at the same time the *haut monde* was not above copying the half-world, particularly where fashionable dress was concerned. But though the two worlds might on the surface seem indistinguishable, there was nevertheless a chasm fixed between them. There was a bridge over this chasm, but it led in one direction only: it was easy enough for a woman from the *haut monde* to fall and find herself in the *demi-monde* but no return journey was possible, no way for a *demi-mondaine* to climb her way into high society, no matter what riches she might amass or works of charity she might undertake.

Where the definition proffered by Dumas *fils* departs most significantly from the general usage of the term is in his insistence that the *demi-mondaine* does not accept money for her favours, that she 'clings to this basic premise: "We give, we do not sell" ',[6] and she is thus distinguished from the courtesan, for whom love is a financial transaction. In fact, despite Dumas *fils*' best efforts, the *demi-mondaine* and the courtesan have always been virtually indistinguishable, and whatever else may remain in doubt about the women known as Marie Duplessis, Cora Pearl, La Païva and La Présidente, their willingness to accept money from the men in their lives (though in varying degrees, La Présidente presenting a markedly different case from the other three) is not in question.

Of these four women Marie Duplessis was the first to die, in 1847 at only twenty-three years old. She thus missed out on the golden age of the French courtesan, though can perhaps be seen as its most significant forerunner. That age was the era of the Second Empire, the eighteen years from 1852 to 1870 when France was ruled by Louis Napoleon Bonaparte, the Emperor Napoleon III, who was both the step-grandson and the nephew of the first Napoleon. (Napoleon III's mother, Hortense Beauharnais, was both the daughter of the Empress Josephine by her first husband, and the wife of Napoleon I's brother, Louis.) The ostentation and delight in show of that era, along with the at least apparent prosperity, provided a perfect setting and encouragement for the opulent lifestyle of the pampered and glamorous courtesan, a type of which Cora Pearl and La Païva were notorious and highly successful examples. There was also always an element of the ersatz, the not-quite-real, about the world of Napoleon III and his court. The Second Empire drew its legitimacy from the First, itself resulting from the extraordinary personal power and charisma of Napoleon I, and much of the court ceremonial and protocol of the Second Empire was merely an imitation of that of the First. The supportive, if supercilious and patronising, comment of the *Illustrated London News* in August 1852 set the tone for what was to be the prevailing judgment of the Second Empire and its 'showiness':

When Louis Napoleon was first heard of we had little respect for the man, and no expectation that he would succeed. Five years ago an outcast and an adventurer, forbidden even to tread the soil of France and now the controller of its fate, his success is the greatest marvel in the modern political world, full as that is of strange occurrences . . . If France can be guided to peace and kept tranquil by shows, shows may in the end be as useful to

them as Parliaments . . . A theatrical Empire in France will be a
pleasant show for the rest of Europe, if the French be satisfied by
the representation, and their Emperor seek popularity and
power only in pyrotechnical victories.[7]

Thus the imperial court could be seen as mirroring and sharing some
of the essence of the *demi-monde*, not only in its ostentation but also in
its shadowiness, its sense of unreality and its flair for imitation, and the
women, like La Païva, who rose to startling prominence through an
accumulation of wealth about whose origins it was best not to
enquire too closely shared some of the characteristics of the Emperor
who had arisen out of a lifetime of exile and relative anonymity to
claim what he considered to be the inheritance of his uncle and step-
grandfather.

This book is not only about the lives of four courtesans but also
about the legends surrounding them, the images made of them
largely through the writings of others, both their contemporaries
and subsequent commentators and historians. It is a truism that much
of what we know, or think we know, about nineteenth-century
women comes from the writings of men, and the case of these four
women is no exception. The most well-known of the memoir
writers of this period of French history were the Goncourt brothers,
Edmond and Jules, who every night wrote up in their Journal their
impressions of the people they had encountered and the events they
had witnessed during the day. They occasionally attended the soirées
of La Païva and La Présidente, and their comments, with their
habitual attendant elements of misogyny, anti-semitism and general
disapproval of everyone apart from themselves, have coloured the
way these women have been seen ever since. An equally vituperative
diarist was Count Horace de Viel Castel, an official at the Louvre and
a regular visitor at the soirées given by Princess Mathilde, cousin of
Napoleon III, where he picked up all the gossip. He added to the
construction of the negative image of La Païva in particular. Other
memoirists usually had their own axes to grind, especially those
writing in the aftermath of the collapse of the Second Empire and

looking round for someone to blame. Those society women who wrote diaries for publication used them partly as a vehicle to express their disapproval of the *demi-mondaines*, in an attempt to clarify the distinction between this half-world and their own respectable sphere, while the few *demi-mondaines* who produced their memoirs were concerned not only to justify themselves but to see off the competition of their fellow courtesans. In all these accounts objective truth, if there is indeed such a thing, was in short supply. And then there were the novelists, playwrights and poets who used what they knew, or imagined, of the life of this or that courtesan in the service of their art.

I have chosen these particular four women to write about as they were subject more than most to the image-making of others, and of themselves. They each became the stuff of legend, both within their own lifetimes and subsequently, and their stories demonstrate the addiction to myth-making which is a part of human life and discourse. Any account of a life is a story, affected by the interpretation, style and point of view of the teller and all previous tellers, and the accounts given of the lives of these women demonstrate this fictionalising process particularly clearly, and none more so than those devoted to Marie Duplessis who became the prototype of the virtuous courtesan through her portrayal as Marguerite Gautier in the novel by Alexandre Dumas *fils*, *La Dame aux camélias*. Her identification with this romantic heroine affected all subsequent judgments and even physical descriptions of her, with the result that the 'real' Marie (who was also in part a fabrication of her own making) slipped into the shadows. The image she has become is almost entirely constructed of the words of others, the only words we have direct from her consisting of one or two brief letters, the main evidence of her way of life being a stash of invoices found after her death.

La Païva, born Thérèse Lachmann, is surrounded by a horde of unlikely legends through which she has attained the status of a fairy-tale character, the evil witch luring young men to part with their wealth by casting a spell of incomprehensible sexual magic upon them. The stories that were told about her attest both to her unusual power and to the prejudices of the storytellers, prejudices against women, Jews and foreigners, all of which Thérèse embodied, along with an infuriating (to the onlooker) ability to make money and a delight in showing it off. Again, words which have come down to us from her own pen are very few and mainly concern practical arrangements, but she did make a very clear statement of her own in the design and building of her opulent *hôtel* in the avenue des Champs Elysées, which still stands and continues to convey a strong impression of this remarkable woman.

Apollonie Sabatier, also known as La Présidente, was the subject of two particular image-making exercises, first as *La Femme piquée par un serpent* (The Woman Bitten by a Snake), a sculpture based on a cast of her body by Auguste Clésinger, and then as *la très-Chère, la très belle* (the Dearest, the most beautiful) of the poet Charles Baudelaire's *Les Fleurs du mal*. Both of these artistic endeavours had a profound effect on Apollonie's life and on the way she has been viewed by her own and subsequent generations. Again, we have little to go on as far as her own words are concerned, though the fragments which remain of her letters to Baudelaire convey a clear sense of her generosity of character and something of the spirit which drew so many men of letters and the other arts to her.

Cora Pearl is the only one of these four women to have written her own account of her life, to take the power of fabrication completely into her own hands, for Cora's memoirs present the version of her life which she wants us to have. Yet she too was subject to the myth-making of others, a myth-making again contaminated by prejudice, particularly against foreign women who profited from the foibles of Parisian men. The descriptions, both physical and moral, given by their contemporaries of all four women were also heavily influenced by prevailing stereotypes of prostitutes, as codified by Dr Parent-Duchâtelet in his highly influential text, first published in 1836, *De la Prostitution dans la ville de Paris considérée sous le rapport de l'hygiène publique, de la morale et de l'administration* (On prostitution in the city of Paris from the point of view of public hygiene, morality and administration).

In looking at the lives and legends of Marie Duplessis, Cora Pearl, La Païva and La Présidente, I will attempt to distinguish each life from the legend, while being aware that this may not always be possible, that to strip away the legend completely may be to leave little of the life. The two have become so thoroughly intertwined, so hard to tell apart, that these women truly inhabit a *demi-monde*, a twilit half-world where the image is frequently taken for the reality and nothing is quite what it seems.

---

1 Alexandre Dumas *fils, Théâtre complet, avec Préfaces inédites*, Vol.II, Calmann Lévy, Paris, 1895, p.11

2 Ibid.

3 Ibid.

4 Ibid.

5 Maxime Du Camp, *Paris: ses organes, ses fonctions et sa vie jusqu'en 1870*, G. Rondeau, Monaco, 1993, p.351 (first published between 1869 and 1875)

6 Alexandre Dumas *fils, Théâtre complet, avec Préfaces inédites*, Vol.II, p.12

7 *Illustrated London News*, No.575, Vol.XXI, Supplement, Saturday, 21 August 1852

CHAPTER ONE

Prostitutes and Prostitution in Nineteenth-century Paris

T HE HIGHLY PAID courtesan of the *demi-monde* represented the pinnacle of a continuum of women who traded their bodies and their company for financial reward in mid-nineteenth century France. Throughout much of that century Paris enjoyed one of the most regulated systems of prostitution in the world, a system envied by the authorities of many other capital cities. Dr Michael Ryan, a member of the Royal Colleges of Physicians and Surgeons and Senior Physician to the Metropolitan Free Hospital, expressed this envy as far as London was concerned in his *Prostitution in London*, published three years after Dr Parent-Duchâtelet's work and drawing heavily upon it:

> As prostitution has ever existed, and will ever exist, in all countries, the French police regulations are intended in every way to diminish the nuisance caused by it, and to regulate the houses devoted to it. The regulations in France, are well calculated to repress crime, while those in this country, are most defective, and hence the frequent murders and robberies, in brothels, so often recorded in the public papers.[1]

The French system was based on the belief of the inevitability, even the necessity, of prostitution combined with the desire to discipline the prostitute, to keep the whole phenomenon contained and subject to authority. As Dr Parent-Duchâtelet put it, 'Prostitutes are as inevitable in a great urban centre as are sewers, roads and rubbish dumps. The attitude of the authorities should be the same in regard to the former as to the latter.'[2] The ideal was considered to be the creation of an enclosed world of prostitutes, a sort of distorted mirror image of the enclosed world of the nun, in which the women concerned would be good 'workers', doing as they were told, and contributing to the stability of society by absorbing the excess sexual energy of men, while remaining invisible to the bulk of the population. It was believed that registration with the police and tight control over the activities of prostitutes would result in the containment of syphilis, a great scourge of the nineteenth century, as well as in the maintenance of stable married life. This was essentially a European attitude, carried to its logical conclusion in the French system of regulation; an entirely different attitude prevailed in New York, for instance, where the emphasis was on the desire to stamp out prostitution altogether. Dr Ryan quotes from an address delivered by the Reverend Mr M'Dowall, Chaplain to the New York Magdalen Asylum, in May 1832 in which he had declared that 'the grand effort of those who would promote reformation, should be directed to arresting, and, if possible, reclaiming, those wretched females, who are the pest and nuisance of society, though equally the objects of our compassion and abhorrence'.[3]

Parent-Duchâtelet's research was conducted and published during the reign of Louis Philippe, a period also known as the July monarchy. The ethos of this monarchy centred on the maintenance of political and social stability and, in the early years of his reign, Louis Philippe's naturally conservative outlook was strengthened by a number of workers' demonstrations – such as the revolts of the Lyonnais weavers in 1831 and 1834, which were brutally suppressed – and by several attempts on his life. Little was done to address the growing social problems arising out of the Industrial Revolution, the workers in the slums having to fend for themselves while the middle and upper classes made money out of them and went dancing and dining on the proceeds. Disease, especially cholera, was rife among the urban population; the cholera epidemic of 1832, which lasted from mid-February to nearly the end of September, claimed the lives of 18,402 Parisians. The glittering façade of Paris masked an under-world of poverty and disease, a dislocation which was a marked feature of Second Empire life but whose seeds were sown during the July monarchy, where the contrasts between rich and poor also provided a natural setting for the growth of prostitution and for the rise of the courtesan.

The backbone of the French system was the registration of prostitutes, a registration which could be entered into voluntarily or enforced following an arrest. Registered prostitutes or *filles soumises* (literally, submissive or compliant whores) had to submit to various regulations, including mandatory health checks for venereal disease, while unregistered ones (*insoumises*) operated outside the law. A *fille soumise* either worked independently, in which case she was known as a *fille libre* or *isolée*, or as a *fille en carte* (because of the obligatory identity card which detailed the dates of her medical inspections as well as any infringements of the rules), or in a strictly regulated and supervised brothel known as a *maison de tolérance* or *maison tolérée*, where she would also live. This latter type of prostitute was known as a *fille de maison* or a *fille de numéro*, by virtue of the number she was given when she was entered in the brothel-keeper's book, though it may also have referred to the fact that the authorities required brothels to display their street numbers in a large size over the door. At the top of the hierarchy were the first- and second-class *maisons*, intended for an aristocratic or bourgeois clientèle, and generally to be found in the centre of Paris, in the area around the Opera House in the rue Le Peletier. Such establishments were lavishly furnished, with thick carpets, mirrors and statuary, and an abundance of mythological motifs in the decorations on ceilings and walls.

Prostitutes who worked independently in Paris were hemmed in by a network of petty restrictions, designed to prevent the innocent and the virtuous from being offended by the too obvious presence of vice which was tolerated only so long as it could be kept invisible except to those who knew where to look, and which increased the difficulties of carrying out their trade. In particular, prostitutes were forbidden to solicit or even appear in the street or other public places before seven o'clock in the evening and after ten or eleven at night. Neither were they supposed to draw attention to their trade by dressing or behaving provocatively. One way in which such restrictions were circumvented was through the use of intermediaries or procuresses who, while appearing to carry on a legitimate business as, for instance, clothing merchants or outfitters, would also be making appointments for a number of prostitutes from whose profits they would take a cut. Such women were likely to have previously been prostitutes themselves and could now, by their very presence alongside younger women in the streets, indicate, to those men who knew the signs, the availability of the latter; they could also direct the interested passer-by to the nearest brothel. 'The more severe the regulations of the police are made, the more important to their class these women become.'[4] The extent to which a prostitute could get away with soliciting varied from area to area of Paris. Alphonse Esquiros, a phrenologist and social commentator who took up and developed some of Parent-Duchâtelet's theories in his *Les Vierges folles* (The Foolish Virgins), first published in 1840, and who, unusually for such commentators, was endowed with a sense of humour, presents a vivid picture of these differences in describing how an old hand might instruct a new recruit:

> In the area of the Bourse, the Chaussée d'Antin and boulevard de Gand, the prostitute should walk along the pavement, discreetly beckoning with her eyes when appropriate; around the Palais Royal and in the streets of Saint-Honoré, Montmartre, Richelieu and Saint-Denis, she should whisper in a man's ear; in the Latin Quarter, she should address him as '*tu*' and call a spade a spade; finally, in the Cité, in the rue de l'Hôtel-de-ville and elsewhere, she should accost the passers-by boldly, seize their protesting arms and drag them to her by force, even at the risk of being elbowed sharply in the chest.[5]

The most convenient arrangement for a prostitute would be to have a roster of regular clients, obviating the need for her to solicit for new ones. A *fille en carte* might have an arrangement whereby a group of gentlemen bought her services *en bloc*, dividing up among themselves who would visit her on which day. Such an arrangement could also be advantageous for the men concerned by lessening the risk – or at least the fear – of contracting a venereal disease, by confining sexual activity within a closed circle of acquaintances.

A distinction was made between those women who registered voluntarily and those registered by the authorities. Voluntary registration was a simple procedure, involving a woman going to the Prefecture of Police armed with her birth certificate and asking to be registered. She would be questioned by the assistant head of the bureau and asked to declare her matrimonial status, the professions of her parents and whether she had any children. She would then undergo a medical examination at the police dispensary. The minimum age at which a girl might legally apply for registration was sixteen. Compulsory registration might be the result of a police raid, of the sort so feared by Emile Zola's Nana in his novel of that name:

> Moreover, Satin inspired [Nana] with an awful fear of the police. She was full of anecdotes about them . . . In the summer they would swoop upon the boulevard in parties of twelve or fifteen, surrounding a whole long reach of sidewalk and fishing up as many as thirty women in an evening . . . [Nana] saw herself hustled and dragged along, and finally subjected to the official medical inspection. The thought of the official armchair filled her with shame and anguish . . .[6]

The compulsory health check, or *contrôle sanitaire*, was detested by prostitutes who, no less than other women of the period, experienced medical examination of the sexual organs as an assault on their modesty. The 'armchair' Nana dreads so much refers to the adapted table on which the women were examined. The doctors preferred to use an ordinary table, with a raised plank at one end for the woman to rest her feet on, but so many prostitutes were in the habit of wearing big hats which they did not want to be squashed as they lay back, that a kind of reclining armchair was devised so that they could remain partially sitting up. The dispensary where the checks were carried out was originally located in the rue Croix-des-Petits-Champs not far from the Louvre and the Tuileries, moving in 1843 to the courtyard of the Prefecture of Police on the quai de l'Horloge on the Ile de la Cité, and it was open from eleven in the morning until five in the afternoon, every day except Sunday. The checks were carried out at speed; on average during the Second Empire, fifty-two women would be examined in one hour. Independent prostitutes were required to attend for the check twice a month, while doctors visited the *maisons de tolérance* to carry out the checks every week.

If a *fille insoumise* arrested during a police raid, or a *fille soumise* attending for her routine check-up, was found to be suffering from a venereal disease, she would be sent to the prison-hospital of Saint-Lazare where she could be detained until she was cured. Registered prostitutes could also be taken there for infringements of the rules. Saint-Lazare was a source of terror, reputed to be filthy as well as harsh, and women were continually devising ways of disguising any tell-tale symptoms of disease, always trying to keep one step ahead of the examining authorities. Some such device, at which Dr Ryan will do no more than hint, appears to have been a form of cup inserted into the vagina and covering the cervix, as it also had the effect of appearing to stop menstrual bleeding:

> It is necessary to abstain from details; but I may mention that this invention has often served to conceal their maladies, and has thus enabled them to elude the watchfulness of the police; and they have also employed it in the hospital to simulate cures, and recover their liberty; but these tricks are now well known, and no longer deceive the persons who are charged with the sanitary *surveillance*.[7]

If, on her first arrest, a *fille insoumise* turned out to be healthy, she would probably be released, while a second arrest was likely to lead to immediate registration. Unless she was in a position to call on some influential protector prepared to vouch for her and to state that she was not after all a prostitute, it would be in the woman's best interest to comply at this point, as refusal to be registered would only result in further detention and investigation.

A further type of institution devoted to the prostitute, in addition to the brothel, the hospital and the prison, was the refuge where she could go to repent and be, to some extent, rehabilitated. Convents had originally provided such a refuge but they had been abolished at the time of the Revolution, and the only institution available to the repentant prostitute at the time of Parent-Duchâtelet's researches was the refuge of the Good Shepherd, founded in 1821 by an association devoted to the education of prostitutes. A woman had to be aged between eighteen and twenty-five to be admitted here, and there was a disturbingly high mortality rate caused, or so Parent-Duchâtelet considered, by the extreme change the prostitute had suddenly to make from her previously unstructured life into this new one of an ordered austerity, involving getting up at five o'clock every morning followed by long hours in chapel: 'they jumped, so to speak, from one extreme to another, and without the least transition'.[8]

Parent-Duchâtelet estimated the number of prostitutes in Paris in 1836 as approximately eighteen thousand,[9] one half of whom were kept women or *femmes galantes*, over whom the police had no jurisdiction because they carried on their affairs in private.

No one, says [Duchâtelet], can deny that these women are really prostitutes; they propagate fatal diseases and precocious infirmities, more than all the others, and they may be considered to be the most dangerous beings in society. The police cannot, however, treat them as prostitutes, for they all have a residence, pay taxes, and conform, apparently, to the rules of decency; consequently, they cannot be refused the outward tokens of respect which are due to virtuous women.[10]

Somewhere between the prostitute and the kept woman came the *grisette*, an untranslatable word which originally referred to a costume of inexpensive grey fabric worn by working-class women but which by 1835 was also being used to denote 'a flirtatious young female worker of loose morals'. Indeed, as early as the seventeenth century, La Fontaine was using the word in this sense:

> A *grisette* is a treasure today,
> For without any effort at all,
> Or accompanying her to a ball,
> You'll easily go the whole way.
> Say what you like, she'll ask nothing of you,
> The only hard thing is finding one who'll stay true.[11]

A *grisette* would be in employment, most probably as a dressmaker, milliner or florist, and, bearing out Parent-Duchâtelet and Ryan's opinion that the most common cause of prostitution was 'an insufficiency of wages',[12] she would supplement her income by taking a paying lover. (A working man's wage at the time averaged three to four francs a day – approximately the equivalent of six to eight pounds sterling at today's values – but women earned only half that amount.) There might well be three men in her life: the mature lover whom she would see on weekdays and who topped up her meagre wages; her young and not so rich lover with whom she would enjoy recreation on Sundays; and the working man of her own class whom she would eventually marry.[13] The money earned by this sort of light-hearted prostitution would go towards luxuries the *grisette* could not otherwise afford, and provide some spice in her life before she settled down to the grind of being a working-class wife and mother. Henri d'Alméras writes of the *grisette* that her job provided her daily bread, while love represented the dessert.[14]

On a higher level than both the *grisette* and the common prostitute were those women known colloquially as *lorettes*, the name initially awarded by Nestor Roqueplan[15] to the superior class of prostitute who tended to live in the new houses built near the church of Notre Dame de Lorette (consecrated in 1836), midway between the boulevard des Italiens and Montmartre. (The congregating of such women in this area was a result not only of its proximity to the fashionable cafés and restaurants of the *grands boulevards* where they would go to meet their clients, but also of the low rents of the rapidly constructed, already rather damp housing.) Some of these women would be unable to avoid police registration, while others were able to use both their lifestyles as outwardly independent women and the influence of well-connected clients to keep them off the official lists. Once having been registered, it was not easy to get one's name removed from the list of prostitutes, but it could be done, with persistence and the right connections. Some *lorettes* were separated women, who had perhaps married above their class but subsequently 'fallen'; they nevertheless remained at a higher level and able to command a higher price than the ordinary prostitutes of the street or brothel. The author of *Scènes de la vie de Bohème*, Henry Murger, described the *lorette* as 'an impertinent hybrid, a mediocre beauty, half-flesh, half-unguent, whose boudoir is a counter where she slices pieces of her heart, as though they were roast beef'.[16] Their lives could be complicated, necessitating careful organisation in order not to confuse the appointments of various lovers and to avoid clashes. As Julien Teppe puts it:

> all this required precautions and careful book-keeping. The hairdresser, the pedicurist and the inevitable 'piano mistress' – in reality, her *éminence grise* – completed the universe of the *lorette*, who was also bombarded by her supplier of all kinds of outfit and jewellery. And so, dressed up to sail the high seas of intrigue, all she had to do was inspire tender – and profitable – feelings.[17]

Some *lorettes* aspired to be actresses, while some dreamt – and some, like Thérèse Lachmann who became La Païva, attained their dream – of becoming great courtesans. Parent-Duchâtelet also identifies a class of women he calls '*femmes à parties*', who gave dinners and soirées at which they hired themselves out as attractions amidst the gaming-tables.

The measure by which the level reached by a woman paid for sex could be judged was not only the amount of money she could command but the degree of choice she could exercise in the selection of her clients. The lowest prostitute had to take whatever was on offer; the élite of the *demi-monde*, the renowned courtesan, had an almost infinite number of aspirants to pick from. She might make her choice mainly on the grounds of which man had the most disposable income, rather than because of any personal characteristics, but the choice was hers to make. That, at least, is the rosy side of the picture. The other side was that the more money the courtesan had lavished upon her, the more she spent and the more her expenses grew. It was often part of her side of the bargain to spend, rather than save, the money given her by a wealthy protector, for the conventions of the age demanded that the mistress of a man of the world be an ostentatious status symbol, not someone to be hidden away in a secluded apartment. And so the courtesan would come to depend on a high income and then, with the inevitable ending of a particular relationship, her debts would quickly accumulate and she would need to find an equally wealthy replacement as soon as possible. It was a lifestyle which, once embarked upon, was no easier to abandon than that of the common prostitute, and few *demi-mondaines* succeeded in making adequate provision for old, or even middle, age.

The words used to denote the various classes of prostitute and courtesan tell us something about the attitudes of those who employed them towards the women thus labelled. Most noticeable is the number of words taking their provenance from the farmyard or the zoo, words which inevitably belittle the women to whom they are applied, lending them the characteristics of birds or animals, dehumanising and depersonalising them. At best the men using these terms are regarding these women as pets, and at worst as ravening beasts. One of the dictionary definitions of *grisette*, for instance, is 'a species of warbler, lark, duck, weevil and butterfly'; applying this epithet to the young female worker who takes a paying lover emphasises her triviality and lack of value – she is the little bird or butterfly a middle-class man can amuse himself with for a while. Slightly more substantial than the *grisette* was the *cocotte*, a child's word for 'hen' or for a piece of paper folded to resemble a hen, and applied to a professional courtesan. A frequently used animal word for a courtesan was *biche*, literally 'doe' though also used of a small bitch. *Chameau*, literally 'camel', colloquially 'cow' or 'bitch', was used of a heartless woman out to exploit men, in contrast with *camélia* which denoted the loving prostitute of whom Marie Duplessis – or, rather, the fictionalising of her in *La Dame aux camélias* – became the prototype. A word which sounds like one of these animal or bird words, but is not, is *cocodette*, the feminine version of *cocodè*, a name given in the first instance by the young and dissipated Duke de Gramont-Caderousse to a few of his intimates among the fast set, addicted to gambling, horses and duels.[18] *Cocodettes*, who often had to be booked far in advance and were valued as an adornment, were sometimes married women who nevertheless had all the luxury and allure of a professional courtesan.[19] Such women who maintained their connections with high society while acquiring some of the habits of the *demi-monde* might also be termed *demi-castors*, a word which originally referred to hats made half of beaver and half of wool.

From the mid-1850s courtesans were sometimes disparagingly referred to as *Filles de marbre*, the name of a play by Théodore Barrière and Lambert Thiboust, first performed in the Vaudeville Theatre on 17 May 1853. The protagonist of the first act is a sculptor, Phidias, who creates marble statues of the famed courtesans of Ancient Greece, Laïs, Aspasia and Phryne. He subsequently falls in love with his marble creations, who remain cold and inert. The moral of the story is demonstrated by the arrival of the rich man who commissioned the statues; he offers them money and luxury, at which the marble women turn their heads towards him. The rest of the play is set in contemporary Madrid and Paris, and tells the story of an artist seduced by a heartless courtesan. For a while he returns to his senses, his mother and his virtuous fiancée. But at the end of the play he has a vision of the marble statues – and drops dead. Such a play would have depended for its success on the audience being able to recognise characteristics, or thinking it could recognise characteristics, of certain contemporary courtesans in the portrayal of the marble statues.

The women of the uppermost ranks, the most desirable *demi-mondaines*, were also often referred to by the epithets *grandes* or *hautes* – *grandes cocottes*, for instance, rather than simple *cocottes*. The pseudonymous writer 'Zed' refers in his *Le Demi-monde sous le Second Empire* of 1892 to *grandes abandonnées* (the great abandoned ones), while Frédéric Loliée in his *Les Femmes du Second Empire* of 1907 uses the term *grandes horizontales* (literally, great horizontals, or women flat on their backs). Collective expressions for the great *demi-mondaines* included *la haute galanterie* (literally high gallantry, chivalry or intrigue, and colloquially the top rank of kept women) and *la Haute Bicherie*. The greatest of the great were also known collectively as *La garde* (properly used to refer to the Imperial Guard); these were the top twelve or so courtesans, the aristocracy of the *demi-monde*. At various stages in their careers, Cora Pearl and La Païva would both have been considered as members of *La garde*. Others included Marie Colombier, Hortense Schneider, Blanche d'Antigny, Léonide Leblanc, Anna Deslion and Marguerite Bellanger (who became one of Napoleon III's mistresses). Yet even at this exalted level, the pejorative animal vocabulary could not be escaped, for such women were also known as *lionnes* – queens of beasts, certainly, but still beasts.

Respectable mothers feared that these beasts would devour their sons, breaking their hearts while eating up their fortunes. The men themselves, along with the medical and police authorities, were more afraid of the danger of contracting syphilis, which could lead to madness and early death. By the end of the nineteenth century as many as 20 per cent of the entire population of Paris was affected by the disease. Dr Michael Ryan, for one, did all he could to increase this fear, in the hope of influencing behaviour, by his description of the symptoms:

> In many cases there is partial or total destruction by ulceration or sloughing off of the virile member, and of the female genitals, of the soft palate, of the cartilages of the nose, there are warts on the glans penis, or labia pudendi, various abscesses, pustules, and fissures, in different parts of the body; there are nervous,

neuralgic, and rheumatic pains, falling off of the hair, phthisis or general breaking up of the constitution, and very frequently death closes the scene.[20]

Courtesans and experienced prostitutes could go some way to allay the fear of syphilis by the use of condoms, which carried the added benefit of helping to avoid pregnancy (though Drs Ryan and Parent-Duchâtelet both seem to have believed that a pregnant prostitute was a particularly enticing proposition to many men). In the early part of the nineteenth century condoms – known to the French as *redingotes anglaises* ('English overcoats') and to the English as 'French letters' – were made of sheep gut with a ribbon used to close the open end and, though they also began to be made of vulcanised rubber in the late nineteenth century, they were still being made of animal skins and silk in Europe right into the twentieth. From the 1820s condoms could be purchased from certain shops in the gallery of the Palais Royal, and later in the century they were available in tobacconists or brothels for fifty centimes.

For those courtesans and prostitutes who did not want their way of life interrupted by the advent of a child – and these were most of them – other methods of contraception were also available, although coitus interruptus remained the most common. Vaginal sponges represented one option, some acting merely as barriers while others delivered chemical agents to the vagina. The insertion of a small, damp sponge tied to a ribbon was recommended by English birth controllers and was declared by the French, if accompanied by a douche or the use of a bidet, to be a woman's best protection. Douching itself was increasingly popular, particularly in France (where foreigners were always struck by the ubiquity of the bidet, an invention which had emerged some time in the late seventeenth century). Women douched with various mineral and vegetable solutions, including one which consisted simply of cold water though more often a little vinegar or alum would be added. By the middle of the nineteenth century commercial douches were readily available in pharmacies and were also sold via respectable mail order catalogues, purportedly for purposes of hygiene.

If all the precautions of condoms and douching failed, there remained the emmenagogues – drugs used for the purpose of bringing on late or missing periods. Many newspapers carried small advertisements for women's medicines and, though no one could openly advertise drugs that would induce abortions, they could freely mention remedies for 'irregular' periods. The dividing line between contraception and abortion (or the inducement of miscarriage) was hazy, and herbal teas, purgatives and suppositories were all employed to keep women 'regular'. Patent remedies guaranteed to cure irregular periods began to edge out the traditional remedies, but even the new concoctions were based on traditional emmenagogues, such as aloes, iron, savin, ergot (from rye), rue, tansy, quinine and pennyroyal. And for most women abortion remained a back-up method of birth control.

Abortion had been made illegal in France in 1791. The Napoleonic law codified in 1810 did not, however, punish pregnant women if the drugs they used were self-administered. On the other hand, anyone who assisted or advised them on which drugs to take – whatever their medical status, from physician to midwife – would be guilty of a criminal act. Seven years later the law was amended to apply also to women who brought about their own abortions. But despite the prohibitions in France and other countries, it was possible throughout Europe to obtain information about which drugs were effective for inducing abortions. In 1805, two years after the Ellenborough Act made abortion illegal in Great Britain, the *London Dispensatory* was published. This guide to drugs was based on the official *London Pharmacopœia*, and the items it names suggest that most drugs used for abortion and contraception were sold in chemists' shops. The 1818 edition of the *London Dispensatory* included some references to birth control, however vague. Using language in such a way as not to appear to be proffering advice, an American guide to drugs published in 1836 contained the information that ergot was popularly used by midwives in parts of Germany, France and Italy to induce contractions of the uterus. The guide warned that this could be dangerous. In short, the guides published in the early nineteenth century all indicate that during the period when abortion was criminalised the means of bringing about abortions were commonly known and available. A survey of newspapers in Great Britain during one week in the mid-nineteenth century showed that a hundred of them contained thinly disguised advertisements for abortion; and in France, by the end of the century, claims were being made that between one hundred thousand and five hundred thousand abortions were carried out every year.

When children were born to prostitutes their chances of survival beyond infancy were not high, both because they may have already been infected in the womb with venereal disease and because the mother's precarious way of life and uncertain income did not provide the optimum background for health and stability. It was also a part of the conventional wisdom of the time that prostitutes would make hopeless mothers anyway, by virtue of their innate fecklessness and childishness. In addition to documenting the regulations governing prostitution in Paris and describing the outward circumstances of the women concerned, Dr Parent-Duchâtelet had devoted some space in his *De la Prostitution dans la ville de Paris* to the moral and physical characteristics of prostitutes, assembling a number of stereotypes which had already obtained wide currency in society and thereby ensuring that they continued to be influential for some time to come. Dr Ryan drew upon Parent-Duchâtelet's descriptions to determine whether the same stereotypes applied to prostitutes in London and concluded that, by and large, they did. Neither doctor, however, agreed with everything that was popularly said about prostitutes and listed some of the common beliefs in order to contradict them.

One of the generally accepted stereotypes concerned the mental and emotional immaturity of the prostitute. She was seen as something of a child, who had not yet learnt how to assimilate the values of society as a whole. She was supposed to have rejected work in favour of pleasure, and thus everything about her was perceived as demonstrating this rejection: her laziness, her love of idleness, the shape of her day. The fact that she might be exhausted after hours of plying her trade did not seem to be taken into account to explain her 'laziness', which was considered to be a prime cause for women taking to prostitution in the first place. Quoting Parent-Duchâtelet, Ryan declares: 'it is the desire of procuring enjoyments without working, that causes many young women to leave their places, or to refrain from seeking others when out of service. The laziness, carelessness, and cowardice of prostitutes have become almost proverbial.'[21] It was also believed that women were propelled into prostitution by vanity, 'and the desire of being finely dressed . . . particularly in Paris, where simplicity in dress is actually a subject of reproach, and shabbiness is still more despised'.[22] Both doctors are clear that these are not the primary causes of women turning to prostitution, however, according that honour to poverty and, in many instances, to a first incident of 'seduction' (or what one might sometimes more accurately call rape). One of the reasons for the poverty of women, Parent-Duchâtelet believed, was that men had been usurping jobs more suitable for that sex, such as waiting in restaurants and serving in shops.[23] Further characteristics attributed to the prostitute were instability, turbulence and agitation, qualities demonstrated by her frequent changes of address, as well as by her love of dancing, her sudden shifts of mood and her inability to concentrate. 'Their volatile and changeable turn of mind is so great, that nothing can fix their attention, which is distracted by the most trifling occurrence.'[24] The prostitute symbolised disorder, excess and improvidence, a rejection of the established order. The types of 'excess' identified included a willingness to be carried away by various enthusiasms, an over-fondness for alcohol and food, a tendency to talk all the time and frequent outbursts of anger. Very few prostitutes, it was thought, knew how to save money; they indulged in useless expenditure, particularly on perishable items such as flowers, and they easily acquired a passion for gambling. 'There are three things in the world that prostitutes love most,' wrote Alphonse Esquiros, 'the sun, flowers, and their hair.'[25]

A particular fear, one clearly discernible in Zola's depiction of Nana and her friend Satin, is that prostitutes had a predilection to love one another instead of loving men. This fear seems to have exercised the Parisian authorities more than those in London, as Dr Ryan

sounds rather surprised by his French colleague's findings on this
score:

> [Parent-Duchâtelet] next alludes to those who from a depraved
> and unnatural taste, select their lovers from persons of their own
> sex. These are called *tribades*, and are numerous when long
> confined in prisons. They are despised and hated by all other
> prostitutes, but their vice prevails to such an extent, that,
> notwithstanding the regulation of the police, which obliges
> every woman to sleep in a separate bed, M. Duchâtelet estimates
> them at less [*sic*] than one-fourth of the entire number of
> prostitutes.
>
> These disgusting and monstrous unions, are much more
> frequent than is generally imagined.[26]

Lesbianism was perceived as a huge threat to the social order of which
properly regulated heterosexual prostitution was otherwise seen as
representing a safeguard. (It is, I hope, a measure of the gulf between
attitudes of the 1830s and those of the early twenty-first century that I
must confess to having no idea what Dr Ryan is talking about when
he concludes his comments on *tribades* thus: 'It has been remarked
that these women are more frequently pregnant than ordinary
prostitutes; and this circumstance has become the subject of jokes
in the prisons. The explanation must be apparent to every one
conversant with human nature.'[27])

On what was perceived to be the positive side, other qualities
attributed to fallen women included an attraction to religious piety
(despite the tendency not to go to church) – 'Many of them refrain
from all religious duties, on account of their unworthiness; though
most of them are anxious for religious consolation when dangerous
or fatal illness assails them';[28] an attachment to young children
(despite, or maybe because of, being incapable of rearing their
own); and a nostalgia for their native countryside (many of them
having made their way to the big cities from the villages where they
had been born). They were also perceived as having a great sense of

solidarity with and charity towards other marginalised elements in society, as well as towards those of their own kind who had fallen on hard times. 'In times of scarcity, a great number of these women, have given a loaf of bread a week, or even a day, to old people, to those in bad health, and also to poor families in their neighbourhood.'[29]

Parent-Duchâtelet mentioned only two physical stereotypes, which were to be repeated endlessly: plumpness of figure, ascribed to greed, laziness and the taking of many warm baths, as well as to the clients' preferences, and a raucous voice, which he believed to be caused by social origin, abuse of alcohol and exposure to cold rather than by, as popular prejudice would have it, the practice of oral sex. Dr Ryan went to some lengths to convince his readership that the genital organs of prostitutes were not, as was commonly supposed, any different from those of the general population of married women. Alphonse Esquiros drew up a more detailed physical stereotype of the prostitute:

> Natural prostitutes, if one may express oneself thus, are in general of a powerful and Herculean race. Everything about them speaks of eager appetites: their chest is wide and generous, their pelvis ample, their flesh abundant and firm to the touch; their face radiates highly developed sensual energies; the large and devouring mouth, the flaring nostrils, the deep and rather raucous breathing – there is no element of their physical characteristics which does not indicate an inexhaustible need for material pleasures.[30]

Esquiros did not share Parent-Duchâtelet's views on the inevitability of prostitutes; rather he regarded them as a section of the human race at a lower stage of development than other women, and believed that the continuing progress of humankind would eventually lead to the end of this phenomenon. He agreed, however, that among the main causes of prostitution were poverty and ignorance, though he also thought that heredity played a not inconsiderable part: 'conceived in the midst of an orgy, most of them have prostitution in the blood'.[31]

He also believed that some of them were governed by an over-whelming need to keep eating, such that no ordinary worker's wage could ever buy enough food to satisfy their appetite; this, he thought, was caused by a particular cerebral organ called 'alimentivity'.[32]

Though in many respects the life of the successful *grande horizontale* was a far cry from that of her less fortunate sister, the common prostitute or *fille publique*, the characteristics attributed to the latter were also in large measure attributed to the former and, no matter what dizzy heights women such as Marie Duplessis and La Païva eventually attained, they were never free from these stereotypes which have coloured nearly every subsequent description and judg-ment of them. They were also in a double bind, for they could be condemned both for conforming and for not conforming to type, either for reinforcing the popular prejudice of the archetypal pros-titute (as Marie did perfectly), or for having the temerity to behave differently and attempt to live outside the accepted classifications (as did La Païva). In both cases the reality became overlaid by the stereotype, so that it became very difficult, maybe even impossible, for both their contemporaries and subsequent generations, to see these women clearly.

The assumption underlying much of what has been summarised in this chapter – of both the regulations governing prostitutes' lives and the stereotypes attributed to them – was the weakness of women, of all women. Not only were prostitutes themselves viewed as having been drawn to their way of life through laziness, greed, vanity and inability to cope with poverty in any other way, but even so-called virtuous women were in danger, through their own inherent weakness, of being contaminated by the example of their fallen sisters if prostitution were allowed to be practised openly, without the protecting walls of the brothel or the rules against open solicitation and display. 'The wide road is too tempting for feminine fragility, women have thrown themselves down it; ask the bosses why they search in vain for workers, ask the artists why it is so difficult to find models; unregistered prostitution has seized them and will not let them go.'[33] The virtuous woman needed protection, not only because she might be shocked at witnessing depravity but, even worse, because she was likely to be tempted into abandoning virtue herself. The splendidly attired, ostentatiously wealthy courtesan was viewed as a particular source of temptation to the virtuous, protected but less dazzling wife, and this is one reason for the disquiet evinced by some contemporary writers such as Maxime Du Camp when describing the *demi-monde* and the difficulty of telling it apart from the *haut monde*.

---

1 M. Ryan, *Prostitution in London, with a comparative view of that of Paris and New York*, H. Baillière, London, 1839, p.72

2 A.J.B. Parent-Duchâtelet, *De la Prostitution dans la ville de Paris*, J.B. Baillière, Paris, 1836, p.513

3 M. Ryan, *Prostitution in London*, p.221

4 Ibid., p.59

5 Alphonse Esquiros, *Les Vierges folles*, P. Delavigne, Paris, 1842, pp.97–8

6 Emile Zola, *Nana*, The Modern Library, New York, 1928, pp.309–11

7 M. Ryan, *Prostitution in London*, pp.64–5

8 A.J.B. Parent-Duchâtelet, *De la Prostitution dans la ville de Paris*, p.549

9 Mr Talbot, Secretary of the London Society for the Prevention of Juvenile Prostitution, reckoned that there were as many as eighty thousand prostitutes operating in London at this time, while the Rev Mr M'Dowall of the New York Magdalen Asylum expressed horror at his estimate of ten thousand existing in New York.

10 M. Ryan, *Prostitution in London*, p.58

11 Quoted in Julien Teppe, *Vocabulaire de la vie amoureuse*, La Pavillon, Paris, 1973, p.115

12 M. Ryan, *Prostitution in London*, p.47

13 See Henry Knepler (ed.), *Man about Paris. The confessions of Arsène Houssaye*, Victor Gollancz, London, 1972, p.74

14 Henri d'Alméras, *La Vie parisienne sous le Second Empire*, Albin Michel, Paris, 1933, p.217

15 See S. Kracauer, *Jacques Offenbach ou le secret du Second Empire*, Editions Bernard Grasset, Paris, 1937, p.92

16 Quoted in Julien Teppe, *Vocabulaire de la vie amoureuse*, p.117

17 Julien Teppe, *Vocabulaire de la vie amoureuse*, p.117

18 See S. Kracauer, *Jacques Offenbach ou le secret du Second Empire*, pp.242–3

19 See Julien Teppe, *Vocabulaire de la vie amoureuse*, p.119

20 M. Ryan, *Prostitution in London*, p.402

21 Ibid., p.43

22 Ibid.

23 A.J.B. Parent-Duchâtelet, *De la Prostitution dans la ville de Paris*, p.97

24 M. Ryan, *Prostitution in London*, p.50

25 Alphonse Esquiros, *Les Vierges folles*, p.135

26 M. Ryan, *Prostitution in London*, p.56

27 Ibid., p.57

28 Ibid., p.50

29 Ibid., p.53

30 Alphonse Esquiros, *Les Vierges folles*, p.46

31 Ibid., p.35

32 Ibid., p.46

33 Maxime Du Camp, *Paris: ses organes, ses fonctions et sa vie jusqu'en 1870*, p.351

CHAPTER TWO

The Life of Marie Duplessis

MARIE DUPLESSIS WAS born Alphonsine Plessis on 15 January 1824 in the village of Saint-Germain-de-Clarfeuille near Nonant in Lower Normandy, the younger daughter of a travelling pedlar called Marin Plessis and his wife Marie, née Deshayes, who had married below herself and disastrously. In the year of Alphonsine's birth Charles X, a Bourbon, was enthroned as king of France, succeeding his elder brother Louis XVIII. The eldest brother of the three had been Louis XVI, executed in 1793. Louis XVIII had been restored to the throne by the allies after the defeat of Napoleon I in 1814. He had to flee when Napoleon returned to France from his exile on Elba and was restored a second time in 1815 after Napoleon's final defeat at Waterloo. Charles X, an ultraroyalist, would have liked France to return to the ways of the *ancien régime,* as it was before the Revolution of 1789.

Marin Plessis was the illegitimate son of a priest and a prostitute. He abused his wife – particularly after the birth of Alphonsine, whom he had wanted to be a boy – until she could stand it no longer. She left to work as a maid to an English woman in Paris, hoping to be able to send for her two daughters once she was able to afford to do so. This never happened, as she died when Alphonsine was six, and the daughters, especially Alphonsine (her sister Delphine was two years older), were left at the mercy of their father. Delphine was sent to live with an uncle, where she remained until she was sixteen and was then apprenticed to a laundress. Initially Alphonsine lived with her mother's cousin, Madame Agathe Boisard, who was a farmer's wife and already had three children of her own. She stayed with the Boisards for several years, despite their poverty and the refusal of Marin Plessis to contribute anything to her upkeep. Eventually, however, Alphonsine, who as a young girl was already pretty and a source of temptation to men (Romain Vienne, who, though an unreliable and inventive biographer, demonstrates a degree of insight into Alphonsine's character, claims that she was abused by male workers from the age of eleven and a half[1]), became too much for Agathe Boisard to handle. There was a scandalous incident involving a farmhand – according to Vienne, Alphonsine seduced the seven-teen-year-old boy against his will[2] – and she was sent back to her father.

Marin placed her, like her sister, as an apprentice to a *blanchisseuse*, which can be loosely translated as 'laundress'. Such an apprenticeship involved long hours of hard and repetitive physical labour. Emile Zola gave a detailed description of a laundress's establishment in his novel *L'Assommoir*, from which it is possible to reconstruct an idea of Alphonsine's working life at this time.[3] First, piles of dirty linen would be sorted and washed, the actual washing sometimes being done at a communal washroom by a washerwoman, a lower level of worker than the *blanchisseuse*. Much of the work of a *blanchisseuse* consisted of ironing, which would be done at a large table covered with a heavy blanket, itself covered with calico. Several irons were heated on the large cast-iron stove, and it would be the job of the apprentice to keep this stove filled – always being careful not to over-fill it – with coke. The room where the *blanchisseuses* worked would also be full of clothes hung up on wires to dry. On the floor there would be an earthenware pan, containing starch into which the linen would be dipped before being ironed. The *blanchisseuse* herself and her older employees would be busy ironing intricate objects such as caps, shirt-fronts, petticoats and embroidered drawers, while the apprentice could be put to work on the plain items, the stockings and handkerchiefs. The ironing would be done standing up around the table, a flat brick alongside each worker on which to place the hot iron. Work could go on until late at night, particularly on Saturdays, so that the customers could have their clean clothes to wear on Sunday.

Such was Alphonsine's life when she was aged about thirteen to fourteen. Then one Sunday, her father, who had remained in touch with her, took her to visit an elderly acquaintance of his, a bachelor in his sixties or seventies by the name of Plantier. But more than taking her to visit, Marin Plessis left Alphonsine with Plantier; possibly he even sold her to him. For a while she attempted to continue her work with the *blanchisseuse* while spending Sundays and Mondays with Plantier. She was dismissed, however, when her employer realised the situation and Alphonsine returned full-time to Plantier. She was resourceful enough to escape from him after a few weeks and to find herself a job in an inn at Exmes in Normandy, where she lived as a maid-of-all-work for several months. This period of relative tranquillity was again disrupted by the arrival of her father, who this time placed her with an umbrella merchant. After two months of selling umbrellas, Alphonsine was once again removed by her father. There followed a fortnight about which little is known but much has been suspected. Alphonsine refused to talk about it to her biographer Romain Vienne, and the only thing which is known for certain is that Marin took his daughter to live with him for two weeks in a hovel where there was room for only one bed and not many ways of keeping warm. And afterwards the neighbours talked. At least so it has been surmised from the sudden departure, in 1839, of Marin and Alphonsine Plessis for Paris.

On arrival in the capital, Alphonsine was left by her father with some more cousins of her mother, the Vitals. Madame Vital found work for her, initially again as an apprentice laundress, but then as something more to her taste in the shop of a dressmaker, Mademoiselle Urbain, in the rue du Coq-Héron, not far from the Palais Royal. At the time Alphonsine was placed as an apprentice there, early in 1839, she was fifteen years old. The apprentices worked from seven o'clock in the morning until eight at night, for six days a week, and learnt such skills as decorating dresses with lace and embroidery. Mademoiselle Urbain supervised her young apprentices as closely as she could, knowing, as did the forewoman in the shop where Nana was apprenticed in Zola's *L'Assommoir*, 'the dangers that a girl ran in the streets of Paris'.[4] It would be an unusual establishment where at least one or two of the girls were not following the customary practices of the *grisette*. And after Alphonsine's life in the countryside, the city of Paris, where gaslight had been introduced in the late 1820s and the first omnibuses had appeared in 1828, must have seemed a place full of life, movement and adventure. The reign of Charles X had been ended in 1830 by the July Revolution, the ultraroyalists having provoked the opposition of the middle classes, who desired more participation in the government of the country. The insurrection had begun on 26 July and led to the installation of a provisional government three days later and the abdication of Charles X on 2 August. Louis Philippe, previously the Duke d'Orléans, was proclaimed king on 31 July and officially acceded to the throne on 9 August. He had formerly been a part of the liberal opposition to Louis XVIII and Charles X and found his support in the discontented upper middle classes. His reign, known as the July monarchy, marked the triumph of the wealthy bourgeoisie; Louis Philippe was himself known as the 'citizen king' because of his bourgeois manners and dress. Many former officials of Napoleon I's Empire were also returned to positions of influence. The increase in the political power of the bourgeoisie coincided with a growth in their spending power, and money began to take over from birth in determining one's place in society.

According to Nestor Roqueplan, Alphonsine's chief interest on her arrival in Paris was food, in particular the fried potatoes sold from stalls in the street. Roqueplan recalled the first time he saw the girl he later recognised as the courtesan Marie Duplessis: it was near the Pont Neuf, and she was nibbling at an apple while eyeing hungrily the potatoes sizzling in a skillet. He bought her a large portion of the fried potatoes, which she ate greedily, having thrown away the despised apple.[5]

For about six months all went well. Alphonsine lived as well as worked at Mademoiselle Urbain's premises, and spent most Sunday afternoons with her relatives the Vitals. Then one Sunday in summer her life took on a new aspect. Alphonsine and two other apprentices, Hortense and Ernestine, had planned a trip by omnibus into the country, to the royal château of Saint Cloud which was a few miles from Paris, on the left bank of the Seine. But it began to rain and, instead of setting off for Saint Cloud, the three girls sheltered in the galerie Montpensier beneath the arcades of the Palais Royal while discussing how to spend their free time. As usual they were hungry, and they decided that they had just enough money between them to eat in a modest restaurant frequented by the local shopkeepers. There they were approached by the owner of the restaurant, a Monsieur Nollet, who offered them a bottle of wine on the house. Further- more, after hearing what their plans had been, he invited them to accompany him to Saint Cloud on the following Sunday. And so the next week the three girls set off with him in a hired carriage for the country. For two of the girls this represented a pleasant, but isolated event, just an unexpected treat; for the third, it marked the beginning of a new phase of existence.

Quite who seduced whom, who exploited whom, is debatable: Alphonsine, with her precocious sexual experience, was an easy prey for a man with a certain amount of sophistication on the look-out for a young and pretty mistress, while she was quick to realise that, if she played her cards right, Nollet was in a position to offer her a way out of a life of drudgery and relative poverty. Events progressed rapidly. Within a month Monsieur Nollet had installed Alphonsine in a small apartment in the rue de l'Arcade and given her three thousand francs (about six thousand pounds in today's terms) for her initial needs.

Alphonsine demonstrated no intention of merely supplementing her income in the manner of a *grisette* or of ever returning to her occupation as a dressmaker. Dressed in her new finery, she went to say farewell to Mademoiselle Urbain and her former fellow appren- tices, but did not, at least according to Romain Vienne, make any further appearance at the Vitals': 'She didn't dare present herself at her cousin Vital's, but she wrote to ask her forgiveness, and to let her know that she intended to visit her on Sunday morning. She didn't have to wait long for a reply: "If you ever set foot in my house again, I'll chase you out like the vermin you are." [6] Her tastes very soon outstripped the abilities of any potential working-class husband to pay for them or even the resources of a bourgeois lover such as Monsieur Nollet to satisfy them. The few dresses and jewels and relatively modest sum of money with which he provided her awoke the desire for more and more luxury. Nollet retired from the scene, having realised he could not keep up with Alphonsine's expenditure, upon which she had a brief liaison with a young man called Valéry and several others besides. But the pivotal point of her transformation from a young kept woman with a very dubious background into the highly prized (and priced) courtesan was her liaison with Agénor de Guiche, *le beau Agénor*, who makes an appearance in the lives of most of the nineteenth-century Parisian *demi-mondaines*. He has also caused a degree of confusion among historians because of his multiple names: as eldest son of the Duke de Gramont, he bore the title of Duke de Guiche until succeeding his father, when he himself became the Duke de Gramont; the family were also known as the princes of Bidache, and were one of the most ancient and illustrious houses of the French nobility. The only thing Agénor lacked was wealth (or at least enough of it to maintain a long-term relationship with a high-spending courtesan), as the Gramonts had lost much of their fortune at the time of the Revolution.

When Agénor took up with Alphonsine he was twenty-one years old and she was sixteen. He had just left the Polytechnic after two years of studies in which he had not particularly excelled, and he had also just embarked on an army career which would be brief and not particularly glorious. Seriously smitten by Alphonsine, and interested in more than just going to bed with her, he decided he wanted to bring her up to his own level of education and refinement. So he arranged for her to have good teachers, paying for piano and dancing lessons for her. Alphonsine improved her writing and reading skills, amassed a library (by the time of her death she owned some two hundred books, ranging from the novels of Walter Scott, through Rabelais and Rousseau, to Michaud's voluminous *Biographie univer-*

selle and Burette's *Histoire de France*), took lessons in deportment and decorum and became skilled in the art of conversation. During this time of Pygmalion-like transformation, Nestor Roqueplan encountered her again, this time in the Ranelagh pleasure gardens:

> One evening, I felt myself being tapped on the shoulder by a tall young man, fresh as a lily and with the blond curls of a Cupid, the Duke de . . ., the bearer of a great name, a name often illustrious and never insignificant; hanging on to his arm was a charming person, elegantly dressed, who was none other than my greedy girl from the Pont Neuf, and whom he was exhibiting with an inventor's satisfaction.[7]

Agénor spent something in the region of ten thousand francs on Alphonsine in three months. There was a break in their relationship before the end of 1840, when he left for England. On his return the liaison was struck up again, though by this time he was not enjoying exclusive rights (if indeed he ever had). But his effect was lasting, Alphonsine having taken readily to the process of education which he had initiated. And to mark her transformation, she changed her name from Alphonsine Plessis to Marie Duplessis.

She was not unusual, among the *grisettes* and courtesans of Louis Philippe's reign, in deciding to change her name; it was also a very common practice among the ranks of ordinary prostitutes. The choice of a new name (ones chosen frequently included Ninette, Niniche and Nana) could serve both to add a touch of glamour and to depersonalise the prostitute, so that she could feel she was merely performing a role, disconnected from her real self. There was also often a desire to disconnect herself from her previous life and from her family, either out of shame or from a desire to escape and not be easily traced. Parent-Duchâtelet emphasises the need in many cases for prostitutes to conceal their identities in order to avoid pursuit by the courts or the police, as well as their desire not to be recognised by family and erstwhile friends.[8] In Alphonsine Plessis's decision to change her name to Marie Duplessis there was undoubtedly an element of this urge to escape her past, and to reflect the remaking of herself in her name. It has also been asserted[9] that she chose the name 'Marie' in honour either of her mother (Marie, née Deshayes) or of the Virgin Mary. A more likely candidate would be Mary Magdalene, patron saint of the repentant prostitute and whose church of La Madeleine Marie was supposed to have visited on many occasions. One also cannot help being struck by the fact that the name 'Marie Duplessis' is not so very far removed from 'Marin Plessis'; perhaps it was the shadowy figure of her depraved father whom Alphonsine was honouring, or at least unconsciously connecting herself with, in the choice of this particular name. He had been the first to teach her, in leaving her with the old man Plantier, that her sexuality could be used as a source of income. It was a lesson she learnt well and to full effect, proving, in this respect at least, that she was indeed her father's daughter.

In June 1840 Marie had taken up with the young Viscount de Méril, who was the first to introduce her to the delights of Spa, the internationally fashionable watering place near Liège in Belgium. It was here that she discovered her predilection for gambling, a fascination which greatly increased her expenditure. The affair with de Méril, who was attached to the Ministry of the Interior, lasted for more than a year and resulted in Marie giving birth to a son, in Versailles, in May 1841. The child was placed by Méril with a nurse in the provinces, but later died of pneumonia. (That, at least, is one version of the story. Another is hinted at in the assertion that in 1869, many years after Marie's death, a young man by the name of Judelet visited her sister Delphine and asked to see a picture of Marie. She showed him the portrait by Vidal, which remained in her family until 1960, and Judelet, it was said, bore a marked resemblance to the woman depicted in it.)[10] A month after the birth of Marie's son her father, Marin Plessis, died of syphilis, aged fifty-one, in the hamlet of Ginai in the canton of Exmes. There had been no further contact between father and daughter since her arrival in Paris.

Marie made it her trademark to be pale, mysterious and rather distant in public, though she could be quite different with a few acquaintances in her own drawing room. At times she could seem excessively exuberant. She enjoyed singing risqué songs, accompanying herself on the piano, dancing madly and drinking too much champagne. Romain Vienne gives a detailed description of her appearance:

> She was tall and slim, fresh as a spring flower; her bodily beauty perhaps lacked that fullness so appreciated by the Turks, those rich curves without which there is no perfection. A painter would have chosen her as a model, a sculptor never. But she was deliciously pretty. Her long, thick, black hair was magnificent, and she arranged it with inimitable skill. Her oval face with its regular features, slightly pale and melancholy when calm and in repose, would suddenly come to life at the sound of a friendly voice or a warm and sincere word. Her head was child-like. Her sweet and sensuous mouth boasted a display of dazzlingly white teeth. Her hands and feet were so slender that her fingers could almost seem too long. The expression of her large black eyes, with their long lashes, was penetrating, and the softness of her glances gave rise to dream.[11]

Marie's propensity for lying represented the only obvious scar from her dreadful upbringing. The following anecdote is repeated endlessly: 'She had an obsession with lying – I say obsession rather than flaw, because her lies were nearly always harmless. One day when someone asked her why she lied, she replied: "Lying whitens the teeth." '[12]

Marie had many lovers, some of them concurrently, others in rapid succession. Early in 1842 she was living at 28 rue de Mont-Thabor, near the rue de Rivoli, and her expenditure demanded that she keep a constant supply of men able to pay the bills. Hippolyte de Villemessant tells how seven members of fashionable Paris decided to club together to purchase her favours, since she was so expensive to maintain (as mentioned in Chapter 1, this was a not uncommon practice). To inaugurate this arrangement they bought Marie a present: a dressing table with seven drawers so that they could each have one in which to keep their things. In the early days Marie's management of her multiple lovers sometimes went adrift. Shortly after Agénor de Guiche's return from England she made the mistake of taking him for a drive in the blue carriage which had been given to her by another lover, Fernand de Montguyon. The latter saw them, and Marie had much explaining to do. Montguyon was a dissipated young man who gave Marie money to spend on lace and satin and took her to dine in fashionable restaurants such as Tortoni's in the boulevard des Italiens. In addition to the blue carriage, he gave her a dog which she called Tom and used to take for walks in the Bois de Boulogne. Subsequently she managed her affairs better and took care not to offend those who were paying the bills. Agénor was at this stage what was known as an *amant de cœur* – that is, his and Marie's relationship was not a monetary transaction (he could no longer afford for it to be) but a matter of genuine affection and mutual enjoyment. A letter she wrote to Agénor when he was in London in July 1842 demonstrates how fond she was of this particular lover. It also attests to the presence in the background of a man of more substantial means – 'the General' – who has become an obstacle to Marie and Agénor's affair:

> my angel I am very sad I'm very fed up at not seeing you . . .
> I've been pestered since you left by the General who is
> absolutely determined that I should receive him and that I
> should be with him as in the past he should not have changed his
> conduct towards me we would have been so happy if he hadn't
> come to surprise us our life was so well organised . . . tell me
> everything you are thinking what you are doing tell me also that
> you love me. . . . I love you more tenderly than ever I kiss you a
> thousand times on your mouth and all over.[13]

A tactful *amant de cœur* always had to know when to withdraw and had to guard against inappropriate jealousy. Zola portrays one such liaison in *Nana*: '[Clarisse] had seen Madame Bron giving the letter to

Simonne's young man, and he had gone out to read it under the gas-light in the lobby. 'Impossible tonight, darling – I'm booked.' And with that he peaceably departed, as one who was doubtless used to the formula. He at any rate knew how to conduct himself.'[14]

Marie subsequently moved to a more comfortable apartment in the rue d'Antin, acquired for her by a new lover, Count Edouard de Perrégaux. Edouard's grandfather was Jean Frédéric de Perrégaux, a financier who was made a senator by Napoleon Bonaparte and who became the first regent of the Bank of France. His son, Charles Bernardin, was made a count during the Empire. Edouard had fought in Africa against Abd-el-Kader, the great opponent of France's conquest of Algeria, and had acquitted himself very well. Afterwards, however, his conduct deteriorated. He contracted debts, which increased on his return to France. On the death of his father, he found himself with a very large fortune at his disposal. He proceeded to dispose of it as fast as he could, becoming involved in all the high life of Paris. On 3 April 1842 he was admitted to the Jockey Club, the exclusive haunt of the sporting aristocracy, located on the corner of the boulevard des Capucines and the rue Scribe; the annual sub-scription was a thousand francs. He first encountered Marie at a masked ball at the Opera House in the rue Le Peletier, the tradition of masked balls having been revived there in 1839, such events being held every Saturday evening during the carnival time before Lent. Edouard and Marie were intrigued by one another, and Edouard rapidly dropped another courtesan, Alice Ozy, in order to take up with her.

The apartment in which he installed her at 22 rue d'Antin comprised a drawing room, boudoir, dining room and two bed-rooms. The windows, and Marie's bed, were curtained with muslin and silk. Marie ordered her goods and services from a wide range of providers: wines from Madame Tisserant, just opposite in the rue d'Antin; cakes delivered by Rollet from the passage de l'Opéra; glacé fruits from Boissier; mint pastilles from Gouache in the boulevard de la Madeleine. Edouard would join in the consumption of all these luxuries, not stopping to make the calculation that by spending at the rate of three thousand francs a month, which was the absolute minimum Marie required to live on, he would rapidly use up his already depleted fortune.

Marie's daily routine involved getting up at about eleven o'clock in the morning or even later, and having a light breakfast, followed by about twenty minutes' piano practice. She would then read for half an hour or so, before starting on the lengthy process of deciding what to wear, changing her outfit several times until she was satisfied. She might also be visited by outfitters, menders, suppliers and a hair-dresser. When all these matters of dress were completed, she would order her carriage and go for a drive, probably to the Bois de Boulogne (which was not yet the landscaped attraction it would become under Napoleon III but which still provided plenty of *allées* for walking along). She would return home towards the end of the afternoon and would then be 'at home' to visitors – not necessarily only lovers or clients, for sometimes these visitors would include poor women or prostitutes hoping for a hand-out from their more fortunate sister and, at least according to Romain Vienne,[15] if she could help them she would. Then it would be time to dress for the evening, to go to the theatre or to go dancing at somewhere like the newly opened Bal Mabille, an enormous garden in the allée des Veuves (now part of the avenue Montaigne), near the Champs Elysées, transformed in 1840 into an enchanted grove by Mabille the dancing teacher. Here, under oil lamps hung from the trees, men watched famous female dancers perform, or couples danced together while an orchestra played. The first Mabille's sons subsequently introduced gaslight, installing five thousand standard lamps, an illuminated sign over the entrance and even little gas jets in the groves for lighting cigarettes. Then would come dinner, and sooner or later Marie would return to her apartment, usually accompanied by a lover. And once she had serviced this paying client and seen him safely off the premises, her *amant de cœur* might arrive and keep her amorously occupied until the early hours of the morning.

Unsatisfied with these few hours at night, wanting Marie to himself and to be with her all the time, Edouard rented a house for her in the countryside at Bougival with the intention of freeing her from this daily round of Paris – and from the exigencies of other men. Here for a few weeks the couple enjoyed a pastoral idyll, though they also made regular excursions into Paris to attend the Opéra and to eat at the Café Anglais or the Maison Dorée. The Café Anglais had opened at 13 boulevard des Italiens in 1822 and consisted of two floors, divided into twenty-two private rooms, while the Maison Dorée or Maison D'Or, with its gilt balconies, opened in 1840 and contained a large room overlooking the street, as well as a number of private rooms. These were just two of the best known of the numerous cafés and restaurants situated on and around the boulevard des Italiens and which enjoyed a flourishing trade. Marie was flattered by Edouard's exclusive passion for her and willing to reciprocate his love as far as she was able and for as long as he was able to continue supporting her. All he wanted to do was keep her happy, and he fell out with his family and friends as Marie continued to dissipate his fortune. It was around this time that Marie began to show signs of illness, coughing blood for the first time.

Then, on their return from a two-month stay in Baden, Edouard realised that he could no longer afford to keep on the house in Bougival. Marie felt she had been deceived as to the extent of Edouard's fortune, and realised that she again needed to find other protectors to support her way of life. Or, as Vienne puts it, 'It was then that she noticed, by the sudden cooling of her sentiments, that she had loved him only superficially, in the intoxication of deceitful hopes; that she had been the dupe of lying appearances, and that she had built her projects on shifting sand.'[16]

Edouard did not make a complete break with Marie, but she returned to dispensing her charms elsewhere. Lovers of all ages were continually arriving at the rue d'Antin. They included Edouard Delessert (a son of the Prefect of Police who would later become a man of letters and a great traveller, his mother Valentine was for many years the mistress of Prosper Mérimée), the Baron de Plancy, Roger de Beauvoir the well-known *boulevardier* and dandy, and Montjoyeux, as well as men who had already enjoyed her favours, such as Montguyon. One of her most notable lovers was Henri de Contades, who was descended from an eighteenth-century marshal of France, Erasme de Contades. Henri had married his cousin Sophie de Castellane when she was eighteen years old, and embarked on his affair with Marie a few years after the wedding. By this time Sophie had already had several affairs herself. Marie also managed to seduce Sophie's brother, Pierre de Castellane. When Henri de Contades died in 1858, Sophie married again and became the virtuous Madame de Baulaincourt.

Another of Marie's lovers, and the most significant for her future reputation, was Alexandre Dumas *fils*; their liaison began in September 1844 and lasted for nearly a year. Alexandre, the illegitimate son of Alexandre Dumas *père* and a serving girl, first saw her in the company of Eugène Déjazet at the Théâtre des Variétés. Eugène was the son of a famous actress, Virginie Déjazet, who provided her adored and spendthrift son with whatever he wanted. The two young men were both twenty years old, the same age as Marie. They were introduced into Marie's apartment through the agency of Clémence Prat, a dressmaker who also acted as a procuress and who lived next door to Marie.

Alexandre, who as a young man did not have the resources even to begin to support Marie, became an *amant de cœur*. It was not a role he found easy. To begin with he was received only between the hours of midnight and six o'clock in the morning. Later he was allowed to join her in her box in the theatre, or at a restaurant. Sometimes she would send him an affectionate little note in the morning, telling him where to meet her, or that he might accompany her during her afternoon drive or walk. But he did not like being only one lover among many and, as one of the more impecunious ones, having no right to do anything about it. He became jealous, dissatisfied with the few hours allotted to him; he did not like to see another man escorting his mistress to the Opéra. After two months they were quarrelling and Alexandre began to distance himself, though the affair struggled on for a further nine months. A short note which Marie sent to him around this time demonstrates her desire to maintain a relationship and is couched in the reasonable tone of a courtesan attempting to keep a young *amant de cœur* in a sensible frame of mind (she addresses him by his initials of 'AD'):

> Dear Adet, why haven't you told me how you are and why don't you write frankly to me? I think you should treat me like a friend. So I hope for a word from you and I kiss you fondly, like a mistress or like a friend, whichever you prefer. In any case I will always be devoted to you.
>
> Marie[17]

Eventually Alexandre felt he could go on no longer. He sent her a note, appearing to end the affair, dated 'midnight' on 30 August 1845. This is a letter redolent of the pain of a young man in love, but also of the hurt pride of the unhappy *amant de cœur* (and containing a certain amount of self-dramatisation):

> My dear Marie. I am neither rich enough to love you as I would like nor poor enough to be loved as you would like. So let us both forget – you a name which must mean hardly anything to you – me a happiness which has become impossible to bear. There is no point in telling you how sad I am – for you already know how much I love you. So farewell – you have too great a heart not to understand the reason for my letter and too good a nature not to forgive me for it. A thousand memories. AD[18]

Meanwhile, during her affair with Alexandre, in the late autumn of 1844 or early in 1845, Marie encountered an elderly gentleman in the spa town of Bagnères. This octogenarian was Count Gustav Ernst von Stackelberg, a former Russian ambassador to Vienna. He claimed to be a widower, and to have been struck by Marie's likeness to his deceased daughter. He offered to become Marie's protector, hoping to save her from the life she was leading. In fact, Count von Stackelberg was not a widower; his wife the Countess was alive and well, living in the rue de la Chaussée-d' Antin, just the other side of the boulevard des Capucines from where Marie lived, and where she held receptions every Friday for diplomats and other foreigners. She died in 1868, having survived her husband by eighteen years. He did indeed have a daughter who had died – Elena, who died in Karlsruhe in 1843 – though she was not his only daughter as he seems to have implied. He was in fact the father of eleven children. Earlier in his life Stackelberg had been known as an 'executioner of virgins', and he was said to keep with him a list of all his conquests. It seems unlikely that his intentions towards Marie were quite as pure as he made out.

Count von Stackelberg set Marie up in style at 11 boulevard de la Madeleine (the present number 15). Her apartment was on the mezzanine floor and comprised a drawing room, a smaller room leading off to the left, and a boudoir, these three rooms sharing five windows which looked out on to the boulevard. The dining room and a large bedroom overlooked the inner courtyard. Stackelberg also provided her with furs, diamonds, horses and carriages. As household staff, Marie enjoyed the services of a coachman, a cook and a chambermaid. There were also providers of various services from outside such as mending and laundry, a hairdresser from Dezoutter in the rue Saint-Honoré who attended her every day, a chiropodist who also cared for the feet of Louis Philippe's court and of famous dancers, a saddler and coachbuilder who looked after the upkeep of the carriages, and a vet. At one time she also had a groom and a footman. She usually had food brought in for lunch, and sometimes for dinner or supper, from the nearby café Voisin. Alternatively she would eat out, often with guests, at the Maison Dorée. She had changed from the days when she voraciously ate a portion of fried potatoes on the street, generally choosing for herself sweet things like biscuits, macaroons and iced meringues; when she was accompanied the order might be for chicken and salad, invariably with wine. She also kept herself well supplied with chocolates and sweets. She used only one toilet water, called 'L'Eau du harem', supplied by Geslin. She also used copious quantities of cold cream.

According to the account given by Romain Vienne, Marie

claimed to spend an average of five hundred francs a day, making a total of about a hundred and eighty thousand francs a year.[19] Such a figure was surely an exaggeration; even to approach it, Marie must have been spending constantly. (As a comparison, schoolteachers were paid three hundred francs a year, priests a thousand, copying clerks one thousand three hundred, and government ministers ten or twenty thousand.) The rent for the apartment in the boulevard de la Madeleine amounted to approximately three thousand two hundred francs a year, payable in quarterly instalments. Another major expense was the upkeep of a carriage and horses; there were also the servants' wages to be paid. Otherwise money was dispensed in a constant trickle on clothes, food, drink and all kinds of luxuries – though Marie was also the recipient of many gifts for which she did not have to pay. The prices for individual items of food which she ordered do not in themselves sound exorbitant – asparagus for three francs, a bottle of champagne for six, a duck for a hundred centimes, an omelette for twenty-five, two dozen oysters or a cutlet for one franc fifty – but to order in fresh every day meant that the bills mounted up and up. Likewise the cost of individual items of dress does not seem high in itself, the material costing more than the labour – Marie paid over one hundred and seventy-four francs for forty-one metres of muslin in November 1842, while having a silk dress made for only twelve francs, and buying a ready-made one at Hirtz *fils* in the rue Française for eighty francs – but her purchase of new things was so constant that the expenditure became vast. And then all these items would require upkeep – cleaning, repairs or dyeing; the cleaning of a long shawl, for instance, cost fifteen francs while three dresses were taken away and cleaned for thirty-six. Pockets and collars were ordered in from tailors, and sewn on by women hired for the purpose; Marie also bought large numbers of hats (which could cost up to eighteen hundred francs each) and pairs of shoes or boots, and ordered chemises and gloves by the dozen. Though many men bought jewels for her, she also bought some for herself, or paid to have them repaired or mounted. Likewise she bought certain items of furniture herself – though the most valuable pieces tended to be bought for her – and she paid the repair bills. Then there were the housekeeping staples, such as candles, matches, cognac and cakes, in addition to heating costs; in December 1842, for instance, Marie paid forty francs for a delivery of firewood and seventy-five centimes an hour to the man who chopped it for her in the cellar.

In addition to the items acquired in the traditional manner, the suppliers arriving at the apartment with their wares or the purchaser dealing directly with the tailor or other craftsman, there was the temptation provided by the new style of shop which had begun to emerge in the 1840s, the *magasins de nouveautés* or fancy goods stores. These were precursors of the modern department store, and towards the end of the decade such shops began to appear everywhere in Paris. They dealt in such things as silks, woollens and other fabrics, shawls, lingerie, hosiery and gloves, and they gradually brought about an end to practices which had done nothing to increase sales, such as the obligation for anyone entering a shop to buy something and the custom of lengthy bargaining over a sale as there were no fixed or marked prices. The most famous of these new stores included the Petit Saint-Thomas in the rue du Bac, the Grand Condé in the rue de Seine and, most conveniently for Marie, the Trois Quartiers on the corner of the boulevard de la Madeleine and the rue Duphot, just a few doors up from her apartment. Here she bought all kinds of items of interior decoration, such as bedspreads, pillow cases and curtains, and paid an extra charge to have them delivered.

Marie was dependent on Count von Stackelberg's willingness to continue to provide her with enough money to cover her rent and all her other expenses, a willingness which lessened as the months went by and it became clear that she had by no means abandoned all her other men in favour of him. As her expenses were consistently and inevitably higher than any budget a protector might try to impose, it seemed absolutely necessary from Marie's point of view to maintain a number of wealthy clients; a single one would never be enough, or not for long. Neither could her need for entertainment be provided solely by the regular visits of an octogenarian, no matter how generous he might be.

Marie loved the theatre and was nearly always to be seen in her box at a first night, the tickets automatically being sent to her by the theatre management, who knew her habits. She would also attend every notable exhibition or concert, and it was at a concert that she first saw the composer and pianist Franz Liszt, who was performing at the Théâtre des Italiens on 16 April 1845. He had split up with his mistress and the mother of his children, Marie d'Agoult, the previous year, and had just returned from a phenomenonally successful concert tour of the major cities of France. Liszt was introduced to Marie later that year by Dr David Ferdinand Koreff, a society doctor who prescribed dubious cures for his wealthy female clientèle who included, besides Marie herself, both Liszt's mother Anna and his ex-mistress. Liszt was subsequently a guest at a number of soirées held by Marie in the boulevard de la Madeleine, where he entertained the other guests on the piano. Marie became very attached to him.

Liszt stayed in Paris for several months, but then had to return to Weimar where he had been *Kapellmeister* since November 1842. Marie wanted to go with him. He dissuaded her, but did suggest she might meet him in Pest (modern Budapest) in the spring after he had given some concerts in Vienna and Prague and said he would then take her to the coasts of the Bosphorus. In a letter to Marie d'Agoult dated 1st May 1847 Liszt gave his own, brief account of what Marie Duplessis had said to him and how he had responded:

> she told me . . . fifteen months ago: 'I shall not live; I am an odd girl and I shan't be able to hold on to this life which I don't know how not to lead and that I can equally no longer endure. Take me, take me anywhere you like; I shan't bother you. I sleep all day; in the evening you can let me go to the theatre; and at night you can do with me what you will!'
>
> I have never told you how strangely attracted to this delightful creature I became during my last visit to Paris. I had told her that I would take her to Constantinople, for that was the only reasonably possible journey I could get her to undertake . . .[20]

The plan never materialised.

And then, on 21 February 1846, Marie Duplessis married Count Edouard de Perrégaux at the Kensington Register Office in London. She had obtained a passport from the Prefecture of Police on 25 January which had described her as 'Mlle Alphonsine Plessis, person of private means, living in Paris at 11, boulevard de la Madeleine' and provided the following additional details: '22 years old, height one metre 65 centimetres, light brown hair, low forehead, light brown eyebrows, brown eyes, well-made nose, medium-sized mouth, round chin, oval face, ordinary complexion'. On 3 February she obtained a visa from the Ministry for Foreign Affairs, and she and Edouard set off for London. The entry in the marriage register upgrades Marie's father Marin Plessis to the status of 'gentleman' and awards him the Christian name of 'Jean'. The address for both Edouard and Marie is given as 37 Brompton Row, Kensington.

Husband and wife never lived together after this mysterious marriage. It was perfectly regular according to English law, and Edouard could have made it valid for France by having it properly announced according to article 170 of the Civil Code. Instead he abandoned his wife immediately after the wedding and let her return alone to Paris. Marie kept the surname Duplessis but began to use the title of Countess for certain business matters. (Some of the invoices found after her death were made out to Madame la Comtesse du Plessis, de Plaissy or other orthographic variations.) With the help of a specialist she designed her own coat of arms, using part of the arms of her husband, and had them emblazoned on her carriage, her linen and her silverware.

Marie was already gravely ill by the time of her marriage. She had been consumptive for years, a condition which cannot have been helped by her life of excess and by her peculiar diet, with its emphasis on snacks and sweets. Towards the end of her life she lived ever more feverishly. On 16 June 1846 she was present at a grand official ball in Spa. Her gambling had become extremely reckless, and she had left a mountain of debts behind her in Paris. She also travelled to Baden, Wiesbaden and Ems that summer, accompanied only by her maid, desperately seeking health but growing ever weaker. She returned to

Paris in mid-September. Stackelberg, tired of her deceptions, had lessened the frequency both of his visits and of his financial offerings. Between March 1846 and January 1847 there were nineteen instances of Marie having recourse to a pawnshop. She also took the precaution of having various valuables removed from her apartment to prevent her creditors seizing them, her friend Julie being entrusted with the task of renting other apartments in the passage Tivoli, the rue de la Chaussée d'Antin and the rue des Dames in which to store items of furniture, ornaments and jewellery. Meanwhile the seven gentlemen who had shared Marie's favours removed their belongings from the communal dressing table. The only men who did not desert her during her final illness were Pierre de Castellane, Olympe Aguado and Edouard Delessert.

The invoices from her last months detail a litany of doctors' visits. Dr Manec of the Salpetrière paid her thirty-nine visits between 18 September and 19 November. Drs Chomel and Louis, the latter a professor at the Hôtel-Dieu, were called in for special consultations. The services of Dr Koreff, to whom Marie owed fourteen hundred francs, were dispensed with (she claimed that he was poisoning her). It later transpired that he was indeed hastening her end by the daily administration of a centigramme of strychnine. Her habitual consultant was a Dr Davaine, one of the most reputable medical specialists in Paris, to whom she showed her gratitude by giving him, some time before she died, a miniature of herself. He paid her three visits in September, thirty-seven in October, forty-four in November, thirty-five in December, thirty-nine in January and eight in February (by the end he was visiting her two or three times a day). Prescriptions she was given by Drs Davaine and Chomel in November 1846 included refreshing drinks, goats' milk, calming potions, grilled meat, fish, eggs and vegetables. She was advised only to go out in mild weather, to talk little and to sleep on a horsehair mattress. None of this did any good. Meanwhile, one by one her old friends fell away and her debts accumulated. She was cared for by her maid, Clotilde, who also tried to protect her from her creditors – despite being one of them herself. In the final weeks deliveries from suppliers were made not to the apartment but to the *concierge*, Pierre Privé, who paid for them out of a sum advanced to him by Clotilde. They included the delivery of a half-bottle of champagne, urgently requested by Marie, costing two francs. Another time she ordered a 'camphor cigar', believed to be of benefit to the respiratory system.

Marie's last appearance in public, in either December 1846 or January 1847, was to attend the theatre. She died at three o'clock on the morning of Wednesday, 3 February 1847, aged just twenty-three. Her funeral took place two days later at the church of the Madeleine, a few hundred yards from her apartment. The mourners included Montjoyeux; Tony, the famous supplier of horses to elegant Paris; Romain Vienne, who signed the register at the Madeleine as a witness; and several prostitutes who had been helped by Marie in the past. The funeral expenses came to one thousand three hundred and fifty-four francs, and it is possible that some of Marie's erstwhile lovers clubbed together to cover them. Her obsequies may also have benefited from the flowers and decorations provided for a grander ceremony, the other funerals taking place that day at the Madeleine being for the Countess d'Augier, the Count d'Escherny and an old man called Monsieur Ducamp de Bussy, who lived in the same building as Marie. The coffin was followed from the Madeleine to the cemetery of Montmartre by Edouard de Perrégaux, who appeared overcome with remorse; behind him came Olympe Aguado, whose twentieth birthday it had been on the day Marie died, and Edouard Delessert. Marie was initially buried in an unmarked temporary grave, and then exhumed and reburied in a permanent plot where a stone bearing the words 'Here lies Alphonsine Plessis' and the dates of her birth and death was erected, under the orders of Edouard de Perrégaux, on 16 February. That day happened to be Mardi Gras and, while the exhumation and reburial were taking place, a carnival procession was winding its way down the butte Montmartre, the revellers in masks and fancy dress undeterred by the falling rain.

1 Romain Vienne, *La Vérité sur la dame aux camélias*, Paul Ollendorff, Paris, 1888, p.13

2 Ibid., p.14

3 See Emile Zola, *Drunkard*, tr. Arthur Symons, Elek Books, London, 1958, pp.128–46

4 Ibid., p.332

5 Nestor Roqueplan, *Parisine*, J. Hetzel, Paris, 1869, pp.64–5

6 Romain Vienne, *La Vérité sur la dame aux camélias*, p.44

7 Nestor Roqueplan, *Parisine*, pp.65–6

8 A.J.B. Parent-Duchâtelet, *De la Prostitution dans la ville de Paris*, p.127

9 See Joanna Richardson, *The Courtesans: The demi-monde in 19th-century France*, Phoenix Press, London, 2000, p.99

10 See ibid.

11 Romain Vienne, *La Vérité sur la dame aux camélias*, pp.105–6

12 Gustave Claudin, *Mes Souvenirs. Les boulevards de 1840–1870*, Calmann Lévy, Paris, 1884, p.40

13 Quoted in catalogue of the sale of a book collector, Jacques Launay, at Drouot's on 6 December 1984

14 Emile Zola, *Nana*, p.175

15 Romain Vienne, *La Vérité sur la dame aux camélias*, p.221

16 Ibid., p.131

17 Quoted in Micheline Boudet, *La Fleur du mal: La véritable histoire de la dame aux camélias*, Albin Michel, Paris, 1993, p.187

18 Quoted in catalogue of the sale of a book collector, Jacques Launay, at Drouot's on 6 December 1984

19 Romain Vienne, *La Vérité sur la dame aux camélias*, p.189

20 Franz Liszt, *Selected Letters*, tr. and ed. Adrian Williams, Clarendon Press, Oxford, 1998, pp.249–50

CHAPTER THREE

La Dame aux camélias

ON 9 FEBRUARY 1847 a notary, Monsieur Ducloux, accompanied by a Monsieur Nicolas Ridel, had made an inventory of the possessions and personal effects of the late Marie Duplessis, and on Thursday, 18 February an announcement of the sale of her goods appeared in *Le Moniteur des Ventes*. Viewing commenced at noon on the following Tuesday and the auction took place, in her apartment on the boulevard de la Madeleine, from Wednesday, 24 to Saturday, 27 February. Much of fashionable Paris attended the sale, fascinated to see the interior of an apartment few would have deigned to enter during the courtesan's life. Among items up for sale were furniture, including pieces in rosewood and marquetry, wardrobes, beds, tables, dressing tables, armchairs, other chairs, mirrors and a piano by Ignace Pleyel, curios, including clocks and candelabras, clothes, silverware, diamonds, other jewels, curtains, carpets, books, pictures, horses and a carriage and its accoutrements. Despite the pecuniary difficulties she had been in before her death, which had led to her selling or pawning many of her more expensive clothes, Marie left a wardrobe of about a hundred and fifty articles, including dozens of pieces of lingerie, twenty-seven peignoirs, more than thirty gowns, masses of lace, boas and shawls. She also left a stash of invoices stuffed in a drawer, detailing the myriad purchases she had made over several years from dressmakers, milliners, restaurants, pastrycooks, florists, booksellers and other suppliers.

The sale realised just over eighty-nine thousand francs, of which nearly fifty thousand went to her creditors, who had been waiting for her to die in order to claim at least some of what was owing to them. One of her dissatisfied creditors was Dr Koreff, who had sued her executors for unpaid medical bills.[1] He even requested Franz Liszt's support in the case against them, but Liszt replied (in a letter of 12 February 1847, Dr Koreff having wasted no time after Marie's death in pressing his claim) that he was unable to help, and that he had not even known Marie at the time of the medical treatment in question (May to June 1845). The remainder of the proceeds of the sale went to her sister Delphine, who now lived in Saint-Evroult-de-Montfort and was married to a man named Paquet. Delphine had been present at neither the death nor the burial of her sister.

The brief, turbulent, extravagant and finally tragic life of Marie Duplessis seems to match almost too perfectly the stereotype of the prostitute drawn up by Dr Parent-Duchâtelet and repeated by Dr Ryan and others. She is a textbook case, the ideal illustration of what could happen to a vulnerable young girl on the streets of Paris. She even managed to die of the right disease to please the moralists and social reformers, for Dr Ryan wrote of consumption or 'phthisis' that 'this direful, and I believe incurable disease . . . is often accelerated by venereal excesses'.[2] This belief came about because of the change in breathing patterns observed during the sexual act; it was thought that this must be harmful to the respiratory organs, so that a surfeit of 'erotic spasms'[3] was likely to be among the causes of consumption.

'Insufficiency of wages', Drs Parent-Duchâtelet and Ryan had declared, was the chief cause of prostitution, and Marie fits neatly into this diagnosis. Her work as an apprentice had provided her with a roof over her head and enough food to prevent her from starving, but she was constantly hungry and pleased to accept a portion of fried potatoes from the first man to offer them to her. Then the doctors remind us that a first case of 'seduction' is nearly always a contributory factor, and again Marie is the perfect exhibit. Left to fend for herself from an early age, she was probably abused by farmhands, was given to an elderly man to service his sexual needs and may have been abused by her own father as well. She had no moral upbringing of any kind. Seeing in Monsieur Nollet an opportunity to acquire expensive dresses for herself, instead of having to repair those belonging to other women, there was no need for an inner struggle. Vanity won the day because there was no opposition, no reason to refuse Nollet's proposition.

All that cannot be argued with. Marie's case merely proves that Parent-Duchâtelet and Ryan got at least part of their diagnosis right. What is more suspect, what leads one to question whether descriptions of Marie's behaviour and character are a reflection of preconceived ideas about the nature of the prostitute or courtesan rather than the depiction of a real person, is the way she appears to fit the prescribed mould temperamentally, the way even her smallest character trait seems to match the stereotype. The prostitute was supposed to be immature and rather child-like; Marie's head, according to Vienne, resembled that of a child. In particular, descriptions of Marie accord with the characteristic traits ascribed to the prostitute of instability and agitation, the sudden shifts of mood and inability to concentrate. Gustave Claudin wrote of her in his memoirs: 'her times of nervous gaiety were always quashed by sudden fits of sadness. She was whimsical, capricious and foolish, adoring today what she had hated yesterday, and vice versa.'[4] Marie's constant enemy was *l'ennui*. She seemed always to be searching for new experiences and for an elusive happiness, a characteristic interpreted, according to Parent-Duchâtelet's diagnosis, as 'a sign of an interior discomfort and proof that [prostitutes] are searching everywhere for a happiness which eludes them'.[5] Romain Vienne wrote: 'When she was bored with a protector, or tormented by the fever of her temperament, she would obey the sudden impulses of her heart and nerves, and seek consolation in a passing love which, more often than not, lasted as long as roses last, but which allowed her to expend her energy and sensibility.'[6] In Marie's case the stereotypical instability and 'agitation' seemed to be intensified by premonitions of an early death, as reported again by Claudin and Vienne, both writing some time after that death and claiming that they are writing of their memories. Claudin declares: 'Marie Duplessis was slim and pale and had magnificent hair which reached right down to the floor. Her delicate

beauty and fine skin, with its tracery of small blue veins, indicated that
she was consumptive and would die young. She had a presentiment
about this.'[7] Vienne elaborates on Marie's need for instant gratifica-
tion:

> Refusing to be shackled, she tolerated no obstacles to her
> desires, and obeyed only her whims of the moment, like a
> spoilt child. If she had a sudden urge to leave for some seaside
> resort, she would immediately put the plan into execution; so
> much the better if her protector or, failing him, a lover agreed to
> accompany her; if not, she would set off with her chambermaid.
> The good which the thermal waters should do her was one
> reason which she was justified in invoking; but that motive was
> only a pretext for the opportunity to satisfy her ruling passion –
> for gambling. At Hombourg, Baden or Spa, her boldness in
> risking considerable sums, and her calm expression, whether she
> was winning or losing, would disconcert the most intrepid
> gamblers and the most daring risk-takers.[8]

Gambling was, of course, considered to be another typical vice of the
prostitute.

Equally striking are the number of positive stereotypical traits of
the prostitute attributed to Marie. She was known to be pious,
frequently visiting the Madeleine to pray, and among the personal
effects found after her death was an order for a prie-dieu covered in
velvet fixed with gilt nails. She also had a reputation for good works
and was believed to give away as much as twenty thousand francs a
year to charity.

If prevailing conventional views about the nature of the prostitute
contributed to the myth of Marie Duplessis and went some way to
veil the reality from sight, then the contribution made by Alexandre
Dumas *fils* to this process was even greater. He had received the news
of Marie's death several days after the event, on 10 February, having
been abroad for some time with his father and unaware that Marie
was suffering the final stages of her illness. He was back in Paris in

time to attend the sale in the apartment where he had previously been received as a lover, and immediately afterwards he wrote the eighty-eight lines of verse which became the last poem in his collection *Péchés de jeunesse* (Sins of Youth). The poem was preceded by a blank page bearing only the initials 'M.D.'. It begins with a recollection of the ending of his affair with Marie – 'We quarrelled; I can't remember why' – and goes on to lament the fact that he can now never make up the quarrel. He alludes to having revisited the apartment where he had previously spent such happy hours with Marie, and he remembers their love-making, in which the feverish heat generated by illness mingles with sexual ardour:

> Do you remember those nights when, a burning lover,
> Your desperate body contorted beneath kisses,
> Consumed by that ardent fever, you found
> The longed-for sleep in your exhausted senses?

He ends his poem by paying tribute to those few mourners who accompanied Marie on her final journey:

> You who loved her and who followed her
> Were not like the dukes, marquesses or lords
> Who prided themselves on maintaining her life
> But saw no pride in accompanying her death.[9]

Alexandre subsequently lost no time in transmuting what he had known of Marie Duplessis into his novel *La Dame aux camélias*, in which Marie is transformed into the 'prostitute with a heart of gold', Marguerite Gautier. Published in 1848, it is the work which made his name. He also adapted it for the stage, as a play which opened at the Vaudeville Theatre on 2 February 1852. The final transmutation of Marie's story is in the form of Verdi's opera *La Traviata*, based on *La Dame aux camélias* and premièred in Venice on 6 March 1853.

La Dame aux camélias tells the story of Armand Duval, a young man who, at the opening of the novel, is racked with remorse over his treatment of a young woman, Marguerite Gautier, who has recently died. Armand, like Alexandre, was away from Paris at the time of the death and learning of it has come as a horrible shock. The narrator, also a young man who had known Marguerite, at least by sight (for what young man about Paris would not have known this beautiful young courtesan?), attends the sale of her effects (Dumas *fils* places this in the apartment in the rue d'Antin, where Marie lived when he first knew her, rather than in the boulevard de la Madeleine) and there he buys a copy of Prévost's novel *Manon Lescaut*, belonging to Marguerite and inscribed by Armand Duval with the words 'Manon to Marguerite, Humility'. Armand discovers on his return to Paris that the young man has bought this book and he comes to ask if he may have it back.

Thus the stage is set for the telling of Armand's story, which he begins by giving the narrator a letter to read. In this letter, which is from the dying Marguerite, she regrets that she will never see Armand again and directs him to go on his return to her friend Julie. There he will receive a journal which Marguerite has been writing and which will explain certain past events to him. There follows a gruesome scene in which the narrator accompanies Armand to the exhumation of Marguerite's body, which is in the first stages of putrefaction.

Armand subsequently falls ill, but during his convalescence he starts to tell the narrator his story, beginning with his first encounter with Marguerite Gautier, which replicates Alexandre's own first encounter with Marie Duplessis, at the Théâtre des Variétés with a friend. Armand is fascinated by the vivacious and restless young woman with her multiplicity of lovers who is already exhibiting symptoms of the disease which will kill her, and he becomes her *amant de cœur*, a role he finds no easier than did Alexandre himself. This relationship, however, soon develops into a more overwhelming love than Alexandre ever seems to have enjoyed with Marie, and Marguerite begins to abandon her other, paying, lovers for him. She even gives up the elderly duke who has been paying most of her bills, and she and Armand retreat to a country house at Bougival, as had Marie and Edouard de Perrégaux. For a time they live there without concerning themselves for the future, but then Armand discovers that Marguerite has been selling off her jewellery and other luxury items in order to maintain their way of life, now that he has become her exclusive lover. She tells Armand that she never wants to return to her former life as a courtesan and that her plan is to sell off all the material goods she has accumulated over the last few years, settle all her debts and use the surplus to buy an apartment in which she and Armand can live. He agrees to her plan and then, unknown to her, visits his lawyer to request that arrangements be made to transfer his income to her.

Meanwhile Armand has been avoiding communicating with his father and his sister, aware that they would be disturbed by the course his life has taken. The lawyer having warned Monsieur Duval senior of the way events seem to be progressing, the father, who cannot believe that Marguerite's motives in the affair are other than venal, arrives to remonstrate with his son. Armand refuses to give up Marguerite. His father's next line of attack is to appeal directly to Marguerite herself, and he arrives in Bougival one day when he has ensured that Armand will be away in Paris. He persuades Marguerite that if she really loves Armand she will give him up, both for the sake of his own future and for that of his sister, who is engaged to be married but whose fiancé will call the wedding off unless his future brother-in-law stops being a cause of scandal for living with a courtesan, even if she wants to be an ex-courtesan.

Marguerite, who longs to be able to perform a redeeming act which will bring her the respect of people like Monsieur Duval and his virtuous daughter, agrees. She realises that Armand loves her too much ever to leave her voluntarily and so, for love of him, she resolves to make him hate her – and she does this by returning to her life as a courtesan and her former lovers. Her ploy works so well that Armand does indeed come to hate her and, whenever he happens to meet her in Paris, he is spiteful and contemptuous towards her. The pain this gives her contributes to the downward path of her health, and she becomes more and more ill.

The couple do have one final night of passion, on the occasion of Marguerite visiting Armand to ask him to stop tormenting her (she never explains to him why she left, knowing that this would make him abandon his father and sister and return to her) and in that night they make love with a fever and a depth they have never before attained. On the next day, overcome by jealousy at the thought of Marguerite with other men, Armand commits his cruellest act towards her by leaving some money at her house to pay her for the night before. He never sees her again. He departs on his travels, and while he is away she dies. The journal which she writes during her last days has explained everything to him, and he is overcome with remorse at having so misunderstood, mistrusted and hurt this girl who had loved him so much that she had sacrificed all her chances of happiness, and even life itself, for what she believed to be his own good.

Because Dumas *fils* had used certain well-known aspects of the life and character of Marie Duplessis in his portrayal of Marguerite Gautier, while changing or inventing other aspects, and because his novel, and then his play, became so popular so quickly, it very soon became impossible to disentangle the myth from the reality, to know whether various descriptions of her are based on genuine memories of Marie or whether they have become entirely overlaid with the image of Marguerite. The hair is one case in point; did Marie really have thick, almost black hair as so many memoirists claim to remember and with which Dumas *fils* endows Marguerite Gautier, or was the description on her passport of 'light-brown hair' closer to the mark? The trademark camellias are another point at issue: Dumas *fils* claimed to have invented this touch himself – that Marguerite Gautier wore or carried white camellias every day, except for four or five days in the month, when they were exchanged for red ones – and that Marie Duplessis had never been known in her lifetime as '*la dame aux camélias*'.[10] Romain Vienne, however, claims that she was indeed given this sobriquet, by a female employee of the Opéra.[11] Marie certainly bought camellias on several occasions, this being confirmed by invoices from a florist called Ragonat in the rue de la Paix. In any event, these flowers became such a powerful symbol, prostitutes capable of falling in love being henceforth known as *camélias*, that they were taken up by commentators and 'remembered' as a salient feature of Marie's life. Nestor Roqueplan, writing towards the end of the 1860s, introduces camellias into this romanticised description of the dead Marie:

> The beauty of this young girl now she was dead was another marvel. She had been so well adorned by the touching taste of her friend, with a coquette's tenderness! Her head was encircled by Alençon lace; her joined hands held a bouquet of camellias, her favourite flower, from the centre of which rose a crucifix, indulgently uniting with this frivolous emblem of a life of dissipation.[12]

If it has been assumed that the fictional Marguerite Gautier was to all intents and purposes a portrait of the real-life Marie Duplessis, much speculation has surrounded the identity of the 'real' Armand Duval, whom she loved so much. In a letter he wrote to the actress Sarah Bernhardt on 28 January 1884, Dumas *fils* claimed this identity for himself; this letter accompanied his gift to the actress, for her portrayal on stage of Marguerite Gautier, of a special copy of *La Dame aux camélias* into which he had pasted his letter to Marie of 30 August 1845, breaking off the relationship. Alexandre certainly used some aspects of his own affair with Marie, including this same letter, in writing his novel and he also gives his hero Armand Duval his own initials, so that he is able to use the affectionate nickname 'Adet'. Yet he also made use of what he knew about Marie's relationships with other men such as Agénor de Guiche and particularly Edouard de Perrégaux; he would have learnt some of the details directly from Marie herself (the most intense phase of her affair with Edouard was over before Alexandre entered her life, and an *amant de cœur* made the perfect confidant), and possibly from Edouard, who could well have needed someone to talk to after Marie's death. Thus Armand Duval became to some extent a composite of Alexandre Dumas *fils* and Edouard de Perrégaux.

But this is a novel, not a biography, and all the characters have necessarily undergone the transformations of fiction. Where *La Dame aux camélias* departs from reality entirely is in the motives ascribed to the heroine. Whereas Marguerite is persuaded to give up Armand by his father, for his own good and to ensure the happy and respectable future of his sister, Marie's relationships with both Edouard and Alexandre broke down over issues of money – neither young man could afford to maintain the exclusive relationship with her that they both desired, because she was too expensive. Marguerite goes on loving Armand to the end, despite all his mistreatment of her, and the clear implication is that it is the circumstances of life, rather than any defects in her own character, that have forced her to lead a life of immorality and excess. This is Marie as Alexandre might have wished her to be, not as she really was. Nevertheless there are glimpses of a real person, of the restless, dissolute and difficult girl who may have been Marie, particularly in the early parts of the narrative. Hervé Maneglier has suggested[13] that Alexandre wrote the book as a form of expiation, in remorse at the way he had abandoned Marie, who had died too soon to be able to forgive him or to tell him of her forgiveness – and maybe there is an element of this in his idealised portrait. On the other hand, he also recognised a good plot when he saw one, and knew how to use the young woman's short life and romantically early death to good effect. For this novel, despite all its idealisation and over-romanticism (the exhumation scene is particularly grisly, for instance, and ignores the fact that this was a perfectly standard procedure) is still tremendously affecting and this fact, combined with Marie's conformity to the more appealing aspects of the stereotypical prostitute – her reputed religiosity, her charitable donations and her love of small animals – contributed to the mythologising of her into the type of the saintly courtesan, the acceptable face of the fallen woman.

Among the characteristics ascribed to Marguerite Gautier by her creator, and deemed to have been those of Marie Duplessis by those who wrote about her, was a relative simplicity of dress (despite the number of items in her wardrobe), her preference for light, pastel shades and the grace with which she knew how to drape a cashmere shawl around her slim body. In the poet and dramatist Théodore de Banville's account, this simplicity of dress becomes symptomatic of Marie's innate 'chastity' and distinction: '. . . this young girl whose gracious and pure face beneath her simply arranged hair, whose long swan-like neck and large, gentle and dreamy eyes gave us, despite everything, a sense of chastity, and whose slim, lithe body seemed so comfortable in her close-fitting and unadorned dress, with a plain cape whose shape was suitable only for a nun or a duchess!'[14] Dumas *fils* himself stated explicitly in the preface to his play of *La Dame aux camélias* that he had based Marguerite Gautier on Marie Duplessis, and he also refers to her 'distinction': 'She was one of the last and only courtesans with a heart . . . She possessed a natural distinction, she dressed with taste and moved gracefully, almost with nobility.'[15] Romain Vienne offers more of the same: 'The way she walked was so imposing, with a style of such decorum and reserve, that everyone would watch her go by with a surprise mingled with admiration and respect.'[16] The myth grew up that Marie was particularly discreet about her profession, that she never flaunted herself, that during her drives down the Champs Elysées or to the Bois she would sit, alone and as near invisible as possible, in the recesses of her carriage (certainly this is how Dumas *fils* described Marguerite Gautier).

This supposed aspect of Marie's character was reinforced by the account given by Madame Judith of the Comédie Française, who records in her memoirs[17] that Marie came to visit her during the actress's illness, having first sent bouquets anonymously, out of modesty. Madame Judith writes that she was greatly impressed by Marie's charm, by her melancholy black eyes and beautiful silken hair, but above all by this modesty, so unexpected in a renowned courtesan. After her recovery, Judith visited Marie in her apartment in the boulevard de la Madeleine, which she describes as 'embalmed' with flowers and rather like being in a museum, with Marie demonstrating the knowledge and passion of a connoisseur about each piece of furniture and ornament. She asserts that Marie told her she was not really happy, that she had entered on this life because of her irresistible need for luxury and that she had desired to experience the 'refined pleasures of artistic taste'. Marie went on to declare, according to Judith, that she had been in love, but that her love had never been reciprocated, and that courtesans were wrong to have a heart. She then began to cough, accusing sadness of killing her, whereas happiness would have made her well. Madame Judith further recounts that one day she encountered Marie in the Bois and invited her to get out of her carriage and walk with her, which she duly did. This was a great mark of friendliness – not to say condescension – on Madame Judith's part, and it was duly noticed and remarked upon, with disdain or approbation, depending on the attitude of the onlooker. Marie later repaid Madame Judith for her gracious gesture by warning her off about a man scheming to marry her for her money. The memoirist goes on to get the year of Marie's death wrong, which hardly inspires confidence in the accuracy of her highly romanticised account.

The way such sentimentalising can lead to the widening of the rift between reality and myth is demonstrated in the description of Marie's last days given by John Forster, the close friend and bio-grapher of Charles Dickens, writing in the mid-1870s. Much of this account, presumably gleaned from the 'talk' in Paris to which he alludes, is pure invention:

> Not many days after I left, all Paris was crowding to the sale of a lady of the demi-monde, Marie Duplessis, who had led the most brilliant and abandoned of lives, and left behind her the most exquisite furniture and the most voluptuous and sumptuous bijouterie. Dickens wished at one time to have pointed the moral of this life and death of which there was great talk in Paris while we were together. The disease of satiety, which only less often than hunger passes for a broken heart, had killed her. 'What do you want?' asked the most famous of the Paris physicians, at a loss for her exact complaint. At last she answered: 'To see my mother.' She was sent for; and there came a simple Breton peasant-woman clad in the quaint garb of her province, who prayed by her bed until she died. Wonderful was the

admiration and sympathy; and it culminated when Eugène Sue bought her prayer-book at the sale.[18]

Yet despite all this exaggeration, sentimentality and confusion of Marie Duplessis with Marguerite Gautier, there remains a kernel of truth, a part of the real Marie, which genuinely impressed onlookers – an innate quality unusual, to say the least, in a woman with her way of life and her background. For only a few days after her death, well before Dumas *fils* had been able to present his version of her, an obituarist wrote of her in *L'Epoque* in terms which draw attention to that 'distinction' so frequently commented upon by others:

> A woman has just died who was once one of the most irascible and most charming of those foolish virgins who fill a whole capital with the noise of their commotion and their loves . . . At the very least you know this woman by name, even if you have never met her: she was called Marie Duplessis. She had received from God the kind of elegance and distinction which would make a great lady envious. Gracefulness came as naturally to her as scent does to a flower. Like Diana Vernon in *Rob Roy*, slender and beautiful, Marie was burning to live yet seemed to run towards death.[19]

The adulation aroused by Dumas *fils*' novel and play was by no means universal. The anonymous 'Chroniqueuse' who provided monthly accounts of Paris life for readers in England wrote in November 1860, when *La Dame aux camélias* was produced at the Gymnase Theatre, of 'that detestably vulgar piece'.[20] Neither did the cantankerous diarist Count Horace de Viel Castel, who saw the play when it first opened, have anything good to say about it or its author:

> This play is a disgrace to the era which supports it, to the government which tolerates it and to the public which applauds it . . .
>
> Alex. Dumas the younger is a young good-for-nothing, for

whom, it must be said in his defence, everything has been lacking: family example, moral instruction, honest companions. All he has ever seen at his father's house are prostitutes. He and his father frequently share the same mistresses and wallow in the same orgies . . .[21]

It was no doubt with such critics in mind that A.D. Vandam defended Dumas *fils* and his subject. He also underlines the fact that options were limited for a young woman of Marie's class who desired to earn more than subsistence wages:

> The world at large, and especially the English, have always made very serious mistakes, both with regard to the heroine of the younger Dumas' novel and play, and the author himself. They have taxed him with having chosen an unworthy subject, and by idealizing it, taught a lesson of vice instead of virtue; they have taken it for granted that Alphonsine Plessis was no better than her kind. She was much better than that, though probably not sufficiently good to take a housemaid's place and be obedient to her pastors and masters, to slave from morn till night for a mere pittance, in addition to her virtue, which was ultimately to prove its own reward — the latter to consist of a home of her own, with a lot of squalling brats about her, where she would have had to slave as she had slaved before, without the monthly pittance hitherto doled out to her.
>
> She was not sufficiently good to see her marvellously beautiful face, her matchless graceful figure set off by a cambric cap and a calico gown, instead of having the first enhanced by the gleam of priceless jewels in her hair and the second wrapped in soft laces and velvets and satins; but, for all that, she was not the common courtesan the goody-goody people have thought fit to proclaim her.[22]

Marie's early death, of what mistakenly came to be viewed as a fashionable, romantic disease (the very word 'consumption' conjuring

up the image of someone languorously wasting away, while occasionally coughing a little blood), was another factor which contributed
to her idealised portrayal. Combined with the misconception which
equated her with Marguerite Gautier, it enabled her to be seen as a
tragic heroine. As early as 1867, according to Dumas *fils*, Marie's grave
was becoming a place of pilgrimage, particularly for women. Later in
the century, the Countess Néra de la Jonchère put fresh camellias on
her tomb every day for many years. In 1950 Edith Saunders, a
biographer of Dumas *fils*, found out that her rather daunting *concierge*
was in the habit of taking flowers to Marie's tomb every Sunday. Even
today, the tomb is seldom without some floral tribute.

The story of Marie's life and death also provided ideal subject
matter for moralists, who could draw the inference that she brought
her early, painful death, abandoned by former lovers and plagued by
creditors, on herself as a direct result of the sinful excesses of her life.
John Forster indicated that Dickens had toyed with the idea of using
Marie's story in this way, and he was not alone. The legend of Marie
Duplessis fitted as neatly into stereotypes about the most appropriate
death for a courtesan as into those pertaining to a prostitute's life:
'Though she may have been no more than a *fille de joie*, according to
the moralists, or a *fille de tristesse*, as Michelet says when speaking of
her sort, death made of her a martyr. She endured a long and painful
agony during which she repented and begged forgiveness from
heaven for having loved pleasure.'[23]

It is striking that, in this case of a young woman whose biography is
so overlaid with stereotypes, fiction and moralising, and of whom it is
very difficult to catch more than glimpses of the actual person, several
of the books which have been dedicated to her life claim to be the
'true' or 'real' story. First off the mark was Romain Vienne with his
La Vérité sur la dame aux camélias (The Truth about the Lady of the
Camellias), published in 1888. Vienne claims to have been a childhood friend of Marie's, and much of what he relates is supposed to
have come direct from her own account in conversations with him.
He was, however, writing many years after her death, and his
narrative (in which he further confuses the issue by disguising the

names of the men involved with Marie) is undeniably coloured by
the idealisation which had gone on since then. He is dazzled by the
image which he himself has helped to create:

> If I have decided to write the story of Marie Duplessis, whom I
> have known since her earliest infancy, and who was worthy of a
> better fate, it is because she was not at all like the common run of
> courtesans, and because she was the heroine neither of extra-
> romantic affairs, nor of sensational scandals, nor of crazy duels;
> because she shone with a dazzling lustre, in a world apart where,
> by a combination of superior qualities, by her beauty, her mind,
> her distinction and her beneficence, she had managed to make
> an exceptional place for herself.[24]

Charles A. Dolph in 1927 also claims to be writing about the 'real' lady
of the camellias[25] and Micheline Boudet, writing in 1993, maintains
the tradition with her title *La Fleur du mal: La véritable histoire de la dame
aux camélias* (Flower of Evil: The True Story of the Lady of the
Camellias). Boudet's work is more scholarly and factual than anything
that has gone before, but she makes her own contribution to the myth
of Marie by building up the short-lived liaison (if that is even what it
was) with Franz Liszt into an affair of far more significance than the
only real evidence – Liszt's affectionate, but brief, mention of her in his
letter to Marie d'Agoult – would appear to justify. Boudet's reason for
doing this is the attempt to find some plausible explanation for Marie's
sudden, apparently unpremeditated, marriage to Count Edouard de
Perrégaux; Boudet suggests Marie married Edouard in order to
achieve respectability so that she could join Liszt in Weimar as a
legitimate countess rather than as a courtesan with a scandalous
reputation, no fit companion to the worthy *Kapellmeister*.[26] This seems
to me quite as far-fetched as any other aspect of Marie's legend.

   After divesting her of legend and stereotyping, is there anything
left of the 'real' Marie Duplessis, or is she too closely bound up with
her own legend for such divesting even to be possible? A particularly
interesting aspect of Marie which can be discerned, and which makes

the disentangling of reality and legend doubly difficult, is the use she herself made of the myth of the ideal courtesan, the way she contributed to the building up of her own legend. This is noticeable in the account Madame Judith gives of their meeting, for instance; if the actress's memory serves her correctly, then Marie fed the kind of information to her that chimed with her own sentimental preconceptions of the life of a courtesan – luxurious but melancholy, loving and never loved, forever seeking an elusive happiness while dying romantically of misery. Such an account suggests that Marie was adept at playing to her audience, living up (or down) to their expectations and reaping the rewards of their sympathy and, in the case of wealthy men, their money. An ability to dramatise and sentimentalise her own life is also apparent throughout the narrative provided by Romain Vienne, if it is indeed based on what Marie told him. And if Count von Stackelberg fabricated aspects of his own life story the better to persuade Marie to accept him as a protector, it is more than likely that she was playing the same game herself, exaggerating her desire to be a reformed character, if only he would provide the money for her to do so. Vienne relates the story of Marie being approached by a 'Baron de Ponval', who pressed his suit by presenting her with a box of twelve oranges, each wrapped in a thousand-franc note. If such a character existed, this was not his real name, but Vienne takes this opportunity to have Marie deliver a speech, a kind of apologia for her way of life and her attitude towards the men who made it their business to fund it – and this is a speech which does have the ring of psychological truth:

Baron, I follow an unpleasant profession; but I must not leave you ignorant of the fact that my favours are very expensive. I spend, on average, five hundred francs a day, and sometimes I indulge in extravagant expenditure which doubles this figure. Therefore my protector needs to be very rich to cover my household expenses and to satisfy my many, varied and strange caprices. At present I am approximately thirty thousand francs in debt, which is very reasonable for me. I find nothing alarming about this figure, and don't mind admitting that it is sometimes higher. There it is, it's an obsession I have, along with plenty more; it is not my fault, after all; it is not I who dance too fast, it is the violins who can't keep up. When my current debts have been paid, I will lose no time in contracting new ones to justify the old and so as not to get out of the habit; it is stronger than I . . .

In addition, I must point out to you that, in my lover's company, I wear only those outfits which his generosity has provided. As for the old ones, I either make them into relics or give them as presents to those less fortunate than myself . . .

I think these confidences are sufficient to explain to you why I always have new outfits; they do honour to those who love me. I am always frank: I intend to remain, at all times, absolutely free in my movements and mistress of my fancies; I give the orders, I do not receive them; I have no desire at all to be compelled to receive a lover whenever he expresses the wish to see me. I have also the misfortune to believe neither in promises nor in fidelity; it is enough to tell you that I acknowledge sincerity only when it has been proved to me.[27]

Thus one aspect of Marie's character which comes over very clearly from her way of handling to her own advantage the expectations of the people she encountered, despite all the myth-making and embellishment – and even because of them – is her manipulativeness. Marie had a gift for telling her hearers what they wanted to hear, as well as what could prove useful for herself; neither should one forget her prescription for white teeth. She also had an innate cleverness, further attested by the speed with which she assimilated the education in culture and decorum provided for her by Agénor de Guiche among others. Moreover, the very fact that this young man wanted to offer her some education, desired to raise her to his own level, suggests that he found in her far more than a girl he paid for sex, that he saw qualities in her which made him desire her companionship. Likewise what we know of her relationships with Alexandre Dumas *fils*, Franz Liszt and Agénor himself, through the few letters which survive, suggests that this girl was not only capable of inspiring love but of loving – even if that love was inconsistent and needed the buttress of financial comfort (she was, after all, still very young) – and that for all her undoubted vanity and extravagance, and despite the exaggerations of her idealised portrait, she was indeed 'not the common courtesan the goody-goody people have thought fit to proclaim her'.[28] Marie also comes across as very sexy, knowing how to ensnare a succession of men of all ages, her seductiveness all the more effective for being understated, her lifelong promiscuity veiled beneath a beguilingly virginal appearance. The young men who featured prominently in her life all longed to make her their own, but she eluded them, flitting like a butterfly from one man to the next, from one experience to a new one. Edouard de Perrégaux went to the lengths of marrying her, but even that could not hold her still. The most obvious explanation for her marriage, it seems to me, was that this was yet another new experience for her, involving the thrill of a clandestine trip to another country and further evidence of her power over this young man, as well as the material benefits of the right to a title (and surely being able to call herself 'countess' was another amusing game for Marie, who cannot have helped but be amazed at the distance she had travelled from her childhood of being dragged from pillar to post by her feckless father). Stable married life can have held little attraction for this restless girl, and whatever she said to Edouard immediately after their marriage was sufficient to drive him away.

In the end it was Alexandre Dumas *fils* who thought he had finally pinned Marie down by capturing her in fiction. But the very nature of fiction and the questions it raises about its relation to reality have ensured that the real Marie remains as elusive and as beguiling as ever, endlessly fascinating and enigmatic, a young woman whose very short, dissolute and extraordinarily full life became a symbol of a paradoxical purity and against whom the lives of other courtesans would be judged.

---

1 See Alan Walker, *Franz Liszt, Vol. 1: The Virtuoso Years, 1811–1847*, Alfred A. Knopf, New York, 1990, p.391

2 M. Ryan, *Prostitution in London*, p.312

3 Ibid.

4 Gustave Claudin, *Mes Souvenirs*, p.40

5 A.J.B. Parent-Duchâtelet, *De la Prostitution dans la ville de Paris*, p.118

6 Romain Vienne, *La Vérité sur la dame aux camélias*, p.144

7 Gustave Claudin, *Mes Souvenirs*, p.40

8 Romain Vienne, *La Vérité sur la dame aux camélias*, pp.223–4

9 The poem is reproduced in Christiane Issartel's *Les Dames aux camélias de l'histoire à la légende*, Chêne Hachette, Paris, 1981, p.62ff

10 Alexandre Dumas *fils, Théâtre complet*, Vol.1, p.8

11 Romain Vienne, *La Vérité sur la dame aux camelias*, p.222

12 Nestor Roqueplan, *Parisine*, p.68

13 Hervé Maneglier, *Les Artistes au bordel*, Flammarion, Paris, 1997, p.100

14 Théodore de Banville, *La Lanterne magique. Camées parisiens. La Comédie Française*, G. Charpentier, Paris, 1883, p.254

15 Alexandre Dumas *fils, Théâtre complet*, Vol.1, p.8.

16 Romain Vienne, *La Vérité sur la dame aux camélias*, pp.216–17

17 Paul Gsell (ed.), *Mémoires de Madame Judith de la Comédie Française et Souvenirs sur ses contemporains*, Jules Tallandier, Paris, 1911, pp.221–9

18 John Forster, *The Life of Charles Dickens*, Cecil Palmer, London, 1972–4

19 Quoted in L. Graux, *Les Factures de la dame aux camélias*, Paul Dupont, Paris, 1934, p.75

20 La Chroniqueuse, *Photographs of Paris Life*, William Tinsley, London, 1861, p.335

21 Comte Horace de Viel Castel, *Mémoires sur le règne de Napoléon III (1851–1864)*, Vol.2, Chez Tous Les Libraires, Paris, 1884, pp.34–6

22 A.D. Vandam, *An Englishman in Paris (Notes and Recollections)*, Chapman & Hall, London, 1893, pp.110–11

23 Gustave Claudin, *Mes Souvenirs*, p.41

24 Romain Vienne, *La Vérité sur la dame aux camélias*, p.58

25 Charles A. Dolph, *The Real 'Lady of the Camellias' and Other Women of Quality*, London, 1927

26 Micheline Boudet, *La Fleur du mal*, pp.203–5

27 Romain Vienne, *La Vérité sur la dame aux camélias*, pp.189–91

28 A.D. Vandam, *An Englishman in Paris*, p.111

CHAPTER FOUR

The Creation of La Païva

I N 1819 A DAUGHTER was born to a Jewish couple living in Russia. The parents' names were Martin and Anna-Marie Lachmann, Martin being of Polish origin and Anna-Marie, whose maiden name was Klein, possibly being of German extraction. Life was not easy for Jews in Imperial Russia in the first part of the nineteenth century. The partitions of Poland in 1792, 1793 and 1795 had brought some four hundred thousand Jews into the Russian Empire and, in spite of their remarkable culture and talents, most of these Jews were poor, partly owing to the discrimination long practised against them and partly because of the economic decline of eighteenth-century Poland.[1] From the outset the Russian government was concerned not only to integrate them, but also to protect other nationalities against them. When the Moscow merchants petitioned in 1791 to be shielded from their competitors, the government responded with a decree forbidding Jews to settle in the capital cities of Moscow and St Petersburg. This decree became the basis for the creation of the Pale of Settlement, which extended from the Baltic to the Black Sea and included Belarus, the Ukraine and Moldova. Various regions of Russia, including those of the Volga, the Urals, Siberia, Moscow and St Petersburg, were not within the Pale and only certain categories of Jews (such as lawyers, doctors and craftsmen who belonged to guilds) were officially allowed to live there. Up to the middle of the nineteenth century, the Jews in the Russian Empire suffered both from popular prejudice and from the government's inability to match its aspirations to integrate them into society with practical measures. The Jewish Statute of 1804, for instance, admitted Jews without restriction to education at all levels; or, if they wished, they could set up their own schools provided the pupils were taught Russian, Polish or German. In reality, however, Russian schools of any kind were so few and far between that very few Jews were able to take advantage of them. Furthermore, conversion to the Orthodox Church became a pre-condition for Jews to enjoy the normal rights of Russian subjects, and the vast majority chose not to convert.

The daughter born to the Lachmanns was given the names Esther Pauline; she later chose to change her first name to Thérèse, signifying from an early age her fascination with France and the French. Nothing is known for sure about her childhood and youth. It has been generally asserted that she was born in the 'Moscow ghetto'[2] without much close enquiry as to whether there was such a place in the early nineteenth century. If the Lachmann family did indeed live in Moscow and live there legally, Martin Lachmann must have been a craftsman belonging to a guild, and thus one of the better off among the Jewish community. Alternatively, the family may have been living illegally in an area of Moscow near the present-day Rossiya Hotel which was the centre of Jewish settlement there, and where there were always Jews living, either legally or illegally. A third possibility is that they did not live in Moscow at all, as the evidence that Thérèse (or Blanche, as she later called herself) was born there comes from the certificate of her third marriage, which contains other misleading information. It may have been that, to the average Frenchman, a Russian in Paris inevitably came from either Moscow or St Petersburg, anywhere else being too remote to be countenanced.

Her father was probably a clothing merchant or a craftsman, the family may have lived in Moscow, and it has been asserted that Thérèse was baptised at the age of seven.[3] No firm evidence has been found to support this assertion but, if there is any truth in the rumour, it would suggest that her parents were unusual among their community in being prepared to renounce their ancestral faith, at least on behalf of their daughter, and that they may have wanted to provide her with some opportunity to lead a broader life than they themselves had been able to, and to try to ensure that some form of education was available to her. The theory that the Lachmanns did not adhere closely to Jewish tradition in the upbringing of their daughter is supported by the fact that she was not already married by April 1835, when new legislation for Jews came into force which, among other things, forbade marriages under the age of eighteen for the groom and sixteen for the bride. By this time Thérèse was already going on sixteen, and in most Jewish families in eastern Europe it was traditional for children to be married between the ages of thirteen and sixteen and for them to reside in the paternal home. The age restrictions in the new code were a reflection of Austrian and Prussian practices designed to restrict population growth among the Jews.

If Martin Lachmann had a broader outlook on life than many of his fellow Jews in Russia – an outlook which he passed on to his daughter – it may have been gained through his activity in the export trade. Jewish merchants travelled annually in large numbers to fairs abroad, particularly to the one held in Leipzig, to buy merchandise and export products such as furs and skins. The legislation of April 1835 also allowed certain classes of merchant to visit the two capitals and the sea ports, as well as the big fairs of Nizhny Novgorod, Kharkov and other Russian cities, for wholesale buying and selling. If the family was not already living in Moscow, it is possible that Thérèse accompanied her father on one of these business trips to the capital, for it was in Moscow that she married on 11 August 1836. She was seventeen; her husband was a twenty-six-year-old tailor called François Hyacinthe Antoine Villoing. Antoine, as he was known, was of French extraction and had been born in Paris. Though it is not known how he came to be in Moscow, there was nothing unusual about his presence there; there were many Frenchmen in Moscow at that time, and French was the language most commonly used in society. If Thérèse had not previously been baptised, she would now have had to convert, as the wedding was celebrated in an Orthodox church.

The main attraction that Antoine Villoing held for Thérèse

Lachmann was his French nationality. He had connections in Paris and at some point would return there – sooner rather than later, if Thérèse had her way. Paris was known throughout Europe not only as a fashionable and sophisticated city, but as a place where Jews as well as Gentiles could have an opportunity to succeed and enjoy the good life. Thérèse believed that Paris could offer her a far brighter future than any prospects she had in Russia, and that marrying Antoine Villoing would be the first step in attaining her goal.

But Antoine was in considerably less of a hurry to leave Moscow than was Thérèse, who in 1837 gave birth to a son, also called Antoine. Her family may have expected that she would now settle into the role of wife and mother, but less than a year later Thérèse left for Paris – without husband or child. It is more than likely that she found another man to take her there; there were plenty of Frenchmen of various sorts living in Russia, working as actors, tutors, or musicians, and Thérèse had great powers of persuasion, not to mention a seductive presence. Antoine had served to inflame her imagination with the desire for another life; perhaps through him she had obtained some glimpse of that inviting city portrayed by Maxime Du Camp in the opening words of his comprehensive study *Paris: ses organes, ses fonctions et sa vie jusqu'en 1870*:

> Throughout my life as a traveller, I have seen many capital cities, some being born, some growing, some flourishing, others dying or dead, but I have seen no other city produce as great an impression as Paris or so clearly convey the sense of a tireless, nervous people, equally active during sunshine or by gaslight, breathless for its pleasures and its business affairs, and with the gift of perpetual motion.[4]

But Antoine had fallen short of providing this new life for her. And so Thérèse took matters into her own hands.

It is not known by what route she travelled to France, nor whereabouts she settled on arrival in Paris. But it is not hard to work out how she earned her living. It may be that she had imagined, as she later hinted, that with the knowledge she had already acquired of French, German, Russian and Polish, she could become a teacher. But at this stage she had no veneer of culture or any idea of how to live in Paris. While she was learning, her only marketable asset was her body, and it was very marketable: 'With her large rather prominent eyes which shone with a conquering flame, her full red lips, her firmly delineated bosom and her generous curves, she was armed with all she needed to stimulate the sensuality of men.'[5] Alphonse Esquiros paints a picture of the kind of fate most likely to befall a girl such as Thérèse:

> A young peasant girl arrives in Paris, bringing with her her figure, her innocence and her seventeen years. Ambition has brought her from the countryside; Paris has been described to her as a magic city where lovely clothes and a comfortable life await young girls. She books into a hotel which has been recommended to her. The expenses of the journey have emptied her small purse; but she easily obtains credit. She spends the first few days looking for work.[6]

No work is forthcoming, her debts mount, and she begins to despair. Meanwhile, she notices that men are continually arriving to visit other young women in the 'hotel'.

> And then one day the landlady, seeing that the girl is desperate and doesn't know where to turn, makes it clear to her that all she has to do is fulfil certain duties towards the house. At last – but too late – the unfortunate girl realises the nature of the trap she has fallen into. Weary and exhausted from searching, in a strangle-hold from the obligations she has contracted, she yields . . .[7]

If something like this did indeed happen to Thérèse, and she began her life in Paris in a *maison de tolérance*, she had the energy and determination not to stay there for long. Instead she exercised all her powers of attraction, as well as her prodigious willpower, to persuade one or several of her clients to help her buy her way out of the brothel and establish herself in a matter of months as an independent, higher class of prostitute.

This early period of her life in Paris was not one on which Thérèse ever chose to dwell, and little is known of her until in 1841, at the age of twenty-two, she set off for the spa town of Ems in Prussia. Ems, or Bad Ems, had been one of Europe's most famous spas since the late seventeenth century and was an ideal venue for making conquests. For her to be in a position to enter the social world of Ems, Thérèse's first two or three years in Paris must have been sufficiently lucrative to have enabled her to acquire respectable clothes and at least fake jewellery. In Ems her fortunes rose to a new level, for it was here that she encountered the pianist Henri Herz.

Henri (or Heinrich) Herz was born in Vienna on 6 January 1808. He was a child prodigy, performing in public and composing from the age of eight. In April 1816 he was admitted to the Paris Conservatoire, and in the 1830s and 1840s he became one of the most famous virtuosos and popular composers in Paris. A. Marmontel, a professor at the Conservatoire (and something of an amateur phrenologist) describes his physical appearance thus:

> Henri Herz's physiognomy is of the Israelite type; the forehead is prominent, the nose aquiline, the bright, wide open eyes suggest clarity of thought and benevolence. The mouth is accentuated, framed by firm lips, and the chin is rounded. There is nothing that is not straightforward and candid in this face with its decisive lines; there are no distinguishing characteristics, apart from the habit of holding the head slightly to one side with a questioning look. His height is a little above average; his rhythmic gait betrays a slight tendency to limp.[8]

At the age of thirty-eight, when Thérèse met him, Herz was at the height of his virtuosity and charm. He had been delighting young women in particular with his performances in Paris, London, Berlin and Vienna; nor did he refrain from seducing them when he had the chance. He spoke several languages fluently and was very wealthy.

It is clear from the style in which he couched his memoir about his tour of America that Herz was a man of 'sensibility', given to high-flown expressions of emotion and displays of enthusiasm. Thérèse, recognising this quality in him, deployed her powers of seduction by swooning at one of his concerts, thus ensuring that he noticed her and was attracted to her. Her genuine love of music played its part in the development of their relationship, and what began as piano lessons ended with Thérèse moving in with Henri in Paris where, in 1842, he became professor of piano at the Conservatoire. He was also involved in the running of his family's piano factory and owned a concert hall in Paris, the Salle Herz.

Thérèse Villoing and Henri Herz lived together for several years in what was then the eleventh (and is now the ninth) arrondissement in the rue de Provence, near the Salle Herz which was situated at 48 rue de la Victoire. More than just living together, they passed themselves off as married, Thérèse having cards printed for Monsieur and Madame Herz. At the same time she chose to change her first name to Blanche, partly, as in the case of Marie Duplessis, to mark a break with her past, to dissociate herself from the woman who had been Thérèse Villoing, and to remove herself symbolically from the life of prostitution which she had been following until then. For what could be purer, or whiter, than 'Blanche'? According to the reminiscences of a former pupil of Henri's brother Jacques, however, her underskirts were not always as white as they might have been at this period, her hems having been trailing in the mud.[9] Her skills at remaking herself became more refined as time went on.

The mysterious origins of this woman – she seemed to the onlooker to have come out of nowhere, after having perhaps been glimpsed in the streets of Paris as a twenty-year-old *lorette* – provided fertile ground for speculation, as did her prodigious powers of attraction, which were almost as mysterious as her origins. She herself fed the speculation, both to cover up what could be considered a not very interesting or a sordid background and to add to her aura of exoticism. And so she spread around the rumour that she was not a Lachmann at all, but the illegitimate daughter of Prince Konstantin Pavlovich, a grandson of Catherine the Great. Neither did she discourage the romanticising of the journey she had made from Moscow to Paris, a tale which included the rumour that she travelled via Constantinople where she had become the head of a harem.

The *raison d'être* for such a rumour was partly an attempt to explain her undeniable, but indefinable, sexual allure – she must have learnt the arts of seduction somewhere exotic, went the reasoning. She was not conventionally beautiful, yet she exerted some kind of power which many men seem to have resented at the same time as being in thrall to it. Physical descriptions of her are noticeable for their similarity to that of the stereotypical prostitute given by Alphonse Esquiros, with his suggestion of large, well-shaped breasts, a sensual face and, in particular, flared nostrils.[10] Marcel Boulanger writes, for instance (not that there is any evidence that he ever saw her), that Thérèse's 'nose was strange, broken at the end like a Kalmuk's, and her large nostrils quivered indecently'.[11] He also describes her as resembling the sort of female devil Cossacks might gallop away with, or a gipsy reading the tarot, and asserts that she had enormous shining eyes, like those of a dragonfly, and that her body was light, arched and wild, poised to spring like a female faun.[12] Frédéric Loliée writes of her in her youth (this again can only have come from conjecture and hearsay) as possessing 'an extraordinarily slim figure, a Grecian, not to say English-style bosom . . . luxuriant hair of bronze hue, a face more expressive than fine and superb slightly prominent eyes'.[13]

Thérèse (or rather Blanche as she now was) travelled with Henri on various of his concert tours, including to London, where he was always very warmly received. The couple enjoyed mixing with artistic society there, and Blanche added a knowledge of English to her accomplishments. Through Henri, Blanche also met various musicians, journalists and literary men in Paris, including Richard Wagner, Hans von Bülow, the pianist and son-in-law of Liszt, the novelist, poet and journalist Théophile Gautier and the editor and newspaper proprietor Emile de Girardin. Such connections sowed the seeds of her career as a hostess. Blanche used Henri to educate herself musically and culturally; she learnt much about how to conduct herself in society – and she learnt how not to handle money. Blanche also had a daughter by Henri, named Henriette, who was entrusted to the care of Henri's brother Jacques and his wife. She was a delicate child, and Jacques Herz decided to send her to Switzerland where he owned property near Berne.

Stories were circulated about Blanche at every stage of her life, usually in an attempt to denigrate her out of resentment at her arrogance and success (her demeanour could not have been further removed from that of the 'modest' courtesan, Marie Duplessis), and her period as Madame Herz was no exception. The stories often arose from some factual incident and were then embellished. The most famous story of the Herz period concerns a reception at the Tuileries, to which Henri Herz had been invited by Louis Philippe and the Queen. Herz attempted to take his 'wife' with him but, unfortunately for Blanche, enquiries had been made into her background and marital status and, as she stood in the queue at the foot of the stairs, a member of the palace staff approached her and, on establishing her identity, asked her to leave. According to Frédéric Loliée, she was so enraged that she broke her fan and threw the pieces in Herz's face for having been unable to prevent her from sustaining such an insult.[14]

By 1846 living with Blanche was beginning seriously to deplete Henri's resources. Business was also going badly and, in consultation with Jacques, he decided to liquidate the piano manufacturing business and to embark on an extensive concert tour of America, on which he would charge very high fees in order to recoup his losses and rebuild some capital. This time he decided that Blanche would not be coming with him but that she should be entrusted, along with Jacques, with the business of the liquidation and management of Henri's other affairs in Paris. He promised to send large amounts of money to her from America, both for her to live on and to pay the staff. It was envisaged that the concert tour would last for six months.

On 2 November 1846 Henri embarked at Liverpool on the

steamer *Caledonia* which was to take him to Boston. Years later, this is
what he wrote about his departure:

> Armed with a good piano – my tool, – with an overnight bag
> and one small suitcase, I left for the new world as others might
> leave Paris to watch the fountains play at Versailles.
>
> I bade farewell to old Europe with a heart full of the feverish
> yearning, mingled with vague fears and melancholy, which is
> the traveller's first and perhaps most delightful emotion.
>
> For I was leaving relatives, friends and land! – but going to see
> America, to live a life replete with enticing dangers, over this
> liquid world called the Ocean; I was going to enjoy a new sky,
> breathe in the scents of unfamiliar vegetation, tread the myster-
> ious ground discovered by the genius of Columbus – and these
> were noble and poetic compensations for the tranquil pleasures
> of the sedentary life.[15]

In the event, Henri stayed in America for five years. He was
accompanied everywhere by his piano, which continually posed
immense logistical difficulties, and he crossed both North and South
America several times, giving more than four hundred concerts.

Meanwhile Blanche and Jacques got on with the work of liquidat-
ing the piano factory. Blanche quickly proved to Jacques that she was
a skilled businesswoman when it came to raising money and calling in
debts. He was less impressed by the fact that she spent the money at
least as fast as she raised it, and he was disturbed by the constant arrival
of new gowns and jewellery. Moreover, creditors kept arriving,
demanding settlement of unpaid bills in the name of Madame Herz.
Jacques decided to inform Henri about her overspending; the latter
wrote a few mildly remonstrative letters to Blanche, about which she
groaned but which had no effect whatsoever on her behaviour.

Jacques had not yet informed his brother of Blanche's other
misdemeanours – of what a good time she seemed to be having
in his absence. Eventually, however, the truth broke. A servant who
had been sacked by Blanche decided to tell Jacques that she and Henri

were not legally married. This was the last straw for Jacques, who informed his brother of everything Blanche had been getting up to, both financially and in other areas. The fact that Henri made no attempt to patch things up with Blanche, but immediately stopped sending her further money and decided to extend his American tour, suggests that some of 'Madame Herz's' exploits involved other men. Perhaps he had also found other women in America who were as prepared as Blanche had been to swoon over his performances. There were terrible scenes between Blanche and Jacques. The latter demanded that she vacate the apartment in the rue de Provence and refused to let her have any further contact with any member of the Herz family, including her own daughter.

Blanche and Henri Herz never met one another again. Their daughter Henriette died at the age of twelve, having never really known either parent. Henri continued to be a pianist adored by his public. On his return from America in 1851 he re-established the piano factory and also co-founded with Jacques and their elder brother Charles a school for pianists, the Ecole Spéciale de Piano de Paris. He clearly continued to attract young women: 'The number of women pianists trained at Henri Herz's school is considerable and forms a brilliant cohort. Unfortunately for music, most of the girls who dedicate themselves to virtuosity soon renounce it in favour of the austere duties of the family.'[16] The instruments made in the Herz factory were regarded by his contemporaries as equal to those of Erard and Pleyel, and one of his pianos won first prize at the Paris Exposition of 1855. His compositions consist largely of variations and fantasies on themes by other composers, but they also include eight piano concertos, as well as various dances, salon pieces and exercises.

So in late 1846 or early 1847 Blanche (who for the time being retained her expropriated surname of Herz) found herself almost back where she had started, in the position of having to find herself a protector, or several, of being well off for a few months or even weeks at a time and then, in between lovers, having to pawn her jewellery and find some cheap accommodation. The identities of her protectors at this period are unclear. She may at some point have been involved with Agénor de Guiche, and she certainly became a well-known figure in the *demi-monde*. A story related in the Journal of the Goncourt brothers in 1863, some sixteen years after it was supposed to have happened, involves an encounter between Blanche and Théophile Gautier, who was already a friend of hers.

The story goes that Blanche was ill and in financial difficulties. She had only been able to find a very cheap hotel to stay in, the Hôtel Varlin on the rue des Champs Elysées, where she had a modest room on the fourth floor. She asked Gautier to visit her there and, in a feverish state, adumbrated her plans for the future to him. She declared that she would one day build the most beautiful house in Paris – 'just there' – pointing out of the window toward the avenue des Champs Elysées. Théophile was unconvinced, though he did not tell Blanche so. This rather hand-to-mouth existence came to an end, probably in 1848, partly through the agency of another courtesan, Esther Guimont, who spoke on Blanche's behalf to Camille, a well-known milliner and purveyor of fashionable clothes, whose client Blanche had been during her liaison with Herz. Camille herself occupied a position on the fringes of the *demi-monde* as what was commonly known as an *ogresse* or, more accurately, *entremetteuse* – that is, she acted both as a procuress and as a facilitator, being prepared to extend sufficient credit to a woman of Blanche's calibre and obvious pulling power to enable her to be dressed as befitted a fashionable woman of the world (or the half-world) and thus to enter the circles where the truly wealthy might be found. Such women understood the value of appearances, in this world of display and ostentatious finery, and knew that to appear wealthy was the first step in becoming so. To this end, an *ogresse* would even supply her client with ready cash – not only for spending, but as a final touch to help create the illusion of being an expensive woman, of the sort that a man of the world would be drawn to and desire to possess. This was the service Camille agreed to perform for Blanche, whose potential she had already assessed during her days as the consort of Henri Herz.

Appropriately attired and bejewelled by Camille, with a 'float' to keep herself going for a few weeks, and determined to make enough money to be able to save so as to avoid the humiliating necessity of having to depend in the future on the whims of a succession of men, Blanche decided that her field of operations should be London. This was a shrewd move on her part. As his reign had gone on, Louis Philippe had become increasingly unpopular. Since 1847 there had been a food crisis in France, due to a series of poor harvests, and there was much poverty in the country. Factories were closing and workers being laid off. This economic recession spread discontent among an already miserable working class, a discontent exploited by numerous secret revolutionary societies, while on the right the King had to contend with both the Legitimists, who wanted the restoration of the Bourbon line, and the Bonapartists. Louis Napoleon Bonaparte had already made two unsuccessful attempts at staging an insurrection, one in October 1836 when he had tried to persuade the garrison at Strasbourg to rise up in support of him and another in August 1840 when he had attempted to take Boulogne. After this second effort he had been sentenced to 'permanent imprisonment' at the fortress castle of Ham, but in May 1846 he had escaped and gone to live in London. Meanwhile Louis Philippe had himself contributed to the evocation of glorious memories of the name of Napoleon both by inaugurating the statue of Napoleon I on top of the Vendôme column in July 1833 and by arranging for the return of his remains from Elba; they were translated to the Invalides, amidst great pomp and ceremony, on 15 December 1840.

The ferment of opposition to Louis Philippe increased throughout 1847 and was formalised in a series of banquets held to promote demands for electoral reform. The banning of one of these banquets, planned for 22 February 1848, led to disturbances, barricades in the streets of Paris and, two days later, the abdication of the King. The Second Republic was proclaimed on 26 February and on 2 March Louis Philippe left for exile in England, where he died on 26 August 1850. But the February Revolution, as it became known, did nothing, at least initially, to improve the economic situation. Blanche realised that Paris was not currently the best place to be for a woman in need of men prepared to lavish their riches upon her. Neither were other regions of continental Europe much more likely to yield the appropriate fruit, in this year of revolutions and popular unrest. By contrast, the ruling classes in London were relatively free of anxiety. Moreover, Blanche was already acquainted with London through her visits there with Henri Herz; she had herself been accepted there as Madame Herz. It was thus the obvious place for her to go.

Little is known for sure about Blanche's stay in London, except that it was entirely successful in its objective. It is said that she appeared one evening, luxuriantly attired, in a box at Covent Garden, and that all male eyes were immediately drawn to her. The most widely spread rumour as to her conquests concerns Lord Edward George Geoffrey Smith Stanley, the 14th Earl of Derby. He was very rich, a man about town and a dandy, yet also a most serious gentleman and a connoisseur of all types of pleasure. Married to a daughter of Lord Skelmersdale, he came second in precedence only to the Earl of Shrewsbury. He was a member of the Tory party and for a long time the right-hand man of Sir Robert Peel. He was himself three times prime minister – in 1852, from 1858 to 1859, and finally from 1866 to 1868. English through and through, this lover of pictures and books, of horse-racing, hunting and women knew how to combine business, duty and pleasure, and it is reputed that for a while Blanche came into the latter category. He possessed a large amount of land in Lancashire as well as considerable property in Ireland and he would, by today's standards, have been a multi-millionaire.

Lord Derby was by no means Blanche's only conquest; judging by the wealth with which she returned triumphantly to Paris, she must have had many rich lovers during her brief sojourn in London. Another rumour typical of the kind which surround her life concerns this money-making expedition: she was supposed to have returned by way of Moscow with a consumptive young prince in tow, who conveniently died and left her all his money. There is no evidence to substantiate this rumour and there are no candidates for the identity of the prince. On her return to Paris Blanche took up residence at 30 place Saint-Georges, near the church of Notre Dame de Lorette, in an unusual *hôtel*, or mansion, decorated with gothic sculptures, which had created a sensation when it was built in 1840 by the architect Renaud. There she received men who could afford her, if and when she chose. She also began to invest the money she had amassed, ensuring that she would never again be penniless.

A few months after the February Revolution Prince Louis Napoleon Bonaparte had also returned to Paris from London and was elected to the National Assembly. In December 1848 he defeated General Louis Eugène Cavaignac in the presidential elections by an overwhelming majority, his success being due both to his prestigious name and to his rather vague politics which allowed people of different parties and persuasions to see him as being on their side. As President of the Second Republic he was limited by law to one term of office, but he soon began to strengthen his position, taking special care to conciliate powerful conservative forces such as the Church.

On 16 June 1849 a notary's clerk arrived at the place Saint-Georges to inform Blanche that François Hyacinthe Antoine Villoing had died in Paris, on the previous day, of cholera. (A cholera epidemic had broken out in March of that year. It lasted until the end of the summer and claimed over sixteen thousand lives.) It is not known how long Antoine Villoing had been in Paris, or precisely what his relations had been with his wife. Clearly the notary had been made aware of her existence and knew where to find her. The notary's clerk also informed her that her son was currently at the boarding school run by the Frères des Ecoles chrétiennes at Passy. Blanche subsequently provided Antoine junior with an allowance of two hundred and fifty francs a month, just enough for him to live on as a schoolboy and later as a medical student. Blanche never saw him herself, the allowance being remitted to him via an official intermediary. He died of tuberculosis at the age of twenty-five.

One day soon after the death of her husband one of Blanche's friends from the literary and artistic circle she had been cultivating since the time of her liaison with Herz introduced her to a Portuguese gentleman who was already well known in the fashionable world. His

name was Albino Francesco de Païva-Araujo, and Blanche took note
of him. He had a reputation as something of a Don Juan, passionate
about gambling and women. Dressed by the best tailors, he was tall
and dark and sported a fine moustache, trimmed in a style similar to
that of the President, Louis Napoleon. He had not been in Paris long,
but was already well established in the crowd of fashionable spend-
thrifts. It was believed that he was the heir to a great fortune; he was
forever talking about the money he would one day inherit from his
mother. In fact, by the time he met Blanche he had already spent
most of it.

Albino Francesco de Païva-Araujo had been born in 1827 in
Macao, a Portuguese possession in the Far East, and was the only
son of a rich businessman who had died there in 1842. Francesco was
in Paris when he learnt of his father's death, being at the time a
boarder at the same school in Passy which the young Antoine
Villoing was to attend a few years later. On the death of her husband,
Francesco's mother left Macao and returned to live in Portugal
where, at eighteen, Francesco rejoined her. He had studied as little
as possible at school, having decided that his wealth made it unnecessary for him to follow a profession. As soon as he had attained his
majority he asked his mother for his inheritance and, after a little
prevarication, she agreed.

Francesco's first port of call was Bad Ems, where he sustained
severe losses in the casinos. Then, arriving in Paris, he moved into a
luxurious apartment at 2 rue Rossini, near the main boulevards and
the Opera House. He became a regular at the casinos, restaurants and
theatres, and also took to styling himself 'Marquess'. (The assumption
of a spurious title was not uncommon among foreigners arriving to
live in Paris; they believed it improved their creditworthiness and
helped them become established in society.)

The shrewd Madame Herz soon noticed that the 'Marquess' de
Païva was on the path to ruin, that he was crippled with debts, having
to borrow constantly, giving as his guarantee the property which he
claimed to possess in Porto and Macao. She realised that this was only
bluff, and she also began to lend him money herself. Before long

Païva found himself at her mercy, with no one knowing that she was partially funding him. It was as though he were being drawn into a spider's web. When Blanche felt that Francesco could no longer hold off his creditors or even the forces of the law, she offered him an escape route. She would pay off his debts and provide him with a monthly allowance so that he could have the appearance of independence. In return, he would marry her. He agreed.

The marriage contract was signed on 4 June 1851 in front of a notary, Monsieur Noel. Giving the same address as Francesco – 2 rue Rossini – Blanche was careful to stipulate that all the furniture in that apartment belonged to her. The civil wedding ceremony took place in the town hall of the eleventh arrondissement, while the religious ceremony was celebrated on 5 June at the Pensionnat des Frères in Passy. (One cannot help wondering whether the young Antoine Villoing caught a glimpse of his mother at this point.) The witnesses were Théophile Gautier, a painter called Barclay who lived at Passy, the secretary of the Portuguese Legation and a notary public. The marriage was announced in the Paris newspapers on the following day.

During that same year, after the defeat in the Assembly of a constitutional amendment which would have allowed Louis Napoleon to serve as President for more than one term, he and his closest advisers began to make plans for a *coup d'état*. This took place on 2 December 1851, various Assembly leaders having been arrested during the night of the 1st. Once again there were barricades in Paris and about two hundred people were killed in clashes with the army. A plebiscite conducted on 20 and 21 December overwhelmingly endorsed the Prince President's action, and a new constitution was promulgated on 14 January 1852 which gave him dictatorial powers and created a Council of State, a Senate and a Legislative Assembly all subservient to him. In November another plebiscite was held, this time to seek the people's approval for the re-establishment of the Empire. That approval was forthcoming, and on 1 December 1852 Louis Napoleon was proclaimed the Emperor Napoleon III.

A distant cousin of Blanche's new husband was the Portuguese chargé d'affaires; he remained in this post during the Second Empire until he committed suicide in Berlin in 1868. Francesco held no office but this did not worry Blanche any more than the fact that his title was fictitious; she adopted for herself the name of Marchioness de Païva with no less aplomb than Louis Napoleon had adopted that of Napoleon III. This had been her aim in marrying the 'Marquess', and for ever afterwards she was known as 'La Païva'. Having attained her object, Blanche became less inclined to keep bailing her husband out. After two years at the most, she advised him to return to Porto and plead his cause with his mother. She made it clear that she herself wanted nothing more to do with him. And so, with no resources or credit remaining to him in Paris, the *soi-disant* Marquess de Païva returned to Portugal. He carried beautiful English suitcases with him, but they were virtually empty. He left behind a few debts which Blanche refused to settle.

The story of this marriage and of Païva's subsequent dismissal was strange enough in itself to give rise to embellished accounts and fanciful descriptions of what may have gone on between the couple. Viel Castel most famously exercised his imagination on this score:

The day after the wedding, when the newly weds woke up, Madame de Païva spoke more or less as follows to her satisfied lover:

'You wanted to sleep with me, and you have managed it by making me your wife. You have given me your name, and last night I performed my duty. I have acted as an honest woman, I wanted a position, and now I have it, but you, Monsieur de Païva, all you have for a wife is a whore, you cannot present her anywhere, you cannot receive anyone; we must therefore separate, you to return to Portugal, and I to remain here, a whore, with your name.'

Païva, ashamed and confused, followed his wife's advice, and hid the memory of his regrettable adventure in the solitude of a Portuguese castle.[17]

His mother did agree to pay off his debts, but she could not forgive him for his marriage. She refused to fund him to the extent he considered necessary, and in future they barely saw one another. He lived in a small house on the edge of his mother's estate. He only left it by night, and spent his days sleeping and eating. A valet would bring him meals from his mother's kitchen.

Blanche de Païva continued to live alone in the place Saint-Georges, the most sought-after of courtesans, at a time when the city of Paris was beginning to enjoy some of its most scintillating years. There were those, such as Victor Hugo, who predicted doom for the Second Empire from the start, as well as those who were conscious of the less benign aspects of Napoleon III's dictatorship – principally, the muzzling of all opposition – but these concerns were not shared by the majority. As Gustave Claudin recalled in his *Souvenirs*: 'If the Empire did not grant much liberty, it offered on the other hand a great deal of security. It dissatisfied the liberals who concerned themselves with politics, but the dissatisfaction was not general, and was not felt at all by those, of whom there are so many in this world, who dream above all of a quiet and happy life and who worry little about politics.'[18]

The ruthlessness with which Blanche had cast off her spendthrift husband once he had served her purposes contributed to her image as a heartless and mercenary woman. She never, it was believed, allowed herself the luxury of sentiment, and in much of what has been written about her one can detect the fear and bewilderment of men in the face of a powerful woman who somehow knew how to get the better of them and who could not be manipulated.

She took care to armour-plate her heart, in order to make herself inaccessible to all emotion. In the course on which she was embarked, nothing could make her hesitate, no force in the world was capable of bending her inflexible will. Entirely devoted to her aim, she remained the self-interested and cold woman, who knows only one thing: money – because for her, money was everything and she knew that through it she could triumph and obtain all the rest. Her constant preoccupation was to be rich in order to be in control.[19]

A marked element of anti-semitism, as well as a general mistrust of foreigners and of foreign women in particular, cannot be denied in some of the judgments made on Blanche de Païva by her contemporaries and by later commentators. There is no escaping the anti-semitism of mid-nineteenth-century Paris, despite the official acceptance of Jews. Count Horace de Viel Castel noted in his diary on 19 August 1853, for instance: 'Since I've been in a position to see the Jews close up, I can understand the edicts of our kings who used to banish them. Today we are more than ever their prey, France's money passes through their hands.'[20] The tendency to ascribe certain characteristics (or supposed characteristics) of La Païva to her 'race' continued long after her death. One commentator who does so is Georges Montorgueil, writing in 1911:

> This Païva's physiognomy is of a singular complexity. A parvenue courtesan, she is not however representative of her class. She presents a unique phenomenon, which is not connected to time or place, but to race. It is the wandering and victorious Jew. No similarity between her and the pretty free spirits of the Second Empire, alluring and fidgety, obsessed with those bodies for which men went mad, queens of the fête, prodigal with the gifts of their beauty and projecting, across the splendours of the régime, the brazen laugh of la Belle Hélène. Madame de Païva did not know how to laugh. She moved towards her goal, proud and mysterious, coldly calculating. She had a powerful instinct of domination, the hidden spring of her life.[21]

Blanche did demonstrate a singular determination to achieve the goals she set herself, chief among then being to attain financial independence, and this single-mindedness as well as her most un-stereotypical ability to manage money (after the early débâcle and learning experience of the Herz finances) made a deep impression on her contemporaries and on subsequent male commentators in particular, who have generally viewed this woman as unusually ambitious and unnaturally strong in willpower. Emile Le Senne presents the standard picture when he writes:

> Her understanding of the social order was simple, to her way of thinking there were only two categories of people: the haves and the have-nots. And what was the point of living in wretchedness and poverty while others lived in opulence?
>
> She possessed an unbounded ambition in whose service she placed a will of iron.
>
> She was convinced that for something to happen, it was enough to want it, firmly and fiercely. Power is will.[22]

Or, as Georges Montorgueil has it in his preface to Le Senne's book: 'There was no place for a sudden impulse in this foreign woman's soul; she left nothing to chance or to the imagination; for her everything was deliberate and willed. She slept with a compass under her pillow and, naturally prudent, she never lost the north.'[23]

1 See Geoffrey Hosking, *Russia: People and empire 1552–1917*, HarperCollins, London, 1997

2 See, for instance, Marcel Boulanger, *La Païva*, Editions M-P. Trémois, Paris, 1930, p.13 and Joanna Richardson, *The Courtesans*, p.50

3 Marcel Boulanger, *La Païva*, p.13

4 Maxime Du Camp, *Paris: ses organes, ses fonctions et sa vie jusqu'en 1870*, p.7

5 Comte Fleury and Louis Sonolet, *La Société du Second Empire*, Vol.4, 1867–1870, Albin Michel, Paris, 1913, p.358

6 Alphonse Esquiros, *Les Vierges folles*, p.87

7 Ibid., p.89

8 A. Marmontel, *Les Pianistes célèbres: silhouettes et médaillons*, A. Chaix & Cie, Paris, 1878, p.36

9 See Frédéric Loliée, *La Païva*, p.31

10 Alphonse Esquiros, *Les Vierges folles*, p.46

11 Marcel Boulanger, *La Païva*, p.16

12 Ibid.

13 Frédéric Loliée, '*La Païva*'. *La Légende et l'histoire de la Marquise de Païva*, Editions Jules Tallandier, Paris, 1920, p.13

14 Ibid., p.34

15 Henri Herz, *Mes Voyages en Amérique*, Achille Faure, Paris, 1866, pp.3–4

16 A. Marmontel, *Les Pianistes célèbres*, p.39

17 Comte Horace de Viel Castel, *Mémoires sur le règne de Napoléon III (1851–1864)*, Vol.4, 1885, p.39

18 Gustave Claudin, *Mes Souvenirs*, p.222

19 Emile Le Senne, *Madame de Païva: Etude de psychologie et d'histoire*, H. Daragon, Paris, 1911, p.10

20 Comte Horace de Viel Castel, *Mémoires sur le règne de Napoléon III (1851–1864)*, Vol.2, 1884, p.231

21 Georges Montorgueil, Preface to Emile Le Senne, *Madame de Païva*, p.ix

22 Emile Le Senne, *Madame de Païva*, pp.7–8

23 Georges Montorgueil, Preface to Emile Le Senne, *Madame de Païva*, p.xiii

CHAPTER FIVE

La Femme piquée par un serpent

I N FEBRUARY 1822, in the town of Mézières in the southern Ardennes, Sergeant André Savatier, of the 47th Infantry Regiment garrisoned in this town, made a declaration, part of which read as follows:

> [he] has before these persons here present freely and voluntarily declared that he is responsible for the pregnancy of Miss Marguerite Martin aged twenty-four years, a washerwoman living at Pont-de-Pierre, in the district of Mézières, the daughter of Charles Théodore Martin, deceased, a distiller at Mézières, and of Marie Jeanne Plumat, his wife, the said Miss Marguerite Martin being about seven and a half months pregnant by him, that he is not and never has, any more than has the said Miss Martin, been engaged in the bonds of matrimony . . .[1]

This was not the first time the beautiful young washerwoman Marguerite Martin had been pregnant. Her first child, Joséphine, had been born of an unknown father on 26 April 1819 but had died in early infancy. The outcome of the pregnancy referred to in Sergeant Savatier's declaration was another daughter, born on 7 April 1822 and christened Aglaé-Joséphine – though the bearer of this name would later assert that her mother had wanted to name her Apollonie, but that the officiating priest would not agree to such an unchristian name. She would also assert that her father was not after all Sergeant Savatier, but rather the Viscount Louis Harmand d'Abancourt,

Prefect of the Ardennes from 1819 to 1823. The story goes that Marguerite worked as a laundress in the house of the rich and married d'Abancourt, who seduced her and subsequently persuaded Savatier to become the expected child's official father. D'Abancourt, who represented Ardennes in the Chamber of Deputies from 1824 to 1831, was forty-eight at the time of Aglaé's birth. He died in 1850, when she was twenty-eight, but there is no record of his having anything further to do with his daughter once he had resolved the paternity issue and ensured that Marguerite was provided for through the arrangement with Sergeant Savatier.

Savatier, who could neither read nor write but who had been made a chevalier of the Legion of Honour for his exploits in the Napoleonic Wars, seems not to have objected to this further award of a young and attractive woman, along with her offspring. His military status precluded an immediate marriage, but did not stop the couple living together. Savatier's wartime experiences had taken their toll physically; he suffered from various infirmities, including fits of uncontrollable trembling. Nevertheless he still represented a more secure future than the (at least) twice-seduced and fatherless Marguerite Martin may have dared hope for.

In 1825 the family, already increased by a boy, Alexandre, moved with Savatier's regiment from Mézières to Paris. Sergeant Savatier finally obtained permission to marry Marguerite, and the marriage ceremony took place in the town hall of the sixth arrondissement when Aglaé-Joséphine was three and a half years old. In 1827 Savatier was awarded a retirement pension of four hundred francs a year, and the family returned to Mézières where it was easier to make ends meet than in Paris and where another boy, Louis, was born in 1828. The final addition to the family was Irma Adelina, known as Bébé and later as Adèle, who was born on 6 September 1832. Shortly afterwards Sergeant Savatier died, and Marguerite moved with her children back to Paris. Some years later she married again, her second husband, Mathieu Cizelet, also being a former soldier. The family settled in the outskirts of the city, in what was then the village of Les Batignolles (and is now an area of Paris near the Porte de Clichy), where Marguerite supplemented the household's income by taking in sewing.

By the time she was fifteen, in 1837, Aglaé-Joséphine was helping her mother to keep house, doing some of her paid work and looking after her five-year-old sister, Bébé. She had inherited her mother's beauty, and was the kind of girl people were drawn to. The headmistress of a local *pensionnat* offered to take her as a pupil at a reduced rate. This headmistress also realised that Aglaé was very musical, and arranged for her to have free piano and singing lessons. She was a sociable girl and also used to attend dances organised by local societies. At one of them, during carnival time, she dressed in the traditional costume of a peasant woman from La Bresse, in which costume she was painted by two young students of Delaroche, Auguste Blanchard and Charles Jalabert. She was tall and well-proportioned, with exquisite hands and luxuriant copper-coloured hair which glinted when it caught the light. She began to frequent artists' studios as a model, and became involved in bohemian life. When she was sixteen she had an affair with a wealthy young man called James de Pourtalès. Had she been a prudent character she might have married him and had an easy life thereafter, but Aglaé demonstrated early on her tendency to follow her heart rather than her head, and the relationship with Pourtalès foundered when she fell in love with Prosper Derivis, a young opera singer at the start of his career and therefore impecunious. Aglaé seems to have enjoyed this bohemian existence for the next few years, still living for the most part with her mother but involved in a series of liaisons, while studying music – though how seriously is open to debate – and obtaining some work as an artist's model. She seems to have lived on the fringes of the *demi-monde* – half in and half out of this half-world – enjoying its freedoms while not being dependent on it for her daily bread. Her mother clearly had a very *laisser faire* attitude to the bringing up of her daughters and, unlike many other parents of her time, never disowned them whatever they did.

Aglaé's rather unsettled, if carefree, way of life changed in 1846, at the age of twenty-four, when she accepted as her protector the wealthy industrialist and patron of the arts Alfred Mosselman. Alfred, who was twelve years older than Aglaé, came from an old bourgeois Belgian family; his sister Fanny had married the Belgian ambassador Charles Le Hon and was also the mistress of Auguste de Morny, the illegitimate half-brother of Louis Napoleon Bonaparte. From 1832 to 1837 Alfred was himself an attaché at the Belgian Legation, and in 1835 he married Eugénie Gazzani, a daughter of the receiver-general of the finances of the Eure in Upper Normandy, by whom he was to have four children between 1836 and 1845. His father was a banker and the owner of some very prosperous mining enterprises in Belgium, and in 1837 Alfred left the diplomatic service to concern himself with the family business which, on 24 May of that year, was constituted as a Belgian company under the name of the Société des Mines et Fonderies de zinc de la Vieille-Montagne. Its first president was Charles Le Hon and the principal administrators were Auguste de Morny (until 1857) and Alfred Mosselman. As a patron of the arts, Alfred was particularly fond of Romantic painting, and he frequented the circle of writers and artists who used to meet in the apartment of Fernand Boissard – musician, painter, art collector and man of letters – at the Hôtel Pimodan on the quai d'Anjou on the Ile Saint-Louis. This was where the *club des haschichins* used to meet at which Charles Baudelaire and Théophile Gautier, among others, experimented with the effect of eating hashish in the form of green jelly. Aglaé was also acquainted with this artistic circle, though there is no record of her having joined in the hashish-eating episodes, and it was at the Pimodan that she first met Alfred Mosselman. He may have caught his first glimpse of her from the Pimodan's balcony as she was returning with two girlfriends from a swimming lesson in the cold-water swimming pool for ladies, newly constructed at the end of the island.[2] Aglaé allowed Alfred to set her up in a second-floor apartment at 4 rue Frochot in the quartier Bréda, not far from Notre Dame de Lorette and an area renowned for its kept women. Around this time she changed her first name from Aglaé-Joséphine to Apollonie, the name she claimed should have been hers from the beginning and which she valued for its classical resonances and its suitability for a woman playing the role of muse to a circle of men. She also made a slight change to her surname, altering the 'v' to a 'b'; this reflected her desire both to distance herself from her adoptive father, Sergeant Savatier, and to dispense with the connection to *savate*, a word meaning an 'old used slipper', hardly appropriate for a beautiful young woman. From now on she was most often known as Madame Sabatier.

The rue Frochot leads off from what is now the place Pigalle and in Apollonie's day was the barrière Montmartre. It is an area which continues to be associated with sex and prostitution, while the avenue Frochot, with its gated access at forty-five degrees to the *rue* of the same name, provides an oasis of tranquility. Number 4 rue Frochot itself is now a three-star hotel. The building was constructed in 1838, and Apollonie's apartment consisted of seven rooms: an antechamber, drawing room, dining room, two bedrooms, a large bathroom and a kitchen, and then a large balcony looking out on to the gardens of the private and secluded avenue Frochot. Alfred furnished the apartment with care, he and Apollonie choosing many pieces from antique dealers on the Ile Saint-Louis. The table in the dining room was wide and rectangular, large enough to seat a dozen people, and the square-backed chairs were upholstered in olive green velvet. In the evening, light came from Louis XVI candelabra attached to the walls and from a polished brass chandelier, and in the day the apartment was filled with sunlight. The garnet-red fabric on the walls provided a fine background for the array of pictures, Delft plaques and plates acquired for his mistress by Alfred. The drawing room was to the left of the dining room, and its windows opened on to a view of the street. Everywhere there were rich hangings, pouffes, cushions, rugs and drapes. The apartment was reached by a narrow staircase and through a double door. The quartier Bréda was an area not only of kept women, but also of artists and writers. Apollonie's neighbours included Théodore Rousseau the landscape painter, Théodore Chassériau who had recently decorated the chapel of Sainte-Marie-l'Egyptienne in the church of Saint-Merri, the painter Eugène Delacroix, the composer Hector Berlioz, the poet and short story writer Gérard de Nerval, Théophile Gautier, the impersonator Henri Monnier, and the writers Henry Murger and Maxime Du Camp. Her nearest neighbour was the painter Eugène Isabey, the windows of whose second-floor studio at 5 avenue Frochot looked directly into Apollonie's.

In order to keep his relationship with Apollonie relatively discreet, Alfred found it useful to employ his friend Fernand Boissard as a confidant and go-between. Thus Apollonie maintained her links with the habitués of the Hôtel Pimodan, who included the painter Ernest Meissonier, already a firm friend of Apollonie's, along with his wife Emma. There were even those who thought that Apollonie was Boissard's, rather than Mosselman's, mistress, but he was living with Maryx (or Marix), a young and striking Jewish woman who modelled for the artists Ary Scheffer and Paul Delaroche.

The first few months in the rue Frochot marked the beginning of a significant time for Apollonie, released from any need to earn her own living. She further developed her artistic sense and discrimination, absorbing knowledge and ideas from the men around her. Alfred Mosselman made an excellent mentor, cultivating her taste to match his own while according her freedom to pursue her independent interests as well. She settled into what was in many ways a very easy life.

One thing has always been rather bewildering about accounts of the beginning of Apollonie's liaison with Alfred Mosselman, and that is the apparent ease with which she gave up what several writers have portrayed as a promising singing career to become his mistress[3] (even though there is no particular reason why she could not have been a professional singer as well as a wealthy man's mistress; several women of the period, such as Hortense Schneider and Alice Ozy, combined quite happily the dual roles of actress and courtesan). At one moment, according to these writers, Apollonie was studying under a very eminent singing teacher indeed, Madame Damoreau-Cinti, one of the foremost opera singers of her day and a professor at the Paris Conservatoire, and the next she had abandoned all idea of a musical career and was entirely contented to be only a kept woman, a *femme galante*. It has even been frequently asserted that she first met Alfred Mosselman, not at the Hôtel Pimodan or among their mutual friends, but at a charity concert which he was backing and at which Apollonie herself was singing, in order to gain experience of professional performance, alongside another pupil of Madame Damoreau-Cinti, Madame Ugalde, who went on to enjoy a distinguished solo career. Even stranger, then, that Apollonie should abandon her singing just when her career appeared about to blossom. Was meeting Alfred Mosselman really such an overwhelming experience that all other thoughts and aspirations flew out of her head?

What we have here in fact is a case of mistaken identity. There was in Paris another singer by the name of Madame Sabatier who turns up in various concert notices between 1839 and 1849 and whose maiden name was Bénazet. She was two years older than Apollonie and married Louis François Sabatier at the church of Saint-Eustache in 1839. This Madame Sabatier did indeed sing in a charity concert at the Salle Herz with Madame Ugalde on 15 February 1847, and maybe Alfred Mosselman heard her there – but he had already installed his Madame Sabatier in the rue Frochot some months previously. Apollonie herself was an excellent amateur singer, as evidenced by the fact that in subsequent years composers such as Ernest Reyer were happy to accompany her in an informal setting, but it is unlikely that she was ever the pupil of anyone as illustrious as Madame Damoreau-Cinti and she made no great sacrifice of ambition in accepting Alfred Mosselman as her protector.

The exaggeration of Apollonie's singing talents is only one of the pieces of false information concerning her life before the beginning of her liaison with Alfred. An unsubstantiated assertion made, in the first instance, by Louis Mermaz[4] and repeated by both Claude Pichois[5] and Joanna Richardson,[6] is that she had an affair with Ernest Meissonier, travelling with him to Italy in 1840. The fact that Meissonier was already – and happily – married, however, should not be taken as evidence one way or the other, as he had very clear views on what an artist's wife should be expected to put up with:

The woman who marries an artist ought to realise that she is entering on a life of self-sacrifice. An artist's wife must not understand fidelity in the ordinary humdrum sense of the term . . . Even if the matrimonial horizon should be darkened by fleeting storms, it should be her part to restore peace and good will. If you have not the courage to include these items in your matrimonial budget, do not marry an artist![7]

The images of Apollonie Sabatier created out of mistaken or misleading information, images of her as a professional singer or as a more promiscuous young woman than she probably was, have something of a life of their own alongside the real woman and go on existing despite evidence to the contrary. They had, however, no particular effect on her in her lifetime, unlike the most powerful image created of her at this period of her life, an image very much based on reality – at least on physical reality. The annual exhibition of contemporary art, the Paris Salon, included among its exhibits in 1847 a sculpture by Auguste Clésinger entitled *La Femme piquée par un serpent*. It represented a naked, supine woman, ostensibly having been bitten by a snake, but who really appeared to be in the throes of orgasm. The model for this sculpture was Apollonie.

It was Alfred Mosselman who had commissioned the statue of his mistress from Clésinger, whose studio he had visited to be shown his works in progress. Auguste Clésinger was the son of a sculptor from Franche-Comté and had himself taken up sculpture at an early age. The start of his career had been fraught with financial difficulties – he had either too few commissions or too little marble – but by 1843 he had a studio in Paris in the rue de l'Ouest near the cemetery of Montparnasse, and a couple of years later his reputation was steadily growing. His supporters included Alexandre Dumas *père* and Emile de Girardin. It was *La Femme piquée*, however, which brought him celebrity.

Another item of misinformation repeated by various writers, such as Louis Mermaz, Jean Ziegler and Henri Troyat, was that Apollonie had also had an affair in her earlier days with Clésinger. In some accounts there is confusion between Clésinger and Meissonier, and in any event there is no evidence to back up either assertion.

The process of creating *La Femme piquée* began with the making of a cast, and Apollonie was initially resistant to the whole idea. She did not, however, have a great deal of choice in the matter, once Alfred Mosselman had decided that this was what he wanted and Auguste Clésinger had determined on the technique he intended to use. It cannot have been a particularly pleasant experience for her, involving, as it did, having each part of her body in turn encased in plaster. Although the skin would be protected with oil, the sensation as the plaster cooled would have been very oppressive. After the casts had been made the sculptor assembled the pieces into the required position, making various adjustments and corrections where necessary. Some attempt was made to preserve Apollonie's anonymity, in that the head was sculpted separately and was not copied from her own. Then Clésinger created a marble statue based on the cast, and it was this statue which was exhibited in the 1847 Salon, as was a bust Clésinger also made of Apollonie, entitled *Bust of Mme A.S.*

La Femme piquée par un serpent is now on permanent display in the Musée d'Orsay, lying at one end of the central hall of sculptures. This marble statue of a naked woman consumed by sexual ecstasy – both the snake wrapped around her ankle and the title were added as afterthoughts, in an attempt to disguise the overt sexual nature of the piece – continues to draw the crowds. *La Femme piquée* is beautiful, tactile, enticing – and it is as though a living, breathing woman is lying or, rather, writhing there. People reach out to touch her – the marble is deteriorating because so many have done so – and it is as though they are touching an actual young woman. Apollonie herself – the roundness of her buttocks, the fullness of her breasts, the curve of her stomach and the shapeliness of her legs – seems to be stretched out on that plinth, exposed in all her seductiveness and vulnerability. Every detail of her anatomy is revealed for public inspection, and no attempt has been made to distance her by awarding her some mythological name. In 1847 the blatancy of this naked display riveted the attention of both public and critics, who were divided according both to their moral standpoint and to their beliefs as to what constituted art.

Théophile Gautier was supportive, writing about *La Femme piquée* in *La Presse* on 10 April 1847:

> A young sculptor, M. Clésinger, who is now a great sculptor and has at his first attempt irresistibly captured the attention of artists, poets and public, has had the audacity, unheard of in our time, to exhibit without any mythological title a masterpiece which is neither goddess, nymph, dryad, orcade, drowned sprite nor oceanide, but quite simply a woman . . . There has been no such original work of sculpture for a long time . . . The quivering body is not sculpted, but moulded; it has the texture and bloom of skin.[8]

The aspects of the sculpture which Gautier singled out for praise – the lack of mythological title, the lifelikeness of the body – were precisely what more orthodox critics such as Gustave Planche took exception to.

> Clésinger's work does not have the character of a sculpted figure, but of a moulded one. The model has various imperfections, paltry details which serious art disdains and ignores and which M. Clésinger has not known how to efface. He has reproduced the folds of the stomach, because the plaster reproduced them. He has preserved the flexion of the toes of the left foot which signifies nothing other than the habit of wearing ill-fitting shoes, etc. etc.[9]

Clésinger did not allow critics such as Planche to dishearten him, and the overwhelming reaction of the public was enthusiastic.

This was a momentous year for Auguste Clésinger, for not only did he attain notoriety with his Salon exhibit but in May he married Solange Dudevant, the daughter of the writer George Sand. On 8 June Sand's lover, the musician Frédéric Chopin, wrote to his family in Poland, deploring Solange's choice of husband and including the following remarks:

> The statue which Clésinger exhibited recently represents a naked woman in a particularly indecent pose – so much so that *in order to justify it,* he had to add a snake around one of the statue's legs. It's alarming how this statue squirms. The truth of it is that it was commissioned by Mosselman (the brother of Madame Lehon, the former Belgian ambassadress whom I've often mentioned to you) and it represents his mistress – his and plenty of other men's, because *she's a kept woman who's very well known in Paris.*[10]

It is clear from Chopin's remarks that, despite the attempts which had been made at anonymity, those who knew Alfred Mosselman and Apollonie Sabatier knew perfectly well that she was the subject of *La Femme piquée*. And this knowledge, the sense that she was spread out naked for them all to view, while also being displayed as the property of Alfred Mosselman, would have a profound effect on how the men whom she gathered around her in the rue Frochot would relate to her, – men unable to forget, for all Apollonie's apparent unattainability, this sight of her naked body in its sexual pleasure, an image calling forth a response which was a curious mixture of reverence and contempt.

1 Quoted in Jean Ziegler, *Gautier-Baudelaire: un carré de dames*, A.G. Nizet, Paris, 1977, p.78

2 See Léon Séché, *La Jeunesse dorée sous Louis-Philippe*, Mercure de France, Paris, 1910, pp.272–3

3 See, for instance, André Billy, *La Présidente et ses amis*, Flammarion, Paris, 195, pp.19–20 and Joanna Richardson, *The Courtesans*, p.108

4 Louis Mermaz, *Madame Sabatier. Apollonie au pays des libertins*, Editions Rencontre, Lausanne, 1967, p.11

5 Claude Pichois, *Baudelaire*, tr. Graham Robb, Vintage, London, 1991, p. 205

6 Joanna Richardson, *Baudelaire*, John Murray, London, 1994, p. 151

7 V.C.O. Gréard, *Meissonier, Part II: The Artist's Wisdom*, William Heinemann, London, 1897, pp.181–2

8 Théophile Gautier, *Correspondance générale*, Vol.3, ed. Claudine Lacoste-Veysseyre, Librairie Droz, Geneva/Paris, 1988, p.174

9 A. Estignard, *Clésinger: sa vie, ses œuvres*, Librairie H. Floury, Paris, 1900, pp.51–2

10 Quoted in Jean Ziegler, 'Alfred Mosselman et Madame Sabatier', *Bulletin du Bibliophile*, 1975, p.371

CHAPTER SIX

Salons

A LETTER FROM Théophile Gautier to Apollonie Sabatier, dated 19 October 1850 and supposedly posted from Rome, begins as follows:

> President of my heart,
>   This filthy letter, intended to replace Sunday's dirty talk, is long overdue, but that's the fault of the filth and not of the writer. Modesty reigns in these solemn but ancient places, and I'm very sorry I can't send you more than this shit-stained and not very spermatic mess . . .[1]

This long and rather tedious letter borders on the pornographic but is more scatological than anything else – full of bums, arses, cunts and haemorrhoids. The reader is treated to such things as a description of the author getting an enormous erection from the effect of the jolting of a poorly sprung carriage, and it ends in the vein in which it began:

> Present my most erectible indecencies to Mlle Bébé – heh! heh! – and my condolences to Fernand's spinal cord, myelitous to the third degree. If this document were not so frivolous and bum-wiperish [*torcheculatif*], I would ask you to present my affectionate greetings to Alfred, but I dare not pay homage against that wall.[2]

It is generally agreed that this is not the finest work of Gautier the poet, reviewer, belles-lettrist and apostle of 'art for art's sake'.

The reference to 'Sunday's dirty talk' suggests that this letter was intended to be read aloud at one of the regular Sunday evening gatherings which took place at the rue Frochot. Ever since Apollonie had taken up residence there, a group of literary, musical and artistic men – many of whom were already part of Alfred Mosselman's circle or were old acquaintances from the Hôtel Pimodan – had begun to form around her, and she soon developed the habit of inviting them to dinner on Sunday evenings. It was Alfred who proposed, after one particularly enjoyable Sunday, that these dinners should become a weekly event, and his offer was accepted with enthusiasm. The selected guests agreed to attend regularly, with the proviso that if another pressing engagement or reason for non-attendance arose, they could cancel by sending a note.

The list of regular guests at these Sunday evenings reads like a roll call of the intellectual élite of mid-nineteenth-century Paris. Théophile Gautier, famed for his bohemian taste in clothes which could encompass a rose-pink doublet and green slippers, was there from the start, as was Louis de Cormenin, son of the Viscount Louis-Marie de Cormenin who had been one of the most celebrated pamphleteers during the reign of Louis Philippe, writing under the pseudonym of 'Timon'. The twenty-three-year-old Louis had accompanied Gautier on his trip to Italy (during which he was supposed to have written the famous letter) and he had for some time been assisting him in the writing of his theatre criticism for *La Presse*. If Gautier had to leave before the end of a play, or if he missed it altogether, then Cormenin would write a draft review which would need little correction, as he was skilled at copying the style of his master. Cormenin married in 1854, after which his visits to the rue Frochot became less frequent. Other regular guests at the Sunday evenings included the painter Eugène Emmanuel Amaury-Duval, the sculptor Auguste Préault, Henri Monnier, the lithographer, writer and inventor of the satirical character Monsieur Joseph Prudhomme, Edouard Delessert (last encountered accompanying Marie Duplessis's coffin to Montmartre), Roger de Beauvoir, the critic Paul de Saint-Victor, the novelist, playwright and journalist

Edmond About, Charles de la Rounat, Fernand Boissard and Ernest Meissonier. Charles Jalabert (one of Apollonie's early portraitists) and the sculptor Christophe came because they were neighbours. Several of the regular guests were initially introduced by Gautier, such as the painter Ernest Hébert (who, with his olive skin, yearning eyes, long dark hair and bushy beard, was said to resemble his own paintings) and Julien Turgan, a doctor at the hospital of the Pitié, who would soon give up medicine for journalism. Gautier also introduced a young composer from Marseilles called Ernest Reyer, who had just arrived in Paris after a long stay in Algeria. Reyer was strongly influenced by Hector Berlioz, whom he succeeded as music critic of the *Journal des débats*. He was normally the only pianist present and he would generally sit down at the piano to accompany his hostess in song, or to play some of his own, or others', compositions. Along with Meissonier and Hébert, Reyer provided a link between Apollonie's salon and the world of official and academic art, of honours and worldly recognition.

Maxime Du Camp, a childhood friend of Louis de Cormenin who had introduced him to Gautier in January 1848, returned to Paris on 3 May 1851 from a tour of Egypt, Palestine, Greece and Italy in the company of Gustave Flaubert. Flaubert himself stayed on for a while in Italy, having arranged to meet his mother in Rome. On Du Camp's return, he was taken by Gautier and Cormenin to the rue Frochot where he was immediately adopted as one of the inner circle. From then on a place was always laid for him on Sunday, on Apollonie's left. He had a reputation as a womaniser who had gone through a string of affairs. If he made any advances to Apollonie, she was skilled enough to turn them down without giving offence. Du Camp was one of the best informed of Apollonie's guests, in terms of both literary and worldly matters. He and she were exact contemporaries (his date of birth was 8 February 1822) and they delighted in the fact that he had been born on St Apollonie's day. Shortly after he joined Apollonie's circle he was followed by his close friend Frédéric Fovard, a lawyer, who soon found himself taking on the legal business of various members of the group.

Gustave Flaubert was a more irregular guest than many of the others, because he spent much of his time writing at his family home of Croisset, about seven miles from Rouen. But from 1855 he developed the habit of living in Paris for six months at a time, renting an apartment at 42 boulevard du Temple. He was always warmly received at Apollonie's dinner table and given an open invitation to attend. A very hard and slow worker who refused most distractions, he nevertheless rarely missed a Sunday evening at the rue Frochot when he was in Paris. And whenever he was in attendance he was likely to be accompanied by his acolyte, the poet Louis Bouilhet.

The novelist and dramatist Ernest Feydeau had to angle for an invitation, though subsequently he became a regular guest. As he confesses himself: 'I found my friends were being very slow to introduce me to Madame S . . ., so I decided to introduce myself, and was no less well received for that.'[3] In addition to the regular guests, for whom the table would be laid in advance, there were also occasional guests brought by one of the regulars. Such visitors included Eugène Delacroix and Paul Joseph Chenavard, an artist from Lyons, who was particularly welcome for his outstanding skills as a conversationalist. Another occasional guest was Gérard de Nerval, who was brought by Gautier (the two men had been fellow students at the Lycée Charlemagne) in between two periods in a mental hospital. (De Nerval committed suicide in January 1855, an upsetting event for many of Apollonie's friends.) The distinguished critic and writer Charles Augustin Sainte-Beuve, known to enjoy good food, was also sometimes in attendance. And from time to time Gautier would bring people who happened to be passing through Paris, such as the Cuban singer Maria Martinez.

Women were greatly outnumbered by men. The singer Ernesta Grisi, Gautier's long-term companion and the mother of his two daughters, would sometimes accompany him (she was a good friend of Apollonie's in her own right). The courtesan Alice Ozy was occasionally present, though she and Apollonie tended to keep some distance between themselves. An undated letter from Alice to Théophile Gautier reads:

> Have I told you that I'm giving a little soirée on Sunday 10th? and that I'm counting *on you*. You'll be coming from Mme Sabatier's. I can't invite her again as she's already turned me down but if she would like to come with you she'll be very welcome. The 10th without fail.[4]

Alice had first made the acquaintance of Gautier during the time of her liaison with Edouard de Perrégaux (who had abruptly left her for Marie Duplessis); at one period she had even had a brief liaison with Gautier as well.

Apollonie's sister Adèle, or Bébé, who had followed her sister's example in changing her surname to Sabatier, was quite often present on a Sunday evening. In 1848, at the age of only sixteen, Bébé became the mistress of Fernand Boissard, a development which initially came about through his need for consolation after his previous mistress, Maryx, had left him for a Danish diplomat. In April 1849 she and Boissard moved into a house together near the rue Frochot, and in December Bébé gave birth, at her sister's house, to a daughter, Fernande Ernesta Jeanne Sabatier (known as Jeanne). Boissard, contrary to the expectations of all their friends, refused to acknowledge the child as his, though at Ernest Meissonier's insistence he did agree to make some financial provision for her. Apollonie and Meissonier acted as godparents at the baptism at Notre Dame de Lorette on 12 February 1850. Bébé spent the next two years still hoping to marry Boissard, who kept stringing her along despite the fact that he was already becoming involved with a young woman called Edwina Broutta. Edwina was the same age as Bébé but belonged to a different world. She came from a wealthy family and was a musician, both qualities which appealed to Fernand Boissard who proposed to her in February 1852. The future looked uncertain for Bébé, who for the next few years continued to live in the shadow of her elder sister.

Another occasional visitor was Elisa de Lucenay, who would be a lifelong friend of Apollonie's, noted for smoking and for wearing a large number of bracelets. Elisa Nieri (sometimes spelt Gnerri or Gnierri), a friend of the Italian revolutionary *Carbonari* and admirer of Orsini (an Italian patriot who attempted to assassinate Napoleon III, whom he saw as an obstacle to revolution, outside the Opéra on 14 January 1858), was sometimes in attendance; a friend also of La Païva's, she and Apollonie used to go to the theatre together on occasion. Apollonie's closest female friend was Emma Meissonier, but she preferred to visit when Apollonie was alone. They corresponded incessantly about clothes and recipes, exchanged confidences and gossiped about their acquaintances. There were plenty of times when Apollonie was the only woman present on a Sunday evening, surrounded by a crowd of admiring men. Alfred Mosselman was nearly always in attendance, his infrequent absences occasioned by business trips.

When Mosselman inaugurated the Sunday evenings as a regular weekly event, the gathering decided to elect a 'President'; they chose Henri Monnier, as the most senior man present. Gautier suggested that they also needed a female President, and so 'La Présidente' became Apollonie's title and it was used frequently by the guests. (Her intimate friends, including Mosselman, also knew her as Lili or Lilette.) Monnier, however, was never known as 'Le Président'. The other regular guests, as well as certain other literary figures about whom they talked but who never made an appearance at the rue Frochot, also received nicknames over the course of time. Thus Victor Hugo was always referred to as *'le père Hugo'*, Sainte-Beuve was known as *'l'oncle Beuve'*, while Flaubert went by the title of *'le sire de Vaufrilard'*. Bouilhet was known as 'Monseigneur', because of his bishop-like paunch and dignified bearing. And Mosselman was referred to among the group as 'Mac-Ha-Rouilh'. Feydeau, who supplies this list of nicknames in his book about Gautier, states that no one had any idea why Mosselman was given this strange-sounding name, but it is noticeably similar to the word *'maquereau'* which was used to denote a *maquignon* or trader of women and in modern parlance is equivalent to 'pimp'. This word was sometimes abbreviated to '*mac*', '*macque*', '*maca*', or '*macchoux*'. The feminine version, '*maquerelle*', referred to a woman who recruited prostitutes from such places as hospitals and railway stations; it is a term used in this way by Parent-Duchâtelet. Thus in awarding this particular nickname to Alfred Mosselman, the habitués of the rue Frochot were making a rather more than tacit allusion to his status as Apollonie's purchaser.

Apollonie soon proved her ability to provide a congenial atmosphere for her guests where they could relax, say what they thought, and enjoy the company of a woman who did not expect to be treated with deference merely on account of her sex. Looking back on his life, Ernest Meissonier paid eloquent tribute to her gifts as an intelligent and sensitive hostess:

> She had a supreme talent for attracting famous men about her, and for organising a salon, in which it was always a pleasure to find one's self. Refined, subtle and genial, smiling and intelligent, admirably balanced, excelling in all she undertook, she adored light, gaiety, sunshine. They were part of herself, indeed. For a weary, busy man it was an exquisite rest and refreshment to find her always the same, always equable, a true refuge from the cares of life, which she gracefully banished for you.[5]

Every Sunday this almost exclusively male group would come to dinner at six o'clock and stay on into the evening, these evenings becoming a cherished weekly ritual. According to Pierre de Lano, Apollonie shared this gift for putting men at their ease with other women of the period: 'The woman of the Second Empire, while inspiring violent desire, allowed Don Juan to relax in her presence. She accorded him the liberty of his brains – if I can put it that way – and he would forget himself, through her and for her, in all the brilliance of his speech, if he was witty, in all the simple charm of conversation, if he was just a chatterer.'[6] Feydeau recorded that Madame Sabatier showed no particular preference for any of her guests, treating them all the same and so dispelling any sense of rivalry.[7] (François Porché's comment on this apparent lack of preference is that each man could interpret her rather mocking laugh as being directed at one of the others.[8]) Food and drink were always excellent *chez* La Présidente, who herself had a zest for eating and drinking. Sunday had been chosen as this was generally the day for seeing friends in Paris; the Goncourt brothers received on Sunday morning, Flaubert and Du Camp were also 'at home' during the day – in fact, many guests would come on from Du Camp's *hôtel* in the rue du Rocher to the rue Frochot.

Many of the guests were already well acquainted with one another, so that there was little need for introductions and breaking of ice. Gautier and Cormenin worked together, Bouilhet could usually be found anywhere that Flaubert went, Maxime Du Camp knew everybody. The *Revue de Paris*, a journal inaugurated in 1850 by Gautier, Du Camp, Arsène Houssaye and Cormenin, could be seen as having been born in the rue Frochot, as it was here that these four first discussed the idea.

Sometimes the guests would play charades, a pastime very much in vogue. At other times they might read to one another. One evening a fancy dress party was held. Théophile Gautier came dressed as a Turk, Gustave Flaubert as a Red Indian with a kitchen utensil for a tomahawk, Maxime Du Camp as a Hindu, Louis Bouilhet as a Chinese-speaking cleric in a cassock, and Ernest Reyer as a chimpanzee. Another memorable evening was 27 March 1859, when Gautier returned from a long visit to Russia. He arrived back in Paris that evening and rushed straight to the rue Frochot without even going home first to change, startling and delighting the other guests by his sudden and unexpected appearance in a fur hat and voluminous overcoat just as they were sitting down to their soup. (Feydeau provides the added detail that it was a macaroni consommé, sprinkled with parmesan.)[9] More often than not, the Sunday evenings were passed in discussion, smoking, drinking and drawing. The artist Gustave Ricard sketched La Présidente among her guests, and Gautier drew her profile in pastel. She had an

Official portrait of the Emperor Napoleon III by Franz Xavier Winterhalter.
Napoleon III ruled France from 1852 to 1870; his rise and fall was mirrored
in the lives of the ostentatious courtesans who flourished during his reign.

Miniature of Marie Duplessis. Romain Vienne described how 'Her oval face with its regular features, slightly pale and melancholy when calm and in repose, would suddenly come to life at the sound of a friendly voice or a warm and sincere word.'

Watercolour of Marie Duplessis at the theatre, by Camille Roqueplan. Marie loved the theatre, and was regularly to be seen in her box at a first night.

Photograph of Alexandre Dumas *fils* by Gaspard Félix Tournachon, known as Nadar. Alexandre, who was one of Marie's *amants de cœur*, immortalised her in his novel and play *La Dame aux camélias*.

Portrait of the pianist and composer Franz Liszt by Henri Lehmann.
Marie Duplessis developed a grand passion for Liszt, and dreamt of
running away with him but nothing came of the relationship.

Watercolour of Apollonie Sabatier by Vincent Vidal. Before becoming the
mistress of Alfred Mosselman, Apollonie spent some of her time working as
an artists' model, and always enjoyed the company of artists and writers.

L'Atelier du peintre (The Artist's Studio) by Gustave Courbet.
Apollonie is shown looking on (wearing a shawl).

The Recital by Ernest Meissonier. Apollonie appeared repeatedly in the paintings
of Meissonier, a life-long friend. Here she is shown standing on the right.

Above: Photograph of the poet Charles Baudelaire
by Nadar. The poet's tortured relationship with
Apollonie Sabatier inspired several of the poems
in his major work *Les Fleurs du mal*.

Right: *Polichinelle* (Mr Punch) by Ernest Meissonier.
Originally painted on a door panel in Apollonie's
apartment in the rue Frochot, this little figure seems
to encapsulate the lascivious way in which so
many men gazed on 'La Présidente'.

Photograph of the Duke de Morny by Eugène Disdéri. Auguste de Morny, one
of the many conquests of Cora Pearl, was the Emperor's illegitimate half-brother
and a central figure in the political, business and cultural life of the Second Empire.

Portrait of Napoleon Joseph Charles Paul Bonaparte, known as Prince Napoleon, by Hippolyte Flandrin. Prince Napoleon, cousin of the Emperor, was another of Cora Pearl's significant conquests. Cora described him as 'an angel to those who pleased him ... demon, roué, madman, unhesitating insulter towards others.'

album which she would pass around for people to write or draw whatever they liked in it.

Ricard, whom Apollonie had first met at the Hôtel Pimodan, also produced a more serious portrait of her entitled *La Dame au petit chien* (The Lady with the Little Dog). Apollonie was very fond of this portrait, in which she is depicted wearing a black velvet Venetian dress with cherry-coloured satin sleeves. The little dog on her lap was brought back for her from Italy by Alfred Tattet, a friend of two other Alfreds – Mosselman and de Musset. Just as *La Femme piquée* made Clésinger's reputation, so *La Dame au petit chien*, which was exhibited at the Salon of 1850, marked a turning point in Ricard's career. He subsequently became one of the most highly regarded portraitists of his time. Apollonie hung this portrait in the middle of a panel in her drawing room.

Other works of art in Apollonie's apartment included another portrait of herself, this time by Meissonier, a pastel drawing by Rosalba, a landscape with animals by Karel Du Jardin, two small Franck *le jeunes*, a copy of a portrait of Philippe IV by Velasquez, a copy of a portrait of a man by Van Dyck (both copies having been made by Wagrez *père*), a watercolour, an etching and two sketches by Meissonier, a study of a red-haired girl by Ricard, a group of people walking in the Tuileries gardens drawn in two colours of crayon by Célestin Nanteuil, a landscape at Fontainebleau by Boissard, nymphs by Camille Fontallard and dogs by Hayrault. On a white plinth stood the bust that Clésinger had made of her, and beneath the portrait of her by Ricard stood a violetwood piano, chosen at Erard's by Ernest Reyer. But what Apollonie prized above all was a piece of Sèvres porcelain, a biscuit figure by Falconet, of a seated woman entitled *Vénus adolescente et pudique*.

On a door panel in Apollonie's boudoir Meissonier had painted a *Polichinelle* (Mr Punch), a favourite motif of his (he painted a whole series of them on the staircase of his own house at Poissy). The expression on the face of this little figure – cheerfully lascivious, with a wicked glint in his eye as he views the inhabitant of the boudoir disrobing – is in keeping with the way most of the men around Apollonie gazed on her, at least in their imagination and in recollection of the naked orgasmic body of *La Femme piquée*. It also fitted in well with the bawdy talk for which Apollonie's salon was famous. It was nearly all talk, and there is no evidence that talk led to action. The men who gathered in the rue Frochot seemed to experience a *frisson* at being able to 'talk dirty' in the presence of a woman who would neither pretend to be shocked nor make any demands on them, who – unlike their wives or their potential wives, for several of them were married while others would eventually become so – had stepped over the borders of respectability and into the *demi-monde*, and yet retained an aura of unavailability by virtue of belonging to Alfred Mosselman, whose identity as her possessor was acknowledged in his nickname of Mac-Ha-Rouilh. His presence also sanctioned the lewd talk, for if he did not object to it going on in the presence of his mistress, how could she? It could lead nowhere: there is no suggestion that Apollonie had sexual relations with her guests or that she was even tempted to do so – she seemed genuinely fond of Alfred and content to be his mistress. And so the salon at the rue Frochot provided an outlet for a frankly adolescent streak in many of the literary and artistic men who met there each week. Gautier expresses the need for such an outlet in an undated letter to Apollonie in which he laments: 'I have a huge sack of filth to empty; I haven't said anything indecent for three weeks.'[10] This is not to say that some of the men did not fantasise about what might happen if Alfred Mosselman were removed from the scene; Gautier clearly had a soft spot for Apollonie, as did Gustave Flaubert, and Julien Turgan once revealed his feelings in a letter to Ernesta Grisi: 'In the event of my death, be so good as to tell La Présidente that I would have loved her if there had been a way. That won't compromise her much, and it will make me happy. Don't talk about it until I'm well and truly rotting in a nice cemetery.'[11]

It is likely that on at least one occasion the evening's entertainment consisted of a reading of Gautier's scatalogical 'Lettre à la Présidente' alluded to at the beginning of this chapter. Such readings were not confined to the rue Frochot; the Goncourt brothers make mention in their Journal of an evening in December 1857 when Paul de Saint-Victor read the letter to a group of men including Henry Murger, Emile Augier, the journalist Gustave Claudin, the composer Victor Massé and the Goncourts themselves. This was the first time that the brothers had heard the letter, though they had previously known of its existence. Though it was clearly intended to be read aloud in this way and its humour is very male, the fact it was ostensibly addressed to a woman, and a woman who was sometimes present when it was read aloud, provided an extra thrill for the men who listened to it so avidly. In a way it was the literary equivalent of Clésinger's sculpture; though of far less artistic value, it too presented Apollonie as a sexual, though essentially passive, being, delivering up an image of her being sexually pleasured in public.

When Théo, as Gautier was known by his friends, was not flirting or indulging his delight in smut, his dealings with Apollonie generally concerned tickets to concerts and plays. As a prolific critic he was very useful to his friends as a dispenser of free tickets; he also found that good company could relieve the tedium of having yet another event to review. The first known letter from Théo to Apollonie is dated 4 February 1849:

Dear Présidente
　I'm in despair. I'm dining at Ronconi's, having been invited yesterday; Ernesta has a concert at the Winter Gardens and, if it isn't too cold, I'll send her to you and then come and collect her in the evening, which will allow me to contemplate your countless delights. Don't expect anyone after half past six. I don't know what time the music will finish.
Yours ever
Théophile Gautier[12]

In a letter of Thursday, 15 March 1849 Théo invited Apollonie to accompany him that evening to a masked fancy dress ball at the

Winter Gardens to celebrate Mi-Carême (mid-Lent, when the rigours of these weeks could be briefly abandoned in a return to a carnival atmosphere). *La Presse* advertised this ball as follows:

> The piquant programme of this carnival night promises a masked ball such as has not been seen for a long time in Paris. There will be polkas of flowers and birds, followed by burlesque quadrilles of animals and fish, by our best dancers. At two o'clock, the quadrille from *Hell*, with devilry and general illumination of the gardens.[13]

Théo rarely gave much notice of his invitations, usually offering a ticket to something on the day on which it was taking place. On Sunday, 15 April 1849 he offered Apollonie a ticket for a concert by Berlioz that evening: 'I'll come to collect you so that your presence will lighten up this musical entertainment for me.'[14] On 8 October he invited her to share a box with him and Ernesta Grisi to see 'la Zélie' dance; 'la Zélie' may possibly have been Ernesta's older sister, Carlotta, to whom Théo was sentimentally attached for the whole of his life.

A kind of low-level bawdiness pervades most of Théo's letters to Apollonie; it became so habitual that it really cannot be taken to mean very much – it was just a style of writing, as in the following short note:

> My dear Lili,
>   Don't forget that you're grazing in my dump this Wednesday with Mlle Virginie Huet. The casseroles are steaming and the macaroni is turning horny, like virile members under the grill. If Alfred is with you, bring him too and that's final.[15]

At other times he is more explicit, as in this letter of 2 June 1854 which refers to his failure to secure Apollonie a seat for the first performance of his ballet *Gemma*: 'You know I adore you and I'm ready, like a large King Charles' spaniel, to lick between your fingers and your buttocks, and your gusset. I needn't mention the clitoris, that goes without saying and is understood.'[16] But even this is not intended as an actual proposition; the sex is all on paper. Some of the letters, however, contain a hint that, if Apollonie were not already so decidedly 'taken', Théo might have ventured on a physical relationship with her:

> My dear Présidente
>   I'm sending you this little pastel daub which would be prettier if your image showed through it, but you know it has passed to the feather duster, which is better for the mahogany than for the picture. Try to find a place for it among your knick-knacks, and believe me your most devoted friend (for want of anything better).[17]

And often, despite all the bawdy talk, a genuine concern and affection shines through in even the briefest of notes, as in the following one of 10 December 1854, on the occasion of a performance of Berlioz's *L'Enfance du Christ*:

> My dear Présidente,
>   I know you want to hear Berlioz's music: here's a numbered seat in the stalls. Ernesta has the other and will make her own way to the salle Herz.
>   Much love; rejoice your ears as you rejoice my eyes.[18]

Théo's erotic fantasies became a reality, at least briefly, with Bébé, who never seems to have shared her sister's inaccessibility. As he put it, in a note accompanying tickets for a box at the Théâtre Français: 'Let Bébé know; you are my love, she is my vice, and I will be happy to dream a winter night's Dream between your two charming realities.'[19] Théo and Bébé had a short-lived affair in the autumn of 1853, at a time when they both needed cheering up.

It is noticeable that, though from about 1850 Théo invariably addresses Apollonie as '*tu*' in his letters to her, she never deviates from calling him '*vous*' in the surviving letters from her. She did not appear to object to his use of '*tu*', but neither did she find it appropriate to respond in kind. Gautier was known to address almost everyone as '*tu*'; such familiarity was one of his hallmarks. One might have expected Apollonie to respond as familiarly to such a long-standing and dear friend, but she maintains a respectful distance, at least in her correspondence, with Théo as with others of her male acquaintance. Her great-great-nephew Thierry Savatier stresses how much of an equal Apollonie was among the men of her circle – we might almost say she was 'one of the boys'; but such deference on her part makes one wonder whether she was exercising quite as much choice in her relationships and in the manner in which they were conducted to be consistent with such a viewpoint. She also retained a certain timidity, despite all her social contacts, and had a tendency to blush and stammer on meeting a friend unexpectedly.[20]

In a letter she wrote to Théo some time during the first half of 1852 Apollonie strikes a particularly deferential tone, and is apologetic over some request she had previously made which he had not been able to fulfil. This letter also conveys a flavour of her need for distraction; not every day was Sunday, and for much of the rest of the week Alfred Mosselman had either to be at work or with his family. There is something of the caged bird in Apollonie's situation, as she waits to be visited by Alfred, invited to the theatre by Théo (whose approval she requires before going to visit the singer Maria Martinez, in case this is an inappropriate thing for a *demi-mondaine* to do), or taken out by one of her circle.

> My dear Théo, I'm going about it a bit better this time. Forgive me for having troubled you over something which I should have seen was impossible. It won't happen again. So if you can let me have anything at all for the show this evening, I'll be most grateful. I must admit that I get very bored in the evenings, and it would be more than your life's worth to see me turning into a fish, which is bound to happen very soon because I yawn hugely until bed-time. Such is my sad situation, don't put your slave to any bother, make mine run along instead and give her Mme

Martinez's address. I want to pay her a visit, but only if you think that wouldn't be indiscreet.

Clara told me that you came by the other evening. I'm really cross not to have been here, but I was dressed up and wanted to make the most of my outfit. If I don't see you before, I'll see you on Thursday, and do bring la Mariquita. We'll dine together. Remember me to Ernesta when you write to her.

Fondest regards

La Présidente[21]

The following extract from a letter by Théo to Ernesta Grisi, dated 7 May 1852, suggests that the relationship between Apollonie and Alfred Mosselman was not always easy and that Apollonie was as ready to flirt as men were willing to seduce her with words; it also mentions Madame Herz (despite the fact that Blanche was by now the Marchioness de Païva):

> Bébé has a *monsieur* who has furnished an apartment for her at 27, rue d'Aumale . . . and who gives her enough money; the morganatic marriage was celebrated about a fortnight ago; the P[résidente] is perhaps a little jealous of her sister's success but she's putting a brave face on it and continues to show a lot of cleavage and to cavort about on sofas. Besides she is always charming to me and the best person in the world . . . Mosselman appears to have had it up to the ears with the Présidente, and it is even rumoured that he has another mistress. Alice [Ozy] is playing the role of the page in *La Vie de Bohème* and Madame Herz is putting on white powder from the love of pastel shades . . .[22]

The correspondence of Blanche de Païva with Gautier, who also knew him as 'dear Théo', could not be more different in tone from that of Apollonie. Though her notes also largely concern arrangements about theatre tickets, they contain no hint of deference (and she is often in a position to offer him a ticket, rather than always being a suppliant like most of his friends). In his letters to her, unusually for him, he invariably addresses her as '*vous*'. The idea of indulging in any 'dirty talk' with her would be unthinkable.

They were friends long before she became 'La Païva', many of her notes to him being signed 'Blanche Herz'. One of the few sympathetic comments made about Blanche by her contemporaries is contained in the reminiscences of Gautier's mistress Maria Mattei, preserved in the Collection Spoelberch de Lovenjoul at the Bibliothèque de l'Institut in Paris:

> On the death of his mother whom he adored, T.G. was deeply upset. He was always grateful to Madame de Païva who used to arrive on horseback to collect him and would seek to distract him by riding with him in the Bois de Boulogne. She wouldn't say a word to him but in this way helped pull him out of his sorrow by forcing him to come out of himself without noticing. This delicate way of handling his grief had greatly touched him.[23]

Théo's mother died on 26 March 1848. Though it is difficult to work out quite how this ties in with Blanche's sojourn in London around this time (for which, however, we have no precise dates), there is certainly the ring of truth about this account; Blanche was known to be an able horsewoman and this practical, non-sentimental way of handling grief and caring for her friend seems in character. Neither would there have been any reason for Maria Mattei to invent such a sympathetic anecdote about another woman's relationship with her former lover. There in the friendship Blanche enjoyed with Théo a sense of equality entirely absent from his relationship with Apollonie (and this had nothing to do with their relative ages as Blanche was only three years older than Apollonie and pretended in later life to be younger; Théo himself had been born in 1811 and was thus eight years older than Blanche and eleven years older than Apollonie). Blanche trusted Théo, as is clear from a letter she wrote to him on 9 December 1850:

Could you, my dear Théo, do me the service of furnishing yourself with *someone or other* for tomorrow Tuesday at three o'clock. I will come and collect you and take you to the notary Maître Noël to be my witness to the deed that you know about.

You will easily understand why, apart from you my true friend, I prefer to have in my confidence someone who knows me little if at all.[24]

This is a very tantalising note, with its mysterious mention of 'the deed that you know about' and which Blanche clearly did not wish anyone else to know about. Maître Noël was the same notary before whom the marriage contract with Païva had been signed; possibly 'the deed' related to dealings with Païva, or it may have concerned her son by Villoing, whose existence this courtesan with her cachet of exclusivity would indeed have wanted to keep secret.

Some of Blanche's notes to Théo are inviting him to call:

Thursday morning

My dear Théo,

I'm in need of a good gossip for a few hours, in other words you would give me great pleasure by coming to see me

B. Herz

PS. I'll be in all day[25]

and

Monday morning

How are you, my dear Théo, are you able to come out and see me if not I warn you I'm determined to break into your house so choose

Sincerely yours
B. Herz[26]

and, from the period after her second marriage:

My dear Théo,

If you've nothing important to do, I'd be very pleased if you were to come and have dinner with me today of course it wouldn't prevent your doing something else with your evening

Bl. de Païva[27]

Blanche did not trouble herself overmuch about punctuation.

She also established regular soirées, and several of Apollonie's guests (including, of course, Gautier) were hers too. But the characters of these two salons were very different. Blanche held two evenings each week: on Fridays there would be only ten guests, on Sundays twenty. Men such as Paul de Saint-Victor, Arsène Houssaye, Augustin de Sainte-Beuve, Edmond About and Théo himself would have to decide which hostess to grace with their presence on a Sunday evening, or possibly they would manage to dine in one place and join the after-dinner conversation in the other.

In 1848 Paul de Saint-Victor had been secretary to the poet and politician Alphonse de Lamartine and had subsequently become a journalist. Charming and very handsome, he was passionate about art and loved to discuss philosophical questions. A great traveller, when in Paris he lived at 49 rue de Grenelle in a ground-floor apartment full of art objects, paintings and ornaments, all mixed up in wonderful disarray. He and Blanche were very dissimilar but got on very well, becoming great friends and confidants. Arsène Houssaye, who turns up in most social gatherings and at most artistic events of the period, was appointed in 1849 as general administrator of the Comédie Française, a post he held for seven years. In 1875 he became director of the Théâtre Lyrique. He was, in turn and sometimes concurrently, a novelist, poet, non-fiction writer, playwright and historian, excelling at none of these things. The balls and fancy dress parties he gave at his *hôtel* were particularly spectacular. Among La Païva's regular guests were also Léon Gozlan, a brilliant chronicler who had been Balzac's secretary, and Jules Lecomte, who could be relied upon to know everything about what was what and who was who in Paris. Emile de Girardin was also a frequent presence, keeping Blanche up to date in political matters and enlivening the dinners with a steady stream of anecdotes.

La Païva was an exacting hostess who expected stimulating conversation from her guests. Houssaye reports that her friends were given *carte blanche* to bring other guests to her dinners, but that people incapable of talking entertainingly would not be invited a second time.[28] In common with Madame Sabatier's salon, as indeed with every other salon of the period, the vast majority of the guests were male. Only one woman was regularly invited to La Païva's soirées, and that was Roger de Beauvoir's wife, Aimée, formerly Mademoiselle Doze of the Comédie Française.

The food and wine Blanche provided were of the best; never, Houssaye declares, were artists and men of letters more royally fêted.[29] Théo was her chief adviser on whom to invite and her chief arbiter on questions of style. Two other regular guests were a Monsieur de Reims, who was the emissary in France of the Duke d'Aumale and who acted as Blanche's financial adviser, and Dumont de Montcel, a connoisseur of good food and wine who served as her 'taster'. Théo was also gifted with a prodigious appetite and a strong appreciation of wine. He was known for drinking only water during a meal, leaving all the wine until he had finished eating, when he would sample every label on offer, becoming ever more voluble. There are some reports that, despite Théo's best efforts, conversation could become stilted at La Païva's – partly because of the high standards she demanded, though possibly also because the guests were at times more interested in eating and drinking than in talking. Neither were the topics chosen for conversation consistently high-minded; everyone enjoyed discussing their minor ailments, as well as indulging in gloomy prognoses about the future. Eugène Delacroix records that he attended one of La Païva's soirées on 2 May 1855. He claims not to have enjoyed himself very much, finding both the company and the conversation 'useless' and 'insipid' and the atmosphere 'pest-laden'.[30]

Despite all La Païva's efforts at artistic and intellectual sophistication, and despite La Présidente's natural abilities as a hostess and the quality of the guests that both these women invited, in a sense neither was more than a superior *femme à partie*, the sort of kept woman for whom, according to Parent-Duchâtelet, 'beauty alone was not enough; they had to have in addition the graces and charms of a cultivated mind. In general, to be admitted *chez elles*, a man would have to be introduced by one of the regular visitors to their gatherings.'[31] Several of the men who frequented the salons of La Présidente and La Païva were also regularly received by a hostess of a rather different order, at least in worldly terms: her Imperial Highness (as she was styled when her cousin Louis Napoleon became Emperor in 1852) the Princess Mathilde.

In 1840, at the age of twenty, Laetitia Wilhelmina Mathilde Bonaparte had been married off to the rich, but dissolute and sadistic, Russian Count Anatole Nikolayevich Demidov. It was a disastrous marriage which was ended by separation in December 1845. As Demidov's wife, however, Mathilde was able to settle in the France of Louis Philippe despite the law banning all Bonapartes, and to live there comfortably after the separation, on an annual allowance of two hundred thousand roubles secured for her by the Tsar. She never saw her husband again. An ardent Bonapartist, Mathilde worked for Louis Napoleon's political success before his election as President in December 1848, and from 1849 until his marriage to Eugénie de Montijo in January 1853 she served as his hostess at the Elysée and Tuileries palaces. On the restoration of the Empire she received an additional income of two hundred thousand francs per year (later increased to five hundred thousand), with which she purchased her country estate of Saint Gratien, near Lake d'Enghien, an hour's journey from Paris. Her personal life was not so very far removed from that of a *demi-mondaine* – except for the crucial differences that during her long-term liaison with the married Count Emilien de Nieuwerkerke she never had to ask him for money and her imperial status ensured her respectability and her place in high society. Nieuwerkerke was a sculptor who, under Mathilde's aegis, became Director of Museums and eventually Superintendent of Fine Arts.

Princess Mathilde was the most distinguished hostess of Second

Empire Paris, giving not only dinners and receptions but fancy dress balls and theatrical soirées. She also held a special celebration every year to mark the Emperor's birthday. L. de Hegermann-Lindencrone wrote in a letter of 1865: 'The Princesse Mathilde receives every Sunday evening. Her salons are always crowded, and are what one might call cosmopolitan. In fact, it is the only salon in Paris where one can meet all nationalities. There are diplomats, royalties, imperialists, strangers of importance passing through Paris, and especially all the celebrated artists.'[32] Princess Caroline Murat is fulsome in the praise of her relative, and describes how she divided up her guests over various evenings:

> Dignified as Imperial Highness, the niece of two emperors, and the cousin of a third, she had more illustrious family connections than the Emperor himself, and she had the ambition and the faculty to rule. She must have been uncommonly beautiful in her young womanhood; she was still very handsome when I saw her first, and she always remained a woman of distinguished presence. Unquestionably she was the most cultured and talented of all the Bonapartes; and she was probably one of the most cultured women in France during her time. Her salon was a court in itself. Begun during the reign of Louis Philippe, it had no equal in the nineteenth century for length of ascendancy. For fifty years it was an important institution, the home and centre of Parisian intellect stamped with her own strongly-marked individuality. Her great wealth enabled her to extend unlimited hospitality, and to make her home the meeting-place of the choice spirits of the day . . .[33]

Although she was at home to her friends every evening, her companions differed in type with the days of the week. Sundays she reserved for current invitations and new introductions. Tuesdays were set aside for the reception of official personages, and Wednesdays, for her chosen intimates who were always exclusively artists. The Sunday soirées at the Rue de Courcelles were especially popular, attended by crowds of distinguished men and women, whose names remain familiar to a later generation.[34]

One of the Princess's most regular guests was Maxime Du Camp, who seems to have enjoyed praising La Présidente *chez* La Princesse and reporting back on La Princesse to La Présidente. Other men known to frequent both the *haut monde* and the *demi-monde* in this way – for men, unlike women, could maintain an easy traffic between the two worlds (though the Princess was not particularly delighted when her guests were prepared to forfeit time they could have spent with her by visiting courtesans and kept women) – included Edmond About, Emile Augier, Gustave Flaubert, the painter Jean-Léon Gérôme, Emile de Girardin, the Goncourt brothers, Charles Augustin Sainte-Beuve (who in the 1860s was considered by Princess Mathilde her literary adviser and an intimate friend), the historian, philosopher and critic Hippolyte Taine – and, of course, the ubiquitous Théo.

---

1 Jean-Jacques Pauvert, *L'Erotisme Second Empire*, Carrère, Paris, 1985, p.115

2 Ibid., p.132

3 Ernest Feydeau, *Théophile Gautier: souvenirs intimes*, E. Plon, Paris, 1874, pp.154–5

4 Théophile Gautier, *Correspondance générale*, Vol.12, 2000, p.164

5 V.C.O. Gréard, *Meissonier, Part II: The Artist's Wisdom*, p.219

6 Pierre de Lano, *L'Amour à Paris sous le Second Empire*, H. Simonis Empis, Paris, 1896, p.8

7 Ernest Feydeau, *Théophile Gautier*, p.167

8 François Porché, *Baudelaire et la Présidente*, Gallimard, Paris, 1959, p.140

9 Ernest Feydeau, *Théophile Gautier*, p.195

10 Théophile Gautier, *Correspondance générale*, Vol.6, 1991, p.89

11 Quoted in Jean Ziegler, *Gautier-Baudelaire: un carré de Dames*, p.88

12 Théophile Gautier, *Correspondance générale*, Vol.4, 1989, pp.9–10

13 Quoted in Jean-Jacques Pauvert, *L'Erotisme Second Empire*, p.103

14 Théophile Gautier, *Correspondance générale*, Vol.4, p.105

15 Ibid., Vol.12, p.172

16 Ibid., Vol.6, p.36

17 Ibid., Vol.12, p.207

18 Ibid., Vol.6, p.97

19 Ibid., p.172

20 See André Billy, *La Présidente et ses amis*, p.47

21 Théophile Gautier, *Correspondance générale*, Vol.5, 1991, p.61

22 Quoted in Jean Ziegler, *Gautier-Baudelaire: un carré de Dames*, pp.100–2

23 Théophile Gautier, *Correspondance générale*, Vol.4, p.507

24 Ibid., p.272

25 Ibid., p.352

26 Ibid., p.353

27 Ibid., Vol.12, p.165

28 Arsene Houssaye, *Les Confessions. Souvenirs d'un demi-siècle 1830–1880*, Vol.5, E. Dentu, Paris, 1891, pp.336 and 338

29 Ibid., p.336

30 *The Journal of Eugène Delacroix*, tr. Walter Pach, Grove Press, New York, 1961, p.461

31 A.J.B. Parent-Duchâtelet, *De la Prostitution dans la ville de Paris*, p.175

32 L. de Hegermann-Lindencrone, *In the Courts of Memory 1858–1875 from Contemporary Letters*, Harper & Brothers, New York and London, 1912, p.68

33 Princess Caroline Murat, *My Memoirs*, Eveleigh Nash, London, 1910, pp.70–1

34 Ibid., p.74

CHAPTER SEVEN

Les Fleurs du mal

Duración the fourteen or so years of Apollonie Sabatier's
liaison with Alfred Mosselman, only one man seems to have
seriously disturbed her equilibrium and aroused in her the desire for
more than a passing flirtation or 'cavorting on the sofa'. That man was
the poet Charles Baudelaire. They had first encountered one another
in the early 1840s when Baudelaire was living at the Hôtel Pimodan,
and from 1851 he had been a regular guest at the Sunday soirées in the
rue Frochot, having been brought there, like so many others, by
Théophile Gautier.

Over the next few years Baudelaire, who was a year older than
Madame Sabatier, wrote a series of poems inspired by her and sent
them to her, one by one, often with a note or letter, always in
disguised, cramped handwriting and anonymously. The first of
these notes, which accompanied the poem *A une femme trop gaie*
(later retitled *A celle qui est trop gaie*) was dated 9 December 1852
and read:

> The person for whom these lines have been written, whether
> they please or displease her, even if they appear totally ridiculous
> to her, is very humbly *implored* not to show them to *anyone*.
> Profound sentiments have a modesty which desires not to be
> violated. Is not the absence of a signature a symptom of this
> invincible modesty? He who has written these lines in one of
> those states of reverie into which he is often plunged by the
> image of the one who is their object has loved her deeply,

without ever telling her so, and he will *forever* feel for her the most tender sympathy.[1]

A une femme trop gaie is a curious poem to send to someone who is 'loved deeply'. The title itself contains implied criticism – the woman is *too* cheerful – and though the narrator of the poem begins by praising '[her] head, [her] air, [her] every way',[2] by the end of the fourth stanza the ambivalence of his feelings is starkly declared: 'I . . . hate you even as I love!'[3] The poet resents the woman's cheerfulness, her beauty and her liveliness – while simultaneously loving them – because they contrast too strongly with his own 'apathy', just as do sunshine and the signs of spring which make him want to destroy a flower in order to punish the 'insolence' of nature. The poem ends in masochistic fantasy as the poet expresses the desire to creep up on the woman when she is asleep, to bruise her breast, to carve a wound in her 'joyous' flesh and then to infuse his blood between the 'lips' of this wound. (In the later, published, version of the poem he changed 'blood' to 'venom' and explained that this was meant to signify the poet's melancholy.)

This was not the first time that Apollonie had read a poem addressed to or about herself. Théophile Gautier had published *Poème de la Femme*[4] in the *Revue des Deux Mondes* on 15 January 1849. That this poem concerns Apollonie is clear from a stanza which was omitted from the final version and which reads:

> She resembles thus contorted
> Clésinger's marble statue
> 'The woman bitten by the asp'
> But that art cannot ape.

The Clésinger statue is also indirectly alluded to in a stanza which Gautier included in the final version:

> Her head stretched out, tilting back;
> Panting, thrusting out her breasts,

> She falls on to the cushions,
> In the arms of her cradling dream.

The whole poem is a pæan to female beauty and sexuality as embodied in this particular woman. A year later another poem, *A une robe rose*, appeared in *L'Artiste*; it begins 'How I like you in this dress/Which so perfectly undresses you' and ends with an expression of unsatisfied desire. Then on 1 February 1853 his poem *Apollonie*, in which the poet rhapsodises about her name, was published in the *Revue de Paris*. So Apollonie was used to being apostrophised in verse, and on receipt of the first anonymous poem and short letter which Baudelaire sent her she may have done no more than smile and put them away in a drawer. It is unlikely that she analysed the poem in depth, or paid much attention to its edge of venom, accepting it simply as another tribute to her beauty and gracious hospitality, taking at face value the 'most tender sympathy' declared in the letter.

On 3 May 1853 Baudelaire sent Apollonie the poem which was to become *Réversibilité* and which at that stage had no title. This poem too is redolent of resentment and, though the poet ends by imploring the prayers of the 'angel full of happiness, joy and light' whom he is addressing, the sense throughout is that he wants this angel to experience anguish instead of gladness, hatred instead of kindness, fevers instead of health, and wrinkles instead of beauty. In other words, he wants his idol to experience some of the pain of the one who idolises her. He also sent in May the poem which begins '*Quand chez les débauchés*' (later given the title *L'Aube spirituelle*) which contains none of the ambivalence of the two earlier poems but which entirely idealises the object of his devotion so that she becomes a 'dear Goddess' and not a woman at all. This poem was sent with a prefatory sentence written in English: 'After a night of pleasure and desolation, all my soul belongs to you.'

Still in May, on Monday the 9th, he sent another poem, beginning '*Une fois, une seule*' and later called *Confession*, along with a letter:

Truly, Madame, I ask a thousand pardons for this idiotic anonymous versifying, which reeks horribly of childishness; but what can I do? I am self-centred like children and invalids. I think about the people I love when I suffer. In general, I think of you in verse, and when the lines have been written, I cannot resist the desire to show them to the person who is their object. At the same time, I hide myself, like someone who is extremely afraid of ridicule. Is there not something essentially comic in love? – particularly for those who have not known it.

But I swear to you that this really is the last time I will expose myself thus; and if my ardent friendship for you lasts as long again as it has already, before I say a word to you about this, we will both be old.

However absurd all this seems to you, believe that there exists a heart which you would be cruel to mock, and where your image lives always.[5]

'*Une fois, une seule . . .*' recalls a time, the only time, when the poet walked with his beloved, her arm resting on his. She talks to him and reveals a more plaintive side of herself than hitherto, speaking of the hard work involved in being a beautiful woman and of her awareness that beauty and love will both come to an end. (In later life Apollonie was to recall to friends a walk arm in arm with Baudelaire along the terrace of the Tuileries gardens beside the Seine one evening.)

There followed a silence of several months, until 7 February 1854, when a further letter accompanied the poem '*Ils marchent devant moi, ces Yeux extraordinaires*' (later to be called *Le Flambeau Vivant*):

I do not believe, Madame, that women in general realise the full extent of their power, be it for good or for evil. Without doubt, it would not be sensible to instruct them all about this. But in your case one risks nothing; your soul is too rich in kindness to leave room for *self-satisfaction* and for cruelty. Besides, you have doubtless been so showered, so saturated with flattery that only one thing can flatter you in future, and that is to learn that you do good – even without knowing it – even when asleep – simply by being alive.

As for this *cowardly anonymity*, what shall I say, what excuse shall I plead, if it is not that my first error necessitates all the others, and that it has become a habit. Imagine, if you like, that sometimes beneath the pressure of an unyielding affliction I cannot find comfort except in the pleasure of writing verses for you, and that afterwards I am obliged to reconcile the innocent desire to show them to you with the horrible fear of displeasing you. – That is what explains *the cowardice*.

Is it not true that you think as I do, – that the most delicious beauty, the most excellent and adorable creature – such as yourself – cannot desire a better compliment than the expression of gratitude for the good she has done?[6]

The accompanying poem apostrophises the beloved's eyes which, the poet declares, save him from 'all the snares and deadly sins'[7] and lead him in the path of the Beautiful. Another poem and letter followed swiftly, on 16 February:

I do not know what women think of the adoration of which they are sometimes the object. Certain people maintain that they must find it absolutely natural, and others that they must laugh at it. They therefore imagine them as either conceited or cynical. But it seems to me that benevolent souls cannot be other than proud and happy at their beneficent action. I do not know whether I will ever be granted the supreme sweetness of talking to you myself of the power which you have acquired over me, and of the perpetual radiation which your image creates in my mind. I am simply happy, for the present, to swear to you again that never was love more disinterested, more ideal, more penetrated with respect than the one I nourish secretly for you, and which I will always hide with the care commanded by this tender respect.[8]

The poem accompanying this letter was '*Que diras-tu ce soir, pauvre âme solitaire?*', in which the poet addresses his own heart and soul, asking what they wish to say to 'the most beautiful, the best, the most dear' one. They reply that they will dedicate their pride to the task of singing her praises, and at the end of the poem the 'phantom' of the beloved is given the following words to utter: 'I am beautiful, and I ordain that for love of me you will love only the Beautiful; I am the guardian Angel, the Muse and the Madonna!'

Monday, 8 May 1854 brought another poem, *A la très-Chère, à la très-belle* (later called *Hymne*), and another letter:

It is a long time, Madame, a really long time since these verses were written. Always the same deplorable habit, reverie and anonymity. Is it the shame of this ridiculous anonymity, or the fear that the verses are bad, that ability has not attained the level of the sentiments, which has made me so hesitant and timid this time? I have no idea. I am so afraid of you, that I have always hidden my name, thinking that an anonymous adoration – clearly ridiculous in the opinion of all those physical worldly boors we could consult on the subject – was, after all, almost innocent, could be no trouble, could disturb nothing, and was infinitely morally superior to a foolish, conceited pursuit, to a direct attack upon a woman who has already placed her affections – and perhaps her duties. Are you not – and I say it with some pride – not only one of the most loved, but also the most deeply respected of all creatures? I want to give you a proof of this. Laugh at it – a lot, if you find it funny – but don't talk about it. Do you not think it natural, simple and human, that a man in love should hate the fortunate lover, the possessor? That he should find him inferior and gross? Well, a while ago, chance had me meet *him*; how can I express to you – without comedy, without making your naughty, always cheerful, face laugh? – how happy I was to find him to be likeable and a man who could please you. My God! do not so many subtleties suggest folly? To conclude, to explain to you my silence and my ardour, an almost religious ardour, I will tell you that when my being is mired in the blackness of its natural spite and stupidity, it dreams profoundly of you. From this stimulating and purifying reverie something good is generally born. You are for me not only the most appealing of women – of all women – but also the dearest and most precious of superstitions. I am an egoist, I make use of you. Here is my miserable bum-wipe. How happy I would be if I could be certain that these high conceptions of love had some chance of being welcomed in a secret corner of your adorable mind! I will never know.

Forgive me, I ask nothing more of you.[9]

The fact that Baudelaire mentions meeting Mosselman in this letter has led one writer, Armand Moss, to speculate that Baudelaire was not, after all, one of the regular guests at the rue Frochot by this time; but he could merely have meant that this was the first time he had had a *tête-à-tête* with Mosselman. It should also be remembered that he was still retaining his disguise, and so might not have wanted Apollonie to realise that he was one of her regular guests. *A la très-Chère, à la très-Belle* or the 'bum-wipe' (*torche-cul*), an expression more in keeping with Gautier's epistolary style and which strikes a jarring note in the midst of these high-minded sentiments, is a hymn of praise to the poet's 'incorruptible love' and marks the completion of this particular phase of Baudelaire's poetic inspiration. It would be more than three years before Madame Sabatier heard from her secret admirer again.

In June 1855 the journal *La Revue des Deux Mondes* published, under the title of *Les Fleurs du mal*, eighteen of Baudelaire's poems, including three of those addressed to Apollonie: *Réversibilité, Confession* and *L'Aube spirituelle*. There could therefore have been no further genuine question of anonymity. There were no developments, however: Apollonie's life continued entirely as before, though she was seeing rather less of Baudelaire as he was no longer living nearby in the rue Pigalle but was leading a nomadic existence, moving from hotel to hotel partly in order to evade his creditors.

The complete collection of *Les Fleurs du mal* was published two years later, on 25 June 1857. On 16 July it was impounded at the printer's in Alençon, and both Baudelaire and his editor, Poulet-Malassis, were charged with offending public and religious morals. On Tuesday, 18 August, two days before the trial was to take place, Baudelaire sent Apollonie a special copy of the book, printed on laid paper, bound in green half morocco, and with the words '*A la Très belle, à la Très bonne, à la Très Chère*' inscribed on the fly-leaf, along with the following letter:

Dear Madame

You didn't believe for one moment, did you, that I could have forgotten you? I have been keeping a special copy for you since it was published, and if it is clothed in a costume so unworthy of you, it is not my fault, but that of my binder, from whom I had ordered something far more spiritual.

Would you believe that the wretches (I speak of the examining magistrate, the prosecutor etc.) have dared to condemn, along with other passages, two of the pieces written for my dear Idol (*Tout entière* and *A Celle qui est trop gaie*)? This last is the one which the venerable Sainte-Beuve declares the best in the volume.

This is the first time I have written to you in my real hand-writing. If I were not overwhelmed with business and corre-spondence (the hearing is the day after tomorrow), I would use this occasion to ask your forgiveness for so much folly and childishness. But in any case, have you not taken sufficient revenge, especially through your little sister? Oh, the little monster! She horrified me one day when we met and she burst out laughing in my face and said: *are you still in love with my sister, and are you still writing her those wonderful letters?* I realised, first, that when I had wanted to hide myself, I had not made a very good job of it and, secondly, that beneath your charming face, you conceal a not very charitable soul. Lechers are *in love*, but poets are *idolatrous*, and I think your sister is not of the sort to understand eternal things.

Allow me then, at the risk of entertaining you also, to renew those protestations which so entertained that little fool. Imagine an amalgam of reverie, liking and respect, with a thousand serious childishnesses, and you will have an inkling of the very sincere something which I do not feel able to define any better.

To forget you is impossible. Poets are said to have existed who have lived their whole lives with their eyes fixed on one cherished image. In fact I believe (though I am too biased) *that fidelity is one of the signs of genius.*

You are more than an ideal and cherished image, you are my *superstition.* When I do something really stupid, I say to myself: *My God! if only she knew!* When I do something good, I say to myself: *This brings me closer to her – in spirit.*

And the last time that I had the happiness (despite my own best efforts) to meet you! – for you do not know how careful I am to avoid you! – I said to myself: how remarkable it would be if this carriage was waiting for her, perhaps I had better go another way. And then: *Good evening, sir!* I went off, repeating all the way: *Good evening, sir!* trying to imitate your voice.

I saw my judges last Thursday. They are not merely not handsome, they are abominably ugly; and their souls no doubt resemble their faces.

Flaubert had the Empress on his side. I am lacking a woman. And then a few days ago, the bizarre thought took hold of me that perhaps you could, through certain relationships and maybe complicated channels, get a word of sense into one of those dense heads.

The hearing is for the day after tomorrow, Thursday morning . . . [details of the judges are included here]

But I want to put all these trivialities on one side.

Remember that someone is thinking of you, that there is nothing trivial about his thought, and that he bears a bit of a grudge against you for your malicious *high spirits.*

I beg you most ardently to keep to yourself in future all that I may confide in you. You are my constant Companion, and my Secret. It is this intimacy, in which I have been playing opposite myself for so long, which has made me bold enough to use such a familiar tone.

Farewell, dear Madame, I kiss your hands with all my Devotion.

Charles Baudelaire

All the verses between page 84 and page 105 belong to you.[10]

This last remark of Baudelaire's assigns some further poems to Apollonie in addition to the ones he had already sent her: *Tout entière, Harmonie du soir* and *Le Flacon*. His reference to 'certain relationships and maybe complicated channels' through which she might be able to influence the judges probably referred to Alfred Mosselman's links with Auguste de Morny. Unfortunately this was the worst possible time to ask Mosselman to intercede with Morny, since the two men had fallen out at the beginning of this year over Morny's callous dropping of Mosselman's sister, the Countess Le Hon, on the occasion of his marriage to a Russian princess. Apollonie may nevertheless have succeeded in getting an introduction to one of the judges, De Belleyme – possibly through Charles Jalabert, who was painting a portrait of the judge at this time – but, if so, nothing came of her intervention. At the trial on 20 August the charge of religious immorality was dropped but that of offending public morals was upheld. Baudelaire was fined three hundred francs, but this was subsequently reduced to fifty after the direct intervention of the Empress. Poulet-Malassis was fined two hundred francs and ordered to delete six poems judged to contain 'obscene or immoral passages or expressions'.

Baudelaire's letter of 18 August drew, for the first time, a response from Apollonie. (She could hardly have responded to the earlier letters as she did not officially know where they came from.) The sequence of events is difficult to establish with certainty, as the letters that Apollonie wrote to Baudelaire have not been preserved in their entirety. A fragment remains of a reply she wrote to him on 29 August, from which it can be inferred that they had met on the previous Thursday, the 27th. Prior to that meeting, Apollonie had been agitated:

Today I am calmer. I have been more aware of the influence of our Thursday evening. I can tell you, without you taxing me with exaggeration, that I am the happiest of women, that I have never been more aware that I love you, that I have never seen you more handsome, more adorable – quite simply, my divine friend. You can strut about, if that pleases you, but don't go and look at yourself, for, whatever you do, you will never manage to give yourself the expression which I saw on you for a second. Now, whatever happens, I will see you always thus, this is the Charles that I love; you may with impunity tighten your lips and draw together your eyebrows without me worrying, I will close my eyes and I will see the other you . . .[11]

On 31 August Charles wrote again to Apollonie, quoting (in italics) certain phrases from a letter she had written to him (perhaps the same one as that from which the fragment quoted above remains) which make it clear that, in writing at least, she had offered herself to him. It is also clear from this letter that they had met on the previous evening as well:

I have torn up this torrent of childishness piled on my table. I did not find it serious enough for you, dear beloved. I take up your two letters again, and write a new reply.

I need a little courage for that; for my nerves are giving me great pain, enough to make me cry out, and I woke up with the inexplicable moral uneasiness which I had when I left you yesterday evening.

. . . *absolute lack of modesty.*

That makes you even dearer to me.

It seems to me that I have belonged to you since the first day I saw you. You will make of that what you will, but I am yours heart, soul and body.

I urge you to keep this letter hidden, unhappy woman! – *Do you really know what you are saying?* There are people whose job it is to put in prison those who do not pay their bills of exchange; but no one punishes the violation of pledges of friendship and love.

I said to you yesterday: You will forget me; you will betray me; the one who amuses you now will end by boring you. And today I add: it is only he who, like an imbecile, takes seriously the things of the soul who will suffer. You see, my beautiful darling, that I have *odious* prejudices where women are concerned. In short, I do not have *faith*. You have a beautiful soul but, all things considered, it is female.

Look how over the course of a few days our situation has been shattered. First, we are both possessed by the fear of grieving an honest man who is fortunate enough still to be in love.

Then we fear our own storm, because we know (I especially) that there are difficult knots to untie.

And finally, just a few days ago, you were a divinity, which is so comfortable, so beautiful, so inviolable. And now you're a woman. And if I'm unfortunate enough to acquire the right to be jealous! oh! what horror in even thinking of it! for with a person such as you, whose eyes are full of smiles and charm for everyone, one would suffer martyrdom.

The second letter bears a seal whose solemnity would please me if I were really sure that you understood it. *Never meet or never part!* [original in English] That means for certain that it would be much better never to have met, but that having met, one should not part. On a letter of farewell, this seal would be very droll.

In the end, let whatever will happen, happen. I am something of a fatalist. But what I know for sure is that I have a horror of passion – because I know it, with all its ignominies; and now the beloved image which dominated all the fortunes of life has become too seductive.

I dare not reread this letter too much; I would perhaps be obliged to change it; for I greatly fear distressing you; it seems to me that I must have let something of the unpleasant side of my character show through.

I hate the thought of making you go to that dirty rue J.-J.-Rousseau. For I have plenty of other things to say to you. So you must write to tell me a way.

As for our little project, if it becomes possible, let me know a few days in advance.

Farewell, dear beloved; I'm a little cross with you for being too charming. Just remember that when I carry away the scent of your arms and your hair, I also carry away the desire to return to them. But what an unbearable obsession!

Charles

I will in fact take this myself to the rue J.-J.-Rousseau, in case you go there today. That way it will reach you sooner.[12]

The rue Jean-Jacques-Rousseau was the location of the central post office, from which letters could be collected. Armand Duval in *La Dame aux camélias* also makes use of it.

What remains of Apollonie's reply to the above letter clearly shows how much this whole exchange is hurting her:

Look, dear, do you want me to tell you what I think, a cruel thought which hurts me greatly? It is that you do not love me. That is why you have these fears, these hesitations to contract a liaison which, in such conditions, would become a source of annoyance for you and a continual torment for me. Do I not have the proof of this in a sentence from your letter? It is so explicit that it makes my blood run cold. *In short, I do not have faith.* You do not have faith! But in that case you lack love. What can one say to that? Is it not clarity itself? Oh my God! How this idea makes me suffer and how I would like to weep on your breast! I feel as though that would comfort me. Be that as it may, I will not change my mind about our meeting tomorrow. I want to see you, if only to try out my role of friend. Oh why did you seek to see me again?

Your very unhappy friend[13]

A few days later, after Charles had been trying to avoid a further meeting, Apollonie wrote again:

What comedy or rather what drama are we playing? For my mind does not know what conjectures to draw and I will not hide from you that I am very anxious. Your conduct has been so strange for some days, that I no longer understand anything. It is much too subtle for a clumsy creature of my calibre. Enlighten me, my friend, I ask only to understand what deathly chill has blown out this beautiful flame. Is it simply the effect of wise reflections? They have come rather late. Alas! is it not all my fault? I should have been grave and thoughtful when you came to me. But what do you want? When the mouth trembles and the heart beats, sensible thoughts fly away . . .

I am not in the habit of criticising what my friends do. It seems that you are terribly afraid of finding yourself alone with me. That is however so unnecessary! You can do what you like about it. When this whim has passed, write or come to me. I am indulgent, and I will forgive you for the pain you are causing me.

I cannot resist the desire to say a few words to you about our quarrel. I had told myself that my conduct should be entirely dignified, but before a whole day has passed my heart is already lacking the strength and besides, Charles, my anger is entirely legitimate! What am I supposed to think when I see you flee my caresses, if not that you are thinking about that other one, whose soul and dark face come to place themselves between us? In the end, I feel humiliated and let down. If I did not respect myself too much, I would insult you. I would like to see you suffer. For I am burning with jealousy, and reason is not possible in such moments. Oh, dear friend, I hope you will never suffer from it.

What a night I have spent and how much I have cursed this cruel love!

I have waited for you all day. . . . In case you come to my house on a whim tomorrow, I should warn you that I will only be in from one to three o'clock, or, in the evening, from eight until midnight.

Good day, my Charles. How is what remains of your heart? Mine is calmer. I have reasoned with it firmly in order not to bore you too much with its weaknesses. You'll see! I will learn how to make it descend to the temperature you desire. I will definitely suffer, but to please you, I will resign myself to bearing all possible sorrows.[14]

On this (incomplete) correspondence a vast edifice of speculation and commentary has been constructed. It has been asserted that Charles and Apollonie slept together at least once (some have even assumed that the 'rue J.-J.-Rousseau' referred to a seedy hotel rather than to a post office)[15] and there are those who have asserted that the relationship collapsed because Baudelaire was impotent.[16] There is no evidence that this latter was the case, and the only evidence for the existence of a physical relationship of any kind, however brief, lies in certain phrases such as Charles's reference to 'the scent of your arms and your hair' and Apollonie's protests in her final letter about Charles now 'fleeing her embraces'. She herself attributes this rejection, at least in part, to his involvement with another woman, Jeanne Duval, a mulatto actress with whom he had been involved, on and off, since 1843 when he had encountered her playing a *soubrette* role in a small theatre on the Left Bank. (For years Apollonie kept a portrait of Jeanne drawn by Baudelaire; she hid it in her copy of *Les Fleurs du mal* and wrote underneath it 'His ideal!') Yet she also admits that what is going on is incomprehensible to her, and here she gets to the nub of the problem – or at least of one of the problems, for Baudelaire's misogyny is another powerful force which cannot be ignored.

The poems that Baudelaire sent to Madame Sabatier between

December 1852 and May 1854 were precisely that – poems. They were formal, stylised, worked on until they were complete in every respect, in rhyme, rhythm and imagery. One cannot assume that the 'I' of the poem is the living, flesh-and-blood Monsieur Charles Baudelaire himself, even though, for ease of expression, one talks about 'the poet' saying this or that. Likewise, one cannot make too close an identification between the 'you' of a poem and an actual woman, between Apollonie Sabatier and the muse into which Baudelaire transformed her. However, undercutting that sense of distance, that stylisation, were the accompanying letters which appear to be saying, if at times ambiguously, more than 'this is the image I have made out of my perception of you' or 'this is how my poems are made' – to be saying, at least between the lines, 'I love you.' That, in any event, judging from her subsequent reaction, is how Apollonie read them, and one can hardly blame her for it.

That sad question in one of her letters – 'Oh why did you seek to see me again?' – is the cry of a woman who has suffered in the past and then recovered from her suffering. It is a protest at having a wound reopened. It suggests that she had believed herself to be in love with the poet who wrote such strangely passionate letters and poems to her in 1853 and 1854, who refused to reveal himself even though she had realised who he was, who was therefore not inviting any response from her and who, she presumed, would continue to love her and thus to write to her. Then the letters and the poems had stopped arriving. For a while she would have gone on expecting them – there had been a fairly lengthy gap before – but eventually she must have realised there would be no more. She continued to say nothing to their author, not even when some of the poems were published – apart from, according to Baudelaire, 'Good evening, sir!' – but felt some degree of abandonment or, at the very least, wonder as to why such ardour had apparently ceased. (It has been suggested that the poems came to an end because Baudelaire, while still attached in some way to Jeanne Duval, was in the process of taking up with another woman, Marie Daubrun, an actress who was also the mistress of Théodore de Banville. It may also simply have been the case that the poems on this particular theme, with this particular inspiration, had, to the poet's mind, been satisfactorily completed.)

And then, three years later, there is suddenly another letter, with renewed protestations of love, and actually signed. Apollonie did not take the time to dissect this letter in a literary critical manner, to detect all its ambiguities or to consider whether his motives were merely that he wanted her to intervene in his trial. Instead she thought, 'Charles does still love me after all, and now that he has revealed himself, I can tell him that I love him too.' Her response to him suggests that she thought he would now become her *amant de cœur*. The horror this response inspired in the poet is perfectly clear in his letter of 31 August, even though it is combined with a reluctance to abandon his ideal, unfleshly love and hence a desire not to lose the real woman completely. So he appears to be hanging on to her, wanting to make plans for some future 'project' together, while at the same time not being able to respond to the love she is offering – which would involve loving the woman and not just the image he had created for his own use.

Apollonie misread the situation partly through not understanding the complicated workings of a poet's mind – through never having read the letters carefully enough – and partly through attributing higher motives to Baudelaire's renewed correspondence with her than were actually in operation. She was also a romantic who liked the idea of this hitherto secret love, which she interpreted according to her own romantic notions. But, in addition to these misunderstandings, there is the convoluted nature of Baudelaire's feelings about women. His ambivalence is at its starkest in his relation to Apollonie: he loves and he hates, he adores the female idol yet the woman herself disgusts him. One phrase in particular in his letter of 31 August is brutally dismissive – '*Te voilà femme maintenant*' ('. . . just a few days ago, you were a divinity . . . *And now you're a woman.*') Several reasons have been advanced for Baudelaire's misogyny, including his complicated relationship with his mother by whom he felt abandoned when she married his stepfather, General Aupick, and it has been noted that his relationship with Jeanne Duval also revolved around his attraction to what simultaneously revolted him. (Jeanne, to whom Baudelaire was irresistibly physically attracted, mocked his work, argued with him, poisoned his cat and frequently took other lovers.) In a sense, his relationship with Apollonie was a mirror image of his relationship with Jeanne. In Jeanne's case, he is drawn towards what he loathes, whereas with Apollonie he finds himself loathing that towards which he is drawn. That enduring poetry should have been produced out of this conflict may be some consolation in an abstract sense, but can have been little more than a source of bewilderment to the women concerned.

The ambivalent, dualistic, even schizophrenic nature of Baudelaire's feelings about women is apparent from his essay published in 1863, *The Painter of Modern Life*, in the section entitled 'Woman'. He writes of woman as the Being for whom, but especially through whom, artists and poets create their work; that she is not merely the feminine gender of man but is 'rather a divinity, a star that presides over all the parturitions of the male brain'.[17] He goes on to say: 'She is a sort of idol – stupid, maybe, but dazzling'[18] – and he also seems to prefer his idols clothed, liking 'the muslins, the gauzes and the great, iridescent clouds of the stuffs that envelop her'.[19] In this essay Baudelaire is a poet writing about an artist, Constantin Guys, and trying to give some explanation of the sources of creativity in modern life; and so, as in his poetry, he is treating woman as image rather than reality, and it would be to misread him as much as Apollonie did to reduce what he writes here to a simple tract of his 'views on women'. But in an earlier essay or, rather, collection of aphorisms, *My Heart Laid Bare*, his fundamental misogyny comes across more baldly:

> Woman is the opposite of the Dandy. That is why she should be regarded with disgust.
> Woman is hungry, and she wants to eat; thirsty, and she wants to drink.
> She feels randy, and she wants to be————.
> Fine characteristics!
> Woman is 'natural' – that is to say, abominable.

Moreover, she is always vulgar – that is to say, the opposite of the Dandy.[20]

The *pièce de résistance* of this catalogue of misogynistic aphorisms is: 'I have always been amazed that women are allowed to enter churches. What sort of conversations can *they* have with God?'[21]

Baudelaire's attitude towards women, though extreme and blatantly expressed, was not particularly unusual for his time and place. Some of Meissonier's comments about the nature of the relationship between men and women are only more courteously phrased versions of the same contempt. He considered, for instance, that 'Man should educate woman, and form her nature from the very outset.'[22] And the Goncourt brothers declared that they regarded women – apart from those with a great deal of education – as evil and stupid animals, fit only for breeding.[23] Most men, however, managed somehow to balance their scorn and their adoration, to enjoy showing off their extravagantly dressed wives and mistresses at the same time as inwardly despising them – or else they managed the balance by worshipping their wives and despising their mistresses. Baudelaire could not achieve this balance and, when Apollonie forced him to realise that his idol was also a woman, she inadvertently destroyed the possibility of any further serious relationship between them.

Following the crisis, Baudelaire's attendance at the Sunday soirées became patchy as he continually found excuses not to be present. He had in any event not been a regular visitor for some time. But he could never entirely relinquish his imaginary muse, and from time to time would send her presents. On Tuesday, 8 September he sent her a note about seats for *King Lear*, and another one on the same subject two days later. On Sunday the 13th he sent a note excusing himself from dinner, and on Friday the 25th he wrote to her about an inkwell he had bought for her (which he admitted looked rather better in the shop window than up close). On 17 November he sent her another note, with some books. The following year, on Sunday, 3 January, he was still excusing himself from dinner. On Tuesday the 12th he wrote to her about Mosselman having caught sight of him, looking rather ill. On Sunday, 2 May he again sent her a note with a book. Two years later, on 15 May 1860, he published in *La Revue contemporaine* a new poem, *Semper Eadem*, also inspired by Apollonie, in which he seems to acknowledge that his feelings for her have been based on a lie, but a lie with which he nevertheless wants to intoxicate himself. There is even a suggestion of resentment that she will not allow him to remain in his state of dream. In fact, at the height of this saga Apollonie was as carried away by a dream as was Charles, imagining him to be quite other than he was, believing that he loved her in a way that could find fulfilment in an ordinary sexual liaison. They were both behaving as Apollonie describes in her first letter to him – closing their eyes and seeing 'the other you', the other they each desired to see and not the reality at all.

Perhaps Baudelaire had Apollonie in mind when he wrote of the relations between the sexes in his notes entitled *Years in Brussels*: 'A matter in which God has shown an infinite cunning is in contriving two creatures so deeply strange to one another that every step they take in their mutual dealings may be a false one.'[24]

---

1 Baudelaire, *Correspondance*, ed. Claude Pichois, Vol.1, Gallimard, Paris, 1973, p.205

2 Charles Baudelaire, *The Flowers of Evil*, tr. James McGowan, OUP, Oxford, 1998, p.87

3 Ibid., p.89

4 Théophile Gautier, *Emaux et camées*, ed. Claudine Gothot-Mersch, Gallimard, Paris, 1981, pp.29–30

5 Baudelaire, *Correspondance*, Vol.1, p.225

6 Ibid., p.266

7 Charles Baudelaire, *The Flowers of Evil*, p.87

8 Baudelaire, *Correspondance*, Vol.1, p.267

9 Ibid., pp.275–6

10 Ibid., pp.421–3

11 Quoted in André Billy, *La Présidente et ses amis*, pp.131–2

12 Baudelaire, *Correspondance*, Vol.1, pp.425–6

13 Quoted in André Billy, *La Présidente et ses amis*, pp. 132–3

14 Ibid., pp.133–5

15 E.g. François Porché, *Baudelaire et la Présidente*, p.214 and Louis Mermaz, *Madame Sabatier*, p.177

16 E.g. François Porché, *Baudelaire et la Présidente*, pp.215–19

17 Charles Baudelaire, *My Heart Laid Bare, and Other Prose Writings*, tr. Norman Cameron, Weidenfeld & Nicolson, London, 1950, p.59

18 Ibid.

19 Ibid., p.60

20 Ibid., p.176

21 Ibid., p.191

22 V.C.O. Gréard, *Meissonier, Part II: The artist's wisdom*, p.181

23 Robert Baldick (ed. and tr.), *Pages from the Goncourt Journal*, OUP, London/ New York/Toronto, 1962, p.18

24 Charles Baudelaire, *My Heart Laid Bare, and Other Prose Writings*, p.217

CHAPTER EIGHT

Rebuilding

NAPOLEON III WILL always be remembered for the great rebuilding project he and his Prefect of the Seine, Baron Haussmann, put into operation: it was designed to transform Paris into a modern capital city to rival London, which the Emperor had come to know well during his time of exile. A programme of public works and an alliance of government and private enterprise transformed the infrastructure of streets, drains, sewers and water supply, and the physiognomy of Paris was permanently altered by the creation of new arteries, buildings and parks.

Baron Haussmann and the Emperor worked closely on this great project of transformation, meeting on an almost daily basis. Haussmann styled himself *artiste démolisseur*, and in the creation of his vision he cleared away much of medieval Paris. He was a devotee of the straight line and prepared to demolish anything which got in the way of it. Five new bridges were built over the Seine – the Pont Napoléon (now the Pont National), the Pont de la Gare (now the Pont de Bercy), the Pont du Point du Jour (now the Pont d'Auteuil), the Pont de l'Alma and the Pont de Solférino – and six others were rebuilt. A number of monumental buildings were erected, including four major theatres, fifteen churches, seventy schools, half a dozen town halls (*mairies*), two major railway stations (the Gares du Nord and d'Austerlitz) and six huge barracks (including the Prefecture of Police). Perhaps the most ambitious scheme was the massive expropriation and demolition of property on the Ile de la Cité and the erection of the new public edifices which reduced the population there from fifteen thousand to five thousand and changed the heart of the city.

One of the greatest improvements designed by Haussmann was the introduction of a new and elaborate sewerage system, for which Paris became famed, and which largely ended the outbreaks of cholera which had regularly decimated the population. The provision of new and improved open spaces represented another aspect of the trans-formation of the city, enhancing it as a place of relaxation and enjoyment as well as of work. The development of the Bois de Boulogne was one of the Emperor's pet projects, inspired by his fond memories of Hyde Park. Work began on it during the spring of 1853, even before Haussmann's appointment in June of that year; the two lakes, the roadway around them and the adjoining lawns had been completed by 1854, the Longchamp racecourse was inaugurated in April 1857 and the Bois had assumed its present aspect by 1858. Work also commenced in the late 1850s on the Bois de Vincennes, near a more crowded part of Paris. Occasionally during the rebuilding process trees were transplanted from one place to another; in 1859, for example, a number of sixty-year-old chestnut trees were removed from the neighbourhood of the Entrepôt des Vins in order to make way for the new boulevard Saint-Germain, and were replanted in the Champs Elysées.

There was a negative side to the monumental building works, in that thousands of poorer people were pushed out to the edges of the city as their old houses were demolished and they were unable to afford the higher rents of the new properties constructed in their place. La Chroniqueuse recorded in 1859 that fifth-floor apartments which had previously cost sixty to seventy pounds a year to rent were now priced at a hundred and sixty to two hundred pounds and that, as a consequence, many English people were also now leaving.[1] The bourgeoisie had already moved out of the central areas, seeking healthier and more salubrious living space on the outskirts. The problems were exacerbated by the growth in the population of Paris, itself partly a result of the influx of artisans and labourers to work on the rebuilding project. Permanent emigration from the countryside to Paris increased dramatically throughout the second half of the century and the capital gained 121,000 inhabitants between the years of 1851 and 1856 alone,[2] but an administration preoccupied with buildings for the wealthy offered very few incentives for the provision of working-class housing. The gap between rich and poor widened considerably during this period of apparent prosperity, and Haussmann's splendid façades hid an appalling world of slums and tenements. Orleanist and Republican opposition tried to exploit the discontent arising from these negative aspects of the rebuilding of Paris, but they met with little success until towards the end of the 1860s, when Haussmann's unorthodox financial methods, which involved the creation of a hidden debt of about half a billion francs and a complicated system of deferred payments, came to light.

This was an age of enormous expansion: of communication, through the railway system, telegraph lines and shipbuilding; of scientific development, including the work of Louis Pasteur, and advances in fields as diverse as aluminium and margarine manufacture. Gaslight, which had gradually been replacing oil lighting throughout Paris in the 1840s, was viewed, along with the railway, as a symbol of human and industrial progress. By the 1850s three thousand new gas lamps had been installed in the streets, and the boulevards were fully gaslit by 1857. Many streets were lit all night. Electric lighting was tried out in the Tuileries gardens for the first time in May 1859. There was a sense of rapid progress, of the constant discovery of new things and new experiences to savour – as well as the *ennui* associated with the overloaded, jaded palate.

Those unable to afford the high rents may have been leaving Paris or moving to the outskirts, but meanwhile the city was acting as a magnet for foreign or provincial visitors with money to burn. As La Chroniqueuse reported in November 1859:

They are all here – England, Russia, Austria, Germany, Italy, Spain, in fact, all the world is represented in a *réunion* in the *salons* of our *élite*; and wealth, that great ruler of us all, lends its aid to magnify and decorate this assemblage of the great and the powerful of all lands. A Parisian *salon* cannot be equalled in this respect, for Paris is the centre of fashion. Here the Goddess of Pleasure has erected her temple, and here must come her worshippers.[3]

Two world fairs were held in Paris during the Second Empire, which did much to advertise the city to the world and to encourage this influx of visitors. The first of these, the Paris Universal Exposition of 1855, was designed to commemorate forty years of peace in Europe since Waterloo as well as to demonstrate that Paris was at least the equal of London where, four years previously, the Crystal Palace Exhibition had inaugurated a series of world fairs. The Paris Exposition, which was opened by Napoleon III and his cousin Prince Napoleon on 15 May, incorporated the fine arts as well as agriculture and industry. The exhibition was financed by the government and had been planned by an imperial commission under the general supervision of Prince Napoleon who, despite being away fighting in the Crimea from April 1854 to February 1855, proved an able and energetic administrator. Most of the leading lights in its planning were heavily influenced by the doctrines of Saint-Simon, with his emphasis on the transformation of society and the improvement of the lot of the masses through the development of science and industry under government sponsorship.

The main body of the Exposition was housed in the specially built Palais de l'Industrie on the site now covered by the Rond Point of the Champs Elysées, while the fine arts exhibits were displayed in the separate Palais des Beaux Arts, built in the French Renaissance style by Hector Lefuel in the avenue Montaigne. In the Rotonde du Panorama, built in 1838 and situated between the Seine and the Palais de l'Industrie, to which it was linked by a walkway, were displayed the imperial jewels and examples of decorative art from the imperial residences. The Palais de l'Industrie itself, which was not quite as large as the Crystal Palace, was one of the first buildings in Paris to be constructed largely of iron and glass, though it was also given a stone facing. It was inadequately ventilated, which led to some discomfort during the hot summer of 1855, despite the use of muslin screens.

There were twenty-four thousand exhibitors (some eleven thousand of whom were French) from thirty-four countries. The original intention to celebrate forty years of peace had been overturned by the Crimean War – France and England had declared war on Russia on 27 March 1854 – but Russia was nevertheless invited to participate. The offer was declined, but Russian traders were issued with passes and Russian officers who were prisoners of war in France were allowed to attend on their word of honour that they would not try to escape. And in August Queen Victoria, along with Prince Albert and two of their children, visited Paris, staying for nine days as the guests of the Emperor and Empress. As allies against Russia, England and France were enjoying their best relations in years, and crowds lined the boulevards to cheer the Queen, who, in addition to visiting the Exposition, explored some of the other pleasures Paris had to offer: 'The Queen, Prince Albert and their children drove around Paris in a hackney carriage and in the strictest incognito; they made purchases in several shops.'[4]

Shops had been developing at a great pace, a development in line with the epoch's emphasis on the value of appearances and material possessions. One of the world's first modern department stores and the quintessential example of this phenomenon, the Bon Marché, was founded by Aristide Boucicaut, the son of a hatter who had arrived in Paris in 1835. He had initially found employment at the Petit Saint-Thomas store, where he gained the reputation of being a brilliant buyer and seller. Retiring in 1852, he used his savings to enter into partnership with the owner of what was then a tiny shop, Au Bon Marché, at the corner of the rue de Sèvres and the rue du Bac. Over the next eleven years he introduced all the characteristic features of what would come to be the modern shopping experience, including entry without obligation to buy, the marking of prices, the right of return and refund, and the offering of a great variety of merchandise seductively displayed in the relevant departments. Another large store, catering for a wealthier clientèle than that of the Bon Marché, was the Grand Magasin du Louvre; opened in July 1855, it took up the whole ground floor of the Hôtel du Louvre, which had been especially constructed in the place du Palais Royal in preparation for the Exposition. Luxuriously appointed, with salons and a buffet, the store eventually took over the entire premises and the hotel moved to a site across the street.

Visitors to Paris could also enjoy the many theatres and several opera houses which each had their distinct characteristics. Three of the opera houses – the Opéra, the Théâtre Lyrique and the Opéra Comique – presented works in French, while the Théâtre Italien was so called because the performances there were given in Italian. The Opéra Comique catered particularly for the bourgeoisie, the Théâtre Lyrique for working people and artists, while the Opéra's clientèle were primarily members of the aristocracy and the intellectual élite. Particularly associated with the Second Empire are the operettas of Jacques Offenbach, who opened his Bouffes Parisiens on 5 July 1855 in the small theatre he had discovered and renovated, with the patronage of Prince Napoleon and Auguste de Morny, on the Champs Elysées. The programme for the first night included a musical farce by Offenbach himself, themes from Rossini, and a romantic idyll and prologue by Ludovic Halévy, who subsequently worked closely with Offenbach as a librettist.

The Exposition was officially closed by the Emperor on 15 November. Forty thousand people attended the closing ceremony at which Berlioz conducted his cantata *L'Impériale* with twelve thousand performers, Prince Napoleon bestowed ten thousand awards, and Napoleon III decorated forty artists, including thirteen foreigners, with the Legion of Honour. The Exposition had summarised many of the dominant ideas of the nineteenth century: the belief in an indefinite material and moral progress, the assumption that the development of science and industry would bring wisdom and happiness, and hope for the rapprochement of classes and peace in Europe. The Paris Exposition in its totality had been almost twice the size of its London predecessor, and some half a million foreign and provincial visitors were thus introduced to the splendours of the Empire and to a Paris whose transformation at the hands of Napoleon III and his Prefect of the Seine was well under way.

In the mid-1850s Napoleon III's fortunes were at their highest. The Crimean War had ended in victory for the French and British on 18 January 1856 and two months later, early on the morning of Sunday, 16 March, the birth of Napoleon and Eugénie's son, to be known as the Prince Imperial, was announced by a hundred and one cannon salvos. He was baptised in Notre Dame on 14 June. The tapestries on the wall were embroidered with golden bees, the Napoleonic symbol, and a representative of the Pope performed the ceremony.

During this time of imperial confidence, the fortunes of businessmen and entrepreneurs such as Alfred Mosselman also flourished, and he continued to maintain Apollonie Sabatier in her apartment in the rue Frochot. Had he wanted to, he could have married her, as his wife died in July 1856, at the age of only forty-two, at her house in Viroflay. According to her death certificate, Alfred's address at the time was 6 passage Sandrié in Paris; the couple had been living apart for several years.

Though by virtue of her position as Alfred's mistress Apollonie belonged firmly to the *demi-monde*, her lifestyle was quite different from that of a great courtesan. She lacked for nothing, since all the physical comforts she needed were provided for her by Alfred – she had plenty of money for clothes, her apartment was furnished with taste and the food she served was excellent. But there was no sense of her being 'on the make', of staying with him for the sake of money, or of playing him off against other lovers to increase her revenue. She did not even own a carriage, but went by hired cab whenever Alfred did not provide a means of transport for her. Her only luxury items were paintings, sculptures and other ornaments, given to her either by Alfred or by the artists themselves. And apart from the possible exception of Baudelaire, and despite all the bawdy talk, Apollonie did not dispense her sexual favours elsewhere during the time of her lengthy liaison with Alfred.

The second half of the 1850s saw significant developments in the life of her sister Bébé. In 1854 she had become involved with a young cavalry officer, Ulric Fallet, who was five years older than her, and on

5 July of that year he officially recognised her little girl, Jeanne, as his own. This was his first step in uniting himself with Bébé (now usually called Adèle), whom he could not yet marry because of his status as an officer in the Imperial Guard. (Adèle's story at this time bears an uncanny resemblance to that of her mother before her.) For the next ten years they lived together without being married, during which time they produced four children. Their first son, whose date of birth is unknown, died before 1858. In the spring of that year Ulric took Adèle with him to Egypt when he was posted there on a military mission. In two letters to her sister, whom she addresses as '*ma chère Ananas*' ('my dear Pineapple'), Adèle writes of her pain at not being able to be presented by Ulric as his legitimate wife. On 23 March 1859 Adèle gave birth to a second son in Paris, who also died at only a few months old. (Maxime Du Camp wrote a letter of condolence to Apollonie about this, lamenting poor Bébé's 'bad luck' with her sons.)[5] Their next two children survived, and Ulric and Adèle were finally married on 2 July 1864. They were rarely in France, as Ulric was generally serving abroad.

Apollonie was also closely involved with other members of her family, her mother and her two brothers, Alexandre and Louis; the latter was a house painter, while Alexandre was a sailor. In 1854 Alexandre was diagnosed as a consumptive and could no longer go to sea. He came to live at 9 rue Neuve-Bréda, very near the rue Frochot, and Apollonie did her best to look after him. On the advice of Julien Turgan she consulted a Dr Cabarrus, a homeopathic doctor specialising in illnesses of the respiratory tract. He had an excellent reputation, particularly among singers and literary men, and immediately responded to Apollonie's request for help. He prescribed various potions for Alexandre and refused all payment (which suggests the appeal Apollonie held for men, and how they desired to do her favours). But it turned out to be too late to help Alexandre, whose condition deteriorated rapidly. He was taken to his mother's house, which at that time was in the village of Montfermeil, a few miles to the east of Paris, where he died in June at the age of thirty-one. Apollonie had been very fond of him, and she was much distressed.

Théophile Gautier continued to write to Apollonie in his usual tone, a notable letter being the long one he sent her from St Petersburg on 10 January 1859:

> Next to my little nest and my brood, the only thing that I miss about Paris is your sparkling laugh and your gaiety shining through the intellectual bacchanalia of Sunday. I miss also the aromatic sachet, more fragrant than Solomon's perfume mountains, hidden beneath your divine armpit, and your back of Paros mica against which I rub myself with the secret desires of a luxuriating cat. I think about it often, and sometimes I think about it with only one hand; the other wanders, and the altar of memory receives the libations of solitude . . .
>
> Whether or not you tickle in my honour the little pink clitoris nestling in gold and fleece, I will love you just the same, light of my eyes, smile of my lips, caress of my soul . . .[6]

Gustave Flaubert had also been in the habit of writing flirtatious letters to Apollonie for many years, finding in her an outlet for some otherwise repressed urge to engage in a rather schoolboyish lubricity. At times he seems almost to have indulged in a fantasy lesbian relationship with her, in which he not only made sapphic allusions but attributed female characteristics to his own anatomy. In the summer of 1859, for instance, he wrote her a letter[7] full of sexual innuendo in which he pictures her swimming in the Seine, the river simulating the act of love beneath her like a 'tribade' (from the Greek *tribein*, 'to rub', and used at the time for 'lesbian', as seen in the work of Parent-Duchâtelet), and wishing that he could himself be that river. Later in the same year he writes[8] that he has had so little sexual activity of late that, were he not in the habit of washing himself every day, his virginity would grow back, the membrane re-forming. He also reveals himself as a foot fetishist, longing to make 'obscene caresses'[9] in the eyelets of Apollonie's boots. (He was, at the time of writing, about to turn thirty-eight, being just a little older than Apollonie herself.)

Then, some time in the spring or summer of 1860, everything changed, for Alfred Mosselman left Apollonie. All appeared to be as usual at the end of January, when a letter from Théo to Maxime Du Camp mentioned that La Présidente and 'Macarouille' would be dining with him on the following Tuesday.[10] But on 31 March, in a letter to Gustave Flaubert, Louis Bouilhet mentions trouble between Alfred and Apollonie, and laments the likely repercussions for himself and his friends, commenting that Apollonie's salon is the only agreeable place in Paris.[11]

One of the reasons, possibly the main reason, for the break-up was Alfred's infidelity and his affair with a woman eighteen years Apollonie's junior, one Laurentine Bernage. Apollonie was by this time thirty-eight years old and, though still attractive, not quite the same proposition as a mistress as she had been at twenty-four. The Mosselman family finances may also have been going through a difficult patch. Whatever the reasons for the ending of the liaison, Alfred did not intend to abandon Apollonie entirely, offering her a not inconsiderable allowance of six thousand francs a year. She, however, refused it, and in so doing demonstrated again how different she was from the run of kept women in Paris. Her pride was hurt, and more than her pride. She had been very happy with Alfred, and her relationship with him had also meant that she was surrounded by many friends. If she had thought about the future at all – and she had a tendency to take life as it came, living only from day to day – she had imagined that her relationship with Alfred would continue indefinitely. Apollonie had never pressed him for marriage, assuming that the terms of their relationship made it unnecessary as well as unlikely. She appears to have thought that they were committed to one another, despite the absence of legal bonds, and his desertion came as a complete shock: her world was turned upside down. The break was total, and meant that Alfred no longer saw their mutual friends, as is clear from a letter he wrote to Théo in June 1864:

Since I no longer have the opportunity, as in the past, of seeing you and hearing you talk of everything with so much charm, I want at least to tell you that the memory has remained with me of many things which serious people would be very embarrassed to remember.

I hope not to die before being able to read your admittance speech to the Academy; I will do my utmost to go and hear you.

Remember me to your daughters who I hear are tall, beautiful and clever.

My respects to Ernesta, my friendship to you

A. Mosselman[12]

Rather than accept money from a man who had rejected her emotionally and sexually, Apollonie, with her usual aplomb and determination to make the best of things – she had shown her resilience in her recovery from the Baudelaire incident – resolved to support herself. The means she chose was the painting and repairing of miniatures, a very popular genre of the period and one in which she had previously been instructed by Ernest Meissonier; he had been sufficiently impressed by her artistic abilities to allow her to share his studio on her frequent visits to his and Emma's house at Poissy during the 1850s, where he had also painted her on numerous occasions. (Meissonier rarely painted women, but he enjoyed using Apollonie as a model; not only was she beautiful, but she was also patient and good company during sittings.) The quality of her work and the recommendations of her friends meant that she was able to make a small living in this way, but it never amounted to a great deal. She had some success, nevertheless, and even had four small oil portraits accepted for exhibition in the Salon of 1861. Du Camp gave them a positive mention in his review of that year's Salon, while he is dismissive of most of the other portraits exhibited.[13]

For the first few months after the rupture life at the rue Frochot carried on much as normal, the only difference at the Sunday soirées being the absence of Alfred. Before long, however, Apollonie's reduced financial circumstances began to take effect. She realised that she needed both to reduce her expenditure considerably and to sell much of what she had acquired during her years with Alfred. On

13 December 1861 a sale was held of her ornaments and valuables at the Salle des Ventes; Maxime Du Camp mentioned in a letter to Flaubert that he had spent the whole day there.[14] (Flaubert had continued his sexual banter with Apollonie during that year, having written on 31 January that he would love to see her 'new moon' – that is, her naked bottom; he writes that he would cover it with kisses, eat it and let himself expire upon it.)[15] Among the items for sale were the Clésinger bust and the Falconet *Venus*, which Apollonie particularly hated having to relinquish. They also included Meissonier's *Polichinelle* which he had himself, at Apollonie's request, removed from her door panel, and made the necessary adjustments to enable it to be sold as a separate painting. All Apollonie decided to keep was the portrait by Ricard and a few other works by her friends. The sale raised some forty-three thousand francs.

The letter from Du Camp to Flaubert on 13 December 1861 contains more news of Apollonie than a simple account of the sale; he tells his friend with some glee: 'I've seen La Présidente who has taken up with a young 22-year-old composer who makes up in love what he can't give her in money . . .'[16] This young man was Elie Miriam Delaborde, a pianist who was also the illegitimate (though unacknowledged) son of the eccentric and reclusive composer Charles Valentin Alkan, a friend of Chopin and others in the circle of George Sand. Elie Miriam had been born in Paris on 8 February 1839 and was therefore indeed twenty-two in 1861 – seventeen years younger than Apollonie.

No one knows why Elie Miriam took or was given the surname 'Delaborde', though there may have been a connection with the George Sand circle as this was the maiden name of Sand's mother. Delaborde's own mother was Lina Eraîm Miriam, a *rentière* ('woman of independent means') living in Paris. She may have been a pupil of Alkan's, she was of high social standing and she was already married. The period of Elie Miriam's birth and early childhood coincides with Alkan's first extended absence from the concert platform, which was to last for six years. Lina Eraîm is cited in Alkan's will, which is the only known official intimation that he had anything to do with her.

From a legal point of view Elie Miriam seems never to have existed, though he pursued a distinguished musical and artistic career and led a highly colourful private life. Like his father, he favoured the *pédalier* (a piano with a pedal board attached) and he was also a composer. In contrast to Alkan, however, his character was extrovert and urbane; he toured widely as a virtuoso, he painted a little and counted both Manet and Bizet (with whom he shared a passion for swimming and possibly also for Bizet's wife) among his friends. Apollonie was involved in helping to launch his career, and they may have spent some time together in Italy, in a villa owned by the Marquess Raimondi in Mosino, near the city of Villa Guardia.

However enjoyable her liaison with this young man, it could do nothing to improve her financial position and in 1862 Apollonie moved into a smaller, four-room apartment in the rue de la Faisanderie, near the Porte Dauphine entrance to the Bois de Boulogne. This was a newly built area which had rapidly become rather fashionable. The apartment was a little dark for her taste but she still managed to make it attractive and, as recorded by Théo's daughter, Judith, she did her own cooking there while singing to herself.[17] The rent for this apartment was five hundred and fifty francs a year, as compared to twelve hundred francs for the rue Frochot. Flaubert wrote her a sympathetic letter during that year, counselling her against despair and reminding her that one never knows what will happen next – such an attitude helps one to sleep, and the wind may change during the night.[18]

Few of the friends whom Apollonie had entertained in more prosperous times visited her with anything like such regularity now that she was in straitened circumstances. Several of them found the conviviality they had previously enjoyed in the rue Frochot in a new institution, the *dîners Magny*, an exclusively male dining club inaugurated in November 1862 which met on alternate Mondays at Magny's restaurant in the rue Contrescarpe Dauphine. One might have imagined that the men who had enjoyed flirting with and writing suggestive letters to Apollonie over many years would have been only too ready to translate their words into actions once Alfred

Mosselman had ceased to be her protector; instead Mosselman's absence removed the safety net from these men's transactions with her and, if anything, most of them avoided her company now that she was free to respond to them (another indication, perhaps, that Baudelaire's reactions were not so very unusual). But one man from the old days did venture on a more complete relationship with her at this period, and that was the Englishman Richard Wallace.

Richard was the illegitimate son of the fourth Marquess of Hertford, though Lord Hertford never acknowledged his paternity during his lifetime. (In this way his situation is remarkably parallel to that of Elie Miriam Delaborde vis-à-vis Alkan, and one wonders whether Apollonie was particularly drawn to men whose fathers would not acknowledge them, just as the Viscount Louis Harmand d'Abancourt had never acknowledged her.) Her new companion was born Richard Jackson, and changed his name to Wallace (his mother's maiden name) in 1842, when the fourth Marquess attained to the title and made Richard his secretary. The two men worked together closely at the Marquess's chosen profession of art collector, Richard living with him either at his apartment in the rue Lafitte or at his small château of Bagatelle in the Bois de Boulogne. (According to the Goncourt brothers, one of the fourth Marquess's claims to fame was that it was he who dubbed the area of the main boulevards between the Maison d'Or, the Opéra in the rue Le Peletier, the Café Anglais and Tortoni's 'the clitoris of Paris'.)

It was Richard Wallace, acting on behalf of Lord Hertford, who purchased Meissonier's *Polichinelle* at the sale in December 1861. He and Apollonie had known each other since the Hôtel Pimodan days, when Richard had been a member of the bohemian circle which used to gather there, and it has even been suggested that they had first had an affair in 1844. The evidence for this supposition rests on a document written by Apollonie to Richard between 1871 and 1874, part of which is preserved in the manuscripts department of the Bibliothèque Nationale. Entitled *Souvenirs de ma mère* (Memories of My Mother), it reads as follows:

It is in our blood, my mother's and mine, to be devoted to the people of your nation for my mother saved the lives of two of your compatriots.

The first time, she was twelve or thirteen years old. I believe it was during the battle of Fleurus.[19] She was very well liked by a nice old surgeon who, seeing how good she was at bandaging the wounded, took her with him to do the dressings while he operated. One day, a young English officer was brought in, as handsome as an angel. His shoulder had been shattered by a bullet. The little girl took a liking to him and wanted to take special care of him, which provoked the reproaches of the old doctor who, not having enough people to tend all the unfortunate wounded men with which the house was teeming, would not permit her to spend more time on this one than on the rest. But, drawn by some mysterious need of her heart, she didn't want to leave him day or night. On the second day, she saw her invalid was worse; his shoulder was terribly swollen. It seemed perfectly natural to her to probe the wound, feel the hard body of the bullet and extract it. She had seen this operation performed so many times before! In short, by dint of loving care, she managed to save him. As he was a prisoner of war, he was put on a cart to be taken away. The little girl surrounded him with as much hay as possible to lessen the jolts of the vehicle, then the poor wounded man took her hand, pressed it to his heart and mouth, said her name, the only word of French he knew, putting into his expression all the loving acknowledgment he felt, and then they separated. The little girl wept for her invalid but, at heart, she was happy to have saved him. I have always wanted to tell you this little story which moved me to tears, but then, as I had so little time in which to look at you, I concerned myself solely with that and forgot my little stories.

The other one took place in the rue des Dames, in Batignolles, where my mother was living. She was by the window. Suddenly a man dashed into the street. He was as

white as a corpse. He had been pursued all the way from the
Gare Saint-Lazare by French workers armed with shovels and
sticks, intent on killing him. She rushed out and took the
wounded man, a poor English mechanic, almost by force as
he didn't quite know whether she intended to save him or hand
him over, hid him in her house and comforted him. Then she
went outside and misled the madmen by telling them that she
had seen the man running away through the gardens. It seems
that at this time French workers had sworn to kill any foreign
worker brought in amongst them. This was in 1844. Do you
remember that year, my friend? For me, it is present in my
thoughts as though it were yesterday.[20]

This document is of interest for the flavour it gives of Apollonie's
rather sentimental nature, but it seems slim evidence on which to
posit an affair between herself and Richard Wallace in 1844, even
though she does remind him of that year with affection. She could by
invoking this date simply be recalling a time when they were both
young – Richard was four years older than Apollonie – and enjoying
the company of friends and stimulus of new ideas. Whether or not
this relationship amounted to more than friendship at that early stage,
they were likely to have encountered one another at various times
over the years. Richard, for instance, was a regular visitor to the
Meissoniers' house at Poissy, as were Apollonie and Alfred Mosselman. On occasion he may also have attended her Sunday salon. And
when Apollonie was preparing for her sale in December 1861,
Richard would have been the ideal man to turn to for advice, as
he was eminently placed to know what was likely to fetch a good
price in the art collecting world.

At some time in the early 1860s Apollonie and Richard travelled
together to the Isle of Wight on Richard's grandmother's yacht (even
though Apollonie never greatly enjoyed travelling, disliking the
separation from material comforts and her bathroom). In addition
they made a trip to Belgium and Holland to visit the museums there,
and they may also have stayed in Italy together. During this period

Richard could live comfortably on the salary he received from the Marquess of Hertford, though he was by no means wealthy in his own right. He and Apollonie did not enjoy an exclusive relationship, as Richard also had a long-term mistress, Amélie Castelnau, who worked in a *parfumerie* and by whom he had had a son in 1840. To what extent Apollonie was seeing Elie Miriam Delaborde at the same time as Richard Wallace, or for how long either liaison lasted, is impossible to determine, but a note in the margin of the Wallace Collection's copy of a book by Bernard Falk called *Old Q's Daughter* ('Old Q' was the fourth Duke of Queensbury and believed himself to be the father of the third Marquess of Hertford's wife) asserts that Richard Wallace would have married Apollonie but cut short his relations with her because of an escapade she had with an artist in Italy. The note was written by Robert Cecil, Assistant to the Director of the Wallace Collection from 1946 to 1979, and states that this information came from D.S. MacColl, Keeper of the Collection from 1911 to 1924, who was married to a granddaughter of Adèle (Bébé) Sabatier.[21] Whether this 'artist' was Elie Miriam Delaborde or some other man is unclear. What is clear is that Apollonie never again settled into a semi-permanent relationship of the type she had enjoyed with Alfred Mosselman.

When in Paris she continued to entertain, though on a much reduced scale, and she was also a regular guest at Théophile Gautier's house in Neuilly. The Goncourt brothers, who had first met her at the rue Frochot and subsequently at Théo's birthday party on 31 August 1862, encountered her again on the evening of 16 April 1864 and wrote on their return home their famous description of her as a *'vivandière de faunes'*, literally a 'sutler of fauns, or satyrs' and sometimes translated as a 'camp-follower for fauns'.[22] This is a phrase which has been often repeated but never adequately explained; possibly the Goncourts were not entirely clear themselves what they meant by it. They excelled throughout their lives at denigrating the people around them, and this insult they dreamt up for Apollonie is also insulting to the men she had entertained throughout her life thus far, the supposed 'fauns', who were also supposed to be friends, or at least acquaintances, of the Goncourt brothers. In addition they declared her to be rather common, with a coarse manner.[23] This may have referred to her liking for, or at least acceptance of, lewd talk. When this volume of their Journal was published and Apollonie read it, she exclaimed, 'So that's what happens when you invite people to your house!' and threw it on the fire.

In 1866 Apollonie left her ground-floor apartment in the rue de la Faisanderie and moved into a newly constructed building at 5 rue Pergolèse, near the Porte Maillot. The annual rent there was eight hundred and fifty francs, which suggests she was managing her finances rather well to be able to afford to move. In the same year she needed to call upon all her customary tact in managing her relationships with Théophile Gautier and Ernesta Grisi, both friends she valued deeply, when Théo suddenly left Ernesta around the time of their daughter Judith's marriage to Catulle Mendès, a marriage about which he had the deepest forebodings. Apollonie continued to maintain close contact with members of her family, receiving frequent visits from Bébé's daughter Jeanne who had settled in Paris on her marriage to a doctor called Emile Zabé. She also saw her old friend Elisa de Lucenay – she of the bangles and cigarettes – nearly every day. Elisa had married Jean-Baptiste Bressant, a well-known member of the Comédie Française, and the couple lived at 53 rue Spontini, just the other side of the avenue de l'Impératrice from Apollonie's address. Unfortunately, after having been persuaded by Bébé to invest in a shipping business in 1865, Apollonie lost much of the proceeds of her auction two years later when the business collapsed as a result of France's ill-fated intervention in Mexico. (This had involved the attempt to place a Habsburg prince, Maximilian, on the throne, and ultimately led to a humiliating withdrawal by French troops and the execution of Maximilian.) The collapse left Apollonie in considerable financial difficulty, and at one point she had to ask Meissonier for a loan of a thousand francs. He proffered it without hesitation; Gustave Ricard also willingly lent her money.

In 1867 Alfred Mosselman died, at the age of fifty-seven. He and Apollonie had not met again since the break-up. Charles Baudelaire also died in 1867, of syphilis. Contrary to some romantic reports,[24] Apollonie was not with him when he died on 31 August; she was in Como, either with Richard Wallace or with some other lover.

---

1 La Chroniqueuse, *Photographs of Paris Life*, pp.149–50

2 See Kristin Ross, 'Shopping' in Emile Zola, *The Ladies' Paradise*, University of California Press, Berkeley/Los Angeles/Oxford, 1992

3 Chroniqueuse, *Photographs of Paris Life*, p.173

4 Comte Horace de Viel Castel, *Mémoires sur le règne de Napoléon III (1851–1864)*, Vol.3, p.179

5 Quoted in André Billy, *La Présidente et ses amis*, p.185

6 Jean-Jacques Pauvert, *L'Erotisme Second Empire*, pp.170–1

7 Ibid., pp.31–2

8 Ibid., p.62

9 Ibid., p.63

10 Théophile Gautier, *Correspondance générale*, Vol.7, 1992, p.210

11 Gustave Flaubert, *Correspondance générale*, Vol.III, 1991, p.904

12 Théophile Gautier, *Correspondance générale*, Vol.8, 1993, p.313

13 Maxime Du Camp, *Le Salon de 1861*, A. Bourdilliat & Cie, Paris, 1861, pp.166–7

14 Gustave Flaubert, *Correspondance*, Vol.III, p.842

15 Ibid., p.143

16 Ibid., p.842

17 Judith Gautier, *Le Collier des jours. Le Second Rang du collier*, Félix Luven, Paris, 1909, p.184

18 Gustave Flaubert, *Correspondance*, Vol.III, pp.218–19

19 More commonly known as the battle of Ligny, this took place on 16 June 1815

20 BNF, Département des manuscrits, dossiers de Jacques Crépet et Jean Ziegler

21 From letter of 3 January 1997 from Robert Wenley of Wallace Collection to Gérard de Senneville, copy in Wallace Collection's file on Madame Sabatier

22 Robert Baldick (ed. and tr.), *Pages from the Goncourt Journal*, p.98

23 Ibid.

24 See Léon Séché, *La Jeunesse dorée sous Louis-Philippe*, Mercure de France, Paris, 1910, pp.293–4

CHAPTER NINE

The Hôtel Païva

W HEN BLANCHE DE Païva was not receiving a wealthy client at her *rez-de-chaussée* in the place Saint-Georges, she would be discussing her business investments with an adviser, purchasing some new item of jewellery (precious stones and jewels being one of her passions) or preparing herself for an evening at the theatre. In her case, this usually meant the Opéra (where she hired a box for every Monday and Wednesday) or the Théâtre Italien; she scorned the more low-brow entertainments of opéra bouffe or light comedy. She was particularly fond of the operas of Verdi and never missed a première of his, so would have been present at the Théâtre Italien on 23 December 1854 for *Il Trovatore*, at the Théâtre Lyrique on 24 December 1863 for *Rigoletto* and at the same theatre on 27 October 1864 for *La Traviata*, the opera based on *La Dame aux camélias*. She would always be accompanied by one of her entourage, such as Théophile Gautier, Jules Lecomte or the famous music critic Pier Angelo Fiorentino, and on entering her box would cause a sensation by the luxury of her attire.

Throughout the Second Empire the Opéra remained in its old building on the rue Le Peletier, joined to the boulevard des Italiens by a covered passageway. Facilities and seating were far from adequate, though the company was regarded as one of the best in the world. The Emperor was not himself passionately fond of music, but did attend fairly often as a ceremonial gesture; he realised, however, that a new and splendid opera house would increase national prestige and enhance his new city. Accordingly a competition was held in 1860 for the design of a new house, and it was won by a young architect called Charles Garnier. His creation, the first stone of which was laid in July 1862 but which was not completed until 1875, encapsulates the baroque style which he called 'Napoleon III' and which was essentially a mélange of styles from every era, elaborate, imitative and ostentatious.

Blanche had hoped that her marriage to the Marquess de Païva would lift her out of the ranks of courtesans and into the sphere of respectability, but in order to leave her profession behind she needed a regular income from other sources. Her investments went some way to providing it, but she needed to keep increasing them in order to fund her desired way of life, and that meant continuing to accept clients (and charging them very high fees for her services). Wealth was a prerequisite; no man could even think of propositioning La Païva if he were not extremely rich, and the difficulty of obtaining her favours gave rise to legends. There was the story, for instance, of a young man whom Emile Bergerat claims[1] to have been Adolphe Gaiffe, a friend of Baudelaire's and Gautier's whose family fortunes had known better days; Viel Castel narrates the tale irresistibly, in the style of a fairy story:

> One of these suitors, at the end of his tether, told her bluntly that he was determined to sleep with her; he said it to her, and wrote so well and so often that one morning she took him aside and spoke to him as follows:
>
> 'You really want to sleep with me, you've set your heart on it and it's become your *idée fixe*; we must therefore get it over with, so that we can have some peace with one another afterwards. What can you offer me? You are poor, you possess bonds to the value of thirty thousand *livres*; I love money, I can never get enough of it, yet I still have more than you; I want to make you buy the favour you request – do you have ten thousand francs?'
>
> 'No,' replied the petitioner.
>
> 'You have answered well, because if you had said that you did

possess ten thousand, I would have asked you for twenty. But as you do not have ten thousand francs, bring me that amount; we will burn it, and I will be all yours for as long as this fire of ten thousand francs lasts.'

The lover bowed and said:

'Until tomorrow, marchioness.'

The next day the marchioness, seated on the couch in her boudoir, was emblazoned at her most coquettish; a marble pedestal table, like an antique altar, seemed to await a victim; the air was perfumed, and daylight barely penetrated the thick curtains which draped the windows.

The lover, decorated not with pennants but with twelve thousand-franc notes drawn on the bank of France – for he had desired to render his sacrifice the more complete – approached the goddess.

La Païva, without changing her position and with the smile and expression of an amorous viper, felt the twelve thousand francs, found them adorable and, arranging them on the marble table-top in such a way that they would burn one after the other, set fire to the first.

The young man flew at once into La Païva's arms and, dispensing with preliminaries, attained his goal immediately, profiting from his good fortune in the manner of a man who knows the value of time.

The notes were burnt up; the satisfied lover and the smiling Païva, rumpled and mocking, found themselves face to face and, while they were adjusting their clothing, the knight, in response to the courtesan's scornful glances, said to her:

'You poor thing, I've made a fool of you; my friend Aguado did such a good job of photographing the notes that you were taken in.'

At these words, La Païva sprang like a panther towards the imprudent man. Neither Camilla nor Hermione in their rages could compare with the anger of the duped courtesan. Had it not been for the court of assizes, she would have stabbed or strangled the insolent man. As it was, she had to make do with stabs of the tongue in place of the dagger; with them she was unstinting, bombarding with terms of abuse the satisfied one who was no longer a lover, and who brushed the dust from his knees as he left.[2]

Such a reaction from La Païva accords with what would have been expected of such a woman by anyone familiar with Parent-Duch-âtelet's descriptions: 'Anger is a frequent emotion in these women who, in such a state, display a truly remarkable energy of body and soul: they produce a flood of words which, by their nature and originality of expression, result in an eloquence which belongs only to this class.'[3] Whatever the truth concealed in this story, such encounters were rendered unnecessary by the arrival in Blanche's life of one man, eleven years her junior: the Count Guido Henckel von Donnersmarck.

He was descended from a very old family from Upper Silesia, one of the most ardent centres of Prussian nationalism and, in the nineteenth century, a very rich mining area. The property of the Henckels covered many thousands of acres, consisting of vast forests and agricultural land but also – and more importantly as regards their wealth – mines and factories. The family's main residence was the castle of Neudeck, in Tarnowitz, on the border of Poland and Silesia; it was a fortress castle, complete with dungeon, moat and ramparts, and it had belonged to them since 1623. The family motto was *Memento vivere* ('Remember to live').

Guido, born in 1830, was the youngest child of a family of four – two boys and two girls. His father, a difficult man, disliked both his daughters and gave all his affection to his elder son, a delicate boy. In 1847 Guido obtained permission to visit Paris, in the company of an old family servant who was French by birth. He was still there in 1848 at the outbreak of the February Revolution; Tarnowitz was not spared the repercussions which spread throughout most of Europe, and the peasants and workers there staged a revolt. Guido's father, who was most disturbed by these developments, was then struck by the additional blow of his elder son's death. At this point he decided to hand over the running of his business interests to Guido, who was accordingly recalled from Paris. When he arrived at Neudeck he found a crowd of demonstrators surrounding the castle, preventing the family from leaving. He passed this first test of his management ability with flying colours, talking to the protestors until they agreed to withdraw.

This accomplished, he dedicated himself to the running of the family business, undertaking a major overhaul of all its enterprises. He travelled far more than had his predecessors, both to acquire new ideas and for public relations purposes. He tended to spend the summer in Tarnowitz while the winter would find him in Berlin, moving in court and political circles, hearing much and giving away little, always with an eye to defending his own interests. His business activities also brought him into contact with French and Belgian entrepreneurs. In particular, he formed an association with the largest producer of zinc in the world – the Belgian company of Vieille Montagne, the family business of Alfred Mosselman.

As a young man, Guido was considered very handsome. He had a long face and large eyes, and bore himself in an aristocratic manner, with more the air of a romantic poet than that of a businessman.

This, then, was the man La Païva encountered in the mid-1850s, when she was just over thirty-five years old. He was introduced to her by Bamberg, the Prussian consul in Paris, who sometimes dined in the place Saint-Georges. Blanche and Guido immediately struck up a rapport. They were united by a love of money and a passion for its pursuit, but there was far more to it than that. Guido was fascinated by Blanche, and he would talk about her with ardour until his death. He loved everything about her: her appearance, her manners, her wit, her ease in society, her sexual knowledge and her business acumen. How much the fascination was reciprocated is an open question. There are those – both contemporary and later commentators[4] – who are convinced that Blanche was incapable of love, that self-interest was the only motivating force in her life. Others[5] are convinced that for Guido Henckel von Donnersmarck she experi-

enced genuine, long-lasting passion. What is certainly clear is that her
liaison with Guido was exclusive, and ended the necessity for her ever
to receive another client. His business affairs also provided her with an
interest and purpose in life which may previously have been lacking;
together they formed a real partnership and became one of the most
well-known couples in Second Empire Paris. And it seemed that, as
far as Guido was concerned, Blanche had no past.

After meeting Blanche Guido began to travel regularly between
Paris and Neudeck, where he placed directors to run the business
during his absences. And money flowed into the place Saint-Georges,
where he took up residence with Blanche. She was gradually
introduced by Guido into the running of his business affairs; he
was surprised and delighted by how quickly she learnt how it all
worked and what the problems and pitfalls were, and by her ability to
suggest ways forward. The experience she had gained in the management of her own finances – and the hard lessons she had learnt
through her disastrous attempts to manage, or undermine, Henri
Herz's business interests – now bore fruit. She was also able to extend
Guido's acquaintance with all the pleasures of Paris, and played a
valuable role in helping him acquire an edge of sophistication and a
sense of *savoir faire*.

In 1857 Viel Castel wrote of this unlikely couple:

> La Païva is at least forty years old, she is painted and powdered
> like an old tightrope walker, she has slept with everyone, yet her
> German is thirty-six at the most.
>
> La Païva's bedroom must conceal mysteries which alone hold
> the key to these extravagances of immorality.[6]

The actual ages of the couple at the time of Viel Castel's entry in his
diary were thirty-eight and twenty-seven. This age gap was Blanche's
principal worry at the time she took up with Guido, and she took
steps to disguise it, convincing him – and the authorities – that she
had been born in 1826 (which would have made her ten years old at
the time of her first marriage and eleven at the birth of her son).

Guido never questioned this assertion, always believing that she was only four years older than he was.

On 11 July 1855 Blanche de Païva had purchased, for the sum of 406,640 francs, a plot of ground situated at 25 avenue des Champs Elysées. This had become a particularly fashionable area to live in, eclipsing the old faubourg Saint-Germain. Other people who acquired land on or around the Champs Elysées included Prince Napoleon, who had a neo-Pompeian palace built for himself which was officially opened on 15 January 1860 (Théophile Gautier composed a special prologue for the occasion); Emile de Girardin, who chose to build in the Roman style; the Count de Quinsonas, who went for a Gothic castle; and Jules de Lesseps, who had a Tunisian château constructed. Blanche intended to build a *hôtel* to rival all these in magnificence. The plot having been acquired, and Henckel von Donnersmarck ready to finance Blanche's great project, she looked around for a suitable architect to realise her vision. She found him in Pierre Manguin, who was a little over forty years old when he was put in touch with her at her request. She had noticed his work at the Universal Exposition of 1855.

The work of designing, building, decorating and furnishing what became known as the Hôtel Païva took ten years to complete. Blanche was closely involved in the process from the beginning, absorbing architectural principles from Manguin with her habitual ease of assimilation. The marble and onyx were carved on site, as though the building under construction were a medieval cathedral rather than a nineteenth-century private mansion. In consultation with Manguin, Blanche chose the artists and craftsmen she wanted to work on each aspect of her magnificent dwelling. She was not interested in collecting antique objects but in commissioning new ones, and thus became a significant patron to a number of artists just embarking on their careers. To paint the ceiling in the main drawing room, the *grand salon*, she selected Paul Baudry, who had won the Prix de Rome in 1850. The son of a shoemaker from La Roche-sur-Yon, he had received a scholarship enabling him to study at the Ecole des Beaux Arts but had known poverty and even wretchedness. On his return from Rome he had attained some success but not enough to make him very well known. La Païva's commission gave him a chance to make his reputation; he went on to paint the foyer of Garnier's new Opéra. Dalou, the artist chosen by La Païva to produce the sculptures which would occupy the corners of the *grand salon*, had only just ceased to be a student when she commissioned him. He was living in poor accommodation in the rue Gît-le-Cœur, with barely enough money to afford to eat every day. The commission from La Païva transformed his life: she not only provided a showcase for his talents but paid her artists well.

By the final months of the great project Blanche was growing impatient, longing to move in. She would arrive on horseback most afternoons, after her ride in the Bois, to measure progress and encourage – or bully – the workers.

The result was dazzling, overwhelming, its ostentation entirely in keeping with the spirit of the age. Baudry's ceiling in the *grand salon*, whose five tall windows overlooked the Champs Elysées, showed Day chasing away Night; the model for Night was said to be La Païva herself.[7] One of the statues gracing the huge fireplace of red and white marble was also taken to be a representation of the mistress of the house. The other drawing rooms were hung with crimson damask, specially woven at Lyons at vast expense. There was a *salon des griffons* containing a black marble fireplace, and a music room boasting *médaillons* by Picou. Throughout the whole house there was a profusion of gold, ornamentation, hangings, statues and paintings. The dining room looked out on to an inner courtyard, and bore an inscription on the wall: '*Mange ce qui est bon, bois ce qui est clair, et ne parle que de ce qui est vrai*' ('Eat what is good, drink what is clear, and only talk of what is true.') This room had four double doors decorated by the painter Ranvier with pastoral and hunting motifs and was dominated by a fresco on the ceiling, painted by Dalou, of Diana asleep on a stag. The staircase (adorned with statues of Virgil, Petrarch and Dante) and the bath were made of onyx. The first floor housed La Païva's bathroom, bedroom and boudoir, as well as a room for Henckel von Donnersmarck. La Païva's bed, inlaid with rare woods and ivory, stood in an alcove below a ceiling on which was portrayed Aurora, goddess of the dawn. Each item of furniture was a masterpiece in itself – such as the sideboard in the dining room, with its friezes reminiscent of della Robbia's singers.

Blanche de Païva and Guido Henckel von Donnersmarck finally moved into their new abode in 1866, though the finishing touches were not completed until two years later when all the items of furniture were finally installed (this was because some of the items they had commissioned were on display in the Universal Exposition of 1867). Here La Païva continued to hold her twice-weekly dinners, lavishing hospitality on the chosen few. The reputation of her *hôtel* was enhanced by the fact that very few people ever saw inside it during the time she lived there. Paul Baudry even had difficulty persuading her to admit the jury for the Emperor's prize to see his paintings, judging from a letter he wrote in desperation to Théophile Gautier in May 1869.[8] It was partly in order to avoid rejection and a reminder of her past life that Blanche limited her invitations to the select group of her friends; no respectable woman from the *haut monde*, for instance, would deign to set foot inside the showy residence of a famous courtesan even if she was now an ex-courtesan, and Blanche pragmatically took the view that it was preferable to reject than to be rejected. She also preferred to invite only those people she found amusing, enlightening or useful. The effect of the restricted admittance to the Hôtel Païva was to produce an aura of fascination around the building, as though it were the magical palace of an enchantress – or of a witch. Fabulous stories abounded; it was said, for instance, that La Païva's bed was flanked by two enormous safes, for her money and her jewels.

There was even a story put around that the Emperor turned up one day, overcome by curiosity to see inside the famous *hôtel*. This was supposed to have taken place after a celebrated incident at the Théâtre Italien, where La Païva had managed to hire the stage box directly opposite the imperial box. On this particular occasion the Emperor remarked to his aide de camp that he wished the Empress were equipped with a Japanese screen like the one La Païva was using to shield her eyes from the glare and heat of the footlights. This remark was unwisely conveyed to Blanche who, never one to miss an opportunity, promptly had her screen sent round to the imperial box. The Empress disdained even to notice it, which *hauteur* rather embarrassed, so it was said, the Emperor. Arsène Houssaye takes up the tale:

> A few days later, when the marchioness was alone in her *hôtel*, one of her manservants brought her a card inside an envelope from a gentleman who had declined to give his name and who wished to see Mme de Païva. She tore open the envelope and read the handwritten name: 'Napoleon III'.
>
> As nothing ever astonished her, she went forward nonchalantly to meet the Emperor, who offered her his fist, in the manner of Louis XIV, in order to conduct her into the drawing room. He was curious to see at last this *hôtel* of which the whole world was talking, although no one apart from the marchioness's twenty-four friends had set foot inside it.
>
> He was no great connoisseur, but he marvelled in front of everything at the exquisite taste of the mistress of the house. He insisted on climbing the onyx staircase. On the first floor, he was no less enchanted by all the furnishings, all the works of art, directing admiring glances everywhere, including at the marchioness who, as always, was covered in jewels like a reliquary.[9]

This was still not the end of the story. A few days later, after midnight at the Friday dinner party, while the hostess and her ten guests were partaking of tea and iced coffee, a servant suddenly announced portentously: 'His Majesty the Emperor!' Everyone stood to attention in amazed silence, as La Païva stepped forward to greet the illustrious visitor. According to Houssaye, 'Napoleon III stretched out his hands like Jesus stilling the waves',[10] and asked for the discussion to continue as before. Unsurprisingly, however, conversation now became stilted though the Emperor kept showering

compliments on various of the guests, including Gautier and Delacroix. He then spent some time staring at the ceiling and twiddling
the ends of his famous moustache. Then finally he began to complain
about how annoying life was at the Tuileries, at which point, says
Houssaye, 'we recognised Vivier, king of the comedians, the spitting
image of Napoleon III'.[11]

La Païva was said never to have forgiven Vivier for this trick;
incapable of laughing at her own expense, and desiring that no one
should better her in ostentatious display, she hated being either
deceived or upstaged. The Emperor, on the other hand, was
believed to have been amused when he heard about it and soon
afterwards Vivier, who was also a famous horn player, was decorated. Whether it was the actor or the Emperor who made the first
visit has never been clarified; Houssaye implies[12] that it was indeed
the Emperor, but then he is rarely to be trusted when it comes to
matters of fact. That the court was aware of Blanche de Païva and
her magnificent *hôtel* is clear from the memoirs of Princess Murat,
who writes that La Païva's 'establishment in the Champs Elysées,
where none but men were admitted, was kept up with the most
insolent luxury'.[13] It is the word 'insolent' which is the most telling
here, suggesting that high society was by no means indifferent to the
activities and self-display of the ex-courtesan which was such an
effective parody of their own.

The life of the court featured its own cycle of entertainments.
Annually between the New Year and the beginning of Lent, the
Emperor and Empress would give four grand balls to which several
thousand guests would be invited. A great object for the occasional
visitor would be to make his or her way into the *Salle des Maréchaux*,
in which the imperial quadrille was danced. La Chroniqueuse
conveys an idea of the brilliance of these occasions in her report
of the ball given on 11 January 1860:

The skilful arrangement of the mirrors in the apartment, which
reflected a hundred-fold the persons and objects contained
therein; the brilliant lights which made the diamonds of the

ladies sparkle and glow like very fire upon the snowy bosoms of the fair wearers; the many and various uniforms; and, last of all, the exquisite court costume worn by the French gentlemen, made one of the grandest *coups-d-œil* that can possibly be imagined.[14]

During carnival time there was usually a fancy dress ball held at the Tuileries, to which invitations would be restricted to those who had previously been presented at court. There they would dance to the music of Waldteufel, Strauss and Offenbach.

During Lent there was no dancing, but there were four concerts, organised by the court chamberlain Bacciochi and the composer Auber, chapel master at the Tuileries. The court spent the spring and most of the summer in the great châteaus of Fontainebleau and Saint-Cloud, the latter often used for entertaining royal visitors from abroad. In the summer they would move to Biarritz near the Spanish border for a few weeks of informality at the Villa Eugénie, a small retreat Napoleon III had built for the Empress.

From 1856, in late October or early November the focus would shift to Compiègne, some fifty miles north of Paris near a beautiful forest famous for its game. The court would remain there for a month to six weeks. Invitations to Compiègne were greatly prized; several hundred guests selected by the Empress from various classes and professions, including artists, would be invited for four days at a time (known as a *série*), and a special train ran from the Gare du Nord at 2.33pm to take them. Once at Compiègne, the entertainment was both plentiful and compulsory. In addition to hunting, guests were expected to play charades, dress up and perform in plays, as well as sparkle in conversation at every meal-time, all in the presence of the imperial couple. The expense could also be daunting, as the women were expected to wear new outfits twice a day, while the men had to appear for dinner in court dress.

Though no acknowledged *demi-mondaine* would ever find her way to Compiègne, it was not unknown for the Emperor to invite his mistresses there, particularly if, like the Countess Walewska, they were married to some other member of the establishment. (Her husband, Count Walewski, was an illegitimate son of Napoleon I.) The Emperor had several mistresses during the course of his marriage as well as many more casual sexual encounters with women procured for him by Count Bacciochi. Prior to his marriage he had already fathered several illegitimate sons, and had enjoyed a liaison of many years' standing with an English woman known to posterity as 'Miss Howard'. One of his longer-term mistresses during the 1860s was Marguerite Bellanger, whose original name was Julie Lebœuf. After working as a hotel chambermaid in Boulogne she had run off to join a circus, becoming an acrobat and a bareback rider. The Emperor, who had first encountered her at Saint-Cloud where she had been brought to the imperial hunt as the guest of a young army officer, was particularly impressed by her ability to do a variety of things while standing on her hands. He bought her a house on the rue des Vignes in Passy, but pensioned her off in 1866 with a Prussian husband and a house in the country.

In the grand house on the Champs Elysées it was said to be very cold (despite the efficient and innovatory central heating system which was still working well in 2001) and Blanche was supposed to like having her hair done with all the windows wide open, even in the middle of winter. This was all part of the mythology surrounding La Païva, which made her appear like some inhuman character who had swept in from the frozen wastelands of Siberia, cold-blooded, needing neither physical nor emotional warmth.

Unsurprisingly, the source for some of the exaggerated stories about Blanche can be traced to the Journal of the Goncourt brothers, whom Théophile Gautier introduced to the Hôtel Païva and its owners on Friday, 24 May 1867. As usual the brothers wrote up their experiences in misanthropic style, describing their hostess as resembling a provincial actress, with false hair and a false smile, and the dining room as being like a private room in an expensive restaurant. They claimed that all the guests were ill at ease, that Paul de Saint-Victor in particular sat twisting his hat out of discomfort at being unable to think of anything to say. They declared that they felt 'that horrible chill which characterizes the houses of tarts playing at being ladies'.[15] Nevertheless they returned for more of the same the following Friday, relating that on this occasion the table's centrepiece did not arrive until six o'clock when everyone was required to admire it and marvel at the cost. In their opinion, the only piece of art in the building worth admiring was Baudry's ceiling.

They also give an unflattering description of La Païva herself: her flesh white, her nose with its flattened end and pronounced nostrils, wrinkles which appeared black in the gaslight, her straight mouth a line of red lipstick in a face whitened by rice powder, with a horseshoe-shaped furrow on either side. They describe how, after coffee, they all went to sit in the small walled garden, from where they could hear the sounds of music drifting in from the nearby Bal Mabille, and where all the guests began to feel the cold – to which their hostess, with her bare shoulders, seemed quite impervious. There was nothing of conventional femininity about her, none of the usual softness – or consideration for her guests – which the brothers expected from a woman, but they could not help observing, despite themselves, that La Païva was far from stupid. She kept surprising them with reflections drawn from her life as a practical business-woman, by her ideas and axioms from her own experience and by a dry originality. They found the latter not to their taste (*antipathique*), and suspected that it came from her race and religion as well as from the prodigious heights and depths of her life to date.[16] She would on occasion appear to be absent in spirit from her guests, thinking about something to which they had no access, but when she was fully present she could always keep up with the conversation of her intellectual male companions. She read the most important news-papers in several languages, kept up to date with all the latest literature and music, and would astonish those around her by the depth and breadth of her knowledge.

The Goncourts returned on 3 January 1868, a snowy day. The celebrated historian, philosopher and critic Hippolyte Taine ('whom one runs into at all the great courtesans' houses'[17]) was dining there for the first time. The brothers stress again how cold seemed to be La

Païva's natural element – she was 'like a sort of monster from a Scandinavian myth' – and they also mention how she expounded on her theory of willpower. She believed, she said, that people can do anything if they seriously set their minds to it, and that the unfortunate only remain that way because at heart they have chosen so to remain. Taking herself as a case in point, she claimed at one time to have cut herself off from human society and even food for three years in order to concentrate on attaining her objective.[18] The Goncourts were there again on 14 February, as was Théophile Gautier, among others. Their comments on this occasion relate to the impossibility of pouring oneself a glass of water reddened with a little wine in La Païva's establishment, because all the jugs and carafes were so enormous ('crystal cathedrals') that they could only be lifted by a servant; they also say there was generally a commotion if one requested anything not on the 'programme'. They allege that Théo sat rather nervously next to his hostess, afraid of burning her robe with his cigar, but that he was nevertheless a wonderful talker and not at all verbally constrained in La Païva's presence.[19] They were there again a few weeks later, on Good Friday, when the conversation ranged from God to astronomy. In May they allude to those fascinating safes reputed to live on either side of her bed, in which she kept her silver, gold, diamonds, emeralds and pearls, and between which she dreamt – or had nightmares.[20]

Though much of what the Goncourts write is exaggerated and decidedly hostile, there is a vestige of truth behind some of their observations. That Blanche and Henckel enjoyed showing off their wealth is evident, and other guests besides the Goncourts have commented on how admiration of all the opulence was expected. This was the price to be paid for accepting Blanche's hospitality, but most of the guests do not seem to have found it too high a price to pay – they did, after all, keep coming back for more. And Blanche continued to expect high standards of conversation from her fellow diners, though a certain degree of post-prandial somnolence seems to have been accepted as well. But deferential charm was not part of her arsenal in her dealings with men, and she kept the assembled company on their toes. A letter from Théo, dated 14 January 1868, alludes to the need to be witty at her gatherings:

> He apologises for not having been able to attend the last two Fridays, but at this coming one he will resume, come hell or high water, his place on her right hand: 'If I am ill, you'll just have to let me lie down after dinner, as they did at Ida's [the wife of Alexandre Dumas *père*] to keep me fresh until the bourgeois people left. But at this banquet of Plato, I dare not say Aspasia, there are only clever people. One must be brilliant from the soup onwards. If I am dull, you will forgive me this once.'[21]

Arsène Houssaye found everything to his satisfaction: 'Never was talk more lively and unpredictable. I think this sumptuous table, supplied by the greenhouses of Pontchartrain, a royal castle, with grapes, cherries and peaches even when it was snowing, served just as well to stimulate the mind as did the frugal table of Mme de Maintenon.'[22] Not only could men of letters and the other arts eat and drink here to their hearts' content; they could also discuss their ideas and aspirations in a select company which – provided the Goncourt brothers were absent – was sympathetic and discreet.

Not content with owning a luxurious and well-appointed mansion in the centre of Paris, in the mid-1860s Guido had bought for Blanche the sixteenth-century château of Pontchartrain from Count Osmond for two million francs. This château, thirty-five kilometres to the west of Paris on the road to Rambouillet, had an eminent history. Louise de la Vallière, one of the *maîtresses en titre* of Louis XIV, had once lived there, and the park had been designed by Le Nôtre. The Osmond family, particularly Count Osmond's mother, had been revered by the local villagers, amongst whom there was some disquiet when the rumour got around that the Count had sold the castle and land – including the location of his mother's tomb – to a foreign woman of dubious reputation. The Count himself had not been concerned about the credentials of his purchasers. Having gambled away most of his fortune, all he had wanted was a quick sale for the best possible price. The proceeds did tide him over for a while, though he squandered some of them in 1866 by giving a famous ball at which all Paris danced until dawn. And so, for at least the second time in her life, Blanche de Païva profited from the fecklessness of a hopeless gambler and spendthrift.

On her arrival in Pontchartrain she had intended to follow the convention of paying introductory visits to neighbouring land-owners. She decided against continuing this practice, however, upon receiving an icy reception from Count Rougé, whose property bordered her own. The local workforce was eventually won round owing to La Païva's efficient management of the estate (though some of the villagers were scandalised by her masculine riding attire), but the aristocracy remained aloof and hospitality at Pontchartrain, as at the Hôtel Païva, was therefore restricted to her own circle of Parisian friends. The only exception to this was the local priest, a man named Got, who visited her frequently and esteemed her company.

Legends accrued around La Païva's life at Pontchartrain as around every other aspect of her life, often originating in gossip inspired by curiosity and a lack of concrete information. Some rumours were spread by disgruntled former staff, such as a certain Ballard who had been her steward until dismissed for insulting her. It was said that she was obsessive over the tidiness of the grounds, that she fined her staff if they allowed so much as a fallen leaf to remain on the ground when she made her daily inspection, and that she lurked in the alleyways to catch and fine anyone, including guests, caught walking on her private path. There was also the legend of the servant whose only task was to open and shut the château's one hundred and fifty windows. He began his work at six in the morning, carried on till midnight each night, and eventually dropped dead from exhaustion. Then there was the story that one day, having been thrown by her horse, La Païva took a pistol from her belt and shot the animal dead. This story was told to Frédéric Loliée[23] by the Count de Prémio-Real, who had it from his father Auguste Dreyfus-Gonzales, a later owner of Pontch-artrain – and so on and so forth.

The greenhouses at Pontchartrain were a particular source of pride to Blanche; it was through these that she kept her Parisian table supplied with out-of-season fruits as alluded to by Houssaye, proving herself ahead of her time in doing what has since become commonplace. It has been said that she had the magic gift of always being a step ahead, of possessing and enjoying things before anyone else knew they existed.[24] She also had a special bath designed and made for her at Pontchartrain, commissioned from Pierre Manguin and sculpted by Donnadieu out of a single block of Algerian yellow onyx. Donnadieu received an award for this extraordinary item at the 1867 Universal Exposition.

1 Emile Bergerat, *Souvenirs d'un enfant de Paris*, Vol.2, Bibliothéque Charpentier, Paris, 1912, pp.300–1

2 Comte Horace de Viel Castel, *Mémoires sur le règne de Napoléon III (1851–1864)*, Vol.4, pp.41–2

3 A.J.B. Parent-Duchâtelet, *De la Prostitution dans la ville de Paris*, p.142

4 See, for example, Joanna Richardson, *The Courtesans*, p.82

5 See, for example, Janine Alexandre-Debray, *La Païva, 1819–1884: ses amants, ses maris*, Librairie Académique Perrin, Paris, 1986, p.117

6 Comte Horace de Viel Castel, *Mémoires sur le règne de Napoléon III (1851–1864)*, Vol.4, p.68

7 See Charles A. Dolph, *The Real 'Lady of the Camellias' and Other Women of Quality*, p.79

8 Théophile Gautier, *Correspondance générale*, Vol.10, 1996, p.335

9 Arsène Houssaye, *Les Confessions. Souvenirs d'un demi-siècle 1830–1880*, 1885, p.95

10 Ibid.

11 Ibid., p.99

12 See Arsène Houssaye, 'L'Ancien Hôtel de la Marquise de Païva' in *Un Hôtel célèbre sous le Second Empire*, Paris, n.d., p.18

13 Princess Caroline Murat, *My Memoirs*, p.87

14 La Chroniqueuse, *Photographs of Paris Life*, p.231

15 Robert Baldick (ed. and tr.), *Pages from the Goncourt Journal*, p.128

16 Edmond et Jules de Goncourt, *Journal. Mémoires de la vie littéraire*, Vol.2: 1866–1886, Fasquelle & Flammarion, Paris, 1956, pp.87–8

17 Robert Baldick (ed and tr.), *Pages from the Goncourt Journal*, p.134

18 Ibid.

19 Edmond et Jules de Goncourt, *Journal. Mémoires de la vie littéraire*, Vol.2, p.134

20 Ibid., p.149

21 Theophile Gautier, *Correspondance générale*, Vol.10, 1996, p.24

22 Arsène Houssaye, *Les Confessions. Souvenirs d'un demi-siècle 1830–1880*, 1891, p.336

23 Frédéric Loliée, '*La Païva*', p.154

24 Frédéric Loliée, *Les Femmes du second empire. La Fête impériale*, Librairie Félix Juven, Paris, 1907, p.139

CHAPTER TEN

The English Beauty of the French Empire

P ART OF THE reason for the stir Blanche de Païva made in Paris, for the controversy she aroused and for the hostile opinions formed about her – particularly after the collapse of the Second Empire – was that she was foreign. She was seen as having come from abroad to lay siege to the rich young men of Paris, and as such she represented a danger to the whole of French society. Another woman viewed in the same light was 'The English Beauty of the French Empire',[1] the woman who called herself Cora Pearl.

She was born in Plymouth, probably in 1835, the second daughter of Frederick William Nicholls Crouch and his wife Lydia (née Pearson). The child was named Emma Elizabeth and years later people who claimed to know would variously give her original name as Emma Crutch,[2] Emma Cruch,[3] Emma Chruch[4] and even Emma Church.[5] Her father was a musician, and his chief claim to fame was that he composed the popular song 'Kathleen Mavourneen'; he styled himself 'Professor'. His wife also gave singing lessons, in between her numerous pregnancies and struggling to run the household. The tumult of daily life can be imagined. As Emma herself put it: 'I was born to hear a great deal of noise, if not to make it; there was in my case a kind of predestination to clatter.'[6]

Her father was full of grandiose stories about his childhood successes: he had been playing in a theatre orchestra at the age of nine, he said, and was a choirboy at both St Paul's Cathedral and Westminster Abbey. The *New Grove Dictionary of Music* entry for Frederick Nicholls Crouch (born in London on 31 July 1808) describes him as a cellist, singer and composer. He studied music with his father Frederick William Crouch (who was the author of a *Complete Treatise on the Violoncello*, published in 1826) and his grandfather William Crouch, who was organist of Old Street church in London. At the age of nine he was indeed playing in the orchestra of the Royal Coburg Theatre (later the Old Vic). He entered the Royal Academy of Music in 1831 but left in June of the following year; during his time there he was also a cellist at the King's Theatre and in other orchestras, including Queen Adelaide's private band. He moved to Plymouth after 1832, working there both as a professional singer and as a travelling salesman. His famous song 'Kathleen Mavourneen' was composed between about 1835 and 1838. He gave occasional lectures on the songs and legends of Ireland, became a supervisor at the music publishers D'Almaine, and was thought to have contributed to advances in zincography, an engraving process.

In 1847 he left his first family and two years later, when Emma Elizabeth was about fourteen, he went to New York as a cellist, probably in order to escape creditors in the wake of a lawsuit (he had twice been declared bankrupt, and before leaving England had contracted the first of four bigamous marriages). Perhaps unsurprisingly in the circumstances, Lydia Crouch told her children that their father had died.

In the United States Crouch undertook several, mostly unsuccessful, musical enterprises, conducting, singing and teaching in Boston, Portland, Philadelphia, Washington and Richmond. He served as a trumpeter in the Confederate Army during the Civil War, and then settled in Baltimore as a singing teacher. In 1881 he was working as a varnisher in a factory; a testimonial concert was given for him in Baltimore in 1883.

An unattributed biographical notice of Crouch preserved in the Manuscripts Department of the British Library contains no mention of his first family. The impression conveyed is of a man unable to stick at any one thing, always chasing rainbows – including going off to El Dorado to prospect for gold – and having to support another (his fourth?) family of wife and five children. The notice concludes with the unlikely story of a devoted American disciple petitioning to change his surname from Marion to Crouch, in order to 'adopt' Crouch as his father and provide for him and his family. Thus, it is alleged, his days of penury were miraculously ended.

Not long after Crouch's flight to America, his wife Lydia took a lover. Her daughter Emma, now in her early teens, did not get on with him and it was decided to send her away to a convent school in Boulogne. She remained there for several years, returning to England in about 1854.

Much of what we know – or think we know – about Emma Crouch comes from her own memoirs, which were published in French shortly before her death and translated into English in the same year. We are thus presented with the picture of her which she wanted us to see, as well as with her view of her contemporaries – in particular, of her numerous lovers. At times, the memoirs are more obfuscating than enlightening. Details are given in non-chronological order and names are disguised – frequently, though not always, transparently. And, throughout, the author maintains the fiction that she was born in 1842, making herself about seven years younger than she actually was.

The French version of the *Mémoires* contains as its frontispiece a reproduction of a Certified Copy of Emma's supposed birth certificate, giving her date of birth as 23 February 1842. It is quite clearly a forgery (though it served her well in her life and even afterwards; her entry in the *Dictionary of National Biography*, for instance, gives this as her date of birth, and the year is also repeated in the *New Grove* entry about her father). What has been changed on this copy is the date (1841 has been changed to 1842) and the first name ('Emma' has been written over 'Louisa'). The original certificate, doctored in this way by Emma, records the birth of her youngest sister, Louisa Elizabeth, on 23 February 1841. The English version of the memoirs, which claims to be the 'Authentic and Authorised Translation from the Original', contains a printed version of the forged certificate. Not content with merely presenting this falsification, the author has the temerity to draw attention to it as a proof of her 'honesty': 'what I affirm is that I speak the truth, having no reason to hide it; the proof is that I begin by my date of birth, a thing that very few women would consent to reveal'.[7] From the start, Emma is poking fun both at her readers and at all those who were taken in by her – but also, and more engagingly, at herself.

But the author of her memoirs was not alone in treating her life story as a pretext for misinformation, embellishent and sheer invention. The English version is prefaced by a 'Press Notice', which is representative of the myth-making of much of what was written about this woman, using a skeleton of a few facts on which to hang a morality tale, demonstrating how the wicked invariably come to a bad end:

> Twenty years ago, says a correspondent, the equipage of Cora Pearl was one of the sights of Hyde Park. The loungers by the rails threw a double intensity into their stare when her carriage passed with its perfect horses and irreproachable liveries. Great ladies were accused of dressing 'after' the celebrity. When she went to Paris and shortly after made her *début* at the Bouffes, the theatre was filled to overflowing with the ladies of the demi-monde and 'personages' titled and untitled. Never did a *première* excite so much curiosity. Certain of the boxes sold at 500f. each, and orchestra stalls fetched 150f. Before then Cora Pearl was well known to Parisians as an Amazon, a female Centaur . . . This is the woman who has just died in the most squalid poverty in a small room in the Rue de Bassano . . . When Madame Christine Nilsson was in America some years ago, on one occasion she sang 'Kathleen Mavourneen' as an encore. After the performance, a wretched-looking poverty-stricken man threw himself at her feet and thanked her with tears for singing so exquisitely his song, the child of his brain. This was Crouch, reduced to such straits that he was almost unable to command the price of a meal. Something was done for him in the way of getting up a subscription, and an American reporter, getting hold of the old man, elicited from him a story of almost life-long

reverses, which went the rounds of the English press at the time. Among other things he stated that he was the father of Cora Pearl. During the last few years her poverty was as great as his. She was often seen in the Champs Elysées, gazing at the house where she once had lived, her dress faded and worn, but the red-dyed hair as conspicuously brilliant as of old; the rouged cheeks and artificially whitened brow giving her at a little distance a factitious air of youthfulness. The disdainful look had deserted her face, and wrinkles were seen, at a near approach, under the rouge. An air of fretful misery had replaced them. The ravages of a terrible disorder were reflected in her face. Her life was an antithesis, of which her death served to dot the i's and cross the t's . . .

A Paris correspondent telegraphs: About 20 persons only attended the funeral of the late Cora Pearl. Several of her former admirers joined in a subscription to pay the expenses of the burial, amounting to £32. Fifty francs was sent by the secretary of a very great personage to buy a five years' grave. A Protestant clergyman officiated out of charity. The deceased wished it to be known that she blamed nobody but herself for her final misery.[8]

The memoirs themselves begin with an explanation of the author's intent; she puts herself forward as a sort of social historian: 'I publish these memoirs because I think they will be interesting, and because they will put once more before the eyes of the world the society of the Second Empire.'[9] Emma is at her most attractive here, in her candour and in her refusal to indulge in self-pity: 'I have had a happy life; I have squandered money enormously. I am far from posing as a victim; it would be ungrateful of me to do so. I ought to have saved, but saving is not easy in such a whirl of excitement as that in which I have lived. Between what one ought to do and what one does there is always a difference.'[10] She makes no mention of her father having run off to America. She claims to have been close to him, that he died when she was only five years old and that she never came to know her mother well. (Quite apart from the fact that her father did not die, one has to remember to make an adjustment of several years every time she mentions her age; an added difficulty is that she is inconsistent in how many years she is subtracting.) She writes that she was sent to France for eight years, and that on her return she went to live with her grandmother (named as 'madame Waats' in the French version), 'and my remaining parent I only saw during an occasional visit, until considerations of delicacy forbade my being received in her house or that of any member of my family'.[11]

The memoirs turn next to one of the defining moments of Emma's life, as a result of which she lays claim to lasting psychological scars. 'Since the day of which I now write I have preserved an instinctive hatred against men. Among them I have reckoned many friends – too many, perhaps – and some sincere well-wishers for whom I had a frank and sincere affection. But the *instinctive* feeling of which I speak has never left me. The impression has remained ineffaceable.'[12] Emma recounts that she used to spend all week at her grandmother's, playing cards with her in the afternoons and reading to her in the evenings. It is thought[13] that she actually worked at this time as an apprentice milliner in Regent Street, but this is not the version of her life Emma chooses to give. On Sundays, she claims, she would visit her mother, accompanied by a maid. Her mother, who does not appear to have been desperate for Emma's company, would send her to church, where the servant would leave her to go for a walk. Dislike of her stepfather continues to be significant in determining her actions (though the following is not included in the English version):

I was not yet fourteen; I was still in a short dress and wore my hair in schoolgirl plaits. I was quite a good girl, and not overly shy. I had an extremely clear complexion. I usually went back to Mummy's after the service. Sometimes I went back to Mrs Waats'. It depended a bit on my stepfather's mood. When he was out, I stayed all day with my sisters.[14]

Then Emma tells the story of how one Sunday the maid does not arrive to collect her after church, so she sets out alone and is accosted by a man, whom she takes to be thirty-five to forty years old. He offers to treat her to cakes; she, totally innocent and unsuspecting, is proud to be out on her own. 'And I followed the gentleman. Why shouldn't I have followed him? I wasn't depraved – no, not at all – or even curious. And yet I did say to myself: "This is quite funny!" not out of defiance – I didn't know a thing – but with one of those little feelings of astonishment which make you smile – inside.'[15] The man takes Emma into some sort of drinking den, possibly near Covent Garden, and gives her gin. She awaits her cakes in vain, and finally falls asleep on her chair. 'The next morning I found myself by the side of the man in his bed. It was one more child ruined – wickedly, bestially. I have never pardoned men, neither this one nor the others who are not responsible for his act.'[16]

This route into prostitution was not, according to Dr Michael Ryan, uncommon in mid-nineteenth-century London. In fact he alludes to a case very similar to that described by Emma Elizabeth Crouch:

A child, aged fourteen years, had lately applied to the [London] Society [for the Prevention of Juvenile Prostitution] . . . for protection. She was decoyed, at the age of twelve years, while passing to or from a Sunday school, into a brothel, and such was the influence gained over her, that, though she left not her home, she continued her visits to this abominable abode for about two years, unknown to her friends or relations.[17]

In the account Emma gives, however, there is no return to the family home. She claims that for her the experience felt like the end of the world and that she knew her old life was over. 'I didn't know what to think. It all felt like a dream. I was honestly expecting to wake up with a start. Yet I also felt that it was all up with me and that I would never again set foot in my grandmother's or Mummy's house.'[18] She refuses the offer her seducer makes for her to stay with him and go round London together, but accepts five pounds with which she decides to rent a room. She wastes no time worrying about the effect of her disappearance on her family. 'I would be telling a lie if I said that the pain of separation from my family made me cry. I had lived far away from them for too long and, on my return from Boulogne, couldn't help but see myself, through force of circumstance, like a child sent back from the wetnurse at the age of thirteen.'[19] Despite the trauma she has endured, Emma relishes her forced independence. 'I preferred the boarding-school to my family; but, even inexperienced as I was, I felt that independence was better than either. Moreover, was it not a real satisfaction to be able to say to myself "I am at home, in a home of my own"?'[20] The French version names the man (though the English does not): 'I never saw the wolf of my story again; it seems he was a diamond merchant by the name of Saunders.'[21]

Though much in Emma's attempt to portray herself as a Little Red Riding Hood figure, cruelly seduced in her innocence, has to be discounted – if it really happened after her return from Boulogne she would have been nearer twenty than fourteen, for instance, and probably nothing like as innocent as she makes out – there is some psychological truth here, at least, some trace of reality. Something happened to turn Emma from either her grandmother's companion or an apprentice milliner into a prostitute – for this is what 'renting a room' is a euphemism for here – and to explain why she never returned home. The fact that such things were known to happen, that other girls were decoyed into brothels or unwittingly raped, makes it neither more nor less likely that it actually happened to Emma. She could easily have heard or read about such an incident happening to someone else and decided to incorporate it into her own story. Nor was it uncommon for a family to reject a daughter who had 'fallen', even when the fall was not at all of her own making. Yet Emma's decision, as here recounted, to make an independent life for herself does seem precipitate. There is clearly much fictionalising going on here, and a condensing of the narrative. Yet there also lurks the shadowy figure of the distrusted, possibly abusive, stepfather. It is impossible to determine what part he may have played in the events which led to Emma's taking up a life of prostitution, but to a modern sensibility elements of this story – an adolescent girl sent away from home after her mother has acquired a new lover, that girl then proving unwilling to return home when he is around, her fanciful narrative of a rape scene by a man who might or might not have been called Saunders, and her total abandonment of and by her family – sound suspicious, to say the least. The words of Alexandre Dumas *fils* have a resonance in Emma's, as in Marie Duplessis's, life: 'The courtesan's excuses are ignorance, an absent or depraved family, bad examples, lack of education, religion and principles, and *always and above all a first error*, often involving a relative, sometimes the brother or father (see the statistics at the police headquarters), a mother who sold them, finally poverty and everything that goes with it.'[22]

The memoirs now turn to the first stage of the transformation of Emma Elizabeth Crouch into Cora Pearl:

> I was not long in making the acquaintance of a young man, Bill Blinkwell, proprietor of some Dance-Rooms. Well brought up, naturally sentimental, he conceived for me a very tender feeling. We spoke French together. He had a way of saying, 'Ma chère Cora!' which sometimes went to my heart. For I had taken the name of Cora Pearl from no particular reason, but purely from fancy.[23]

Emma makes it sound as though 'Cora Pearl' was the first name which came into her head, and maybe it was. Yet it is also a sign that she desired to escape her past, in particular her family, and choosing a name quite different from her birth name helped her to cover her traces effectively. She also enjoyed the play on words, making of herself a gem strung on a chain of lovers, though she affected to despise men who kept repeating the pun, especially when they accused the pearls around her neck of being as false as the Pearl who wore them. 'Bill Blinkwell' or, in the French version, 'William Bluckel', was actually Robert Bignell, proprietor of the Argyll Rooms, also known as the Argyll Theatre and the New Private

Saloon Theatre, just off Regent Street, and where Emma/Cora had been plying her trade. Still amending her age, she claims: 'He was twenty-five years old; I was fifteen. He loved me madly, and I was rather pleased with him.'[24] According to Cora, he even proposed, but 'I replied that I never wished to marry, for I detested men too much ever to obey one of them.'[25] Nevertheless, for the purpose of paying a visit to Paris together she allowed him to obtain a passport in which she was described as his wife.

In Paris Bignell introduced her to all the usual haunts of the tourist. 'We stayed at the York and Albion Hotel. The day after our arrival my "husband" took me upon the Arc de Triomphe, into the sewers, into the vaults of the Panthéon, to the fountains of the Tuileries, where we saw the gold fish.'[26] Cora may have been misremembering or embellishing here, as the sewers only really became a tourist attraction towards the end of the 1860s, whereas she arrived in Paris in the mid- to late 1850s. In any event, she enjoyed herself immensely. After a month, Robert told her it was time to return home; he had work to attend to. But Cora had other plans; she seized the joint passport and threw it on the fire. Robert realised he was defeated, paid the hotel bill and left. Cora knew whom to blame: 'What I had done was perhaps ill, but it was so spontaneous. It was his fault after all, poor boy! It is a mistake to bring your wife to Paris, when your property is London Dance-Rooms.'[27]

Cora Pearl's first Parisian lovers were undistinguished, as was the area of eastern Paris in which she lived, the Cité des Bluets. She subsequently lived in the place du Havre, followed by the rue Le Peletier and the rue Grange Batelière, all the while moving up the fashionable scale and closer to the area of operations of the highest class of courtesan. But, reading between the lines of her memoirs, she began as a common prostitute, most probably a *fille en carte* – that is, working independently rather than in a brothel. Cora records that the first 'acquaintance' she made in Paris was a sailor called d'Aménard. He had no money but was amusing and, when he set sail, promised to marry her on his return. She told him she would wait for him, but neither meant what she said nor expected to see him again, for 'a sailor is flotsam, an empty cask, a gangplank on which it would be reckless to count!'[28] Cora went on to use the services of a procuress: 'Then I was put in touch with Roubise, who was highly esteemed in her world and who procured many clients for me.'[29] One of these clients was a man Cora calls Delamarche; she claimed to be fond of him, but the relationship could not last as he had no money: 'But, in his case too, the heart was more wealthy than the wallet, and he spent both with the best will in the world. When the wallet is empty, the heart is full. What can you do then? Find shelter in the fields. That's what he did.'[30]

Before long Cora's career took off and she began to acquire the kind of lovers she wanted, men with sufficient wealth to make her wealthy too. She attracted them not only by her sexual prowess and striking appearance (her naturally red or dyed yellow hair and athletic physique seemed to fascinate the French, attracting and repelling in equal measure), but by her intelligence, her wit and her humour. As her 1930s' biographer, Baroness von Hutten, put it: 'She knew . . . how to make bored men laugh.'[31] She was also in the right place at the right time: 'However it came about, she appeared in Paris, at a time when the Second Empire was at its height of luxury, of pleasures and of power, and she knew how to please the men of leisure who follow women – if you will excuse this hunting term – like hounds track animals.'[32] Cora called the string of lovers she acquired her 'golden chain'. As in the case of Marie Duplessis, it is very difficult to work out exact dates for Cora's many affairs, both because various accounts conflict and because several of the liaisons were concurrent. Others were very short-lived.

Once she could afford it, she took a fine house at 61 rue Ponthieu (parallel with the avenue des Champs Elysées) which she shared with another courtesan, Caroline Hassé. The Count de Maugny, the man behind the pseudonym of 'Zed', recalled seeing Caroline at the establishment of Cellarius the dancing master, and described her as 'a splendid creature with thick golden hair and ample curves: a tall, beautiful person, cheerful and pleasant, glowing with freshness, youth and luxury'.[33] The relationship between the two women was not always harmonious – naturally enough, for they were in competition. 'Zed' also tells a particularly malicious story about Cora's attitude towards Caroline. One day, he relates, the house caught fire: 'By chance I was walking past at the moment of the fire. I went into the courtyard to see what was going on, and what did I find? Cora at the window, in her chemise, shouting at the top of her voice to her stable hands: "I'll sack the first person who takes a bucket of water to that cow upstairs!" ' [34]

Cora had a long-term liaison with the man she calls 'Lassema' (a thin disguise for Victor Masséna); it lasted, according to her, for six years though was run concurrently with many others. Masséna, the third Duke of Rivoli and later the fifth Prince of Essling (and a grandson of Napoleon's great marshal), bought her dresses by Worth and Laferrière, and jewels from the rue de la Paix. He also maintained her servants, including her brilliant and profligate chef, Salé. 'He [Masséna] was unquestionably one of the first links in my chain of gold. Heir of a great name of the First Empire, rich, correct in his bearing, he was still most thoughtful, most anxious to please, most adorable, and, I should add, the man who received the least in return.' [35] Masséna was very jealous, Cora says, of 'Adrien Marut' – that is, Prince Achille Murat, another aristocratic lover and, at the time Cora met him, still only a teenager.

Achille was the youngest brother of Princess Caroline Murat. Both had been born, along with another brother and sister, in the United States during the time when everyone with Bonaparte connections was in exile. (Prince Joachim Murat, Caroline and Achille's grandfather, had been the brother-in-law of Napoleon I and became the King of Naples.) The Murats had arrived in Paris in October 1848 after the overthrow of Louis Philippe and some two months before the election of Louis Napoleon as President of the Republic. Prince Achille was the first man to make Cora the present of a horse. Unfortunately he had financial problems:

But he was as much in debt as in love, and that's saying a good deal. At the end of his resources, afraid of Papa who was also very fond of his little comforts, but who had a rather quick hand though an excellent heart, little Adrien ran to pour out his woes on the Emperor's breast. The latter forgave him, paid his debts and was so kind as to dispatch him to Africa.[36]

Some years later, in 1865, Prince Achille foolishly became embroiled in a dispute Cora had with a horse-dealer who had claimed that she owed him money. Prince Achille agreed to sign a certificate stating that she had already paid the money in question, which was untrue. The Republican journalist Henri Rochefort publicly criticised Prince Achille for this, who responded by challenging Rochefort to a duel. The latter suffered a slight wound in the thigh in the ensuing contest (which took place in the riding school at St Germain) and was most annoyed to find himself the subject of gossip, the popular rumour being that he had fought the duel over Cora herself. He was not at all averse, however, to having been seen in combat with a relative of the Emperor.

Next Cora tells us about 'le duc Citron', with whom, she says, she had another fairly long-lasting affair, punctuated by his absences from Paris. This is a transparent pseudonym for William, Prince of Orange, elder son and heir of the King of Holland. He was called Citron, a nickname he hated, by many of his friends. A weak and self-indulgent character, he was a great friend of the dissipated Duke de Gramont-Caderousse who died of consumption and exhaustion at the age of thirty in September 1865, a year in which, despite the improvements in public hygiene and sanitation, there was another cholera epidemic in Paris; at nearly four and a half thousand the fatalities were still high, but represented a marked improvement on previous figures. Cora may have had a very brief liaison with Gramont-Caderousse as well, but he was far more heavily involved with another courtesan, the actress Hortense Schneider, by whom he had a child. Whenever else Citron may have been in Paris, and thus renewing his acquaintance with Cora, he is recorded as visiting the court in January 1860 and he was one of the many foreign royal figures present during the

Universal Exposition of 1867. Cora makes it clear that her relationship with him was entirely mercenary:

> The last time that I saw him I was in a low-neck dress. He asked
> to come to my house. I refused, fearing I might have some
> reason to regret yielding too easily.
> He insisted.
> 'I offer you five blue bank-notes.'
> He came.[37]

Cora's name also came to be associated with two of the most
significant figures of the Second Empire. The first of these was the
Duke de Morny, already encountered as a business associate of Alfred
Mosselman and as the lover (in both cases until 1857) of his sister, the
Countess Le Hon. So central was Auguste de Morny to the history of
the Second Empire, so famed for having a finger in every pie, that
even the mention of his name could affect share prices:

> In the eyes of many people happy to depend for their informa-
> tion on the radical newspapers from the time of the Empire, M.
> de Morny spent his life in debauchery and speculation; the
> famous *Morny's mixed up in it* acquired currency everywhere,
> and so great is Parisian credulity that no small financial society or
> newspaper could be founded, no theatre or mildly significant
> shop could open without someone rushing to spread the
> rumour: *Morny's mixed up in it*, in an effort to entice share-
> holders.[38]

He was born Auguste Demorny in 1811, the illegitimate son of
Hortense Beauharnais, herself the daughter of the Empress Josephine
and the mother of the future Napoleon III (who was three years old
when Auguste was born). His real father was Joseph, Count de
Flahaut, and his official father a Prussian officer named Demorny. He
was brought up by Flahaut's mother, Madame de Souza, and watched
over by Flahaut from afar. His own mother never saw him after his

birth, and Louis Napoleon knew nothing of his half-brother's existence until after Hortense's death in 1837. Auguste began his career in the army, and was decorated for saving the life of a general. By 1835 he had resigned his commission and become a man-about-town, funding himself partly through his affair with Countess Le Hon. After appropriating the title 'Count' for himself and adjusting his name to de Morny he soon proved himself to be a skilled and unscrupulous businessman who knew how to make everything, including his own appearance and facial expression, work in his favour:

A trim figure, very refined features, eyes with an expression subtle and diplomatic in its indecision, a pleasantly oval-shaped head, unmarred by its premature baldness, a posture dignified and reserved without being stiff, reminiscent of that of members of the English aristocracy: such was M. Morny.[39]

He first became involved in politics during the reign of Louis Philippe, but remained somewhat on the sidelines until the election of Louis Napoleon as President of the Second Republic in December 1848, at which point he arranged a meeting with his half-brother through a mutual friend, Count Bacciochi. From then on, he was never far from the centre of power.

Princess Caroline Murat was a great admirer of Morny's:

In the early years of the Empire, the Duke de Morny was, without doubt, 'the king of fashion, of elegance, of refinement'. He looked a grand seigneur, his manners savoured of the old *régime*. . . . He acquired great influence with the Prince-President, with whom, by his position, he was a great favourite. He was also what people call lucky in all he undertook. Had it not been for his clever conception and manoeuvring, I doubt if the *Coup d'Etat* would ever have taken place . . .

In politics he was clever, calmly resolute, inflexible, but with a certain charm of manner, a rare delicacy and *finesse*, which served to gain his ends. He was the Emperor's most intimate adviser, and his friendship with the Empress guided her influence from the wrong direction as long as he lived.[40]

Though Morny was undoubtedly involved in the *coup d'état* on 2 December 1851, his fellow conspirator Emile de Maupas would not accord him quite the central position which Princess Murat (who had clearly fallen prey to Morny's charms) ascribed to him. According to Maupas, Louis Napoleon's feelings for his half-brother were never straightforward. Sometimes he appeared intimate towards him, sometimes markedly distant, but he was always somewhat distrustful. Consequently, though the Prince-President never concealed from Morny the fact that he was considering a *coup d'état*, he did not let him know the date and exact plans until just before the event, for fear that this arch-speculator might let the cat out of the bag.

Morny remained at the heart of Napoleon III's administration for the rest of his life. He was Minister of the Interior from 1851 to 1852, ambassador to Russia from 1856 to 1857, and President of the Corps Législatif from 1854. Whereas he had previously lived in a building adjoining the Countess Le Hon's *hôtel*, this latter post brought him, along with his salary of a hundred thousand francs, lodgings in the Palais Bourbon. Here he was able to live in the style to which he had always aspired, holding brilliant gatherings of the most distinguished members of Parisian society in the fields of politics, science and the arts. In 1857 he married his Russian princess, the delicately beautiful Sophia Troubetskaya, unceremoniously discarding Countess Le Hon, who had by this time been his mistress for some twenty years. Both the Emperor himself and the senator Eugène Rouher became involved in subsequent attempts to placate the Countess (who was also the mother of Morny's daughter, Louise), and an indemnity of three and a half million francs was paid to her out of the privy purse. It cannot be unconnected that it was during this same year that Morny ceased working alongside the Countess's brother, Alfred Mosselman, in the running of the Société de la Vieille-Montagne.

Morny fulfilled his duties as President of the Corps Législatif with aplomb, while still finding time to manage his many business affairs which included an involvement in the sugar beet industry, banking, the development of the railway system, the construction of the Suez Canal and the proprietorship of newspapers. He was also a developer and speculator – this was what really made him rich – and was the prime mover behind the creation of the resort town of Deauville. A member of the Jockey Club (founded by an uncle of Richard Wallace, Lord Henry Seymour), he played a major part in the establishment of horse racing in France at Longchamp and Deauville. In 1862 he was made a duke. He was an epicure and a gourmet, an amateur of painting and the theatre, and was said to have written the libretti for several operettas. The only one of these to have survived – M. *Champfleury restera chez lui*, written in 1860 and set to music by Offenbach – was in fact drafted by Halévy with a few interpolations from Morny.

Maxime Du Camp relates that, while Morny was one of the wittiest men he knew in private or in a small gathering, he was quite incapable of improvised public speaking, having to write down all his speeches to the Corps Législatif in advance and read them out, word for word.[41] Nevertheless, once installed in his official seat he exuded an absolute authority. His facial expression betrayed a constant lassitude, and he could rarely be bothered to finish his sentences – unless, exceptionally, he considered his interlocutor to be of equal intelligence to himself. He led an extremely well-ordered life, even allotting specified hours to relaxation. At whatever time he arrived home, he would get on with his work. People who had left him in the middle of the night would be amazed the next morning to find him well informed on subjects about which he had known little the previous evening. When he was dissatisfied with his health he would take a 'blue pill', a remedy which may have shortened his life by leading to the development of stomach ulcers. (Made of mercury with glycerin and honey of rose, 'blue pill' or 'blue mass' was widely used in the nineteenth century both as an anti-depressant and as a purgative; Abraham Lincoln was another user of it, until he realised it put him in a bad mood.) Maupas, who as Minister of Police must have worked closely with Morny, sums him up, somewhat dismissively, thus:

> To be precise, one could say of M. de Morny: he was a man of extreme elegance and rare *savoir-faire*; he was courageous always, skilful and strong when he felt like it; in business affairs he was adventurous and not entirely honest; but his name and his deeds made a great stir. That was his ambition, and he had the satisfaction of achieving it.[42]

Cora refers to Morny as 'Moray' in her memoirs and relates that she first met him while skating in the Bois one December. He subsequently invited her to his *résidence* and also bought her a white Arab pony, having admired her riding ability. Her description of him fits in well with those of other observers, and she esteemed him as much as she esteemed any man:

> My host embodied the type of the perfect gentleman. Sometimes he seemed to let himself go, but he always recovered himself. No one could turn a compliment better than he; yet his compliments were never bland: he hated banality. He even knew how to make a reproach sound obliging, so that there was pleasure in being scolded by him. He was one of those who do not grow old, and who always remain alive in one's memory. A passionate lover of the arts, he was particularly interested in the theatre. He worshipped Musset: and no one was surprised by that. Those who resemble one another esteem one another. He could have written a comedy between hosting a diplomatic reception and delivering an official speech. When he was at home, the most agreeable pastime, in those happy moments when I was able to see him, was to listen to him talk with his inexhaustible verve, his subtle jests, his expert and unpretentious criticism. He was charming, sitting at the piano in his purple velvet suit. He played with much feeling, and crooned with exquisite taste.[43]

Apollonie Sabatier. This engraving by Mathey is based on an
1854 oil painting by Apollonie's friend and mentor Ernest Meissonier.

Portrait of Apollonie Sabatier by Gustave Ricard: *La Dame au petit chien* ('The Lady with the Little Dog'). This was one of Apollonie's favourite portraits of herself, and it helped establish Ricard's reputation when it was exhibited at the Paris Salon of 1850.

Photograph of the prolific journalist, critic and poet Théophile Gautier by Nadar. Gautier, known as Théo to his friends, was an indispensable member of the entourages of both La Païva and La Présidente, and the most accomplished practictioner of the 'dirty talk' for which Apollonie's soirées were famed.

Photo: Martin Dudley

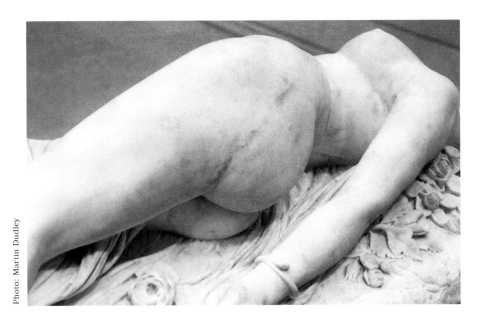

La Femme piquée par un serpent (The Woman Bitten by a Snake) by Auguste Clésinger, exhibited at the Paris Salon of 1847, and for which Apollonie was the model. The realism of this scuplted woman, clearly in the throes of orgasm, provoked a lasting effect on the way men related to Apollonie.

Blanche de Païva consistently refused to have her portrait painted, and this engraving (above left) is one of the very few, possibly the only, extant image of her face. Aware that she was not a conventional beauty, Blanche preferred to exhibit her power and wealth through the opulence and magnificence of the mansion she had built for herself, the Hôtel Païva. Prouder of her body than she was of her face, she did nothing to counteract the rumours that she was herself the model for some of the figures on display in the Hôtel, such as this one (above right) on one of the mantelpieces.

La Païva's bath (left) and the onyx staircase (right) at the Hôtel Païva.

The ceiling of the salon of the Hôtel Païva, painted by Paul Baudry, was considered
by the Goncourt brothers to be the only work of real artistic merit in the Hôtel.
The model for the figure of 'Night' was reputed to be La Païva herself.

Above: An engraving after Henri Grevedon of the celebrated
pianist Henri Herz. As Herz's 'wife', the future Blanche de Païva
became a well-known figure in Parisian artistic circles and
succeeded in depleting Herz's wealth until she was thrown out
of the house by his brother.

Right: Caricature of Count Guido Henckel von Donnersmarck by
Sem. Henckel von Donnersmarck, La Païva's third husband and
an assured source of wealth for her, was viewed by many Parisians
as the archetypal dour and bearded Prussian – particularly
in the aftermath of the Franco-Prussian War.

Cora Pearl, 'the English Beauty of the French Empire', adorned with her favourite bracelet which was attached by a chain to her finger. She was particularly proud of her beautiful hands.

Cora wearing a crinoline, that most voluminous and ostentatious of Second Empire fashions. Though it could look elegant in a pose such as Cora's, it presented problems in the fields of locomotion, seating capacity and fire prevention.

An image of Cora Pearl that belies the description given of her by 'Zed':
'English by birth, character and appearance, she had the head of a City worker,
neither good nor bad, fiery blonde, almost red, hair, a vulgar and unbearable accent,
a raucous voice, exceedingly common manners and the tone of a stable boy.'

Morny died on 10 March 1865, at the age of only fifty-four. His premature death has been attributed by some to his habit, common among fashionable Parisians, of taking not only blue pills but also arsenic, reputed to be a youth preserver. Cora was believed to indulge in the same remedy. In Princess Murat's opinion Morny's death was a disaster for the Empire:

> There is little doubt that the death blow to our prosperity was the passing away of the Duke de Morny in 1865. He was the heart and soul of the Empire. He alone held firm against the all-invading influence of the Empress; an influence always so sinister for France. His loss was irreparable. He died under the treatment of the English physician, his doctor and friend, and, I believe, medical man to the English Embassy, who administered very freely blue pill to an already weakened constitution.[44]

Maxime Du Camp relates how on his deathbed Morny instructed one of his secretaries (Montguyon, one of Marie Duplessis's former lovers) to burn all his private letters.[45] The process was begun, but then the chimney caught fire, so the letters had to be flushed down the water closet instead, with the aid of buckets of water and a broom handle – and so letters from actresses, duchesses, marchionesses, *grisettes*, ambassadresses and princesses all went floating off into the sewers of Paris. Another version is that all of his private papers were seized after his death, on the express orders of the Empress;[46] Morny may, of course, have anticipated this eventuality and so arranged for the really private documents to be disposed of before his death – which he insisted on referring to as his 'departure'. He left not only a grieving widow – for the Duchess de Morny had become very attached to him, despite her peculiarities and his affairs – but a two-year-old daughter who would one day attain notoriety in her own right as 'Missy', the lover of Colette. Morny's tomb dominates one of the crossroads in the cemetery of Père Lachaise, a miniature temple to the self-made man, ensuring that his ennobled name is as prominent in death as it was in life.

The other most noteworthy man to have been one of Cora's lovers was, as far as outward appearance was concerned, the antithesis of the suave and urbane Auguste de Morny. In intellect, however, he was more than Morny's equal and he too was central to the life of the Second Empire. This man was Prince Napoleon Joseph Charles Paul Bonaparte, cousin of the Emperor and brother of Princess Mathilde.

Contemporary memoirists rarely have a good thing to say about Prince Napoleon, particularly as regards his manners; Viel Castel, as usual, does not mince his words: 'The Prince is always, whatever he's doing, the same man, lifeless, coarse and badly brought up, detested by all who come near him.'[47] The Prince also offended the delicate sensibilities of La Chroniqueuse:

> The time was, and that not many years ago, when the name prince and gentleman were synonymous terms; now, *au contraire*. I don't think any *gentleman* would ride through the streets of Paris in an Imperial *calèche* with a cigar in his mouth and a straw hat stuck rakishly on the front of his head, his legs (don't be shocked, ladies, it is quite true) stretched out on the front seat, and his arm thrown over the back of the carriage![48]

Anna Bicknell, a English governess in the imperial household, was equally scathing:

> The physical likeness [to Napoleon I] was wonderful, but the expression was totally different. In the good portraits of Napoleon I, the clear eyes have a singularly piercing glance, at once conveying the idea of a commanding genius. With the same cast of features, there was something peculiarly low and thoroughly bad in the face of Prince Napoleon, which recalled in a striking manner the stamp of the worst Roman Caesars.[49]

She goes on: '. . . never were natural gifts so misapplied or so wasted. He could bear no restraint, no interruption in his life of sensual pleasures, and he never persevered in anything that he undertook, when any personal sacrifice was required to carry it out.'[50]

In her memoirs Cora refers to Prince Napoleon as 'Duke Jean', sometimes calling him 'Jean-Jean', a transparent disguise for the Prince's nickname of 'Plon-Plon'. She relates that during their first assignation he took her to drink milk at a farm near Meudon, ten miles from Paris, where the Prince had a château and where Cora had been hunting with Achille Murat. The visit to the farm lasted about an hour. 'An expert in agricultural matters, as in so much else, the Duke obligingly undertook my rural education.'[51] Cora was in no hurry to grant the Prince, or 'the Duke', sole rights over her, but the fact that he was able to pay far more than her other current conquests gave him a distinct advantage:

> At that time de Rouvray was my 'friend'. He cared about me perhaps more from tenderness of heart than from the desire to show off. On several occasions he encountered the Duke at my place and, unless I am much mistaken, benevolence was not really what they felt for one another. Godefroy, as Barberousse euphemistically called him, was another of my regulars. In this trio of performers or dilettantes, it was naturally the Duke who, destined by his high calling to produce the highest note, made it heard the most acutely.[52]

Even so, Cora insists that she remained in control: 'Far from feeling with him the least embarrassment, at the end I mastered him. He bent with good grace, and only revolted when spurred by pride and jealousy. With him, as with all the others, I took care to assert my independence.'[53] The Prince did hold a trump card, however, which even Cora admits threatened her much-vaunted independence, and that was the power to have her deported. And so, with this ultimate threat in mind, Cora, who had been pretending to have a twisted ankle in order to explain her avoidance of the Prince while she had been playing the field with other men, realised that it was to her advantage at least to appear to be faithful to him: 'For the time being, it was my interest to submit. I, therefore, got on my legs again, and went to sign peace.'[54]

Cora is one of the few people to say anything agreeable about the Prince: 'He was only rough externally. A very little knowledge of him revealed his real delicacy of manner.'[55] Astute and observant as ever, she realised that he could be a quite different person, depending on whom he was having dealings with: 'My first impression concerning the Duke has never been modified. This man was an angel to those who pleased him. His voice was agreeable, his laugh frank, his conversation witty, and at need playful; angel, I repeat, to those who pleased him; demon, roué, madman, unhesitating insulter towards others.'[56] Yet even Cora alludes to how difficult he could be and refers to habits which would certainly have been considered coarse and ill-mannered: 'He was in the habit of putting his feet upon a chair, and often complained of the tyranny of stiff waistcoats. Though of very moderate appetite at his meals, he sometimes had fits of hunger. On such occasions he would buy a roll at the first baker's shop he came to, put it in his pocket and munch pieces of it as he was walking along';[57] and 'It was an awful penance to him to go to the Tuileries on reception days. He never concealed what an annoyance to him were what he called the mummeries of etiquette.'[58]

In the real duties of public life, however, away from the 'mummeries of etiquette', the Prince could cut an impressive figure. His intelligence made a deep impression on the people around him, as did his oratorical skills:

> When he was on the rostrum, as in his intimate surroundings, he demonstrated his powerful faculties. Almost without preparation, with the help only of his daily meditations, he would let no argument escape him which might serve his cause. Without concerning himself with method, he would throw himself into the discussion with the passion of his nature, and if he didn't succeed in convincing, because he too often made himself the defender of lost causes, he would succeed in obtaining applause for his talent, even from those who would condemn his principles.[59]

The Prince was a skilled administrator, as he had demonstrated in his role as president of the commission of the 1855 Universal Exposition. He also assimilated new ideas at speed and with enthusiasm so that scholars, inventors and exhibitors of all sorts could communicate with him easily. Despite the disparagement regularly meted out to Prince Napoleon in court circles the Emperor always stood by his cousin, tending to treat him as the child prodigy of the family. The Prince himself was very conscious not only of his imperial status, but also of the fact that he would always remain subservient to his cousin. There had been a time when he might have expected to succeed to the imperial throne, but such hopes were dashed when the Emperor married (it was noted that the Prince looked sulky at the wedding) and even more so when the Prince Imperial was born. Prince Napoleon never seemed to find quite the right outlet for his undoubted talents, which led to frustration and a degree of irascibility. He was known for flying into terrible rages when he was crossed, particularly if he felt he was being slighted in any way.

Cora gives an entertaining and enlightening picture both of Prince Napoleon's enthusiams and preoccupations and his tendency to get worked up about them, and of her own more prosaic concerns. One can almost hear the Prince pontificating while Cora waits impatiently for him to finish:

> Don't let him get started on America! It's there that the art of travel is practised with intelligence! Whereas our own railways are stagecoaches. Moreover, in France the real sovereign – the only authority in no danger of being assassinated – is routine. That's why the most intelligent nation remains backward, it's our lack of initiative, despite all attempts at improvement, and there's no willingness to profit from the progress which actually took place a long time ago.
>
> I would be saying to myself: 'If he carries on like this, we'll miss the Bouffes!'[60]

Cora sums up the Prince well, and not without a touch of humour:

> We never talked politics. It was evident, however, that the
> Duke had a perfect admiration for Napoleon I. For at heart he
> was very Bonapartist, but in a fashion of his own. He wrote
> concerning the First Empire, and gave himself up to patient
> literary researches. He was an excellent judge, a profound
> thinker, an indefatigable worker; and, at the same time, was
> good-natured, a friend to men and animals, much taken up with
> dogs and horses.[61]

On 30 January 1859, at the age of thirty-six, Prince Napoleon had
married the sixteen-year-old Princess Clotilde, daughter of King
Victor Emmanuel of Savoy. It was a match made for political reasons,
this being a period of constantly shifting allegiances among the
various European powers over the future of Italy, and it was clear
from the outset that the couple were unsuited. Clotilde was a very
devout and serious young woman, said to speak five languages
fluently as well as knowing Greek and Latin, and was completely
out of sympathy with the party-going and frivolity of the Second
Empire. La Chroniqueuse described her appearance, after having
encountered her at an exhibition of Ary Scheffer's paintings in May:
'To those who may feel interested I will state that she is not pretty,
and not excessively *distinguée*; in figure she is *petite*, her hair is auburn,
and her nose decidedly *retroussé*; still she seems very modest, even
retiring, and in this forms a striking contrast to her ladies of honour,
who, from their supercilious airs, might by the inexperienced be
taken for the Princess herself.'[62]

At the beginning of that month war had been declared on Austria,
which had attacked Piedmont a few days previously. Shortly after the
victory of the French and Sardinians at the battle of Solférino towards
the end of June, and partly through shock at the enormous bloodshed
resulting from this battle, the Emperor Napoleon suddenly deserted
his Sardinian ally and made a separate peace with Austria at Villa-
franca. La Chroniqueuse, however, considering that her readers were

more likely to be interested in a princess's personal appearance than in international politics, continued her scrutiny at the Opéra in September when she wrote of Clotilde: 'She has, what is very rare among French ladies, a beautiful complexion, and I honestly believe does not make any use of any of the preparations for the skin with which Paris is filled. Her hair is light, rather inclined to be red; but her shoulders and neck are superb, and can vie successfully with those of the Empress. She is decidedly not pretty, having an over-hanging brow, which makes her look ill-tempered.'[63] The imperial governess Anna Bicknell pitied the Princess for having to put up with her awful husband, but even she had to admit that the marriage was not easy for either party. She also calls into question Clotilde's reputation as a scholar:

[Princess Clotilde] was, and is still, a princess of medieval times, a Saint Elizabeth of Hungary, neither very highly educated nor very clever, caring only for her religious practices and her works of charity. She soon ceased to pay much attention to her toilet, reaching even the point of carelessness, which greatly annoyed her husband. It must be acknowledged that the devotion of the Princess Clotilde went perhaps beyond what was quite judicious, but no one had any influence over her, and what she considered her duty was performed with a sort of gentle, placid stubbornness which allowed of no expostulation . . . During the Empire, even in her early youth, no one dared to show the least familiarity in her presence; but the stiff decorum of her circle did not make home life particularly agreeable. During the day, her ladies accompanied her to the churches, where they unwillingly awaited her pleasure for hours; in the evening they were seated round a table with their work, while the Princess herself diligently plied her needle, speaking very little and not encouraging any one else to do so.[64]

There was no attempt made to disguise the nature of the relationship between Prince Napoleon and Cora (and neither did she by any means represent his only extra-marital adventure). She was given free access to the Palais Royal, the official residence of the Prince and Princess and their children, where, if Cora is to be believed, the affair was conducted in close proximity to the family:

> I had a key which gave me access from a side street. I sometimes slept in a room next to the apartments of Madame X, a companion of the Duchess. The return of the latter presented no obstacle to our meetings. I would dine immediately after her, in the same room, and served by the same butler. While taking my meal, I would hear the Duchess talking and the children playing in the next room.[65]

Cora's next sentence, however, has been far less frequently quoted, and is not even included in the authorised English version: 'I was always aware of that and it embarrassed me.'[66] Princess Clotilde had presumably come to some sort of accommodation over her husband's infidelities, though in the first months of the marriage she had protested at his behaviour and attempted to change it. La Chroniqueuse had reported the following event on 28 September 1859:

> A very unpleasant, but not wholly unexpected, affair has occurred in high quarters. The Prince N. left Paris about ten days ago to travel in Switzerland. His Royal and Imperial spouse, hearing that the suite of her husband comprised other persons than those strictly necessary to keep up the state of a prince, resolved to join him without further delay. Her unexpected arrival at Geneva angered her lord and master beyond control, and he asked the lady by whose authorisation, and by what right she dared follow him. 'The right that every wife has to join her husband,' she replied; 'but since my presence is so obnoxious to you, I will return to my father, whose love for me will prevent his considering State interests before the happiness of his child.' So saying, the young Princess C. left the Prince.[67]

Yet the marriage survived, and Clotilde attracted much sympathy:

> She was almost a saint, and bore her domestic trials with so
> much dignity and quiet superiority that she compelled the
> respect of her husband and his associates, and the admiration
> of the rest of the world . . . She moved, grave and irreproach-
> able, amidst the levity and frivolity of the second Empire; it was
> a piteous sight to see her at the theatre, her head slightly
> drooping, her eyes vaguely fixed on the stage, her thoughts
> evidently far away, always silent, always solitary.[68]

At one time Cora appears to have been conducting simultaneous
affairs with Prince Napoleon (while attempting to convince him that
she was faithful to him), Paul Demidov (the nephew of Princess
Mathilde's estranged husband Anatole) and Demidov's compatriot
Narischkin. She was expert at playing them off one against the other,
ratcheting up the value of the presents that each would give her. She
also had a liaison with Khalil Bey, an imposing blue-spectacled Turkish
gentleman, the former Ottoman ambassador in St Petersburg. He was
one of the wealthiest and most lavish of her lovers; arriving in Paris in
the late 1860s, he startled even the jaundiced Parisians with his oriental
magnificence and enormous expenditure. Cora writes approvingly of
him – particularly as, according to her, he knew how to treat a *demi-
mondaine* with respect; she changes his name by only one letter in her
memoirs (he becomes Khadil rather than Khalil):

> One of the most extraordinary men in my opinion was old
> Khadil-bey. He appeared to me like a character out of the
> *Thousand and One Nights*. His *hôtel* was splendid. All the marvels
> of the Orient came together there. A magical conservatory,
> enchanted apartments. In spring he received in his salon; during
> winter in his garden . . .
>
> The master was the most striking aspect of the whole *hôtel*, a
> charming and lovable curiosity. Majestic in his whole person, his
> majesty excluded neither grace nor playfulness. He loved like an
> artist and entertained in grand style. He cultivated beauty in all

its forms, and was himself a type of beauty, and even more of bounty . . .

He was one of those men – and they are rare – who would think themselves dishonoured if they had, I don't say shown, but even conceived the slightest contempt for a woman they had received in their house, and whose smile they had tenderly and magnificently rewarded.[69]

Cora enjoyed luxuriating in this Moorish-style mansion in the avenue Montaigne, rented fully furnished to Khalil Bey by Jules de Lesseps: 'I bathed in the pink marble basin, I slept long hours on the couches, breathing the scent of flowers, and dreaming of enchanted places; and when I awoke, the reality appeared more beautiful than the dream.'[70] There were games to play at Khalil Bey's too, and one afternoon the high-spirited Cora indulged herself. There is a sense in her narrative of a harem-like atmosphere; a number of 'ladies' were present during the following scene:

One evening before tea, the maid requested the ladies to wait a few moments. Khadil-bey was having a nap. I noticed a box of toys on the table. I could see no reason for not opening it, and I have always loved poking around in things: this curiosity has often got me into trouble. The box contained all sorts of games. Skittles, shuttlecocks, dominos, rackets. I had had, since time immemorial, a huge desire to play skittles. Without more ado, I got down on the floor and started playing. I had been abandoning myself to this exercise for some minutes, fairly energetically, I must admit, when in came Khadil, and the ball, vigorously thrown by me, hit him right in the legs. Highly embarrassed by my clumsiness, I made haste to pick up the skittles and put them back where they belonged.

'Take this box away,' he instructed a maid. That was all his revenge.

We had tea, we chatted.

On getting home, the first thing I saw was the box. Sculpted

all over in ivory. Valued at 4,800 francs. Khadil had had it taken
to my house during the evening.[71]

This rather suggests that the unsentimental Cora had the gift valued
on receipt.

If Cora managed her multiple lovers with comparative ease, she
showed far less skill in the management of her finances. In fact she did
not attempt to manage them at all, constantly spending far more than
the considerable sums she was given by Prince Napoleon and others
(the Prince bought her two *hôtels* – one at 101 rue de Chaillot and
another in the rue des Bassins – as well as providing her with an
allowance of twelve thousand francs a month), a prey to unscrupulous
servants and 'friends of friends' more than happy to indulge themselves at her expense. She admits that she ran out of money on more
than one occasion: 'How many times I've ended up without a
farthing! I remember being in this fortunate position in Baden. I
was due to rejoin Lassema, who had set off a few days before me for
Paris. I had to pawn my diamonds in order to make the journey.
Money slipped through one's fingers with a speed you can't imagine.'[72] She was consistently extravagant and realised, at least in
retrospect, that she was as consistently cheated: 'In order to know the
price of goods, one must know the value of money; I have not the
least idea what a louis [the equivalent of twenty francs] is worth.
Tradesmen, nay, even financiers had charge of my education in such
matters, and the information they impart is one-sided.'[73]

Cora's costliest servant was her chef, Salé, who ran up an enormous
bill during one of her stays in Baden and was clearly running a part-
time business from her kitchen, charging the bills to her and taking
the profits himself. Cora describes the situation vividly:

In addition to his important role in the kitchen, Salé did the
shopping himself and handed in his accounts, which he sim-
plified as much as possible into round figures.

The long addition of his culinary contrivances was hypnotic:
one didn't wake up until the total.

Lassema and I were about to leave. We went down into the kitchen.

The first thing to strike us was a row of five beautiful chickens, plus some enormous quarters of cooked beef – a whole display of cold meats. A real roast meat shop. And I don't just mean that's what it resembled.

'So who is all this for?' I asked Salé.

He replied imperturbably: 'For the Duke.'[74]

In 1864 Cora rented the château de Beauséjour on the banks of the Loiret, a few miles from Orléans. Here she imported a large bronze bath, made specially by Chevalier of Paris, and engraved with her monogram of three intertwined Cs. She spent an enormous amount of money entertaining, inviting groups of people to stay, in a semi-deliberate parody of the imperial *séries* at Compiègne. Cora was always an extravagant hostess: 'In the winter at my suppers I used to have the fruit brought on table embedded, instead of in moss, in Parma violets which had cost me fifteen hundred francs. I believe no guest of mine can reproach me with my lack of attention. I always made it a point of honour to faithfully fulfil my duties as mistress of the house.'[75] In Vichy, where she stayed with Masséna for two weeks, she entertained day and night, to the extent that she likened her villa to a hotel: 'My *White Horse* hotel was always open to friends, and to friends of friends. It was this entirely friendly addition which put a deplorable strain on my budget. There was dancing in the morning, and dancing in the evening! Everything skipped about at my place: both people and money.'[76] Cora's, or rather Masséna's, hospitality was abused by people she hardly knew: 'There are some hungers which are never satisfied. I'm far from complaining about it, but I would have preferred to restrict myself to feeding my friends. I didn't even know the names of most of my guests; and it was these anonymous appetites which afforded me a very expensive satisfaction.'[77] Cora justly remarks on her value to the local economy:

My presence at Vichy was an era of blessedness for the suppliers. One day, at ten o'clock, I met my faithful Salé carrying half a sheep on his shoulder.

'What have you got there?'

'You can see very well, Madame, it is half a sheep.'

'Why half a sheep?'

'Madame, they don't sell it in smaller quantities.'

It must be a joy for an artist to cook in a country where life is interpreted generously: 30,000 francs-worth of food in a fortnight.[78]

The guests at Vichy played at *tableaux vivants* and charades; two of them, according to Cora, vented their spleen at having come off badly in a game of charades by spreading the rumour that their hostess had made an unsuccessful play for the Emperor who happened to be staying in Vichy at the same time. Cora herself denied having made any attempt to seduce him. There was the occasional mishap as a result of the high spirits of her guests, as in the case of one 'Castelnar', a short-sighted elderly gentleman who tried to climb in through a window and got stuck: 'His rather voluminous stomach bounced against the window jamb, he lost his footing and found himself suspended from the hook, from just below the waist.'[79] This was not the only example of tomfoolery among Cora's guests, much of it being orchestrated by Achille Murat: 'My worthy chef was not the only one to play tricks. There was a spirit of all sorts of eccentricities in the air. You would have taken them for a group of schoolboys on holiday. The ones who looked the most serious were the craziest. They would go running through the streets in the evenings, changing the shop signs and smashing the streetlamps.'[80]

Cora also lost money through gambling, particularly in Monte Carlo, where her most disastrous gambling exploit took place and where she seems to have resorted to petty burglary in order to get home:

In short, I lost seventy thousand francs in eight months. A nice way of discharging my obligations towards my suppliers – so polite and deferential as long as they knew or believed me to be rich, so hard and merciless, so insolent afterwards! Nevertheless they were paid; just a little late, that's all. But for the moment I had absolutely nothing. I owed the hotel seven hundred francs. They kept my luggage.

All the same I returned to Paris. I had to. But how? Here's the best, the glorious part of the story. I took five hundred francs from the cashdesk, for the journey. Being poor, I travelled like the poor. There was no reason to blush about that. And yet I visited this same year, during my stay, some very great ladies who have since . . . But then it was all part of the game.[81]

1 Emma Elizabeth Crouch, *The Memoirs of Cora Pearl*, George Vickers, London, 1886, title page

2 In *The Pretty Women of Paris*, 1883, in Captain Bingham's *Recollections of Paris*, 1896, and in Henry Vizetelly's *Glances Back through Seventy Years*, 1893

3 In Philibert Audebrand's *Petits Mémoires d'une stalle d'orchestre*, 1885, in Henri Rochefort's *The Adventures of My Life*, 1896, in S. Kracauer's *Jacques Offenbach ou le secret du Second Empire*, 1937, and in Henri d'Alméras' *La Vie parisienne sous le Second Empire*, 1933

4 In Pierre de Lano's *L'Amour à Paris sous le Second Empire*, 1896, and in Zed's *Le Demi-monde sous le Second Empire*, 1892

5 In Maurice Allem's *La Vie quotidienne sous le Second Empire*, 1948

6 Emma Elizabeth Crouch, *The Memoirs of Cora Pearl*, p.5

7 Ibid.

8 Ibid., frontispiece

9 Ibid., p.1

10 Ibid., p.2

11 Ibid., p.5

12 Ibid., pp.6–7

13 See Polly Binder, *The Truth about Cora Pearl*, Weidenfeld & Nicolson, London, 1986, p.20

14 Emma Elizabeth Crouch, *Mémoires de Cora Pearl*, Jules Lévy, Paris, 1886, p.16

15 Ibid., p.18

16 Emma Elizabeth Crouch, *The Memoirs of Cora Pearl*, p.10

17 Michael Ryan, *Prostitution in London*, p.167

18 Emma Elizabeth Crouch, *Mémoires de Cora Pearl*, p.20

19 Ibid., p.26

20 Emma Elizabeth Crouch, *The Memoirs of Cora Pearl*, p.13

21 Emma Elizabeth Crouch, *Mémoires de Cora Pearl*, p.26

22 Alexandre Dumas *fils*, *Théâtre complet*, Vol.1, p.33

23 Emma Elizabeth Crouch, *The Memoirs of Cora Pearl*, pp.13–14

24 Ibid., p.14

25 Ibid., p.15

26 Ibid., p.16

27 Ibid., pp.17–18

28 Emma Elizabeth Crouch, *Mémoires de Cora Pearl*, pp.37–8

29 Ibid., p.38

30 Ibid.

31 Baroness von Hutten, *The Courtesan. The life of Cora Pearl*, Peter Davies, London, 1933, p.20

32 Pierre de Lano, *L'Amour à Paris sous le Second Empire*, p.105

33 Zed, *Le Demi-monde sous le Second Empire. Souvenirs d'un sybarite*, Ernest Kolb, Paris, 1892, p.63

34 Ibid., p.64

35 Emma Elizabeth Crouch, *The Memoirs of Cora Pearl*, p.19

36 Emma Elizabeth Crouch, *Mémoires de Cora Pearl*, p.39

37 Emma Elizabeth Crouch, *The Memoirs of Cora Pearl*, pp.25–6

38 Hippolyte de Villemessant, *Mémoires d'un Journaliste, Vol.3: A Travers Le Figaro*, E. Dentu, Paris, 1873, p.341

39 Vicomte E. de Beaumont-Vassy, *Les Salons de Paris et la société parisienne sous Napoléon III*, Ferdinand Sartorius, Paris, 1868, pp.200–1

40 Princess Caroline Murat, *My Memoirs*, pp.179–80

41 Maxime Du Camp, *Souvenirs d'un demi-siècle*, p.227

42 C.E. de Maupas, *Mémoires sur le Second Empire*, Vol.1, E. Dentu, Paris, 1884, pp.294–5

43 Emma Elizabeth Crouch, *Mémoires de Cora Pearl*, pp.51–2

44 Princess Caroline Murat, *My Memoirs*, p.179

45 Maxime Du Camp, *Souvenirs d'un demi-siècle*, p.235

46 W.H. Holden, *The Pearl from Plymouth*, British Technical and General Press, London, 1950, p.56

47 Comte Horace de Viel Castel, *Mémoires sur le regne de Napoléon III (1851–1864)*, Vol.3, 1885, p.180

48 La Chroniqueuse, *Photographs of Paris Life*, pp.100–1

49 Anna Bicknell, *Life in the Tuileries under the Second Empire*, T. Fisher Unwin, London, 1895, p.64

50 Ibid., p.65

51 Emma Elizabeth Crouch, *Mémoires de Cora Pearl*, p.113

52 Ibid., p.121

53 Emma Elizabeth Crouch, *The Memoirs of Cora Pearl*, p.59

54 Ibid., p.69

55 Ibid., p.80

56 Ibid., p.59

57 Ibid., pp.76–7

58 Ibid., p.77

59 C.E. Maupas, *Mémoires sur le Second Empire*, Vol.2, p.122

60 Emma Elizabeth Crouch, *Mémoires de Cora Pearl*, pp.124–5

61 Emma Elizabeth Crouch, *The Memoirs of Cora Pearl*, p.60

62 La Chroniqueuse, *Photographs of Paris Life*, p.31

63 Ibid., p.113

64 Anna Bicknell, *Life in the Tuileries under the Second Empire*, pp.78–80

65 Emma Elizabeth Crouch, *Mémoires de Cora Pearl*, p.129

66 Ibid., p.130

67 La Chroniqueuse, *Photographs of Paris Life*, pp.129–30

68 A Cosmopolitan, *Random Recollections of Court and Society*, Ward & Downey, London, 1888, pp.148–9

69 Emma Elizabeth Crouch, *Mémoires de Cora Pearl*, pp.189–90

70 Ibid., p.191

71 Ibid., pp.191–2

72 Ibid., pp.67–8

73 Emma Elizabeth Crouch, *The Memoirs of Cora Pearl*, p.34

74 Emma Elizabeth Crouch, *Mémoires de Cora Pearl*, pp.65–6

75 Emma Elizabeth Crouch, *The Memoirs of Cora Pearl*, p.51

76 Emma Elizabeth Crouch, *Mémoires de Cora Pearl*, pp.73–4

77 Ibid., p.75

78 Ibid., p.79

79 Ibid., p.77

80 Ibid., p.79

81 Ibid., p.69

CHAPTER ELEVEN

Putting on a Show

T HE AMBITION ATTRIBUTED to the Duke de Morny by Emile de Maupas to 'make a great stir' could equally be seen as the ambition of the great courtesans, and certainly of both Cora Pearl and La Païva. Quite apart from their natural propensity to be noticed, they used several methods to achieve that ambition; both methods and ambition were in tune with the spirit of the age, for the ethos of the Second Empire was itself grounded in the importance of display, of showing its grandeurs to the world, of achieving those 'pyrotechnical victories'[1] which the *Illustrated London News* had predicted for it at the outset. Certain words occur again and again in descriptions of the Second Empire, nouns such as *fanfreluches* (trimmings, frills and so on), *frivolité, luxe, réclame* (fame, or publicity) and *l'effet*, adjectives such as *fastueux* (lavish, sumptuous) and *tapageur* (loud, flashy or blatant), and the verb *paraître* (to appear – with its double meaning of being visible and things not being quite what they seem). The overall impression conveyed is of froth and frivolity, of the world as a stage-set, of the supreme importance of the show.

One of the first things an individual needs to do when setting out to make a stir and to put on a show is – as we have seen in the case of each of these *demi-mondaines*, as indeed of that of Auguste Demorny in his detaching of the 'de' – to choose an appropriate name. The importance attached to names was not a phenomenon peculiar to the Second Empire, though that era was permeated by the resonance of the name 'Napoleon'. (An element which adds to the confusion in sorting out Bonaparte family history was Napoleon I's insistence that all his male descendants should have 'Napoleon' included in their names; there was also a preponderance of the names Louis, Jerome and Charles in various combinations. Louis Napoleon's elder brother, for instance, who died in 1831, was called Napoleon Louis, while Prince Napoleon, or to give him his full name Prince Napoleon Joseph Charles Paul, who was the son of Prince Jerome, was himself also known as Jerome by the family.)

For the woman desiring to be noticed her physical appearance is even more important than her name, and Second Empire fashions in dress provided ample opportunities for display. This was an age of ostentation, when the urge to compete for attention could on occasion take on ridiculous proportions. Ostentation in female attire attained its apogee in the crinoline which, despite its impracticality, enjoyed a long dominance. Originally a sort of horse-hair stuffing which enlarged the hips, it became refined over time into a metal cage over which the skirts were spread. Above this a woman would typically wear a corset which squeezed the waist and emphasised the bust. Under the cage, which could sway unpredictably to reveal the legs, pantaloons were worn. The crinoline posed problems in the areas of transport (there was no room for men in carriages alongside the voluminous skirts of their female companions), safety (the flaring skirt was particularly susceptible to fire), and accommodation. The theatre at Compiègne, which comfortably held eight hundred in Louis Philippe's day, was crowded with five hundred during the Second Empire. The proportion of women to seats in churches altered too, causing church authorities to worry about decreased revenue.

Maxime Du Camp tells how in October 1856 the Gymnase put on a play entitled *Les Toilettes tapageuses* and how the lead actress, according to the satiric intent of the piece, wore a ludicrously large crinoline. The morning after the first night, however, various society ladies were making enquiries about copying it, and within a few days the crinoline worn in the fashionable world was twice as large as before.[2] The Paris correspondent of the *Illustrated London News* lamented in January 1860: 'The prediction of the decrease in the amplitude of ladies' dresses in 1860 still remains unrealised, and the generally-condemned crinoline has not yet been compelled to hide its diminished head. We cannot tell to what we ought to attribute this persistence in enormous proportion, unless it be the ordinary difficulty of suppressing a bad custom.'[3] Princess Pauline Metternich, wife of the Austrian ambassador and a friend of the Empress's, is credited with having brought about the crinoline's gradual demise; in 1861 she gave a ball for which the invitations specified that ladies were not to wear them. The Empress, however, continued to wear hers until the last years of the Empire.

When women finally gave up their crinolines and became 'deflated', they did not necessarily abandon wearing yards and yards of material. La Chroniqueuse writes of the fashion for trailing dresses, which sound nearly as impractical as the crinoline (and these fashions certainly provided a boost to the textile industry): 'It appears that the Imperial fiat has gone forth as regards crinoline, as I observe some of our *élégantes* already walking up and down the Champs Elysées, like Dorothy Draggletail, performing the ignominious office of street-sweeper, with silks at twelve shillings a yard. Rather an expensive broom, you will say, but "*que voulez vous,*" these ladies must be in the fashion.'[4]

Male fashions were less capricious. Particularly in vogue during the Second Empire were knee breeches which showed off a man's calves, and cylindrical top hats, known vulgarly as stove pipes (*tuyaus de poêle*). Gloves were less to be worn than to be carried.

The most famous *couturier* of the Second Empire, the founder of modern Parisian *haute-couture*, who dressed both society women and *demi-mondaines*, was an Englishman, Charles Frederick Worth (the French, according to La Chroniqueuse, pronounced his name 'Monsieur Voss').[5] Born in Lincolnshire, he was apprenticed at thirteen to Swan and Edgar in Piccadilly. Fascinated by the Paris fashions which he had studied in magazines, he set off for the French capital in 1846, at the age of twenty-one, with no knowledge of the language and a hundred and seventeen francs in his pocket. He found a job at Gagelin and Opigez, a fashionable fabric retailer in the rue de

Richelieu, married a former Gagelin *demoiselle de magasin*, was soon creating costumes for her to model and was allowed to establish a dressmaking department. In 1858 he accepted the offer of a wealthy Swedish friend to set him up in business at 7 rue de la Paix. To begin with, he catered to a moderately well-off middle class clientèle, but his great opportunity came in 1860 when he persuaded Princess Metternich to buy one of his gowns. The Princess proceeded to recommend Worth to the Empress, and his career became meteoric. After 1864 he made all of the Empress's evening dresses, and by 1867 he had a workforce of twelve thousand and was dressing the nobility and royalty of France, Russia, Austria, Spain and Italy. Even Queen Victoria bought several gowns from him, as did the wives of American millionaires.

Apollonie Sabatier was fascinated by clothes but held herself rather aloof from conventional fashion, preferring to create her own style. She enjoyed wearing original outfits, which were sometimes designed especially for her by artist friends. Her dress sense was not infallible, however, as is clear from a letter Théophile Gautier wrote to Ernesta Grisi on 8 November 1856:

> . . . on the subject of the Présidente, she outdid herself at the first performance of the Bouilhet. She was wearing a ridiculous headdress – one of those frightful basin-shaped caps, the colour of chocolate, with feathers, ribbons and other extravagant trimmings. I think she managed to make herself look ugly, something very difficult to achieve . . .[6]

Ernesta replied: 'as for Mme Sabatier I think she's going crazy at the idea that she's getting older, she shouldn't worry, no one will copy her weird outfits.'[7]

If Apollonie was known for her 'weird outfits', Cora Pearl and La Païva were both renowned for their extravagant, not to say excessive, use of make-up. Jean Philippe Worth, son of the couturier, describes Cora's appearance succinctly: 'Her teeth were incomparable, but her make-up was shockingly overdone, and she looked much better at a distance.'[8] She was nevertheless credited with a degree of originality and an occasionally successful audacity in her self-ornamentation: 'She was the first person to colour her hair yellow and to think of making her eyelashes iridescent, of illuminating her eyes, making her forehead shimmer and powdering her flesh with silver, frost, snow, milk, stars and pearls.'[9] Powder, made of various starches and mixed with other substances such as talc, magnesia and oxide of zinc, and applied with a hare's foot or a puff made of swan's down, was a compulsory element in the arsenal of any lady of fashion. Cora's originality seems to have lain in what she added to the powder to create her special effects.

The habit of dyeing her hair seems to have provoked particular fascination and spawned much imitation: 'And then, oh unsurpassed glory! Cora Pearl introduced to the world the tincture, thanks to which a brunette can give herself the pleasure of hearing a poet compare her hair, dyed red or pink, to a Bengal rose or to a crimson veil.'[10] The turning of her hair yellow may conceivably have been a mistake, or at least achieved by accident rather than design. A known recipe for dyeing the hair black involved the use of nitrate of silver, water and sulphuret of potassium, but if the sulphuret was not fresh it would have the effect of turning the hair yellow rather than black. (It was not only women who practised the art of hair-dyeing; it was noticed that, when the Italian patriot Orsini was guillotined in March 1858, his hair, which had been raven-black at the time of his arrest two months previously, was now iron-grey. His supporters claimed that he had gone grey as a result of the treatment meted out to him in prison, but G.W. Septimus Piesse, the author of *The Art of Perfumery & the Methods of obtaining the Odours of Plants, with instructions for the manufacture of perfumes for the handkerchief, scented powders, odorous vinegars, dentifrices, pomatums, cosmetics, perfumed soap etc.*, published in 1862, is convinced that the real reason was that during his incarceration he was deprived of his habitual hair-dye.) A less drastic method of achieving a golden glow was to sprinkle the hair with *poudre d'or* or golden powder. The Empress Eugénie was the first woman to appear thus glittering, at a festival in 1860. The best (and most expensive) sort of *poudre d'or* consisted of crushed gold leaf, though a similar effect could be created using powdered bronze.

Cora was also very fond of jewellery, nearly always wearing broad gold bracelets on her arms and wrists, a necklace, flowers in her hair, and jewellery or flowers in her corsage. Usually she wore a broad belt, pulled as tight as possible, to emphasise her waist. She also often wore a ring on the third finger of her right hand, attached by a slim chain to a bangle on her wrist. She was exceedingly proud of her elegant hands, and had models or casts of them spread around as ornaments in her drawing room.

Though Cora could undoubtedly overdo the make-up and overall presentation, she had the natural performer's ability to amuse, and her exaggerated self-display served as an effective ploy to get herself noticed in her chosen milieu. She is even reputed to have dyed her dog blue to match her outfit – or, according to Mrs Burton Harrison, a young American woman visiting Paris from Virginia in 1867 – yellow to match her hair.[11] The element of humour was missing from La Païva's ostentation, however, and her abundant use of make-up was never admired but only derided. Never considering her face to be her best feature (she avoided having portraits painted of herself for this reason), she mistakenly believed that heavy make-up would improve her appearance and, as she grew older, wore more and more of it. Jean Philippe Worth commented on her overuse of kohl, made at the time from Indian ink dissolved in rosewater and applied with a fine camels' hair brush: 'I did not see her until she was no longer young and her beauty was already on the wane. And I am afraid that I did not appreciate it. Her eyelids were shockingly blackened, and this, combined with the prominence of her eyes, made her look fierce and hawklike.'[12]

Both Cora Pearl and La Païva may have been over-lavish in their personal adornment, but then not much store was set by subtlety in the society in which they flourished. In this era of conspicuous consumption, women paraded their finery and men paraded their women. As Alexandre Dumas *fils* put it:

Women were luxuries for public consumption, like hounds, horses and carriages. There was fun to be had in taking a girl who, eight days earlier, had been selling fish in the market or pouring drinks for early morning bricklayers, and covering her with velvet and rattling her about in a carriage; one no longer set any store by wit, gaiety, or spelling; rich today, you could be ruined tomorrow, so in the meantime you'd better have supper with this or that famous woman . . .[13]

Part of the transaction between a courtesan and her rich protector was that she was to act as a status symbol, to declare to the world that he could afford to keep an expensive mistress and that he knew how to do so in style. And in the case of those who consorted with the highest class of courtesans, there was the *cachet* to be obtained in showing off that one had been chosen out of an array of suitors for the privilege of being allowed to pay for the favours of a particular woman. And, as Dumas *fils* pointed out, in this era of speculation, of opportunities for investment in roads, railways, property development and the new telegraph system, when fortunes could be made and lost within the space of a few weeks, it was considered better to spend the money one had while one still had it, and to enjoy being seen to be rich, at least for a while.

If men used courtesans as status symbols, the courtesan could always respond in kind. The rank a courtesan had reached could be measured by the social standing of her clients and Cora, for instance, is careful whom she selects out of her many clients to include in her memoirs. She mentions the odd sailor or impoverished young man in her early days, partly for comic effect, but the bulk of her narrative is concerned with the Massénas, the Mornys, the dukes and the princes, to convey the impression of her own significance through her contact with these significant men.

Cora, happy to play along with contemporary society's preconceptions about women, to be paraded as an expensive status symbol and to be amply financially rewarded for being a 'sex object', would spend much of her day on an elaborate beauty routine. 'From the moment of getting up it would be, first, a manicure, intimate attentions with all their arsenal, then the arrival of the linen-keeper or outfitter and a natter with her, a visit from the jeweller, billets-doux to be dispatched in all directions, and serious matters. All that would take until about four o'clock or half-past four.'[14] Then she would go out, probably for a drive down the Champs Elysées or in the Bois de Boulogne (the Emperor and Empress being in the habit of taking their drive around the lake earlier in the afternoon, the *demi-mondaines* generally saved their display until later). She might also visit an establishment such as Worth's in the afternoon, or receive a client, perhaps even several.

The evenings could include visits to the theatre and to a fashionable restaurant, particularly to one of the private rooms in an establishment such as the Café Anglais. Another, more select, restaurant frequented by Cora was the Petit Moulin Rouge (no relation to the Montmartre cabaret) which was located off the Champs Elysées and boasted, in addition to its main entrance, a secret door in a side street for the use of diners requiring the strictest privacy. There were large dining rooms on the ground floor, while the usual *cabinets particuliers* were located on the two upper floors. The renowned chef Escoffier began working at the Petit Moulin Rouge on Easter Monday 1865 and in his memoirs recalls the use Cora made of the establishment, likening her ability to fleece young men to the art of pigeon plucking:

> The same evening, in a private dining room close to the one reserved by the Count de Paris, Cora Pearl could be found dining with a young lord, or perhaps I should say a young pigeon. This beautiful woman, who is far from forgotten, was particularly talented in the art of plucking these little birds so beloved by sensitive women. She took care to find them just as they left the nest, ready to fly alone, and then lavished her charm upon them until they were completely picked clean. Then, considering the deal closed, she turned to someone else.[15]

Escoffier invented a dish named after her: Noisettes d'Agneau Cora.[16] The noisettes of lamb were to be sautéed and then placed inside freshly cooked artichoke hearts, intended as a pun on '*cœur d'artichaut*', a term used to designate the kind of man who falls in love with every girl he meets (and thus likely to fall prey to Cora's pigeon-plucking charms). It has frequently been asserted[17] that on one occasion Cora had herself served up naked on a huge silver platter in the room known as the Grand Seize at the Café Anglais, where she is also said to have exposed her breasts at a women's dinner party – which suggests that she enjoyed display for the sake of it, and not just to attract a potential client. Another courtesan, Marie Colombier, refers to this event, and to Cora's inventive use of make-up, in her memoirs:

> At a dinner party of women, in the Grand Seize of the Café Anglais, it was only possible to find one criticism which could be made of these goddess-like breasts: it was claimed that she must have put make-up on them, because the pale pink which coloured her nipples looked as though it had been stolen from wild rose petals.[18]

Cora's aptitude as a horsewoman was another important aspect of her self-display; horse-riding had long been considered a particular strength (or foible) of the English, though the women of Paris had been becoming increasingly fond of it since the early 1830s. It is not without a touch of professional jealousy that Marie Colombier alludes to Cora's talents in this direction, and to the supposed effect such a sport had on her physique:

> Cora Pearl personified what can be termed the English style of courtesan. She was above all a sportswoman, riding a horse like a jockey, wielding her crop with a swagger; she had bandy legs, which gave her, when she walked, the rolling gait of a stable lad; and, to complete the resemblance, she drank a lot and often; but her bust was beyond reproach, her bosom marvellous and worthy of being moulded by some illustrious artist of antiquity.[19]

Cora was renowned not only for riding on horseback but also for running a splendid carriage, and she was determined to outclass any rivals in the drives or rides around the Bois. Her competitors in the aristocratic world included the *équipages* of Princess Metternich (an imitation of whose famous bright yellow livery was worn by Cora's jockeys, while her *calèche* was upholstered in sky-blue), Madame Musard (an American), the Countess de Pourtalès, the Marchioness de Gallifet (the wife of one of Cora's conquests), Madame de Contades and the Duchess de Persigny, while in the *demi-monde* her chief rivals included Blanche d'Antigny (who had at one time been a rider in the circus), Giulia Barucci (reputed never to have refused herself to a member of a fashionable club) and La Païva, who was herself an able horsewoman. Nestor Roqueplan wrote admiringly of both Cora's horsemanship and her management skills in this area. He is influenced by ideas about racial stereotypes, ascribing the small stature and gravity of her grooms to their Englishness:

All Paris knew Cora Pearl. She was a centauress; she created the amazon.

She was the first to appear in our elegant promenades on a real horse which she rode with unequalled distinction and skill, or in carriages which the most refined people considered models in terms of their design and colour, just as they admired her so well-matching pair, the style and standard of her harness, her livery and her servants, whose smallness and good manners contrasted with their gravity.

No one who knew about horses could ever have confused Cora Pearl with the awkward centauresses who sometimes tried to compete with her. Clumsy efforts, soon abandoned! Poor stables, bad drivers; cardboard horses, arrangements just for show; incomplete and fleeting chic.

Cora Pearl's stables generally consisted of a dozen horses groomed and looked after by English servants, who do not laugh, a favour never obtained by the spendthrift and disorganised tarts who aspire to be amazons, who pay their people badly and let them play cards in their apartment.

For Cora Pearl, the horse is not only a luxury, it is an art; it is not only an art, it is an enterprise. A visit to her stables makes one realise how ridiculous sums can be spent in all seriousness under this one item of a fantastic budget. It is a form of rational insanity.[20]

Between 1863 and 1868 Cora bought more than sixty horses; in the space of three years she spent ninety thousand francs with one horse-dealer alone. This scale of expenditure was all part of the show.

Though Julian Osgood Field's *Uncensored Recollections* could equally be called 'Unreliable Recollections' and contain more than an element of anti-semitism, they do capture something of Cora's spirit, the liveliness of her presence and her delight in display (as well as presenting an amusing picture of the dumbstruck reactions of a couple of adolescent English public schoolboys when confronted with her):

I knew Cora Pearl very well, although, of course, not in her zenith . . . She was an amiable, but very stupid woman, and very fond of playing coarse, silly monkey tricks. I remember lunching at her house once in the Rue des Bassins when she put her hand into a dish of cutlets or something and put a large dripping piece of whatever it was on the head of Ferdinand Bischoffscheim. He took it very meekly and smiled a weak semitic smile through the veil of thick sauce that covered his face. But the Duke of Hamilton, who was there, seeing her put her hand into the dish again, cried: 'Damn you, Cora, if you put that on my head, I'll strangle you.' Cora shrieked with laughter – that was her idea of fun. Speaking of her and the Duke of Hamilton (who, although almost old enough to be my father, was my bosom chum), I saw a very funny thing years before that at Baden Baden. Cora was gracefully sailing into the Kursaal, all dressed in white satin and white lace, covered with diamonds and pearls, on the arm of Salamanca, the Jew banker of Madrid . . . when they were very politely and firmly stopped by an official with a big gold chain round his neck, and Cora was told her presence would cause a scandal and she must retire. I, with two other English boys from my school, was standing by, and I remember remarking that the train of Cora's dress was so extravagantly long that it had not yet entirely got into the room when she was forced so to speak to double back and retire. We callow chickos, of course, thought all was now over, and the eclipse final. But not a bit of it; lo and behold! within half-an-hour Cora and her red hair and white jewels and her interminable white dress, again appeared in the doorway triumphant, for this time being on the arm of the Duke of Hamilton (whose hair, by the way, almost matched hers in colour), whose mother was a Princess of Baden, her progress was unimpeded; in fact, all the Casino officials bowed to the ground as she advanced. I very distinctly remember how I (little beast) swelled with pride as I went forward and was warmly greeted by the duke and Cora, and how I was envied by my companions. Cora delighted – positively revelled in the most wild and reckless extravagance, and no doubt she was quite right, for in her special profession it is more than half the battle to keep in the limelight and have all the drums incessantly beating. Prince Napoleon sent her once a huge vanload of the most expensive orchids. She gave a supper party, strewed the orchids over the floor and dressed as a sailor, danced the hornpipe, followed by the Can-can over them.[21]

Cora's extraordinary reputation was summed up by Zed in his book about the *demi-mondaines* of the Second Empire. Some of what he says is hearsay, or memory mixed with a good dose of invention and exaggerated by repetition – if the infamous book in which she was supposed to have recorded the performance of her clients ever existed, for instance, it has never been discovered. But his sense of bewilderment – precisely what was it about this woman which ensnared so many rich and powerful men? – was shared by many, particularly among the French, whose bewilderment included the fact that Cora was an Englishwoman and hence, almost by definition to a fashionable Parisian, deficient in matters of style and taste:

I humbly admit that hers was a success I never understood, that it must be noted, as it did exist, but there is no justification for it. To me, she represents a stain on what was, taken all in all, a scintillating group, refined and aristocratic, of the gallant women of her epoch and from whom she differed absolutely in every respect. She was a personality apart, a specimen of another race, a bizarre and astonishing phenomenon. And perhaps this is what explains her notoriety and was the cause of her prestige.

English by birth, character and appearance, she had the head of a City worker, neither good nor bad, fiery blonde, almost red, hair, a vulgar and unbearable accent, a raucous voice, exceedingly common manners and the tone of a stable boy.

But she rode extremely well and her admirers assured us that she was perfectly shaped, that her body was a marvel. I acknowledge that there was some truth in this opinion, for I was allowed to see her, as were my comrades, in the costume of Eve before the fall, a costume of which she was particularly fond and which was often her version of a dressing gown in which to receive visitors.

Cora led her lovers by the nose and was not at all hesitant to address the most violent and offensive words to them in public. She spared them in nothing and for nothing and made their lives very hard . . . None of which prevented her from dragging behind her chariot princes of the blood, one of whom – a future king, if you please – made her a present of a pearl necklace of phenomenal value, as well as noblemen of the highest rank, very popular young men, and very estimable men of all sorts. What hidden lure, what secret potion did she have that she was able to live it up, for twenty years, to the tune of fifty thousand francs a month, to have jewels, outfits and carriages like no other, to stun and astound Paris?

She swallowed up money and, moreover, like the far-sighted daughter of Albion that she was, she was systematic, very systematic. One day we discovered at her house an amazing register, divided into three columns. In one column were inscribed the names of her clients, most of whom were our friends or known to us; in the second, alongside each name, the date of their visit; in the third . . . the price the pilgrim had paid for the hospitality received . . .

There was even, God forgive me, a comment column in the fatal register. Not too pleasant for some, the comments![22]

Cora's most blatant moment of self-display, of literally putting on a show, came on 26 January 1867 when she made her début as Cupid in Offenbach's operetta *Orphée aux enfers* at the Théâtre des Bouffes Parisiens. According to her own account she was approached by the producer and asked if she could sing, as he was lacking someone to play Cupid and time was getting short. She claimed to know the part off by heart, though admitted to having had no formal singing lessons. These were arranged for her, and she was coached for the part by 'Collinvert, the teacher and husband of the great singer Urbine' who, as Cora puts it, 'drummed my role into me at speed, singing with me, miming with me, helping me with the pauses, and finally initiating me into all the little tricks which served me so well during the flaunting of my perhaps rather unorthodox Cupid'.[23] This was no mean undertaking, for though the part of Cupid is short, it is virtuosic and most untrained singers would have had no hope at all of mastering it. Cora had inherited some musical ability from her parents, she had a quick wit which would undoubtedly have helped, she had a sense of adventure which made the opportunity hard to refuse, and she knew that her appearance could probably carry the day even if her singing and acting skills lacked finesse. The men in the audience on the first night included a selection of Cora's past and present lovers: Prince Napoleon was there, as were the Princes Achille Murat, Narischkin and Troubetskoy, Khalil Bey, the Duke de Rivoli, Mustapha Pasha and the Prince de Sagan. The *demi-monde* was also there in force. Cora had considered that a normal dressing room was insufficient for her needs, and Prince Napoleon had had an adjoining apartment adapted for her use. Access from it to the theatre was via a door inserted for the occasion, and the exit was by way of a private staircase. This also made the apartment a very convenient trysting place for the Prince during the weeks devoted to rehearsal and performance.

As the curtain went up for the second act there was Cora, asleep on Mount Olympus. The critics are united that, as an actress and singer, she was not a resounding success. But they were all struck, as she (and the producer) had known they would be, by what she was wearing: very little, apart from a mass of jewels. Philibert Audebrand recalls: 'Cora Pearl appeared on the stage half-naked, singing quite brightly with a funny little Anglo-Saxon accent the couplets which begin: *I am Love*. That evening the Jockey Club filled the house in force. All the armigerous names to be found in the Golden Book of the French nobility were there, in white gloves and holding ivory lorgnettes . . . It was a success of sorts.'[24] Marie Colombier fulminated about 'those circumflex legs' and laughed at Cora's pronunciation: '*Je souis Kioupidone*',[25] while Paul Foucher wrote of the 'profound mockery' contained in the enthusiasm of the audience and complained about Cora's 'hip-swaying sincerity'.[26] The *Illustrated London News* managed a more measured response:

> Mdlle. Cora Pearl, the dashing *Amazone* of the Bois de Boulogne, made her début the other evening at the Bouffes Parisiennes, in the part of Cupid in 'Orphée aux Enfers'. She was one blaze of diamonds − diamonds in her hair, round her neck, on her tiny cloak, round her arms, round her waist, and round her ankles. She displayed great nervousness, and sang much of her part with her eyes closed. The reception she met with, however, was most enthusiastic.[27]

Foucher too noted that Cora kept her eyes closed for much of her performance − either she was indeed nervous or this was her interpretation of Cupid's blindness. One of the other singers taking part in this performance was Madame Ugalde, who twenty years previously had performed at a charity concert with the other Madame Sabatier. Her professionalism, her 'voice changed by the rigours of a hectic career, but in accents inspired by genius',[28] could not help but emphasise the amateur nature of Cora's efforts. Nevertheless Cora made her exit in style, kicking up her heels to display her diamond-studded soles (and much besides). Captain the Hon. D. Bingham spoke for many of the men present when he wrote: 'I remember little of the performance, except that Cupid played with great self-possession, that she was not much encumbered with garments, and that the buttons of her boots were large diamonds of the purest water.'[29]

Cora managed a dozen performances before a group of students decided to disrupt the event in protest at the role being given to a foreign courtesan with no professional acting or singing experience; their hissing and whistling became too loud for her to continue. Cora's own comment on her theatrical adventure is succinct:

I played twelve times in a row. My band of friends brought the house down. At the end I was hissed. I left the boards without regret, and with no desire to tread them again.
Such is glory.[30]

Later that year Paris put on its own show: the Universal Exposition of 1867 was opened on 1 April by the Emperor's small son, the Prince Imperial, who was then eleven years old. After weeks of rain, the day was crisp and clear. Planning had begun four years earlier, again under the aegis of Prince Napoleon, and the aim was to demonstrate to the world (in the wake of the London Exhibition of 1862) that the quality of French industry was in no way inferior to that of Great Britain and that Paris could justly be viewed as a universal model.

The Exposition occupied the entire site of the Champ de Mars on the left bank of the Seine, opposite the Butte de Chaillot which was levelled in preparation. The main exhibition building, of whom the chief engineers were Gustave Eiffel and Jean Krantz, covered almost forty acres; it was a vast structure of oval design, with concentric rings of galleries surrounding a central garden. Hydraulic lifts carried visitors from the ground floor to the roof, where there were walkways offering splendid views. The oval galleries represented themes, while the transverse avenues divided the building into national sections.

The central theme was 'The history of labour and its fruits'; the Exposition was also intended to symbolise the prosperity and material achievements of the Second Empire, to show off the new Paris and to state the case for economic liberalism. The arts as well as industry were represented, the fine art exhibits including paintings and sculptures from fifteen countries, executed between 1855 and 1867 and representing the largest collection of contemporary art ever assembled. Unfortunately, the process of selection ensured the imposition of official taste and avant garde painters, including Camille Pissarro and Paul Cézanne, were therefore rejected. Edouard Manet's submissions were not even sent on to the jury; he responded by organising his own exhibition, as did Gustave Courbet, just outside the Exposition grounds.

This was the first Exposition both to have national pavilions and to offer a carnival atmosphere. Every French wine district had its own exhibits and cellar, while cafés and restaurants offering a variety of international cuisines encircled the main building and opened on to the outer gardens. The French pavilion, a miniature palace, was used as a lounge for the imperial family and their guests, who included the brother of the Emperor of Japan, the Kings of Belgium, Greece, Portugal and Sweden, Tsar Alexander II of Russia (the target of an assassination attempt at Longchamp on 6 June), King William I of Prussia, the Khedive of Egypt, the Sultan of Turkey, the Queen of Württemberg and the Emperor of Austria. Prince Napoleon also made use of a room for himself, as alluded to by Cora Pearl:

When we wanted to meet at the Universal Exhibition, we always went there separately. The Duke had there a room fitted in the Turkish fashion, where I found him every day at the same hour. He often brought papers there so as to waste as little of his working time as possible. He examined with extreme pleasure the smallest details relating to foreign manufactures, particularly machines which had to do with new applications of electricity.

Many times I have seen him draw portions of machinery, and note upon his drawings any novel points, concerning which he would afterwards have prolonged interviews with the exhibitors. The subject of aërial navigation interested him equally. He had a large collection of engravings representing balloons of all kinds.[31]

At the heart of the Exposition was the machinery gallery, which included a display of Prussian military might which the French would have done well to take note of – a gigantic fifty-ton Krupp cannon made of steel which could fire shells weighing a thousand pounds.

By May the Exposition was in full swing and people began to flock to Paris from all over Europe. Maxime Du Camp, writing from a rather jaundiced post-Empire perspective, noted that Paris was also subject to a vast influx of prostitutes at this time, that the Exposition 'drew from the four corners of the world all the fallen women, or those who wanted nothing more than to fall'.[32] He even appears to suggest that the authorities deliberately brought in such women, to encourage the visitors to have a good time and lavish their money on the entertainments of all varieties which Paris had to offer. There were more and more shops to enjoy, new department stores opening in the second half of the 1860s including the Printemps near the Gare Saint-Lazare, La Samaritaine between the Pont Neuf and the rue de Rivoli, and the Grand Bazar de l'Hôtel de Ville. In 1863 Aristide Boucicaut had bought his partner's interest in the Bon Marché and four years later issued the first French mail order catalogue for the benefit of provincial customers. Then in September 1869 the foundation stone of a new and magnificent building for the Bon Marché was laid; the architects were L.A. Boileau and Gustave Eiffel, both pioneers in the use of iron and glass in functional architecture. The fashionable restaurants were also continuing to flourish: the owner of the Café Anglais, for instance, was able to afford the life of a country gentleman and to pay his celebrated chef, Adolphe Dugléré (whom Rossini named 'the Mozart of French cooking'), twenty-five thousand francs a year.

The great ceremony for the distribution of prizes by the Emperor was held on 1 July in the Palais de l'Industrie before twenty thousand invited guests. The Exposition was closed after seven months on 3 November; more than eleven million visits had been recorded. The buildings were immediately demolished and the Champ de Mars returned to its former state.

The aim of Parisians and visitors alike was summed up by the courtesan Marguerite Bellanger in her *Confessions*: 'To have fun, fun and more fun was everyone's preoccupation.'[33] There is a sense of glitter – of *poudre d'or* – about Second Empire Paris at its zenith, accompanied by an underlying disquiet that all that glitters may not really be gold. 'Celebrities sprang up like mushrooms and shrivelled even before the sun went down. One lived fast, feverishly. What did tomorrow matter so long as today was exhilarating?'[34] As the English governess Anna Bicknell put it: 'Paris was a sort of fairyland, where every one lived only for amusement, and where every one seemed rich and happy. What lay underneath all this, would not bear close examination – the dishonorable acts of all kinds, which too often were needed to produce the glamour deceiving superficial observers.'[35] Not all non-Parisians were so judgmental; Dr Thomas W. Evans, for example, Napoleon III's American dentist and a man highly valued in court circles throughout Europe for his anaesthetic skills, clearly liked what he saw and enjoyed the emphasis on the outward show:

It was a society full of movement and originality, of unconventionality, and gaiety, and charm. The admirable taste, the artistic sentiment and distinction shown by those who best represented it, especially in everything relating to manners, and dress, and the outward appearance of the person, found expression in a word which was then frequently used to symbolise the sum of all these mundane elegancies. The women of those days were not more beautiful than are the women of the Republic; but the women of the Empire had *chic*.[36]

Arsène Houssaye wrote of the self-confidence of the best years of the Empire: 'no black specks on the horizon; the peacefulness of luxury and of money: one lived just for the sake of living – from day to day. One spoke in the Chamber merely to demonstrate one's eloquence. We were afraid of nothing, we thought we dominated the world, never had Paris been so widely acknowledged as the universal capital.'[37] Count Horace de Viel Castel, however, could be predicted to see the dark side and to see it before most other people; his final diary entry, dated 27 August 1864, three months before his death, was doom-laden: 'We are in decline, and what was young in the Emperor's entourage is growing old, and what was not yet corrupted four years ago is now corrupted absolutely.'[38]

The Second Empire saw the beginning not only of modern French industry, finance and social reform, but also of modern poetry, painting and fiction. Official recognition of some of these developments had to wait for a later period, however; Maxime Du Camp noted in his *Souvenirs d'un demi-siècle* that this was a time when literature and art were scorned, when only what was practically and immediately useful was valued, that taste was debased and fashions ridiculous.[39] Light opera drew the crowds more than any other form of entertainment and Offenbach triumphed with a string of operettas, most notably *Orphée aux enfers* at the Bouffes in October 1858, *La Belle Hélène* at the Variétés in December 1864, and *La Vie parisienne* at the Théâtre du Palais Royal in October 1866. This last work particularly captured the spirit of Paris during the heady days leading up to the Exposition of 1867, the chorus expressing the delight with which visitors flocked to the city to experience all the pleasures it had to offer:

> We come running, we hurry
> To know, oh Paris,
> To know the intoxication
> Of your days and of your nights.
> All the enraptured foreigners
> Rush towards you, oh Paris![40]

During the Exposition itself another Offenbach operetta, *La Grande Duchesse de Gérolstein*, was playing at the Variétés, and visitors from all parts of Europe were amused by this satire about an absurd German principality.

And more than the art and literature, the plays, operas and fireworks, more even than the monumental building works and the Expositions, it was the women, and particularly the women of the *demi-monde*, who were the main source of fascination for visitors to the city, and who gave Second Empire Paris its lasting reputation:

> As I have already observed, the things as well as the people of the Second Empire provoke an extreme curiosity in the public, and the political or historical facts which marked this epoch are by no means the only reason for this curiosity. It is aroused quite as much, if not above all, by the gossip of the period, and one can hardly mention the reign of Napoleon III without mouths puckering in malicious smiles and eyes winking mischievously. By gossip, one means primarily, in effect, the question of love – which was, it must be admitted, under the Second Empire, one of the most important questions on the agenda, not only of the Tuileries, but also of the salons and the elegant boudoirs.[41]

The final great official spectacle of the Second Empire was the opening of the Suez Canal on 16 November 1869, the celebration of one of the greatest engineering achievements of the nineteenth century. Constructed over the course of ten years, the Canal provided the first direct maritime route between the Mediterranean and the Red Sea and was largely the result of the combined efforts of Ferdinand de Lesseps and Napoleon III. It was opened by the Empress Eugénie and de Lesseps on board *L'Aigle*, leading a flotilla of sixty-seven ships carrying representatives of the European powers on a voyage from Port Said to Suez. Amidst the celebrations, both here and back in Paris where Verdi's *Le Bal masqué* was opening at the Théâtre Lyrique, there was no presentiment of how near the end was:

Ask all these society women whom they envy. There will be only one reply: Cora Pearl. In frivolous society, which is not – let this be understood – synonymous with French society, but which cuts across it like a cotillion, with its flashiness and smiles, the women's coquetry, the men's intoxication, they are all so blind that no one sees silhouetted on the walls of the room the shadow of Bismarck . . .[42]

---

1 *Illustrated London News*, No. 575 Vol.XXI, Supplement, Saturday, 21 August 1852

2 Maxime Du Camp, *Paris: ses organes, ses functions et sa vie jusqu 'en 1870*, p.680

3 *Illustrated London News*, No.1014 Vol.XXXVI, Saturday, 28 January 1860

4 La Chroniqueuse, *Photographs of Paris Life*, p.189

5 Ibid., p.156

6 Théophile Gautier, *Correspondance générale*, Vol.6, 1991, p.247

7 Ibid., p.252

8 Jean Philippe Worth, *A Century of Fashion*, tr. Ruth Scott Miller, Little, Brown & Co., Boston, 1928, p.103

9 Gustave Claudin, *Mes Souvenirs*, p.248

10 Théodore de Banville, *La Lanterne magique*, p.272

11 Mrs Burton Harrison, *Recollections Grave and Gay* (electronic edition), Charles Scribner's Sons, New York, 1911, p.253

12 Jean Philippe Worth, *A Century of Fashion*, p.110

13 Alexandre Dumas *fils*, *Théâtre complet*, Vol.1, pp.23–4

14 Zed, *Le Demi-monde sous le Second Empire*, p.30

15 Auguste Escoffier, *Memories of My Life*, tr. Laurence Escoffier, Van Nostrand Reinhold, New York, 1997, p.13

16 Ibid., p.14

17 See, e.g., Claude Blanchard, *Dames de cœur*, Editions du Pré aux Clercs, Paris, 1946, p.26

18 Marie Colombier, *Mémoires. Fin d'Empire*, Flammarion, Paris, 1898, p.306

19 Ibid.

20 Nestor Roqueplan, *Parisine*, pp.60–1

21 Julian Osgood Field, *Uncensored Recollections*, Eveleigh Nash & Grayson, London, 1924, pp.55–8

22 Zed, *Le Demi-monde sous le Second Empire*, pp.52–5

23 Emma Elizabeth Crouch, *Mémoires de Cora Pearl*, pp.294–5

24 Philibert Audebrand, *Petits Mémoires d'une stalle d'orchestre*, Jules Lévy, Paris, 1885, p.222

25 Marie Colombier, *Mémoires*, p.307

26 Paul Foucher, *Entre Cour et jardin. Etudes et souvenirs du théâtre*, Amyot, Paris, 1867, pp.432–3

27 *Illustrated London News*, No.1411 Vol.L, Saturday, 2 February 1867, p.102

28 Paul Foucher, *Entre cour et jardin*, p.433

29 Captain The Hon. D. Bingham, *Recollections of Paris*, Vol.1, Chapman & Hall, London, 1896, p.61

30 Emma Elizabeth Crouch, *Mémoires de Cora Pearl*, p.295

31 Emma Elizabeth Crouch, *The Memoirs of Cora Pearl*, p.75

32 Maxime Du Camp, *Paris: ses organes, ses fonctions et sa fie jusqu 'en 1870*, p.351

33 Marguérite Bellanger, *Confessions*, Librairie Populaire, Paris, 1882, p.11

34 C. Simond (ed.), *Paris de 1800 à 1900, Vol.II, 1830–1870*, Librairie Plon, Paris, 1900, p.431

35 Anna Bicknell, *Life in the Tuileries under the Second Empire*, p.118

36 E.A. Crane (ed.), *The Memoirs of Dr Thomas W. Evans. Recollections of the Second French Empire*, Vol.1, T. Fisher Unwin, London, 1905, p.139

37 Arsène Houssaye, *Les Confessions. Souvenirs d'un demi-siècle 1830–1880*, Vol.1, 1885, p.6

38 Comte Horace de Viel Castel, *Mémoires sur le règne de Napoléon III (1851–1864)*, Vol.6, 1884, p.331

39 Maxime Du Camp, *Souvenirs d'un demi-siècle*, p.136

40 Meilhac and Halévy, *Théâtre*, Vol.4, Calmann Lévy, Paris, c.1904, p.385

41 Pierre de Lano, *L'Amour à Paris sous le Second Empire*, p.3

42 C. Simond (ed.), *Paris de 1800 à 1900, Vol.II, 1830–1870*, p.432

CHAPTER TWELVE

The Collapse of Empire

O N NEW YEAR'S DAY 1870, all the usual festivities took place at
the court of the Tuileries. At eleven o'clock in the morning
the imperial family luncheon was attended by Prince Napoleon and
Princess Clotilde, Prince and Princess Murat, Princess Mathilde and
other relatives. The guests also included the Emperor's old friend and
physician Dr Conneau (who had helped him escape from the fortress
of Ham in 1846), members of the palace staff such as the Chamberlain, the Master of Ceremonies and the Prince Imperial's tutor,
General Bourbaki of the Maison Militaire and Marshal MacMahon.
During the course of the day a number of visitors came to pay their
respects, including Baron Haussmann, the Count de Nieuwerkerke
and the President of the Corps Législatif, Monsieur Schneider. The
favourite ladies of the court were also very much in evidence,
including the Princess Metternich and the Marchioness de Gallifet.
The *Illustrated London News*' report of the day read as follows:

> Shortly after the conclusion of mass in the chapel of the
> Tuileries the Emperor, proceeding to the throne-room, re-
> ceived the congratulations of the Corps Diplomatique, to
> whose address he replied in the ordinary conventional terms,
> professing to see in it 'a new proof of the good relations
> existing between France and foreign Powers,' and expressing a
> hope that the new year would tend to increase concord and
> the advancement of civilisation.[1]

The immediate event which triggered the Franco-Prussian War later that same year is known to posterity as the Hohenzollern candidacy. Prince Leopold of Hohenzollern-Sigmaringen, the nephew of the Prussian King William and a brother of King Ferdinand of Romania, agreed in the spring of 1870 to a request by the Spanish government to pose his candidacy for the Spanish throne, vacant since the overthrow of Queen Isabella in September 1868. Although Prince Leopold was initially reluctant to become a candidate and the Prussian king viewed the Hohenzollern candidacy with misgivings, his Chancellor, Otto von Bismarck, was taking an active interest in the matter – hoping, in fact, to provoke a war with France as part of his plan to bring about a unified German empire by rallying the south German states to Prussia's cause against the French. The intention was for the Cortes, Spain's lower house of legislature, to hold a secret election to ratify the candidacy, but there were delays, and in the process France got wind of what was going on. (It so happened that at the time of the Hohenzollern candidacy the French Foreign Minister was Agénor, Duke de Gramont – formerly Duke de Guiche – the erstwhile lover of Marie Duplessis and probably of Blanche de Païva, and once characterised by Bismarck as the 'stupidest man in Europe'.)

On 6 July the French Foreign Minister declared to the Corps Législatif that France would not tolerate a Prussian prince on the Spanish throne, and France's minister in Berlin, Count Vincent Benedetti, was instructed by Agénor de Gramont to go to Bad Ems to try to persuade King William to advise Leopold to withdraw his candidacy. The King, however, was reluctant to take the initiative in a matter that constituted a personal decision by Leopold and supposedly did not concern the Prussian government. In the event it was the Prince's father who decided to withdraw the candidacy. The French were further incensed, however, when King William refused to give a guarantee that he would not authorise such a candidacy in the future.

Bismarck then stepped into the picture, by editing King William's account to him of the discussions at Bad Ems (known to history as the Ems telegram) and publishing it on the evening of 13 July in a way calculated to ignite both French and German chauvinism and to precipitate a war he was confident of winning. France fell into the trap and on 19 July declared war on Prussia. The French Minister of War, Marshal Edmond Lebœuf, exuded confidence, and both French hopes and the calculations of Europe's military experts held that the Napoleonic professionalism of the French army would prove irresistible, this despite the facts that the French standing army had remained at its pre-1866 strength of under four hundred thousand men and that France continued to lack an effective system of mobilisation and trained reserves.

On 21 July the Corps Législatif adjourned, on the 23 July the Empress was appointed Regent, and on the 28th July the Emperor, in great pain from a gallstone which had been plaguing him for years (he often used to wear make-up on public occasions, to disguise how ill he felt), left for the front from his private railway station at Saint-Cloud and the next day assumed control of the French forces at the garrison town of Metz. The French mobilisation was chaotic: complacency led them to make far less effective use than the Germans of such relatively new technical developments as the railway and the telegraph system. (Though there may have been disarray in matters of strategic military importance, other priorities were not overlooked. On 25 July Escoffier, the chef at the Petit Moulin Rouge, accompanied by his assistant Bouniol, was drafted to Metz to serve as *chef de cuisine* to the second section of the General Staff.)

Unrealistic French joy and over-confidence at going to war soon vanished, although censorship prevented the French people knowing the true course of events until early September. On 4 August the Germans had crossed the border into Alsace. They defeated the French at Wissembourg, pushing back the troops under Marshal MacMahon's command to Châlons-en-Champagne and forcing a wedge between these troops and those of General Bazaine, centred on Metz. The Germans then began to advance towards Paris, while the attempt by Napoleon III and MacMahon to rescue Bazaine led to an encounter between the French and the Germans at Sedan.

The battle of Sedan began on 30 August. On the afternoon of 1

September, recognising the impossibility either of defending the besieged city or of escaping from it with his army, Napoleon III ordered the raising of the white flag – a task undertaken by a former lover of Cora Pearl, Prince Achille Murat. On the following day the Emperor met with the Prussian King and his chief minister, Bismarck, to sign the instrument of surrender.

First word of the disaster reached Paris by telegraph at about six o'clock on the evening of 2 September, and was conveyed to the Empress. The Corps Législatif met on the following afternoon, the Chief Minister admitting the defeat but concealing its full extent. Shortly after they had adjourned a telegram was received from Napoleon III, confirming the events at Sedan. The Council of Ministers was unable to agree on a course of action, beyond informing Paris of the situation and calling the Corps Législatif to convene at noon on 4 September.

Crowds were now gathering in various parts of the city, and the collapse of Empire followed swiftly. A mob had invaded the Palais Bourbon, preventing the Corps Législatif from resuming its sitting. Léon Gambetta and Jules Favre, republican lawyers and statesmen who had long been known for their opposition to the imperial regime, then led most of the mob and part of the Corps Législatif across Paris to the Hôtel de Ville, where at about four o'clock in the afternoon a republic was proclaimed. Meanwhile the Senate had been meeting under the presidency of Eugène Rouher and had voted unanimous support for the Bonaparte dynasty. During the course of the afternoon a huge crowd assembled around the Tuileries palace. Inside, the Empress Eugénie was being advised to leave by her friends the Austrian and Italian ambassadors, and by the Prefect of Police. Accompanied by a maidservant, she succeeded in slipping away from the palace unobserved and took refuge in the home of the imperial family's dentist, Dr Thomas W. Evans, where she spent the night. On 5 September, while Eugénie quietly left Paris in Evans' carriage and Napoleon III arrived at Wilhelmshöhe to begin his captivity, the Corps Législatif was dissolved and the Senate abolished.

Blanche de Païva had left for Silesia some weeks previously. Her position was not an easy one, for the man with whom she shared her life was not only a prominent Prussian industrialist but had close links with Bismarck's administration. Despite rumours of impending war, life had continued as usual in Paris until the summer of 1870: La Païva was still giving her usual Sunday dinner parties for twenty guests at the end of June. Then in early July Guido Henckel von Donnersmarck, who was well apprised of the situation between France and Prussia, impressed the urgency of departure on his mistress. Blanche did not wish to leave Paris but bowed to Guido's insistence. Accompanied by him, she travelled by train to Silesia and arrived at the old castle of Neudeck, where she had never enjoyed staying.

Blanche had visited Guido's property in Silesia several times during the course of her relationship with him. On the first occasion that he had taken her to Tarnowitz she had immediately appreciated the importance of this enormous property and of its industrial and mining concerns, and had understood the actual and potential power of her lover. She had been less impressed, however, by its lack of material comforts and by heavily Germanic interior decoration. Before long she had persuaded Guido to have the whole place rebuilt, and this time she chose as her architect a man with close imperial connections – Lefuel, who had worked on the completion of the Louvre for Napoleon III. Furthermore, she insisted that the plans be closely based on those of the Tuileries. As with the Hôtel Païva, she wanted the edifice to reflect her self-image, to speak loud and clear of the importance she attached to herself and to demonstrate her power to have whatever she chose. Work began on the building of the new castle in 1870 and was not completed until 1874.

Having safely deposited Blanche at Neudeck, Donnersmarck set off for Berlin whither he had been summoned by Bismarck. (He did not expect hostilities to last long, having laid a wager with Emile de Girardin that the victorious Prussians would be marching past Girardin's mansion near the Arc de Triomphe a month after the declaration of war.) He enlisted with the army, and proceeded to play a prominent role on the Prussian side throughout the war, being appointed temporary Prefect of Lorraine on 23 August.

During the war Blanche did not forget her tenants at Pontchartrain, arranging for the provision of a monthly pension and foodstuffs
for all the women whose husbands had been conscripted to fight for
the French. After the war and during the period of Prussian occupation, Guido invited General von Thann to establish his residence
there. Blanche persuaded Guido to ensure that the local villagers were
exempted from paying war taxes; on her eventual return the response
towards her was far more positive than it had been previously.

Cora Pearl kept herself busy during the war in her usual fashion,
enjoying a liaison with Baron Abel Rogniat. After her extravagance had
succeeded in ruining him, he retired to Civitavecchia in Italy where he
founded a soap factory. She also corresponded with Prince Napoleon,
reproducing in her memoirs various letters which she claims to have
received from him. In a letter of 15 September he seems to be expressing
the hope that all is not yet over for France and the Empire:

Dear P.,

I have just received your letter of the 7th. I do not know how
it came to me from Florence. I have arrived here with much
difficulty, passing again through France. I have been with my
family for some days. The disasters have been great, but they do
not astonish me. I have no plans yet, and it will be impossible to
make any for some days; it will be necessary to await the result of
the Attack on Paris. For two days we have had no communications. I do not even know whether this letter will reach you.
My head is well, but I suffer much from my legs. What events
during the last few weeks! Come what may, we must hope. I
have known so many misfortunes of late that I have become
very calm. Your letter gave me great pleasure, my poor P.

They have even detained my shirts at Paris, where everything
has been sequestrated. That, however, does not affect me much.

I want you to go to England and live in some quiet nook for a
few weeks, while the present storm blows over. We must have
calm and patience, and wait. *It cannot be for long.* Write to me
often, and give me your exact address.

I am very poor, very disgusted, but not cast down. I feel for the country much more than for myself. What does oneself matter after all – life is short; but we must struggle as much as possible. Let us hope always for better times. Write to me. I embrace you.[2]

The Prince's optimism was misplaced, though his resilient attitude served him well in the years of exile which followed. The siege of Paris by the Prussians began on 19 September. On that day Cora succeeded in getting eight of her horses out of Paris, pretending that they were being taken out for exercise. Later on she, like many other women of both the *haut* and the *demi-mondes*, played an active part in nursing the wounded, turning her *hôtel* in the rue de Chaillot into a field-hospital. (The Baroness de Ladoucette did the same thing with her house in the same street as Cora's, as did the Baroness de Rothschild in the rue Lafitte and the Duchess de Galliéna in the rue de Varennes.) Everything, Cora writes, was done at her expense. 'The doctor of the committee had only to give orders and his time. I even paid the funeral expenses. My fine linen sheets were turned into shrouds. Eight beds constantly occupied. Well dressed, more than decently fed, I do not think that my guests had any reason to complain of me. All this cost me twenty-five thousand francs.'[3]

Apollonie Sabatier's fortunes now took a distinct turn for the better, despite all the political and military turbulence going on around her: two days before the siege commenced, Richard Wallace arranged for her to receive an annual income of twenty-five thousand francs. On the death of the fourth Marquess of Hertford on 25 August he had inherited an immense fortune, along with the château of Bagatelle and the art collections housed in the *hôtel* at 29 boulevard des Italiens, and, despite the ending of their amorous relationship, Richard had not forgotten Apollonie. That she did not refuse this gift, as she had refused money from Alfred Mosselman after their break-up, suggests that either the years of relative poverty had weakened her resolve to fend for herself, or that there had been anger and resentment in her refusal of Alfred's offer which were absent from her relations with Richard.

It was prudent for Apollonie to accept the offer of a reliable income in 1870. She was by this time forty-eight years old, and knew that the likelihood of finding any other way to make sufficient money to live on comfortably was remote. (It would certainly have been unwise to hope for any financial assistance from her other lover of the 1860s, the eccentric Delaborde; he was currently giving a series of concerts in London, accompanied by a retinue of a hundred and twenty-one parrots and cockatoos.) Wallace's action was in keeping with his habitual generosity – during the siege he had also donated money for an ambulance service, opened a hospital in his own house, distributed food and firewood, and was the first to subscribe to a fund for the relief of families who had lost their houses through shelling. It also shows him as a man who believed in honouring his promises; according to Flaubert, he had promised Apollonie at the time of their affair that he would provide for her should he ever become rich. He must also have retained respect and affection for her, despite the breaking off of their liaison, and wanted her to be able to live the rest of her life in security and in the style she liked.

On 29 October Count Henckel von Donnersmarck was appointed Prefect of Metz. This was the same day on which Prussian troops entered the garrison town, which had been holding out under General Bazaine since the fall of Sedan. (After the fall of Metz, Marshal MacMahon was also taken prisoner and transferred to a villa in Wiesbaden; his staff officers were lodged nearby. Once again Escoffier was commandeered to cater for them.)

By the third month of the siege, near-starvation conditions were existing in Paris. According to Edmond de Goncourt, whose younger brother Jules had died of syphilis on 20 June, meat and even vegetables cost more than anyone could afford, and half a pound of horsemeat represented two people's rations for three days. The staples of cheese and potatoes were nowhere to be found, and most people subsisted on a diet of coffee, wine and bread.[4] At the end of December and beginning of January three elephants from the zoo were slaughtered for food. Charles Garnier's new opera house, still unfinished at the fall of the Empire, was being used as a munitions store. Throughout all the disturbances the theatres did not go dark, but opened or closed from day to day, depending on outside events. The cold was so intense in the dimly lit auditoria that actors and spectators could hardly see one another through the condensation of breath.

On 18 January 1871 William I, King of Prussia, was crowned Emperor of Germany in the Hall of Mirrors at Versailles. On the same day Edmond de Goncourt recorded in his diary:

> It is no longer a case of a stray shell now and then as it has been these last few days, but a deluge of cast iron gradually closing in on me and hemming me in. All around me there are explosions fifty yards away, twenty yards away, at the railway station, in the Rue Poussin, where a woman has just had a foot blown off, and next door, where a shell had already fallen the day before yesterday. And while, standing at the window, I try to make out the Meudon batteries with the aid of a telescope, a shell-splinter flies past me and sends mud splashing against my front door.[5]

The siege ended with an armistice and the capitulation of Paris on 28 January. On the following day Count Henckel von Donnersmarck travelled from Metz to Versailles to see Bismarck, who invited him to stay to lunch.

A note dated 3 February 1871 from Prince Napoleon tells Cora: 'The other day my poor servants and whippers-in from Meudon, where they had been taken prisoner, were sent back here to Mayence! It reminded me of our lovely hunts. I thought about you a lot.'[6] As for Cora herself, she professed to be annoyed that her efforts on behalf of the wounded during the siege had done nothing to rehabilitate her in the eyes of society or the authorities. The gulf between the world of respectability and the *demi-monde* could not be bridged by mere acts of charity on the part of the *demi-mondaines*, or by anything else. In Cora's indignant words, 'I did not even receive a diploma.'[7] She demanded an indemnity of fifteen hundred francs because of the trouble and expense she had gone to and, after appealing to the courts, was awarded it. In later life, she seemed to regret having let her pique at being treated differently from society ladies propel her into taking this action: 'Were it to be done again, I should not appeal to the law. It was troubling it about a very trifling matter. Very polite, the law, all the same. I would rather have taken the slight with a cheerful heart. There are some things about which one is sorry to have been annoyed; this is one of them. A certificate – a mighty fine thing. The best diploma is the gratitude of the people.'[8] Richard Wallace, on the other hand, received more than a diploma; he was honoured in both France and Britain, being made a commander of the Legion of Honour in the former and awarded a baronetcy by the latter.

On 12 February the National Assembly convened in Bordeaux and Adolphe Thiers became premier five days later. (And on 15 February Richard Wallace married his long-term mistress, Amélie Castelnau, the mother of his son Edmond, who had served in the cuirassiers during the war.) Preliminary peace talks were held on 26 February. Three days earlier, when the preliminaries to peace were being discussed, the men deputed by Bismarck to examine the financial clauses of the treaty with Thiers were the Berlin banker Bleichroeder and Henckel von Donnersmarck. The latter had become very useful to Bismarck, because of his knowledge both of international affairs and the French way of life, with footholds in the intellectual and social life of Paris as well as in the world of high finance. Bleichroeder put forward the figure of three thousand million francs as the war indemnities which France should pay. Henckel, better informed about French resources and how much the country could afford, suggested that a figure of not less than six thousand million would be more appropriate. No decision was taken immediately but, in order to continue the discussion, Bismarck asked Henckel to stay with him. Then on 6 March they took the express train together to Metz, where Bismarck stayed with Henckel at the Prefecture. The war indemnity was eventually fixed at five thousand million francs.

Meanwhile Blanche de Païva was continuing to supervise the building work at Neudeck, staying informed about what Guido was doing from a distance. She kept a low profile at this time, aware of the precariousness of her position. France was the country she had chosen to live in and to which she wanted to return as soon as possible, and yet her partner was heavily involved, in his role as a loyal Prussian and adviser to Bismarck, in bringing about the humiliation of that country. By this time Guido was forty years old: no longer the tall, slim young man of the 1850s, he had put on weight, grown his beard and acquired a rather ponderous manner. He had an aura of calm self-assurance, the result of wealth and success. Blanche herself was now fifty-one, though continued to present herself to the world – including Guido – as only forty-four. But documents are easier to forge than faces and by 1870 she was losing such beauty as she had previously enjoyed, though she went on trying to reproduce it by an abundant use of make-up. She had also grown fat, and wore a variety of different-coloured wigs. Yet there is no trace of Guido ever having been interested in another woman during his relationship with Blanche. During the 1860s Bismarck had even offered to find a wife for him, saying he was prepared to introduce him to a charming young relative of his. But Guido was interested only in Blanche.

On 1 March the Prussians rode in triumph into Paris, as part of the arrangement made between Bismarck and Thiers (who had resolved to endure the triumphal entry in exchange for not having to cede additional territory to Prussia). Despite it being a beautiful sunny day, there was hardly anyone out on the streets to greet them or watch them ride by, and the statues representing the cities of France in the place de la Concorde were draped in black. No newspapers were published that day and no public transport was running. The shops were closed, as were the shutters of nearly all the houses. Only one café was open, the café Dupont at the Rond Point of the Champs Elysées, and it paid for its temerity when it was ransacked later during the Commune.

Later in the day the Kaiser reviewed his troops at Longchamp and then they marched down the Champs Elysées, preceded by fifes and drums. The Kaiser had returned immediately to Versailles, while Bismarck accompanied the troops only as far as the Arc de Triomphe. Legend has it that the only building in the Champs Elysées to be open and illuminated was the Hôtel Païva, and that Count Henckel von Donnersmarck was standing in full dress uniform on the steps to salute his comrades as they rode by, thereby giving a slap in the face to France and to French public opinion.[9] The more prosaic truth is that some time between 1 and 3 March Henckel, who was staying with Bismarck at Versailles, rode to Paris and, while he was there, visited the Hôtel Païva to check that it had survived the war and the siege intact. It is likely that he put on some lights inside the house, which thus provided a contrast with other buildings in the street. It was perhaps not the most tactful thing to do, nor the most sensible time to choose to visit Paris, but the fact that no reprisals were ever taken against the Hôtel Païva suggests that the Parisians did not view this act as the great affront which it became in some later embellished accounts.

As part of the peace terms provisionally accepted by the French the Prussians withdrew from Paris two days after entering it, and so on 3 March they retreated back up the Champs Elysées. Again, hardly anyone came out to watch. On 7 March Bismarck stopped on his way back to Germany at the Prefecture in Metz, to have dinner and a long conversation with Henckel von Donnersmarck.

On 18 March there was a revolt in Paris, when the National Guard of the city refused to disarm and submit to the Thiers regime. Thiers fled to Versailles and on 26 March the Parisians elected a municipal council; two days later the Commune was officially installed. While the victorious Prussian troops affected neutrality outside the city, the Versailles troops loyal to Thiers began their own siege of Paris on 11 April. Fighting intensified over the course of the next five weeks.

France had no choice but to sign Bismarck's harsh peace terms of the Treaty of Frankfurt, which included the loss of Alsace and part of Lorraine, on 18 May. The defeat of the Commune, in what came to be known as the 'bloody week' (*La Semaine sanglante*), began on 21 May. The Versailles troops entered the city, despite the desperate defence put up by the Communards, who erected barricades, shot hostages (including the Archbishop of Paris and the *curé* of the Madeleine) and set fire to the Tuileries palace, the Hôtel de Ville and the Palais de Justice. The severe reprisals that followed the final defeat on 28 May resulted in more than eighteen thousand Parisians dead and almost seven thousand deported. Count Henckel von Donnersmarck, despite the offer from Bismarck of a post in his cabinet, elected to return to his business affairs and to his life with Blanche in Paris.

The humiliating defeat of the Franco-Prussian War, the subsequent Prussian occupation of parts of French territory and the annexation of Alsace-Lorraine had noticeable effects on the French psyche. There was a desire to find someone and something to blame. An obvious target was Napoleon III and his Empire, and writers in the 1870s indulged in much moralising about the most noticeable manifestation of that Empire which had been so easily shattered by Bismarck: the showy, shallow and extravagant *vie Parisienne*, epitomised by the opulent, brash lifestyles of the most famous courtesans who now found themselves the scapegoats for all the ills of France. J. de l'Estoile, writing in 1871, epitomises this form of post-Empire paranoia:

> When, after the fall of Bonaparte, public feeling was troubled by the disastrous state of our finances, the first thought to enter everyone's head was to wonder where all the missing gold had gone . . .
>   . . . you naive people, your gold promenaded under your noses for twenty years, around the lake of the Bois de Boulogne, the spoils of the Imperialists, feasting to the music of Offenbach! The garnish of decadence, familiar to Parisians, had ruined the country, and blind Paris took a malicious pleasure in seeing [*sic*] the daily parade of the bitches who were consuming France.[10]

This moralising reactionary goes on to spell out his agenda clearly: 'To make woman moral is to create society; for to make woman moral is to make the mother, and good mothers make real men, patriots, citizens of strong nations, members of well ordered societies, which nothing can cause to disappear, of which nothing can jeopardise the fate.'[11]

It is an indication both of how deeply affected the French were by the events of the war and its aftermath, and of how different Apollonie Sabatier was seen to be from the typical *demi-mondaine*, to find her good friend (and womaniser) Maxime Du Camp also infected with post-Empire paranoia. In his monumental work, first published between 1869 and 1875, *Paris: ses organes, ses fonctions et sa vie jusqu'en 1870*, he attributes many of the ills of contemporary society to prostitution, professing to see it as a gangrene arising from the lower depths of society, invading the entire social body during the Second Empire. This desire of both the conservative and liberal bourgeoisie to repress sexual activity, seen as a flood about to engulf society, resulted in intense repression of prostitutes between 1872 and 1877, and the introduction of new by-laws in October 1878. The exaggerations in Emile Zola's portrayal of Nana (a composite figure and type of the courtesan, in the creation of whom Zola drew on stories of Cora Pearl, La Païva and others) reflect the extent to which he too was influenced by this anxiety. In one of his harshest diatribes, he likens a woman such as Nana to a disease-carrying fly:

> Muffat was reading slowly Fauchery's article entitled 'The Golden Fly', describing the life of a harlot, descended from four or five generations of drunkards, and tainted in her blood by a cumulative inheritance of misery and drink, which in her case has taken the form of a nervous exaggeration of the sexual instinct. She has shot up to womanhood in the slums and on the pavements of Paris and tall, handsome, and as superbly grown as a dung-hill plant, she avenges the beggars and outcasts of whom she is the ultimate product. With her the rottenness that is allowed to ferment among the populace is carried upwards and rots the aristocracy. She becomes a blind power of nature, a leaven of destruction, and unwittingly she corrupts and dis-

organises all Paris, churning it between her snow-white thighs as milk is monthly churned by housewives. And it was at the end of this article that the comparison with a fly occurred, a fly of sunny hue, which has flown up out of the dung, a fly which sucks in death on the carrion tolerated by the roadside, and then buzzing, dancing, and glittering like a precious stone, enters the windows of palaces and poisons the men within by merely settling on them in her flight.[12]

Zola also, in common with many other post-Empire writers, continued to reiterate the stereotypes catalogued by Parent-Duchâtelet nearly half a century earlier, dwelling on the prostitute's instability and talkativeness, her taste for alcohol, her love of food and passion for gambling, her propensity towards laziness, lying and anger. On the positive side, the emphasis remained on her sense of solidarity, her love of children, animals and flowers, her modesty when confronted with the medical profession and, above all, her religiosity.

Despite the depressing forecasts of the moralisers, in many respects life did carry on as before after the Empire, yet a certain spontaneity and unselfconscious enjoyment had departed and there was less money to throw around. As Marie Colombier put it in her memoirs: 'We still love, but we no longer have fun. We still get drunk, but the cocktail has replaced the champagne.'[13]

1 *Illustrated London News*, No.1575 Vol.LVI, Saturday, 8 January 1870

2 Emma Elizabeth Crouch, *The Memoirs of Cora Pearl*, pp.81–2

3 Ibid., pp.169–70

4 Robert Baldick (ed. and tr.), *Pages from the Goncourt Journal*, p.181

5 Ibid., p.182

6 Emma Elizabeth Crouch, *Mémoires de Cora Pearl*, p.158

7 Emma Elizabeth Crouch, *The Memoirs of Cora Pearl*, p.170

8 Ibid., pp.170–1

9 See, e.g., Marcel Boulanger, *La Païva*, p.72 and Joanna Richardson, *The Courtesans*, p.63

10 J. de l'Estoile, *Les Courtisanes du Second Empire*, Office de Publicité, Brussel, 1871

11 Ibid., p.27

12 Emile Zola, *Nana*, p.246

13 Marie Colombier, *Mémoires*, pp.314–15

CHAPTER THIRTEEN

La Femme de Claude

O N TUESDAY, 28 October 1871 Count Guido Henckel von Donnersmarck married Blanche de Païva at the Eglise Evangélique de la Rédemption, the Lutheran church in the rue Chauchat. He had been pressing Blanche to marry him since 1863. The problem had been that she was still married to the Marquess de Païva. Divorce, which had been possible in France from 1792 to 1816, was not permitted again until 1884, and so the only possible way out was to obtain an annulment, a long and complicated process. Neither Blanche nor Guido ever made any allusion to their friends about the negotiations which went on over several years with the Papal nuncio; it was important not to allow gossip to compromise their chances of success. Guido, who had contacts everywhere including in Rome, first broached the matter of an annulment of the marriage between Francesco de Païva and the widow Villoing in 1865. In 1871 his lawyers finally managed to persuade the Sacred Congregation of the validity of the case, and the marriage was annulled, as far as the Church was concerned, on 16 August.

A further complication was that the burning of the Hôtel de Ville by the Communards had destroyed the records of the civil marriage between Blanche and Païva, and Guido therefore had to approach the Portuguese consulate to get the necessary documents drawn up to effect the annulment of the civil marriage. These formalities were duly completed on 26 September, and Blanche returned to Paris and her beloved *hôtel* to make the preparations for the wedding ceremony. She first had to abjure Roman Catholicism (as she had previously abjured both Judaism and Russian Orthodoxy) and promise her allegiance to the Lutheran Church, and then the German ambassador had to be petitioned to authorise the marriage.

Blanche was fifty-two years old, though the wedding certificate gives her year of birth as 1826 (and her place of birth as Moscow). Her father's occupation is recorded as 'capitalist' and Villoing's as 'banker'. The witnesses to the marriage were Count Léon Henckel von Donnersmarck from Nassenheld in Prussia, Blanche's architect Hector-Martin Lefuel, and two old friends – Julien Turgan and the 'taster' Dumont de Montcel. As a wedding present Guido gave Blanche the three-row diamond necklace which had previously belonged to the Empress Eugénie and which she had been forced to sell. This was Blanche's apotheosis.

Despite this marriage and the publicity attendant upon it, the new Countess von Donnersmarck never escaped her sobriquet of 'La Païva'. It had taken on a life of its own, becoming a defining aspect of the woman who had chosen it, the axis of legend, the encapsulation of the image of the *grande horizontale*. The story of this name, of its refusal to detach itself from the woman who had adopted it, clinging to her long after she had renounced all legal claim to it, illustrates how those who dedicate their lives to the presentation of a particular image, who use their freedom to create that image, may ultimately find that they lose their freedom through it too, that the image takes over and offers no escape.

Once reinstalled in Paris and with the wedding festivities completed, the woman who was always to be known as La Païva proceeded to resurrect her salon, which would in future include a sprinkling of political men such as the German ambassador, the Prince of Hohenlohe. The presence of such guests could not help but add fuel to the fire of innuendo which would surround La Païva and her husband to the end of her life and beyond.

To the moralising which went on in France after the collapse of the Second Empire was added the fear of espionage, the reason again being the attempt to find some explanation for the rapid and total defeat of France and its subsequent fall into chaos. The popular imagination saw spies round every corner, and what better place to find them than the Hôtel Païva whose foreign occupants – one a fiendish Jewess who thrived on cold and the other a bearded Prussian closely allied with Bismarck – still showed off their opulence in a most unrepublican manner? Allegations that Blanche and Guido were spies, or at least that they were suspected as such and therefore asked to leave France, have been repeated so often[1] that they have acquired the patina of truth, though no real evidence supporting these allegations has ever existed – and the couple were not in fact asked to leave France. Guido's very taciturnity has told against him, as guests remembered him – or those who were never invited imagined him – sitting there week by week listening to the conversations of the men surrounding his mistress. 'The presence of the coldly formal Silesian who covered the expenses of these showgrounds did nothing to dissipate the sense of unease hovering in the room, no matter how courteous his welcome, how engaging his diplomat's smile tried to be.'[2]

But what can these writers and artists have been discussing that was of any substantive interest to the Prussians, since the conversations generally revolved around art, artists, women and digestion? Marcel Boulanger has suggested that La Païva would pass on information from Arsène Houssaye or Emile de Girardin on the state of mind of the Parisians and on opinions at court, gossip which would be backed up with facts from Guido.[3] He also alleges that she simultaneously urged the Prussians on to war whilst reassuring the French that war would never come.[4]

Such assertions accord her far more power than she ever had, and also ignore the professionalism of the Prussian spy network which did undoubtedly contribute towards the rapidity with which the French were defeated. Amateurs like La Païva would hardly be necessary to the Prussians. Neither is there any evidence that Blanche ever betrayed negative feelings about France, the country in which she had chosen to live and make her name. Moreover, there is nothing in French police files to implicate either Blanche or Guido in spying activities, despite the fact that a Prussian of Guido's importance would have been under close surveillance.

In 1872 Blanche's former husband, the Marquess de Païva, shot himself. The years since he had returned to his mother's estate in Portugal had not been happy. He had left Porto in 1860 and moved to Braga, where he had earned some money teaching French at the college of Madre de Deus and to a foreign family. This work had enabled him to save enough money to return to Paris, which he finally did in 1872, harbouring the illusion that all his old friends would be both pleased to see him and prepared to lend him the funds he considered necessary to re-establish himself through gambling. In other words, his experiences of the last few years had not changed him. He did succeed in borrowing money for a few weeks, until his friends grew tired of funding him, for what he won one day he would lose the next. In early November Païva wrote to a former friend, requesting a final loan of two thousand francs. He then sat in his hotel at 114 rue Neuve-des-Mathurins, awaiting a response. It came after two days, and was negative.

This was the end for Païva, who went upstairs and shot himself in the chest. Even in suicide he was unsuccessful: he lingered on for several hours, dying at the Beaujon hospital at nine o'clock on the evening of 8 November. His death certificate read: 'Death certificate of Aubin-François de Païva-Araujo, of no profession, aged forty-five years, married to (no information available), said deceased born in Lisbon (Portugal).'[5] The minister for Portugal paid the expenses of his burial at Père Lachaise; no one attended the funeral.

Païva's mother was still alive and, when she was informed of her son's death, was also told of the extent of his most recent debts. She was forced to sell her property in order to pay them off, and thereafter retired to a small house on the outskirts of Porto, supported by a small allowance paid to her by her sister.

In addition to running her salon in Paris and to spending time managing her investments, Blanche Henckel von Donnersmarck also made frequent visits to Neudeck to supervise the continuing building works. The Countess's own apartments were to be sumptuously decorated, and a whole wing was to be devoted to guest rooms as the Henckels anticipated entertaining on a grand scale. They continued to hold receptions and to make public appearances in Paris, though from time to time they were forcibly reminded of their unpopularity. There was a story put around by Xavier Feuillant and repeated by Frédéric Loliée, among others, that La Païva was hissed by the audience when she appeared at a performance of Offenbach's *La Périchole* in May 1872 and that Thiers, the President of the Republic, then had to make reparations by inviting her to dinner.[6] In fact *La Périchole* was not performed after the war until 25 April 1874, when a new version was staged. Xavier Feuillant had himself, however, hit Count Henckel in the face with his riding crop in the Champs Elysées, and it was as a result of this incident that Thiers had asked the Prefect of Police, Léon Renault, to visit the Count and Countess to apologise and smooth things over. The Henckels had already indicated that they did not want this unpleasantness to be blown up into the status of a diplomatic incident.

Thiers had begun to give large dinners, followed by soirées, first at Versailles and then at the Elysée Palace, and he decided it would be politic to invite the Henckels to one of these, both to keep the German ambassador happy and to soothe the Henckels for the affronts that a section of Parisian society was determined to mete out to them. Emile Bergerat, who married Théophile Gautier's younger daughter in 1872, claimed to have first encountered La Païva around this time, at a Wagnerian concert held in the photographer Nadar's salons. In one of the most extreme descriptions of her ever produced, he writes that she resembled both an automaton and a vampire, who had spent her life sucking the blood of various men and now, at the age of sixty-five – an exaggeration of at least ten years – had the Siegfried-like Henckel in tow. He adduces the fact that her origins were obscure as further evidence of her evil, other-worldly nature, mentioning the hypotheses that she may have been Circassian or Irish, and the conclusion of Adolphe Gaiffe that she was the progeny of a witch and a broomstick. He declares that she was only ever in love with her money, and that she hated dogs, cats, birds and children.[7]

Alexandre Dumas *fils* would seem inclined to agree with Bergerat.

The former's youthful experiences appear to have left him with a bitter and puritanical attitude towards women, particularly courtesans, and he was also seriously affected by post-Empire paranoia. He launched an implicit attack on La Païva and her husband in his strange play *La Femme de Claude*, which opened at the Gymnase on 16 January 1873. Claude, a virtuous Frenchman and cuckolded husband, has invented a cannon whose deterrent effect will be the salvation of France and may even put an end to war altogether. He is assisted in his work by his adopted son, Antonin; these two alone know the secret formulae of Claude's invention. When the play opens Claude's wicked wife, Césarine, has just returned to his house three months after having run away with her lover. The lover has abandoned her, and she has had an abortion. It is made clear that she had previously already committed the 'unforgivable' sin of not having loved her illegitimate child (she had originally tricked Claude into marrying her in an attempt to cover up this particular lapse). Claude describes his wife thus: 'She is always in need of new sensations to make herself believe that she is alive, for she is more dead than those whose death she has already caused.'[8]

A man called Cantagnac arrives on the scene. He speaks with a Marseillais accent, but is really a foreign spy (Prussian, as is made clear in the preface). He is ostensibly there to discuss the sale of Claude's property (for his patriotic inventions are on the point of bankrupting him), but his real intention is to steal the secret of Claude's cannon. He means to do this by blackmailing Césarine, the assumption being that if Claude were to find out about the abortion he would hand her over to the courts. Césarine's way of getting at the secret will be to seduce Antonin who, foolish youth, is in love with her. The other characters in the play include Rebecca and her father Daniel, who are about to leave to go searching for the lost tribes of Israel. Rebecca is in love with Claude, but hers is a 'pure' love, which is why she is leaving with her father, never to return. Claude himself has been too damaged by his former love for Césarine to love anyone or anything except his cannon and his country. Finally there is Edmée the servant girl, given to listening at keyholes. She it is who eventually reveals the fiendish plot to Claude.

Césarine's first thought had been to pretend repentance and get Claude to agree to forgive her again (in advance of knowing all she has done), a promise which, if once made, she believes he would stand by even when informed of the 'crime' of her abortion. Claude, however, does not believe in Césarine's repentance and is immovable. He utters what is intended to be the real indictment of Césarine:

> No! this woman does not love me, neither me, nor anyone else. Did she not leave behind for ever not only love, but humanity, when she could not love her child? Do I owe anything to such a mother other than indifference and her daily bread, and is not such a woman no more than the form of a human being, more alien to me than the least of the dumb animals, who are hard-working and useful?[9]

In the face of Claude's upright self-righteousness and hostility, Césarine determines to exact revenge. She is trying to wrest the secret manuscript from Antonin when Claude appears and shoots her dead. The play ends with Claude telling Antonin (who drops to his knees in gratitude) to get back to work.

Dumas *fils* attempted to explain his intentions in writing this play and to justify its ending in his preface, in which he ostensibly addresses a critic who has taken him to task for apparently suggesting that a husband has the right to murder his unfaithful wife. The playwright has clearly fallen prey to an overwhelming fear of the fallen woman. He relates a vision he had while contemplating the state of the nation, during which he 'saw a huge bubbling welling up in the crucible; and . . . out came a colossal Beast with seven heads and ten horns, and on its horns ten diadems . . . and above each of the seven [*sic*] diadems, in the middle of all sorts of blasphemous words, there blazed this word, bigger than all the others: Prostitution.'[10] Dumas goes on to explain that this 'Beast' was 'none other than a new incarnation of woman', who, after thousands of years of slavery, had decided to revolt and finally get the better of man. An imaginary speech she makes to mankind, and which Dumas 'overhears', shows how she intends to go about this:

> You will no longer have a mother, you will no longer have a wife, you will no longer have a daughter, you will no longer even have a mistress; you will no longer have anything except the incessant and implacable sensation which will slacken your muscles, discolour your blood, poison your bones, cloud your reason, annihilate your will and extinguish your soul; for I will no longer resist you, and that will be my revenge; but you will possess no more of me than my rouge, my white and my black, my false hair, my rice powder and my perfumes, my surfaces in fact, which I will make you adorn and adore, which you will show in public and brag about in a loud voice. My inner being will remain obscure and closed to you; you will never penetrate it . . .[11]

Dumas then writes that, having heard what the Beast was saying to herself, he made a point of following her around and of identifying her beneath her disguises of 'the great lady, the wife, the mother, and the girl, whose functions she does not accept, but whose clothes and bearing she borrows'.[12] And in identifying the Beast, Dumas asserts, he also became aware of the mortal danger France was in by 1870: 'She it was who showed me, before anyone else had seen them, the barbarians marching towards Paris, the triumph of the populace, and the ruins in the midst of which we have been stumbling for two years.'[13] Ultimately, of course, it is all the Beast's fault: '. . . it is to the Beast that we owe [the harsh lesson], for it was she who began to dissolve our vital elements, by undermining little by little morality, faith, family, work . . .'[14] Having dealt with the evils of this new incarnation of woman, Dumas turns his attention to the dangers inherent in the Prussian who still lurks in the midst of French society:

> Look at this man who prowls around your father's house, your dear home, breached, dilapidated and mortgaged, the remains of

which you are forced to sacrifice to your work and your mission. This man gets right inside; he has an open expression and an outstretched hand; he understands you, he loves you, he offers you his friendship and his wallet; he shares your hopes, he wants to be associated with your work and your retaliation . . . It is the neighbour, it is the false friend, it is the stranger, it is the hater, it is the spy who has slipped, over the years, into your family, and who, while all the time playing with your children, being saucy with the maid, talking to you of his blonde fiancée waiting at home, has been copying your locks, your accounts and the plan of your house . . .'[15]

Dumas *fils*, in building himself up to his final peroration, is at pains to stress the dire consequences of the Prussian spy joining force with the wicked woman, and he becomes frenzied as he seeks to justify his hero's action:

Claude does not kill his wife, the author does not kill a woman, they both kill the Beast, the vile, adulterous, prostituted, infanticide Beast, who undermines society, dissolves the family, soils love, dismembers the fatherland, enervates man, dishonours woman, whose face and appearance she takes, and who kills those who do not kill her.[16]

He concludes by uttering a clarion call to patriotic Frenchmen: '. . . it is no longer appropriate to be clever, light, libertine, mocking, sceptical and playful; enough of that . . . God, fatherland, work, marriage, love, woman, child, all that is serious, very serious, and rises up before you. Either all that must live or you must die!'[17]

La Païva ensured the failure of *La Femme de Claude* by recruiting a cabal from among her supporters. The effort was probably unnecessary, as the public did not like the play anyway. The press was also negative about it, hardly surprising given both the quality of the play and the number of journalists who were good friends of Blanche's. The ravings of Dumas *fils* may be the most extreme example of post-

Empire paranoia, but they do serve to point up the underlying reasons behind the hostility felt towards Blanche by so many contemporary and later commentators. These include her foreignness, her alliance with an influential Prussian and the suspicion that she was a traitor to France, her history as a promiscuous woman who knew how to take advantage of weak men and, in particular, her 'unnaturalness', her lack of conventional femininity and her rejection of the 'redemptive' gift of motherhood. Despite her best efforts at concealment, the fact that she had given birth to two children whom she had ostensibly abandoned was known and held against her.

Count Henckel von Donnersmarck, still apparently unaware of the extent to which he was viewed as the hated Prussian, now made a significant error of judgment. Bismarck had decided that on 1 February 1874 the new subjects of the German Empire would be called to elect to the Reichstag in Berlin fifteen deputies, of whom four would be for Lorraine and four for Alsace. This gave the election great importance and people throughout Europe, particularly in France and Germany, would await the result with heightened emotions. The annexed populations resolved that, in order to make their protests as vehement as possible, they would shelve their normal differences, conservatives and democrats working side by side on this occasion. Nowhere was this determination stronger than in Metz where the diocesan bishop, Mgr Dupont des Loges, was chosen as the candidate. He was accepted with enthusiasm by the public as champion of the French cause. Despite this obvious popular support, however, the committee of the German colony of Metz decided to field a candidate against the bishop.

The committee may have felt they had to do this, or there may have been pressure on them to do so. What is less explicable is Count Henckel von Donnersmarck's decision to agree to be the candidate. He seems to have imagined that the economic power and influence which he wielded in the locality, where he had invested heavily, would guarantee him the popular vote. And so he set about campaigning, offering the voters various benefits should he win.

The result of the election on 18 February was embarrassing for

Guido, who polled only 2,346 votes, all these coming from civil servants and German immigrants. Even his own workers at Ars sur Moselle had refused to vote for him. Mgr Dupont des Loges was duly elected deputy for Metz, with 13,054 votes. This seems to have been one occasion on which the astute Blanche either failed to offer sensible advice to her husband, or he refused to take it. In any event, in both Alsace and Lorraine the successful candidates were only protestors. After the first session of the Reichstag, during which the deputy for Saverne made a solemn protest against the enforced annexation of Alsace-Lorraine, the eight deputies for the region left the building and never returned.

This unfortunate incident did not dampen the Henckels' taste for politics, and throughout the 1870s they tried to assist in bringing about a Franco-Prussian rapprochement. Their efforts were tinged with a degree of naivety, as neither of them ever seemed to grasp the extent of French mistrust and dislike of Prussians in general and of themselves in particular. Nevertheless Blanche did have some success in entering the political arena, if only by securing from 1876 Léon Gambetta, the French Minister of the Interior, as one of her regular Friday evening guests. Whenever a large number of guests was present, Gambetta would restrict himself to discussions of literature; once most had departed, and only a few diplomats and the Henckels remained, the talk would become political. Emile de Girardin, one of the first literary men to return regularly to the Hôtel Païva after the war, was also interested in bringing about closer links between France and Germany, arguing for this in the daily paper *La France*, the editorship of which he had resumed in 1874. The idea behind this hoped-for rapprochement seems to have been that, if France allowed Bismarck to make other territorial conquests, he might agree to return Alsace-Lorraine. It also seems, however, that this was largely wishful thinking. In the spring of 1878 the Henckels were plotting to contrive a secret meeting between Bismarck and Gambetta to negotiate about Lorraine, but it never happened. Either Count Henckel von Donnersmarck was not as important as he liked to think he was and Bismarck only took notice of him when it suited his own interests, or Gambetta realised Bismarck was only toying with him and decided it would be unwise to proceed. There is no trace after the summer of 1878 of relations of any sort between Bismarck and Gambetta. The latter continued to dine frequently at the Hôtel Païva, however, and to charm the other guests, who would generally include representatives of all the French political parties.

The last years of La Païva's life were difficult. On 12 January 1880 she made her will, leaving everything to her husband. If he were to predecease her, then half of her fortune was to go to help the arts and artists in Paris. That year her health began to deteriorate rapidly, but she kept believing that she would recover, trusting to the attentions of the French and German doctors Count Henckel urged her to consult. The Count also suggested that she should try a change of air, and so she visited Baden and Berlin as well as continuing to make trips to Silesia. But she was unhappy away from Paris, for she missed her old friends as well as her *hôtel*. Then, as more of them began to die – both Paul de Saint-Victor and Emile de Girardin died in 1881 – even Paris became less of a solace. At least there were still plays, concerts and operas to sustain her interest (though the last performance at the Théâtre Italien had taken place on 15 December 1878, after which the theatre was turned into a bank). But then the doctors counselled, and Guido agreed, that the excitement of life in Paris only worsened her state of health, and Blanche was persuaded to retire to Neudeck until she recovered. Guido assured her that the Hôtel Païva would be ready and waiting to welcome her again as soon as she was better. In late autumn 1882 Blanche set off, accompanied by the still adoring Guido, for Neudeck.

For a while she did feel better in her luxurious new castle, glad to rest after the strain of life in Paris. Soon, however, she began to feel bored. She had Guido for company, but longed for the stimulating conversation with which she had taken care to surround herself for most of her life. There was no one to talk to at Neudeck, only nurses and doctors who told Guido that guests would be injurious to his wife's health. So the sumptuous guest wing remained uninhabited. For exercise Blanche was allowed to go for drives in the area around the castle and to take very slow walks in the lanes around Tarnowitz. She had had to abandon horse-riding while still in Paris, when her obesity – the heart disease she was suffering from caused her body to swell – had prevented her from mounting even the most docile of horses.

She had four personal maids whose job it was to try to cover up the ravages of old age and sickness. Each day she took a series of baths to try to counteract the acidity of her blood. She tried everything in the attempt to regain her lost attractions, but nothing prevailed – not the daily walks, nor the careful diet, nor the attentions of her doctors. She also began to suffer from a constant fear of robbery or assassination. Her cardiac trouble confined her more and more to her bedroom and finally to her bed. Then she had a stroke. Suddenly she seemed to have become a very old woman.

Blanche died at Neudeck on 21 January 1884, at four o'clock in the afternoon. She was buried in the Henckel von Donnersmarck family vault. Guido, overcome by grief, declared at the funeral that he would never remarry. Her death merited only a brief mention in the Paris press.

Even after her death La Païva continued to be the stuff of legend, the most detailed account of the following story being given by Emile Bergerat.[18] Despite his declaration at the funeral, a little over three years later Guido did remarry. Bergerat reports that Guido told his new wife, in true Gothic horror fashion, that she was free to go wherever she pleased in his castle, with the exception of one room which he kept locked and which he forbade her to enter. At certain times he would lock himself into this room and stay there for hours; he never told anyone what he was doing there and would emerge in a very strange mood to go galloping off through the woods. But one day, when he was out on one of these mysterious gallops, his wife happened to notice that he had left the key in the lock of the forbidden room. Curiosity overcame her; she turned the key, opened the door – and screamed. Hours later she was found by the servants in a dead faint on the floor – while dancing up and down like a life-sized puppet in a huge jar of embalming fluid was the body of La Païva, from whom the poor widower could not bear to be parted, even by death.

In June 1888 Count Henckel von Donnersmarck sold the château of Pontchartrain to the financier Auguste Dreyfus-Gonzales. More attached to the Hôtel Païva, he had briefly thought, shortly after Blanche's death, of transporting it stone by stone to Germany. He had asked the architect Rossigneux to look into the possibility of this project, but it ultimately proved too difficult to undertake. In December 1891 Guido took his wife Catherina to Paris for the first time, where he was amazed to find she hated the *hôtel*, which she declared was too small and completely uninhabitable. What she did not say, but which was more to the point, was that it was completely impregnated with the character of Guido's first wife; no successor to La Païva could possibly be happy there. And so Guido sought a purchaser, finding one in 1893 in a Berlin banker and racehorse owner. During the Exposition of 1900 an erstwhile chef from the imperial court of Russia, Monsieur Cubat, became the tenant and installed a restaurant there but, despite the sumptuous décor extolled in the promotional book *Un Hôtel célèbre sous le Second Empire*, the restaurant did not succeed. Monsieur Cubat also took insufficient care with various alterations he made, bequeathing major problems to the subsequent owners a few decades later. In 1904 the building was acquired by the Travellers' Club.

The Hôtel Païva not only still stands at 25 avenue des Champs Elysées, the sole surviving example of a private Second Empire mansion, but has now been listed as an historic monument and, as such, is in receipt of state funding to ensure it can be maintained in good repair. Major work had to be carried out during the 1970s and 1980s as one of the ceilings was in danger of collapsing entirely after damp had got into the supporting beams. It now belongs to the Travellers' Club in perpetuity. It has thus retained something of the exclusive *cachet* its founder intended; (male) members from around the world can stay there, while it is open to the public for guided tours only on certain Sunday mornings. The booklet for sale in the foyer describes Blanche's beloved *hôtel* as 'one of the most magnificent examples of French 19th-century architecture',[19] and a comment made by a tourist – 'It's just like Napoleon III's apartments in the Louvre' – would undoubtedly have delighted her.

Blanche's building project in Silesia did not fare so well. In 1922, when the province of Silesia was attached to Poland, Neudeck changed its name to Swerklianec. Twenty-three years later the great castle of Swerklianec was entirely destroyed by fire. All that remained were the ruins of the chapel and part of the park.

---

1 See, e.g., Marcel Boulanger, *La Païva*, p.68

2 Frédéric Loliée, *La Païva*, p.192

3 Marcel Boulanger, *La Païva*, p.68

4 Ibid., p.70

5 Quoted in Janine Alexandre-Debray, *La Païva, 1819–1884*, p.76

6 See Frédéric Loliée, *La Païva*, pp.242–3 and Marcel Boulanger, *La Païva*, pp.82–3

7 Emile Bergerat, *Souvenirs d'un enfant de Paris*, Vol.2, pp.295–302

8 Alexandre Dumas *fils*, *La Femme de Claude*, Michel Lévy Frères, Paris, 1873, p.19

9 Ibid., p.75

10 Ibid., pp.xli–xliii

11 Ibid., p.xliv

12 Ibid., p.xlv

13 Ibid., p.xlvi

14 Ibid., pp.xlix–l

15 Ibid., pp.liv–lvi

16 Ibid., pp.lxxv–lxxvi

17 Ibid., p.lxxviii

18 Emile Bergerat, *Souvenirs d'un enfant de Paris*, Vol.2, pp.302–3

19 D.S. Neave in P. Fleetwood-Hesketh, *Hôtel Païva*, Editions Champflour, Marly-le-Roi, 1994, p.23

CHAPTER FOURTEEN

Last Years

THE RELATIONSHIP BETWEEN Cora Pearl and Prince Napoleon continued for some time after the Franco-Prussian War, though their meetings were of necessity infrequent and rarely took place in Paris. In his letters, wrote Cora, 'he . . . gave me the most loving advice and, although very dejected himself, he raised my spirits'.[1] A note from him when he was in Paris for several days, having received permission for a short visit, gives a flavour of what life was like for a Bonaparte in post-Empire France:

> It would make me very happy to see you, but where? *that is the question*? [original in English] Impossible at my place. As for yours, I find it rather repellent, that *hôtel* . . . Do you understand? In addition I am watched a lot, although I'm a simple bourgeois, and the press are very irritatingly interested in my doings. I would hate to cause you any embarrassment with those you're seeing or in your affairs. The best thing would be to go this evening to the Bois de Boulogne. The weather's so warm. If a walk suits you, I can be in front of the Jardin d'Acclimatation at half past eight when I can kiss you and we can talk while we walk. Let me know.[2]

Other letters make it clear that the Prince's relations towards Cora had now taken on an almost avuncular tone:

> Look, don't give up: you must be brave and sensible. I can assure you that I'm in just as much difficulty myself, but

one must struggle on. Lessen your expenses as much as you can . . .

Tell me what you're doing and how you are. What are these pains you've got? Your pretty face swollen – the thought of that upsets me. I keep busy enough, despite being alone and sad, as you can imagine. I would like to see you again as well; when? where? Recent events force me to take a rather prudent course as I am horribly *spied on*. But I'm still stubborn and determined.[3]

The Prince spent much of the rest of his life wandering around Europe. During 1871 he visited London several times, living for a while at 108 Lancaster Gate and at other times staying incognito, as the Count de Moncalieri, at Claridge's. The following episode, which Cora does not date specifically but which probably occurred after the siege of Paris and before the Commune (this being the most likely time for Cora to have left Paris for a while), has been much quoted:

After 1870 I went to London, where the Duke was to join me *incognito*, and engaged a grand suite of rooms at the Grosvenor Hotel, where, by the way, I returned after my expulsion.

One morning the manager came up and said to me: 'You are Mdlle Cora Pearl?'

To which I replied: 'What is that to you?'

'I cannot allow you to remain here,' he retorted.

'But I have paid a month in advance for the rooms on the first floor.'

'That will be for the expense you put the hotel to.'

That is the way in England.

I was compelled to seek another hotel, only I did not pay in advance. The Duke arrived a week afterwards, but this time he objected to stay in the hotel; there were some Germans on the ground floor. He rented a house for five weeks for £1,000.[4]

After their stay in London they went together, according to Cora, to Switzerland. She relates an incident which occurred there, involving some young men only too ready to rejoice at the misfortunes of a Bonaparte. Cora's response suggests that she was as fond of the Prince as she was of any man, and that she appreciated him for his dignity almost as much as for his money:

> He suggested boating one day. We had rowed a few yards out when a boat with some young men in it passed ours.
>
> 'Halloa!' said one, pointing out the Duke to his comrades, 'look at him, that's he!'
>
> 'He has forgotten his big sword!' said another.
>
> Coarse and pointed rudeness like this is very painful. Had one of the blackguards been within reach of my hand, I would have slapped his face with pleasure.
>
> The Duke said nothing. It was on that beautiful lake that, perhaps for the first time, I felt happy in being his friend.
>
> When we landed, after our excursion, the same individuals once more began insulting him, but from a distance. The weather was fine, the lake limpid, and the Duke very calm; and I took his arm.[5]

Cora and the Prince are also reported to have toured the west of England together, where she was sometimes mistaken for Princess Clotilde and fêted accordingly. There is even a story that they visited Dublin, where the Lord Mayor mistook her identity and asked to call and pay his respects. (The trustworthiness of Pierre de Lano's account of this alleged incident is somewhat called into question, however, by his locating Dublin in Scotland.)[6]

In 1872 when Cora was about thirty-seven, though still maintaining the pretence of being only thirty, a young man in his mid-twenties called Alexandre Duval fell in love with her. Alexandre's father Louis, originally a Paris butcher, had built up a chain of restaurants known as the Bouillons Duval. An early version of the fast food outlet, there were a dozen such establishments in Paris by the time of Louis' death in 1870. The restaurants were characterised by clean marble tables, attended by neat and efficient waitresses, and clients could choose from a printed fixed-price menu. A complete meal, with wine, would cost less than two francs. Alexandre had inherited this business along with a large personal income, which he began rapidly to deplete through his infatuation with Cora. In addition to giving her such extravagant gifts as a book whose leaves consisted of a hundred banknotes of a thousand francs each, he had been paying for the upkeep of 101 rue de Chaillot and of a country house at Maisons Lafitte. He had also given Cora several carriages and horses, including some which had been purchased from the former imperial stables. Before long he ran out of money; his family prudently refused to give him any more, and Cora – now that he was no longer useful to her – refused to see him, giving orders to her servants that he was no longer to be admitted. The desperate Alexandre kept begging to be let in and then, during the afternoon of Thursday, 19 December, having spent most of the morning wandering the streets in the rain, turned up with a gun, forced his way past the servants and shot himself in front of Cora. The wound was severe but not fatal – the bullet entered below his lung, just missing his stomach and lodging in his back. There were those who said Cora's only concern was the mess his blood was making of her carpets.

Alexandre was eventually nursed back to health by his family, but the post-Empire authorities were not prepared to turn a blind eye towards the ruin and near-death of a young Frenchman through the agency of a foreign courtesan, and Cora received a visit from the Prefect of Police who gave her to understand that she was to leave France immediately. Cora herself was astute about the reaction of high society to her expulsion, and implies that some of those who most applauded it were her erstwhile clients who felt they could not now be seen to support her:

Those whom it is the done thing to call honest people could not but applaud the expulsion of 'a person of my sort'. For them the trial was judged in advance. The majority of those who approved of the punishment inflicted on me were themselves 'honest people': they held tightly to this designation, which they would not however have been afraid to lose in deigning to pay me a visit or two. But they would have been afraid to show a little sympathy for a woman who had fallen on hard times. I went down in their estimation precisely because of my disgrace. Other times, other rules![7]

On 14 January 1873, a week after the death of the ex-Emperor Napoleon III in exile in England, *Le Figaro* published a list of Cora's creditors. Her debts included the sums of four thousand five hundred francs owed to a building contractor, three hundred francs to a publisher, six thousand six hundred and twenty-five to a dressmaker, five thousand four hundred and forty to a linen draper and over two thousand five hundred to a firm of cutlers. These creditors attempted to take advantage of Cora's enforced absence by seizing the contents of 101 rue de Chaillot under a law applicable to alien debtors. She successfully resisted this seizure of her goods, through her lawyer Monsieur Lefoullon, on the grounds that she was still a property-owner in Maisons Lafitte and Paris, which was her normal place of residence despite the temporary banishment. In February 1873 she sold 101 rue de Chaillot to another courtesan and took refuge for a while in Monte Carlo with her friend Caroline Letessier, who was being kept at the time by the son of the Prince of Monaco. From there Cora moved on to stay at Caroline's villa in Nice, and then travelled on to Milan where she succeeded in finding Prince Napoleon.

The Prince went on sending money to Cora whenever he could, for as long as he could. As he explained, however, 'If I do not write you oftener, it is because I should like to send you the wherewithal to make you happy; and it is not always possible.'[8] He had long ago given up any exclusive claim on her, and sometimes wished her well in making money from other men.[9] In 1874 he reached a decision that a definitive change in his relations with Cora was necessary. From what she quotes as his final letter it is clear that this change included the cessation of financial aid and probably the end of any sexual relationship (the two, of course, always going together as far as Cora was concerned):

> In the face of duty, no hesitation is possible! I make up my mind against you, and against myself for what is necessary. You understand my motives. I have a life of labour which must not be frittered away in dissipation, nor be under the sway of pleasure. You have always been charming, and you please me much; but with time, you will feel I could not act otherwise. I send you a last present which may be useful to you. I shall not see you for a few days: but later I shall shake you by the hand, and kiss you with great joy if you like, my dear Cora.[10]

Prince Napoleon lived on for another seventeen years, dying in exile in Rome in 1891.

As women like Cora became unable, both because of the inevitable ageing process and the changes in the social climate, to command the high prices they had previously charged and thus to enjoy a luxurious lifestyle, their lives began to be rewritten as morality tales, the wicked supposedly coming to a satisfyingly bad end. Zola provided the pattern in his novel *Nana*, first published in 1880, portraying in the death of Nana from smallpox just as the Franco-Prussian War breaks out the only fitting conclusion, according to the moralisers, for women of her type:

> Nana was left alone, her face upturned in the light from the candle. What lay on the pillow was a charnel-house, a heap of pus and blood, a shovelful of putrid flesh. The pustules had invaded the whole face, so that one pock touched the next. Withered and sunken, they had taken on the greyish colour of mud, and on that shapeless pulp, in which the features had ceased to be discernible, they already looked like mould from the grave. One eye, the left eye, had completely foundered in the bubbling purulence, and the other, which remained half

open, looked like a dark, decaying hole. The nose was still suppurating. A large reddish crust starting on one of the cheeks was invading the mouth, twisting it into a terrible grin. And around this grotesque and horrible mask of death, the hair, the beautiful hair, still blazed like sunlight and flowed in a stream of gold. Venus was decomposing. It was as if the poison she had picked up in the gutters, from the carcases left there by the roadside, that ferment with which she had poisoned a whole people, had now risen to her face and rotted it.

The room was empty. A great breath of despair came up from the boulevard and filled out the curtains.

'To Berlin! To Berlin! To Berlin!'[11]

Though he did not have the satisfaction of seeing her rotting in death, Henri Rochefort makes the ageing Cora sound as disgusting as possible, with 'her negress lips, her little grey eyes, and her dripping nose'.[12] He also attributes the following sentiments to an older and, it is implied, wiser Alexandre Duval:

> . . . one night while we were at the theatre together, we saw the ugly profile of the old wreck peering out of a box, and my friend whispered to me furiously –
>
> 'When one thinks that I lay for three months between life and death on account of that disgusting harridan, whom I wouldn't touch today with a pair of tongs, well – well, I wonder where my head was!'[13]

Pierre de Lano was another commentator who relished the chance to describe a Cora gone to seed: 'After having fled [Paris], she returned there, but she became sinisterly isolated, poor, stripped of almost everything, a lugubrious shadow, badly dressed, atrociously painted, left with only the memory of her splendour of yesteryear.'[14] 'Zed' also paints an exaggeratedly gloomy portrait of Cora's life after the Duval affair; he goes so far as to trace the start of her decline to January 1867 and her appearance on stage as Cupid:

This was her Waterloo. From this moment, despite new and scandalous amorous exploits, despite the mad passion she inspired in a nice young chap who tried to kill himself for her, despite the expulsion which ensued, despite the publicity, she steadily declined and ended by falling into disrepute and ridicule. One saw her only from time to time, caked in make-up and poorly rigged out, looking like something from an old puppet show. This brought down on her one day, in the guise of a funeral oration, this cruel epigram on the part of her former friend Emilie Williams, with whom she had fallen out: 'Get lost, you old clown!'

Shortly afterwards, she disappeared from circulation altogether.[15]

The reality was not quite so gruesome. Cora had indeed succeeded in returning to Paris after her banishment in 1872 and she did lead a precarious existence, returning to the ups and downs of her early life as a prostitute. That Cora was, at least during certain phases of her life, officially registered as a *fille soumise* is attested to by the fact that she, unlike either La Païva or La Présidente or indeed most of the grand courtesans, merits an entry in *The Pretty Women of Paris* which is subtitled 'a complete Directory or Guide to Pleasure For Visitors to the Gay City' and was privately printed in 1883 at the Press of the Prefecture of Police 'by subscription of the members of the principal Parisian clubs'. One of its sources is clearly the register of prostitutes compiled by the police and kept at the Prefecture. The entry for Cora includes the standard observations about her and is written in a generally approving tone:

Pearl, Cora

6, rue Christophe Colomb

One of the most celebrated whores of her time. She has charmed a generation of votaries to Venus, and still goes on undaunted. Her real name is simply Emma Crutch, and she hails from Portsmouth in Great Britain. No supper party was complete without her society, and she was once served up naked, with a sprinkling of parsley, upon an enormous dish, borne by four men . . . An accomplished horsewoman, her stables were as handsome as her apartments. She never thought of counting her money, and gold ran through her fingers like water . . . Now she is poor, almost friendless, and up to her neck in debt, but she has not lost her merry disposition. No woman was ever so really good-hearted and generous when she had money, and none of her old lovers speak of her except in terms of praise. Her features are not pleasing; her hair is dyed fair, but her teeth are magnificent and healthy; and her skin is of dazzling milky whiteness. When undressed, she is a picture, and her flesh is yet hard and cool, although she is quite forty now. She has never omitted using cold water, and is continually drenching her frame with an enormous sponge. To these ablutions and healthy exercise on horseback, we may ascribe the marvellous preservation of her bodily beauty. Every man of any note for the last fifteen years has passed a few hours with Cora, and time flies quickly in her company . . . There is a great lack of all ceremony about her, and she never took a penny from any man unless he cared to offer it. She is a jolly good fellow, and consequently will die in poverty and misery, as all unselfish people do, whether respectable men and women, or only simple-minded whores, like poor old Emma Crutch, who after sleeping in black satin sheets, embroidered with the arms of the Empire, now sheds tears of joy when an amateur slips a bank-note in her hand.[16]

One thing Cora did not lose was her sense of humour, her ability to laugh both at the men she encountered and at the scrapes she got herself into. A liaison she contracted late in her life was with a doubtful character from the Balkans, a former Serbian soldier, whom she calls 'the Prince of Hersant'. He sounds rather strange, to say the least:

He professed a great admiration for the plays of Dumas *fils*.

He said to me after a performance of *La Dame aux camelias* which we had attended together. 'That story is my own, provided you make Marguerite Gautier into a man, and old man Duval into a mother-in-law.'

I could never imagine what his story might be. Sometimes it occurred to me that the worthy man was completely off his head. At other times I had suspicions about his princely status. I wondered – afterwards I repented, but one spends one's life repenting, only to fall back into the old error – I wondered whether I might be dealing with a crook.[17]

The dénouement was predictable:

He spent a fortnight with me, without giving me anything. Finally, at the beginning of the third week, he did it . . . or rather he did me, for he never came back. His disappearance coincided with that of a very valuable brooch, given to me by Duke Jean [Prince Napoleon].

I didn't go to the prefecture to lodge a request for restitution. I didn't want to be thought too friendly with M. de Hersant.

He was a bargain-basement prince, and a chevalier . . . of ingenuity![18]

On 24 and 25 May 1877 Cora sold her silver and other items at Drouot's, the auction house. The catalogue listed two hundred and thirty-two pieces, mostly from the eighteenth century. Quite a large sum was raised, most of which went to pay creditors. She continued to receive clients in the apartment she had moved to at 23 avenue des Champs Elysées, over the premises of Georges Pilon the coachbuilder and next door to the Hôtel Païva. There is no record of the two women having anything to do with one another. It was while she was living here that Cora claimed to have received the attentions of a lovelorn poet – only one among many, according to her.

I cannot pass over in silence the more or less platonic loves, the troubadours who came to scratch at the guitar below my windows.

The most sentimental was quite a young man: blond beard with black eyes, a type of beauty which I must say I don't admire that much in a man. He wore a round and remarkably tall hat, and a tailcoat with completely unbelievable tails: over this outfit, an overcoat which hardly reached his calves. I was living in the avenue des Champs Elysées. It was three o'clock, and it was pouring with rain.

My poet – he couldn't have been anything other than a poet – walked up and down a couple of times, crossed the road, and went straight to a bench, situated just opposite my window; he then opened his umbrella, spread it out upside down, took out his pencil and sharpened it, his eye trained on my window, behind which I was standing in my dressing gown, watching his carryings-on. Without doubt, he was dreaming up poetry, and preparing to write me an ardent ode. I didn't miss one of his gestures, and I felt sorry for him. His hand moved feverishly. Three times the pencil broke under the strain of his vigorous scribbling, three times he sharpened it again. The song was ended and the poet soaked, thanks to his umbrella which was still open but had not for an instant covered his head. He stood up, blew me a languorous kiss, stowed away his billet-doux, and finally went away, though not without turning round more than ten times. Was it a dream? I was for a while tempted to believe so, as I received no verse of any kind in the post. Perhaps the poor devil didn't have enough left in his wallet for a stamp. Perhaps, and this must have been the case, he did indeed deliver his poem into my newspaper box, where it got mixed up with all the others which I received every day.[19]

In 1881 Cora visited Monte Carlo, the setting for a pathetic story related by Julian B. Arnold in his memoir *Giants in Dressing Gowns*. Arnold claims that he encountered Cora in a destitute state one night and took her back to his villa, where two bachelor friends – 'a tall Scotchman and a short-statured Irishman'[20] – were staying with him. There they gave Cora a good dinner and a bed for the night. Mr Arnold continues the tale:

> That night I was reading alone in the library of the villa. The armchair in which I was seated had its back to the door, so that when later it was opened softly I supposed that one of my friends had entered, and I did not look up from my book but continued reading. Presently I heard the voice of Cora Pearl, 'Forgive my disturbing you.'
>
> Glancing up from my book, I discovered that the lady of the voice was standing directly in front of me. She was wearing a man's dressing-gown much too long for her and obviously appropriated from the wardrobe of the tall Scotchman. Hastening to rise from my chair, I found my embarrassment not lessened when she incontinently let fall to her feet the dressing-gown, which fell in crumpled folds around her ankles, leaving her as unencumbered as Venus arisen from the foam![21]

This display was intended, says the author, to demonstrate that, whatever else Cora might have lost, she still had a beautiful body.

In 1883 Cora was involved in litigation (which she lost) with a Madame Perron, a dealer in lingerie and clothes with a shop at 46 rue de Provence, over a bill for thirty-two thousand francs, and with a Monsieur Denugent over a bracelet. Captain Bingham asserts in his *Recollections* that Cora was robbed of over twenty thousand pounds towards the end of her life, forcing her into abject poverty.[22]

One of the ways in which Cora kept herself entertained during her last years was by the study of Volapük, an artificial language and the precursor of Esperanto invented in 1879 by a German priest called Johann Martin Schleyer. It spread first to Austria, where it awakened considerable interest, the first society for its propagation being formed in Vienna in 1882. Until 1884 its adherents outside the German-speaking countries were very few and far between. In 1885 Dr

Auguste Kerckhoffs, a professor at the School of Higher Commercial Studies in Paris, published several articles, lectures and treatises on Volapük. This caused a great sensation in France, and it must have been at this stage that Cora took up the study of the language, demonstrating that she still had a keen interest in life and a certain irrepressibility, no matter what her personal circumstances. In 1884 she had sold her *Mémoires* to the publisher Jules Lévy as a way of raising some much-needed cash. In his book published a year before Cora's death, Philibert Audebrand writes as though she were already dead. Perhaps he thought she was:

> Although everything passes as quickly as a lightning flash, Paris has not forgotten this Englishwoman with the red chignon who came to us from London at the same time as Louis Bonaparte. It is not without serious motives that I link these two names. The britannic Phryne was one of the brightest stars in the firmament of the Second Empire. It is unanimously acknowledged that she was for twenty-five years the prototype of the modern courtesan.[23]

Cora died painfully, of cancer of the intestines, in a third-floor flat at 8 rue de Bassano at two o'clock on the morning of 8 July 1886, four months after the publication of her *Mémoires*. She had only been living in the rue de Bassano, not far from the locus of her days of triumph in the rue de Chaillot, for the last few months. Her final domicile was nothing like as squalid as some accounts would suggest, for all the apartments in that building comprised three bedrooms, two reception rooms and a kitchen. She did, however, from time to time have to send out her housekeeper, Eugénie Laforet, on begging expeditions to former lovers. Cora's death was reported at the Prefecture by Eugène Picot, a costumier of 4 rue Gustave Courbet. She was buried two days later, under her original name of Emma Elizabeth Crouch, in grave number 10, row 4, of the Batignolles cemetery. No tombstone was erected. Notices of the sale of her effects at the Hôtel Drouot appeared in *Le Journal des Arts* on 24 September and 1 October. The items are said to have included a considerable amount of false hair and a blonde wig. Her father, Frederick Nicholls Crouch, survived her by ten years, dying in Portland, Maine on 18 August 1896.

Cora's unmarked grave has long since disappeared. Batignolles cemetery is one of Paris's municipal cemeteries; out by the Porte de Clichy, behind the Lycée Honorée de Balzac which is itself surrounded by barbed wire, and partly underneath a road bridge, it is no tourist attraction. Perhaps her spirit lingers in the rue Ponthieu, where the house she once shared with Caroline Hassé is now a block of expensive apartments at the back of the Galerie des Champs, one of the Champs Elysées' exclusive shopping arcades. But what really remains of Cora are her memoirs, which she ends in characteristically clear-sighed and ironic fashion:

> It is finished – my memoirs have come to an end – many others are at the beginning or in the middle of theirs. There will always be attractive graces, just as there will always be princes and diplomats, idlers and capitalists, gentlemen and swindlers. Were I to begin my life over again I should be less a madcap perhaps, and also more respected; not because I should be more worthy of esteem, but because I should be more careful. Am I to regret my present position? Yes, if I consider how poor I am. No, if I take into account what a quiet life would have cost me.
>
> If louis are made to roll, and diamonds to glitter, I cannot be reproached with having perverted from their normal uses these noble things. With the latter I glittered, the former I set rolling. It was according to the rule, and all my sin has been a too great respect for the rule, rendering to the currency what belonged to Cæsar, and to my creditors that which had ceased to belong to me. Honour and justice are satisfied. I have never deceived anybody, because I have never belonged to anybody. My independence was all my fortune, and I have known no other happiness; and it is still what attaches me to life; I prefer it to the richest necklaces, I mean necklaces which you cannot sell, because they do not belong to you.[24]

Apollonie Sabatier's life after the war and the Commune was placid in comparison with those of Cora Pearl and La Païva. With her new-found prosperity, courtesy of Richard Wallace, she moved in 1871 from the rue Pergolèse to a six-roomed apartment on the third floor at 13 avenue de l'Impératrice. (Everyone continued to call the street by this name even though it had been officially renamed the avenue Ulrich, and changed again in 1875 to the avenue du Bois. It is now the avenue Foch.) She also had the use of a stable in the courtyard. The rent was three thousand five hundred francs a year, more than four times what she had been paying in the rue Pergolèse. She was able to employ a cook and a maid, and hired a small landau by the month to take herself and her three dogs for walks in the Bois de Boulogne.

Apollonie used some of Wallace's benefaction (the income was transmitted to her through Wallace's agent, Emile Levasseur) to help support her remaining family, particularly her mother. Wallace himself (now Sir Richard) moved to Hertford House in London in 1872, taking with him from Paris many of his finest works of art. (In 1871 he had added to his own collections by buying those of the Count de Nieuwerkerke, Princess Mathilde's former lover.) In 1872 he also funded the installation of a hundred water fountains in Paris, after a design by the sculptor Le Bourg. Between 1872 and 1875 he had major alterations made at Hertford House, including the provision of purpose-built display galleries on the first floor, but he hung *Polichinelle*, the painting which had once been a door panel in Apollonie's apartment in the rue Frochot, in one of his own rooms, rather than in the gallery of modern art along with the other paintings by Meissonier.

In her new apartment Apollonie decided to resume her Sunday soirées, but the brilliance of those earlier days could not be recaptured. The guests had changed; some were dead, others ageing and not always wishing to be reminded of the fact. Apollonie herself had grown plump – or *plantureuse*, the French word expressive of spreading flesh – with the passing years; only her hands retained their former beauty. Paul de Saint-Victor came to visit her, and

Ernest Reyer attended a few of her dinners. She saw Flaubert for the last time on 6 January 1872 at the première of *Aïssé*, for which he had sent her tickets. After that they drifted apart, through age, indifference and forgetfulness. Since the mid-1860s she had sustained her links with her former life mainly through the agency of Théophile Gautier and the dinner parties which he held every Thursday at his home in Neuilly. These Thursdays had become as much of an institution as Apollonie's Sundays had once been. The guests would arrive at about four or five o'clock in the afternoon and stay for dinner and beyond. As with her Sundays, some people were always welcome at Théo's Thursdays, while others were specially invited. Apollonie herself was a regular, but she was not well acquainted with many of the younger people who frequented them.

On 15 May 1872 she attended the wedding of Théo's younger daughter Estelle to Emile Bergerat in the church of Saint-Pierre in Neuilly. Less than six months later Apollonie was among the mourners at Théo's funeral, an event which was as significant as any in marking the end of an era. Théo had been much tried and depressed by the events of the war and its aftermath; as he saw his beloved Paris shelled during the siege, then ransacked and burned during the last days of the Commune, he grew noticeably older and began to lose his zest for life. He also experienced the tiredness of the lifelong journalist, unwilling to start all over again to build up sources of income (it has been estimated that over the course of twenty years he earned no more than twenty thousand francs for his books and plays and a hundred thousand francs from his journalism), particularly as he had for the first time attained some financial security with his appointment as Princess Mathilde's librarian in 1868. (Mathilde herself had taken refuge in Belgium after the collapse of the Empire; she returned to Paris and Saint-Gratien in 1872 and continued to provide hospitality to writers and artists until the end of her life.) His health was also in decline; he had grown stout and had difficulty walking. He was no longer the sparkling, witty Théo who enlivened every gathering; he spoke little and was enthusiastic about nothing. On his death on 23 October the doctor diagnosed cardiac arrest, but his friends felt he had died of tiredness and grief.

On the day of his funeral a large crowd of those friends gathered outside his house in the rue de Longchamp. The church at Neuilly was too small to hold all the mourners; there were more people outside than congregation within. Many old friends from the Pimodan and rue Frochot days were there, including Auguste Préault, Paul Chenavard, Ernest Reyer, Paul de Saint-Victor and Théodore de Banville. More recent friends included the artists Gustave Doré, Paul Baudry and Puvis de Chavannes. Ernesta Grisi was there, with Judith and Estelle. There is no record of La Païva having been present, however. After the funeral a cortège of three hundred people made its way to Montmartre, and crowds lined the route. At the cemetery a crowd of several thousand were waiting to see Théo laid to rest.

A few months later the painter and portraitist of Apollonie, Gustave Ricard, also died, suddenly of a heart attack; he was not yet fifty. He too had been complaining of tiredness and of feeling old; he preferred to visit Apollonie when she was alone and had taken to avoiding the Sunday dinners.

Early in 1873 Apollonie made another trip to Italy, this time in the company of an old friend, Madame Delabarre. They spent a fortnight in Rome where they encountered Paul Baudry in the Sistine Chapel, attached to some scaffolding and copying one of Michelangelo's sybils in preparation for the work he was to carry out in Garnier's new opera house. (That year the old Opera House in the rue Le Peletier burned down, an event which finally galvanised the authorities of the Third Republic into agreeing to fund the completion of the new building. Garnier handed over the keys – all one thousand nine hundred and forty-two of them – on 30 December 1874, and the Opéra Garnier opened on 5 January 1875 with a gala evening of operatic and balletic extracts. The event was attended by dignitaries from all over Europe, including the Lord Mayor and Aldermen of London.)

Edmond Richard, who on his death left extensive – if not always trustworthy – biographical notes about Apollonie which have been preserved in the municipal library of Fontainebleau, claims that he was introduced to her in 1875 when he was twenty-eight and she was fifty-three. The introduction was made, he said, by his friend, and her nephew by marriage, Dr Zabé (whose daughter would one day marry D.S. MacColl, the Keeper of the Wallace Collection). Apollonie was still attractive despite her amplitude. Her naturally auburn or chestnut hair showed hardly a trace of grey, her eyes were lively and her mouth nearly always smiling, though her cheeks and jowls were becoming rather heavy. Her hands were still covered in rings, and her voice retained its musical tone. She attributed her increased weight to the fact that she now drove to the Bois instead of walking. She had left the avenue de l'Impératrice in the spring of 1874 and was living at 168 avenue d'Eylau (now the avenue Victor Hugo) in Passy, still in the same locality in which she had lived since leaving the rue Frochot.

Richard, who from the evidence of correspondence he left actually met Apollonie some time before 1875, became her final lover. He was an orphan, the eldest of a poor family, and had carved out quite a successful career in railway administration while also harbouring an interest in literature. He encouraged Apollonie to recount her reminiscences to him and he in turn kept her informed on all the latest developments in Parisian life. Richard consoled her somewhat for her faded glories, while he received a kind of reflected glory from her and her history.

Number 168 avenue d'Eylau consisted of a whole house on two floors, containing a dozen rooms. A small courtyard separated the house from the stable, the coach house and the coachman's quarters. A shaded garden full of flowers sloped down to the rue Spontini. The windows of the drawing room, which extended for most of the length of the ground floor, opened on to this garden, which was also overlooked by the basement kitchen. Apollonie's bedroom was on the first floor, the bed being raised on a small platform. The dining room, decorated with tapestries from Beauvais, fronted the avenue d'Eylau. This room could easily seat a dozen guests, but only six to eight would now attend on Sundays. Pride of place on the walls was reserved for those works of art Apollonie had kept with her through all her changes of abode and fortune: the portraits of herself by Ricard and Meissonier, the painting by Boissard, a drawing by Jalabert, and a watercolour and sketch of *Polichinelle* by Meissonier.

She now only saw her old friends from time to time. Ernest Reyer, always in good spirits, was one of her most regular visitors. The sculptor Christophe sometimes came to dinner and once had a long conversation with Apollonie about how *La Femme piquée* was made. Paul de Saint-Victor came from time to time and continued to provide Apollonie with theatre tickets when she asked for them. Meissonier visited only occasionally. Ernesta Grisi frequently came to see her, as did Bébé's daughter Jeanne and her husband Emile Zabé. Apollonie also gathered some new friends around her, who would come regularly to play cards and talk. Some of them, notably Monsieur and Madame Worms, were introduced by her old friend Madame Bressant, née Lucenay; Gustave Worms was also an actor who eventually took Jean-Baptiste Bressant's place at the Comédie Française. Both men were celebrated actors in their day, and through them Apollonie was kept very much abreast of developments in the theatre. Never having greatly enjoyed her own company, she gave small dinner parties several days a week and continued to keep open house on Sundays.

In 1880 Maxime Du Camp came to the avenue d'Eylau to see Apollonie, who had written to congratulate him on his election to the Académie Française. They had a long talk, which left her in tears and him greatly moved. In October of that year Paul de Saint-Victor informed her about a Belgian gentleman with a great enthusiasm for Théophile Gautier, who was in the process of collecting as many of Théo's manuscripts as possible with a view to writing a history of his works. This man was the Viscount Spoelberch de Lovenjoul. He had a passion for the great French writers of the nineteenth century and had spent his life collecting documents relating to Balzac, Gautier, Musset, Sainte-Beuve and George Sand. He had asked Saint-Victor to find out whether Madame Sabatier would be prepared to sell him her letters from Théo. She refused absolutely, and neither was she prepared to lend them to him. All she would allow was that the Viscount could consult them in her house. The staid Belgian was rather nervous about meeting her, having acquired the impression that she was a flamboyant courtesan in the style of Cora Pearl. Nevertheless he duly presented himself at 168 avenue d'Eylau, where he was shown into the drawing room by a maid. Apollonie was doing her knitting. Edmond Richard was also present. Apollonie had already got out the letters which she thought would interest the Viscount, and Edmond was deputed to read them aloud. And so, over the course of several evenings, he read out Théo's scatological epistles, while the Belgian sat there dumbfounded and La Présidente got on with her knitting.

During the 1880s Apollonie left the house in the avenue d'Eylau and moved to Neuilly-sur-Seine, first to 32 boulevard de la Saussaye and then to 48 rue de Chézy, a two-storey house surrounded by a garden on the corner of the boulevard Eugène. The drawing room, dining room and bedroom were on the ground floor; on the first floor Apollonie created a studio where she carried on with her painting. Here she spent the remaining years of her life, living quietly, continuing to enjoy the services of a coachman to drive her and her little dogs to the Bois for their daily walk, a chambermaid, and a cook to enable her to receive guests on Sundays. These guests included some of the younger generation of artists, such as Tony Robert-Fleury. Edmond Richard would come for long visits. Apollonie continued to support her elderly mother, providing her with a monthly allowance and visiting her regularly (she lived in a small single-storey house in Bois-le-Roi). Her brother Louis was now dead and Apollonie kept in close contact with his two children, Richard and Marie Marguerite.

Augustin Thierry, great-nephew of the famous historian of the same name, describes in *Le Temps* of 23 August 1932 a visit he made to Madame Sabatier in Neuilly, in the company of a schoolfriend of his who was also her nephew, a few months before her death. He describes her as having become very fat and lost all her beauty – apart from her still lovely eyes and hands. He talks of her reminiscing, particularly about Baudelaire, 'showing off her treasures',[25] as he puts it – the letters from Baudelaire. It does not appear to have occurred to the youthful Thierry that she was exhibiting the Baudelaire letters for their sakes, rather than for her own. She would have known perfectly well that it was her identity as the poet's muse which interested them; they would hardly be fascinated in a rotund and ageing woman for herself.

Apollonie died of influenza, during the epidemic which had broken out in Paris the previous month, on 3 January 1890. Her nephew Eugène Fallet, a lieutenant in the dragoons, and Edmond Richard registered her death. The official insisted that her real name of Aglaé-Joséphine Savatier be used on the certificate. She was buried in the cemetery at Neuilly, her headstone bearing the name 'Apollonia'. Her funeral, on a cold, damp day, was sparsely attended; among the mourners was the old, white-bearded figure of Ernest Meissonier.

She was survived by her mother, who died nearly a year later on 1 December 1890, at the age of ninety-four. Sir Richard Wallace also died in 1890, at Bagatelle, where he had returned alone in 1887 after the death of his son, leaving Lady Wallace in London. Apollonie's younger sister, Adèle or Bébé, had moved to El Biar in the suburbs of Algiers, where her husband, a retired colonel, possessed not inconsiderable vineyards. She had not been able to be present during her sister's illness or death, but had arrived in time for the funeral and then spent several months living in the house in the rue de Chézy, sorting out Apollonie's affairs and attending to their mother. Her husband died in December 1897, while she herself lived on until 10 July 1905.

In 1897 Lady Wallace bequeathed Sir Richard's art collections to the British nation; the Wallace Collection at Hertford House opened its doors to the public in 1900 and continues to be one of London's most treasured museums. The Meissonier door panel from Apollonie's apartment is on permanent display.

---

1 Emma Elizabeth Crouch, *Mémoires de Cora Pearl*, p.155
2 Ibid., p.159

3 Ibid., pp.160–1

4 Emma Elizabeth Crouch, *The Memoirs of Cora Pearl*, pp.90–1

5 Ibid., pp.92–3

6 Pierre de Lano, *L'Amour à Paris sous le Second Empire*, p.111

7 Emma Elizabeth Crouch, *Mémoires de Cora Pearl*, pp.268–9

8 Emma Elizabeth Crouch, *The Memoirs of Cora Pearl*, p.94

9 Ibid., p.97

10 Ibid., pp.101–2

11 Emile Zola, *Nana*, tr. George Holden, Penguin, Harmondsworth, 1972, p.471

12 Henri Rochefort, *The Adventures of My Life*, tr. Ernest W. Smith, Edward Arnold, London and New York, 1896, p.108

13 Ibid., p.110

14 Pierre de Lano, *L'Amour à Paris sous le Second Empire*, p.119

15 Zed, *Le Demi-monde sous le Second Empire*, p.55

16 Anon, *The Pretty Women of Paris*, Paris, 1883, pp.153–4

17 Emma Elizabeth Crouch, *Mémoires de Cora Pearl*, p.335

18 Ibid., p.337

19 Ibid., pp.341–3

20 Julian B. Arnold, *Giants in Dressing Gowns*, Macdonald, London, 1945, p.41

21 Ibid., p.42

22 Captain The Hon. D. Bingham, *Recollections of Paris*, Vol. 1, p.61

23 Philibert Audebrand, *Petits Mémoires d'une stalle d'orchestre*, p.220

24 Emma Elizabeth Crouch, *The Memoirs of Cora Pearl*, pp.187–8

25 Quoted in André Billy, *La Présidente et ses amis*, p.257

Seen and Unseen

A MIDST THE CATALOGUE of stereotypes, the listing of the usual prejudices of the time about the causes for women turning to prostitution, Alphonse Esquiros in his book *Les Vierges folles* suddenly casts a beam of unexpected light:

> All the same, the real cause of prostitution, in our opinion, is neither poverty, nor idleness, nor ignorance, nor incapacity, nor love: it is man.
>
> If there were not men who buy, there would not be women who sell themselves . . .[1]

Amidst all the glamour of the courtesan, there is a tendency to forget that money is being exchanged for sex. This is partly because so much else enters into the transaction as well: La Païva, La Présidente, Marie Duplessis and even Cora Pearl provided their male companions with far more than sex in return for the maintenance of their lifestyles. It is also an aspect of the *demi-monde* that the actual nature of the transaction is veiled, semi-deliberately; when the common prostitute solicits, it is clear that what is on offer is sex, but when a *demi-mondaine* is looking for a protector, or even just a client, she is offering a whole package in which the sexual act is implicitly included but may be the one thing which is not overtly displayed – or, when it is displayed, it is done so in a statue, or on stage, or in stylised half-joking, half-erotic letters. In other words, it is all part of the show. There are signs that sex is what the transaction is fundamentally about – signs in the clothes she chooses to wear and, in particular, in her elaborate bed, sometimes designed to resemble a goddess's throne. We hear much talk about the proceeds of the sexual transaction, and the rewards for having sold one's body are expected to be ostentatiously paraded; but the actual sex stays hidden in the alcove. In a sense she is selling far more than is the prostitute, for she is not much interested in a one-off transaction, involving only her body and only for an hour or so; the whole package she has to offer is herself – and 'if there were not men who buy' she would not be able to do so.

Cora Pearl was insistent that she was at all times exercising her independence, though even she admitted this independence had to be tempered when faced with something like the threat of expulsion from France. She makes it sound as though she chose to live the way she did; she certainly – usually – gives the impression of enjoying herself. Yet there is also a suggestion in her memoirs that she devoted her life to taking revenge on men because of what one man did to her when she was young, that she was determined to exploit men because she had herself first been exploited. Something similar was at work in La Païva's life. On her arrival in Paris she had had no choice but to prostitute herself. Having realised this, she applied all her efforts to reach a level of prostitution where she could make vast sums of money, and finally attained her aim, through capturing Henckel von Donnersmarck, of being able to leave the life of a courtesan behind altogether. Her enormous reserves of willpower enabled her to turn the tables on men, coming to dominate where initially she had been dominated – yet she also came to be dominated by the need for money. Though she might have preferred another route than prostitution originally, she came to realise that the only way open to her to acquire the wealth she desired was to avail herself of the wealth of men.

At this point there is a very narrow dividing line between the *demi-monde* and the *haut monde*, and that is marriage. If La Païva resented not being received into respectable society – and it has been said that she resented it very much – part of the reason was her recognition that plenty of women in that society were quite as mercenary, quite as self-seeking, quite as determined to entrap a man for his money as she was; the difference was that they had managed to get a rich man to marry them – and to marry them before they had time, or the need, to commit that first 'error' from which there was no way back. What had made the difference for these women was that they had been born into families of high enough class and income for them to be in the right market to attract a wealthy man prepared to marry them. In his preface to *La Dame aux camélias* Dumas *fils* expressed how this mere difference in circumstance could lead to a lifelong difference of reputation:

> A girl with no education, no family, no profession and no bread, possessing nothing at all apart from her youth, her heart and her beauty, sells it all to a man foolish enough to clinch the deal. This girl has sealed her dishonour and society excludes her forever.
>
> A well-brought-up girl, born to a conventional family, with just about enough to live on, and clever and determined, gets herself married to a man old enough to be her father or even her grandfather, whom she doesn't of course love, but who is immensely rich. She buries him after a month (there have been recent examples). This girl has made a good marriage, and society receives her with open arms, as wife and widow.[2]

La Païva, who had had to struggle every inch of the way, knew that many of the women who looked down their noses at her, who would have refused to enter her *hôtel* had she deigned to invite them, were no better than her in their hearts and souls; as far as she was concerned, they had just had it easier, and had no right to judge her, particularly as most of them could not hold a candle to her in terms of intelligence. That high society remained obstinately closed to her, despite her marriages to an ersatz marquess and then to a genuine count, can only have increased her resentment and maybe also her bewilderment.

La Païva was by no means alone among *demi-mondaines* in being frustrated in her attempt to rejoin, or join for the first time, the world of respectability. Another courtesan who made a determined effort to do so was the woman known in her heyday as Mogador. She had been renowned as a dancer at the Bal Mabille and also appeared in 1845 as an equestrienne in a circus at the new Hippodrome. One of her lovers was a scion of one of the oldest families in France, Lionel de Chabrillon; the couple loved one another but in 1852 Lionel set off to make his fortune in Australia. Meanwhile Mogador went into the theatre and enjoyed some success at the Théâtre des Variétés.

Lionel then returned to France, having lost what little money he had, where he proposed to Mogador, offering her a future as the wife of the French consul-general in Melbourne. She accepted, they were married in January 1853, and soon afterwards sailed for Australia. Mogador, who had reverted to her original name of Céleste, under-took charitable work in Australia and played the role of respectable wife. Ill health necessitated her return to France after three years. Lionel joined her on leave but had to return to Australia in July 1859. He became ill during the voyage and died in December, at the age of forty. Céleste struggled to survive without him, and eventually made a successful writing career for herself, producing twelve novels and many plays and operettas.

Nothing, however – neither her life of respectability with Lionel, nor her literary or charitable activities – could redeem her in the sight of French society, to whom she always remained the notorious Mogador. When she arranged for a home for war orphans from Alsace and Lorraine to be built on her own land, she was not allowed to attend the inauguration on 22 August 1877. *Le Figaro* commented on her situation in 1885:

Poor woman, she has attempted the hardest thing on earth: rehabilitation. The public has a habit of classifying people. It rarely lets them change their original classification. The Com-tesse Lionel de Chabrillon, widowed after five years of marriage, has been trying to kill Mogador for more than thirty years. She has never managed to do so.[3]

Apollonie Sabatier, unlike her sister Bébé, appears never to have been particularly interested in becoming respectable; she threw away her chances of marriage at least twice, once in her youth with James de Pourtalès and later with Richard Wallace. Alfred Mosselman, despite the apparent security and happiness of their fourteen-year liaison, did not treat her well. Neither of them seems to have considered at the outset what agreeing to live as a kept woman might mean for her long-term future and, when he had the option to marry her, he did not take it. But I doubt whether this worried Apollonie unduly; she appears to have been a genuine free spirit, despite the efforts made to contain her in sculpture and poetic image.

Marie Duplessis, like both Cora Pearl and La Païva, began by being exploited by men and ended by exploiting them too. The men retained the ultimate power, however, for they could leave her whenever it suited them, with no ill consequences for themselves, whereas she needed them to maintain her way of life. The story of a disagreement she had with one of her lovers illustrates her power-lessness well:

> Marie had arrived at her lover's house at two o'clock without having forewarned him, and the Count had replied through his valet that he was out. She knew for certain he was not, and her vanity was cruelly hurt by this slight.
>
> On the following day, Marie was taking her usual drive in the Champs Elysées, in an uncovered barouche. The Count, who was on horseback, rode up to greet her. She averted her head and said to her driver, with a cold and mocking air:
>
> 'Tell the Count I am not in.'[4]

'The Count', however (he was the Count de Grandon), held all the cards as he was the one currently paying the bills. Marie had therefore to swallow her pride and capitulate, at least for the time being – their reconciliation only lasted for about a month. The desertion of her lovers when she became ill left her no way out from poverty, other than to sell what they had previously given her or provided her with the money to buy. As was the case with Cora, her independence was illusory, like so much else in the shadowy world of the *demi-mondaine*.

That Cora, Blanche and Marie were skilled sexual performers must be beyond doubt, even though the delivery of the actual sex act was only part of their allure. The impression conveyed of Marie is that, at least with some of her lovers, she enjoyed sex. For Cora and Blanche it was first and foremost a financial transaction; there is something in Blanche's determination to cease being a courtesan that suggests that she came to dislike, even hate, it. Her faithfulness to Henckel was made up of genuine affection and possibly sexual attraction, of relief at no longer having to engage in sex with anyone else, and pragmatism. Having attained her goal of possessing a secure source of wealth, she would never be foolish enough to jeopardise it. Cora had the reputation of being business-like and would be no more sentimental about sex than she was about anything else; she could be amused by her partners, and even liked a few of them, but she made it quite clear that love never came into it and one imagines that fairly speedy sex would suit her purposes best. 'I can honestly say,' she wrote, 'that I have never had an *amant de cœur*. That is explained by that very sentiment which has always inspired me with an instinctive horror of the stronger sex . . . as for what is conventionally termed blind passion or fatal attraction, no! Luckily for my peace of mind and happiness, I have never known them.'[5] Apollonie, on the other hand, was interested in relating to men and not just in having sex with them, for money or any other reason. This is obvious in many of her actions, from her rejection of Alfred's further support of her when their relationship fundamentally altered, to her willingness to attempt to be Baudelaire's friend, rather than his lover, when it became clear that he was rejecting her sexual advances.

There is no equivalent word for a male version of a courtesan, the masculine version '*demi-mondain*' never being used, but if there was one man of the Second Empire to whom the term might have been applied, that man was Auguste de Morny. There are many similarities between him and the *demi-mondaines* of this book, from the circumstances of his birth, the slight change he made to his name and his adoption of a spurious title, to his financial dependence for many years on a married woman, the Countess Le Hon. Where he differed from the *demi-mondaines* was in the attitude society took towards him and the fact that nothing he had done in his life, no disreputable act, no exchange of love or sex for material comfort, was ever held against him or prevented him attaining high office and moving in the most elevated circles. Morny was admired for some of the very qualities for which La Païva was abhorred – ambition, willpower and determination to succeed, energy, an eye for the main chance and the use of other people to satisfy his own ends. His long and well-publicised liaison with the Countess Le Hon did nothing to damage his prospects. The only criticism he engendered was for ending the affair, not for having it; he even worked alongside his mistress's husband and brother in the direction of the Société de la Vieille-Montagne.

The case of Morny is but one illustration of the unbridgeable gap between the experiences and opportunities of men, and those of women, in Paris in the mid-nineteenth century. Morny wanted money and power; so too did La Païva. Morny had a number of routes he could take to reach his goals, and he used all of them: the love of rich women, speculation, business, the army and high political office. Most of those routes were closed to La Païva. She proved herself an able business woman and a shrewd investor, but she could only get into the position of being able to exercise her talents in those arenas through the agency of men, initially by selling her body for the highest price possible and then by finding a man prepared to dedicate himself and his wealth to her, whatever her past may have been. In this, Henckel was remarkable, for most men would have been too blinded by prejudice to see in her more than the archetypal, irredeemable courtesan, and too overcome by fear that her past would contaminate their own future to agree to ally themselves with her in this way.

The only other route open to women ambitious of wealth was through the stage. Certain figures stand out from this time, such as

Rachel, the great *tragédienne*, who did manage to command enormous fees at least for a short period (during a year touring Russia in 1853–4 she netted four hundred thousand francs for herself and one hundred thousand for her troupe), Hortense Schneider, the heroine of many an operetta and, later, Sarah Bernhardt. In many cases, celebrated actresses also had lovers who paid for the privilege. Those who were highly talented were less denigrated than other *demi-mondaines*, but still remained outside the realm of genuine respectability.

A man like Morny could move easily between worlds, entertaining a courtesan before going to a meeting with the Emperor, drafting the libretto for an operetta in between sittings of the Legislative Assembly. He could join in the ostentation of Empire, play his part in all the ceremonial and the show, but also enjoy genuine and far-reaching power and influence. The *horizontales* were allowed the ostentation, but it was supposed to be only that. The show was hollow. They were supposed to know their place, to know that they were ornamentation, trinkets, to be easily discarded when the time came. They were not supposed to seek power, not supposed to be noticed for themselves rather than for the men who had enabled them to be noticed, not supposed to display their superior wit, not supposed to attempt to get into a court reception at the Tuileries or to build vast houses on the Champs Elysées and then ostentatiously refuse to let anyone in. The impossible was demanded of the *demi-mondaine* – that she should both display herself and not be seen. They were supposed to be like Marie Duplessis, or like the legend of her – available when required, seductively conscious of sin so that she seemed simultaneously to be displaying herself and shrinking from display, and conveniently and discreetly dying before becoming old enough to be a source of embarrassment to erstwhile lovers. Here is where the courtesan and the common prostitute find common ground: despite the demand that the courtesan should flaunt her acquired wealth ostentatiously to be an obvious status symbol for the man who has provided that wealth, she is simultaneously supposed to remain invisible, just as prostitution is supposed to be contained and invisible to those who do not already know where to look, so that the 'innocent' may be protected while the men who enjoy the services of the fallen woman may forget about her on their return to the world of high society and their legitimate concerns of business and politics. Charles Baudelaire could have been speaking for most of his peers when he declared to Apollonie Sabatier: 'I am an egoist, I make use of you.'[6]

Such a world of double standards, of ostentation combined with secrecy, is mirrored in the physical nature of Second Empire Paris subjected to 'Haussmanisation', the glittering façades designed to conceal the slums, great wealth co-existing alongside extremes of poverty, and that wealth itself of the here-today-gone-tomorrow variety. Moreover, in this world where sex is dressed up and flaunted, while being simultaneously hidden and discreet, the sewers become a tourist attraction, the dark side of the city there to be gazed upon, always provided it is controlled and packaged acceptably.

Yet despite all the constraining elements placed upon these women – *horizontales* at the highest level of prostitution, subject to received ideas about their nature, even about their physical appearance, expected to remain in their shadowy half-world, grateful for the attentions lavished upon them and not seeking to exercise undue power and influence – the personalities of Marie Duplessis, Cora Pearl, La Païva and La Présidente were all of sufficient strength and individuality that they could not ultimately be contained. Something of their true natures shines through all the myth-making to which they were subject, notwithstanding the difficulty of seeing them without the distortions of contemporary stereotypes about prostitutes and women in general. Had they lived a century or so later, Marie's ability to manipulate the men around her by creating the image they desired or expected to see, Cora's wit, acerbity and abilities of self-expression and self-display, La Païva's business acumen, drive and cultivation of artists, and La Présidente's gifts for friendship and for putting guests at their ease would surely have found other outlets than those available to them under the July monarchy and the Second Empire. Even before the deaths of Blanche, Cora and

Apollonie, things had begun to change for women: Paris's first *lycée* for girls, for example, opened in September 1883. That these women made of their lives as much as they did when they did, all four coming from nowhere to make their marks not only on the *demi-monde* but on the world beyond that half-world, where they became the stuff of legend even though they were not allowed to intrude on it in their lives, demonstrates their remarkable qualities, including those of resilience, creativity and power to act upon the imagination. 'Like a track of perfume, these women have left behind them a strange and unforgettable tradition of invincible tenderness, of daring independence, of hughty caprice or wild dissipation, which seems a long extension of the intoxicating hours of the eighteenth century.'[7]

---

1 Alphonse Esquiros, *Les Vierges folles*, p.42

2 Alexandre Dumas *fils, Théâtre complet*, Vol.1, p.19

3 Quoted in Joanna Richardson, *The Courtesans*, p.136

4 Romain Vienne, *La Vérité sur la Dame aux camélias*, p.116

5 Emma Elizabeth Crouch, *Mémoires de Cora Pearl*, pp.299–300

6 Baudelaire, *Correspondance*, Vol.1, p.276

7 Frédéric Loliée, *Women of the Second Empire*, tr. Alice M. Ivimy, John Lane, London and New York, 1907, pp.xviii–xix

Select Bibliography

On Marie Duplessis

The most recent work on Marie Duplessis is also the best – that by Micheline Boudet, a former member of the Comédie Française; a detailed and readable biography, whose only idiosyncrasy is the undue weight given to Marie's liaison with Franz Liszt. Prior to Boudet, the most informative work was that by Christiana Issartel. Romain Vienne is fascinating for some of his insights into Marie's character, though his whole account is romanticised and his factual detail is not reliable.

Boudet, M., *La Fleur du mal: La véritable histoire de la dame aux camélias*, Albin Michel, Paris, 1993
Dolph, C.A., *The Real 'Lady of the Camellias' and Other Women of Quality*, London, 1927
Graux, L., *Les Factures de la dame aux camélias*, Paul Dupont, Paris, 1934
Gros, J., *Alexandre Dumas et Marie Duplessis*, Louis Conard, Paris, 1923
Issartel, C., *Les Dames aux camélias de l'histoire à la légende*, Chêne Hachette, Paris, 1981
Saunders, E., *The Prodigal Father. Dumas Pére et Fils and 'The Lady of the Camellias'*, Longmans, Green & Co., London/New York/Toronto, 1951
Vienne, R., *La Vérité sur la dame aux camélias*, Paul Ollendorff, Paris, 1888

On Cora Pearl

The best writer on Cora Pearl remains Cora Pearl herself, particularly in the French version of her memoirs. The so-called memoirs 'edited' by William Blatchford, which contain far more erotic passages than Cora ever wrote, are in fact a spoof, 'William Blatchford' being the pseudonym for Derek Parker, editor of *Poetry Review* from 1965 until 1970 and current editor of the Society of Authors' journal *The Author*. Despite the fact that the author admitted to the hoax at the time of publication (as reported in the *Sunday Times* on 3 April 1983), the book is still classified as 'biography' both in the catalogue of the British Library and on the shelves of the London Library. W.H. Holden and Baroness von Hutten are both worth consulting. B. Narran's strangely titled book is a not very good novel.

Binder, P., *The Truth about Cora Pearl*, Weidenfeld & Nicolson, London, 1986

Blatchford, W., (ed.), *The Memoirs of Cora Pearl*, Granada, London/Toronto/Sydney/New York, 1983

Crouch, E.E., *Mémoires de Cora Pearl*, Jules Lévy, Paris, 1886

Crouch, E.E., *The Memoirs of Cora Pearl* [authentic and authorised translation from the original], George Vickers, London, 1886

Holden, W.H., *The Pearl from Plymouth*, British Technical & General Press, London, 1950

Hutten, Baroness von, *The Courtesan. The Life of Cora Pearl*, Peter Davies, London, 1933

Narran, B., *Cora Pearl 'The Lady of the Pink Eyes'*, Anglo-Eastern Publishing Co. Ltd, London, 1919

On La Païva

The most informative and reliable book about La Païva is easily that by Janine Alexandre-Debray. Everything prior to her is far too coloured by prejudice and hearsay.

Alexandre-Debray, J., *La Païva, 1819–1884: ses amants, ses maris*, Librairie Académique Perrin, Paris, 1986

Boulanger, M., *La Païva*, Editions M.P. Trémois, Paris, 1930

Fleetwood-Hesketh, P., *Hôtel Païva*, Editions Champflour, Marly-le-Roi, 1994

Houssaye, A., 'L'Ancien Hôtel de la Marquise de Païva' in *Un Hôtel Célèbre sous le Second Empire*, n.d.

Le Senne, E., *Madame de Païva: Etude de Psychologie et d'Histoire*, H. Daragon, Paris, 1911

Loliée, F., *'La Païva.' La légende et l'histoire de la Marquise de Païva*, Jules Tallandier, Paris, 1920

On La Présidente

The most informative book to date on La Présidente is that by Gérard de Senneville; this is likely to be superseded, however, by Thierry Savatier's *Une femme trop gaie: biographie d'un amour de Baudelaire* due for publication during 2003. Savatier's knowledge and scholarship have already been demonstrated in his edition of Gautier's *Lettres à la Présidente*. Prior to Senneville, the most informative book was that by André Billy who was the first to make extensive use of Edmond Richard's notes. Jean Ziegler adds some fascinating detail in his two articles in the *Bulletin du Bibliophile*, while his *Gautier-Baudelaire* is particularly interesting for its section on Apollonie's sister, Bébé. Louis Mermaz's book contains much fantasy. Every writer on Baudelaire includes a section on his relationship with Apollonie and contributes his/her own theories about it: Enid Starkie and Joanna Richardson have the most sensible suggestions to make, while Claude Pichois writes about various liaisons he supposes Apollonie to have had, for which there is no evidence at all.

Billy, A., *La Présidente et ses amis*, Flammarion, Paris, 1945

Gautier, T., *Letter à la Présidente*, Editions Sauret, Monaco, 1993

Gautier, T., *Lettres à la Présidente et poésies erotiques*, ed. Thierry Savatier, Honoré Champion, Paris, 2002

Mermaz, L., *Madame Sabatier. Apollonie au pays des libertins*, Editions Rencontre, Lausanne, 1967

Moss, A., *Baudelaire et Madame Sabatier*, A.G. Nizet, 1978

Pichois, C. (with Ziegler, J.), *Baudelaire*, tr. Graham Robb, Vintage, London, 1991

Porché, F., *Baudelaire et la Présidente*, Gallimard, Paris, 1959

Richardson, J., *Baudelaire*, John Murray, London, 1994

Savatier, T., *Une femme trop gaie: biographie d'un amour de Baudelaire*, CNRS Editions, Paris, 2003

Senneville, G. de, *La Présidente: une egérie au XIXe siècle*, Stock, Paris, 1998

Starkie, E., *Baudelaire*, Victor Gollancz Ltd, London, 1953

Troyat, H., *Baudelaire*, Flammarion, Paris, 1994

Ziegler, J., 'Alfred Mosselman et Madame Sabatier', *Bulletin du Bibliophile*, 1975, pp.266–73

Ziegler, J., *Gautier-Baudelaire: un carré de dames*, A.G. Nizet, Paris, 1977

Ziegler, J., 'Madame Sabatier (1822–1890). Quelques notes biographiques', *Bulletin du Bibliophile*, 1977, pp.365–82

On courtesans in general

Anon, *The Pretty Women of Paris: Their names and addresses, qualities and faults*, Paris, 1883

Blanchard, C., *Dames de Cœur*, Editions de Pré aux Clercs, Paris, 1946

Briais, B., *Grandes Courtisanes du Second Empire*, Librairie Jules, Talladier, Paris, 1981

Decaux, A., *L'Empire, l'amour et l'argent: amours Second Empire*, Librairie Académique Perrin, Paris, 1982

Esquiros, A. *Les Vierges folles*, P. Delavigne, Paris, 1842 (3rd edition)

Griffin, V., *The Mistress: Histories, myths and interpretations of the 'other woman'*, Bloomsbury, London, 1999

Lano, P. de, *L'Amour à Paris sous le Second Empire*, H. Simonis Empis, Paris, 1896

L'Estoile, J. de, *Les Courtisanes du Second Empire*, Office de Publicité, Brussels, 1871

Loliée, F., *Les Femmes du second empire. La Fête impériale*, Librairie Félix Juven, Paris, 1907

Loliée, F., *Women of the Second Empire*, tr. Alice M. Ivimy, John Lane, London and New York, 1907

Parent-Duchâtelet, A.J.B., *De la Prostitution dans la ville de Paris, considérée sous le rapport de l'hygiène publique, de la morale et de l'administration*, J.B. Baillière, Paris, 1836

Richardson, J., *The Courtesans: The demi-monde in nineteenth-century France*, Phoenix Press, London, 2000

Roberts, N., *Whores in History: Prostitution in western society*, HarperCollins, London, 1992

Ryan, M., *Prostitution in London, with a comparative view of that of Paris and New York*, H. Bailliere, London, 1839

Skinner, C.O., *Elegant Wits and Grand Horizontals. Paris – La Belle Epoque*, Michael Joseph, London, 1963

Contemporary memoirs and letters

Adams, H., *The Education of Henry Adams*, 1905

Arnold, J.B., *Giants in Dressing Gowns*, Macdonald, London, 1945

Audebrand, P., *Petits Mémoires d'une stalle d'orchestre*, Jules Lévy, Paris, 1885

Baldick, R., (ed. and tr.), *Pages from the Goncourt Journal*, OUP, London/New York/Toronto, 1962

Banville, T. de, *La Lanterne magique. Camées parisiens. La Comédie Française*, G. Charpentier, Paris, 1883

Baudelaire, C., *Correspondance*, ed. Claude Pichois, 2 vols, Gallimard, Paris, 1973

Baudelaire, C., *My Heart Laid Bare, and Other Prose Writings*, tr. Norman Cameron, Weidenfeld & Nicolson, London, 1950

Beaumont-Vassy, Vicomte E. de, *Les Salons de Paris et la société Parisienne sous Napoléon III*, Ferdinand Sartorius, Paris, 1868

Bellanger, M., *Confessions. Mémoires anecdotiques*, Librairie Populaire, Paris, 1882

Bergerat, E., *Souvenirs d'un enfant de Paris*, Vol.2, Bibliothèque Charpentier, Paris, 1912

Bicknell, A.L., *Life in the Tuileries under the Second Empire*, T. Fisher Unwin, London, 1895

Bingham, D., *Recollections of Paris*, Vol.1, Chapman & Hall, London, 1896

La Chroniqueuse, *Photographs of Paris Life*, William Tinsley, London, 1861

Claudin, G., *Mes Souvenirs. Les boulevards de 1840–1870*, Calmann Lévy, Paris, 1884

Colombier, M., *Mémoires. Fin d'Empire*, Flammarion, Paris, 1898

Contades, Comte G. de, *Portraits et fantaisies*, Maison Quantin, Paris, 1887

A Cosmopolitan, *Random Recollections of Court and Society*, Ward & Downey, London, 1888

Crane, E.A. (ed.), *The Memoirs of Dr Thomas W. Evans. Recollections of the Second French Empire*, 2 vols, T. Fisher Unwin, London, 1905

Daudet, A., *La Doulou. La Vie. Extraits des carnets inédits de l'auteur*, Fasquelle Editeurs, Paris, 1931

Daudet, E., *Les Coulisses de la société parisienne*, 2me série, Paul Ollendorff, Paris, 1895

Delaxroix, E., *Journal*, tr. Walter Pach, Grove Press, New York, 1961

Du Camp, M., *Souvenirs d'un demi-siècle: Au temps de Louis-Philippe at de Napoléon III 1830–1870*, Hachette, Paris, 1949

Escoffier, A., *Memories of My Life*, tr. Laurence Escoffier, Van Nostrand Reinhold, New York etc., 1997

Feydeau, E., *Théophile Gautier: souvenirs intimes*, E. Plon, Paris, 1874

Field, J.O., *Things I Shouldn't Tell*, Eveleigh Nash & Grayson, London, 1924

Field, J.O., *Uncensored Recollections*, Eveleigh Nash & Grayson, London, 1924

Field, J.O., *More Uncensored Recollections*, Eveleigh Nash & Grayson, London, 1926

Flaubert, G., *Correspondance*, Vols II–IV, ed. Jean Bruneau, Gallimard, Paris, 1980–98

Foucher, P., *Entre Cour et jardin. Etudes et souvenirs du théâtre*, Amyot, Paris, 1867

Gautier, J., *Le Collier des jours. Le Second Rang du collier*, Félix Luven, Paris, 1909

Gautier, T., *Correspondance générale*, ed. Claudine Lacoste-Veysseyre, 12 vols, Librairie Droz, Geneva/Paris, 1988–2000

Goncourt, E. and J. de, *Journal. Mémoires de la vie littéraire*, ed. Robert Ricatte, Fasquelle & Flammarion, Paris, 1956

Gsell, P. (ed.), *Mémoires de Madame Judith de la Comédie Française et souvenirs sur ses contemporains*, Jules Tallandier, Paris, 1911

Halévy, L., *Carnets, Vol.1: 1862–1869*, Calmann-Lévy, Paris, 1935

Harrison, B., *Recollections Grave and Gay*, Charles Scribner's Sons, New York, 1911

Hegermann-Lindencrone, L. de, *In the Courts of Memory 1858–1875. From contemporary letters*, Harper & Brothers, New York and London, 1912

Henningsen, *Revelations of Russia: or the Emperor Nicholas and his Empire in 1844 by one who has seen and describes*, Vol.1, Henry Colburn, London, 1844

Herz, H., *Mes Voyages en Amérique*, Achille Faure, Paris, 1866

Houssaye, A., *Les Confessions. Souvenirs d'un demi-siècle 1830–1890*, 6 vols, E. Dentu, Paris, 1885–91

Hyslop, L.B. and F.E. (tr. and ed.), *Baudelaire: A self-portrait. Selected Letters*, OUP, London, 1957

Knepler, H. (tr. and ed.), *Man about Paris. The confessions of Arsène Houssaye*, Gollancz, London, 1972

Leclerc, Y. (ed.), *Correspondances: Gustave Flaubert–Alfred Le Poittevin; Gustave Flaubert–Maxime Du Camp*, Flammarion, 2000

Liszt, F., *Selected Letters*, tr. and ed. Adrian Williams, Clarendon Press, Oxford, 1998

Lonergan, W.F., *Forty Years of Paris*, Fisher Unwin, London, 1907

Maupas, C.E. de, *Mémoires sur le Second Empire*, 2 vols, E. Dentu, Paris, 1884–5

Metternich, Princess Pauline, *The Days That Are No More: Some reminiscences*, Eveleigh Nash & Grayson, London, 1921

Murat, Princess Caroline, *My Memoirs*, Eveleigh Nash, London, 1910

North Peat, A.B., *Gossip from Paris during the Second Empire*, Kegan Paul, Trench, Trübner & Co., London, 1903

Rochefort, H., *The Adventures of My Life*, tr. Ernest W. Smith, Vol.1, Edward Arnold, London and New York, 1896

Roqueplan, N., *Parisine*, J. Hetzel, Paris, 1869

Uzanne, O., *La Femme à Paris. Nos contemporains*, Les Librairies-Imprimeries Réunies, Paris, 1894

Vandam, A.D., *An Englishman in Paris (Notes and Recollections)*, Chapman & Hall, London, 1893

Vandam, A.D., *Undercurrents of the Second Empire. Notes and recollections*, Heinemann, London, 1897

Viel Castel, Comte H. de, *Mémoires sur le règne de Napoléon III (1851–1864)*, Chez Tous Les Libraires, Paris, 1883–5

Villemessant, H. de, *Mémoires d'un Journaliste, Vol.1: Souvenirs de Jeunesse; Vol.3: A Travers Le Figaro; Vol.6: Mes Voyages et mes Prisons*, E. Dentu, Paris, 1872–8

Vizetelly, H., *Glances Back Through Seventy Years*, Vol.II, Kegan Paul, Trench, Trübner & Co., London, 1893

Zed, *La Société parisienne*, La Librairie Illustrée, Paris, 1888

Zed, *Le Demi-monde sous le Second Empire. Souvenirs d'un sybarite*, Ernest Kolb, Paris, 1892

Other works on Paris

d'Alméras, H., *La Vie parisienne sous le Second Empire*, Albin Michel, Paris, 1933

d'Ariste, P., *La Vie et le monde du boulevard (1830–1870)*, Editions Jules Tallandier, Paris, 1930

Burchell, S.C., *Upstart Empire. Paris during the brilliant years of Louis Napoleon*, Macdonald, London, 1971

Cabaud, M., *Paris et les parisiens sous le Second Empire*, Pierre Belfond, 1982

Le Cérémonial Officiel ou les honneurs, les préséances, les rangs et les costumes civils, militaires, ecclésiastiques et diplomatiques, Paul Dupont, Paris, 1868

Christiansen, R., *Tales of the New Babylon: Paris 1869–1875*, Sinclair-Stevenson, London, 1994

Delvau, A., *Les Plaisirs de Paris: guide pratique*, Achille Faure, Paris, 1867

Du Camp, M., *Le Salon de 1861*, A. Bourdilliat & Cie, Paris, 1861

Du Camp, M., *Paris: ses organes, ses fonctions et sa vie jusqu'en 1870*, G. Rondeau, Monaco, 1993

Friedrich, O., *Olympia: Paris in the age of Manet*, Aurum Press, London, 1992

Gasnault, F., *Guinguettes et Lorettes. Bals publics et danse sociale à Paris entre 1830 et 1870*, Aubier, Paris, 1986

Harsin, J., *Policing Prostitution in 19th-century Paris*, Princeton University Press, 1985

Horne, A., *The Fall of Paris: The Siege and the Commune 1870–1*, Macmillan, London, 1965

Manéglier, H., *Paris Impérial: La vie quotidienne sous le Second Empire*, Armand Colin, 1990

Miller, M.B., *The Bon Marché: Bourgeois culture and the department store, 1869–1920*, George Allen & Unwin, London, 1981

Pinkney, D.H., *Napoleon III and the Rebuilding of Paris*, Princeton University Press, Princeton NJ, 1958

Richardson, J., *La Vie Parisienne 1852–1870*, Hamish Hamilton, London, 1971

Richardson, J., *The Bohemians. La Vie de Bohème in Paris 1830–1914*, Macmillan, London, 1969

Séché, L., *La Jeunesse dorée sous Louis-Philippe*, Mercure de France, Paris, 1910

Simond, C. (ed.), *Paris de 1800 à 1900, Vol.II: 1830–1870*, Librairie Plon, Paris, 1900

Sitwell, S., *La Vie Parisienne. A tribute to Offenbach*, Faber & Faber, London, 1937

Sonolet, L., *La Vie parisienne sous le Second Empire*, Payot, Paris, 1929

Tulard, J. and Fierro, A. (eds), *Almanach de Paris, Vol.2: De 1789 à nos jours*, Encyclopædia Universalis, Paris, 1990

Uzanne, O., *Les Modes de Paris: Variations du goût et de l'esthétique de la femme 1797–1897*, L. Henry May, Paris, 1898

Walsh, T.J., *Second Empire Opera: The Théâtre Lyrique, Paris 1851–1870*, John Calder, London, 1981

Worth, J.P., *A Century of Fashion*, tr. Ruth Scott Miller, Little, Brown & Co., Boston, 1928

On the history of France

Allem, M., *La Vie quotidienne sous le Second Empire*, Hachette, Paris, 1948

Bac, F., *Intimités du Second Empire*, 3 vols, Librairie Hachette, Paris, 1931–2

Bellesort, A., *La Société Française sous Napoléon III*, Librairie Académique Perrin, Paris, 1932

Benbassa, E., *The Jews of France: A history from antiquity to the present*, tr. M.B. DeBevoise, Princeton University Press, Princeton NJ, 1999

Bresler, F., *Napoleon III: A life*, HarperCollins, London, 2000

Corbin, A., *Women for Hire: Prostitution and sexuality in France after 1850*, tr. Alan Sheridan, Harvard University Press, Cambridge MA, 1990

Echard, W.E. (ed.), *Historical Dictionary of the French Second Empire, 1852–1870*, Aldwych Press, London, 1985

Fleury, Comte and Sonolet, L., *La Société du Second Empire*, 4 vols, Albin Michel, Paris, 1913

Furet, F., *La Révolution, 2: Terminer la Révolution (1814–1880)*, Hachette, Paris, 1988

Kracauer, S., *Jacques Offenbach ou le secret du Second Empire*, tr. Lucienne Astruc, Editions Bernard Grasset, Paris, 1937

Kurtz, H., *The Empress Eugénie, 1826–1920*, Hamish Hamilton, London, 1964

McLaren, A., *Sexuality and Social Order: The debate over the fertility of women and workers in France, 1770–1920*, Holmes & Meier Publishers Inc., New York and London, 1983

Plessis, A., *The Rise and Fall of the Second Empire, 1852–1871*, tr. Jonathan Mandelbaum, CUP, Cambridge, 1985

Price, R., *Napoleon III and the Second Empire*, Routledge, London and New York, 1997

Smith, W.H.C., *Second Empire and Commune: France 1848–1871*, Longman, London and New York, 1985

Tombs, R., *France 1814–1914*, Longman, London and New York, 1996

Williams, R.I., *The World of Napoleon III 1851–1870*, The Free Press, New York, 1965

Poems, plays and novels

Baudelaire, C., *Les Fleurs du mal*, ed. Enid Starkie, Basil Blackwell, Oxford, 1942

Baudelaire, C., *The Flowers of Evil*, tr. James McGowan, OUP, Oxford, 1998

Barrière, T. and Thiboust, L., *Les Filles de marbre*, Michel Lévy Frères, Paris, 1853

Dumas *fils*, A., *La Dame aux camélias*, tr. David Coward, OUP, Oxford and New York, 1986

Dumas *fils*, A., *La Femme de Claude*, Michel Lévy Frères, Paris, 1873

Dumas *fils*, A., *Théâtre complet*, Vol.I, Michel Lévy Frères, Paris, 1868

Dumas *fils*, A., *Théâtre complet*, Vol.II, Calmann Lévy, Paris, 1895

Feydeau, E., *Sylvie*, E. Dentu, Paris, 1861

Flaubert, G., *L'Education sentimentale: Histoire d'un jeune homme*, Seuil, Paris, 1993

Gautier, T., *Emaux et camées*, ed. Claudine Gothot-Mersch, Gallimard, Paris, 1981

Gautier, T., *Gentle Enchanter* (34 poems), tr. Brian Hill, Rupert Hart-Davis, London, 1960

Guitry, S., *Deburau*, tr. Harley Granville-Barker, Heinemann, London, 1921

Meilhac, H. and Halévy, L., *La Vie parisienne*, Michel Lévy Frères, Paris, 1867

Zola, E., *Drunkard*, tr. Arthur Symons, Elek Books, London, 1958

Zola, E., *Nana*, tr. George Holden, Penguin Books, Harmondsworth, 1972

Zola, E., *Pot Luck (Pot-Bouille)*, tr. and notes Brian Nelson, OUP, Oxford and New York, 1999

Zola, E., *The Ladies' Paradise (Au Bonheur des Dames)*, University of California Press, Berkeley/Los Angeles/Oxford, 1992

Other works consulted

Aretz, G., *The Elegant Woman: From the rococo period to modern times*, tr. James Laver, Harrap, London, 1932

Aron, J.P. (ed.), *Misérable et glorieuse: la femme du XIXe siècle*, Fayard, Paris, 1980

Auriant, *La Véritable Histoire de 'Nana'*, Mercure de France, Paris, 1942

Barry, P.B., *Sinners down the Centuries*, Jarrolds, London, 1929

Benjamin, W., *Charles Baudelaire. A lyric poet in the era of high capitalism*, tr. Harry Zohn, Verso, London and New York, 1983

Dictionary of National Biography, OUP, London, 1973

Dubnow, S.M., *History of the Jews in Russia and Poland from the Earliest Times Until the Present Day*, tr. I. Friedlænder, Vol.1, Jewish Publication Society of America, Philadelphia, 1916

Escudier Frères, *Etudes Biographiques sur les chanteurs contemporains*, Just Tessier, Paris, 1840

Estignard, A., *Clésinger: sa vie, ses œuvres*, Librairie H. Floury, Paris, 1900

Forster, J., *The Life of Charles Dickens*, Cecil Palmer, London, 1872–4

François-Sappey, B., *Charles Valentin Alkan*, Fayard, 1991

Gréard, V.C.O., *Meissonier*, William Heinemann, London, 1897

Henriot, E., *D'Héloïse à Marie Bashkirtseff. Portraits de femmes*, Librairie Plon, Paris, 1935

Hosking, G., *Russia: People and empire 1552–1917*, HarperCollins, London, 1997

Hungerford, C.C., *Ernest Meissonier: Master in his genre*, Cambridge University Press, Cambridge, 1999

Klier, J.D., *Imperial Russia's Jewish Question, 1855–1881*, Cambridge University Press, Cambridge, 1995

Manéglier, H., *Les Artistes au Bordel*, Flammarion, 1997

Marmontel, A., *Les Pianistes Célèbres: silhouettes et médaillons*, A. Chaix & Cie, Paris, 1878

McLaren, A., *A History of Contraception: From antiquity to the present day*, Blackwell, Oxford, 1990

New Grove Dictionary of Music and Musicians, Second Edition, Macmillan Publishers Ltd, 2001

Pauvert, J.J., *L'Erotisme Second Empire*, Carrère, Paris, 1985

Piesse, G.W.S., *The Art of Perfumery and the Methods of Obtaining the Odours of Plants*, Longman, Green, Longman & Roberts, London, 1862

Richardson, J., *Théophile Gautier. His life and times*, Max Reinhardt, London, 1958

Richardson, J., *Judith Gautier. A biography*, Quartet Books, London and New York, 1986

Riddle, J.M., *Eve's Herbs: A history of contraception and abortion in the west*, Harvard University Press, Cambridge MA and London, 1997

Shaw, T., *The World of Escoffier*, Zwemmer, London, 1994

Smith, R., *Alkan. Vol I: The Enigma*, Katin & Averill, London, 1976

Teppe, J., *Vocabulaire de la vie amoureuse*, Le Pavillon, Paris, 1973

Walker, A., *Franz Liszt, Vol.I: The Virtuoso Years, 1811–1847*, Alfred A. Knopf, New York, 1990

Watterson, H., *'Marse Henry': An Autobiography*, Vol.2, George H. Doran Company, New York, 1919

Wyndham, H., *Feminine Frailty*, Ernest Benn Ltd, London, 1929

Useful websites

These recommendations are made with the proviso that web addresses can change, or sites cease to exist. I have, nevertheless, attempted to select sites that are of professional quality and seem likely to last.

The Wallace Collection http://www.the-wallace-collection.org.uk/index.htm
A comprehensive introduction to the Wallace Collection, including reproductions of the exhibits.

The Art Renewal Centre   http://www.artrenewal.org
An on-line museum, featuring reproductions of the works of numerous artists, including many of those mentioned in this book.

Ville de Jouars-Pontchartrain   http://www.mairie-jouarspontchartrain.fr
Includes photograph of château of Pontchartrain, which once belonged to La Païva.

La célèbre baignoire de la Païva   http://perso.wanadoo.fr/sbr/paiva.htm
Photographs and details about the bath made for La Païva at Pontchartrain.

Salons   http://www.aei.ca/~anbou
Site devoted to the history of salons, including a page each on Madame Sabatier and Princess Mathilde.

Charles Baudelaire   http://www.poetes.com/baud
Excellent site devoted to Baudelaire, including texts of poems.

Messieurs de Goncourt   http://membres.lycos.fr/goncourt
Site devoted to Goncourt brothers.

Gustave Flaubert   http://www.univ-rouen.fr/flaubert
Comprehensive site dedicated to Flaubert, maintained by the Centre Flaubert of the University of Rouen.

http://perso.wanadoo.fr/jb.guinot/pages/accueil.html
Another worthwhile Flaubert site.

Théophile Gautier   http://www.mta.ca/faculty/arts-letters/mll/french/gautier
Site dedicated to Gautier, including biography, illustrations and extracts from correspondence.

http://www.llsh.univsavoie.fr/gautier
Another Gautier site, including complete text of *Emaux et camées* (Edition Charpentier 1884)

La Bibliothèque Electronique de Lisieux   http://www.bmlisieux.com
Archive contains many complete texts by nineteenth-century French writers, with
a new one added every month.

Les antres de l'almasty   http://membres.lycos.fr/almasty
More texts by various writers mentioned in this book.

Franz Liszt   http://www.d-vista.com/OTHER/franzliszt.html
An amusing site about the Romantic pianist which even contains an animation in
which Liszt blinks, but also has useful information on life and works.

Napoleon III   http://napoleontrois.free.fr
Excellent and detailed site on the Emperor and the imperial family.

Fondation Napoléon   http://www.napoleonica.org/us/na/na_fondation.html
Dedicated to the history of the First and Second Empires, this is both an academic
and a general interest site.

The Siege and Commune of Paris, 1870–1
                        http://www.library.northwestern.edu/spec/siege
This site contains links to over 1200 digitised photographs and images recorded
during the Siege and Commune.

ExpoMuseum – 150 years of International Expositions
                            http://www.expomuseum.com
Concerns history and future of Universal Expositions, including some photographs
from 1855 and 1867.

La Comédie Française   http://www.comedie-francaise.fr/index.htm
Official site of the Comédie Française, including history and details of past
members.

La Vie parisienne
     http://www.regardencoulisse.com/oeuvres/vieparisienne/vieparisienne.php3
Details about Offenbach's opera (in an e-magazine of musical theatre).

Gallica 2000   http://www.bnf.fr/site_bnf_eng/connaitrgb/gallicagb.htm
Multimedia documents from Bibliothèque Nationale.

Chimères: Petit glossaire de la prostitution
                        http://www.insenses.org/chimeres/glossaire.html
Definitions of words connected with prostitution, courtesans etc.

Handbook of Volapük http://personal.southern.edu/~caviness/Volapuk/HBoV
For anyone wanting to follow in Cora Pearl's footsteps by taking up the study of
Volapük, here it all is.

Index

d'Abancourt, Viscount Louis
  Harmand 97–8, 168
abortion 22–3
About, Edmond 111, 126, 130
d'Agoult, Marie 49, 70
Aguado, Olympe 51, 52
Alexandre-Debray, Janine 318
Alkan, Charles Valentin 166,167, 168
d'Alméras, Henri 16
Amaury-Duval, Eugène Emmanuel
  110
d'Antigny, Blanche 20, 238
anti-semitism 6, 75–7, 94
Arnold, Julian B. 295–6
Audebrand, Philibert 243, 297
Augier, Emile 119, 130

Bacciochi, Count 186, 187, 209
Banville, Théodore de 65, 148, 301
Barucci, Giulia 238
Baudelaire, Charles 100, 133–52, 161,
  172–3, 305, 312, 315, 319, 326
  Fleurs du Mal, Les 6, 133–42, 147–9
  his misogyny 149–51
Baudry, Paul 181–2, 183, 301
Beauharnais, Hortense 3, 208–9
Beauvoir, Aimée de 127
Beauvoir, Roger de 43, 110
Bellanger, Marguerite 20, 187, 247
Bergerat, Emile 176, 273, 281, 300
Berlioz, Hector 101, 160
Bernage, Laurentine 164
Bernhardt, Sarah 63, 314
Bicknell, Anna 214–15, 219, 247

Bidache, Prince of see Guiche,
  Agénor de
Bingham, Captain the Hon. D. 244,
  296
Bignell, Robert 203–4
Billy, André 319
Bismarck, Count Otto von 250,
  254–5, 256, 257, 261, 262–5, 278,
  279–80
Bizet, Georges 167
Blatchford, William see Parker, Derek
Boissard, Fernand 100, 102, 111, 113
Bonaparte, Laetitia Wilhelmina
  Mathilde see Mathilde, Princess
Bonaparte, Louis Napoleon see
  Napoleon III
Bonaparte, Napoleon Joseph Charles
  Paul see Napoleon, Prince
Boucicaut, Aristide 159, 246
Boudet, Micheline 70, 317
Bougival 43, 60–1
Bouilhet, Louis 112, 114, 116, 164
Boulanger, Marcel 82, 271
Bressant, Jean–Baptiste 172, 303
Bressant, Madame see Lucenay, Elisa de
Broutta, Edwina 113
Bülow, Hans von 82

Castellane, Pierre de 44, 51
Castelnau, Amélie 171, 262, 305
Chabrillon, Countess de see Mogador
Chabrillon, Lionel de 310
Chassériau, Théodore 101
Chenavard, Paul Joseph 112, 301

cholera 10–11, 89, 156, 207
Chopin, Frédéric 106–7, 166
Christophe 111, 303
Chroniqueuse, La 67, 156, 157–8, 185–6, 214, 218–19, 220, 231
Citron see Orange, Prince William of
Cizelet, Mathieu 98
Claudin, Gustave 57–8, 93, 119
Clésinger, Auguste 6, 104–5, 106–7
    Bust of Mme A.S. 105, 117, 166
    La Femme piquée par un serpent 6, 104–7, 118, 134–5, 303
clothes and fashion 47–8, 55, 64–5, 68, 86, 230–2, 234
    crinoline, the 230–1
    make–up, 232–4
    male fashions 231
    'trailing dresses' 231
Clotilde, Princess 218–21, 253, 287
Colombier, Marie 20, 237, 243, 267
Commune 264–5
Compiègne 186, 230
Contades, Henri de 44
contraception 21–2
Cormenin, Louis de 110, 111, 116
courtesans
    daily routines 42, 46, 235–6
    diet 46–7, 116, 223–5, 236–7
    terms for 18–20
        abandonnées 20
        biches 19, 20
        camélias 19
        chameaux 19
        cocodettes 19
        cocottes 18–19, 20
        déclassées 1
        demi-castors 19
        demi-mondaines 1–2
        femmes à partie 17, 128
        femmes galantes 15
        filles de marbre 19
        garde, La 20
        grisettes 15–16, 18
        haute galanterie 20
        horizontales 20, 27
        lorettes 16–17
    court life 185–7

Crimean War 159, 161
Crouch, Emma Elizabeth see Pearl, Cora
Crouch, Frederick William Nicholls 195–7, 198–9, 298
Crouch, Louisa Elizabeth 197
Crouch, Lydia 195, 196, 197, 200

Damoreau-Cinti, Madame 102–3
Daubrun, Marie 148
Déjazet, Eugène 44
Delaborde, Elie Miriam 166–7, 168, 171, 260
Delacroix, Eugène 101, 112, 127, 185
Delaroche, Paul 102
Delessert, Edouard 43, 5, 52, 110
Demidov, Count Anatole Nikolayevich 128
Demidov, Paul 221
Derby, Lord see Stanley, Lord Edward George Geoffrey Smith
Derivis, Prosper 99
Deshayes, Marie née 31, 38
Deslion, Anna 20
Dickens, Charles 66, 69
Dolph, Charles A. 70
Donnersmarck, Countess von see Païva, Blanche de
Donnersmarck, von see Henckel von Donnersmarck, Count Guido
Doré, Gustave 301
Du Camp, Maxime 2, 28, 78, 102, 111, 116, 130, 162, 164, 165, 166, 211, 213, 230, 246, 248, 266, 303
Dudevant, Solange 106
Dugléré, Adolphe 246
Dumas fils, Alexandre 44–5, 58–9, 60, 62–4, 67–8, 69, 73, 203, 234–5, 273–4
    Dame aux camélias, La 5, 19, 59–65, 67, 145, 294, 309
    Demi-Monde, Le 1–2
    Femme de Claude, La 274–8
    Péchés de jeunesse 59
Dumas père, Alexandre 44, 68, 104
Dumont de Montcel 127, 270

Duplessis, Marie 3, 5,7, 19, 27, 56–9,
   60, 62–73, 83, 113, 203, 307, 311–
   12, 314, 315, 317
   birth 31
   childhood 31–2
   apprenticeship as laundress 32–3
   early life in Paris 33–5
   beginning of life as courtesan 35–7
   change of name 37–8
   birth of son 38
   flourishing as courtesan 39–49
   marriage 50, 70, 73
   illness 43, 50–2, 56, 68–9
   death 52
   sale of goods 55–6
   physical appearance 32, 38–9, 50,
      57–8, 62–3, 64–5, 68
Duval, Alexandre 287–8, 291
Duval, Jeanne 147, 148, 149–50

Eiffel, Gustave 244, 246
Escoffier, Auguste 236–7, 255, 260
Esquiros, Alphonse 12, 24, 26–7, 79,
   82, 307
Eugénie, Empress 128, 141, 142,
   183–4, 186, 210, 213, 231, 232,
   233, 236, 249, 255, 256, 270
Evans, Dr Thomas W. 247, 256

Fallet, Adèle see Sabatier, Bébé
Fallet, Jeanne see Sabatier, (Fernande
   Ernesta) Jeanne
Fallet, Ulric 161–2, 305
fashion see clothes and fashion
Feydeau, Ernest 112, 114, 115–16
Field, Julian Osgood 239–40
Filles de marbre (play by Théodore
   Barrière and Lambert Thiboust) 19
Flahaut, Count de 208
Flaubert, Gustave 111, 112, 114, 116,
   118, 130, 141, 163, 164, 166, 167,
   260, 300, 326
Forster, John 66–7, 69
Foucher, Paul 243
Fovard, Frédéric 111
Franco-Prussian War 254–8, 265
furnishings 55, 101, 117, 182–3

Gaiffe, Adolphe 176, 273
Gambetta, Léon 256, 279–80
gambling 58, 225
Garnier, Charles 176, 301
Gautier, Estelle 300, 301
Gautier, Judith 167, 172, 301
Gautier, Théophile 82, 86, 91, 100,
   102, 106, 110, 111, 112, 113, 114,
   116, 118, 119–26, 127, 130, 163,
   164–5, 171, 172, 175, 181, 183,
   185, 187, 189, 190, 232, 300–1,
   303–4, 326, 327
   A une robe rose 135
   Apollonie 135
   Lettre à la Présidente 109–10,
      118–19
   Poème de la Femme 134–5
Gazzani, Eugénie 100, 161
Gérôme, Jean-Léon 130
Girardin, Emile de 82, 104, 126–7,
   130, 181, 257, 271, 279, 280
Goncourt, Edmond and Jules de 4,
   86, 116, 119, 130, 151, 168, 171–
   2, 187–90, 260, 261, 326
Gozlan, Léon 126
Gnerri (or Gnierri), Elisa see Nieri, Elisa
Gramont, Duke de see Guiche,
   Agénor de
Gramont-Caderousse, Duke de 19, 207
Grandon, Count de 311
Grisi, Carlotta 120
Grisi, Ernesta 112, 118, 119, 120,
   121, 123, 165, 172, 232, 301, 303
Guiche, Agénor de 36–7, 40, 63, 72,
   86, 254
Guimont, Esther 86

Halévy, Ludovic 160, 211
Hamilton, Duke of 239–40
Hassé, Caroline 205–6, 298
Haussmann, Baron 155–7, 253
Hébert, Ernest 111
Hegermann-Lindencrone, L. de 129
Henckel von Donnersmarck, Count
   Guido 178–81, 182, 183, 189, 190,
   257–8, 260, 261, 262–4, 265, 269–
   71, 272–4, 278–82, 313

Hertford, fourth Marquess of 168, 171, 259
Herz, Jacques 81, 83–5
Herz, Henri 80–1, 82–5, 86, 88
Herz, Henriette 83, 85
hygiene
    cholera 10–11, 89, 156, 207
    contrôle sanitaire 13–14
    see also venereal disease
Holden, W.H. 318
Houssaye, Arsène 116, 126, 127, 184–5, 190, 248, 271
Hugo, Victor 93, 114
Hutten, Baroness von 205, 318

Isabey, Eugène 102
Issartel, Christiana 317

Jackson, Richard see Wallace, Richard
Jalabert, Charles 99, 111, 142
Jockey Club 41, 211
Jonchère, Countess Néra de la 69
Judith, Madame 65–6, 71
July monarchy 10–11, 34, 87

Khalil Bey 221–3, 242
Koreff, Dr David Ferdinand 49, 51, 56

Lachmann, Martin 75, 76–7, 270
Lachmann, Thérèse see Païva, Blanche de
La Fontaine 16
Lano, Pierre de 115, 287, 291
Leblanc, Léonide 20
Lecomte, Jules 126, 175
Lefuel, Hector-Martin 257, 270
Le Hon, Charles 100
Le Hon, Countess (Fanny) 100, 107, 142, 208, 209, 210, 313
Le Senne, Emile 95
Lesseps, Ferdinand de 249
Lesseps, Jules de 181, 222
Letessier, Caroline 289
Liszt, Franz 49, 56, 70, 72, 317, 327
Loliée, Frédéric 20, 82, 83, 191, 273
London 50, 82, 88, 286

love
    amants de cœur 40–1, 44–5
    as expressed by Baudelaire 133–4, 136–9, 140–2, 143–5
    as experienced by Apollonie Sabatier 143, 145–7, 148–9, 152
Louis Philippe 10, 34, 83, 87
Lucenay, Elisa de 114, 172, 303

make-up, use of 232–4
Maneglier, Hervé 64
Manet, Edouard 167, 245
Manguin, Pierre 181, 192
Martin, Marguerite 97–9, 162, 169–70, 305
Martinez, Maria 112, 122–3
Maryx 102, 113
Massé, Victor 119
Masséna, Victor 206, 223–4
Mathilde, Princess 4, 128–30, 253, 300, 326
Mattei, Maria 124
Maugny, Count de see Zed
Maupas, Emile de 210, 211–12, 229
medicine and medical practices
    abortion 22–3
    arsenic as youth preserver 213
    'blue pill' 211, 213
    contraception 21–2
    contrôle sanitaire 13–14
    prescriptions for consumption 51–2
Meissonier, Emma 102, 114, 165
Meissonier, Ernest 102, 103–4, 105, 111, 113, 115, 117, 151, 165, 170, 172, 299, 303, 305
    Polichinelle 117, 166, 168, 299, 305
Méril, Viscount de 38
Mermaz, Louis 103, 104, 319
Metternich, Princess Pauline 231, 232, 238, 253
Missy see Morny, Mathilde de
Mogador 310
money 35, 42, 46–8, 71–2, 289, 307–9, 311–12
    gambling 58, 225
Monnier, Henri 102, 110, 114
Montguyon, Fernand de 40, 44, 213

Montijo, Eugénie de *see* Eugénie, Empress
Montorgueil, Georges 94, 95
Morny, Duke Auguste de 100, 142, 160, 208–14, 229, 312–14
Morny, Duchess de 210, 213
Morny, Mathilde de 213
Moscow 75–8, 88
Moss, Armand 139
Mosselman, Alfred 100–3, 104, 105, 107, 109, 110, 114–15, 118, 120, 122, 123, 139, 142, 152, 161, 164–5, 168, 170, 172, 179, 208, 210, 259–60, 311
Murat, Prince Achille 206–7, 215, 225, 242, 253, 256
Murat, Princess Caroline 129–30, 185, 206, 209–10, 213, 253
Murger, Henry 17, 102, 119

Nadar (Gaspar Félix Tournachon) 273
Napoleon I 3, 31, 87, 214, 229–30
Napoleon III 3–4, 20, 87, 89, 91, 93, 114, 128, 129, 155–6, 158, 160, 161, 175, 183–7, 206–7, 208–9, 210, 217, 218, 225, 236, 249, 253, 255–6, 265, 289, 327
Napoleon, Prince 158, 160, 181, 214–21, 223, 230, 240, 242–3, 244, 245–6, 253, 258–9, 261, 285–7, 289–90, 294
Nerval, Gérard de 102, 112
Neudeck 178, 179, 180, 257, 263, 272, 280–81, 283
Nieri, Elisa 114
Nieuwerkerke, Count Emilien de 128, 253, 299

Offenbach, Jacques 160, 211, 248–9
Orange, Prince William of 207–8
Orsini, Count Felice 114, 233
Osmond, Count 190–1
Ozy, Alice 41, 102, 112–13, 123

Païva, Blanche de (also known as La Païva) 3–4, 5–6, 7, 17, 20, 27, 114, 123–6, 195, 229, 232, 234, 238,
266, 292, 294, 301, 307–9, 311, 312–13, 315, 318, 326
  birth 75
  childhood 76–7
  first marriage 77–8
  early life in Paris 78–80
  relationship with Henri Herz 80–5
  visit to London 86–8
  second marriage 89–92
  life in place Saint-Georges 93–5, 126–8, 175–8
  as consort of Henckel von Donnersmarck 178–85, 187–92, 256–8, 263
  third marriage 269–74, 277–80
  declining years 280–1
  death 281
  physical appearance 79, 82, 123, 180, 184, 187–8, 232, 234, 263, 273, 281
  legends surrounding 81–2, 83, 88, 92, 176–8, 183–5, 187, 189, 191, 281–2
Païva-Araujo, Albino Francesco de 90–3, 125, 176, 269, 272
Païva, Marquess de *see* Païva-Araujo, Albino Francesco de
Parent-Duchâtelet, Dr A.J.B. 6, 9–10, 15, 16, 17, 23–6, 37, 56–7, 115, 128, 163, 178, 267
Paris
  boulevards
    Capucines, des 41
    Italiens, des 16, 40, 43, 259
    Madeleine, de la 41, 46, 48, 55, 65
    Saint-Germain 156
    Saussaye, de la 304
  cemeteries
    Batignolles 297–8
    Montmartre 52, 301
    Père Lachaise 213, 272
  churches
    Madeleine, La 38, 52, 58, 265
    Notre Dame 161
    Notre Dame de Lorette 16, 88, 100, 113

Commune 264–5
hotels and private mansions
  Bagatelle (château) 168, 259, 305
  Hôtel Païva 6, 181–5, 187–90,
    264, 271, 279–80, 282–3,
    294
  Hôtel Pimodan 100, 102, 110,
    133, 168
department stores
  Bon Marché 159, 246
  Grand Bazar de l'Hôtel de Ville
    246
  Grand Condé 48
  Grand Magasin du Louvre 159–60
  Petit Saint-Thomas 48, 159
  Printemps 246
  Samaritaine, La 246
  Trois Quartiers 48
palaces
  Elysée 128, 273
  Palais Royal 35, 220
  Tuileries 83, 185–6, 216, 253,
    256, 257, 265
parks
  Bois de Boulogne 40, 42, 66,
    124, 156, 182, 212, 236, 285,
    299, 304
  Bois de Vincennes 156
pleasure gardens
  Bal Mabille 42, 188, 310
  Ranelagh 37
rebuilding of 155–7
restaurants and cafés
  Café Anglais 43, 236, 237, 246
  Maison Dorée (or Maison d'Or)
    43, 46
  Petit Moulin Rouge 236
  Tortoni's 40
  Voisin 46
siege of 259–61
streets
  d'Antin, rue 41, 60
  l'Arcade, rue de 35
  d'Aumale, rue 123
  Bac, rue du 48, 159
  Bassano, rue de 198, 297
  Bassins, rue des 223, 239

Chaillot, rue de 223, 259, 288,
  289, 297
Champs Elysées, avenue de 6,
  86, 156, 181, 199, 231, 236,
  263–4, 282, 294–5, 298, 311
Chauchat, rue 269
Chaussée-d-Antin, rue de la 45,
  51
Chézy, rue de 304
Christophe Colomb, rue 292
Coq-Héron, rue de 33
Courcelles, rue de 129
Croix-des-Petits-Champs, rue
  14
d'Eylau, avenue 302–4
Faisanderie, rue de la 167
Frochot, rue 100–2, 107, 110–19,
  133, 161, 165, 171
Frochot, avenue 101–2
Grange Batelière, rue 204
l'Impératrice, avenue de 299
Jean-Jacques-Rousseau, rue 145,
  147
Lafitte, rue 168, 259
Le Peletier, rue 11, 175, 204
Montaigne, avenue 158, 222
Mont-Thabor, rue de 39
Neuve-Bréda, rue 162
Neuve-des-Mathurins, rue 272
Paix, rue de la 62, 206, 232
Pergolèse, rue 172
Ponthieu, rue 205, 298
Provence, rue de 81
Rossini, rue 90, 91
Saint-Georges, place 88–9, 179,
  180
Sandrié, passage 161
Spontini, rue 172, 302
Varennes, rue de 259
Veuves, allée des 42
Victoire, rue de la 81
theatres
  Bouffes Parisiens 160, 198, 217,
    242–4, 248
  Gymnase 67, 230, 274
  Italien 49, 160, 175, 183, 280
  Lyrique 160, 175, 249

Opéra Comique 160
Opera House (old) 11, 41, 114,
    160, 175, 301
Opera House (new) 176, 182,
    261, 301
Palais Royal 248
Variétés 44, 60, 248, 249, 310
Vaudeville 19, 59
Parker, Derek 318
Pearl, Cora 3, 6–7, 20, 229, 266, 307,
    308, 312, 315, 317–18
    birth 195
    childhood 195–7
    start of life as prostitute 200–3
    change of name 203
    early experiences in Paris 204–8
    height of career 208, 212–26, 232–
        42, 245–6, 250
    as Cupid in Orphée aux enfers 242–4,
        291
    during Franco-Prussian War and
        siege of Paris 258–9, 261–2
    declining years 285–97
    death 297–8
    memoirs 197–9, 235, 297, 298,
        317–18
    physical appearance 199, 200, 205,
        232–4, 237–44, 291–3, 296, 297
Perrégaux, Count Edouard de 41–3,
    50, 52, 60, 63–4, 70, 73, 113
Pichois, Claude 103, 319
Planche, Gustave 106
Plessis, Alphonsine see Duplessis,
    Marie
Plessis, Delphine 31, 38, 56
Plessis, Marin 31–3, 38, 50
Pontchartrain 190–92, 258, 282, 326
Porché, François 116
Pourtalès, James de 99, 311
Prat, Clémence 44
Préault, Auguste 110, 301
Présidente, La see Sabatier, Apollonie
Pretty Women of Paris, The 292–3
Prince Imperial 161, 244
prostitutes
    lesbianism among 24–5
    maisons de tolérance 11, 79
    registration of 10, 11, 13–15, 17
    repression of 266
    restrictions on 11–12
    stereotypes of 23–7, 56–8, 64, 69,
        82, 178, 267
    types of
        filles de maison 11
        filles en cartes 11–13, 204
        filles insoumises 13–14
        filles soumises 11
        grisettes 15–16, 18
        lorettes 16–17
Puvis de Chavannes 301

Rachel 314
Raimondi, Marquess 167
revolutions
    July (1830) 34
    February (1848) 87–8, 178
Reyer, Ernest 103, 111, 116, 117,
    300, 301, 303
Ricard, Gustave 116–17, 172, 301
    La Dame au petit chien 117, 166,
        303
Richard, Edmond 301–2, 304, 305,
    319
Richardson, Joanna 103, 319
Rochefort, Henri 207, 291
Rogniat, Baron Abel 258
Roqueplan, Nestor 16, 34, 37, 63,
    238–9
Rouher, Eugène 210, 256
Rounat, Charles de la 111
Rousseau, Théodore 101
Ryan, Dr Michael 9, 14, 16, 20–21,
    23–6, 56–7, 201

Sabatier, Adèle see Sabatier, Bébé
Sabatier, Apollonie 3, 4, 6, 7, 266,
    307, 311, 312, 315–16, 319, 326
    birth 97
    childhood 98–9
    life as artists' model 99
    as mistress of Alfred Mosselman
        99–107, 109–23, 130, 133–52,
        161–4, 232
    change of name 100–1

years of comparative poverty
165–8, 170–73
supported by Richard Wallace
259–60, 299–304
declining years 304–5
death 305
physical appearance 99, 104, 105,
106, 123, 232, 299, 302, 304
Sabatier, Bébé 98–9, 109, 113, 121,
123, 140–1, 161–2, 171, 305, 319
Sabatier, (Fernande Ernesta) Jeanne
113, 162, 172, 303
Sabatier, Madame (the singer) 103
Saint Cloud (château) 35, 186, 187
Sainte-Beuve, Charles Augustin 112,
114, 126, 130, 140
Saint-Victor, Paul de 110, 119, 126,
187, 280, 299, 301, 303
Sand, George 106, 166
Savatier, Aglaé-Joséphine *see* Sabatier,
Apollonie
Savatier, Alexandre 98, 162
Savatier, André 97–8, 101
Savatier, Bébé *see* Sabatier, Bébé
Savatier, Irma Adelina *see* Sabatier,
Bébé
Savatier, Louis 98, 162, 304
Savatier, Marguerite *see* Martin,
Marguerite
Savatier, Thierry 122, 319
Saunders, Edith 69
Scheffer, Ary 102, 218
Schneider, Hortense 20, 102, 207,
314
Second Empire
attitudes towards 247–8, 265
characteristics of 3–4, 229, 234–5,
247–9, 315
Second Republic 87, 89
Senneville, Gérard de 319
sex 59, 82, 241–2, 308, 312
abortion 22–3
contraception 21–2
'dirty talk' 109–10, 118–19, 120–1,
163, 166
see also venereal disease
siege of Paris 259–61

spas and resorts
Bad Ems *see* Ems
Baden 43, 50, 58, 223, 280
Ems 50, 80, 90, 254
Monte Carlo 225, 289, 295
Spa 50, 58
Wiesbaden 50
Spoelberch de Lovenjoul, Viscount
303–4
Stackelberg, Count Gustav Ernst von
45–6, 48, 51, 71
Stanley, Lord Edward George
Geoffrey Smith 88
Starkie, Enid 319
Sue, Eugène 67

Taine, Hippolyte 130, 188
Tattet, Alfred 117
Teppe, Julien 17
Thierry, Augustin 304–5
Thiers, Adolphe 262, 263, 264, 273
Traviata, La 59, 175
Troubetskaya, Sophia *see* Morny,
Duchess de
Troyat, Henri 104
Turgan, Julien 111, 118, 162, 270

Ugalde, Madame 103, 243–4
Universal Exposition (1855) 85, 158–60,
181, 217, 327
Universal Exposition (1867) 183, 192,
208, 244–7, 248–9, 327

Vandam, A.D. 68
venereal disease 13,14
syphilis 20–1
Victoria, Queen 159, 232
Viel Castel, Count Horace de 4,
67–8, 92, 94, 176–8, 180, 214, 248
Vienne, Romain 32, 33, 35–6, 39,
42, 43, 46–7, 52, 57–8, 62, 65,
69–70, 71, 317
Villemessant, Hippolyte de 39
Villoing, François Hyacinthe Antoine
77–8, 89, 270
Villoing, Antoine (son) 78, 89, 90,
91, 125

Villoing, Thérèse *see* Païva, Blanche de
Volapük 296–7, 327

Wagner, Richard 82
Walewska, Countess 186
Walewski, Count 187
Wallace, Lady *see* Castelnau, Amélie
Wallace, Richard 168–71, 173, 211,
    259–60, 262, 299, 305, 311
women
    attitudes towards 27–8, 119, 122,
        151, 265–6, 278, 308–9, 313–15
    on the part of Baudelaire 147,
        149–51

on the part of Dumas *fils* 275–7
on the part of the Goncourts 151
on the part of Meissonier 103–4
Worms, Gustave 303
Worth, Charles Frederick 206, 231–2,
    236
Worth, Jean Philippe 232–3, 234

Zabé, Emile 172, 302, 303
Zed 20, 205–6, 240–2, 291–2
Ziegler, Jean 104, 319
Zola, Emile
    L'Assommoir 32, 34
    Nana 13, 24, 40–1, 266–7, 290–1

A NOTE ON THE AUTHOR

Virginia Rounding is a writer and translator living in London. This is her first book.

A NOTE ON THE TYPE

The text of this book is set in Bembo. This type
was first used in 1495 by the Venetian printer
Aldus Manutius for Cardinal Bembo's *De Aetna*,
and was cut for Manutius by Francesco Griffo. It
was one of the types used by Claude Garamond
(1480–1561) as a model for his Romain de
L'Université, and so it was the forerunner of
what became standard European type for the
following two centuries. Its modern form follows the original types and was designed for
Monotype in 1929.

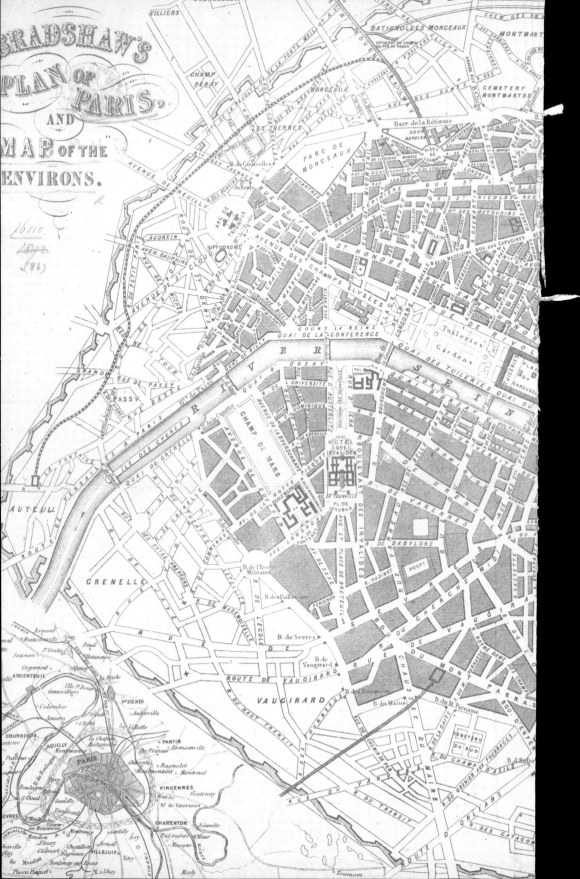